ADMINISTRATIVE
LAW
SECOND EDITION

This book is dedicated to
Professors Albert Melone and William McLauchlan,
who provided excellent role models
at crucial points in my life.

ADMINISTRATIVE LAW

SECOND EDITION

Steven J. Cann

SAGE Publications
International Educational and Professional Publisher
Thousand Oaks   London   New Delhi

For information address:

SAGE Publications, Inc.
2455 Teller Road
Thousand Oaks, California 91320
E-mail@sagepub.com

SAGE Publications Ltd.
6 Bonhill Street
London EC2A 4PU
United Kingdom

SAGE Publications India Pvt. Ltd.
M-32 Market
Greater Kailash I
New Delhi 110048 India

Printed in the United States of America

Cann, Steven J.
    Administrative law / by Steven Cann. — 2nd. ed.
        p. cm.
    Includes bibliographical references and index.
    ISBN 0-7619-0976-1 (cloth)
    1. Administrative law—United States—Cases. 2. Administrative
procedure—United States—Cases. I. Title.
    KF5402.A4C355 1998
    342.73'06—dc21   97-45281

98 99 00 01 02 03 04 8 7 6 5 4 3 2

Acquiring Editor:	Catherine Rossbach
Editorial Assistant:	Kathleen Derby
Production Editor:	Diana E. Axelsen
Production Assistant:	Karen Wiley
Typesetter/Designer:	Danielle Dillahunt
Cover Designer:	Ravi Balasuriya
Print Buyer:	Anna Chin

CONTENTS IN BRIEF

PART III: SUBSTANTIVE ISSUES IN ADMINISTRATIVE LAW

CONTENTS

4. Control of Agencies by Default: The Courts and Administrative Law   94

PART II: THE ADMINISTRATIVE PROCESS

PART III: SUBSTANTIVE ISSUES IN ADMINISTRATIVE LAW

LIST OF CASES

Boldface page numbers indicate cases that appear in full in the text.

PREFACE

Of the courses I teach, administrative law is the most rewarding. One can readily see the fruits of one's labor as students learn about a subject that so many know so little about—the workings of bureaucracy and administrative law. Student evaluations of my course indicate, however, that although students enjoyed the subject matter, they did not appreciate the text. That dissatisfaction, I believe, stems from the fact that many texts are written by lawyers and practitioners without an undergraduate audience in mind. Administrative law is complex, but it does not have to be difficult.

Not only did student feedback indicate that the text was of little help in enhancing understanding, but in my opinion students were not offered enough cases. As a believer in the case method as a pedagogical device, I thought a casebook could be written that would be more student friendly than texts currently on the market. This text, I believe, addresses these points and offers several distinguishing features for both students and faculty.

DISTINGUISHING FEATURES
OF THIS TEXT

Student-Friendly Conceptual Framework. The book is organized around a conceptual framework that contrasts democracy with the administrative state, or "fourth branch of government" (significant policy making by insulated technocrats and bureaucrats).

Illustrative Cases. Each chapter begins with a scenario, or case in point, presented somewhat polemically, to pique students' interest. Each case demonstrates the central point of its chapter, and often the student is referred back to that case to illustrate concepts throughout the chapter.

Balance of Cases. Because it has been my experience that cases are an excellent pedagogical device—students enjoy reading them, for one thing— this text uses cases liberally, more than do most textbooks aimed at an undergraduate/MPA audience. I have tried to find the right balance between too many cases, on the one hand, and too few, on the other (which I find is common in many texts on the market).

More Case Content. In contrast with other texts that use cases, this book also includes more of each case so that students can better grasp what led to the lawsuit and how the Court resolved it. In addition to the introductory cases in point, then, the book presents cases throughout each chapter, and chapters end with several more cases relevant to the chapter material. The cases in the middle of chapters tend to be "classics," whereas the cases at the end of chapters represent more recent decisions on the same points of law.

Summary of Doctrines. Finally, I have included chapter summaries of administrative law doctrines, legal principles, and constitutional tests that students should have gleaned from the cases presented in the chapter and that they should be able to apply to the end-of-chapter cases or to hypothetical cases.

Pedagogical Design. The book is designed to be compatible with a problem-solving pedagogical approach. Questions at the end of cases query students' understanding of doctrines, principles, and constitutional tests and whether the Court applied those doctrines, principles, and tests; modified them; or ignored them. Also, the summary at the end of each chapter is compatible with a pedagogical approach that uses testing by hypothetical cases and requires students to outline. Case text from the courts is presented in a double-column format, which should make for easy reference to specific cases.

THEORETICAL FRAMEWORK

The theoretical framework for this text is the juxtaposition of democracy and the fourth branch of government, the administrative state. Democracy is presented simply as the notion that citizens, either directly or indirectly, ought to have some influence on governmental policy. Each chapter, however, presents the student with examples of the administrative state—decisions and policies made by unaccountable agencies that base those decisions and policies on the expertise of unelected individuals. Delegation of power is presented early in the text so that students become aware of the increasing abdication of congressional responsibility to agencies.

The text further argues that the president, on the one hand, often possesses the will to control bureaucracy but lacks the raw power to do so. Congress, on the other hand, possesses the power but generally lacks the will to exercise it in controlling agencies. Therefore, almost by default, the task of control of the fourth branch of government falls to the courts. Administrative law is the tool at their disposal.

In the last chapter of the book, the student is asked to analyze whether courts are well suited to this task and whether, on the whole, courts have been successful. As former Secretary of Labor Robert Reich indicated, volumes have been written about the inconsistency of judicial review and democracy, but almost nothing has been written about the inconsistency between the administrative state and democracy.

AUDIENCE

This book was written for undergraduate students in administrative law at the junior or senior level. It would also be appropriate for MPA courses because, even at the graduate level, a law school casebook is underused for the price. Because the text includes more cases and more of each case than do typical casebooks not intended for law schools, it should be suitable for prelaw courses.

CONTENT

Part I of the text consists of four chapters establishing the theoretical context. Chapter 1 combines a description of what agencies do and how they do it with a discussion of democracy. Chapter 2 provides a discussion of the ways in which the president attempts to control bureaucracy, beginning with an analysis of the president's constitutional Article II powers and including an analysis of the presidential appointment and removal powers. Here, the discussion focuses on presidential frustration with appointees and the concept of "captivity." Cases are presented and discussed relative to executive removal. The chapter also analyzes other traditional modes of executive control, including a discussion of the concept of "administrative presidency." Finally, the 1990 case of *Dole v. United Steelworkers of America* is presented and discussed. This case does not bode well for presidential control of agency rule making by use of the Office of Management and Budget (OMB). I argue that the Constitution fails to provide the president with the raw power necessary to control bureaucracy and that other mechanisms have not been overly successful.

Chapter 3 provides a similar analysis of Congress except for demonstrating that Congress clearly possesses the raw power to control agency behavior. Because of constituency service, "cozy" or "iron" triangles, group money and elections, and dependency on agencies for information, however, Congress generally lacks the will to exercise genuine control over bureaucracy; that is, Congress has little or no incentive to play the watchdog role or to engage in effective oversight, and there are many disincentives to doing so.

Chapter 4 explores the impediments to judicial control of bureaucracy. It covers the topics of reviewability, exhaustion, primary jurisdiction, ripeness and finality, and standing and concludes with a discussion of the scope of review that courts can apply to different types of agency action.

The administrative process is the subject of Part II. Chapter 5 presents a discussion of bureaucracy and information. It analyzes how agencies get information and what they do with it once they have it. Chapter 6 explores informal agency decision making and subsequent judicial review. Chapter 7 provides an analysis of agency rule making and adjudication.

Part III of the text includes three chapters analyzing specific problems of administrative law. The law of public employment, discussed in Chapter 8, begins the section. This chapter begins with an analysis of the law of public employment in education. Students will readily grasp the concept of "property interest," with tenure as an example. The discussion then extrapolates to public employment more generally. Chapter 9 covers due process of law in contexts other than public employment, and Chapter 10 presents the legal liability of government and individual government employees.

The final chapter summarizes the cases and material from the perspective of judicial control of agencies. Finally, students are exposed to modern examples of agency decision making that are not inconsistent with the concept of "popular control."

ACKNOWLEDGMENTS

This book would not have been possible without the support of, and partial funding from, Washburn University of Topeka, Kansas, which provided both large and small grants that paid for salaries, paper, floppy disks, postage, and other expenses. The university also awarded me a sabbatical leave, which provided the time necessary to complete this project. Besides time and money, a third ingredient—the support of others—contributed to the completion of this text. Of support I had an abundance. My secretary, Cathy Tunnell, typed and edited tirelessly, overcoming any obstacles to the task. I received invaluable support from my law student research assistant, Duane Rogers; my undergraduate research assistants, Tim Merchant and Shawn Beatty; my proofreader, Junie Davis; the staff of the Washburn University Law School Library; and the computer center. My colleagues in the Political Science Department provided valuable input and support. Drs. David Freeman, Marvin Heath, Loran Smith, and Steven Wagner provided helpful suggestions, most of which are included in the book. Of course, the final product would not have been possible without the help of Sage editors and staff, including Catherine Rossbach, Diana Axelsen, Danielle Dillahunt, and Linda Poderski.

Finally, my wife, Rita, not only provided support and understanding but also read most of the chapters as they were written. She may never take a class in administrative law, but she agrees that the subject is much more interesting than the usual images of administrative law connote.

LEGAL LINGO

Lawyers do not write in common English. Legal writing makes heavy use of Latin and has a unique way of citing references. As a layperson venturing into the legal world, you will need help. Any number of good, inexpensive, paperback legal dictionaries are on the market, and you should not attempt to take a substantive legal course (e.g., constitutional law, administrative law) without one.

In any case, for those who will begin to read the first chapter of this book prior to obtaining a law dictionary or supplement, it will be helpful to know that legal citations always consist of three essential elements: the volume number, the reference material, and the page number. Some examples are listed below:

1. The citation 440 U.S. 472 (1979) means that you will find a case (*National Muffler Dealers Association, Inc. v. U.S.*) in Volume 440 of the *United States Supreme Court Reports* (official reporter of U.S. Supreme Court decisions) on page 472, followed by the year. F.Supp is the reporter for U.S. district court cases, and F.2d is the reporter for U.S. circuit court of appeals cases.

2. 5 U.S.C. 551 means Title 5 of the *United States Code* (laws of the federal government), Chapter 551 (the Administrative Procedure Act of 1946). U.S.C.A. stands for *United States Code Annotated* (*annotated* means

that case citations have been included where courts have interpreted the statute).

3. 36 Fed. Reg. 22906 means Volume 36 of the *Federal Register* (publication of federal agencies' rules and proposed rules) on page 22906. This is the rule requiring passive restraint in autos.

4. 29 C.F.R. 17 means Title 29 of the *Code of Federal Regulations,* Chapter 17. The *Federal Register* is sometimes difficult to use because it is a weekly publication that informs interested parties of rules, regulations, or standards that nearly all federal agencies have promulgated that week, and it also provides notice of proposed rules, regulations, or standards on which the various agencies are about to hold hearings. Hence, its best use is on a weekly basis by those who are regulated by agencies or who have business before an agency to keep up on what the agency is about to do and what it has done. All of these weekly rules are compiled by subject matter in the C.F.R.; so, Title 29, for example, deals with labor, and Chapter 17 is the beginning of 1,600 pages of rules, regulations, and standards adopted by the Occupational Safety and Health Administration (OSHA).

Most cases come to the U.S. Supreme Court through a *writ of certiorari* ("cert."), which is a form of appeal by which the higher court can exercise discretion regarding whether to hear the appeal. If the Court decides to hear the appeal, it will issue a writ of cert. requesting the record from the lower court.

Once the Supreme Court decides a case, it has several options: (a) It can *affirm* the lower-court decision, which means the lower court's (or agency's) interpretation or decision or both were correct; (b) it can (but rarely does) *overrule* a lower federal court; that is, the Court rejects a particular interpretation and generally adopts a new interpretation as precedent; or (c) the Court can *reverse* (set aside) a lower-court decision. For a federal court or federal agency, the Court could (but rarely does) reverse the court or agency decision and make the final decision itself. More frequently, however, the Court will reverse a state supreme court, lower federal court, or federal agency decision or interpretation and remand the case to the lower court or agency for a decision not inconsistent with the Supreme Court's interpretation.

The text of the Federal Register and the Code of Federal Regulations can be found on the World Wide Web at the following addresses:

```
http://cos.gdb.org/repros/fr/fr-intro.html
http://www.access.gpo/nara/cfr/index.html
```

PART I

POLITICS, DEMOCRACY, AND BUREAUCRACY

CHAPTER 1

DEMOCRACY AND BUREAUCRACY

By the early 1960s, U.S. autos were getting bigger, faster, and more powerful than ever before. Many states had very lax speed limits. Montana and Wyoming, for example, had no specific speed limits, saying, instead, that the speed was to be "reasonable and prudent" for the weather conditions; on a clear day, ninety miles per hour could be reasonable and prudent. In addition, most of our nation's highways consisted of only two lanes. This combination of events led to increasing and alarming numbers of motor vehicle fatalities—nearly forty thousand in 1960.[1]

CASE IN POINT:
MOTOR VEHICLE MANUFACTURERS ASSOCIATION V. STATE FARM INSURANCE COMPANY, 463 U.S. 29 (1983)

In 1966, Congress decided that more could be done to reduce traffic injuries and fatalities and that it should be done at the national level through the federal power to regulate commerce among the states. Congress then passed the National Traffic and Motor Vehicle Safety Act, whose purpose was to reduce traffic accidents, injuries, and fatalities. Congress also directed the secretary of transportation (or the secretary's delegate) to issue motor vehicle safety standards.

Many agencies are required to set standards, and when they do, they must follow a procedure outlined in Section 553 of the Administrative Procedure Act. The procedure requires that proposed rules, regulations, or standards that agencies are thinking of adopting must be announced to the public and interested parties. The agency must inform the public of the time, date, and place of the hearing on the proposed standard (or rule) and invite public comment before adopting the rule.

In 1967, the secretary of transportation promulgated a rule calling for the installation of seat belts in all motor vehicles, but because of public resistance to "buckling up," traffic fatalities continued to climb despite the fact that cars were now manufactured with seat belts. In 1969, the secretary of transportation promulgated a passive restraint rule (34 F.R. 11148) that would have required motor vehicle manufacturers to install either air bags or automatic seat belts by 1975. In preparation for the 1975 model year, manufacturers chose to install a seat belt with an ignition lock (if the seat belt was not fastened, the car would not start). This safety standard was challenged by Chrysler in the courts and upheld by a circuit court in *Chrysler v. Department of Transportation* (DOT), 472 F.2d 659 (1972). Because of severe negative public reaction to the ignition lock system, Congress amended the Motor Vehicle Safety Act to prohibit the system.

President Gerald Ford's secretary of transportation, William Coleman, Jr., opened new hearings on passive restraints, which resulted first in a one-year delay in the target date (now it would be 1976 before passive restraint was required). Later, the passive restraint rule was rescinded in favor of a pilot program fitting 500,000 autos with passive restraints. President Jimmy Carter's secretary of transportation, Brock Adams, disagreed with the pilot program approach and held new hearings, which resulted in the adoption of "modified rule 208." Rule 208 required the phasing in of passive restraint devices between 1982 and 1984 (the restraint devices specified in the standard were air bags and automatic seat belts). This rule, too, survived a challenge in the courts (*Pacific Legal Foundation v. Department of Transportation,* 593 F.2d 1338 [1979]).

In February 1981, President Ronald Reagan's secretary of transportation, Andrew Lewis, in one of his first official acts, reopened hearings on the passive restraint standard. He, too, delayed the starting date for one year and later rescinded the passive restraint safety standard. State Farm Insurance Company and others challenged Secretary Lewis's rescinding order in court.

Two issues were before the Supreme Court in this case, which you will read in detail in Chapter 7, but suffice it to say here that the Supreme Court reversed the secretary's rescission order and, in effect, ordered him to justify his decision. Because he apparently could not, a new passive restraint safety standard was issued in 1984, calling for air bags or automatic seat belts in all cars manufactured after 1989. By 1988, traffic fatalities had fallen to 19.7 thousand a year.[2]

Questions

1. Is it democratic that Congress recognized a problem and passed a law in 1966 requiring traffic safety standards and then allowed those standards to be thwarted and delayed by agencies until 1989?
2. In your opinion, should the decision to require air bags or automatic seat belts or both be up to Congress to make, or is that more appropriately an agency decision based on expertise? (Is the decision a policy decision, or is it simply an administrative decision implementing congressional action?)
3. Is the standard a good idea or a bad idea? Why?
4. Do you think it is democratic for an unelected, appointed-for-life Supreme Court to substitute its judgment for the judgment of the also unelected secretary of transportation? Why?

DEMOCRACY

If you are like most Americans, you assume that you live in a democracy, but you probably cannot define what that means. Try to define democracy, being concise and definite about what the term means.

Chances are, you did one of two things: (a) You went back to Abraham Lincoln and said, "government of the people, by the people, for the people," or (b) you tried to define it in terms of a process (e.g., elections, political parties). Without belaboring the point, let us consider these typical responses.

Government of the People

It is difficult to imagine what Lincoln had in mind when he said "of the people," but we can put the rest of his phrase to a commonsense test. Presumably, "by the people" means some variant of "the people govern." When was the last time you "governed"? When was the last time you had significant input into a governmental policy? When was the last time you had *any* input into a governmental policy? When was the last time anyone you know had any input into a governmental policy?

You may be saying to yourself, "But people can't really govern. We elect representatives to do that for us." True enough. When was the last time you called your senator or went to Washington, D.C., to see your senator about an issue of concern to you? When was the last time you provided governmental input to any of the following elected officials: U.S. representative, county commissioner, city councilperson, mayor, governor, U.S. president? If you have provided such input, do you think it was a significant force in shaping policy? The notion "by the people" is too simplistic to describe what part (if any) the American people play in shaping policy.

The concept of "for the people" could be difficult to deal with because it would seem possible to govern "for the people" by doing the opposite of what the people want (assuming one could ever assess what the people want). Let us, for now, assume that Lincoln was getting at the notion of governmental responsiveness to citizens' demands. In the late 1970s, more than 75 percent of Americans opposed a Panama Canal Treaty, but we got one. For the past thirty years, 65 percent or more of Americans have favored stronger gun control and doing away with the electoral college.[3] In the case of gun control, a small minority has been able to thwart a policy that the vast majority favors. In the case of the electoral college, although proposed constitutional changes have been introduced in Congress, none have passed. Although some empirical evidence suggests an association between public opinion and public policy,[4] we can say that, in the United States, the people often do not get the policies they want. Indeed, the Founding Fathers invented or refined several ingenious devices whose purposes were to thwart governmental responsiveness to the demands of the masses (e.g., state legislative election of U.S. senators, the electoral college, federalism, and separation of powers—including a judicial branch that later became armed with judicial review). Even conceding that Lincoln's phrase "of the people, by the people, for the people" was an accurate description of American democracy in 1860 (which is doubtful), it does not describe what happens in the United States today.

Democracy as a Process

If you defined democracy by referring to elections and competing political parties, bear in mind that many very authoritarian regimes in the world today have elections and competing parties (e.g., South Korea, El Salvador).

DEMOCRACY DEFINED

One could take a semester course in notions and definitions of democracy, but for our purposes, let us simply say that *democracy* is a form of government in which people have some influence over the policies that affect their lives. This is not an absolute concept in the sense that either you have it or you do not. Rather, it is a continuum, with some countries having a lot of it, and some countries having not very much or none at all.

One could argue, for example, that many parliamentary systems are very democratic because the political parties take divergent and clearly identifiable stands on issues and possess the party discipline to enact their platforms into law. Hence, when a voter votes for a candidate who says, "If elected, I will help my political party bring about X, Y, and Z," that voter has significant influence if his or her party wins a majority of seats in Parliament because the party will enact policies X, Y, and Z. But in the United States, because of separation of powers, federalism, and weakened political parties, even on those rare occasions when a politician or political party takes a definite and clear stand on a policy issue, the result is not predictable. To cite a popular example, look at what happened in 1988 when presidential candidate George Bush said, "Read my lips. No new taxes." In 1992, it may have cost him reelection when, as President George Bush, he was forced to accept a budget compromise containing a significant tax increase.

In any case, although we may not be the most democratic country in the world, we are certainly not the least democratic. If we can agree that a democracy is a form of government in which the people can have an impact on policies that affect their lives, a short discussion addressing how the people do that is in order.

Once a polity gets beyond a certain size (say, several hundred), it becomes impossible for all the people to debate and vote on policies. According to the 1990 census, more than 248 million people live in the United States, so it is unlikely that everyone could have input on every policy. A *republic* is a democratic form of government in which people elect representatives to represent them. Political scientists use the term *linkages* to describe the devices that link the people with their representatives. Those linkages are public opinion, political parties, voting, elections, and interest groups. So, in theory at least, the people influence policy indirectly by the use of linkages with their representatives—who, presumably, reflect constituency demands in debate and votes on policies.

DEMOCRACY AND BUREAUCRACY

How democratic would you think our government was if it were true that 90 percent of "laws" that regulate everyday life were made by nonelected, politically insulated, job-secure, career bureaucrats?[5] What if it were true that the policy-making branch of government (at any level—federal, state, county, or city) passed only broad and vague legislation and then delegated the power to agencies to adopt standards, rules, and policies to fill in the gaps and holes, leaving those agencies with a tremendous amount of discretion? The notion of policy making by agencies and bureaucracies, rather than by popularly elected (and accountable) representatives, is referred to as the "administrative state" or the fourth branch of government.[6]

Specifically, the *administrative state* connotes policy making by bureaucratic or agency expertise, and the *fourth branch* simply means bureaucracy as an organization or structure. The term *fourth branch* implies more than a bureaucracy, however. It implies a bureaucracy coequal with the presidency, Congress, and the courts, and it assumes the policy-making aspect of the administrative state. Apparently, the term *fourth branch* was coined by Justice Robert Jackson in a 1951 case:

> The rise of administrative bodies probably has been the most significant legal trend of the last century and perhaps more values today are affected by their decisions than by those of all the courts, review of administrative decisions apart. They also have begun to have important consequences on personal rights (*United States v. Spector,* 343 U.S. 169). They have become a veritable fourth branch of the Government, which has deranged our three-branch legal theories much as the concept of a fourth dimension unsettles our three-dimensional thinking.
>   Courts have differed in assigning a place to these seemingly necessary bodies in our constitutional system. Administrative agencies have been called quasi-legislative, quasi-executive or quasi-judicial, as the occasion required, in order to validate their functions within the separation-of-powers scheme of the Constitution. The mere retreat to the qualifying "quasi" is implicit with confession that all recognized classifications have broken down, and "quasi" is a smooth cover which we draw over our confusion as we might use a counterpane to conceal a disordered bed.[7]

The concept of "administrative state" implies that the old distinction between policy making and the administration of those policies no longer exists. In the modern, complex, industrial world, policies are initiated, formulated, promulgated, and modified by technocratic experts who hold mid- to high-level positions in America's bureaucracies (federal, state, and local). Although there may be academic squabbles over the degree of power that bureaucracies have acquired, there is virtually no disagreement over the fact that the old dichotomy between policy making and administration is gone and that administrative agencies now perform both functions, fused into one institution. It is a reflection of the administrative state that the secretary of transportation made a policy decision to force automobile manufacturers to install passive restraint systems and the next secretary of transportation re-scinded the rule. The reader should not assume that Secretary Lewis possessed the expertise to make the rescinding decision. That decision was urged by lower-level bureaucrats, probably within the Office of Management and Budget (OMB), who based their recommendations on a cost-benefit analysis. It is equally true that none of Secretary Lewis's predecessors possessed the expertise to recommend (a) passive restraint or (b) specific passive restraints. These recommendations, too, would have come from mid-level bureaucrats who possessed the technical expertise to make them.

Does the existence of the administrative state mean there is no democracy? Not necessarily. If it were true that popularly elected officials exercised considerable control over agencies, then the elements of democracy as we have defined them and outlined them would still exist. In Chapters 2 and 3, the argument is made that neither the chief executive (specifically, the president, but governors and mayors as well) nor legislative bodies (Congress, state legislatures, or city councils) effectively control agencies. What all of this has to do with administrative law is that, almost by default, the job of attempting to control agencies has fallen to the courts, and administrative law is the tool the courts use. The air bag case should make this clear. After readers have digested the cases, concepts, and discussions presented throughout this book, they should be able to reach their own conclusions regarding the state of democracy in the United States. For now, we need to understand the rise of the administrative state.

FROM GEORGE WASHINGTON
TO THE ADMINISTRATIVE STATE

The U.S. polity was founded on certain basic principles, with others evolving early on to form a theoretical framework. The essential components of that framework are as follows: limited government, negative freedom, and laissez-faire economics. *Limited government* is the notion that the powers of government are restricted or limited. Devices such as a written Constitution with a Bill of Rights, the separation of powers, and federalism limit governmental power, which is supposed to be limited to the protection of life, liberty, and/or property. *Negative freedom* is "freedom from." A citizen is free to the degree that no other citizen or government interferes with his or her activity.[8] Thus, where the exercise of governmental power is limited to the protection of life, liberty, and/or property, citizens are truly free. The notion of *laissez-faire economics*—that government should stay out of the economy and allow the free market to determine economic policy—fits hand in glove with the two other notions, negative freedom and limited government.

Although early America had problems such as poverty, poor health, and poor housing, governing elites did not consider the exercise of governmental power to be a proper tool for addressing these problems. In the early 1800s, the United States had a rural population with an agrarian/cottage industry economy. The process of industrialization brings urbanization, and urbanization exacerbates problems such as poverty, poor housing, poor health, crime, hunger, malnutrition, sewage disposal, and alienation, to list just a few. A government based on such concepts as "limited government," "negative freedom," and "laissez-faire economics" (and eventually "social Darwinism") is not an instrument for dealing with such problems.

Eventually, political and social movements began to espouse different positions that challenged the older theoretical framework. Farmers and merchants in the West began to demand that government regulate the rates that businesses (e.g., railroads, grain elevators) charged. Other segments of society began to demand that government take some action to deter child labor and that government take responsibility for educating children. Still others demanded that government take responsibility for a wholesome and edible food supply and that government regulate monopolies. Labor unions began to demand that government pass laws regulating the conditions under which laborers worked. The terms that we use to identify the philosophy that encompasses these calls to governmental action are *positive freedom* and *positive government*. If negative freedom is "freedom from," then positive freedom is "freedom to," and it can generally be achieved with governmental help. *Positive freedom* is the notion that individuals can achieve their fullest potential with governmental help. *Positive government* is the idea that government has a positive role to play in the economy and in people's lives and that it should not be limited simply to protecting life, liberty, and property.[9]

The socialist movement had Otto von Bismarck so concerned for the future of capitalism that, in the 1880s, Germany adopted a social security and national health care system. The British followed suit some twenty years later. In the

United States, the federal government's response to progressive pressure was antitrust legislation and the Federal Trade Commission (FTC). Income taxes and the Federal Reserve Bank were responses to erratic business cycles. Twice, the federal government passed laws against child labor (as did many of the states), but the Supreme Court declared them unconstitutional.

Although it is something of an oversimplification, it can be said that these two philosophies came to a head, after more than fifty years of conflict, in the election of 1932. The philosophy of positive freedom and positive government won out. Although President Franklin D. Roosevelt never used the terms, the first one hundred days of his first administration and the era referred to as the New Deal were the epitome of positive freedom and positive government. Shortly after Franklin Roosevelt became president, a new economic theory compatible with positive freedom and positive government gained credence. That theory was *Keynesian economics* (that government can and should manipulate the demand for goods and services by manipulation of the money supply to lessen the effects of the cycle of inflation and recession/depression). The new public philosophy of positive government, positive freedom, and Keynesian economics replaced the old philosophy of negative freedom, limited government, and laissez-faire economics. If government was now to play a large part in things such as retirement, health care, college education, housing, unemployment, job training, and a clean and safe environment, then government would need to rely on experts to help it deliver services or implement programs (e.g., to recommend safety standards to reduce traffic fatalities). The experts are the public servants who serve in agencies, constituting the situation we have described as the administrative state.

The growth of bureaucracy in the United States closely parallels historical developments. As you would expect from a government founded on the principles of negative freedom and limited government, President George Washington's administration consisted of only a small bureaucracy: the Department of State, the Department of Treasury, the Post Office, the Department of War, and an Office of the Attorney General. One early department was the Army Corps of Engineers (1802), which was created to enhance the flow of commerce through the country. It built the canals. Another early agency was the Patent Office, which was made a federal bureau in 1803; it is necessary in a capitalist society to protect ideas and inventions as a society begins to industrialize. Several cabinet agencies were created after the Civil War, and a few of the first regulatory agencies were created in the clash between the status quo (limited government, negative freedom, and laissez-faire economics) and the progressive movement (positive government and positive freedom). The following is a list of agencies with their dates of creation:

- Department of the Interior, 1849
- Department of Agriculture, 1862
- Department of Commerce and Labor, 1903
- Interstate Commerce Commission (ICC), 1887
- Food and Drug Administration (FDA), 1906
- Federal Trade Commission (FTC), 1914

After the election of President Franklin Roosevelt, a host of agencies were created to help the government deliver services:

- Federal Home Loan Bank, 1932
- Federal Deposit Insurance Corporation (FDIC), 1933
- Tennessee Valley Authority (TVA), 1933
- Federal Communications Commission (FCC), 1934
- National Mediation Board, 1934
- Securities and Exchange Commission (SEC), 1934
- National Labor Relations Board (NLRB), 1935
- Social Security Board, 1935

During World War II, federal bureaucracies nearly ran the country. They did things as diverse as rationing commodities such as gas, butter, and rubber tires and controlling rent prices throughout the whole country.

Despite extensive governmental regulation, the United States relies on the market more than any other industrialized country. For example, we are still the only industrialized country without a national health care system. The market cannot take care of everything, however, and the market has flaws, called *market failures.* The market has no mechanism, for example, to discourage companies from killing rivers and streams by dumping toxic chemicals into them. If it is more profitable to dump toxins into a river than it is to dispose of them safely, then the market dictates that the toxins be dumped. Ditto for clean air and many other aspects of life (e.g., including safer automobiles). If air, water, drivers, workers, and so on are to be protected, then government must do it because the market will not. More agencies were created in the 1960s and 1970s to help with market failures and with new problems that government decided to tackle. These agencies are as follows:

- Department of Housing and Urban Development (HUD), 1965
- Department of Transportation, 1966
- Peace Corps, 1961
- Equal Employment Opportunity Commission (EEOC), 1964

— Environmental Protection Agency (EPA), 1970
— Occupational Safety and Health Administration (OSHA), 1970
— AMTRAK, 1970
— Federal Election Commission, 1971
— Commodity Futures Trading Commission, 1974
— National Transportation Safety Board (NTSB), 1976
— Federal Mine Safety and Health Review Commission, 1977
— Department of Energy, 1977
— Department of Education, 1979

By 1992, the federal bureaucracy, displayed in Figure 1.1, had grown to the point that it consists of the following: (a) an Executive Office of the President, established in 1939, with 1,577 employees spread among thirteen offices and agencies, including the OMB, the National Security Council (NSC), the Council of Economic Advisors (CEA), and the Office of the Vice President (this segment of the bureaucracy is referred to as a *staff agency,* as opposed to a *line agency*; staff agencies have no formal administrative functions, their sole function being to advise the president);[10] (b) fourteen cabinet-level agencies, which employ just over two million people; and (c) sixty independent agencies, governmental corporations, and independent regulatory commissions, hereafter referred to collectively as independent regulatory agencies (IRAs), which employ almost a million workers (997,000). Actually, despite the addition of new agencies and departments, the size of the federal government (in terms of employees) has grown steadily but slowly, compared with the explosive bureaucratic growth at the state and local levels. In 1970, the federal bureaucracy had approximately 2.9 million employees, and in 1988, it had 3.1 million employees. That works out to 7 percent growth over eighteen years, or an average of 0.3 percent per year. State and local bureaucracies, in contrast, grew by 42 percent during the same period.[11] Most people are aware that there is a bureaucracy and that it is large, but they probably cannot explain with much accuracy what bureaucracies do.

WHAT ADMINISTRATIVE AGENCIES DO

Stated simply, agencies (bureaucracies) do everything that all three branches of government do. They make laws (called *rules*), they investigate infractions of those rules, they hold trials to adjudicate infractions of those rules, and they impose sanctions for violations of those rules. Agencies also provide services:

14

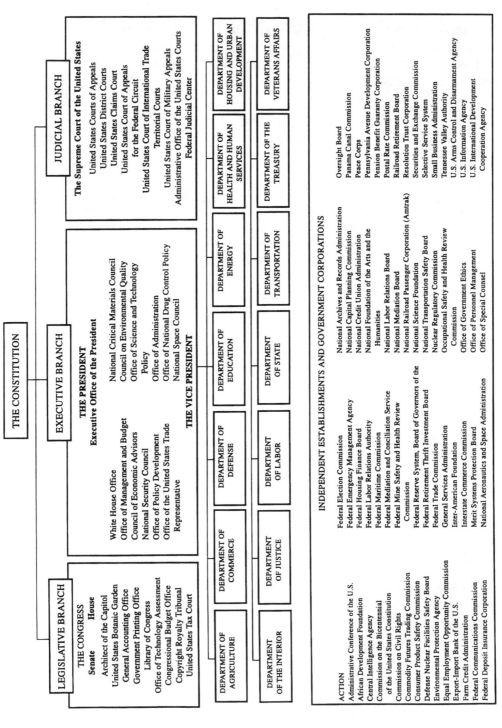

Figure 1.1 The Government of the United States

SOURCE: U.S. Bureau of the Census

They deliver mail, preserve our national parks, maintain veterans hospitals and services, provide disaster relief, issue food stamps, and provide for Social Security. Agencies perform functions as well. For example, bureaus collect revenue and supervise and fund the building of our interstate highway system. One agency, the National Aeronautics and Space Administration (NASA), even sent humans to the moon and brought them back to earth!

Basic to an understanding of agencies is the knowledge that Congress (or the state legislature) is the ultimate source of power. Congress decides whether to create an agency, where it will be located, how long it will live, how much money it will have, and perhaps most important, how much authority it will have and how that authority will be exercised. The term used for this is *enabling legislation.* If a legal question arises concerning an agency's exercise of authority, the courts first look to the Constitution. If no conflict with the Constitution is found, the courts look at the enabling legislation to see whether they can discern legislative intent. Hence, the first principle of administrative law is this: *Always look to the enabling legislation.*

Frequently, Congress creates agencies to deal with pressing problems of the day. Early in the twentieth century, progressive pressure forced Congress to attack the problem of monopolies, which posed a threat to free trade and the market. Congress reacted by passing the Clayton Act in 1914, which made illegal certain business practices recognized as instruments of monopolies. At the same time, Congress passed the Federal Trade Commission Act, which created the FTC and gave it the task of prohibiting "unfair methods of competition" and "unfair or deceptive acts or practices"[12] in interstate commerce. How was the FTC to accomplish this task? Remember that, in 1914, the dominant philosophical framework was still a combination of negative freedom, limited government, and laissez-faire economics and that the notion of an FTC is not compatible with those concepts. It could be argued that although Congress succumbed to progressive pressure to attack monopolies by legislation, Congress was not ready to truly attack the problem by creating an agency with the power to control monopolies. Hence, the FTC was not initially given the power to promulgate rules (that did not come until the early 1970s), nor was it given the power to impose sanctions (it still does not possess such power).[13] The FTC was given the "power" to issue cease and desist orders for "deceptive trade practices" listed elsewhere in legislation. If a company chose not to comply with the cease and desist order, then all the FTC could do was file a suit in federal district court. Today, of course, that means backlog and delay for FTC cease and desist orders.

Many agencies created more recently, however, are provided with a more impressive array of powers than Congress initially provided for the FTC. By the late 1960s, industrial accidents were a leading cause of death in the United States, so again Congress responded to pressure for federal help, in the form of the Occupational Safety and Health Act of 1970. The goal of the act was to reduce the incidence of fatal industrial accidents and to reduce the number of serious industrial accidents. To accomplish this, Congress created OSHA, which describes its duties and responsibilities as follows: "develops and promulgates occupational safety and health standards; develops and issues regulations; conducts investigations and inspections to determine the status of compliance with safety and health standards and regulations; and issues citations and proposes penalties for noncompliance with safety and health standards and regulations."[14]

These powers and duties are typical of most regulatory agencies and even of many cabinet-level agencies at both the federal and state levels today. The enabling legislation creating OSHA is about 17 pages long. The agency has produced 1,658 pages of rules, regulations, and safety standards.[15]

Look again at Figure 1.1 and carefully read the names of the line agencies (cabinet-level departments and IRAs). It will be clear in most cases that the agencies were created to meet a particular problem or to perform a fairly obvious set of tasks. So, what agencies do is attempt to accomplish goals given to them by Congress (e.g., to reduce traffic fatalities and industrial fatalities, to control monopolies) or to accomplish their own goals as implied from congressional direction. Most, but not all, agencies attempt to accomplish those goals by promulgating rules and standards (Chapter 7), investigating infractions of those rules (Chapter 5), adjudicating infractions of those rules (Chapter 7), and, often, imposing sanctions for infractions of those rules. Kenneth Culp Davis, perhaps the foremost authority on administrative law, had this to say about the pervasiveness of public administration in 1958:

> The average person is much more directly and much more frequently affected by the administrative process than by the judicial process. The ordinary person probably regards the judicial process as somewhat remote from his [or her] own problems; a large portion of all people go through life without ever being a party to a lawsuit. But the administrative process affects nearly everyone in many ways nearly every day. The pervasiveness of the effects of the administrative process on the average person can quickly be appreciated by running over a few samples of what the administrative process protects against: excessive prices of electricity, gas, telephone, and other utility services; unreasonableness in rates, schedules, and services of airlines, railroads, street cars, and buses; disregard for the public interest in radio and television and chaotic conditions for broadcasting; unwholesome meat and poultry; adulteration in food; fraud in inadequate disclosure in sale of securities;

physically unsafe locomotives, ships, airplanes, bridges, elevators; unfair labor practices by either employers or unions; false advertising and other unfair or deceptive practices; inadequate safety appliances; uncompensated injuries related to employment; cessation of income during temporary unemployment; subminimum wages; poverty in old age; industrial plants in residential areas; loss of bank deposits; and (perhaps) undue inflation or deflation. Probably the list could be expanded to a thousand or more items that we are accustomed to take for granted.

The volume of the legislative output of federal agencies far exceeds the volume of the legislative output of Congress. The *Code of Federal Regulations* is considerably larger than United States Code. The *Federal Register,* the accumulation of less than one-quarter of a century, fills much more shelf space than the Statutes at Large, the accumulation of nearly a century and three-quarters.[16]

Although not many used the term in 1958, the fourth branch or administrative state was a reality even then. If democracy is a system in which citizens have some input into policies that affect them, and if, increasingly, those decisions are made by bureaucrats rather than by elected officials, then there could be a problem with our democracy. If the president or Congress exercises sufficient control over agencies, then the existence of the administrative state should not be a threat to democracy. An examination of presidential and congressional control of agencies follows in the next two chapters. Before turning our attention to subsequent chapters, however, the student should attempt to ascertain what principles or concepts can be drawn from the case *Motor Vehicle Manufacturers Association v. State Farm Insurance Company,* presented at the beginning of the chapter. For instance, consider the following:

1. Agencies do, in fact, make rules (or set standards) that have significant impact on people's lives, and those rules have the force and effect of law. (The administrative state is a reality.)

2. Often, presidential control over agencies is marginal. (Both President Reagan and his secretary of transportation opposed mandatory passive restraint, but it became policy during Reagan's presidency.)

3. One should always look to the enabling legislation because Congress determines what agencies do and how they must proceed. (In the *State Farm* case, the Court, in fact, decided against the administrator of the National Highway Traffic Safety Administration by turning to the enabling legislation to assess legislative intent.)

4. The courts are the final arbiters in conflicts involving public administration.

SUMMARY

In an attempt to keep things simple but realistic, we have defined democracy as a system in which people have some influence over policies that affect their lives. It is recognized that, frequently, bureaucratic agencies make policies that affect people's lives (the administrative state). If, however, popularly elected officials, such as the president and members of Congress, exercise sufficient control over agencies, then the administrative state is not inconsistent with democracy.

NOTES

1. U.S. Bureau of the Census, *Historical Statistics of the U.S.: Colonial Times to Present,* Part 2 (Washington, DC: U.S. Government Printing Office, 1970), 719.

2. U.S. Bureau of the Census, *Statistical Abstract of the United States,* 111th ed. (Washington, DC: U.S. Government Printing Office, 1991), 78.

3. Robert Weissberg, *Public Opinion and Popular Government* (Upper Saddle River, NJ: Prentice Hall, 1976), 126-32.

4. Robert Erikson, Norman Luttberg, and Kent Tedin, *American Public Opinion: Its Origins, Content, and Impact,* 3d ed. (New York: Macmillan, 1988), 348-51.

5. Kenneth Warren, *Administrative Law in the Political System,* 2d ed. (St. Paul, MN: West, 1988), 108.

6. See Frederic C. Mosher, *Democracy and the Public Service,* 2d ed. (New York: Oxford University Press, 1982), 83-109.

7. *Federal Trade Commission v. Ruberoid Co.,* 343 U.S. 470, 487 (1951) (Justice Jackson dissenting). See also Kenneth J. Meier, *Politics and Bureaucracy: Policymaking in the Fourth Branch of Government* (North Scituate, MA: Duxbury, 1979) and Peter Strauss, "The Place of Agencies in Government: Separation of Powers and the Fourth Branch," *Columbia Law Review* 84 (1984): 574.

8. Sir Isaiah Berlin, "Two Concepts of Liberty," in *Four Essays on Liberty* (New York: Oxford University Press, 1969), 122-34.

9. Ibid.

10. One reason the Iran-Contra Affair was such a fiasco was that a staff agency (the NSC) that is not empowered to accomplish anything assumed the task of selling arms to the enemy and sending the profits to Central America in violation of an act of Congress, whereas line agencies (the Department of State and the Department of Defense), given the authority to sell arms and conduct foreign policy, opposed the scheme.

11. U.S. Bureau of the Census, *Statistical Abstract,* 308, 330.

12. *United States Government Manual 1991/92* (Washington, DC: Office of the Federal Registrar, National Archives and Records Administration, 1991), 600.

13. See, generally, 15 U.S.C. 45. The rulemaking power is granted in 15 U.S.C. 57a.

14. *U.S. Government Manual 1991/92,* 418.

15. 29 C.F.R. 17.

16. Kenneth Culp Davis, *Administrative Law Treatise,* vol. 1 (St. Paul, MN: West, 1958), 7, 8.

CHAPTER 2

EXECUTIVE CONTROL
OF BUREAUCRACY

From Chapter 1, you learned that Congress passes broad and vague pieces of legislation and delegates the power to agencies to write rules, regulations, and standards that provide teeth to the legislation. In any given year, Congress passes fewer than two hundred laws (eighty-eight in 1995). The bureaucracy, however, adopts nearly 5,000 rules, filling 67,715 pages in the *Federal Register*, and it has been estimated that the number of federal bureaucrats writing rules has grown to 122,000.[1]

One primary objective for a chief executive in gaining control over bureaucracy is somehow to control the rule-making power of the agencies. Although the president is the titular head of the federal bureaucracy, Congress creates agencies, gives them rule-making power, and commands them to make rules enforcing legislation. Hence, it is not at all clear whether the president has the constitutional authority to control the rule-making power of agencies.

CASE IN POINT:
DOLE V. UNITED STEELWORKERS OF AMERICA,
110 S.CT. 929 (1990)

The fact that it may be unconstitutional for presidents to control agency rule making mandated by Congress has not stopped modern presidents from attempting to find a way to do it. A more precise history of these attempts is presented later in this chapter, but for now it is enough to know that Presidents Nixon, Ford, Carter, Reagan, and Bush used the Office of Management and Budget (OMB) to exercise control over agency rule making.

President Ronald Reagan, for instance, issued Executive Order 12291. That order required all agency heads to submit proposed rules with an estimated cost to the economy of $100 million or more to the OMB for a cost-benefit analysis prior to beginning the rule-making process.[2] Bear in mind that the OMB is a staff agency, not a line agency, and because its sole legal function is to advise the president, the OMB cannot forbid the promulgation of an agency rule or standard. Because the OMB is so close to the president and the president's advisers, however, OMB disapproval of a proposed rule or standard is tantamount to presidential disapproval (even though the president may not actually be cognizant of all that is going on). Those agency heads or department heads whose jobs depend on continued presidential support are likely to reach a compromise with the OMB.

Presidents Reagan and Bush relied heavily on the Paperwork Reduction Act of 1980 for the statutory authority allowing the OMB to impose its will on agency rule making. The Paperwork Reduction Act was passed to reduce the amount of required paperwork. The administrator of the Occupational Safety and Health Administration (OSHA—an agency within the Department of Labor) proposed a rule called the Hazard Communication Standard, which originally was intended to require all employers to warn their workers about exposure to hazardous substances on the job. Not President Reagan, the president's chief of staff, the secretary of labor, or the director of the OMB wanted to impose the Hazard Communication Standard on business. When the proposed rule was submitted to the OMB as required by Executive Order 12291, the OMB objected, and subsequent to negotiations, OSHA limited the rule to apply only to manufacturing industries. A group of consumer-oriented interest groups and labor unions successfully challenged the narrower rule in court in 1983 and forced OSHA to adopt a new rule that would apply to all work sites in all sections of the economy. The new rule was sent back to the OMB, which again voiced objections, and negotiations between the OMB and OSHA in 1987 produced another modified rule that would not apply to the construction industry. The rule adopted in 1987 was immediately challenged in the courts by the United Steelworkers of America and one of Ralph Nader's organizations. In 1990, the U.S. Supreme Court ruled in *Dole* (for then Secretary of Labor Elizabeth Dole) that the OMB lacked the statutory authority under the Paperwork Reduction Act to block this and other agency rules or standards.[3]

The Court determined that the legislative purpose of the Paperwork Reduction Act was to reduce paperwork that citizens and business had to produce for the federal government. Because the Hazard Communication Standard would produce paperwork intended for workers and not the government, the Paperwork Reduction Act was not applicable. Therefore, the OMB cannot rely on it as a source of authority to block this and similar regulations.

One item in the Republican Party's Contract With America (widely acclaimed as being responsible for the Republican Party capturing control of Congress in the 1994 elections) was to amend the Paperwork Reduction Act. Although Republicans did not campaign on the fact, the reason they wanted to amend the Paperwork Act was to undo or reverse the Supreme Court's decision in the *Dole* case.

The Paperwork Reduction Act of 1995 is one of the few parts of the Contract With America that actually passed both houses of Congress and was signed by President Bill Clinton to become law. The Paperwork Reduction Act referred to in the Case in Point above expired, so Congress passed a new one. The act sets year-by-year targets for the federal government to reduce paperwork (40 percent by 2001). It makes the act applicable to all federal paperwork requirements (addressing the narrow interpretation given to the original act by the Court) and authorizes a bureau within the OMB, the Office of Information and Regulatory Affairs, to exercise control over agency rules with paperwork implications. Thus, presidential control of agency rule making (at least with respect to paperwork) has been restored to the pre-*Dole* state of affairs.

WHY THE PRESIDENT
CANNOT CONTROL BUREAUCRACY

All modern presidents, from FDR to the present, are said to have complained that their worst problem was not the Soviets, not the opposition party, but rather

---

Questions

1. In your opinion, should it be a congressional or an agency decision to decide that workers should be warned about hazardous substances on the job?
2. From reading the preceding description of the *Dole* case, what sense do you get about presidential power to control bureaucracies?
3. If Congress passes a law to meet a problem and then creates an agency to deal specifically with that problem, further instructing the agency to do *X,* should the president interfere with the implementation of *X*? Why or why not?
4. The president has a constitutional mandate to exercise executive power and to see that laws are faithfully executed. What did the Court do to those constitutional mandates in the *Dole* decision?
5. In your opinion, was President Reagan faithfully executing the law as passed by Congress?

---

the very bureaucracy in which the president is supposed to be in charge. After speculation about General Dwight D. Eisenhower's becoming President Eisenhower, Harry Truman is reported to have said, "He'll sit here (Truman would tap his desk for emphasis) and he'll say, 'Do this! Do that!' *And nothing will happen.* Poor Ike—it won't be like the Army. He'll find it very frustrating."[4]

Truman also said, "I sit here all day trying to persuade people to do the things they ought to have sense enough to do without my persuading them. . . . That's all the powers of the President amount to."[5] An aide to President Eisenhower said, "The President still feels that when he's decided something, that *ought* to be the end of it . . . and when it comes back undone or done wrong he tends to react with shocked surprise."[6]

President Lyndon Johnson is supposed to have once said that the only power he had was nuclear and that he could not use it.[7] More recently, President Jimmy Carter complained, "I can't even get a damn mouse out of my office." Apparently, the president's request to remove the mouse got lost in a bureaucratic turf battle between the Department of the Interior, which has jurisdiction over the White House grounds, and the General Services Administration, which has jurisdiction over the White House building (which, of course, sits on the White House grounds).[8]

The public statements of undeclared presidential candidate Ross Perot in the 1992 election campaign epitomize typical American ignorance about presidential power: He said, "It's time to pick up the shovel and clean out the barn." He was referring to the process of U.S. government. At the root of the problem of presidential control over bureaucracy is the fact that the Founding

Fathers did not provide the office of the presidency with either the tools or the processes to "pick up the shovel and clean out the barn."

Most modern presidents have possessed the will to control bureaucracy; they simply have lacked the power. Although Perot should have known better, the misconception about the office of the presidency seems to be widespread, especially among younger generations who grew up getting their news from television. Perhaps it is simply easier to cover the president than it is to cover 535 members of Congress or even, say, 20 or so congressional leaders, but for whatever reason, the media spend an inordinate amount of airtime covering the president. Perhaps this has led people to believe that the office is more powerful than it really is.

Constitutional Powers

It is instructive to examine the list of presidential powers:

1. Article I, Section 7, defines the veto: On January 1, 1997, the president became vested with the *line item veto* (the power to veto or strike specific lines in the budget, a power shared with the governors of two thirds of the states). The president does not possess an *amendatory veto* (allowing the executive to veto [amend] objectional parts of legislation other than budgets). As of the writing of this edition, President Clinton has used the line item veto, and members of Congress have challenged its constitutionality. Many experts believe that it will be declared unconstitutional because it significantly shifts power among the branches of government without an amendment to the Constitution.

2. Article II, Section 1, provides that executive power be vested in the president. You will see shortly that this section does not provide a residual of "executive power" for the president to use.

3. Article II, Section 2, names the president commander in chief and gives him or her power to do the following:
   a. require written opinions from department heads (this is the only reference in the Constitution to the bureaucracy)
   b. grant reprieves and pardons
   c. make appointments (with advice and consent of the Senate)
   d. make treaties (with advice and consent of the Senate)
   e. make appointments during congressional recess

4. Article II, Section 3, states that the president may do the following:
   a. inform Congress of the state of the union
   b. recommend legislation to Congress
   c. on extraordinary occasion convene Congress
   d. adjourn Congress should both houses disagree on adjournment

   e. receive ambassadors
   f. take care that the laws be faithfully executed

These are not the powers of the most powerful executive in the world today. Indeed, those who wrote the Constitution did not intend for the office to be powerful. They intended the president to have only enough power to carry out the wishes of Congress.

Extraconstitutional Powers

It is true, however, that the presidency is more powerful today than the preceding list suggests. That is because Supreme Court decisions have provided the presidency with enormous power in the area of foreign policy. By a combination of historical use and Court decisions, there are also extraconstitutional powers, such as impoundment, executive agreements, executive privilege, and delegation of power.

To understand presidential power today is to recognize a bifurcated presidency: one presidency that, in foreign affairs, is quite powerful and another presidency that, in domestic affairs, requires action by Congress in nearly every situation and hence is significantly weaker.

The Supreme Court recognized and sanctioned a notion referred to as the sole organ theory in cases such as *United States v. Curtis-Wright Export Corporation,* 299 U.S. 304 (1936) and *United States v. Belmont,* 301 U.S. 324 (1937). The *sole organ theory* is the concept that foreign policy must be conducted by one office occupied by one recognizable individual with the authority to speak for the whole nation. Hence, there is no room for fifty individual states to have a voice in foreign affairs, nor is there any room for shared power with Congress. In the *Curtis-Wright* case, the Supreme Court said,

> In this vast external realm [foreign policy] with its important, complicated, delicate and manifold problems, the President alone has the power to speak or listen as a representative of the nation. He *makes* treaties with the advice and consent of the Senate; but he alone negotiates. Into the field of negotiation the Senate cannot intrude; and Congress itself is powerless to invade it.[9]

In the *Belmont* case, the Court sanctioned the practice of executive agreements (legally binding agreements between the president and other heads of state that do not need senatorial approval and hence circumvent the treaty provision in Article II of the Constitution). Finally, Congress has delegated some of its foreign policy powers to the president. For example, in the War Powers Resolution of 1973, Congress delegated to the president its power to declare war, and in the *Curtis-Wright* case, Congress delegated its power to enact embargoes.

The cumulative effect of congressional delegations, executive agreements, and Supreme Court decisions supportive of the sole organ theory renders presidential power almost unchecked in the area of foreign policy. By way of example, Congress had tried to control and limit the use of executive agreements to no avail, so in 1972 it passed a law requiring the president to notify it of each executive agreement (Case-Zablocki Act, 1 U.S.C. § 112b). Modern presidents routinely ignore this law with no consequences, legal, political, or otherwise.[10]

Presidential power on the domestic side is a wholly different story. As you can see from the preceding list of presidential powers, no domestic power is granted solely to the president (except for the pardon power). Again, the extraconstitutional powers of impoundment, executive privilege, and delegation of power have rendered the presidency, on the domestic side, more powerful than the list of constitutional powers suggests.

Impoundment is the idea that the president simply refuses to spend money that has been appropriated by Congress. Generally, when presidential impoundments are challenged in court, the president loses. Congress has attempted to regulate presidential impoundment through the Congressional Budget and Impoundment Control Act of 1974. The president today, however, still manages to impound nearly $12 billion annually.[11]

Executive privilege means that, to enhance presidential decision making, the president (and advisers) may withhold information from Congress and even sometimes from a court of law. The concept is explored more fully in Chapter 5 under the Freedom of Information Act, but suffice it to say here that executive privilege increases power in the White House to the degree that information and control of it is power.

Delegation of power is a concept to which you have already been exposed, but it has not been defined for you. Delegation of power is a topic central to the next chapter on congressional control of agencies. It is simply an instance in which Congress entrusts its constitutional Article I, Section 8, powers to the executive branch. For example, when Congress decides to reduce traffic fatalities or to reduce industrial fatalities, it assigns its lawmaking power to an agency so that the agency can "execute the law." When Congress delegates its power to the president, that enhances the power of the presidency. Congress rarely assigns its power directly to the president, however. Instead, it generally transfers its power to an executive agency (e.g., OSHA, Department of Transportation). The degree to which the president can control agencies is the degree to which presidential power is increased via delegation of power. From the examples of air bag regulation and the Hazard Communication Standard, you should begin to understand that presidential control of agencies is slippery, at best. Richard Neustadt, perhaps the foremost authority on the presidency, argues that presidential power amounts to the power to persuade.[12] This is particularly true on the domestic side.

In the famous *Steel Seizure*[13] case, the Supreme Court addressed an exercise of presidential power that was domestic but had serious foreign policy implications. During the Korean War, the steelworkers union threatened to strike the industry, which had refused to bargain in good faith.[14] President Truman and executive officials tried to get the two sides to settle, but to no avail. With a strike against the entire steel industry scheduled for midnight on April 9, 1952, Truman ordered Secretary of Commerce Charles Sawyer to seize the steel mills and keep them operating. Youngstown Sheet and Tube Company and other steel mills filed suit, and less than two months later the Supreme Court declared Truman's seizure to be unconstitutional. Although the case is fascinating and important, what has come to be most important from this case is Justice Jackson's concurring opinion. Jackson's opinion in the case is important because the modern Supreme Court relies on it when it is called on to assess particular issues of presidential power. Justice Jackson said that presidential power falls into the following three categories:[15]

1. When the president acts pursuant to a congressional delegation of power, the president's power is at a maximum because the president is using all the power of the executive branch plus all the power of Congress.
2. When a president acts and Congress has said nothing on the subject, the president must rely on the powers of Article II of the Constitution to justify the action.
3. When presidential action is "incompatible with the expressed or implied will of Congress, his power is at its lowest ebb."[16]

To emphasize the point, Congress, in the steel seizure scenario, had not forbidden the president from nationalizing or seizing companies. However, a bill had been introduced to grant the president the power to seize important industries during war or emergencies, and this bill died in committee. The Court considered the bill's demise to be the "implied will of Congress" and, therefore, one in which the president had acted counter to congressional will. His power was at its lowest ebb, and the action could not be justified by Article II of the Constitution. Hence, the presidential action was unconstitutional.

THE TOOLS OF
PRESIDENTIAL CONTROL

As indicated earlier, modern presidents have had the will and, perhaps, a strong desire to control bureaucracy but have not met with much success because the raw power (the ability to make one do that which one does not want to do) is not there. Any standard U.S. government textbook provides a list of tools that presidents use in attempting to control agencies.[17] Those tools are appointments, removal, reorganization, issuing executive orders, the budget, and OMB screening of proposed agency rules. Finally, in this section, the concept of "administrative presidency" is analyzed.

Presidential Appointments

A president has the potential to appoint more than 1,300 officials, all of which require senatorial approval.[18] Some of these positions are policy-making positions (e.g., cabinet secretaries), and some are judges, U.S. marshals, ambassadors, and so on. With many of these appointments, the president's choices are constrained by senatorial courtesy. *Senatorial courtesy* requires the president to appoint the choice of the senior senator of the president's party from the state where the vacant seat occurs. Presidential failure to do so is likely to result in the Senate's refusal to confirm. The president is also able to make another 1,140 bureaucratic appointments.[19]

The common assumption might be that, in those situations in which the president can appoint his or her own choice to head an agency, presidential control would be enhanced over that agency. To test this presumption, assume that you have been appointed by your longtime friend and political associate, the governor, to a seat on the Public Utilities Commission. In several weeks, you will be expected to vote on a proposal by the major electric utility company in your state to raise its rates by 35 percent. The utility company has produced a three-volume report with facts, figures, and charts documenting rising costs, rising overhead, and dwindling revenues. A local consumer group has produced a similar document showing that the utility made some poor investments and simply wants to recoup losses at the consumers' expense. Repeated attempts to discuss this with your old friend, the governor, have failed because of your inability to get past the appointment secretary and chief of staff. How will you vote? How and where will you get independent information to help you in casting an intelligent vote? The answer is the same for you as it was for the secretary of transportation when he had to decide how best to reduce traffic fatalities; both you and the secretary turn to the technical experts who work for the Department of Transportation and the Public Utilities Commission (midlevel bureaucrats).

The preceding scenario introduces the concept of "captivity." Because presidential appointees average less than two years at a position and frequently are unfamiliar with the agency or department they are appointed to head, political appointees often become the captives of the midlevel career bureaucrats who have been in the agency for decades. These bureaucrats possess the expertise on which the appointee comes to depend. They also have more political influence and clout than the appointee because they have spent years cultivating a political base with members of Congress and also with powerful interest groups that have a vested interest in what happens at the agency.[20] Perhaps the following quotations will provide the reader with a real grasp of some problems that presidents have with appointees:

> In a real sense, delegation of authority to an operating manager of an entirely unfamiliar field [i.e., secretary delegates to the bureaucrat] means that the secretary serves the bureau chief rather than vice versa.[21]

> [The secretary's] judgement on budget items is, of course, the most important decision he will make in his term of office and is the decision he is usually least well-equipped to make intelligently.[22]

> The President's title, "Chief Executive," is a misnomer. More accurately the president can be described as a "Nonexecutive Chief" for the White House is far from being the command center of the executive branch. Although the president appoints the heads of great operating departments and agencies, the principal resources upon which they depend . . . are derived from acts of Congress. Programs and policies, to the extent that they are implemented, are carried out by tenured civil servants, who were on the job before the incumbent president arrived and who will remain there after he leaves.[23]

> The single most powerful figure in the great pyramid is the bureau chief, who in many substantive ways can frustrate the president's purposes when they diverge from his own. He cultivates ties with pressure groups whose interests his organization serves and [with] the congressional committees that provide him with money and authority. Congressional committees and subcommittees welcome his attentions since all are united in a common purpose, protecting the integrity of the bureau's functions. Presidents sometimes feel so remote from the bureaus that they lose sight of their responsibility to oversee them.[24]

Presidential candidate Ronald Reagan said that, if elected, he would bring about "a new structuring of the presidential cabinet that will make cabinet officers the managers of the national administration—not captives of the bureaucracy or special interests they are supposed to direct."[25]

Presidents Nixon, Ford, and Carter tried to get agencies to move in particular directions and met with little success. More recently, Presidents Reagan and Bush tried to get the bureaucracy to stop moving at all, and although it is fair to say that Reagan enjoyed somewhat more success than either his predecessors or Bush, he was not entirely successful either.[26] The two cases presented so far, *State Farm* and *Dole,* are two examples in which the president (Reagan), his appointed secretaries, the director of the OMB, and his chief of staff were all adamantly opposed to what the agencies wanted to do, and yet passive restraint and the Hazard Communication Standard are the law of the land today. The mere fact that a president appoints a department head whose job security depends on presidential goodwill is not sufficient to enhance presidential control over agencies.

Presidential Removal

Although the Constitution clearly rests the appointment power in the president with senatorial consent, the document is silent on the question of the president's power to remove those he or she has appointed. One might logically assume that because Article II of the Constitution places executive power in the president, the president's ability to remove those who serve in the executive branch would be somewhat unrestricted. Presidential removal power is not that clear, however, and to understand it, we must examine several Supreme Court cases on the subject.

In 1876, Congress passed an act providing for four-year terms for first-, second-, and third-class postmasters and further provided that such postmasters would be appointed and *removed* by the president with the *consent of the Senate.* In 1920, President Woodrow Wilson (or perhaps Mrs. Wilson) ordered the postmaster general to fire a first-class postmaster in Portland (Mr. Myers), but there was no senatorial consent to this firing. Although Myers died, his wife, as administratrix of his estate, sued to recover lost salary. In *Myers v. United States,* 272 U.S. 52 (1926), the Supreme Court said that that portion of the act of 1876 requiring senatorial consent to presidential removal decisions was unconstitutional. The Court reasoned that, without the absolute and unrestrained power to remove those the president has appointed, a president would be unable to (a) exercise executive power or (b) faithfully execute the laws of the United States as required by Article II of the Constitution.

Nine years later, however, the question faced the Court again. This time, President Franklin D. Roosevelt fired William Humphrey, who had been appointed to a seven-year term on the Federal Trade Commission (FTC) by President Herbert Hoover. Actually, FDR asked Humphrey to resign, saying that it was no reflection on Humphrey personally or his performance as a commissioner but that there were deep ideological differences between what FDR believed the FTC should be doing and what Humphrey believed it should do. When Humphrey refused to resign, FDR fired him. The problem this time was that the Federal Trade Commission Act specifies that commissioners may be removed only for "inefficiency, neglect of duty or malfeasance in office." Because, by the president's own admission, Humphrey met none of the criteria for removal, Humphrey sued. Curiously enough, before the case could be settled, Humphrey (like Myers) died. Hence, the case is entitled *Humphrey's Executor v. United States,* 295 U.S. 602 (1935). Two constitutional issues were before the Supreme Court: first, whether the language in the section limiting removal of commissioners for cause was intended to limit the president's power of removal, and second, if so, is that part of the act constitutional? The Court answered in the affirmative on both issues. Congress could restrict the removal power of the president to removal for cause, and that restriction was a constitutional prerogative of Congress.

The Court said that whether the president's power of removal under the executive power in Article II of the Constitution can be restricted by Congress depends on the nature of the office involved. On the one hand, some offices are political and may involve policy making. Such offices are meant to fall under executive control, and in those instances, Congress cannot restrict presidential removal power. On the other hand, some offices have functions that are not political, executive, or policy oriented but, rather, are simply to enforce or implement the law through quasi-judicial or quasi-legislative procedures. The latter offices have as their basis expertise, rather than politics, and were intended from their creation to be politically independent. To these types of offices, the president's removal power does not extend absolutely and may be restricted as in the case here involving the FTC.

> The commission [FTC] is to be non-partisan; and must . . . act with impartiality. It is charged with the enforcement of no policy except the policy of the law. Its duties are neither political nor executive, but predominantly quasi-judicial and quasi-legislative. Like the ICC, its members are called upon to

exercise the trained judgement of a body of experts "appointed by law and informed by experience."[27]

The Role of Law

You are about to read the first case from Supreme Court records presented in this text, but before you do, think about what the Supreme Court does when it decides a case. The main function of the Supreme Court is to resolve issues of constitutional law so that citizens and officials will understand what can and cannot be done under the Constitution or the laws of Congress. Questions such as the following are classic: whether the Constitution forbids capital punishment, whether it forbids abortion, whether it forbids separate schools for black students and white students. Generally, when the Court answers these questions, it establishes a *doctrine*, a legal principle or rule, that will guide behavior in the future in situations involving similar facts.

The student is not exposed to all the cases in an area of law in a text such as this but, rather, to the ones that establish doctrines or legal tests. Often, the text presents a recent or interesting case so that the reader can see how (or whether) the Court applied the doctrine. What would you say is the doctrine in the *Myers* case? Can you identify a doctrine for the *Humphrey* case? Do you believe that the Court overruled the *Myers* doctrine in the *Humphrey* case?

If you said that the doctrine from the *Myers* case was something like, "the President's removal power is absolute," you would be right. The doctrine from the *Humphrey* case is a bit more complicated: The president's removal power is absolute for those offices that are political or executive in nature. Removal power can be restricted for those offices that Congress intended to be free from political control and those offices that perform quasi-judicial or quasi-legislative functions. The Court did not overrule *Myers* in *Humphrey* but, rather, modified it to restrict the area of unbridled presidential removal. For the case that follows (and those throughout the text), think about the following:

1. After you have read the facts, predict how the Court will decide the case, given the doctrine.
2. Ask yourself whether the Court followed doctrine or whether it created a new doctrine or test.
3. Do you understand why the Court decided the case the way it did?

WIENER V. UNITED STATES
357 U.S. 349 (1958)

Justice Frankfurter delivered the opinion for a unanimous Court.

This a suit for back pay, based on petitioner's alleged illegal removal as a member of the War Claims Commission. The facts are not in dispute. By the War Claims Act of 1948, Congress established that Commission with "jurisdiction to receive and adjudicate according to law," claims for compensating internees, prisoners of war, and religious organizations, who suffered personal injury or property damage at the hands of the enemy in connection with World War II. The Commission was to be composed of three persons, at least two of whom were to be members of the bar, to be appointed by the President, by and with the advice and consent of the Senate. The Commission was to wind up its affairs not later than three years after the expiration of the time for filing claims, originally limited to two years but extended by successive legislation first to March 1, 1951, and later to March 31, 1952. This limit on the Commission's life was the mode by which the tenure of the Commissioners was defined, and Congress made no provision for removal of a Commissioner.

Having been duly nominated by President Truman, the petitioner was confirmed on June 2, 1950, and took office on June 8, following. On his refusal to heed a request for his resignation, he was, on December 10, 1953, removed by President Eisenhower in the following terms: "I regard it as in the national interest to complete the administration of the War Claims Act of 1948, as amended, with personnel of my own selection." The following day, the President made recess appointments to the Commission, including petitioner's post. After Congress assembled, the President, on February 15, 1954, sent the names of the new appointees to the Senate. The Senate had not confirmed these nominations when the Commission was abolished, July 1, 1954. Thereupon, petitioner brought this proceeding in the Court of Claims for recovery of his salary as a War Claims Commissioner from December 10, 1953, the day of his removal by the President, to June 30, 1954, the last day of the Commission's existence. A divided Court of Claims dismissed the petition, 142 F.Supp. 910. We brought the case here, because it presents a variant of the constitutional issue decided in *Humphrey's Executor v.*

United States. Controversy pertaining to the scope and limits of the President's power of removal fills a thick chapter of our political and judicial history. The long stretches of its history, beginning with the very first Congress, with early echoes in the Reports of this Court, were laboriously traversed in *Myers v. United States,* and need not be retraced. President Roosevelt's reliance upon the pronouncements of the Court in that case in removing a member of the Federal Trade Commission on the ground that "the aims and purposes of the Administration with respect to the work of the Commission can be carried out most effectively with personnel of my own selection" reflected contemporaneous professional opinion regarding the significance of the *Myers* decision. Speaking through a Chief Justice who himself had been President, the Court did not restrict itself to the immediate issue before it, the President's inherent power to remove a postmaster, obviously an executive official. As of set purpose and not by way of parenthetic casualness, the Court announced that the President had inherent constitutional power of removal also of officials who have "duties of a quasi-judicial character * * * whose decisions after hearing affect interests of individuals, the discharge of which the President cannot in a particular case properly influence or control." This view of presidential power was deemed to flow from his "constitutional duty of seeing that the laws be faithfully executed." The assumption was short-lived that the *Myers* case recognized the President's inherent constitutional power to remove officials, no matter what the relation of the executive to the discharge of their duties and no matter what restrictions Congress may have imposed regarding the nature of their tenure. The versatility of circumstances often mocks a natural desire for definitiveness. Within less than ten years a unanimous Court, in *Humphrey's Executor v. United States,* narrowly confined the scope of the *Myers* decision to include only "all purely executive officers." The Court explicitly "disapproved" the expressions in *Myers* supporting the President's inherent constitutional power to remove members of quasi-judicial bodies. Congress had given members of the Federal Trade Commission a seven-year term and also provided for the removal of a Commissioner by the President for inefficiency, neglect of duty or malfeasance in office. In the present case, Congress provided for a tenure defined by the relatively short period of time during which the War Claims Commission was to operate—that is, it was to wind up not later than three years after the expiration of the time for filing of claims. But nothing was said in the Act about removal. . . . And what is the essence of the decision in *Humphrey's* case? It drew a sharp line of cleavage between officials who were part of the Executive establishment and were thus removable by virtue of the President's constitutional powers, and those who are members of a body "to exercise its judgment without the leave or hindrance of any other official or any department of the government," as to whom a power of removal exists only if Congress may fairly be said to have conferred it. This sharp differentiation derives from the difference in functions between those who are part of the Executive establishment and those whose tasks require absolute freedom from Executive interference. "For it is quite evident," again to quote *Humphrey's Executor,* "that one who holds his office only during the pleasure of another, cannot be depended upon to maintain an attitude of independence against the latter's will."

Thus, the most reliable factor for drawing an inference regarding the President's power of removal in our case is the nature of the function that Congress vested in the War Claims Commission. . . . The Commission was established as an adjudicating body with all the paraphernalia by which legal claims are put to the test of proof, with finality of determination "not subject to review by any other official of the United States or by any court by mandamus or otherwise." The final form of the legislation, as we have seen, left the widened range of claims to be determined by adjudication.

Congress could, of course, have given jurisdiction over these claims to the District Courts or to the Court of Claims. The fact that it chose to establish a Commission to "adjudicate according to law" the classes of claims defined in the statute did not alter the intrinsic judicial character of the task with which the Commission was charged. The claims were to be "adjudicated according to law," that is, on the merits of each claim, supported by evidence and governing legal considerations, by a body that was "entirely free from the control or coercive influence, direct or indirect," of either the Executive or the Congress. If, as one must take for granted, the War Claims Act precluded the President from influencing the Commission in passing on a particular claim, a fortiori must it be inferred that Congress did not wish to have hang over the Commission the Damocles' sword of removal by the President for no reason other than that he preferred to have on that Commission men of his own choosing. . . . Judging the matter in all the nakedness in which it is presented, namely, the claim that the President could remove a member of an adjudicatory body like the War Claims Commission merely because he wanted his own appointees on such a Commission, we are compelled to conclude that no such power is given to the President directly by the Constitution, and none is impliedly conferred upon him by statute simply because Congress said nothing about it. The philosophy of *Humphrey's Executor,* in its explicit language as well as its implications, precludes such a claim.

The judgment is reversed.

Questions

1. Do you believe that the Court created a new doctrine in this case, or did it simply apply the existing law?
2. Wiener won this case (and Eisenhower lost). Can you explain why?

The problem with the Court's doctrine regarding presidential removal is that it rests on a simplistic notion that a clear and distinct dichotomy exists between policy making on the one hand and simple administration of those policies on the other. We know from our discussion in Chapter 1 that that dichotomy no longer exists. The doctrine in *Humphrey* survived for more than fifty years, until the Court decided *Morrison v. Olson,* 487 U.S. 654 (1988), which is included at the end of this chapter. The point relative to a discussion of presidential removal power is that, as a tool of presidential control over administrative agencies, removal power is not always effective—or even available. The *Morrison* case further erodes presidential power in the area of both appointment and removal.

Executive Reorganization

Executive reorganization refers to presidential efforts to shift, combine, or eliminate agencies. All agencies are created and funded by Congress, not the president; therefore, the president lacks the power or authority to modify the jurisdiction or organizational structure of any cabinet-level bureau or an independent regulatory agency. Indeed, under the Reorganization Act, the president may submit a reorganization plan to Congress, transferring functions among agencies. Only if Congress endorses the plan within ninety days does it become effective (a process that is now constitutionally suspect; see Chapter 3). This is how the Environmental Protection Agency (EPA) was created in 1970.[28] The president does, however, possess the power to reorganize the staff agencies, the Executive Office of the President. Look again at Figure 1.1. The president may reorganize without congressional interference, but, of course, it would require a congressional appropriation to continue to operate any reorganized staff agency. In terms of the president's control over agency activity, the "power to reorganize" is not a power at all. The president's ability to reorganize departments depends, as Neustadt said about twenty years ago,[29] on the president's ability to persuade Congress and the heads of agencies involved to do it. In 1980, as a presidential candidate, Reagan made it a campaign promise to get rid of the Departments of Education and Energy. The astute reader will notice that those two agencies still exist today, as healthy as they ever were.

Executive Orders

The president has the ability to issue executive orders. Remember that the Constitution does not give the president a policy-making role; therefore, the most effective executive orders are the ones that execute congressional legislation. For example, the Natural Gas Policy Act of 1978, 15 U.S.C. § 3301-343, authorizes the president to issue executive orders declaring natural gas emergencies during shortages. It also authorizes executive orders allocating gas supplies for high-priority use.[30]

President Reagan's Executive Order 12291, 46 Fed.Reg. 13193 (1981) (referred to in the *Dole* case at the beginning of this chapter) required all executive agencies, "to the extent permitted by law," not to issue rules at all unless the benefits outweighed the costs. Further, it required agencies to prepare an impact analysis of their proposed rules, regulations, or standards. This executive order was not issued pursuant to any congressional action and therefore rests solely for its legal authority on Article II of the Constitution, vesting executive power in the president. The phrase "to the extent permitted by law" suggests that when a conflict arises between an agency attempting to fulfill congressional mandates and Executive Order 12291, the executive order must give way. Congress has, for example, forbidden OSHA to use a cost-benefit analysis in creating safety standards.[31] Therefore, OSHA not only need not, but literally cannot, comply with Executive Order 12291. In *Environmental Defense Fund [EDF] v. Thomas,* 627 F.Supp. 566 (D.D.C. 1986),[32] a federal district court in Washington, D.C., held that an OMB review of cost-benefit impact analysis cannot be used to keep agencies from complying with statutory deadlines.

Much publicity and fanfare accompanied President George Bush's executive order placing a moratorium on all federal agency rules and regulations for ninety days so that existing rules, regulations, and standards could be reviewed.[33] The theory was that those regulations not meeting Bush's approval would be eliminated. From the *State Farm* case in Chapter 1, however, the Court said that a notice and hearing process are required by an agency to rescind a rule. Therefore, it was not certain that those rules that Bush (actually a committee of his advisers headed by Vice President Dan Quayle) disliked would be eliminated. Further, we know from the *Environmental Defense Fund v. Thomas* case just cited that the moratorium executive order could not be used to delay statutory deadlines. Finally, the weight of constitutional evidence suggests that the moratorium could not interfere with agencies promulgating regulations in compliance with a congressional mandate. Indeed, by the administration's own admission, rules required by statute and those likely to benefit the economy would be exempt.[34] What's left? The point is that executive orders are a tool for presidential management but are most effective when "taking care that the laws be faithfully executed."

The Budget

Although some textbooks are entirely devoted to the budget process, to evaluate presidential control of agencies via the budget, the student needs to understand the broad contours of the budget process. By June of each year, the president has developed economic assumptions about the fiscal year to begin in October of the next year. He or she has decided what the total spending will be, estimated revenues, and speculated as to the size of the deficit. All of this is done with the help of the OMB, which then transmits this information to the various bureaus and agencies. They are given spending targets and have until September to submit proposed agency budgets to the OMB. At that point, the OMB may or may not modify agency proposed budgets. The OMB holds budget hearings with the various agencies during the fall, and between December and February, the OMB, the White House staff, and the president develop the president's budget, which is submitted to Congress in February.

Congress has its own counterpart to the OMB called the Congressional Budget Office (CBO), which does its own analysis of the economy, projected revenues, and deficits. On the basis of the CBO, the OMB, and the president's proposed budget, Congress passes a budget resolution, which is a spending limit for the coming fiscal year. This is done by April 15. Next, the House and Senate appropriations committees decide how much to spend on specific programs and how much to give to individual agencies (the congressional side of the budget process is dealt with in more detail in the next chapter).

OMB Screening of Proposed Agency Rules

In a procedure called *sequester,* the OMB issues a report that indicates whether spending limits have been exceeded and recommends withholding funds in specific areas to meet the spending limits. The president must then sequester the funds identified by the OMB.[35]

It is the president's budget in the sense that, if his or her budget calls for $1.4 trillion in spending, Congress will pass a budget with $1.4 trillion in spending, but Congress frequently changes the amounts *within* the budget from the president's proposals. Given that the OMB and its director are close to the president and given the OMB's role in setting agency budgets, it is fair to say that the president exerts significant control over agencies in terms of spending limits. Agencies have a good deal of latitude about how they spend within their budgets, but whether an agency will grow and prosper and start new programs or whether it will simply maintain or even suffer cuts seems to be determined by the OMB in close collusion with the White House staff. In the past, when presidents (or their budget directors) cut an agency's budget, it was not unheard of for the bureau chief to go to Congress to get the cuts restored. President Reagan's first budget director, David Stockman, put a stop to that practice. He let it be known that bureau chiefs who did not preach the administration's line before congressional committees would be transferred to Butte, Montana, or would be required to submit status reports every Monday, Wednesday, and Friday, and so on. More recent budget directors have continued the practice but more subtly. Ours is a government of checks and balances, however, and Congress fought back against budget directors who dealt too high-handedly with bureau chiefs whom Congress (and interest groups) had come to know and respect. When Congress threatened to cut the budget of the OMB under Reagan, the budget director backed off.

Especially after the *Dole* decision, the president may have difficulty directly controlling agency rules via a cost-benefit analysis at the OMB. The president can, however, have an impact on agency rule-making activity more subtly through the OMB's role in the budget process. In that respect, the president can exercise control over agencies through the budget. It is just possible, however (depending on the agency), for Congress to restore OMB-recommended cuts. This could happen because powerful congressional committee chairpersons do not want to see a particular agency suffer cuts or because interest groups that have a vested interest in the agency lobby Congress to restore the cuts. It is also likely that if Congress has exceeded spending caps (and it nearly always does), then the budget director might single out that agency for cuts in the sequester procedure.

Generally, recent presidents (especially Reagan and Bush) have been able to exercise more control over agencies through the budget than have their predecessors. That is because the OMB has become so centralized and influential, not only in the budget process but also in other aspects involving agencies. Not only must agencies submit proposed rules or standards to the OMB for cost-benefit analysis, but agencies must also submit a proposal for congressional legislation to the OMB.

THE ADMINISTRATIVE PRESIDENCY

The fact that the OMB has become so involved in the daily lives of agencies is a natural consequence of a quest on behalf of successive presidents to find a way to control agencies. The quest started with President Richard Nixon, and the concept is called "the administrative presidency."[36]

When President Nixon was elected in 1968, he had an agenda that he wanted to fulfill. He tried to accomplish his goals by submitting legislation to Congress, but his administration was not particularly successful at dealing with Congress. After two years, he decided to try to accomplish his goals by using the bureaucracy, rather than by going through Congress, and he quickly discovered that the chief executive ("nonexecutive chief") does not control the bureaucracy. He was reelected in 1972 with a resolve to find out how to control agencies, but the Watergate scandal unfolded before he could accomplish much.

The reasons why presidents could not control agencies in Nixon's days are as follows: (a) Mid- and high-level bureaucrats who really controlled power and authority (and information and expertise) within bureaucracies were protected by civil service laws (now the Office of Personnel Management), and it was almost impossible to fire them; (b) presidential appointees quickly became the captives of the agencies they were supposed to run and soon displayed more allegiance to the agency than to the president; (c) probably because of the first two reasons, the president had no control over agency promulgation of rules, regulations, and standards (such rules being the essence of the administrative state, it is crucial for a president who would control agencies to control agency rule making); and (d) the president had little control over agency budgets because when the president proposed to cut an agency's budget, the bureau chief, who was protected by civil service laws, could simply go to Congress and get the budget restored.

The key to the administrative presidency, then, is to find ways to counter the effects of civil service laws protecting high-level bureaucrats, counter the effects of captivity, control agency rule making, and gain budgetary control over the agencies. Nixon began to try some of this by executive reorganization. He created "super secretaries" who would be in close presidential contact and have jurisdiction over broad areas of domestic policy within the Executive Office of the President, as well as head their cabinet agencies. Nixon also used the OMB in an attempt to exercise control.[37] Nixon's plan was not in place long enough to assess whether he would have been successful. Actually, Jimmy Carter was the president responsible for creating one major aspect of the administrative presidency, the Senior Executive Service (SES), a modification of the civil service system. Under the system created by Carter, high-level bureaucrats, those who head bureaus or agencies, are given the choice of remaining under the protection of civil service laws or choosing to enter the SES. If they choose SES, they will forfeit civil service job protection in favor of higher pay that would more closely approximate what private industry would pay for a position of such responsibility. Today, about 95 percent of those eligible for the SES have taken the opportunity. This reduces the possibility that bureau chiefs will "end run" the president's budget by going to Congress to restore OMB cuts. Good administrative theories exist for having an SES,[38] but neither President Reagan nor President Bush made effective use of it, except politically, because it provides the White House with more control over senior administrators just below the appointed officials.

President Reagan completed the administrative presidency by taking the following steps:

1. To counter captivity, his political appointments to agencies were based, not on patronage, management skill, or administrative experience, but rather on ideology. No one would be appointed to a position within an agency who did not believe that the federal government was bloated and needed to pare back. Because these appointees did not care whether they got along with their professional colleagues in the agency or, indeed, whether the business of the agency got done, the problem of captivity was pretty well solved.
2. President Reagan made effective use of Executive Order 12291, the Paperwork Reduction Act, and the OMB to control rule-making activity as discussed earlier; this provided more presidential control of agency rule making than ever before.
3. In terms of the budget, President Reagan made very effective use of the OMB.

This combination is the administrative presidency, and it gave Reagan more bureaucratic control than any president has had since civil service laws began in 1883. President Bush did not use ideology in his appointments as much and, as cited earlier, suffered setbacks in the form of Court decisions impairing his use of the OMB to control agency rule making.

This chapter began with the proposition that presidents may have the will to control the fourth branch but lack the power. Some presidents possess more will to control agencies than do others. President Nixon was paranoid about it, President Reagan was committed to it, and President Bush tried to continue in the Reagan mold but was not enough of an ideologue to avoid captivity problems and suffered some setbacks (e.g., the *Dole* decision). Apparently, President Clinton is not concerned about controlling agency regulations. On September 30, 1993, he issued an executive order restoring to the agencies the discretion to write rules and regulations without White House interference (reducing the role of the OMB in the administrative process).[39]

Presidents such as Clinton, who believe in positive government, are not threatened by agency rule making because bureaucracy is the tool of positive government. Presidents who are less enthusiastic about positive government have more reason to try to inhibit agency rule making.

The efforts of the Clinton administration and Vice President Al Gore to "reinvent government" and to "streamline the government" are not aimed at controlling the rule making of agencies but, rather, are concerned with reducing the size of bureaucracy (primarily through attrition), streamlining some procedures (procurement), and combining some agencies.[40]

SUMMARY

Republican presidents (especially since the Reagan "revolution") will tend to be less enthusiastic about positive government and consequently will likely be disposed to attempt to control agency budgets and rule making, but the lack of raw constitutional and statutory power will make it difficult for them to do so. Democratic presidents, like Clinton, will likely be inclined toward positive government. They will not see their own branch of government as an enemy to be slain and hence will be less concerned with controlling agency behavior.

The Constitution makes control of the bureaucracy a shared power between the executive and Congress, but clearly Congress possesses the lion's share of the power.

Presidents do have at their disposal tools that at first glance would appear to provide them with control over agencies, but after closer examination, these tools seem to be flawed. Modern presidents do exercise more control over agencies than did their predecessors, going back to the point in history where civil service became the law (1883). This increased presidential control is a result of the SES and of the increased role of the OMB in the daily activities of agencies. It remains to be seen whether the Supreme Court will sanction further OMB interference with agency rule making.

1. Congress restored the president's ability to use the OMB to control agency rule making with paperwork implications, but that power will likely lay dormant until a Republican president is in the White House.

2. Where Congress attempts to place restrictions on the president's removal power, the test is whether those restrictions are of such a nature that they impede the president's ability to perform his or her constitutional duties—that is, to exercise executive power and see that the laws are faithfully executed (*Morrison v. Olson*).

END-OF-CHAPTER CASES

DOLE V. UNITED STEELWORKERS OF AMERICA
494 U.S. 26 (1990)

Justice Brennan delivered the opinion of the Court, joined by Justices Marshall, Blackmun, Stevens, O'Connor, Scalia, and Kennedy. Justice White dissented, joined by Chief Justice Rehnquist.

Among the regulatory tools available to governmental agencies charged with protecting public health and safety are rules which require regulated entities to disclose information directly to employees, consumers, or others. Disclosure rules protect by providing access to information about what dangers exist and how these dangers can be avoided. Today we decide whether the Office of Management and Budget (OMB) has the authority under the Paperwork Reduction Act of 1980 (Act), 44 U.S.C. § 3501, to review such regulations.

I

In 1983, pursuant to the Occupational Safety and Health Act of 1970 (OSH Act), which authorizes the Department of Labor (DOL) to set health and safety standards for workplaces, DOL promulgated a Hazard Communications Standard. 29 C.F.R. § 1910 (1984). The Standard imposed various requirements on manufacturers aimed at ensuring that their employees were informed of the potential hazards posed by chemicals found at their workplace.

Specifically, the Standard required chemical manufacturers to label containers of hazardous chemicals with appropriate warnings. "Downstream" manufacturers—commercial purchasers who used the chemicals in their manufacturing plants—were obliged to keep the original labels intact or else transfer the information onto any substitute containers. The Standard also required chemical manufacturers to provide "material safety data sheets" to downstream manufacturers. The data sheets were to list the physical characteristics and hazards of each chemical, the symptoms caused by overexposure, and any pre-existing medical conditions aggravated by exposure. In addition, the data sheets were to recommend safety precautions and first aid and emergency procedures in case of overexposure, and provide a source for additional information. Both chemical manufacturers and downstream manufacturers were required to make the data sheets available to their employees and to provide training on the dangers of the particular hazardous chemicals found at each workplace.

Respondent United Steelworkers of America, among others, challenged the Standard in the Court of Appeals for the Third Circuit. That court held that the Occupational Safety and Health Administration (OSHA) had not adequately explained why the regulation was limited to the manufacturing sector, in view of the OSH Act's clear directive that, to the extent feasible, OSHA is to ensure that no employee suffers material impairment of health from toxic or other harmful agents. The court directed OSHA either to apply the hazard standard rules to workplaces in other sectors or to state reasons why such application would not be feasible. *United Steelworkers of America v. Auchter,* 763 F.2d 728, 739 (CA3 1985).

When DOL responded by initiating an entirely new rulemaking proceeding, the union and its copetitioners sought enforcement of the earlier order. The Third Circuit Court of Appeals directed DOL, under threat of contempt, to publish in the *Federal Register* within 60 days either a hazard communication standard applicable to all workers covered by the OSH Act or a statement of reasons why such a standard was not feasible on the basis of the existing record, as to each category of excluded workers. *United Steelworkers of America v. Pendergrass,* 819 F.2d 1263, 1270 (CA3 1987).

DOL complied by issuing a revised Hazard Communications Standard that applied to worksites in all sectors of the economy. At the same time, DOL submitted the Standard to OMB for review of any paperwork requirements. After holding a public hearing, OMB approved all but three of its provisions. OMB rejected a requirement that employees who work at multi-employer sites (such as construction sites) be provided with data sheets describing the hazardous substances to which they were likely to be exposed, through the activities of any of the companies working at the same site. The provision permitted employers either to exchange data sheets and make them available at their home offices or to maintain all relevant data sheets at a central location on the worksite. OMB also disapproved a provision exempting consumer products used in the workplace in the same manner, and resulting in the same frequency and duration of exposure, as in normal consumer use. Finally, OMB vetoed an exemption for drugs sold in solid, final form for direct administration to patients. OMB disapproved these provisions based on its determination that the requirements were not necessary to protect employees. OMB's objection to the exemptions was that they were too narrow, and that the Standard, therefore, applied to situations in which disclosure did not benefit employees. DOL disagreed with OMB's assessment, but it published notice that the three provisions were withdrawn. DOL added its reasons for believing that the provisions were necessary, proposed that they be retained, and invited public comment.

The union and its copetitioners responded by filing a motion for further relief with the Third Circuit. That court ordered DOL to reinstate the OMB-disapproved provisions. The court reasoned that the provisions represented good faith compliance by DOL with the court's prior orders, that OMB lacked authority under the Paperwork Reduction Act to disapprove the provisions and that, therefore, DOL had no legitimate basis for withdrawing them.

The United States sought review in this Court. We granted certiorari to answer the important question whether the Paperwork Reduction Act authorizes OMB to review and countermand agency regulations mandating disclosure by regulated entities directly to third parties. We hold that the Paperwork Reduction Act does not give OMB that authority, and therefore affirm.

II

[1] The Paperwork Reduction Act was enacted in response to one of the less auspicious aspects of the enormous growth of our federal bureaucracy: its seemingly insatiable appetite for data. Outcries from small businesses, individuals, and state and

local governments, that they were being buried under demands for paperwork, led Congress to institute controls. Congress designated OMB the overseer of other agencies with respect to paperwork and set forth a comprehensive scheme designed to reduce the paperwork burden. The Act charges OMB with developing uniform policies for efficient information processing, storage and transmittal systems, both within and among agencies. OMB is directed to reduce federal collection of all information by set percentages, establish a Federal Information Locator System, and develop and implement procedures for guarding the privacy of those providing confidential information. The Act prohibits any federal agency from adopting regulations which impose paperwork requirements on the public unless the information is not available to the agency from another source within the Federal Government, and the agency must formulate a plan for tabulating the information in a useful manner.

Agencies are also required to minimize the burden on the public to the extent practicable. In addition, the Act institutes a second layer of review by OMB for new paperwork requirements. After an agency has satisfied itself that an instrument for collecting information—termed an "information collection request"—is needed, the agency must submit the request to OMB for approval. If OMB disapproves the request, the agency may not collect the information . . .

The promulgation of a disclosure rule is a final agency action that represents a substantive regulatory choice. An agency charged with protecting employees from hazardous chemicals has a variety of regulatory weapons from which to choose: It can ban the chemical altogether; it can mandate specified safety measures, such as gloves or goggles; or it can require labels or other warnings alerting users to dangers and recommended precautions. An agency chooses to impose a warning requirement because it believes that such a requirement is the least intrusive measure that will sufficiently protect the public, not because the measure is a means of acquiring information useful in performing some other agency function.

Petitioner submits that the provisions requiring labeling and employee training are "reporting requirements" and that the provision requiring accessible data sheets containing health and safety information is a "recordkeeping requirement." We believe, however, that the language, structure, and purpose of the Paperwork Reduction Act reveal that petitioner's position is untenable because Congress did not intend the Act to encompass these or any other third-party disclosure rules.

On a pure question of statutory construction, our first job is to try to determine congressional intent, using traditional tools of statutory construction.... Petitioner's interpretation of "obtaining or soliciting facts by an agency through . . . reporting or recordkeeping requirements" is not the most natural reading of this language. The common-sense view of "obtaining or soliciting facts by an agency" is that the phrase refers to an agency's efforts to gather facts for its own use and that Congress used the word "solicit" in addition to the word "obtain" in order to cover information requests that rely on the voluntary cooperation of information suppliers as well as rules which make compliance mandatory. Similarly, data sheets consisting of advisory material on health and safety do not fall within the normal meaning of "records," and a government-imposed reporting requirement customarily requires reports to be made to the government, not training and labels to be given to someone else altogether.

That a more limited reading of the phrase "reporting and recordkeeping requirement" was intended derives some further support from the words surrounding it. The traditional canon of construction, noscitur a sociis, dictates that "words grouped in a list should be given related meaning." The other examples listed in the definitions of "information collection request" and "collection of information" are forms for communicating information to the party requesting that information. If "reporting and recordkeeping requirement" is understood to be analogous to the examples surrounding it, the phrase would comprise only rules requiring information to be sent or made available to a federal agency, not disclosure rules.

The same conclusion is produced by a consideration of the object and structure of the Act as a whole. Particularly useful is the provision detailing Congress' purposes in enacting the statute. The Act declares that its purposes are: "[1] to minimize the Federal paperwork burden for individuals, small businesses, State and local governments, and other

persons; (2) to minimize the cost to the Federal Government of collecting, maintaining, using, and disseminating information; (3) to maximize the usefulness of information collected, maintained, and disseminated by the Federal Government; (4) to coordinate, integrate and, to the extent practicable and appropriate, make uniform Federal information policies and practices; (5) to ensure that automatic data processing, telecommunications, and other information technologies are acquired and used by the Federal Government in a manner which improves service delivery and program management, increases productivity, improves the quality of decisionmaking, reduces waste and fraud, and wherever practicable and appropriate, reduces the information processing burden for the Federal Government and for persons who provide information to and for the Federal Government; and (6) to ensure that the collection, maintenance, use and dissemination of information by the Federal Government is consistent with applicable laws relating to confidentiality, including . . . the Privacy Act." Disclosure rules present none of the problems Congress sought to solve through the Paperwork Reduction Act, and none of Congress' enumerated purposes would be served by subjecting disclosure rules to the provisions of the Act.

III

For the foregoing reasons, we find that the terms "collection of information" and "information collection request," when considered in light of the language and structure of the Act as a whole, refer solely to the collection of information by, or for the use of, a federal agency; they cannot reasonably be interpreted to cover rules mandating disclosure of information to a third party. Because we find that the statute, as a whole, clearly expresses Congress' intention, we decline to defer to OMB's interpretation. *Chevron U.S.A. Inc. v. Natural Resources Defense Council, Inc.,* 467 U.S. 837 (1984) ("If the intent of Congress is clear, that is the end of the matter"). We affirm the judgment of the Third Circuit insofar as it held that the Paperwork Reduction Act does not give OMB the authority to review agency rules mandating disclosure by regulated entities to third parties.

It is so ordered.

MORRISON V. OLSON
487 U.S. 654 (1988)

Chief Justice Rehnquist delivered the opinion of the Court, joined by Justices Brennan, White, Marshall, Blackmun, Stevens, and O'Connor. Justice Scalia dissented, and Justice Kennedy did not participate.

This case presents us with a challenge to the independent counsel provisions of the Ethics in Government Act of 1978. We hold today that these provisions of the Act do not violate the Appointments Clause of the Constitution, or the limitations of Article III, nor do they impermissibly interfere with the President's authority under Article II in violation of the constitutional principle of separation of powers.

I

Briefly stated, Title VI of the Ethics in Government Act allows for the appointment of an "independent counsel" to investigate and, if appropriate, prosecute certain high-ranking Government officials for violations of federal criminal laws. The Act requires the Attorney General, upon receipt of information that he determines is "sufficient to constitute grounds to investigate whether any person [covered by the Act] may have violated any Federal criminal law," to conduct a preliminary investigation of the matter. When the Attorney General has completed this investigation, or 90 days has elapsed, he is required to report to a special court (the Special Division) created by the Act "for the purpose of appointing independent counsels." If the Attorney General determines that "there are no reasonable grounds to believe that further investigation is warranted," then he must notify the Special Division of this result. In such a case, "the division of the court shall have no power to appoint an independent counsel." If, however, the Attorney General has determined that there are "reasonable grounds to believe that further investigation or prosecution is warranted," then he "shall apply to the division of the court for the appointment of an independent counsel." The Attorney General's application to the court "shall contain sufficient information to assist the [court] in selecting an independent counsel and in defining that independent counsel's prosecutorial jurisdiction." § 592(d).

Upon receiving this application, the Special Division "shall appoint an appropriate independent counsel and shall define that independent counsel's prosecutorial jurisdiction." With respect to all matters within the independent counsel's jurisdiction, the Act grants the counsel "full power and independent authority to exercise all investigative and prosecutorial functions and powers of the Department of Justice, the Attorney General, and any other officer or employee of the Department of Justice." The functions of the independent counsel include conducting grand jury proceedings and other investigations, participating in civil and criminal court proceedings and litigation, and appealing any decision in any case in which the counsel participates in an official capacity.

. . . The counsel's powers include "initiating and conducting prosecutions in any court of competent jurisdiction, framing and signing indictments, filing informations, and handling all aspects of any case, in the name of the United States." The counsel may appoint employees, may request and obtain assistance from the Department of Justice, and may accept referral of matters from the Attorney General if the matter falls within the counsel's jurisdiction as defined by the Special Division. Two statutory provisions govern the length of an independent counsel's tenure in office. The first defines the procedure for removing an independent counsel. Section 596(a)(1) provides: "An independent counsel appointed under this chapter may be removed from office, other than by impeachment and conviction, only by the personal action of the Attorney General and only for good cause, physical disability, mental incapacity, or any other condition that substantially impairs the performance of such independent counsel's duties." If an independent counsel is removed pursuant to this section, the Attorney General is required to submit a report to both the Special Division and the Judiciary Committees of the Senate and the House "specifying the facts found and the ultimate grounds for such removal." Under the current version of the Act, an independent counsel can obtain judicial review of the Attorney General's action by filing a civil action in the United States District Court for the District of Columbia. Members of the Special Division "may not hear or determine any such civil action or any appeal of a decision in any such civil action." The reviewing court is authorized to grant reinstatement or "other appropriate relief." Under the Act as originally enacted, an independent counsel who was removed could obtain judicial review of the Attorney General's decision in a civil action commenced before the Special Division. If the removal was "based on error of law or fact," the court could order "reinstatement or other appropriate relief." 28 U.S.C. § 596(a)(3).

The other provision governing the tenure of the independent counsel defines the procedures for "terminating" the counsel's office. Under § 596(b)(1), the office of an independent counsel terminates when he or she notifies the Attorney General that he or she has completed or substantially completed any investigations or prosecutions undertaken pursuant to the Act. In addition, the Special Division, acting either on its own or on the suggestion of the Attorney General, may terminate the office of an independent counsel at any time if it finds that "the investigation of all matters within the prosecutorial jurisdiction of such independent counsel . . . have been completed or so substantially completed that it would be appropriate for the Department of Justice to complete such investigations and prosecutions."

. . . Finally, the Act provides for Congressional oversight of the activities of independent counsel. The proceedings in this case provide an example of how the Act works in practice. In 1982, two Subcommittees of the House of Representatives issued subpoenas directing the Environmental Protection Agency (EPA) to produce certain documents relating to the efforts of the EPA and the Land and Natural Resources Division of the Justice Department to enforce the "Superfund Law." At that time, appellee Olson was the Assistant Attorney General for the Office of Legal Counsel (OLC), appellee Schmults was Deputy Attorney General, and appellee Dinkins was the Assistant Attorney General for the Land and Natural Resources Division. Acting on the advice of the Justice Department, the President ordered the Administrator of the EPA to invoke executive privilege to withhold certain of the documents on the ground that they contained "enforcement sensitive information." The Administrator obeyed this order and withheld the documents. In response, the House voted to hold the Administrator in contempt, after which the Administrator and the United States together filed a lawsuit against the House. The conflict abated in March 1983, when the administration agreed to give the House Subcommittees limited access to the documents. The following year, the House Judiciary Commit-

tee began an investigation into the Justice Department's role in the controversy over the EPA documents. During this investigation, appellee Olson testified before a House Subcommittee on March 10, 1983.

Both before and after that testimony, the Department complied with several Committee requests to produce certain documents. Other documents were at first withheld, although these documents were eventually disclosed by the Department after the Committee learned of their existence. In 1985, the majority members of the Judiciary Committee published a lengthy report on the Committee's investigation. *Report on Investigation of the Role of the Department of Justice in the Withholding of Environmental Protection Agency Documents from Congress in 1982-83,* H.R.Rep. No. 99-435 (1985). The report not only criticized various officials in the Department of Justice for their role in the EPA executive privilege dispute, but it also suggested that appellee Olson had given false and misleading testimony to the Subcommittee on March 10, 1983, and that appellees Schmults and Dinkins had wrongfully withheld certain documents from the Committee, thus obstructing the Committee's investigation. The Chairman of the Judiciary Committee forwarded a copy of the report to the Attorney General with a request . . . that he seek the appointment of an independent counsel to investigate the allegations against Olson, Schmults, and Dinkins.

The Attorney General directed the Public Integrity Section of the Criminal Division to conduct a preliminary investigation. The Section's report concluded that the appointment of an independent counsel was warranted to investigate the Committee's allegations with respect to all three appellees. After consulting with other Department officials, however, the Attorney General chose to apply to the Special Division for the appointment of an independent counsel solely with respect to appellee Olson. The Attorney General accordingly requested appointment of an independent counsel to investigate whether Olson's March 10, 1983, testimony "regarding the completeness of [OLC's] response to the Judiciary Committee's request for OLC documents, and regarding his knowledge of EPA's willingness to turn over certain disputed documents to Congress, violated . . . any provision of federal criminal law." The Attorney General also requested that the independent counsel have authority to investigate "any other matter related to that allegation." On April 23, 1986, the Special Division appointed James C. McKay as independent counsel to investigate "whether the testimony of . . . Olson and his revision of such testimony on March 10, 1983, violated . . . any provision of federal law." The court also ordered that the independent counsel "shall have jurisdiction to investigate any other allegation of evidence of violation of any Federal criminal law by Theodore Olson developed during investigations, by the Independent Counsel, referred to earlier, and connected with or arising out of that investigation, and Independent Counsel shall have jurisdiction to prosecute for any such violation." McKay later resigned as independent counsel, and on May 29, 1986, the Division appointed appellant Morrison as his replacement, with the same jurisdiction.

In January 1987, appellant asked the Attorney General to refer to her as "related matters" the Committee's allegations against appellees Schmults and Dinkins. The Attorney General refused to refer the matters, concluding that his decision not to request the appointment of an independent counsel in regard to those matters was final. Appellant then asked the Special Division to order that the matters be referred to her. On April 2, 1987, the Division ruled that the Attorney General's decision not to seek appointment of an independent counsel with respect to Schmults and Dinkins was final and unreviewable and that therefore the court had no authority to make the requested referral. *In re* Olson, 260 U.S.App.D.C. 168, 818 F.2d 34. The court ruled, however, that its original grant of jurisdiction to appellant was broad enough to permit inquiry into whether Olson may have conspired with others, including Schmults and Dinkins, to obstruct the Committee's investigation.

Following this ruling, in May and June 1987, appellant caused a grand jury to issue and serve subpoenas ad testificandum and duces tecum on appellees. All three appellees moved to quash the subpoenas, claiming, among other things, that the independent counsel provisions of the Act were unconstitutional and that appellant accordingly had no authority to proceed. On July 20, 1987, the District Court upheld the constitutionality of the Act and denied the motions to quash. *In re* Sealed Case, 665 F.Supp. 56 (DC). The court subsequently ordered that appellees be held in contempt for continuing to refuse to comply with the subpoenas. The court stayed the effect of its contempt orders pending expedited appeal. . . .

III

The Appointments Clause of Article II reads as follows: "[The President] shall nominate, and by and with the Advice and Consent of the Senate, shall appoint Ambassadors, other public Ministers and Consuls, Judges of the Supreme Court, and all other Officers of the United States, whose Appointments are not herein otherwise provided for, and which shall be established by Law: but the Congress may by Law vest the Appointment of such inferior Officers, as they think proper, in the President alone, in the Courts of Law, or in the Heads of Departments." The parties do not dispute that "[t]he Constitution for purposes of appointment . . . divides all its officers into two classes." As we stated in *Buckley v. Valeo,* 424 U.S. 1, 132 (1976): "[P]rincipal officers are selected by the President with the advice and consent of the Senate. Inferior officers Congress may allow to be appointed by the President alone, by the heads of departments, or by the Judiciary." The initial question is, accordingly, whether appellant is an "inferior" or a "principal" officer. If she is the latter, as the Court of Appeals concluded, then the Act is in violation of the Appointments Clause. First, appellant is subject to removal by a higher Executive Branch official. Although appellant may not be "subordinate" to the Attorney General (and the President) insofar as she possesses a degree of independent discretion to exercise the powers delegated to her under the Act, the fact that she can be removed by the Attorney General indicates that she is to some degree "inferior" in rank and authority.

Second, appellant is empowered by the Act to perform only certain, limited duties. An independent counsel's role is restricted primarily to investigation and, if appropriate, prosecution for certain federal crimes. Admittedly, the Act delegates to appellant "full power and independent authority to exercise all investigative and prosecutorial functions and powers of the Department of Justice," but this grant of authority does not include any authority to formulate policy for the Government or the Executive Branch, nor does it give appellant any administrative duties outside of those necessary to operate her office. The Act specifically provides that in policy matters appellant is to comply to the extent possible with the policies of the Department.

Third, appellant's office is limited in jurisdiction. Not only is the Act itself restricted in applicability to certain federal officials suspected of certain serious federal crimes, but an independent counsel can only act within the scope of the jurisdiction that has been granted by the Special Division pursuant to a request by the Attorney General. Finally, appellant's office is limited in tenure. There is concededly no time limit on the appointment of a particular counsel. Nonetheless, the office of independent counsel is "temporary" in the sense that an independent counsel is appointed essentially to accomplish a single task, and when that task is over the office is terminated, either by the counsel herself or by action of the Special Division. Unlike other prosecutors, appellant has no ongoing responsibilities that extend beyond the accomplishment of the mission that she was appointed for and authorized by the Special Division to undertake. In our view, these factors relating to the "ideas of tenure, duration . . . and duties" of the independent counsel, are sufficient to establish that appellant is an "inferior" officer in the constitutional sense. . . . This does not, however, end our inquiry under the Appointments Clause. Appellees argue that even if appellant is an "inferior" officer, the Clause does not empower Congress to place the power to appoint such an officer outside the Executive Branch. They contend that the Clause does not contemplate congressional authorization of "interbranch appointments," in which an officer of one branch is appointed by officers of another branch. The relevant language of the Appointments Clause is worth repeating. It reads: ". . . but the Congress may by Law vest the Appointment of such inferior Officers, as they think proper, in the President alone, in the courts of Law, or in the Heads of Departments." On its face, the language of this "excepting clause" admits of no limitation on interbranch appointments. Indeed, the inclusion of "as they think proper" seems clearly to give Congress significant discretion to determine whether it is "proper" to vest the appointment of, for example, executive officials in the "courts of Law." . . .

V

We now turn to consider whether the Act is invalid under the constitutional principle of separation of powers. Two related issues must be addressed: The first is whether the provision of the Act restricting the Attorney General's power to remove the independent counsel to only those instances in which he can show "good cause," taken by itself, impermissibly interferes with the President's exercise of his constitutionally appointed functions. The second is whether, taken as a whole, the Act violates the separation of powers by reducing the President's ability to control the prosecutorial powers wielded by the independent counsel.

A

Two Terms ago we had occasion to consider whether it was consistent with the separation of powers for Congress to pass a statute that authorized a Government official who is removable only by Congress to participate in what we found to be "executive powers." *Bowsher v. Synar,* 478 U.S. 714, 730 (1986). We held in *Bowsher* that "Congress cannot reserve for itself the power of removal of an officer charged with the execution of the laws except by impeachment." . . . Our present considered view is that the determination of whether the Constitution allows Congress to impose a "good cause"-type restriction on the President's power to remove an official cannot be made to turn on whether or not that official is classified as "purely executive." The analysis contained in our removal cases is designed not to define rigid categories of those officials who may or may not be removed at will by the President, but to ensure that Congress does not interfere with the President's exercise of the "executive power" and his constitutionally appointed duty to "take care that the laws be faithfully executed" under Article II. . . . The real question is whether the removal restrictions are of such a nature that they impede the President's ability to perform his constitutional duty, and the functions of the officials in question must be analyzed in that light. . . .

Considering for the moment the "good cause" removal provision in isolation from the other parts of the Act at issue in this case, we cannot say that the imposition of a "good cause" standard for removal by itself unduly trammels on executive authority. There is no real dispute that the functions performed by the independent counsel are "executive" in the sense that they are law enforcement functions that typically have been undertaken by officials within the Executive Branch. As we noted earlier, however, the independent counsel is an inferior officer under the Appointments Clause, with limited jurisdiction and tenure and lacking policymaking or significant administrative authority. Here, as with the provision of the Act conferring the appointment authority of the independent counsel on the special court, the congressional determination to limit the removal power of the Attorney General was essential, in the view of Congress, to establish the necessary independence of the office. We do not think that this limitation as it presently stands sufficiently deprives the President of control over the independent counsel to interfere impermissibly with his constitutional obligation to ensure the faithful execution of the laws.

VI

In sum, we conclude today that it does not violate the Appointments Clause for Congress to vest the appointment of independent counsel in the Special Division; that the powers exercised by the Special Division under the Act do not violate Article III; and that the Act does not violate the separation-of-powers principle by impermissibly interfering with the functions of the Executive Branch. The decision of the Court of Appeals is therefore Reversed.

Justice Scalia, dissenting.

IV

I will not discuss at any length why the restrictions upon the removal of the independent counsel also violate our established precedent dealing with that specific subject. For most of it, I simply refer the reader to the scholarly opinion of Judge Silberman for the Court of Appeals below. See *In re* Sealed Case, 267 U.S.App.D.C. 178, 838 F.2d 476 (1988). I cannot avoid commenting, however, about the essence of what the Court has done to our removal jurisprudence today.

There is, of course, no provision in the Constitution stating who may remove executive officers, except the provisions for removal by impeachment. Before the present decision it was established, however, (1) that the President's power to remove principal officers who exercise purely executive powers could not be restricted, see *Myers v. United States*, 272 U.S. 52 (1926), and (2) that his power to remove inferior officers who exercise purely executive powers, and whose appointment Congress had removed from the usual procedure of Presidential appointment with Senate consent, could be restricted, at least where the appointment had been made by an officer of the Executive Branch. The Court could have resolved the removal power issue in this case by simply relying upon its erroneous

conclusion that the independent counsel was an inferior officer, and then extending our holding that the removal of inferior officers appointed by the Executive can be restricted, to a new holding that even the removal of inferior officers appointed by the courts can be restricted. That would in my view be a considerable and unjustified extension, giving the Executive full discretion in neither the selection nor the removal of a purely executive officer. The course the Court has chosen, however, is even worse.

Since our 1935 decision in *Humphrey's Executor v. United States*, 295 U.S. 602—which was considered by many at the time the product of an activist, anti-New Deal Court bent on reducing the power of President Franklin Roosevelt—it has been established that the line of permissible restriction upon removal of principal officers lies at the point at which the powers exercised by those officers are no longer purely executive. Thus, removal restrictions have been generally regarded as lawful for so-called "independent regulatory agencies," such as the Federal Trade Commission, the Interstate Commerce Commission, and the Consumer Product Safety Commission, which engage substantially in what has been called the "quasi-legislative activity" of rulemaking, and for members of Article I courts, such as the Court of Military Appeals, who engage in the "quasi-judicial" function of adjudication.

It has often been observed, correctly in my view, that the line between "purely executive" functions and "quasi-legislative" or "quasi-judicial" functions is not a clear one or even a rational one. But at least it permitted the identification of certain officers, and certain agencies, whose functions were entirely within the control of the President. Congress had to be aware of that restriction in its legislation. Today, however, *Humphrey's Executor* is swept into the dustbin of repudiated constitutional principles. "[O]ur present considered view," the Court says, "is that the determination of whether the Constitution allows Congress to impose a 'good cause'-type restriction on the President's power to remove an official cannot be made to turn on whether or not that official is classified as 'purely executive.' " What *Humphrey's Executor* (and presumably *Myers*) really means, we are now told, is not that there are any "rigid categories of those officials who may or may not be removed at will by the President," but simply that Congress cannot "interfere with the President's exercise of the 'executive power' and his constitutionally appointed duty to 'take care that the laws be faithfully executed.' " One can hardly grieve for the shoddy treatment given today to *Humphrey's Executor,* which, after all, accorded the same indignity (with much less justification) to Chief Justice Taft's opinion 10 years earlier in *Myers v. United States,*—gutting, in six quick pages devoid of textual or historical precedent for the novel principle it set forth, a carefully researched and reasoned 70-page opinion.

It is in fact comforting to witness the reality that he who lives by the ipse dixit dies by the ipse dixit. But one must grieve for the Constitution. *Humphrey's Executor* at least had the decency formally to observe the constitutional principle that the President had to be the repository of all executive power, which, as *Myers* carefully explained, necessarily means that he must be able to discharge those who do not perform executive functions according to his liking. As we noted in *Bowsher,* once an officer is appointed " 'it is only the authority that can remove him, and not the authority that appointed him, that he must fear and, in the performance of his functions, obey.' " By contrast, "our present considered view" is simply that any executive officer's removal can be restricted, so long as the President remains "able to accomplish his con-

stitutional role." There are now no lines. If the removal of a prosecutor, the virtual embodiment of the power to "take care that the laws be faithfully executed," can be restricted, what officer's removal cannot? This is an open invitation for Congress to experiment. What about a special Assistant Secretary of State, with responsibility for one very narrow area of foreign policy, who would not only have to be confirmed by the Senate but could also be removed only pursuant to certain carefully designed restrictions? Could this possibly render the President "[un]able to accomplish his constitutional role"? Or a special Assistant Secretary of Defense for Procurement? The possibilities are endless, and the Court does not understand what the separation of powers, what "[a]mbition . . . counteract[ing] ambition," is all about, if it does not expect Congress to try them.

As far as I can discern from the Court's opinion, it is now open season upon the President's removal power for all executive officers, with not even the superficially principled restriction of *Humphrey's Executor* as cover. The Court essentially says to the President: "Trust us. We will make sure that you are able to accomplish your constitutional role." I think the Constitution gives the President—and the people—more protection than that.

NOTES

1. Robert Pear, "Aides Urge Bush to Impose Moratorium on Regulations," *The New York Times,* 21 January 1992, A1, national edition; David Rosenbaum and Keith Schneider, "Bush Is Extending Regulatory Freeze With a Fanfare," *The New York Times,* 29 April 1992, A1, national edition.

2. David Rosenbloom, *Public Administration: Understanding Management, Politics, and the Law in the Public Sector,* 2d ed. (New York: Random House, 1989), 378-79.

3. This information comes from Linda Greenhouse, "High Court Decides Budget Office Exceeded Power in Blocking Rules," *The New York Times,* 22 February 1990, A1, national edition. The actual case of *Dole v. Steel-*

workers of America, however, appears at the end of the chapter.

4. Richard E. Neustadt, *Presidential Power: The Politics of Leadership From FDR to Carter* (New York: John Wiley, 1980), 9.

5. Ibid.

6. Ibid.

7. Alan Gitelson, Robert Dudley, and Melvin Dubnic, *American Government,* 2d ed. (Boston: Houghton Mifflin, 1991), 313.

8. Rosenbloom, *Public Administration,* 54.

9. 299 U.S. 304, 319 (1936).

10. Arthur Miller, *Presidential Power: In a Nutshell* (St. Paul, MN: West, 1977), 141-42.

11. Ibid., 257-59.

12. Neustadt, *Presidential Power.*

13. *Youngstown Sheet and Tube Co. v. Sawyer,* 343 U.S. 579 (1952).

14. Alan F. Westin, *The Anatomy of a Constitutional Law Case: Youngstown Sheet and Tube v. Sawyer* (New York: Macmillan, 1958), 2-6, 14-16.

15. 343 U.S. 579, 634-55 (1952).

16. 343 U.S. 579, 637 (1952).

17. For example, see Susan Welch, John Gruhl, Michael Steinman, and John Comer, *American Government,* 3d ed. (St. Paul, MN: West, 1990), 389-94.

18. Ibid., 389.

19. Ibid.

20. Rosenbloom, *Public Administration,* 48-61.

21. Ibid., 60.

22. Ibid.

23. Louis Koenig, *The Chief Executive,* 5th ed. (New York: Harcourt Brace Jovanovich, 1986), 175.

24. Ibid., 177.

25. Richard Nathan, "The Reagan Presidency in Domestic Affairs," in *The Reagan Presidency: An Early Assessment,* ed. Fred Greenstein (Baltimore: Johns Hopkins University Press, 1983), 71.

26. See, generally, Richard Nathan, *The Administrative Presidency* (New York: John Wiley, 1983).

27. 295 U.S. 602, 624 (1935).

28. Earnest Gellhorn and Ronald Levin, *Administrative Law and Process: In a Nutshell* (St. Paul, MN: West, 1990), 61-62.

29. Neustadt, *Presidential Power.*

30. Welch et al., *American Government,* 393.

31. Gellhorn and Levin, *Administrative Law and Process,* 65.

32. Ibid.

33. Pear, "Aides Urge Bush"; Rosenbaum and Schneider, "Bush Is Extending Regulatory Freeze."

34. Pear, "Aides Urge Bush."

35. Information on the budget process was taken from John Harrigan, *Politics and the American Future,* 3d ed. (New York: McGraw-Hill, 1992), 333-42; but for a thorough treatment of the subject, see Aaron Wildavsky, *The New Politics of the Budgetary Process* (New York: HarperCollins, 1991).

36. See, generally, Nathan, *The Administrative Presidency.*

37. Ibid., 53-56.

38. James W. Fesler and Donald F. Kettl, *The Politics of the Administrative Process* (Chatham, NJ: Chatham House, 1991), 158-75.

39. John Cushman, Jr., "President Moves to Loosen Grip of White House on Regulations," *The New York Times,* 1 October 1993, A16, national edition.

40. Gwen Ifill, "Federal Cutbacks Proposed by Gore in Five-Year Program," *The New York Times,* 8 September 1993, A1, national edition; Clifford Krause, "Gore's Efficiency Plan Draws Nods in Congress (for now)," *The New York Times,* 9 September 1993, A1, national edition.

CHAPTER 3

LEGISLATIVE CONTROL OF BUREAUCRACY

What Congress gives, Congress can take away. Or can it? By now, you are familiar with the concept of "delegation of power"; that is, Congress makes a decision to deal with an issue or problem (e.g., traffic or industrial fatalities) and delegates its power to an agency so that the agency can use its expertise to attack the problem. Democratic theory, however, demands that Congress keep track of what the agency is doing and maintain sufficient leverage so that agency rules, regulations, or standards can be undone. One device for maintaining legislative control of agencies is the *legislative veto.*

A legislative veto provision will usually be found in the enabling legislation. It provides that either house of the legislature can pass a resolution undoing an agency rule, regulation, or standard. Since 1932, Congress has attached a legislative veto to nearly two hundred pieces of legislation,[1] and legislative vetoes are common with state legislatures as well. In Chapter 2, for example, you were introduced to the concept of "presidential impoundment of funds." The Congressional Budget and Impoundment Act of 1974 provides that either house of Congress can pass a resolution disapproving a particular presidential impoundment of funds, thus forcing the spending of money that the president would prefer not to spend.

CASE IN POINT:
IMMIGRATION AND NATURALIZATION SERVICE V. CHADHA, 462 U.S. 919 (1983)

The Immigration and Nationality Act is the legislation in which Congress exercised its Article I, Section 8, power "to establish a uniform rule of naturalization" and its implied power to control immigration and deportation. It delegated its power to the Immigration and Naturalization Service (INS) to implement the act. In the act, Congress provided for exemptions from deportation; that is, otherwise deportable individuals can be spared deportation under certain circumstances. One of those circumstances is known as the "extreme hardship" exemption, and it works like this: Once the INS has served notice that it will initiate deportation hearings against an individual, the attorney general of the United States can recommend that the deportation procedure be suspended because of "extreme hardship." Congress therefore delegated some of its power to control immigration to the attorney general, as well as to the INS. Should the attorney general choose to exercise that power by recommending a suspension of deportation, he or she must notify Congress of that recommendation within a specific period of time. Either house of Congress can pass a resolution disapproving the attorney general's recommendation.

Prior to the establishment of this procedure, when Congress (or a member of Congress) wanted to suspend deportation hearings for an individual, someone had to introduce a private bill (a bill passed by both houses of Congress and signed by the president that applies only to one individual, family, or business). The private bill procedure was clumsy and time-consuming, so Congress streamlined the procedure by delegating its power to the attorney general but provided for a congressional veto.

Jagdish Rai Chadha was born in Kenya and entered the United States on a British passport with a student visa. He was allowed to stay in the United States to attend college but stayed beyond the allotted time. The INS held a deportation hearing on Chadha, and the immigration judge found him to be in the country without authorization and declared him to be deportable. The judge suspended the deportation, however, because he found that Chadha qualified for an extreme hardship (generally reserved for immigrants who marry while here and have children who are U.S. citizens). The judge transmitted his recommendations to the attorney general, who made a suspension recommendation for Chadha and sent it to Congress. The attorney general's recommendation languished there for a year and a half (Congress has a certain amount of time to act on legislative vetoes or else the recommendation becomes fact). Almost at the last minute (late 1975), a resolution was introduced in the House of Representatives to veto the suspension recommendations of the attorney general for Chadha and five other immigrants. The veto resolution was never debated, and no recorded vote was taken. It simply stated that the six immigrants did not meet the statutory requirements for the extreme hardship exemption (had lived in the United States for seven years continuously, had good moral character, and would suffer an extreme hardship if deported), and the resolution passed. Because it was a resolution, it did not go to the Senate or to the president for a signature. After passage of the resolution, the INS judge reinstituted deportation procedures for Chadha, and he, along with the five others, was ordered deported. Chadha challenged his deportation in the courts, and the case ended up before the Supreme Court because a court of appeals declared the legislative veto provision to be unconstitutional.

The Supreme Court upheld the appellate court's decision and declared the legislative veto to be unconstitutional in this case. The Court said, "Congress' decision to deport Chadha—no less than Congress' original choice to delegate to the Attorney General the authority to make that decision—involves determinations of policy that Congress can implement in only one way; bicameral passage followed by presentment to the President."[2]

The Court, in its decision, recognized the virtue of the legislative veto as a tool for congressional control of its delegations to agencies and its democratic value in terms of accountability. It also recognized the efficiency of the legislative veto as a substitute for private bills in dealing with the problem of deportation. The Court argued, however, that constitutional principles must be adhered to. The Constitution is very specific in addressing the policy-making process at the federal level. Before a proposal can become law or policy, it must pass both houses of Congress identically (bicameralism) and be presented to the president for his or her signature (presentment). The Constitution is specific as to the four situations that do not require bicameral action by Congress or presentment:

1. The House of Representatives can initiate impeachment.
2. The Senate can try impeachments.
3. The Senate can approve or disapprove presidential appointments.
4. The Senate can approve or disapprove treaties.

Therefore, despite the potential assets of the legislative veto, it is unconstitutional.

Although the Court in this case declared only Section 244 (C)(2) of the Immigration and Nationality Act to be unconstitutional, one might assume that all the other two hundred legislative veto provisions at the federal level, as well as countless state provisions, are all unconstitutional.[3]

Questions

1. If it is difficult to control agency rule making by both the president (e.g., lack of raw power) and congressional veto (e.g., *Chadha*), how democratic do you think the system is?
2. What do you suppose could have been the motive for introducing the resolution in Congress to deny Chadha and the five others residency status?[4]

LEGISLATIVE CONTROL OF AGENCIES

What was said of presidential control of agencies in the previous chapter can be turned on its head for congressional control. Whereas the president possesses the will to control agencies but lacks the power and authority to do so, Congress possesses the power but generally lacks the will to exercise it. Congress rarely exercises truly effective control over agencies. Occasionally, however, when an agency has gone "too far" and upset powerful constituents and interest groups, Congress can and will bring in the reins and control that agency.

In 1964, the Federal Trade Commission (FTC) promulgated a rule that would have required cigarette manufacturers to print a label on the package to the effect that smoking causes death.[5] The rule would have also banned all cigarette advertising that might lead the public to believe that smoking "promotes good health or physical well-being."[6]

When the rule was promulgated, fifty million Americans smoked 549 billion cigarettes for an annual per capita consumption of 4,345 cigarettes. Smokers spent $20 billion on tobacco products, and tobacco was grown in twenty-three states (so forty-six senators were upset by the proposed rule). The tobacco industry employed two million people, paid $22 billion in taxes, and spent billions in advertising (tobacco advertisements accounted for 10 percent to 20 percent of all advertising revenues).[7] The tobacco industry felt sufficiently threatened to have industry presidents, lobbyists, and members of the Tobacco

Institute travel to Washington to see what Congress was going to do about this "problem." Congressional reaction was swift and effective (two characteristics not particularly associated with congressional action). Congress passed, and President Johnson signed, the Cigarette Labeling and Advertising Act of 1965. Packaged as a health and truth-in-advertising measure, the act did require that a warning be printed on cigarette packages. The act also, however, stripped the FTC of its rule-making power in the area of cigarette advertising for four years (the original bill called for a permanent ban) and banned smoking-rule promulgation by any other federal agency (the Federal Communications Commission [FCC] was also considering action). The act by Congress constitutes what is called *federal preemption,* which means that the states were preempted from passing any kind of warning label law (and several states were considering doing just that).[8] The label that was required by Congress in the 1965 act was mild and certainly did not mention death. It read "Caution: Cigarette Smoking May Be Hazardous To Your Health." By contrast, these were the proposed labels that the FTC considered in its 1964 rule-making procedure:

1. "CAUTION—CIGARETTE SMOKING IS A HEALTH HAZARD: The surgeon general's advisory committee has found that 'cigarette smoking contributes to mortality from specific diseases and to the overall death rate.' "
2. "CAUTION: Smoking is dangerous to health. It may cause death from cancer and other diseases."

After passage of the 1965 act, the FTC was forced to rescind its label warning. To ensure peace of mind for important constituents, Congress, in 1970, passed another act continuing the ban on FTC rule making in the cigarette area for two more years.[9] Further, Congress required the FTC to give it six months' advance notice of "any plans it might have . . . to adopt a trade regulation rule affecting cigarettes."[10] It also required the FTC to submit supporting evidence for any such proposed rule along with the notice.

After the FTC promulgated rules unfavorable to other industries—pharmaceutical companies, the insurance industry, used car dealers, undertakers, and television advertising aimed at children—Congress reacted even more harshly than it had in the cigarette controversy,[11] with proposed legislation to do away with the FTC, budget cuts, and legislative vetoes. Congress took away rule-making jurisdiction again, this time with regard to the funeral industry and children's television advertising. The FTC was forbidden to investigate certain areas (agricultural cooperatives) and is now required to engage in cost-benefit analysis (by Congress, as well as by the Office of Management and Budget [OMB]) before it proposes a rule.[12] The astute reader will recognize that the tobacco issue moved from the FTC to the Food and Drug Administration (FDA) in the mid 1990s. The issue has also been taken up by the judicial branch of government.

It may be that Congress is forbidden by the Constitution from vetoing an agency rule by a one-house resolution, but it ought to be obvious that Congress possesses a veritable armory of weapons if it chooses to exercise its power against an agency. The operative phrase in the preceding sentence is "if it chooses." Generally, it does not.

Subgovernments

The case of the FTC is unique because no other federal agency has been singled out and treated so harshly by Congress (although the Central Intelligence Agency [CIA] was spanked by the Foreign Relations Committee after its role in the Watergate/dirty tricks scandal became public). The FTC, despite being one of the oldest regulatory agencies in government, had stepped on the toes of powerful interests and had little or no support from nontobacco members of Congress or nontobacco interest groups. Much more typical of the relationship among agencies, Congress, and interest groups are subgovernments. *Subgovernments* is a term used to describe policy making by a small and intimate triad of governmental agencies, interest groups, and congressional subcommittees. The following are several of the better-known subgovernments: Department of Agriculture (USDA)—House and Senate committees on agriculture—farm interest groups (e.g., Tobacco Growers Association, American Dairy Association); the procurement office of the Pentagon—House and Senate appropriations committees on defense—defense contractors; Department of Veterans Affairs—House and Senate veterans affairs committees—veterans' organizations (e.g., Veterans of Foreign Wars, American Legion, Disabled American Veterans); the Federal Maritime Commission—merchant marine and fisheries committees of the House—merchant marine companies and their trade association.[13] These are subgovernments because they "effectively make most of the routine decisions in a given substantive area of policy."[14] They have been referred to as *iron triangles,* but I prefer the more descriptive term *cozy triangles* (see Figure 3.1).

Some of the coziest triangles are those among the Agricultural Stabilization and Conservation Service and the Commodity Credit Corporation in the USDA, the House and Senate subcommittees on particular commodities (e.g., tobacco, wheat, cotton, soybeans, peanuts), and various interest groups (e.g., National Cotton Council, Soybean Council of America, Tobacco Institute, National Association of Wheat Growers). These agricultural cozy trian-

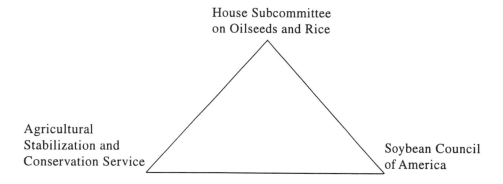

Figure 3.1. Cozy Triangle

gles have quietly produced an array of governmental benefits, such as price supports for each crop: "price support loans [mandated loan rates for commodities grown by farmers who can use their crop as collateral and default if the market price is lower than the loan rate]; acreage and production controls [to keep supplies low and prices up]; mandated target price levels [these generate deficiency income support payments to farmers when market prices fall below target levels]; . . . marketing orders, storage facilities, tax breaks, agricultural research and development, low interest loans";[15] and even in some cases (peanuts and hops) a "licensing" system so that only a privileged few can grow the crop.[16]

The triangles are cozy because the relationship within them is symbiotic; that is, each member of the triangle gets something it needs from the other members.

The agency gets appropriations and new programs from the subcommittee, and the subcommittee gets support and information from the agency. The interest groups get policies and benefits from both the subcommittee and the agency, and the subcommittee gets support, information, and campaign contributions for its members from the interest groups. Meanwhile, the agency gets information and support from the interest groups before Congress and those outside the triangle (e.g., the OMB). The relationships among individuals who work together in the triangle are often personal. They are personal because those who represent the three sides of the triangle tend to enjoy longevity in office and come to know each other well.

The relationships among the partners in the triangle are, as the name suggests, not antagonistic. Rather, they are friendly, cooperative relationships from which all parties benefit. Cozy triangles often exist where the agency or bureau is involved in implementing distributive policies that affect relatively few people. Consequently, they tend to enjoy low visibility and do not gain public attention.

The problem for the FTC in 1964, when it attempted to require the warning label on cigarettes, was that it ran smack into the tobacco cozy triangle and had no triangular relationship of its own for support. Not all substantive policy areas have triangles, and because no coordination exists between triangles, we often end up with Kafka-like situations. For example, the federal government provides generous price supports for tobacco and low excise taxes on cigarettes on the one hand, but on the other hand, the cozy triangle involving the health care industry has seen governmental spending rise to $5 billion a year on cancer research and health problems caused by smoking.[17] This may seem irrational, but if one understands that a good deal of policy gets made in separate and distinct subgovernments, it makes perfect sense. Each triangle (tobacco and health care) is doing what it does best—and doing it very efficiently.

The relationships in these triangles are so cozy that triangles have been referred to as "incest groups."[18] The point is that all the players know each other so well that no part of the triangle is likely to take action that would disturb the equilibrium. Consequently, there is no reason for Congress to exercise its power to control the agencies. Indeed, the existence of triangles often makes it difficult for congressional subcommittees to exercise truly effective and legitimate oversight of the agencies in their triangles.

Whether triangular relationships exist or not, many agencies have clients instead of cozy triangular partners. These clients often are powerful and not shy about protecting their own interests by lobbying Congress on behalf of "their agency." One reason the FDA is apparently having more success against the tobacco interests than the FTC did is that the FDA has powerful clients who can hold senators from tobacco states at bay.

It is testimony to the strength of triangular and client relationships with agencies that the Departments of Education and Energy are still alive and well today and apparently not endangered despite nearly two decades of attack by Republican presidents and presidential candidates and more recently by Republican majorities in Congress. An even better testimony to the staying power of agencies is the National Endowment for the Arts. Even though the agency's budget is less than a pittance of the whole federal budget (it is even a pittance of just the discretionary funding portion of the budget), the agency has become the symbolic whipping boy of Speaker Newt Gingrich, Majority Leader Richard Armey, and the new Republican majorities in Congress who got elected by displaying the will to control government.

The agency's clients are not powerful like the tobacco lobby, and they could not stop the Republican Congress from cutting the agency's budget by 40 percent in 1995. The Republicans promised a "phase out" of the agency by fiscal year 1996, but the agency is making a comeback. It is still funded at only the 60 percent level, but now Majority Leader Armey admits he lacks the votes to kill the agency. Indeed, *The New York Times* headline that introduced the story said "House Panel Praises Endowment for the Arts."[19]

Reelection and Constituency Service

The second reason Congress rarely chooses to exercise its control over agencies is that bureaucrats and their agencies help legislators get reelected. The concept is called "casework" or constituency service. Although average citizens might assume that they sent their senator or representative to Washington to legislate and conduct the nation's business, those citizens would be wrong. Members of Congress perform three tasks: "lawmaking, pork-barreling and casework."[20] Members of Congress spend the least amount of time doing what you would most expect them to do—making laws. They spend a bit more time on pork-barreling and as much time (and resources) on casework as they do on the other two things put together.[21]

Constituency service simply means that the legislator, who will sometime during the fiscal year vote on the agencies' budgets and programs, runs interference for constituents who are having trouble with a federal agency. The congressperson might get requests for help with Social Security problems, veterans benefits, unemployment compensation, the Small Business Administration, the Internal Revenue Service, or immigration problems.[22] Casework helps senators and representatives get reelected because, except for casework, the effects of congressional action are not readily noticeable to the average constituent. How a legislator voted on a particular bill or issue generally has little immediate effect on the constituent (who, by the way, is nearly always ignorant of how the legislator voted or even that a vote was taken). Although the effects of pork barreling are somewhat more noticeable, the constituent may not be aware that the representative's efforts resulted in the post office building they are standing in or that the senator got the money for the dam that created the lake where the constituent can go fishing or boating.

Most constituents, however, have, through casual conversation with a neighbor or family member, heard something similar to this: "So and so was having trouble with the VA, so he called Senator *X*'s office, and within a week the VA was taking care of him."

A Gallup poll in October 1990 showed that only 24 percent of Americans approved of how Congress was doing its job, and yet a month later, in the election of 1990, 98 percent of all House incumbents were reelected, as were 85 percent of all Senate incumbents.[23] According to Susan Welch et al., "Members [of Congress] who served in the 1987-89 Congress were as likely to be absent from the 1989-90 Congress because they died as because they were defeated."[24] Constituents may not like Congress as an institution, but they certainly do like their legislators—and the reason is constituency service. Senators and representatives are aware of this. Most of their staff, both in Washington, D.C., and at home, are assigned to casework.

As with triangles, notice the symbiotic relationship in casework. The legislator needs the bureaucrat because the bureaucrat has the information, expertise, and ability to solve the legislator's (constituent's) problem. The bureaucrat needs the legislator's support for his or her budget and for the program's growth or maintenance (this becomes especially crucial when the bureaucrat's own president is attempting to slash the bureau's funding). Good results with congressional casework can help the bureaucrat protect both budget and programs from the OMB and the White House without the bureaucrat's publicly appearing to oppose the administration. Although bureaucrats are aware of the need for such political trade-offs, they are not as happy about playing the casework game as they are about triangular relationships. That is because when an agency has to put daily business on hold to take care of a particular senator's problem, the service to thousands gets held up for the sake of one.

Sometimes casework leads to legislative activity. The "Notch" case is instructive as an example of how far a member of Congress will go for constituents and for reelection. Retired citizens make up an increasingly large percentage of the population, and they are beginning to vote in increasing numbers, nearly all with similar electoral concerns (they are united, if not homogeneous), and no elected politician wants to risk their wrath. Social Security is designed to provide retirees with approximately 41 percent of wages in their later years. In 1972, Congress amended the Social Security Act to include cost-of-living adjustments (COLAs) twice a year. Every Social Security beneficiary receives an adjustment for inflation twice a year, and in 1972 there was double-digit inflation. The House committee, however, inadvertently created a flaw in the formula for the calculations of COLAs. The flaw created "Bonanza Babies" (those retirees born prior to 1917) and "Notch Babies" (those retirees born between 1917 and 1926).

The mistake in the formula caused Bonanza Babies suddenly to receive 60 percent of their wages instead of the 41 percent. Had that continued, it would have bankrupted the Social Security system. In 1977, Congress adjusted the flawed formula so that those born between 1916 and 1926 would qualify for benefits lower than the benefits of Bonanza Babies until the average would approximate 41 percent again. Congress debated reducing the benefits of the Bonanza Babies, many of whom still receive benefits at the 60 percent level, but thought better of it. But now the Notch Babies are angry. The Notchers do not care that others were overpaid; they believe that their benefits were reduced, and of course, at first, they blamed the Social Security Administration (SSA). After getting nowhere with the SSA, they began to write to their representatives, and the representatives began to pester the SSA. In this situation, the agency cannot help a legislator with casework, so the only response the SSA could give the representatives was that the Notch was created by legislative mistake and can be rectified only by legislation. The following letter to a retirement magazine from a Notch Baby is representative:

> I received the enclosed information from my congressman, noting that since I was born in 1923, I am in the "Notch" years of 1916 to 1926. The Social Security benefits of people born in those years were unfairly reduced. I am greatly disturbed by this and am much surprised that a smart and aggressive politician has not jumped in and protected the senior citizens who are being denied money that is rightfully theirs.
>
> M.C.S., Florala, AL[25]

In an attempt to appease Notch constituents, more than one "smart and aggressive politician" has submitted legislation to extend the adjusted formula to even more citizens who do not deserve more than the 41 percent. In the 102nd Congress, five bills or resolutions were introduced that would require the secretary of health and human services to study the Notch problem and report to Congress on how to fix it (two of these five bills would establish commissions to do the same). Another five bills were introduced simply to provide those in the Notch with more money. Representative Roybal's bill was attached as an amendment to the Enterprise Zone Incentive Act of 1991 but was subsequently ruled out of order. Another concurrent resolution would have made it the sense of the House that "Notch relief" be tied to any tax relief or economic recovery legislation that might pass during that Congress. These various bills and resolutions had 350 cosponsors in the House and 51 in the Senate.[26]

Pork barrel projects accomplish much the same thing as casework does for Congress. The spending of several million federal dollars for a post office, military installation, dam, or water project benefits any local economy. Whether pork barrel money actually translates into votes the way casework does is debatable, but the politicians believe that it does. From the viewpoint of the agency, pork barreling promotes a better relationship than does casework because casework interferes with the agency mission, whereas pork barreling means growth and more money for the agency (e.g., another dam for the Army Corps).

Passage of the line item veto is meant to help control federal spending by providing the president with a tool to attack pork barrel spending.

Unfortunately for the FTC, it has no triangular relationship, it cannot help Congress with casework, and it is not in a position to help a representative bring home the pork, so it was very vulnerable when it took on powerful interests. Congress does have at its disposal tools for controlling the bureaucracy, but because of cozy triangles and dependency on bureaucrats for constituency service, Congress rarely finds it necessary to use those tools in any real sense.

THE TOOLS OF CONGRESSIONAL CONTROL OF BUREAUCRACY

As it would with the presidency, any standard text will list the tools of congressional control: (a) the power to create and organize agencies, (b) the power to control agency budgets, (c) the power to investigate agency activity, and (d) guidance legislation.[27]

The Power to Create and Organize Agencies

Here, it is true that what Congress gives it can (if it chooses) take away. The example of the FTC should make that clear. Generally, it never gets to the point that Congress has to take something away, because Congress often exercises caution in creating an agency. In the enabling legislation, Congress decides several crucial things for an agency. First, it decides the jurisdiction of the agency. In the case of the FTC, Congress later restricted the agency's jurisdiction several times. Second, Congress decides whether the agency will have the power to make rules. Remember from Chapter 1 that the FTC was not originally given the power to make rules; it could only issue cease and desist orders and had no power to enforce those. Even if an agency is given the power to promulgate rules, Congress can make it easy or difficult for the agency to make those rules. Because the FDA, too, would have the potential to step on the toes of powerful interests that Congress would prefer to protect, when Congress established the FDA, it was given the power to make rules, but Congress intended for that to be difficult.

Agencies can make decisions or policy in basically two ways. One is the rule promulgation procedure already referred to in earlier chapters. Here, an agency announces in the *Federal Register* that it is proposing to make a rule, announces a time and place for a hearing, receives input, and makes a decision. The decision is called a *rule,* and it has the force and effect of law. The hearing resembles a city council hearing or a meeting of student government. The second way that agencies can make decisions or policy is through a "quasi-judicial" hearing that looks every bit like a trial. These decisions are called *orders,* and they also have the force and effect of law. Congress provided the FDA with only the quasi-judicial procedure, which is a clumsy, time-consuming, and haphazard way of making policy. As a somewhat famous example, when the FDA wanted to force peanut butter manufacturers to increase the amount of peanuts in peanut butter by 2 percent, the hearing stretched into two decades (1950s and 1960s), generated tens of thousands of pages of testimony, and cost both taxpayers and companies much more than it should have.[28]

Congress also decides whether agencies will have the power to issue subpoenas, whether they will have the power to issue cease and desist orders, and whether they will be able to back them up. The degree to which an agency is likely to be successful in accomplishing legislative goals depends to a large degree on whether Congress intends for it to be successful, as seen by the powers given to the agency in the enabling legislation.

Clearly, Congress did not originally intend for either the FTC or the FDA to be very successful. Congress is more likely to restrict the powers of an agency initially in the enabling legislation than it is to rein in an agency later by restricting jurisdiction or rule-making ability.

The Power to Control Agency Budgets

The Constitution gives Congress the power to tax and spend, and clearly the power to control agency budgets rests here. To understand congressional budgeting and agencies, one must have a passing familiarity with the following concepts: "incrementalism," "budget authorization," and "budget appropriation."

Businesses or institutions smaller than the federal government often tie budget decisions to goals. If a business wants to increase sales, then additional resources go to the sales department. To increase production, one might hire additional help. The federal government does not do budgeting this way. (Indeed, this type of budgeting was forced on government in the 1960s but did not work.) Federal budget decisions are based on *incrementalism,* a process in which this year's budget is simply last year's budget plus inflation and plus, perhaps, a new program or two. Not a lot of soul-searching or analysis is done within either agencies or Congress when it comes to putting together the next year's budget.

Congress has divided its budget process into a bifurcated system of authorizations and appropriations. An *authorization* is the legal authority to spend; an *appropriation* is the actual "giving" of the money. Authorizations are done by the standing committees. For example, the House Agricultural Committee will authorize the USDA to spend a certain amount during the fiscal year. It will also hold hearings on new programs the USDA may be contemplating. The standing committees (and their subcommittees) form cozy triangles with agencies and interest groups.

Each house of Congress has an appropriations committee, and there agencies are actually provided with an appropriation for the fiscal year. Because the appropriations committees are supposed to abide by a spending ceiling recommended by Congress earlier in the year, appropriations are often smaller than authorizations. According to Richard Fenno, appropriations committees are expected to be the fiscal watchdogs and to cut appropriations. Therefore, authorizations always come in high.[29] Appropriations committees are not actually involved in cozy triangles, but members and their staffs maintain regular and close contact with agencies. Under normal circumstances, an agency would prepare a budget that would request an amount of money equal to what the agency had last year plus inflation. The director of the OMB might recommend small cuts, and the agency would try to negotiate with the OMB. If the agency were unsuccessful with the OMB, it would submit its slightly lower request to the standing committee for the authorization. Assuming a fairly cozy triangular relationship, the standing committee might restore the OMB cuts. The appropriations committee might cut the authorization slightly but perhaps not as much as did the OMB. The agency would then end up with not as much as it wanted but more than the president wanted it to have. Finally may come the sequester procedure or even a presidential impoundment. The budgeting process is accomplished through a seemingly interminable series of hearings in the authorization subcommittee, the authorization committee, and the appropriations committee. Bureaucrats who testify at these hearings are questioned about programs, effectiveness, and expectations for the agency.

The Power to Investigate Agency Activity

A good deal of what Congress does is called *legislative oversight,* and the name implies that Congress is aware of what agencies are doing. Hence, it sounds as if the popularly elected officials are controlling the bureaucracy. Actually, the authorization process referred to earlier is a form of legislative oversight, but cozy triangles and constituency service often inhibit effective oversight of this nature. When Congress restricted FTC activity, that, too, was a form of legislative oversight. The kind of oversight that citizens hear the most about is when an agency is called before Congress to explain "administrative irregularities,"[30] such as the purchase of a $60 hammer and a $300 toilet seat by the Air Force (which the agency apparently explained to congressional satisfaction!), the explosion of a space shuttle with astronauts and a civilian aboard, the wholesale failure of savings and loans institutions, and the sale of arms to a Central American rebel group when such sale was forbidden by law.

One could make the initial observation that all these irregularities come to the attention of the press, and to Congress, after the fact. In many instances, Congress is clearly not aware of what the agencies are doing or failing to do. Such oversight is done to show the people that Congress is attempting to control the situation and, it is hoped, to avoid a repeat performance.

Any standing committee has the power to investigate an agency over which it has jurisdiction, but Congress has deemed it necessary to create special committees (Government Operations in the House and Governmental Affairs in the Senate) to investigate agencies. Although investigations by the Government Operations Committee often get good press, they are not effective in terms of controlling agencies. The Government Operations Committee exercises ineffective control because it lacks a significant legislative function, because its members interlock with other standing committees (cozy triangles again), and, finally, because standing committees actually threaten the investigating committees so that the latter "back off."[31]

Perhaps two examples will help demonstrate why congressional investigation of agencies is not effective. When an investigative committee met to find out what happened in the space shuttle *Challenger* disaster, it found four basic things: (a) The O-ring had failed, (b) technicians in both private industry and the National Aeronautics and Space Administration (NASA) were aware of the potential for O-ring failure under the circumstances of the scheduled launch, (c) a warning of the potential failure of the O-ring did not find its way to a high-level NASA decision maker with the power to cancel the launch, and (d) the reason a warning of potential disaster did not reach the appropriate NASA decision maker was that only good news reaches the top of a bureaucratic organization and that those at the top are "protected" against bad news. Even if Congress had cared to legislate against this bureaucratic principle (it did not), it would have been difficult to do so. Consequently, even today, bad news still gets lost somewhere near the top of a bureaucracy.

A second example involves the Contra half of the Iran-Contra scandal. It is clear now that the CIA was involved in selling arms to the Contras at a time when such activity was prohibited by law. In October 1986, the Nicaraguan government shot down a CIA airplane delivering arms to the Contras. The survivor of the aircraft revealed that this had been a CIA operation, and he identified one of the CIA operatives who ran it as Max Gomez. The Senate Foreign Relations Committee immediately called in Mr. Friers (head of the CIA Central American task force) and Mr. George (number-three man at the CIA) to find out whether Gomez worked for the CIA and whether the agency was involved. According to Friers's testimony at George's trial for lying to Congress, they both knew who Gomez really was and that he was indeed with the CIA, but they had lied to Congress.[32] Not only did they lie, but they also then returned to the agency and joked about their perjury.[33] The fact that mid- to high-level bureaucrats control information and expertise has been referred to in this text previously, and although this example may be an extreme case, it graphically illustrates how dependent Congress really is.

In mid-March 1997, President Clinton's nominee to head the CIA, Anthony Lake, withdrew his name from consideration amid allegations that he lied to Congress about arms sales to Bosnian Muslims and that he withheld information from Congress about Chinese influence in the 1996 election.

Some significant oversight is conducted by the investigative agency that works for Congress: the General Accounting Office (GAO). The GAO would have documented that the Pentagon procurement office actually paid $300 for a toilet seat. The problem with oversight by the GAO is that its investigations occur long after the fact and its reports do little to address solutions to problems. It is testimony to cozy triangles and the ineffectiveness of oversight that a bureaucrat from the procurement office could explain such an expenditure to the satisfaction of congressional committee members.

Guidance Legislation

Guidance legislation is a term given to legislation that applies to all agencies, rather than to each agency individually. Examples are the Pendleton Act, the Administrative Procedure Act (APA), the Hatch Act, the Freedom of Information Act (FOIA), and the Sunshine Act.

The Pendleton Act is what you would recognize as the Civil Service Act, and it depoliticized and professionalized bureaucracy. You will come to know the APA well by the time you have finished this course. It is the major legislation that controls and standardizes agency procedure and court review of agency action. The Hatch Act forbids federal employees from contributing money or taking an active part in federal election campaigns. Both the FOIA and the Sunshine Act are amendments to the APA, but they allow citizens to access the information that agencies have (FOIA) and to force governmental policy making to be conducted in open hearings (Sunshine Act). Not too long ago, cozy triangles did their work in closed committee hearings and behind the closed doors of administrative agencies and were not compelled to release pertinent information to the public. The Sunshine Act was passed in 1976 and the FOIA in 1966. Generally, guidance legislation has been beneficial in a democratic context because it has reduced agency discretion and imposed regularized congressional control.

DELEGATION OF POWER

"Congressional power, like chastity, is never lost, rarely taken by force, and almost always given away."[34] As with presidential removal, the Constitution does not address the problem of Congress's giving away its Article I, Section 8, powers. This is probably because the men who drafted the Constitution had all read John Locke, who argued that elected representatives should never give their power to anyone or anything (another institution). The reason is simple: If the citizens elect the representatives and the representatives make the policy, then the people, judging the policies, can hold the representatives accountable. If the representatives have given their power to someone else who does not stand for election, then the people lose accountability and, therefore, democracy. Because the Constitution does not address the question of delegation of power, that question remains for the courts to deal with. Early justices of the Supreme Court also read John Locke, and they articulated a theory of jurisprudence that would become known as the *Nondelegation Doctrine.* That doctrine says it is unconstitutional for the legislature to delegate its power.

As you will see from the following case, although the Supreme Court said the words "nondelegation doctrine," it allowed delegations almost from the beginning. The modern problem in terms of delegation of power is not *whether* Congress should delegate its power, but rather *how* Congress should delegate its power.

HAMPTON V. UNITED STATES
276 U.S. 394 (1928)

Chief Justice Taft delivered the opinion for a unanimous Court.

J. W. Hampton, Jr., & Co. made an importation into New York of barium dioxide which the collector of customs assessed at the dutiable rate of six cents per pound. This was two cents per pound more than that fixed by statute. The rate was raised by the collector by virtue of the proclamation of the President, issued under, and by authority of, section 315 of title 3 of the Tariff Act of September 21, 1922, which is the so-called flexible tariff provision. Protest was made and an appeal was taken.
. . . The case came on for hearing before the United States Customs Court. A majority held the act constitutional. Thereafter the case was appealed to the United States Court of Customs Appeals. On the 16th day of October, 1926, the Attorney General certified that in his opinion the case was of such importance as to render expedient its review by this Court.

. . . The pertinent part of the Tariff Act says that in order to regulate the foreign commerce of the United States and to put into force and effect the policy of the Congress by this act intended, whenever the President, upon investigation of the differences in costs of production of articles wholly or in part the growth or product of the United States and of like or similar articles wholly or in part the growth or product of competing foreign countries, shall find it thereby shown that the duties fixed in this act do not equalize the said differences in costs of production in the United States and the principal competing country he shall, by such investigation, ascertain said differences and determine and proclaim the changes in classifications or increases or decreases in any rate of duty provided in this act shown by said ascertained differences in such costs of production necessary to equalize the same. The President issued his proclamation May 19, 1924. ". . . Now, therefore, I, Calvin Coolidge, President of the United States of America, do hereby determine and proclaim that the increase in rate of duty provided in said act shown by said ascertained differences in said costs of production necessary to equalize the same is as follows: 'An increase in said duty on barium dioxide (within the limit of total increase provided for in said act) from 4 cents per pound to 6 cents per pound.' "

. . . The issue here is as to the constitutionality of section 315, upon which depends the authority for the proclamation of the President and for two of the six cents per pound duty collected from the petitioner. The contention of the taxpayers is twofold—first, they argue that the section is invalid in that it is a delegation to the President of the legislative power, which by article 1, § 1 of the Constitution, is vested in Congress, the power being that declared in section 8 of article 1, that the Congress shall have power to lay and collect taxes, duties, imposts and excises. Their second objection is that, as section 315 was enacted with the avowed intent and for the purpose of protecting the industries of the United States, it is invalid because the Constitution gives power to lay such taxes only for revenue.

[1] First. It seems clear what Congress intended by section 315. Its plan was to secure by law the imposition of customs duties on articles of imported merchandise which should equal the difference between the cost of producing in a foreign country the articles in question and laying them down for sale in the United States, and the cost of producing and selling like or similar articles in the United States, so that the duties not only secure revenue, but at the same time enable domestic producers to compete on terms of equality with foreign producers in the markets of the United States. It may be that it is difficult to fix with exactness this difference, but the difference which is sought in the statute is perfectly clear and perfectly intelligible. Because of the difficulty in practically determining what that difference is, Congress seems to have doubted that the information in its possession was such as to enable it to make the adjustment accurately, and also to have apprehended that with changing conditions the difference might vary in such a way that some readjustments would be necessary to give effect to the principle on which the statute proceeds. To avoid such difficulties, Congress adopted in section 315 the method of describing with clearness what its policy and plan was and then authorizing a member of the executive branch to carry out its policy and plan and to find the changing difference from time to time and to make the adjustments necessary to conform the duties to the standard underlying that policy and plan.

. . . Our Federal Constitution and state Constitutions of this country divide the governmental power into three branches. The first is the legislative, the second is the executive, and the third is the judicial, and the rule is that in the actual administration of the government Congress or the Legislature should exercise the legislative power, the President or the state executive, the Governor, the executive power, and the courts or the judiciary the judicial power, and in carrying out that constitutional division into three branches it is a breach of the national fundamental law if Congress gives up its legislative power and transfers it to the President, or to the judicial branch, or if by law it attempts to invest itself or its members with either executive power or judicial power. This is not to say that the three branches are not co-ordinate parts of one government and that each in the field of its duties may not invoke the action of the two other branches in so far as the action invoked shall not be an assumption of the constitutional field of action of another branch. In determining what it may do in seeking assistance from another branch, the extent and character of that assistance must be fixed according to common sense and the inherent necessities of the governmental coordination.

. . . As Judge Ranney, of the Ohio Supreme Court in Cincinnati, said in such a case: "The true distinction, therefore, is, between the delegation of power to make the law, which necessarily involves a discretion as to what it shall be, and conferring an authority or discretion as to its execution, to be exercised under and in pursuance of the law. The first cannot be done; to the latter no valid objection can be made." Again, one of the great functions conferred on Congress by the Federal Constitution is the regulation of interstate commerce and rates to be exacted by interstate carriers for the passenger and merchandise traffic. The rates to be fixed are myriad. If Congress were to be required to fix every rate, it would be impossible to exercise the power at all. Therefore, common sense requires that in the fixing of such rates Congress may provide a Commission, as it does, called the Interstate Commerce Commission, to fix those rates, after hearing evidence and argument concerning them from interested parties, all in accord with a general rule that Congress first lays down that rates shall be just and reasonable considering the service given and not discriminatory. As said by this Court in *Interstate Commerce Commission v. Goodrich Transit Co.,* 224 U.S. 194, "The Congress may not delegate its

purely legislative power to a commission, but, having laid down the general rules of action under which a commission shall proceed, it may require of that commission the application of such rules to particular situations and the investigation of facts, with a view to making orders in a particular matter within the rules laid down by the Congress."

. . . It is conceded by counsel that Congress may use executive officers in the application and enforcement of a policy declared in law by Congress and authorize such officers in the application of the congressional declaration to enforce it by regulation equivalent to law. But it is said that this never has been permitted to be done where Congress has exercised the power to levy taxes and fix customs duties. The authorities make no such distinction. The same principle that permits Congress to exercise its rate-making power in interstate commerce by declaring the rule which shall prevail in the legislative fixing of rates, and enables it to remit to a rate-making body created in accordance with its provisions the fixing of such rates, justifies a similar provision for the fixing of customs duties on imported merchandise. *If Congress shall lay down by legislative act an intelligible principle to which the person or body authorized to fix such rates is directed to conform, such legislative action is not a forbidden delegation of legislative power* [italics added]. If it is thought wise to vary the customs duties according to changing conditions of production at home and abroad, it may authorize the Chief Executive to carry out this purpose, with the advisory assistance of a Tariff Commission appointed under congressional authority. This conclusion is amply sustained by a case in which there was no advisory commission furnished the President—a case to which this Court gave the fullest consideration nearly 40 years ago. In *Marshall Field & Co. v. Clark,* 143 U.S. 649, the third section of the Act of October 1890 contained this provision: "That with a view to secure reciprocal trade with countries producing the following articles, and for this purpose, on and after the first day of January, eighteen hundred and ninety-two, whenever, and so often as the President shall be satisfied that the government of any country producing and exporting sugars, molasses, coffee, tea and hides, raw and uncured, or any of such articles, imposes duties or other exactions upon the agricultural or other products of the United States, which in view of the free introduction of such sugar, molasses, coffee, tea and hides into the United States he may deem to be reciprocally unequal and unreasonable, he shall have the power and it shall be his duty to suspend, by proclamation to that effect, the provisions of this act relating to the free introduction of such sugar, molasses, coffee, tea and hides, the production of such country, for such time as he shall deem just, and in such case and during such suspension duties shall be lived, collected, and paid upon sugar, molasses, coffee, tea and hides, the product of or exported from such designated country as follows, namely."

Then followed certain rates of duty to be imposed. It was contended that this section delegated to the President both legislative and treaty-making powers and was unconstitutional. After an examination of all the authorities, the Court said that, while Congress could not delegate legislative power to the President, this act did not in any real sense invest the President with the power of legislation, because nothing involving the [expediency] or just operation of such legislation was left to the determination of the President; that the legislative power was exercised when Congress declared that the suspension should take effect upon a named contingency. What the President was required to do was merely in execution of the act of Congress. It

was not the making of law. He was the mere agent of the lawmaking department to ascertain and declare the event upon which its expressed will was to take effect.

[3] Second. . . . It is contended that the only power of Congress in the levying of customs duties is to create revenue, and that it is unconstitutional to frame the customs duties with any other view than that of revenue raising. As we said in the Child Labor Tax Case, "Taxes are occasionally imposed in the discretion of the Legislature on proper subjects with the primary motive of obtaining revenue from them and with the incidental motive of discouraging them by making their continuance onerous. They do not lose their character as taxes because of the incidental motive." And so here the fact that Congress declares that one of its motives in fixing the rates of duty is so to fix them that they shall encourage the industries of this country in the competition with producers in other countries in the sale of goods in this country cannot invalidate a revenue act so framed. Section 315 and its provisions are within the power of Congress.

The judgment of the Court of Customs Appeals is affirmed.

Question

It is obvious in the *Hampton* case that the Court will allow congressional delegations of power under certain circumstances. Those circumstances constitute the Court doctrine or the constitutional test for when a delegation of power is constitutional. Can you state that doctrine?

The Court Applies the Hampton *Test*

The *Hampton* case was decided in 1928, and seven years later the Court struck down two congressional delegations of power. In *Panama Refining Company v. Ryan,* 293 U.S. 388 (1935), the Court declared the following delegation of power to be unconstitutional:

Section 9 * * * (c) of the National Industrial Recovery Act says: The President is authorized to prohibit the transportation in interstate and foreign commerce of petroleum and the products thereof produced or withdrawn from storage in excess of the amount permitted to be produced or withdrawn from storage by any state law or valid regulation or order prescribed thereunder. . . . Any violation of any order of the President issued under the provisions of this subsection shall be punishable by fine of not to exceed $1,000, or imprisonment for not to exceed six months, or both.

From the delegation just quoted, the president delegated to the secretary of the interior the power to promulgate rules to prohibit the interstate shipment of "hot oil" (oil produced and sold in violation of production quotas). The secretary's rule required petroleum producers to file, under oath, a monthly report of their production. The rule also required buyers of petroleum to file similar reports. The Court said that Congress had failed to provide "intelligible standards or principles" or guidelines with the delegation so that administrative discretion could be held in check.

Five months later, the Court held Section 3 of the National Industrial Recovery Act to be unconstitutional in a famous case called the "Sick Chicken Case," *Schechter Poultry Corporation v. United States,* 295 U.S. 495 (1935). Section 3 of the Recovery Act authorized the president to approve Codes of Fair Competition. One of the codes that he approved was called the Live Poultry Code, and he approved it by issuing an executive order. The constitutional problem with the delegation of power here was that Congress had authorized *private* trade associations to create codes of fair competition for their own industry and to present them to the president for authorization. The act did specify a few things of which the president had to be assured before authorizing the code, but the real problem here was not simply the absence of "intelligible standards"; it was a delegation of legislative power to private business groups!

What is now called the Delegation Doctrine says that congressional delegations of power are constitutional so long as they are accompanied by sufficient standards or guidelines so that the executive branch's exercise of legislative power is not unbridled and that, rather, the exercise of such power is channeled and controlled by Congress. The Court has declared that the best way for Congress to channel and control the administrative exercise of legislative power is for the delegation of power to be accompanied by "intelligible standards or principles or guidelines."

The *Benzene* case, which follows, is notable for Justice Rehnquist's concurring opinion. How well do you think the Court applied the Delegation Doctrine to the Occupational Safety and Health Administration's (OSHA's) regulation of benzene?

INDUSTRIAL UNION DEPARTMENT AFL-CIO V.
AMERICAN PETROLEUM INSTITUTE (THE BENZENE CASE)
488 U.S. 607 (1980)

Justice Stevens announced the judgment of the Court and delivered the opinion. Chief Justice Burger concurred, as did Justices Stewart, Powell, and Rehnquist. Justice Marshall's dissent was joined by Justices Brennan, White, and Blackmun.

The Occupational Safety and Health Act of 1970 (Act), 84 Stat. 1590, 29 U.S.C. § 651 et seq., was enacted for the purpose of ensuring safe and healthful working conditions for every working man and woman in the Nation. This litigation concerns a standard promulgated by the Secretary of Labor to regulate occupational exposure to benzene, a substance which has been shown to cause cancer at high exposure levels. The principal question is whether such a showing is a sufficient basis for a standard that places the most stringent limitation on exposure to benzene that is technologically and economically possible.

The Act delegates broad authority to the Secretary to promulgate different kinds of standards. The basic definition of an "occupational safety and health standard" is found in § 3(8), which provides: "The term 'occupational safety and health standard' means a standard which requires conditions, or the adoption or use of one or more practices, means, methods, operations, or processes, reasonably necessary or appropriate to provide safe or healthful employment and places of employment." Where toxic materials or harmful physical agents are concerned, a standard must also comply with § 6(b)(5), which provides: "The Secretary, in promulgating standards dealing with toxic materials or harmful physical agents under this subsection, shall set the standard which most adequately assures, to the extent feasible, on the basis of the best available evidence, that no employee will suffer material impairment of health or functional capacity even if such employee has regular exposure to the hazard dealt with by such standard for the period of his working life. Development of standards under this subsection shall be based upon research, demonstrations, experiments, and such other information as may be appropriate. In addition to the attainment of the highest degree of health and safety protection for the employee, other considerations shall be the latest available scien-

tific data in the field, the feasibility of the standards, and experience gained under this and other health and safety laws."

* * *

Wherever the toxic material to be regulated is a carcinogen, the Secretary has taken the position that no safe exposure level can be determined and that § 6(b)(5) requires him to set an exposure limit at the lowest technologically feasible level that will not impair the viability of the industries regulated. In this case, after having determined that there is a causal connection between benzene and leukemia (a cancer of the white blood cells), the Secretary set an exposure limit on airborne concentrations of benzene of one part benzene per million parts of air (1 ppm), regulated dermal and eye contact with solutions containing benzene, and imposed complex monitoring and medical testing requirements on employers whose workplaces contain 0.5 ppm or more of benzene. . . . On pre-enforcement review . . . the United States Court of Appeals for the Fifth Circuit held the regulation invalid. *American Petroleum Institute v. OSHA*, 581 F.2d 493 (1978). The court concluded that the Occupational Safety and Health Administration (OSHA) had exceeded its standard-setting authority because it had not shown that the new benzene exposure limit was "reasonably necessary or appropriate to provide safe or healthful employment" as required by § 3(8), and because § 6(b)(5) does "not give OSHA the unbridled discretion to adopt standards designed to create absolutely risk-free workplaces regardless of costs." Reaching the two provisions together, the Fifth Circuit held that the Secretary was under a duty to determine whether the benefits expected from the new standard bore a reasonable relationship to the costs that it imposed. The court noted that OSHA had made an estimate of the costs of compliance, but that the record lacked substantial evidence of any discernible benefits. . . .

[1] We agree with the Fifth Circuit's holding that § 3(8) requires the Secretary to find, as a threshold matter, that the toxic substance in question poses a significant health risk in the workplace and that a new, lower standard is therefore "reasonably nec-

essary or appropriate to provide safe or healthful employment and places of employment." Unless and until such a finding is made, it is not necessary to address the further question whether the Court of Appeals correctly held that there must be a reasonable correlation between costs and benefits, or whether, as the federal parties argue, the Secretary is then required by § 6(b)(5) to promulgate a standard that goes as far as technologically and economically possible to eliminate the risk.

Because these are unusually important cases of first impression, we have reviewed the record with special care. In this opinion, we (1) describe the benzene standard, (2) analyze the Agency's rationale for imposing a 1 ppm exposure limit, (3) discuss the controlling legal issues, and (4) comment briefly on the dermal contact limitation.

I

Benzene is a familiar and important commodity. It is a colorless, aromatic liquid that evaporates rapidly under ordinary atmospheric conditions. Approximately 11 billion pounds of benzene were produced in the United States in 1976. Ninety-four percent of that total was produced by the petroleum and petrochemical industries, with the remainder produced by the steel industry as a byproduct of coking operations. Benzene is used in manufacturing a variety of products including motor fuels (which may contain as much as 2% benzene), solvents, detergents, pesticides, and other organic chemicals. 43 Fed.Reg. 5918 (1978).

The entire population of the United States is exposed to small quantities of benzene, ranging from a few parts per billion to 0.5 ppm, in the ambient air. Over one million workers are subject to additional low-level exposures as a consequence of their employment. The majority of these employees work in gasoline service stations, benzene production (petroleum refineries and coking operations), chemical processing, benzene transportation, rubber manufacturing, and laboratory operations. . . .

Benzene is a toxic substance. Although it could conceivably cause harm to a person who swallowed or touched it, the principal risk of harm comes from inhalation of benzene vapors. When these vapors are inhaled, the benzene diffuses through the lungs and is quickly absorbed into the blood. Exposure to high concentrations produces an almost immediate effect on the central nervous system. Inhalation

of concentrations of 20,000 ppm can be fatal within minutes; exposures in the range of 250 to 500 ppm can cause vertigo, nausea, and other symptoms of mild poisoning. Persistent exposures at levels above 25-40 ppm may lead to blood deficiencies and diseases of the blood-forming organs, including aplastic anemia, which is generally fatal.

Industrial health experts have long been aware that exposure to benzene may lead to various types of nonmalignant diseases. By 1948 the evidence connecting high levels of benzene to serious blood disorders had become so strong that the Commonwealth of Massachusetts imposed a 35 ppm limitation on workplaces within its jurisdiction. In 1969 the American National Standards Institute (ANSI) adopted a national consensus standard of 10 ppm averaged over an 8-hour period with a ceiling concentration of 25 ppm for 10-minute periods or a maximum peak concentration of 50 ppm. Id., at 5919. In 1971, after the Occupational Safety and Health Act was passed, the Secretary adopted this consensus standard as the federal standard. . . . The final standard was issued on February 10, 1978.

In its final form, the benzene standard is designed to protect workers from whatever hazards are associated with low-level benzene exposures by requiring employers to monitor workplaces to determine the level of exposure, to provide medical examinations when the level rises above 0.5 ppm, and to institute whatever engineering or other controls are necessary to keep exposures at or below 1 ppm. . . . As presently formulated, the benzene standard is an expensive way of providing some additional protection for a relatively small number of employees. According to OSHA's figures, the standard will require capital investments in engineering controls of approximately $266 million, first-year operating costs (for monitoring, medical testing, employee training, and respirators) of $187 million to $205 million and recurring annual costs of approximately $34 million. The figures outlined in OSHA's explanation of the costs of compliance to various industries indicate that only 35,000 employees would gain any benefit from the regulation in terms of a reduction in their exposure to benzene. Over two-thirds of these workers (24,450) are employed in the rubber-manufacturing industry. Compliance costs in that industry are estimated to be rather low, with no capital costs and initial operating expenses estimated at only $34 million ($1,390 per employee); recurring annual costs would also be rather low, totalling less than $1 million. By contrast, the segment of the petroleum refining industry that produces benzene would be required to incur $24 million in capital costs and $600,000 in first-year operating expenses to provide additional protection for 300 workers ($82,000 per employee), while the petrochemical industry would be required to incur $20.9 million in capital costs and $1 million in initial operating expenses for the benefit of 552 employees ($39,675 per employee). . . .

[3] Any discussion of the 1 ppm exposure limit must, of course, begin with the Agency's rationale for imposing that limit. The written explanation of the standard fills 184 pages of the printed appendix. Much of it is devoted to a discussion of the voluminous evidence of the adverse effects of exposure to benzene at levels of concentration well above 10 ppm.

OSHA did not state, however, that the nonmalignant effects of benzene exposure justified a reduction in the permissible exposure limit to 1 ppm. In the end OSHA's rationale for lowering the permissible exposure limit to 1 ppm was based, not on any finding that leukemia has ever been caused by exposure to 10 ppm of benzene and that it will not be caused by exposure to 1 ppm, but rather on a series of assumptions indicating that some leukemias might result from exposure to 10 ppm and that the number of cases might be reduced by reducing the exposure level to 1 ppm.

In light of the Agency's disavowal of any ability to determine the numbers of employees likely to be adversely affected by exposures of 10 ppm, the Court of Appeals held this finding to be unsupported by the record.

[5] If the purpose of the statute were to eliminate completely and with absolute certainty any risk of serious harm, we would agree that it would be proper for the Secretary to interpret §§ 3(8) and 6(b)(5) in this fashion. But we think it is clear that the statute was not designed to require employers to provide absolutely risk-free workplaces whenever it is technologically feasible to do so, so long as the cost is not great enough to destroy an entire industry. Rather, both the language and structure of the Act, as well as its legislative history, indicate that it was intended to require the elimination, as far as feasible, of significant risks of harm.

[6] By empowering the Secretary to promulgate standards that are "reasonably necessary or appropriate to provide safe or healthful employment and places of employment," the Act implies that, before promulgating any standard, the Secretary must make a finding that the workplaces in question are not safe. But "safe" is not the equivalent of "risk-free." There are many activities that we engage in every day—such as driving a car or even breathing city air—that entail some risk of accident or material health impairment; nevertheless, few people would consider these activities "unsafe." Similarly, a workplace can hardly be considered "unsafe" unless it threatens the workers with a significant risk of harm.

[7][8] Therefore, before he can promulgate any permanent health or safety standard, the Secretary is required to make a threshold finding that a place of employment is unsafe—in the sense that significant risks are present and can be eliminated or lessened by a change in practices.

[10] In this case the record makes it perfectly clear that the Secretary relied squarely on a special policy for carcinogens that imposed the burden on industry of proving the existence of a safe level of exposure, thereby avoiding the Secretary's threshold responsibility of establishing the need for more stringent standards. In so interpreting his statutory authority, the Secretary exceeded his power. . . . The judgment of the Court of Appeals remanding the petition for review to the Secretary for further proceedings is affirmed.

It is so ordered.

Justice Rehnquist, concurring in the judgment.

The statutory provision at the center of the present controversy, § 6(b)(5) of the Occupational Safety and Health Act of 1970, states, in relevant part, that the Secretary of Labor " . . . in promulgating standards dealing with toxic materials or harmful physical agents . . . shall set the standard which most adequately assures, to the extent feasible, on the basis of the best available evidence, that no employee will suffer material impairment of health or functional capacity even if such employee has regular exposure to the hazard dealt with by such standard for the period of his working life." According to the Secretary, who is one of the petitioners herein, § 6(b)(5) imposes upon him an absolute duty, in regulating harmful substances like benzene for which no safe level is known, to set the standard for permissible exposure at the lowest level that "can be achieved at bearable cost with available technology." . . .

Respondents reply that § 6(b)(5) must be read in light of another provision in the same Act, § 3(8), which . . . requires the Secretary to demonstrate that any particular health standard is justifiable on the basis of a rough balancing of costs and benefits. In considering these alternative interpretations, my colleagues manifest a good deal of uncertainty, and ultimately divide over whether the Secretary produced sufficient evidence that the proposed standard for benzene will result in any appreciable benefits at all. This uncertainty, I would suggest, is eminently justified, since I believe that this litigation presents the Court with what has to be one of the most difficult issues that could confront a decisionmaker: whether the statistical possibility of future deaths should ever be disregarded in light of the economic costs of preventing those deaths. . . . Congress, the governmental body best suited and most obligated to make the choice confronting us in this litigation, has improperly delegated that choice to the Secretary of Labor and, derivatively, to this Court. . . . In his Second Treatise of Civil Government, published in 1690, John Locke wrote that "[t]he . . . legislative can have no power to transfer their authority of making laws and place it in other hands." . . . The rule against delegation of legislative power is not, however, so cardinal of principle as to allow for no exception. . . .

This Court also has recognized that a hermetic sealing-off of the three branches of government from one another could easily frustrate the establishment of a National Government capable of effectively exercising the substantive powers granted to the various branches by the Constitution. . . . Later decisions that have upheld congressional delegations of authority to the Executive Branch have done so largely on the theory that Congress may wish to exercise its authority in a particular field, but because the field is sufficiently technical, the ground to be covered sufficiently large, and the Members of Congress themselves not necessarily expert in the area in which they choose to legislate, the most that may be asked under the separation-of-powers doctrine is that Congress lay down the general policy and standards that animate the law, leaving the agency to refine those standards, "fill in the blanks," or apply the standards to particular cases.

These decisions, to my mind, simply illustrate the above-quoted principle stated more than 50 years ago by Mr. Chief Justice Taft that delegations of legislative authority must be judged "according to common sense and the inherent necessities of the governmental co-ordination."

Viewing the legislation at issue here in light of these principles, I believe that it fails to pass muster. . . . In drafting § 6(b)(5), Congress was faced with a clear, if difficult, choice between balancing statistical lives and industrial resources or authorizing the Secretary to elevate human life above all concerns save massive dislocation in an affected industry. That Congress recognized the difficulty of this choice is clear. . . . That Congress chose, intentionally or unintentionally, to pass this difficult choice on to the Secretary is evident from the spectral quality of the standard it selected and is capsulized in Senator Saxbe's unfulfilled promise that "the terms that we are passing back and forth are going to have to be identified."

As formulated and enforced by this Court, the nondelegation doctrine serves three important functions. First, and most abstractly, it ensures to the extent consistent with orderly governmental administration that important choices of social policy are made by Congress, the branch of our Government most responsive to the popular will. See *Arizona v. California,* 373 U.S. 546, 626 (HARLAN, J., dissenting in part); *United States v. Robel,* 389 U.S. 258, 276 (1967) (BRENNAN, J., concurring in result). Second, the doctrine guarantees that, to the extent Congress finds it necessary to delegate authority, it provides the recipient of that authority with an "intelligible principle" to guide the exercise of the delegated discretion. See *J. W. Hampton & Co. v. United States,* 276 U.S., at 409 (1928); *Panama Refining Co. v. Ryan,* 293 U.S., at 430. Third, and derivative of the second, the doctrine ensures that courts charged with reviewing the exercise of delegated legislative discretion will be able to test that exercise against ascertainable standards. See *Arizona v. California,* supra, 373 U.S., at 626 (HARLAN, J., dissenting in part); *American Power & Light Co. v. SEC,* supra, at 106.

I believe the legislation at issue here fails on all three counts. The decision whether the law of diminishing returns should have any place in the regulation of toxic substances is quintessentially one of legislative policy. For Congress to pass that decision on to the Secretary in the manner it did violates, in my mind, John Locke's caveat—reflected in the cases cited earlier in this opinion—that legislatures are to make laws, not legislators. Nor, as I think the prior discussion amply demonstrates, do the provisions at issue or their legislative history provide the Secretary with any guidance that might lead him to his somewhat tentative conclusion that he must eliminate exposure to benzene as far as technologically and economically possible. Finally, I would suggest that the standard of "feasibility" renders meaningful judicial review impossible. . . . A number of observers have suggested that this Court should once more take up its burden of ensuring that Congress does not unnecessarily delegate important choices of social policy to politically unresponsive administrators. Other observers, as might be imagined, have disagreed. . . .

If we are ever to reshoulder the burden of ensuring that Congress itself make the critical policy decisions, these are surely the cases in which to do it. It is difficult to imagine a more obvious example of Congress simply avoiding a choice which was both fundamental for purposes of the statute and yet politically so divisive that the necessary decision or compromise was difficult, if not impossible, to hammer out in the legislative forge. Far from detracting from the substantive authority of Congress, a declaration that the first sentence of § 6(b)(5) of the Occupational Safety and Health Act constitutes an invalid delegation to the Secretary of Labor would preserve the authority of Congress. If Congress wishes to legislate in an area which it has not previously sought to enter, it will in today's politi-

cal world undoubtedly run into opposition no matter how the legislation is formulated. But that is the very essence of legislative authority under our system. It is the hard choices, and not the filling in of the blanks, which must be made by the elected representatives of the people. When fundamental policy decisions underlying important legislation about to be enacted are to be made, the buck stops with Congress and the president insofar as he exercises his constitutional role in the legislative process.

I would invalidate the first sentence of § 6(b)(5) of the occupational Safety and Health Act of 1970 as it applies to any toxic substance or harmful physical agent for which a safe level, that is, a level at which "no employee will suffer material impairment of health or functional capacity even if such employee has regular exposure to [that hazard] for the period of his working life," is, according to the Secretary, unknown or otherwise "infeasible." Absent further congressional action, the Secretary would then have to choose, when acting pursuant to § 6(b)(5), between setting a safe standard or setting no standard at all. Accordingly, for the reasons stated above, I concur in the judgment of the Court affirming the judgment of the Court of Appeals.

Questions

1. Did the Court declare Section 6(b)(5) of the Occupational Safety and Health Act to be an unconstitutional delegation of power?
2. Can you synthesize Justice Rehnquist's argument into a short paragraph? Do you agree with him? Why?

Since the two cases in 1935, the Supreme Court has not declared a congressional delegation of power to be unconstitutional, and it has reviewed some broad and sweeping delegations. See whether you believe that the following delegations of power supply sufficient guidelines so that they channel administrative discretion.

1. A price control administrator is delegated the power to "set generally fair and equitable prices."[35]
2. The Securities and Exchange Commission (SEC) is delegated the power "to prevent an unfair or inequitable distribution of voting power among security holders."[36]

3. The Federal Power Commission (FPC) is delegated the power "to determine just and reasonable rates."[37]

4. The Federal Communications Commission (FCC) is delegated the power to grant broadcast licenses "as the public interest, convenience, or necessity require."[38]

5. The secretary of every federal department is delegated the power "to determine when excessive profits have been realized" and to renegotiate federal contracts with those who realized such profits.[39]

Congress may have reasons for giving away so much unregulated power. Justice Rehnquist refers to some of those reasons in the *Benzene* case: Increasing problems require more areas for regulation; the areas in need of regulation are increasingly technical, and Congress lacks the expertise to be precise in its language; and the subject matter to be regulated may be too broad for Congress to be specific. The point of Justice Rehnquist's concurring opinion, however, is that what was delegated to OSHA was the power to decide which is more important: the life of a worker or industry profits. When Congress, which *is* constitutionally empowered to make such decisions or value judgments, passes this power on to an unelected bureaucrat, the citizens have lost significant control of their democracy. Justice Rehnquist is not the only one to argue that the U.S. Supreme Court should continue to declare every overly broad, vague, and loose delegation of congressional power to be unconstitutional.[40]

Situations like this do not develop independently of historical context. Congress has delegated its power to the executive branch almost from the beginning.[41] Initially, the federal government was small and operated under an ideology (negative freedom, limited government, and laissez-faire economics) that restricted governmental activity. Therefore, Congress felt no particular need to go to great lengths to keep an eye on the bureaucracy. With the onset of the progressive era and the realignment of the 1930s, however, Congress began to enact distributive, redistributive, and regulatory policies,[42] which often require congressional reliance on expertise. This had two consequences: First, it changed the political nature of Congress. As constituents came to rely on entitlements and to expect other benefits, such as pork barrel projects, elected representatives had to spend more time on casework, pork barrel legislation, and building relationships with bureaucrats. Second, because legislative politics had changed, institutional processes changed, too, so cozy triangles developed and legislative oversight became important. Congress developed the legislative veto as one means of exercising its control over the now far-flung and disparate activities of the bureaucracy.

Republican Majorities in Congress
and the Will to Control Bureaucracy

Some of what I have said above about the lack of congressional will to control bureaucracy may not comport with reality for those who watched the Republicans take control of Congress in the 1994 election. The Contract With America and accompanying campaign rhetoric were an attack on governmental status quo, and a good deal of it was aimed at Congress's partner in sin, the bureaucracy. It is certainly true that the Gingrich Republican leadership and those who were elected as freshmen in 1994 are possessed of more of a will to control bureaucracy than are more moderate Republicans and most Democrats. It is also true that it takes 218 votes in the House and 51 in the Senate to exercise more control over agencies, and the 1994 Republic freshmen class and its leadership have not been able to muster the required votes to either pass legislation or pass it over a presidential veto. Very little of the Contract With America got passed in the 104th Congress (1995 and 1996), and prospects for "radical" change do not look good for the Republicans in the 105th Congress either (1997 and 1998).

The Contract With America was, in reality, only a promise to bring certain legislation to the floor of the House for a vote within the first one hundred days of new Republican control of the House, and in that sense the contract was met. Some of it passed the House floor; some did not. The following is an account of what happened to Contract with America legislation that relates to bureaucracy. Welfare reform (Aid to Families with Dependent Children [AFDC], as opposed to the hundreds of other welfare programs) passed. It is unlikely to affect the size or scope of the Department of Health and Human Services (HHS). Indeed, it will, in all probability, produce bureaucratic growth at the state and local levels to deal with poverty in ways that those levels of government have never done before. Some, but not all, agricultural subsidies were legislated out of existence. The line item veto was passed, and that could affect agency budgets. Legislation was passed that prohibits unfunded mandates and that could inhibit agency growth by reducing agency proposals for new programs or regulations.

One section of the contract was entitled "Roll Back Government Regulations" and had three specific legislative proposals. One was the banning of unfunded mandates discussed above. A second was the Paperwork Reduction Act discussed in Chapter 2. A third would impose cost-benefit and risk assessment analysis on all federal agencies before they could propose rules, regulations, or standards. This legislation also included a requirement that any agency action that reduced the value of property would require just compensation.

To impose a cost-benefit procedure on all agencies would require either the amending of the APA or new guidance legislation or amending each individual agency's enabling legislation. This proposal did not pass the 104th Congress. The Supreme Court has already stolen the thunder from the just compensation movement. In three recent cases, the Court has required just compensation to property owners who had been affected by agency regulations (see *Nollan v. California Coastal Commission,* 483 U.S. 825 [1987]; *Lucas v. South Carolina Coastal Commission,* 505 U.S. 1003 [1992]; and *Dolan v. City of Tigard,* 114 S.Ct. 2309 [1994]).

The three cases cited above, however, involved regulations of state or local agencies, whereas the contract and the Republicans are more concerned with federal regulations, particularly as they relate to wetlands. It is no secret that the Supreme Court is more callous in its treatment of state and local units of government than it is in its treatment of a coequal branch of government. Also, the Court was badly divided in the *Nollan, Lucas,* and *Dolan* cases: All were five-to-four decisions. With the real possibility of one or more Supreme Court vacancies during President Clinton's second term, just compensation jurisprudence could take a 180-degree turn. I would look for renewed Republican efforts with regard to just compensation and cost-benefit analysis. The extreme conservative wing of the House Republicans was not replenished by the 1996 elections, however, and if it did not have the votes before, it is unlikely they have them now.

Lest you believe that devices like cost-benefit analysis would be a panacea against the flood of agency rules and regulations, let me remind you that the Army Corps of Engineers has been under imposed cost-benefit analysis for years. The Corps, however, has never seen the water project that it could not get approved by an expert manipulation of the value of the costs and benefits.

Finally, regarding the legislative will to control agencies, remember that such will is closely tied to reelection fortunes. The basic reason Congress has failed to exercise control over agencies is that the incumbents have come to depend on bureaucrats and their clients in cozy triangles, in providing constituency service, and in bringing home the bacon. None of these things became extinct in the 104th Congress, and none face extinction in the 105th. Especially with the demise of the push for term limits, look for incumbents to spend most of their time raising reelection money, taking care of constituents, pork barreling, and continuing dependency on agency expertise.

SUMMARY

The power to control the bureaucracy clearly lies with Congress. For a variety of reasons, Congress rarely exercises effective control over agencies. Subgovernments or cozy triangles inhibit effective control, as does the dependency created in performing constituency service or in obtaining pork barrel legislation. Agency control of information and expertise also mitigates against effective control. Finally, perhaps Congress would feel less compelled to exercise agency oversight on so regular a basis if it would enact tighter, more specific delegations of power. It is not likely to do that, however, because elected representatives dislike making difficult choices, such as whether the health of a worker is more important than the economic health of an industry. Elected officials do not like to go back home and explain to constituents why they voted the way they did on such an issue. It is just too easy now to turn these decisions over to someone else. There is a reason, given our political system, why John F. Kennedy could come up with only sixteen examples of "profiles in courage." [43]

1. Legislative delegations of power to agencies should be accompanied by sufficient standards and guidelines to limit agency discretion. The Supreme Court still says these words but does not enforce them with legislative delegations.

2. One-house legislative vetoes that lack presentment to the president are unconstitutional.

END-OF-CHAPTER CASES

IMMIGRATION AND NATURALIZATION SERVICE V. CHADHA
462 U.S. 919 (1983)

Chief Justice Burger delivered the opinion of the Court, joined by Justices Brennan, Marshall, Blackmun, Stevens, and O'Connor. Justice Powell concurred, and Justices White and Rehnquist were in dissent.

We granted certiorari in Nos. 80-2170 and 80-2171, and postponed consideration of the question of jurisdiction in No. 80-1832. Each presents a challenge to the constitutionality of the provision in the Immigration and Nationality Act, authorizing one House of Congress, by resolution, to invalidate the decision of the Executive Branch, pursuant to authority delegated by Congress to the Attorney

General of the United States, to allow a particular deportable alien to remain in the United States.

I

Chadha is an East Indian who was born in Kenya and holds a British passport. He was lawfully admitted to the United States in 1966 on a nonimmigrant student visa. His visa expired on June 30, 1972. On October 11, 1973, the District Director of the Immigration and Naturalization Service ordered Chadha to show cause why he should not be deported for having "remained in the United States for a longer time than permitted." . . . A deportation hearing was held before an immigration judge on January 11, 1974. Chadha conceded that he was deportable for overstaying his visa and the hearing was adjourned to enable him to file an application for suspension of deportation under § 244(a)(1) of the Act, Section 244(a)(1) provides: "[a] As hereinafter prescribed in this section, the Attorney General may, in his discretion, suspend deportation and adjust the status to that of an alien lawfully admitted for permanent residence, in the case of an alien who applies to the Attorney General for suspension of deportation and—(1) is deportable under any law of the United States except the provisions specified in paragraph (2) of this subsection; has been physically present in the United States for a continuous period of not less than seven years immediately preceding the date of such application, and proves that during all of such period he was and is a person of good moral character; and is a person whose deportation would, in the opinion of the Attorney General, result in extreme hardship to the alien or to his spouse, parent, or child, who is a citizen of the United States or an alien lawfully admitted for permanent residence." After Chadha submitted his application for suspension of deportation, the deportation hearing was resumed on February 7, 1974. On the basis of evidence adduced at the hearing, affidavits submitted with the application, and the results of a character investigation conducted by the INS, the immigration judge, on June 25, 1974, ordered that Chadha's deportation be suspended. The immigration judge found that Chadha met the requirements of § 244(a)(1): he had resided continuously in the United States for over seven years, was of good moral character, and would suffer "extreme hardship" if deported. Pursuant to § 244(c)(1) of the Act, the immigration judge suspended Chadha's deportation and a report of the suspension was transmitted to Congress. Once the Attorney General's recommendation for suspension of Chadha's deportation was conveyed to Congress, Congress had the power under § 244(c)(2) of the Act, to veto the Attorney General's determination that Chadha should not be deported.

The June 25, 1974 order of the immigration judge suspending Chadha's deportation remained outstanding as a valid order for a year and a half. For reasons not disclosed by the record, Congress did not exercise the veto authority reserved to it under § 244(c)(2) until the first session of the 94th Congress. This was the final session in which Congress, pursuant to § 244(c)(2), could act to veto the Attorney General's determination that Chadha should not be deported. The session ended on December 19, 1975. Absent Congressional action, Chadha's deportation proceedings would have been cancelled after this date and his status adjusted to that of a permanent resident alien. On December 12, 1975, Representative Eilberg, Chairman of the Judiciary Subcommittee on Immigration, Citizenship, and International Law, introduced a resolution opposing "the granting of permanent residence in the United States to [six] aliens," including Chadha. The resolution was referred to the House Committee on the Judiciary. On December 16, 1975, the resolution was discharged from further consideration by the House Committee on the Judiciary and submitted to the House of Representatives for a vote. The resolution had not been printed and was not made available to other Members of the House prior to or at the time it was voted on. So far as the record before us shows, the House consideration of the resolution was based on Representative Eilberg's statement from the floor that "[i]t was the feeling of the committee, after reviewing 340 cases, that the aliens contained in the resolution [Chadha and five others] did not meet these statutory requirements, particularly as it relates to hardship; and it is the opinion of the committee that their deportation should not be suspended." The resolution was passed without debate or recorded vote. Since the House action was pursuant to § 244(c)(2), the resolution was not treated as an Article I legislative act; it was not submitted to the Senate or presented to the President for his action.

After the House veto of the Attorney General's decision to allow Chadha to remain in the United States, the immigration judge reopened the deportation proceedings to implement the House order deporting Chadha. Chadha moved to terminate the proceedings on the ground that § 244(c)(2) is unconstitutional. The immigration judge held that he had no authority to rule on the constitutional validity of § 244(c)(2). On November 8, 1976, Chadha was ordered deported pursuant to the House action. . . .

III

A

[12] We turn now to the question whether action of one House of Congress under § 244(c)(2) violates strictures of the Constitution. We begin, of course, with the presumption that the challenged statute is valid. Justice White undertakes to make a case for the proposition that the one-House veto is a useful "political invention," and we need not challenge that assertion. We can even concede this utilitarian argument although the long range political wisdom of this "invention" is arguable. It has been vigorously debated and it is instructive to compare the views of the protagonists. . . . But policy arguments supporting even useful "political inventions" are subject to the demands of the Constitution which defines powers and, with respect to this subject, sets out just how those powers are to be exercised. Explicit and unambiguous provisions of the Constitution prescribe and define the respective functions of the Congress and of the Executive in the legislative process. Since the precise terms of those familiar provisions are critical to the resolution of this case, we set them out verbatim. Art. I provides: "All legislative Powers herein granted shall be vested in a Congress of the United States, which shall consist of a Senate and a House of Representatives." Art. I, § 1. "Every Bill which shall have passed the House of Representatives and the Senate, shall, before it becomes a Law, be presented to the President of the United States; . . ." Art. I, § 7, cl. 2. "Every Order, Resolution, or Vote to which the Concurrence of the Senate and House of Representatives may be necessary (except on a question of Adjournment) shall be presented to the President of the United States; and before the Same shall take Effect, shall be approved by him, or being disapproved by him, shall be repassed by two thirds of the Senate and House of Representatives, according to the Rules and Limitations prescribed in the Case of a Bill." Art. I, § 7, cl. 3. These provisions of Art. I are integral parts of the constitutional design for the separation of powers. We have recently noted that "[t]he principle of separation of powers was not simply an abstract generalization

in the minds of the Framers: it was woven into the documents that they drafted in Philadelphia in the summer of 1787." Just as we relied on the textual provision of Art. II, § 2, cl. 2, to vindicate the principle of separation of powers in *Buckley,* we find that the purposes underlying the Presentment Clauses, and the bicameral requirement of Art. I, guide our resolution of the important question presented in this case. The very structure of the articles delegating and separating powers under Arts. I, II, and III exemplify the concept of separation of powers and we now turn to Art. I.

B

The Presentment Clauses

The records of the Constitutional Convention reveal that the requirement that all legislation be presented to the President before becoming law was uniformly accepted by the Framers. Presentment to the President and the Presidential veto were considered so imperative that the draftsmen took special pains to assure that these requirements could not be circumvented. The President's role in the lawmaking process also reflects the Framers' careful efforts to check whatever propensity a particular Congress might have to enact oppressive, improvident, or ill-considered measures.

C

Bicameralism

The bicameral requirement of Art. I, §§ 1, 7 was of scarcely less concern to the Framers than was the Presidential veto and indeed the two concepts are interdependent. By providing that no law could take effect without the concurrence of the prescribed majority of the Members of both Houses, the Framers reemphasized their belief, already remarked upon in connection with the Presentment Clauses, that legislation should not be enacted unless it has been carefully and fully considered by the Nation's elected officials.

Finally, we see that when the Framers intended to authorize either House of Congress to act alone and outside of its prescribed bicameral legislative role, they narrowly and precisely defined the procedure for such action. There are but four provisions in the Constitution, explicit and unambiguous, by which one House may act alone with the unreviewable force of law, not subject to the President's veto: (a) The House of Representatives alone was given the power to initiate impeachments. Art. I, § 2, cl. 6; (b) The Senate alone was given the power to conduct trials following impeachment on charges initiated by the House and to convict following trial. Art. I, § 3, cl. 5; (c) The Senate alone was given final unreviewable power to approve or to disapprove presidential appointments. Art. II, § 2, cl. 2; (d) The Senate alone was given unreviewable power to ratify treaties negotiated by the President. Art. II, § 2, cl. 2. Clearly, when the Draftsmen sought to confer special powers on one House, independent of the other House, or of the President, they did so in explicit, unambiguous terms. These carefully defined exceptions from presentment and bicameralism underscore the difference between the legislative functions of Congress and other unilateral but important and binding one-House acts provided for in the Constitution. These exceptions are narrow, explicit, and separately justified; none of them authorize the action challenged here. On the contrary, they provide further support for the conclusion that Congressional authority is not to be implied and for the conclusion that the veto provided for in § 244(c)(2) is not authorized by the constitutional design of the powers of the Legislative Branch.

Since it is clear that the action by the House under § 244(c)(2) was not within any of the express constitutional exceptions authorizing one House to act alone, and equally clear that it was an exercise of legislative power, that action was subject to the standards prescribed in Article I. The bicameral requirement, the Presentment Clauses, the President's veto, and Congress' power to override a veto were intended to erect enduring checks on each Branch and to protect the people from the improvident exercise of power by mandating certain prescribed steps. To preserve those checks, and maintain the separation of powers, the carefully defined limits on the power of each Branch must not be eroded. To accomplish what has been attempted by one House of Congress in this case requires action in conformity with the express procedures of the Constitution's prescription for legislative action: passage by a majority of both Houses and presentment to the President.

IV

We hold that the Congressional veto provision in § 244(c)(2) is severable from the Act and that it is unconstitutional. Accordingly, the judgment of the Court of Appeals is Affirmed.

Justice White, dissenting.

Today the Court not only invalidates § 244(c)(2) of the Immigration and Nationality Act, but also sounds the death knell for nearly 200 other statutory provisions in which Congress has reserved a "legislative veto." For this reason, the Court's decision is of surpassing importance. And it is for this reason that the Court would have been well-advised to decide the case, if possible, on the narrower grounds of separation of powers, leaving for full consideration the constitutionality of other congressional review statutes operating on such varied matters as war powers and agency rulemaking, some of which concern the independent regulatory agencies. The prominence of the legislative veto mechanism in our contemporary political system and its importance to Congress can hardly be overstated. It has become a central means by which Congress secures the accountability of executive and independent agencies. Without the legislative veto, Congress is faced with a Hobson's choice: either to refrain from delegating the necessary authority, leaving itself with a hopeless task of writing laws with the requisite specificity to cover endless special circumstances across the entire policy landscape, or in the alternative, to abdicate its law-making function to the executive branch and independent agencies. To choose the former leaves major national problems unresolved; to opt for the latter risks unaccountable policymaking by those not elected to fill that role. Accordingly, over the past five decades, the legislative veto has been placed in nearly 200 statutes. The device is known in every field of governmental concern: reorganization, budgets, foreign affairs, war powers, and regulation of trade, safety, energy, the environment and the economy.

The wisdom and the constitutionality of these broad delegations are matters that still have not been put to rest. But for present purposes, these cases establish that by virtue of congressional delegation, legislative power can be exercised by independent agencies and Executive departments without the passage of new legislation. For some time, the sheer amount of law—the substantive rules that regulate private conduct and direct the operation of government—made by the agencies has far outnumbered the lawmaking engaged in by

Congress through the traditional process. There is no question but that agency rulemaking is lawmaking in any functional or realistic sense of the term. The Administrative Procedure Act, provides that a "rule" is an agency statement "designed to implement, interpret, or prescribe law or policy." When agencies are authorized to prescribe law through substantive rulemaking, the administrator's regulation is not only due deference, but is accorded "legislative effect." These regulations bind courts and officers of the federal government, may preempt state law, and grant rights to and impose obligations on the public. In sum, they have the force of law. If Congress may delegate lawmaking power to independent and executive agencies, it is most difficult to understand Article I as forbidding Congress from also reserving a check on legislative power for itself. Absent the veto, the agencies receiving delegations of legislative or quasi-legislative power may issue regulations having the force of law without bicameral approval and without the President's signature. It is thus not apparent why the reservation of a veto over the exercise of that legislative power must be subject to a more exacting test. In both cases, it is enough that the initial statutory authorizations comply with the Article I requirements. I do not suggest that all legislative vetoes are necessarily consistent with separation of powers principles. A legislative check on an inherently executive function, for example that of initiating prosecutions, poses an entirely different question. But the legislative veto device here—and in many other settings—is far from an instance of legislative tyranny over the Executive. It is a necessary check on the unavoidably expanding power of the agencies, both executive and independent, as they engage in exercising authority delegated by Congress.

V

I regret that I am in disagreement with my colleagues on the fundamental questions that this case presents. But even more I regret the destructive scope of the Court's holding. It reflects a profoundly different conception of the Constitution than that held by the Courts which sanctioned the modern administrative state. Today's decision strikes down in one fell swoop provisions in more laws enacted by Congress than the Court has cumulatively invalidated in its history. I fear it will now be more difficult "to insure that the fundamental policy decisions in our society will be made not by an appointed official but by the body immediately responsible to the people." I must dissent.

BOWSHER V. SYNAR
478 U.S. 714 (1986)

Chief Justice Burger delivered the opinion of the Court, joined by Justices Brennan, Powell, Rehnquist, and O'Connor. Justices Stevens and Marshall concurred, and Justices White and Blackmun dissented.

The question presented by these appeals is whether the assignment by Congress to the Comptroller General of the United States of certain functions under the Balanced Budget and Emergency Deficit Control Act of 1985 violates the doctrine of separation of powers.

I

A

On December 12, 1985, the President signed into law the Balanced Budget and Emergency Deficit Control Act of 1985, popularly known as the "Gramm-Rudman-Hollings Act." The purpose of the Act is to eliminate the federal budget deficit. To that end, the Act sets a "maximum deficit amount" for federal spending for each of fiscal years 1986 through 1991. The size of that maximum deficit amount progressively reduces to zero in fiscal year 1991. If in any fiscal year the federal budget deficit exceeds the maximum deficit amount by more than a specified sum, the Act requires across-the-board cuts in federal spending to reach the targeted deficit level, with half of the cuts made to defense programs and the other half made to nondefense programs. The Act exempts certain priority programs from these cuts.

These "automatic" reductions are accomplished through a rather complicated procedure, spelled out in § 251, the so-called "reporting provisions" of the Act. Each year, the Directors of the Office of Management and Budget (OMB) and the Congressional Budget Office (CBO) independently estimate the amount of the federal budget deficit for the upcoming fiscal year. If that deficit exceeds the maximum targeted deficit amount for that fiscal year by more than a specified amount, the Directors of OMB and CBO independently calculate, on a program-by-program basis, the budget reductions necessary to ensure that the deficit does not exceed the maximum deficit amount. The Act then requires the Directors to report jointly their deficit estimates and budget reduction calculations to the Comptroller General. The Comptroller General, after reviewing the Directors' reports, then reports his conclusions to the President. The President in turn must issue a "sequestration" order mandating the spending reductions specified by the Comptroller General. There follows a period during which Congress may by legislation reduce spending to obviate, in whole or in part, the need for the sequestration order. If such reductions are not enacted, the sequestration order becomes effective and the spending reductions included in that order are made.

Anticipating constitutional challenge to these procedures, the Act also contains a "fallback" deficit reduction process to take effect "[i]n the event that any of the reporting procedures described in section 251 are invalidated." Under these provisions, the report prepared by the Directors of OMB and the CBO is submitted directly to a specially created Temporary Joint Committee on Deficit Reduction, which must report in five days to both Houses a joint resolution setting forth the content of the Directors' report. Congress then must vote on the resolution under special rules, which render amendments out of order. If the resolution is passed and signed by the President, it then serves as the basis for a Presidential sequestration order.

B

Within hours of the President's signing of the Act, Congressman Synar, who had voted against the Act, filed a complaint seeking declaratory relief that the Act was unconstitutional. Eleven other Members later joined Congressman Synar's suit. A virtually identical lawsuit was also filed by the National Treasury Employees Union. The Union alleged that its members had been injured as a result of the Act's automatic spending reduction provisions, which have suspended certain cost-of-living benefit increases to the Union's members. In his

signing statement, the President expressed his view that the Act was constitutionally defective because of the Comptroller General's ability to exercise supervisory authority over the President. . . .

III

We noted recently that "[t]he Constitution sought to divide the delegated powers of the new Federal Government into three defined categories, Legislative, Executive, and Judicial." *INS v. Chadha,* 462 U.S. 919, 951 (1983). The declared purpose of separating and dividing the powers of government, of course, was to "diffus[e] power the better to secure liberty." . . . That this system of division and separation of powers produces conflicts, confusion, and discordance at times is inherent, but it was deliberately so structured to assure full, vigorous, and open debate on the great issues affecting the people and to provide avenues for the operation of checks on the exercise of governmental power.

The Constitution does not contemplate an active role for Congress in the supervision of officers charged with the execution of the laws it enacts. The President appoints "Officers of the United States" with the "Advice and Consent of the Senate. . . ." Art. II, § 2. Once the appointment has been made and confirmed, however, the Constitution explicitly provides for removal of Officers of the United States by Congress only upon impeachment by the House of Representatives and conviction by the Senate. An impeachment by the House and trial by the Senate can rest only on "Treason, Bribery or other high Crimes and Misdemeanors." Article II, § 4. A direct congressional role in the removal of officers charged with the execution of the laws beyond this limited one is inconsistent with separation of powers. "The fundamental necessity of maintaining each of the three general departments of government entirely free from the control or coercive influence, direct or indirect, of either of the others, has often been stressed and is hardly open to serious question. So much is implied in the very fact of the separation of the powers of these departments by the Constitution; and in the rule which recognizes their essential co-equality." The Court reached a similar result in *Wiener v. United States,* 357 U.S. 349 (1958), concluding that, under *Humphrey's Executor,* the President did not have unrestrained removal authority over a member of the War Claims Commission.

In light of these precedents, we conclude that Congress cannot reserve for itself the power of removal of an officer charged with the execution of the laws except by impeachment. To permit the execution of the laws to be vested in an officer answerable only to Congress would, in practical terms, reserve in Congress control over the execution of the laws. As the District Court observed: "Once an officer is appointed, it is only the authority that can remove him, and not the authority that appointed him, that he must fear and, in the performance of his functions, obey." The structure of the Constitution does not permit Congress to execute the laws; it follows that Congress cannot grant to an officer under its control what it does not possess. The dangers of congressional usurpation of Executive Branch functions have long been recognized. "[T]he debates of the Constitutional Convention, and the Federalist Papers, are replete with expressions of fear that the Legislative Branch of the National Government will aggrandize itself at the expense of the other two branches." Indeed, we also have observed only recently that "[t]he hydraulic pressure inherent within each of the separate Branches to exceed the outer limits of its power, even to accomplish desirable objectives, must be resisted."

With these principles in mind, we turn to consideration of whether the Comptroller General is controlled by Congress. The critical factor lies in the provisions of the statute defining the Comptroller General's office relating to removability. Although the Comptroller General is nominated by the President from a list of three individuals recommended by the Speaker of the House of Representatives and the President pro tempore of the Senate, and confirmed by the Senate, he is removable only at the initiative of Congress. He may be removed not only by impeachment but also by joint resolution of Congress "at any time" resting on any one of the following bases: "(i) permanent disability; (ii) inefficiency; (iii) neglect of duty; (iv) malfeasance; or (v) a felony or conduct involving moral turpitude." This provision was included, as one Congressman explained in urging passage of the Act, because Congress "felt that [the Comptroller General] should be brought under the sole control of Congress, so that Congress at any moment when it found he was inefficient and was not carrying on the duties of his office as he should and as the Congress expected, could remove him without the long, tedious process of a trial by impeachment." Against this background, we see no escape from the conclusion that, because Congress has retained removal authority over the Comptroller General, he may not be entrusted with executive powers. The remaining question is whether the Comptroller General has been assigned such powers in the Balanced Budget and Emergency Deficit Control Act of 1985. . . .

VII

No one can doubt that Congress and the President are confronted with fiscal and economic problems of unprecedented magnitude, but "the fact that a given law or procedure is efficient, convenient, and useful in facilitating functions of government, standing alone, will not save it if it is contrary to the Constitution. Convenience and efficiency are not the primary objectives—or the hallmarks—of democratic government. . . ."

We conclude that the District Court correctly held that the powers vested in the Comptroller General under § 251 violate the command of the Constitution that the Congress play no direct role in the execution of the laws. Accordingly, the judgment and order of the District Court are affirmed.

Our judgment is stayed for a period not to exceed 60 days to permit Congress to implement the fallback provisions.

It is so ordered.

MISTRETTA V. UNITED STATES
488 U.S. 361 (1989)

Justice Blackmun delivered the opinion of the Court joined by Chief Justice Rehnquist and Justices Brennan, Marshall, White, Stevens, O'Connor, and Kennedy. Justice Scalia dissented.

In this litigation, we granted certiorari before judgment in the United States Court of Appeals for the Eighth Circuit in order to consider the constitutionality of the Sentencing Guidelines promulgated by the United States Sentencing Commission. The Commission is a body created under the Sentencing Reform Act of 1984. The United States District Court for the Western District of Missouri ruled that the Guidelines were constitutional. *United States v. Johnson,* 682 F.Supp. 1033 (W.D.Mo. 1988).

A

Background

For almost a century, the Federal Government employed in criminal cases a system of indeterminate sentencing. Statutes specified the penalties for crimes but nearly always gave the sentencing judge wide discretion to decide whether the offender should be incarcerated and for how long, whether he should be fined and how much, and whether some lesser restraint, such as probation, should be imposed instead of imprisonment or fine. This indeterminate-sentencing system was supplemented by the utilization of parole, by which an offender was returned to society under the "guidance and control" of a parole officer. Thus, under the indeterminate-sentence system, Congress defined the maximum, the judge imposed a sentence within the statutory range (which it usually could replace with probation), and the Executive Branch's parole official eventually determined the actual duration of imprisonment. Serious disparities in sentences, however, were common.

Rehabilitation as a sound penological theory came to be questioned and, in any event, was regarded by some as an unattainable goal for most cases. In 1958, Congress authorized the creation of judicial sentencing institutes and joint councils to formulate standards and criteria for sentencing. In 1973, the United States Parole Board adopted guidelines that established a "customary range" of confinement. Congress in 1976 endorsed this initiative through the Parole Commission and Reorganization Act, an attempt to envision for the Parole Commission a role, at least in part, "to moderate the disparities in the sentencing practices of individual judges." That Act, however, did not disturb the division of sentencing responsibility among the three Branches. The judge continued to exercise discretion and to set the sentence within the statutory range fixed by Congress, while the prisoner's actual release date generally was set by the Parole Commission.

This proved to be no more than a way station. Fundamental and widespread dissatisfaction with the uncertainties and the disparities continued to be expressed. Congress had wrestled with the problem for more than a decade when, in 1984, it enacted the sweeping reforms that are at issue here.

Helpful in our consideration and analysis of the statute is the Senate Report on the 1984 legislation, S.Rep. No. 98-225 (1983). The Report referred to the "outmoded rehabilitation model" for federal criminal sentencing, and recognized that the efforts of the criminal justice system to achieve rehabilitation of offenders had failed. It observed that the indeterminate-sentencing system had two "unjustifi[ed]" and "shameful" consequences. The first was the great variation among sentences imposed by different judges upon similarly situated offenders. The second was the uncertainty as to the time the offender would spend in prison. Each was a serious impediment to an evenhanded and effective operation of the criminal justice system. The Report went on to note that parole was an inadequate device for overcoming these undesirable consequences. This was due to the division of authority between the sentencing judge and the parole officer who often worked at cross purposes; to the fact that the Parole Commission's own guidelines did not take into account factors Congress regarded as important in sentencing, such as the sophistication of the offender and the role the offender played in an offense committed with others, and to the fact that the Parole Commission had only limited power to adjust a sentence imposed by the court.

The Act

The Act, as adopted, revises the old sentencing process in several ways:

1. It rejects imprisonment as a means of promoting rehabilitation, and it states that punishment should serve retributive, educational, deterrent, and incapacitative goals.

2. It consolidates the power that had been exercised by the sentencing judge and the Parole Com-

mission to decide what punishment an offender should suffer. This is done by creating the United States Sentencing Commission, directing that Commission to devise guidelines to be used for sentencing, and prospectively abolishing the Parole Commission.

3. It makes all sentences basically determinate. A prisoner is to be released at the completion of his sentence reduced only by any credit earned by good behavior while in custody.

4. It makes the Sentencing Commission's guidelines binding on the courts, although it preserves for the judge the discretion to depart from the guideline applicable to a particular case if the judge finds an aggravating or mitigating factor present that the Commission did not adequately consider when formulating guidelines. The Act also requires the court to state its reasons for the sentence imposed and to give "the specific reason" for imposing a sentence different from that described in the guideline.

5. It authorizes limited appellate review of the sentence. It permits a defendant to appeal a sentence that is above the defined range, and it permits the Government to appeal a sentence that is below that range. It also permits either side to appeal an incorrect application of the guideline.

Thus, guidelines were meant to establish a range of determinate sentences for categories of offenses and defendants according to various specified factors, "among others." The maximum of the range ordinarily may not exceed the minimum by more than the greater of 25% or six months, and each sentence is to be within the limit provided by existing law. . . .

D

The Responsibilities of the Commission

In addition to the duty the Commission has to promulgate determinative-sentence guidelines, it is under an obligation periodically to "review and revise" the guidelines. It is to "consult with authorities on, and individual and institutional representatives of, various aspects of the Federal criminal justice system." It must report to Congress "any amendments of the guidelines." It is to make recommendations to Congress whether the grades or maximum penalties should be modified. It must submit to Congress at least annually an analysis of the operation of the guidelines.

We note, in passing, that the monitoring function is not without its burden. Every year, with respect to each of more than 40,000 sentences, the federal courts must forward, and the Commission must review, the presentence report, the guideline worksheets, the tribunal's sentencing statement, and any written plea agreement. . . .

II

This Litigation

On Dec. 10, 1987, John M. Mistretta (petitioner) and another were indicted in the United States District Court for the Western District of Missouri on three counts centering in a cocaine sale. Mistretta moved to have the promulgated Guidelines ruled unconstitutional on the grounds that the Sentencing Commission was constituted in violation of the established doctrine of separation of powers, and that Congress delegated excessive authority to the Commission to structure the Guidelines. As has been noted, the District Court was not persuaded by these contentions. . . .

III

Delegation of Power

[1] Petitioner argues that in delegating the power to promulgate sentencing guidelines for every federal criminal offense to an independent Sentencing Commission, Congress has granted the Commission excessive legislative discretion in violation of the constitutionally based nondelegation doctrine. We do not agree.

[2] The nondelegation doctrine is rooted in the principle of separation of powers that underlies our tripartite system of government. The Constitution provides that "[a]ll legislative Powers herein granted shall be vested in a Congress of the United States," and we long have insisted that "the integrity and maintenance of the system of government ordained by the Constitution," mandate that Congress generally cannot delegate its legislative power to another Branch. We also have recognized, however, that the separation-of-powers principle, and the nondelegation doctrine in particular, do not prevent Congress from obtaining the assistance of its coordinate Branches. Applying this "intelligible principle" test to congressional delegations, our jurisprudence has been driven by a practical understanding that in our increasingly complex society, replete with ever changing and more technical

problems, Congress simply cannot do its job absent an ability to delegate power under broad general directives. Until 1935, this Court never struck down a challenged statute on delegation grounds. After invalidating in 1935 two statutes as excessive delegations, we have upheld, again without deviation, Congress' ability to delegate power under broad standards. See, e.g., *Lichter v. United States,* 334 U.S. 742, 785-786, 68 S.Ct. (1948) (upholding delegation of authority to determine excessive profits); *American Power & Light Co. v. SEC,* 329 U.S., at 105 (upholding delegation of authority to SEC to prevent unfair or inequitable distribution of voting power among security holders); *Yakus v. United States,* 321 U.S. 414, 426 (1944) (upholding delegation to administrator to fix commodity prices that would be fair and equitable, and would effectuate the purposes of the Emergency Price Control Act of 1942); *FPC v. Hope Natural Gas Co.,* 320 U.S. 591, 600 (1944) (upholding delegation to Federal Power Commission to determine just and reasonable rates); *National Broadcasting Co. v. United States,* 319 U.S. 190, 225-226 (1943) (upholding delegation to the Federal Communications Commission to regulate broadcast licensing "as public interest, convenience, or necessity" require). In light of our approval of these broad delegations, we harbor no doubt that Congress' delegation of authority to the Sentencing Commission is sufficiently specific and detailed to meet constitutional requirements. Congress charged the Commission with three goals: to "assure the meeting of the purposes of sentencing as set forth" in the Act; to "provide certainty and fairness in meeting the purposes of sentencing, avoiding unwarranted sentencing disparities among defendants with similar records . . . while maintaining sufficient flexibility to permit individualized sentences," where appropriate; and to "reflect to the extent practicable, advancement in knowledge of human behavior as it relates to the criminal justice process." Congress further specified four "purposes" of sentencing that the Commission must pursue in carrying out its mandate: "to reflect the seriousness of the offense, to promote respect for the law, and to provide just punishment for the offense"; "to afford adequate deterrence to criminal conduct"; "to protect the public from further crimes of the defendant"; and "to provide the defendant with needed . . . correctional treatment."

In addition, Congress prescribed the specific tool—the guidelines system—for the Commission

to use in regulating sentencing. More particularly, Congress directed the Commission to develop a system of "sentencing ranges" applicable "for each category of offense involving each category of defendant." . . . We conclude that in creating the Sentencing Commission—an unusual hybrid in structure and authority—Congress neither delegated excessive legislative power nor upset the constitutionally mandated balance of powers among the coordinate Branches. The Constitution's structural protections do not prohibit Congress from delegating to an expert body located within the Judicial Branch the intricate task of formulating sentencing guidelines consistent with such significant statutory direction as is present here. Nor does our system of checked and balanced authority prohibit Congress from calling upon the accumulated wisdom and experience of the Judicial Branch in creating policy on a matter uniquely within the ken of judges. Accordingly, we hold that the Act is constitutional. The judgment of United States District Court for the Western District of Missouri is affirmed.

Justice Scalia, dissenting.

While the products of the Sentencing Commission's labors have been given the modest name "Guidelines," they have the force and effect of laws, prescribing the sentences criminal defendants are to receive. A judge who disregards them will be reversed. I dissent from today's decision because I can find no place within our constitutional system for an agency created by Congress to exercise no governmental power other than the making of laws. . . .

It should be apparent from the above that the decisions made by the Commission are far from technical, but are heavily laden (or ought to be) with value judgments and policy assessments. This fact is sharply reflected in the Commission's product, as described by the dissenting Commissioner: "Under the guidelines, the judge could give the same sentence for abusive sexual contact that puts the child in fear as for unlawfully entering or remaining in the United States. Similarly, the guidelines permit equivalent sentences for the following pairs of offenses: drug trafficking and a violation of the Wild Free-Roaming Horses and Burros Act; arson with a destructive device and failure to surrender a cancelled naturalization certificate; operation of a common carrier under the influence of drugs that causes injury and alteration of one motor vehicle identification number; illegal trafficking in explosives and trespass; interference with a flight attendant and unlawful conduct relating to contraband cigarettes; aggravated assault and smuggling $11,000 worth of fish." Dissenting View of Commissioner Paul H. Robinson on the Promulgation of the Sentencing Guidelines by the United States Sentencing Commission 6-7 (May 1, 1987) (citations omitted). Petitioner's most fundamental and far-reaching challenge to the Commission is that Congress' commitment of such broad policy responsibility to any institution is an unconstitutional delegation of legislative power. It is difficult to imagine a principle more essential to democratic government than that upon which the doctrine of unconstitutional delegation is founded: Except in a few areas constitutionally committed to the Executive Branch, the basic policy decisions governing society are to be made by the Legislature. Our Members of Congress could not, even if they wished, vote all power to the President and adjourn sine die.

II

Precisely because the scope of delegation is largely uncontrollable by the courts, we must be particularly rigorous in preserving the Constitution's structural restrictions that deter excessive delegation. The major one, it seems to me, is that the power to make law cannot be exercised by anyone other than Congress, except in conjunction with the lawful exercise of executive or judicial power. The whole theory of lawful congressional "delegation" is not that Congress is sometimes too busy or too divided and can therefore assign its responsibility of making law to someone else; but rather that a certain degree of discretion, and thus of law-making, inheres in most executive or judicial action, and it is up to Congress, by the relative specificity or generality of its statutory commands, to determine—up to a point—how small or how large that degree shall be. Strictly speaking, there is no acceptable delegation of legislative power. . . . In the present case, however, a pure delegation of legislative power is precisely what we have before us. It is irrelevant whether the standards are adequate, because they are not standards related to the exercise of executive or judicial powers; they are, plainly and simply, standards for further legislation. The lawmaking function of the Sentencing Commission is completely divorced from any responsibility for execution of the law or adjudica-

tion of private rights under the law. It is divorced from responsibility for execution of the law not only because the Commission is not said to be "located in the Executive Branch" (as I shall discuss presently, I doubt whether Congress can "locate" an entity within one Branch or another for constitutional purposes by merely saying so); but, more importantly, because the Commission neither exercises any executive power on its own, nor is subject to the control of the President who does.

By reason of today's decision, I anticipate that Congress will find delegation of its lawmaking powers much more attractive in the future. If rule-making can be entirely unrelated to the exercise of judicial or executive powers, I foresee all manner of "expert" bodies, insulated from the political process, to which Congress will delegate various portions of its lawmaking responsibility. How tempting to create an expert Medical Commission (mostly MDs, with perhaps a few PhDs in moral philosophy) to dispose of such thorny, "no-win" political issues as the withholding of life-support systems in federally funded hospitals, or the use of fetal tissue for research. This is an undemocratic precedent that we set—not because of the scope of the delegated power, but because its recipient is not one of the three Branches of Government. The only governmental power the Commission possesses is the power to make law; and it is not the Congress. Today's decision may aptly be described as the *Humphrey's Executor* of the Judicial Branch, and I think we will live to regret it. Henceforth there may be agencies "within the Judicial Branch" (whatever that means), exercising governmental powers, that are neither courts nor controlled by courts, nor even controlled by judges. If an "independent agency" such as this can be given the power to fix sentences previously exercised by district courts, I must assume that a similar agency can be given the powers to adopt Rules of Procedure and Rules of Evidence previously exercised by this Court. The bases for distinction would be thin indeed.

* * *

Today's decision follows the regrettable tendency of our recent separation-of-powers jurisprudence, see *Morrison,* supra; *Young v. United States ex rel. Vuitton et Fils S.A.,* 481 U.S. 787 (1987), to treat the Constitution as though it were no more than a generalized prescription that the functions of the Branches should not be commingled too much—how much is too much to be determined, case-by-case, by this Court. The Constitution is not that. Rather, as its name suggests, it is a prescribed structure, a framework, for the conduct of government. In designing that structure, the framers themselves considered how much commingling was, in the generality of things, acceptable, and set forth their conclusions in the document.

I think the Court errs, in other words, not so much because it mistakes the degree of commingling, but because it fails to recognize that this case is not about commingling, but about the creation of a new branch altogether, a sort of junior-varsity Congress. It may well be that in some circumstances such a branch would be desirable; perhaps the agency before us here will prove to be so. But there are many desirable dispositions that do not accord with the constitutional structure we live under. And in the long run the improvisation of a constitutional structure on the basis of currently perceived utility will be disastrous.

I respectfully dissent from the Court's decision, and would reverse the judgment of the District Court.

The sentencing commission guidelines regarding sentencing for drug-related offenses have been under attack since the mid-1980s. The gravamen of this attack is a racial one, that the effects of the guidelines fall harder on black defendants than on white defendants. The mere possession of five grams of crack cocaine will land the first-time offender in federal prison for five years. One would have to be caught with five hundred grams of cocaine powder (hence, more readily meeting the presumption of intent to sell) to receive the same sentence. Because of processing methods, it is less expensive to produce cocaine in crack form; hence, the street value of crack is less than powder. Consequently, powdered cocaine is the drug of choice for the affluent in the suburbs, whereas its less expensive twin (crack) is one of the drugs of choice in the inner city. This particular sentencing disparity contributes to the over-representation of blacks in prison and has been severely criticized by black politicians who sometimes impart racial motives behind the sentencing guidelines. The disparity was originally apparently based on a belief that cocaine in crack form was more addictive than in powder form. A twenty-year study of cocaine addiction has proven that the addictive properties of cocaine are identical regardless of how it is processed or how it is ingested.[44]

NOTES

1. Craig Ducat and Harold Chase, *Constitutional Interpretations,* 4th ed. (St. Paul, MN: West, 1988), 185.

2. 462 U.S. 919, 954-55 (1983).

3. Some are of the opinion that other legislative vetoes might survive court scrutiny and that it may not be dead as a tool of congressional control. See Kenneth F. Warren, *Administrative Law: In the Political System,* 2d ed. (St. Paul, MN: West, 1988), 176-80, esp. p. 80; Michael Saks, "Holding the Independent Agencies Accountable: The Legislative Veto of Agency Rules," *Administrative Law Review* 36 (1984): 41; Daniel P. Franklin, "Why the Leg-

islative Veto Isn't Dead," *Presidential Studies Quarterly* 16 (1986): 491-502.

4. The resolution to veto the attorney general's recommendation of resident immigrant status for Chadha and the other five was done so hastily that the resolution before Congress was not even printed so that the House members could read it. The chair of the House Judiciary Subcommittee on Immigration, Citizenship, and International Law, Mr. Eilberg, said in his oral resolution to Congress that the subcommittee had reviewed 340 "hardship" suspensions and found that Chadha and the other five did not meet the hardship criteria. Evidence even suggests that the rest of Congress did not understand that its vote was a veto of the attorney general's recommendation, 426 U.S. 919, 926 (1983) (n. 3).

5. The material on the FTC and the smoking rule comes from A. Lee Fritschler, *Smoking and Politics: Policy Making and the Federal Bureaucracy,* 4th ed. (Upper Saddle River, NJ: Prentice Hall, 1989), 72.

6. Ibid., 73.

7. Ibid., 6, 18.

8. Ibid., 96-97.

9. The Cigarette Labeling and Advertising Act of 1970, 15 U.S.C. 1331.

10. Fritschler, *Smoking and Politics,* 95.

11. Ibid.

12. Ibid., 96.

13. The material on subgovernments comes from Randal B. Ripley and Grace A. Franklin, *Congress, the Bureaucracy, and Public Policy,* 4th ed. (Chicago: Dorsey Press, 1987).

14. Ibid., 8.

15. Ibid., 114.

16. Congressional Quarterly, Inc., *The Washington Lobby,* 4th ed. (Washington, DC: Congressional Quarterly Press, 1982), 25-27.

17. Ripley and Franklin, *Congress, the Bureaucracy, and Public Policy,* 116-18.

18. Ibid., 10.

19. Judith Miller, *The New York Times,* 14 March 1997, A13.

20. Morris P. Fiorina, *Congress: Keystone of the Washington Establishment* (New Haven, CT: Yale University Press, 1977), 41.

21. Ibid., 41-49. See also James Boyd, " 'Legislate? Who Me?': What Happens to a Senator's Day," in *Inside the System,* 4th ed., ed. Charles Peters and Nicholas Lemann (New York: Holt, Rinehart & Winston, 1979), 99-107.

22. Roger Davidson and Walter Oleszek, *Congress and Its Members* (Washington, DC: Congressional Quarterly Press, 1981), 126.

23. U.S. Bureau of the Census, *Statistical Abstract of the United States* (Washington, DC: U.S. Government Printing Office, 1991), 263. The actual figures are for the 1988 election but are fairly standard from year to year except for the following reapportionment.

24. Susan Wilch, John Gruhl, Michael Steinman, and John Comer, *American Government,* 3d ed. (St. Paul, MN: West, 1990), 338.

25. A letter written to *New Choices for Retirement Living,* June 1992, 86. Any Association for the Advancement of Retired Persons office (or congressperson's local office, for that matter) will have a huge file on the Notch group and will be happy to provide information.

26. See H.R. 85, H.R. 207, and H. Con. Res. 4, all introduced 3 January 1991; H. Con. Res. 30, 11 January 1991; H. Con. Res. 274, 5 February 1991; H.R. 917, 6 February 1991; H.R. 1127, 27 February 1991; S561, 6 March 1991; H.R. 1433, 13 March 1991; S964, 25 April 1991; H.R. 3825, 20 November 1991.

27. Warren, *Administrative Law,* 172.

28. Ibid., 317.

29. Richard F. Fenno, Jr., *Congressmen in Committees* (Boston: Little, Brown, 1973), 193-202, esp. 193-94.

30. Warren, *Administrative Law,* 184.

31. Ibid., 184-87.

32. Neil Lewis, "Ex-Spy Weeps in Iran-Contra Testimony," *The New York Times,* 30 July 1992, A6, national edition.

33. Ibid.

34. David B. Frohnmayer, "The Separation of Powers: An Essay on the Vitality of a Constitutional Idea," *Oregon Law Review,* 52 (1973): 220.

35. *Yakus v. United States,* 321 U.S. 414, 426 (1944).

36. *American Power and Light Company v. Securities and Exchange Commission,* 329 U.S. 90, 105 (1946).

37. *Federal Power Commission v. Hope Natural Gas Company,* 320 U.S. 591, 600 (1944).

38. *National Broadcasting Company v. United States,* 319 U.S. 190, 225-26 (1943).

39. *Lichter v. United States,* 334 U.S. 742 (1948). The list of delegations referred to in notes 35 to 38 is the Court's own list in *Mistretta v. United States,* 488 U.S. 361, 373-74 (1988).

40. Theodore J. Lowi, *The End of Liberalism: Ideology, Policy, and the Crisis of Public Authority* (New York: Norton, 1969), chap. 10.

41. See *The Brig Aurora,* 7 Cranch 382 (1813). Power was delegated to the president to determine whether Britain or France violated the neutrality of U.S. Commerce and if they had not, then sections of an expired 1809 act would be revived; *Field v. Clark,* 143 U.S. 649 (1982), delegated the power to the president to determine whether agricultural products from specific countries were being imported into the United States at a disadvantage to U.S. agriculture. If the president found that to be the case, he or she could raise the tariff on the product from a specific country; as a result of *United States v. Grimoud,* 220 U.S. 506 (1911), the secretary of agriculture was delegated the power to make rules necessary to protect the public forests.

42. Ripley and Franklin, *Congress, the Bureaucracy, and Public Policy,* 21-28.

43. John F. Kennedy, *Profiles in Courage* (New York: Harper & Row, 1956).

44. Christopher Wren, *The New York Times,* 20 November 1996, 1.

CHAPTER 4

CONTROL OF AGENCIES BY DEFAULT

The Courts and Administrative Law

*B*rown v. *Board of Education* was decided in 1954 and mandated an end to government-enforced discrimination in education. Throughout the rest of the 1950s and most of the 1960s, federal courts attempted to force southern states to adopt integrated schools. There was much resistance. In the face of perpetual losses in both litigation and the political arena, the forces favoring segregation in the South began to find subtler ways to avoid the dictates of the Supreme Court's desegregation decisions. One primary tool used in this less overt segregation was the private academy. Discrimination is discussed in more detail in Chapter 8, but for now, suffice it to say that the federal government has more difficulty attempting to redress private discrimination than it does government-enforced discrimination.

CASE IN POINT:
ALLEN V. WRIGHT ET AL.,
468 U.S. 737 (1984)

As local school districts and cities in the South began the process of court-ordered integration of schools, private academies began to flourish. Many of these private academies did not admit black students. They were, however, subsidized by the federal government to the extent that many of them enjoyed tax-exempt status from the Internal Revenue Service (IRS). This meant that contributions to establish these academies and to keep them afloat were deductible from the donor's income taxes.

Parents of black public school children, the Wrights, who lived in the South, sued to try to force the IRS to tighten its regulations so that private academies that discriminate against blacks would lose their tax-exempt status. Although the Wrights did not attempt to enroll their children in a private academy, they and the class of people they represent in this case made two constitutional arguments:

1. That the IRS regulations constitute federal financial aid to racially segregated schools in violation of equal protection.
2. That the IRS regulations encourage the growth and perpetuation of segregated schools and that this results in children's inability to exercise their constitutionally protected right to attend racially integrated schools.

Congress, through the Internal Revenue Code, has forbidden tax-exempt status for schools that discriminate on the basis of race and has delegated to the IRS the responsibility both to promulgate rules defining racial discrimination and to enforce the code. Actually, the IRS has adopted fairly strict guidelines for nondiscrimination, which private schools must prove they can meet before the IRS will grant tax-exempt status. The IRS has also adopted the position, however, that private schools can receive tax-exempt status merely by adopting and certifying a nondiscrimination policy without actually implementing that policy. This latter implementation interpretation the plaintiffs attack.

In Chapter 1, you were introduced to the concept of "administrative state" (policy making by administrative expertise). Chapters 2 and 3 presented the argument that neither the president nor Congress is very successful at controlling the bureaucracy. Thus, if any branch of government is to control bureaucracy, almost by default it will have to be up to the courts. Throughout the rest of this book, you will be able to assess for yourself the degree to which courts have checked bureaucratic power. The current members of the U.S. Supreme Court, however, do not appear to have a propensity to watch too closely over bureaucracy. A 1990 study (that would not have included Justices Thomas, Ginsberg, or Breyer) indicates that, in administrative law cases during the 1986 and 1987 Court term, the Court sided with the agencies in more than 70 percent of cases.[1] Table 4.1 presents a list of sitting members of the Court in 1986-87 and their votes siding with agencies expressed as a percentage of all administrative law cases in which they participated.

Questions

1. Why, do you think, would the IRS go through all the trouble to promulgate strict guidelines for nondiscrimination and require the private academies to adopt nondiscriminatory policies that meet those guidelines and then let the academies off the hook by granting the tax-exempt status without regard to whether the policy of nondiscrimination is ever implemented?

2. Will the courts listen to the Wrights and give them their "day in court"? If you answered yes, you would be wrong, as will be evident later in the chapter.

IMPEDIMENTS TO JUDICIAL CONTROL OF AGENCIES

Courts are not well suited to the task of being watchdog over agencies for any number of reasons, including the following:

1. Most current members of the U.S. Supreme Court (and Reagan/Bush appointees to the lower federal courts) believe that it is not the proper judicial role for unelected judges to play an active role in policy making/implementation.

2. Courts must play a passive role because they must wait for a conflict to come to them in the form of a proper lawsuit. Congress and the president, in contrast, do not have to wait for situations to confront them before they act.

3. Courts in the U.S. judicial system operate under a series of constraints that limit and restrict a court's ability to handle a lawsuit. The field of administrative law has even more constraints than do other areas of law.

Table 4.1   Sitting Members of the U.S. Supreme Court and "Support" Scores in Administrative Law Cases (1986-87)

O'Connor	76.6%
Rehnquist	72.3%
Scalia	67.4%
Stevens	63.8%
Kennedy	62.5%

SOURCE: Richard A. Brisbin, Jr., "The Conservatism of Antonin Scalia," *Political Science Quarterly* 105 (Spring 1990): 13.

The legal source of the constraints just mentioned is found in Article III of the Constitution, which limits the jurisdiction of U.S. federal courts to "cases or controversies." Judges use the phrase "concrete case or controversies," meaning that there must be a real (as opposed to hypothetical or collusive) legal conflict between at least two parties and that all parties must be proper parties before the court. Legal concepts give definition to the case or controversy requirement and constrain court action. Some apply to all lawsuits, and some are specific constraints in administrative law.

GENERAL CONSTRAINTS ON THE EXERCISE OF JUDICIAL POWER

Jurisdiction

Before a court can hear a case, it must have the power to resolve that particular conflict. That power is called *jurisdiction,* and it is conferred on courts by constitutions (state or federal) or by legislatures (state or federal).

Article III of the U.S. Constitution, for instance, confers the jurisdiction on federal courts to hear cases or controversies involving conflicts that may arise under either the Constitution or the laws of the federal government. It goes on to give Congress the power to set jurisdiction for federal courts for cases they can hear on review (called *appellate jurisdiction*). Jurisdiction can be a complicated concept (in some cases, the question before the court is whether that court has jurisdiction to hear the case), but for our purposes here, we can keep it simple. At the federal level, it means that courts can hear cases presenting a claim under the Constitution or under an act of Congress, or, because Congress has delegated to agencies the power to make rules and regulations on behalf of

Congress, one may have jurisdiction arising under a federal administrative rule or action.

Standing

Recall that the discussion in this chapter began with the case of *Allen v. Wright et al.* There, Mr. Wright and the class of people he represented attempted to challenge an IRS decision to allow private academies to receive tax-exempt status after a showing that they had adopted a policy of nondiscrimination even though they had not implemented that policy (and hence still did discriminate).

If you thought Wright could challenge that policy in court, you were wrong. That is because Wright lacks standing to sue.

Standing means that one must be the proper party to bring a suit (or in this case, to challenge an administrative action). How the courts define or interpret the concept of "standing" is important. The narrower the interpretation, the smaller the class of people who can use the courts for redress of an administrative decision or action.

In administrative law, court interpretations about who was a proper party to challenge an administrative action were at first very narrow and constrictive. The U.S. Supreme Court broadened the concept of "standing" in the late 1960s and into the 1970s, but as evidenced by *Allen v. Wright et al.* and *Lujan,* the Rehnquist Court seems to be in the process of narrowing the concept of "standing" again.

Prior to broadening the concept of "standing," the courts applied a test referred to as the *legal interest test.* This meant that one could not challenge an administrative action unless one could show that a legally protected interest had been adversely affected. The fact that one might have suffered economic loss because of an administrative action was not enough by itself. One had to show that economic loss was covered by an existing legal right, such as contract law (breach of contract), property law, probate law, and tort law.

The case that rejected the legal interest test and broadened the class of people who could challenge administrative action was *Association of Data Processing Service Organizations v. Camp,* 397 U.S. 159 (1970). In this case, Mr. Camp, the comptroller of the currency, promulgated the following rule: "Incidental to its banking services, a national bank may make available its data processing equipment or perform data processing services on such equipment for other bank and bank customers." The plaintiff in this case is a trade association of data processing companies that provide data processing services to businesses. Assume for the moment that the businesses and corporations that make up the Association of Data Processing Service Organizations control 75 percent to 90 percent of the market that supplies data processing to businesses. If the national banks are allowed to enter that market, they will cut into the profits of the businesses that belong to the trade association. That reduction of profit is the very definition of economic injury, especially in light of the fact that Section 4 of the Bank Service Corporation Act says, "No bank service corporation may . . . engage in any activity other than the performance of banking services for banks."

Despite the fact that the Administrative Procedure Act (APA) grants standing to challenge an administrative action to a person "aggrieved by agency action within the meaning of a relevant statute," the district court dismissed the suit, saying the Association of Data Processing Service Organizations lacked standing to challenge the comptroller's action. The district court said (and the circuit court of appeals affirmed) that "a Plaintiff may challenge an alleged illegal competition when as complainant it pursues—1) a legal interest by reason of public . . . charter or contract . . . 2) a legal interest by reason of statutory protection."[2] Because in this case no breach of contract or statute conferred a special privilege on the data processors, the lower federal courts, following precedent, dismissed the suit. The Supreme Court reversed, creating a two-pronged test for standing to challenge administrative action.

To establish standing, a plaintiff or petitioner need only show the following:

1. Injury in fact
2. That the action complained of is arguably under the zone of interest meant to be protected by a particular statute

The first prong, injury in fact, means that one challenging an administrative action need only show that the action or decision has caused him or her some definable injury, economic or otherwise (aesthetic, conservational, or maybe even recreational), and it need not be tied to a legal right or interest. The injury may be in the future if it is eminent.

The second prong of the test is tied to the APA, which confers standing on persons aggrieved by agency action "*within the meaning of a relevant statute* [italics added]." That is, the person challenging agency action must argue that (a) he or she has suffered some demonstrable injury from agency action and (b) the agency action falls under a statute that arguably protects the plaintiff from such action. To apply the test in this case, (a) the injury in fact is lost profits and, indeed, a lost contract.

The petitioners not only allege that competition by national banks in the business of providing data processing services might entail some future loss of profits for the petitioners, they also allege that respondent American National Bank and Trust was performing or preparing to perform such services for two customers for whom petitioner Data Systems, Inc., had previously agreed or negotiated to perform such services.[3]

(b) The agency action arguably falls under the zone of interest meant to protect the person challenging the agency action because, in this case, the plaintiffs contend that Section 4 of the Bank Services Corporation Act, which excludes national banks from any service other than banking, underpins this country's long-standing (until the Reagan era and Reaganomics) public policy of strictly limiting banks to banking. Hence, arguably, Section 4 should protect them from the comptroller's policy.

Questions

What result do you get when you apply this two-pronged test to what you know so far about *Allen v. Wright et al.*?

1. Do Mr. Wright or his children suffer some identifiable injury? If you think so, then describe that injury. If you think there is no injury, then explain why not.
2. Is the action complained of by Wright arguably protected by some statute or other law (the Constitution)?

LUJAN V. DEFENDERS OF WILDLIFE
112 S.Ct. 2130 (1992)

Defenders of Wildlife (DOW) is suing Secretary of the Interior Lujan for a declaratory judgment against a rule promulgated by the Department of the Interior (DOI) in 1986. The suit also asks the Court to require the secretary to promulgate a new rule. The Endangered Species Act of 1973 delegates primary enforcement to the DOI. The law requires the secretary to identify endangered species and their habitats. Further, the law requires that all other federal agencies consult with the secretary prior to taking any action that might adversely affect an endangered species or its habitat. In 1979, the DOI promulgated a rule extending the consultation requirement to actions contemplated by federal agencies to be taken overseas. In 1986, the Reagan administration promulgated the rule challenged here that restricts the consultation provision to domestic situations (not to overseas actions). The crux of the plaintiff's (DOW) argument is that the Agency for International Development (AID) lent funds to Egypt and Sri Lanka for water projects that will negatively affect the habitats of elephants, leopards, and crocodiles (all endangered species) and that the AID did so without consulting with the secretary of the interior. Such consultation would have been required prior to the 1986 change in the requirement.

The opinion was written by Justice Scalia and joined by Justices White and Thomas and Chief Justice Rehnquist. Concurring opinions were by Justice Kennedy, joined by Justices Souter and Stevens. Justice Blackmun, joined by Justice O'Connor, dissented.

This case involves a challenge to a rule promulgated by the Secretary of the Interior interpreting § 7 of the Endangered Species Act of 1973 (ESA), 87 Stat. 884, in such fashion as to render it applicable only to actions within the United States or on the high seas. The preliminary issue, and the only one we reach, is whether respondents here, plaintiffs below, have standing to seek judicial review of the rule.

I

The ESA, as amended, seeks to protect species of animals against threats to their continuing existence caused by man. The ESA instructs the Secretary of the Interior to promulgate by regulation a list of those species which are either endangered or threatened under enumerated criteria, and to define the critical habitat of these species.

In 1978, the Fish and Wildlife Service (FWS) and the National Marine Fisheries Service (NMFS), on behalf of the Secretary of the Interior and the Secretary of Commerce respectively, promulgated a joint regulation stating that the obligations imposed by § 7(a)(2) extend to actions taken in foreign nations. The next year, however, the Interior Department began to reexamine its position. A revised joint regulation, reinterpreting 7(a)(2) to require consultation only for actions taken in the United States or on the high seas, was proposed in 1983, 48 Fed.Reg., and promulgated in 1986, 50 C.F.R. 402.01 (1991).

Shortly thereafter, respondents, organizations dedicated to wildlife conservation and other environmental causes, filed this action against the Secretary of the Interior, seeking a declaratory judgment that the new regulation is in error as to the geographic scope of § 7(a)(2) and an injunction requiring the Secretary to promulgate a new regulation restoring the initial interpretation. The District Court granted the Secretary's motion to dismiss for lack of standing. *Defenders of Wildlife v. Hodel,* 658 F.Supp. 43 (Minn. 1987). The Court of Appeals for the Eighth Circuit reversed by a divided vote. *Defenders of Wildlife v. Hodel,* 851 F.2d 1035 (1988). On remand, the Secretary moved for summary judgment on the standing issue, and respondents moved for summary judgment on the merits. The District Court denied the Secretary's motion, on the ground that the Eighth Circuit had already determined the standing question in this case; it granted respondents' merits motion, and ordered the Secretary to publish a revised regulation. *Defenders of Wildlife v. Hodel,* 707 F.Supp. 1082 (Minn. 1989). The Eighth Circuit affirmed. 911 F.2d 117 (1990). We granted certiorari. . . .

[3][4] Over the years, our cases have established that the irreducible constitutional minimum of standing contains three elements. First, the plaintiff must have suffered an "injury in fact"—an invasion of a legally protected interest which is (a) concrete and particularized, . . . and (b) "actual or imminent, not 'conjectural' or 'hypothetical.' " Second, there must be a causal connection between the injury and the conduct complained of—the injury has to be "fairly . . . trace[able] to the challenged action of the defendant, and not . . . th[e] result [of] the independent action of some third party not before the court." *Simon v. Eastern Ky. Welfare Rights Organization,* 426 U.S. 26, 41-42 (1976). Third, it must be "likely," as opposed to merely "speculative," that the injury will be "redressed by a favorable decision."

[5][6][7] The party invoking federal jurisdiction bears the burden of establishing these elements. Since they are not mere pleading requirements but rather an indispensable part of the plaintiff's case, each element must be supported in the same way as any other matter on which the plaintiff bears the burden of proof, i.e., with the manner and degree of evidence required at the successive stages of the litigation. . . .

[8] When the suit is one challenging the legality of government action or inaction, the nature and extent of facts that must be averred (at the summary judgment stage) or proved (at the trial stage) in order to establish standing depends considerably upon whether the plaintiff is himself an object of the action (or foregone action) at issue. If he is, there is ordinarily little question that the action or inaction has caused him injury, and that a judgment preventing or requiring the action will redress it. When, however, as in this case, a plaintiff's asserted injury arises from the government's allegedly unlawful regulation (or lack of regulation) of someone else, much more is needed. In that circumstance, causation and redressability ordinarily hinge on the response of the regulated (or

regulable) third party to the government action or inaction—and perhaps on the response of others as well. The existence of one or more of the essential elements of standing "depends on the unfettered choices made by independent actors not before the courts and whose exercise of broad and legitimate discretion the courts cannot presume either to control or to predict," also *Simon,* supra, 426 U.S., at 41-42, and it becomes the burden of the plaintiff to adduce facts showing that those choices have been or will be made in such manner as to produce causation and permit redressability of injury.

A

[9][10] Respondents' claim to injury is that the lack of consultation with respect to certain funded activities abroad "increas[es] the rate of extinction of endangered and threatened species." Of course, the desire to use or observe an animal species, even for purely aesthetic purposes, is undeniably a cognizable interest for purpose of standing. "But the 'injury in fact' test requires more than an injury to a cognizable interest. It requires that the party seeking review be himself among the injured." To survive the Secretary's summary judgment motion, respondents had to submit affidavits or other evidence showing, through specific facts, not only that listed species were in fact being threatened by funded activities abroad, but also that one or more of respondents' members would thereby be "directly" affected apart from their " 'special interest' in th[e] subject." See generally *Hunt v. Washington State Apple Advertising Comm'n,* 432 U.S. 333, 343 (1977).

[11][12] With respect to this aspect of the case, the Court of Appeals focused on the affidavits of two Defenders' members—Joyce Kelly and Amy Skilbred. Ms. Kelly stated that she traveled to Egypt in 1986 and "observed the traditional habitat of the endangered Nile crocodile there and intend[s] to do so again, and hope[s] to observe the crocodile directly," and that she "will suffer harm in fact as the result of [the] American . . . role . . . in overseeing the rehabilitation of the Aswan High Dam on the Nile . . . and [in] develop[ing] . . . Egypt's . . . Master Water Plan." Ms. Skilbred averred that she traveled to Sri Lanka in 1981 and "observed th[e] habitat" of "endangered species such as the Asian elephant and the leopard" at what is now the site of the Mahaweli project funded by

the Agency for International Development (AID), although she "was unable to see any of the endangered species"; "this development project," she continued, "will seriously reduce endangered, threatened, and endemic species habitat including areas that I visited . . . [, which] may severely shorten the future of these species"; that threat, she concluded, harmed her because she "intend[s] to return to Sri Lanka in the future and hope[s] to be more fortunate in spotting at least the endangered elephant and leopard." When Ms. Skilbred was asked at a subsequent deposition if and when she had any plans to return to Sri Lanka, she reiterated that "I intend to go back to Sri Lanka," but confessed that she had no current plans: "I don't know [when]. There is a civil war going on right now. I don't know. Not next year, I will say. In the future."

We shall assume for the sake of argument that these affidavits contain facts showing that certain agency-funded projects threaten listed species—though that is questionable. They plainly contain no facts, however, showing how damage to the species will produce "imminent" injury to Mses. Kelly and Skilbred. That the women "had visited" the areas of the projects before the projects commenced proves nothing. As we have said in a related context, " 'Past exposure to illegal conduct does not in itself show a present case or controversy regarding injunctive relief . . . if unaccompanied by any continuing, present adverse effects.' " *Lyons,* 461 U.S., at 102, 103. And the affiants' profession of an "inten[t]" to return to the places they had visited before—where they will presumably, this time, be deprived of the opportunity to observe animals of the endangered species—is simply not enough. Such "some day" intentions—without any description of concrete plans, or indeed even any specification of when the some day will be—do not support a finding of the "actual or imminent" injury that our cases require.

Besides relying upon the Kelly and Skilbred affidavits, respondents propose a series of novel standing theories. The first, inelegantly styled "ecosystem nexus," proposes that any person who uses any part of a "contiguous ecosystem" adversely affected by a funded activity has standing even if the activity is located a great distance away. This approach, as the Court of Appeals correctly observed, is inconsistent with our opinion in *Na-*

tional Wildlife Federation, which held that a plaintiff claiming injury from environmental damage must use the area affected by the challenged activity and not an area roughly "in the vicinity" of it.

[14] Respondents' other theories are called, alas, the "animal nexus" approach, whereby anyone who has an interest in studying or seeing the endangered animals anywhere on the globe has standing; and the "vocational nexus" approach, under which anyone with a professional interest in such animals can sue. Under these theories, anyone who goes to see Asian elephants in the Bronx Zoo, and anyone who is a keeper of Asian elephants in the Bronx Zoo, has standing to sue because the Director of the Agency for International Development (AID) did not consult with the Secretary regarding the AID-funded project in Sri Lanka. This is beyond all reason.

B

Besides failing to show injury, respondents failed to demonstrate redressability. Instead of attacking the separate decisions to fund particular projects allegedly causing them harm, respondents chose to challenge a more generalized level of Government action (rules regarding consultation), the invalidation of which would affect all overseas projects. This programmatic approach has obvious practical advantages, but also obvious difficulties insofar as proof of causation or redressability is concerned. As we have said in another context, "suits challenging, not specifically identifiable Government violations of law, but the particular programs agencies establish to carry out their legal obligations . . . [are], even when premised on allegations of several instances of violations of law, . . . rarely if ever appropriate for federal-court adjudication." *Allen,* 468 U.S., at 759-760.

[15] The most obvious problem in the present case is redressability. Since the agencies funding the projects were not parties to the case, the District Court could accord relief only against the Secretary: He could be ordered to revise his regulation to require consultation for foreign projects. But this would not remedy respondents' alleged injury unless the funding agencies were bound by the Secretary's regulation, which is very much an open question.

The short of the matter is that redress of the only injury in fact respondents complain of requires action (termination of funding until consultation) by the individual funding agencies; and any relief

the District Court could have provided in this suit against the Secretary was not likely to produce that action.

[17] A further impediment to redressability is the fact that the agencies generally supply only a fraction of the funding for a foreign project. AID, for example, has provided less than 10% of the funding for the Mahaweli project. Respondents have produced nothing to indicate that the projects they have named will either be suspended, or do less harm to listed species, if that fraction is eliminated.
. . .

[19] We have consistently held that a plaintiff raising only a generally available grievance about government—claiming only harm to his and every citizen's interest in proper application of the Constitution and laws, and seeking relief that no more directly and tangibly benefits him than it does the public at large—does not state an Article III case or controversy.

* * *

We hold that respondents lack standing to bring this action and that the Court of Appeals erred in denying the summary judgment motion filed by the United States. The opinion of the Court of Appeals is hereby reversed, and the cause is remanded for proceedings consistent with this opinion.

It is so ordered.

Justice BLACKMUN, with whom Justice O'CONNOR joins, dissenting.

I part company with the Court in this case in two respects. First, I believe that respondents have raised genuine issues of fact—sufficient to survive summary judgment—both as to injury and as to redressability. Second, I question the Court's breadth of language in rejecting standing for "procedural" injuries. I fear the Court seeks to impose fresh limitations on the constitutional authority of Congress to allow citizen suits in the federal courts for injuries deemed "procedural" in nature. I dissent.

I

Article III of the Constitution confines the federal courts to adjudication of actual "Cases" and "Controversies." To ensure the presence of a "case" or "controversy," this Court has held that Article III requires, as an irreducible minimum, that a plaintiff allege (1) an injury that is (2) "fairly traceable to the defendant's allegedly unlawful conduct" and that is (3) "likely to be redressed by the requested relief." *Allen v. Wright,* 468 U.S. 737, 751 (1984).

A

To survive petitioner's motion for summary judgment on standing, respondents need not prove that they are actually or imminently harmed. They need show only a "genuine issue" of material fact as to standing. Fed.Rule Civ.Proc. 56(c). This is not a heavy burden. A "genuine issue" exists so long as "the evidence is such that a reasonable jury could return a verdict for the nonmoving party." *Anderson v. Liberty Lobby, Inc.,* 477 U.S. 242, 248 (1986). This Court's "function is not [it]self to weigh the evidence and determine the truth of the matter but to determine whether there is a genuine issue for trial." . . .

I think a reasonable finder of fact could conclude from the information in the affidavits and deposition testimony that either Kelly or Skilbred will soon return to the project sites, thereby satisfying the "actual or imminent" injury standard. . . .

I fear the Court's demand for detailed descriptions of future conduct will do little to weed out those who are genuinely harmed from those who are not. More likely, it will resurrect a code-pleading formalism in federal court summary judgment practice, as federal courts, newly doubting their jurisdiction, will demand more and more particularized showings of future harm. Just to survive summary judgment, for example, a property owner claiming a decline in the value of his property from governmental action might have to specify the exact date he intends to sell his property and show that there is a market for the property, lest it be surmised he might not sell again. A nurse turned down for a job on grounds of her race had better be prepared to show on what date she was prepared to start work, that she had arranged daycare for her child, and that she would not have accepted work at another hospital instead. And a Federal Tort Claims Act plaintiff alleging loss of consortium should make sure to furnish this Court with a "description of concrete plans" for her nightly schedule of attempted activities. . . .

I find myself unable to agree with the plurality's analysis of redressability, based as it is on its invitation of executive lawlessness, ignorance of principles of collateral estoppel, unfounded assumptions about causation, and erroneous conclusions about what the record does not say. In my view, respondents have satisfactorily shown a genuine issue of fact as to whether their injury would likely be redressed by a decision in their favor. . . .

In conclusion, I cannot join the Court on what amounts to a slash-and-burn expedition through the law of environmental standing. In my view, "[t]he very essence of civil liberty certainly consists in the right of every individual to claim the protection of the laws, whenever he receives an injury." *Marbury v. Madison,* 1 Cranch 137, 163, 2 L.Ed. 60 (1803).

I dissent.

Questions

1. The Court does not resolve the legal dispute in *Lujan* in the same way it resolved standing in *Camp.* Can you explain why not?
2. Can you find any mention of the "zone of interest" in the *Lujan* case? Can you cite and explain alternative standing tests listed in *Lujan*?

For a recent application of *Lujan* also involving the Endangered Species Act and the DOI but reaching the opposite result, see *Bennett v. Spear,* 117 S.Ct. 1154 (1997).

Two variables are at work in these standing cases. The first is a constitutional separation of power variable that the courts have imposed to restrict the use of the judicial branch as a vehicle for those who would change public policy simply because they disagree with the policy. The second variable relates to the parties involved in the dispute that the Court has been asked to resolve.

In a typical case, an agency has taken some action that adversely affects a business, corporation, industry, interest group, or individual. In the Chapter 1 example, when Secretary of Transportation Lewis revoked a rule requiring all automobiles manufactured in the United States to have a passive restraint system, that decision would have adversely affected the automobile insurance industry. The same can be said for the Chapter 2 example, Secretary Dole's decision to restrict the effectiveness of the Hazard Communication Standard; workers who would not receive the warnings were adversely affected. Ditto, the Chapter 3 examples of Congress's adverse action on Jagdish Rai Chadha and the Secretary of Labor's decision to reduce the ppm of benzene in the air from ten to one that adversely affected petroleum producers' profits.

In situations like those above, standing is not difficult because the injury in fact is obvious and the injured parties can show that a particular statute (or constitutional or common law provision) arguably protects them from the actions the agency has taken (the zone of interest test). The zone of interest test is meant to ensure that ordinary citizens do not attempt to use the judicial branch to change those public policies that we disagree with (we should use the legislative branch). Those who are specifically injured by governmental action (the insurance industry, construction workers, Chadha, and petroleum producers), however, do have standing to challenge the policy in court.

Less frequently, however, situations occur in which governmental action has affected an intervening or third party and that party's action theoretically adversely affects an "injured party." The "injured party" then sues the government agency that started the chain reaction. Such was the case in *Allen v. Wright et al.* and *Lujan v. Defenders of Wildlife* (and also in *City of Los Angeles v. Lyons,* which appears at the end of the chapter).

Wright's complaint is really with private academies that discriminate and only tangentially with the IRS. The Defenders of Wildlife are concerned with the actions of Egypt and Sri Lanka and only more remotely with the AID and the DOI. Basically, plaintiffs in such situations must argue that the governmental action (or inaction) caused another party to take some action (or inaction) that adversely affects the plaintiffs. In these "third party" standing cases, the Court has created a three-pronged test:

1. Is there injury in fact?
2. Is the injury to the plaintiff fairly traceable to the defendant (the agency)?
3. If the Court were to grant the plaintiff the remedy requested, would that redress the plaintiff's injury?

You are already familiar with the first prong, injury in fact. The second prong is referred to as "traceability" and relates to causality; that is, did the actions of the agency "cause" the harm to the plaintiffs? The Wrights could not show that their children were denied their constitutional right to attend desegregated schools because of the implementation interpretation of the IRS. Their injury was not fairly traceable to the IRS.

The third prong of the test is referred to as "redressability" and asks whether the Courts can solve the plaintiff's problem. Although the DOW had traceability problems in its suit against the DOI, the Court concentrated on the redressability problem. To understand redressability, you have to know what remedy the plaintiffs have requested. The DOW was asking the Court to reverse a DOI rule restricting Department of the Interior consultation under the Endangered Species Act (ESA) to domestic projects. Even if the Court were to order the DOI to consult on overseas ESA projects, that would not necessarily ensure that Egypt and Sri Lanka would not proceed with the projects that threaten crocodiles, elephants, and leopards. Hence, according to the Court, the DOW cannot show redressability and lacks standing to sue the DOI.

Although it is an oversimplification, the notion of restricting access to the Courts is a conservative, judicial self-restraint notion, and allowing broader access to the courts is supposed to be a liberal or judicial activism notion. Currently, a majority of the Court could be called "conservative." They are Nixon, Reagan, and Bush appointees (Rehnquist, O'Connor, Scalia, Kennedy, and Thomas), and they have used the added concepts of "traceability" and "redressability" to restrict plaintiffs' ability to gain standing to challenge governmental action (although O'Connor dissented in *Lujan,* she was with the majority in *Allen v. Wright et al.*). In 1996, the Court unanimously applied the three-pronged third-party test to a two-party case. It was not an administrative law case, but a union sued an employer for an alleged failure to notify of an impending plant closure within the required time period (see *United Food and Commercial Workers Union Local 751 v. Brown Shoe Co.,* 116 S.Ct. 1529, 1996).

CONSTRAINTS ON THE EXERCISE
OF JUDICIAL POWER THAT ARE
UNIQUE TO ADMINISTRATIVE LAW

Reviewability

As indicated earlier, the Constitution gives Congress the power to set the jurisdiction of federal courts in terms of the questions it can hear acting as a reviewing court—that is, as a court reviewing the decision of a lower court (or administrative agency), rather than acting as a trial court. Indeed, the ability to manipulate the appellate jurisdiction of federal courts is a powerful tool in the check-and-balance system that Congress uses to check the courts. During the Civil War, for example, Congress withdrew federal court jurisdiction to review habeas corpus petitions from prisoners convicted by military tribunals (*Ex Parte McCardle* 74 U.S. [7 Wall.] 506 [1869]).

In the context of administrative law, there was once a common law presumption of unreviewability regarding the decisions of administrative agencies; that is, it was considered "mischief" for the courts to interfere with the performance of executive functions.[4] Only if Congress specifically authorized judicial review of an agency's action would the courts grant review. In Chapter 7 of the APA, Congress specifically authorized judicial review of nearly all federal agencies' decisions: "A person suffering legal wrong because of agency action, or adversely affected or aggrieved by agency action . . . is entitled to judicial review thereof.[5]

Today, then, nearly all federal agency decisions are reviewable, but it is important to remember that this is the case only because Congress has said so. Indeed, that same section of the APA exempts from judicial review two situations: (a) those in which Congress has precluded judicial review by statute and (b) those in which agency action is committed to agency discretion by law.

The first of these exceptions is referred to as "statutory preclusion of judicial review." The most often cited and litigated example of this preclusion involves the Veterans Administration (VA). In passing the Veterans Benefits Act of 1957, Congress said, "The decisions of the administrator on any question of law or fact . . . providing benefits for veterans and their dependents or survivors shall be final . . . and no . . . court of the United States shall have the power or jurisdiction to review any such decision."[6]

Despite the clarity of the language in the Veterans Benefits Act, the courts have found instances in which preclusion of review does not apply, and the courts have reviewed VA actions. Where a decision of the VA allegedly violated the free-exercise clause of the Constitution, the Court said that statutory preclusion of judicial review did not apply (*Johnson v. Robinson,* 415 U.S. 361 [1974]). In that case, Robinson, a conscientious objector who served his time in alternate service as required by the draft laws, argued that the decision by the VA to deny him benefits violated his free exercise of religion. In a more recent case, the Court decided that the statutory preclusion of review did not apply where a decision of the VA ran counter to another congressional act that applied to all federal agencies.

TRAYNOR V. TURNAGE
485 U.S. 535 (1988)

Traynor and other petitioners in this case are honorably discharged veterans who have not exhausted their education assistance benefits from the VA within ten years following their discharge. In passing the "G.I. Bill," Congress mandated that benefits must be used within ten years of discharge. Veterans may obtain an extension beyond the ten-year limit, however, if they were prevented from using the benefits "by a physical or mental disorder which was not the result of (their) own willful misconduct" (38 U.S.C. § 1662[a][1]).

Traynor, a recovering alcoholic, did not use his benefits within the ten-year limit because of his earlier alcoholism. Turnage, the administrator of the VA, enforced the agency's interpretation that "primary" alcoholism (alcoholism unrelated to an underlying psychiatric disorder) is "willful misconduct" and denied Traynor's application for a waiver from the ten-year limit.

Traynor argued that the VA's decision is prohibited by the Rehabilitation Act of 1973, which forbids federal agencies from discriminating against persons with disabilities solely on the basis of the disability (and alcoholism is considered to be a disability).

The VA argued that the administrator's decisions "on questions of law or fact . . . providing benefits

. . . shall be final . . . and no court of the U.S. shall have the power to review any such decision."

The district court held that judicial review was not foreclosed and invalidated the VA's interpretation relating to primary alcoholism as violating the Rehabilitation Act. The circuit court of appeals agreed on the question of reviewability but found the VA's interpretation relating to primary alcoholism to be rational and reasonable and not in conflict with the Rehabilitation Act.

Justice White wrote the opinion, joined by Justices Rehnquist, O'Connor, and Stevens, and joined in part by Justices Brennan, Marshall, and Blackmun. Justices Scalia and Kennedy took no part in the decision.

We must first consider whether § 211(a)'s bar against judicial review of "the decisions of the Administrator on any question of law or fact under any law administered by the Veterans' Administration providing benefits for veterans" extends to petitioner's claim that the Veterans' Administration regulation defining primary alcoholism as "willful misconduct" discriminates against handicapped persons in violation of the Rehabilitation Act. We have repeatedly acknowledged "the strong presumption that Congress intends judicial review of administrative action." *Bowen v. Michigan Acad-*

emy of Family Physicians, 476 U.S. 667, 670 (1986); see also *Dunlop v. Bachowski,* 421 U.S. 560, 567 (1975); *Barlow v. Collins,* 397 U.S. 159, 166-167 (1970). The presumption in favor of judicial review may be overcome "only upon a showing of 'clear and convincing evidence' of a contrary legislative intent." *Abbott Laboratories v. Gardner,* 387 U.S. 136, 141 (1967) (citations omitted). We look to such evidence as " 'specific language or specific legislative history that is a reliable indicator of congressional intent,' or a specific congressional intent to preclude judicial review that is 'fairly discernible in the detail of the legislative scheme.' " *Bowen v. Michigan Academy of Family Physicians,* supra, at 673.

In *Johnson v. Robison,* supra, we held that the federal courts could entertain constitutional challenges to veterans' benefits legislation. We determined that "neither the text nor the scant legislative history of § 211(a)" provided the requisite "clear and convincing" evidence of congressional intent to foreclose judicial review of challenges to the constitutionality of a law administered by the Veterans' Administration. 415 U.S., at 373-374. In that case, we reasoned that "the prohibitions [of § 211(a)] would appear to be aimed at review only of those decisions of law or fact that arise in the administration by the Veterans' Administration of a statute providing benefits for veterans." 415 U.S., at 367. The questions of law presented in that case, however, arose under the Constitution rather than under the veterans' benefits statute and concerned whether there was a valid law on the subject for the Veterans' Administration to execute. We went on to conclude that the principal purposes of § 211(a)— "(1) to insure that veterans' benefits claims will not burden the courts and the Veterans' Administration with expensive and time-consuming litigation, and (2) to insure that the technical and complex determinations and applications of Veterans' Administration policy connected with veterans' benefits decisions will be adequately and uniformly made," Id., at 370—would not be frustrated if federal courts were permitted to exercise jurisdiction over constitutional challenges to the very statute that was sought to be enforced. We noted that such challenges "cannot be expected to burden the courts by their volume, nor do they involve technical consideration of Veterans' Administration policy." Id., at 373.

The text and legislative history of § 211(a) likewise provide no clear and convincing evidence of any congressional intent to preclude a suit claiming that § 504 of the Rehabilitation Act, a statute applicable to all federal agencies, has invalidated an otherwise valid regulation issued by the Veterans' Administration and purporting to have the force of law. Section 211(a) insulates from review decisions of law and fact "under any law administered by the Veterans' Administration," that is, decisions made in interpreting or applying a particular provision of that statute to a particular set of facts. Id., at 367. But the cases now before us involve the issue whether the law sought to be administered is valid in light of a subsequent statute whose enforcement is not the exclusive domain of the Veterans' Administration. There is no claim that the regulation at issue is inconsistent with the statute under which it was issued; and there is no challenge to the Veterans' Administration's construction of any statute dealing with veterans' benefits, except to the extent that its construction may be affected by the Rehabilitation Act. Nor is there any reason to believe that the Veterans' Administration has any special expertise in assessing the validity of its regulations construing veterans' benefits statutes under a later-passed statute of general application.

Permitting these cases to go forward will not undermine the purposes of § 211(a) any more than did the result in *Johnson.* It cannot be assumed that the availability of the federal courts to decide whether there is some fundamental inconsistency between the Veterans' Administration's construction of veterans' benefits statutes, as reflected in the regulation at issue here, and the admonitions of the Rehabilitation Act will enmesh the courts in "the technical and complex determinations and applications of Veterans' Administration policy connected with veterans' benefits decisions" or "burden the courts and the Veterans' Administration with expensive and time-consuming litigation." Id., at 370. Of course, if experience proves otherwise, the Veterans' Administration is fully capable of seeking appropriate relief from Congress. Accordingly, we conclude that the question whether a Veterans' Administration regulation violates the Rehabilitation Act is not foreclosed from judicial review by § 211(a). We therefore turn to the merits of petitioners' Rehabilitation Act claim.

III

. . . It is thus clear that the 1977 legislation precluded an extension of time to a veteran who had not pursued his education because of primary alcoholism. If Congress had intended instead that primary alcoholism not be deemed "willful mis-conduct" for purposes of § 1662(a)(1), as it had been deemed for purposes of other veterans' benefits statutes, Congress most certainly would have said so.

Petitioners, however, perceive an inconsistency between § 504 and the conclusive presumption that alcoholism not motivated by mental illness is necessarily "willful." They contend that § 504 mandates an individualized determination of "willfulness" with respect to each veteran who claims to have been disabled by alcoholism. It would arguably be inconsistent with § 504 for Congress to distinguish between categories of disabled veterans according to generalized determinations that lack any substantial basis. If primary alcoholism is not always "willful," as that term has been defined by Congress and the Veterans' Administration, some veterans denied benefits may well be excluded solely on the basis of their disability. We are unable to conclude that Congress failed to act in accordance with § 504 in this instance, however, given what the District of Columbia Circuit accurately characterized as "a substantial body of medical literature that even contests the proposition that alcoholism is a disease, much less that it is a disease for which the victim bears no responsibility." 792 F.2d, at 200-201. Indeed, even among many who consider alcoholism a "disease" to which its victims are genetically predisposed, the consumption of alcohol is not regarded as wholly involuntary. See Fingarette, The Perils of Powell: In Search of a Factual Foundation for the "Disease Concept of Alcoholism," 83 *Harv. L. Rev.* 793, 802-808 (1970). As we

see it, § 504 does not demand inquiry into whether factors other than mental illness rendered an individual veteran's drinking so entirely beyond his control as to negate any degree of "willfulness" where Congress and the Veterans' Administration have reasonably determined for purposes of the veterans' benefits statutes that no such factors exist.

In sum, we hold that a construction of § 1662(a)(1) that reflects the original congressional intent that primary alcoholics not be excused from the 10-year delimiting period for utilizing "G.I. Bill" benefits is not inconsistent with the prohibition on discrimination against the handicapped contained in § 504 of the Rehabilitation Act. Accordingly, since we "are not at liberty to pick and choose among congressional enactments . . . when two statutes are capable of co-existence," *Morton v. Mancari,* 417 U.S., at 551, we must conclude that the earlier, more specific provisions of § 1662(a)(1) were neither expressly nor implicitly repealed by the later, more general provisions of § 504.

This litigation does not require the Court to decide whether alcoholism is a disease whose course its victims cannot control. It is not our role to resolve this medical issue on which the authorities remain sharply divided. Our task is to decide whether Congress intended, in enacting § 504 of the Rehabilitation Act, to reject the position taken on the issue by the Veterans' Administration and by Congress itself only one year earlier. In our view, it is by no means clear that § 504 and the characterization of primary alcoholism as a willfully incurred disability are in irreconcilable conflict.

If petitioners and their proponents continue to believe that this position is erroneous, their arguments are better presented to Congress than to the courts. . . .

In 1988, as Congress moved the VA from an independent agency to a cabinet-level agency, it also modified the preclusion of review so that now most (but still not all) rulings of the VA are reviewable.

In fall 1996, Congress revised the Immigration and Naturalization Act in an attempt to restrict immigration into the United States. In doing so, the conservative Republican majorities believed that the Immigration and Naturalization Service (INS) would be a better watchdog over immigration policy than the "liberal" courts. Congress made INS immigration decisions unreviewable to the courts in the area of the granting of political asylum. Fortunately for Francisco Lucas Rodriguez-Roman, his case was reviewed by the federal court before the new immigration law went into effect. Rodriguez so hated the Castro regime that he gave up a career as a teacher to join the merchant marine with the hope that someday he could jump ship in the United States. This he did, but the INS judge denied him political asylum and ordered him deported to face "harsh if not fatal punishment." The INS judge compared Rodriguez's desertion with that of Private Eddie Slovik during World War II (Slovik was the only U.S. soldier executed for desertion in World War II). The court reviewing the INS deportation of Rodriguez reversed, holding that harsh punishment does provide grounds for asylum. At least one member of the court pointed out that had the Rodriguez case hit the courts a few months later, after the new immigration bill, Rodriguez would be on his way back to Cuba because the INS decision would be unreviewable. According to the judge, that surely was not a result intended by the bill's sponsor, Representative Lamar Smith, (R) Texas, who was adamant about denying court review of INS asylum decisions.[7]

If you turn to the Administrative Procedure Act in the appendix of this book, you will notice that Section 564 deals with a procedure called Negotiated Rule-Making (Neg-Reg), which is discussed in Chapter 7. For now, however, if you move forward several pages to Section 570, which is titled "Judicial Review," you will see that Congress has exercised statutory preclusion of judicial review for negotiated rules.

The second exception to general reviewability of agency actions, "agency action committed to agency discretion by law," is even more confusing. This is a classic example of Congress's not doing the job its members get paid in excess of $130,000 a year to do. The statutory logic goes like this:

1. Prior to the APA (1946), most administrative decisions were considered to be unreviewable.
2. Congress intended to change that, for the most part, in 1946 with the passage of the APA.
3. The APA declared that, with two exceptions, all actions and decisions of federal agencies are subject to judicial review in federal court.
   a. First, Congress meant to exempt from judicial review the decisions of agencies for which Congress specifically excluded review in the enabling legislation, such as the VA.
   b. Then, Congress (apparently) intended to exempt another category of agency decisions, but the best it could come up with was to say "where agency action is committed to agency discretion by law."

You may be thinking to yourself, "That doesn't mean much to me, but surely a judge, trained in the law, will understand what Congress meant." You would be wrong. In very few cases have courts had to interpret this clause, but where courts have had to deal with it, the judges have been forced to "guess at its meaning and differ as to its application." Justice Souter's opinion in the case below discusses some of the past decisions in this area.

LINCOLN V. VIGIL
113 S.Ct. 2024 (1993)

Justice Souter delivered the unanimous opinion of the Court.

For several years in the late 1970s and early 1980s, the Indian Health Service provided diagnostic and treatment services, referred to collectively as the Indian Children's Program, to handicapped Indian children in the Southwest. In 1985, the Service decided to reallocate the Program's resources to a nationwide effort to assist such children. We hold that the Service's decision to discontinue the Program was "committed to agency discretion by law" and therefore not subject to judicial review under the Administrative Procedure Act, 5 U.S.C. § 701(a)(2), and that the Service's exercise of that discretion was not subject to the notice-and-comment rulemaking requirements imposed by § 553.

I

The Indian Health Service, an agency within the Public Health Service of the Department of Health and Human Services, provides health care for some 1.5 million American Indian and Alaska Native people. . . . The Service receives yearly lump-sum appropriations from Congress and expends the funds under authority of the Snyder Act, 25 U.S.C. § 13, and the Indian Health Care Improvement Act, 25 U.S.C. § 1601. So far as it concerns us here, the Snyder Act authorizes the Service to "expend such moneys as Congress may from time to time appropriate, for the benefit, care, and assistance of the Indians," for the "relief of distress and conservation of health." The Improvement Act authorizes expenditures for, Indian mental-health care, and specifically for "therapeutic and residential treatment centers." . . .

This case concerns a collection of related services, commonly known as the Indian Children's

Program, that the Service provided from 1978 to 1985. In the words of the Court of Appeals, a "clou[d of] bureaucratic haze" obscures the history of the Program, . . . which seems to have grown out of a plan "to establish therapeutic and residential treatment centers for disturbed Indian children." These centers were to be established under a "major cooperative care agreement" between the Service and the Bureau of Indian Affairs, and would have provided such children "with intensive care in a residential setting."

Congress never expressly appropriated funds for these centers. In 1978, however, the Service allocated approximately $292,000 from its fiscal year 1978 appropriation to its office in Albuquerque, New Mexico, for the planning and development of a pilot project for handicapped Indian children, which became known as the Indian Children's Program. The pilot project apparently convinced the Service that a building was needed, and, in 1979, the Service requested $3.5 million from Congress to construct a diagnostic and treatment center for handicapped Indian children. . . . The appropriation for fiscal year 1980 did not expressly provide the requested funds, however, and legislative reports indicated only that Congress had increased the Service's funding by $300,000 for nationwide expansion and development of the Program in coordination with the Bureau.

Plans for a national program to be managed jointly by the Service and the Bureau were never fulfilled, however, and the Program continued simply as an offering of the Service's Albuquerque office, from which the Program's staff of 11 to 16 employees would make monthly visits to Indian communities in New Mexico and Southern Colorado and on the Navajo and Hopi Reservations. The

Program's staff provided "diagnostic, evaluation, treatment planning and follow-up services" for Indian children with emotional, educational, physical, or mental handicaps. "For parents, community groups, school personnel and health care personnel," the staff provided training in child development, prevention of handicapping conditions, and care of the handicapped child." Congress never authorized or appropriated monies expressly for the Program, and the Service continued to pay for its regional activities out of annual lump-sum appropriations from 1980 to 1985, during which period the Service repeatedly apprised Congress of the Program's continuing operation.

Nevertheless, the Service had not abandoned the proposal for a nationwide treatment program, and in June 1985 it notified those who referred patients to the Program that it was "re-evaluating [the Program's] purpose . . . as a national mental health program for Indian children and adolescents." In August 1985, the Service determined that Program staff hitherto assigned to provide direct clinical services should be reassigned as consultants to other nationwide Service programs, and discontinued the direct clinical services to Indian children in the Southwest. The Service announced its decision in a memorandum, dated August 21, 1985, addressed to Service offices and Program referral sources: . . .

The Service invited public "input" during this "difficult transition," and explained that the reallocation of resources had been "motivated by our goal of increased mental health services for all Indian [c]hildren." Ibid. [FN2]

Respondents, handicapped Indian children eligible to receive services through the Program, subsequently brought this action for declaratory and injunctive relief against petitioners, the Director of the Service and others (collectively, the Service), in the United States District Court for the District of New Mexico. Respondents alleged, inter alia, that the Service's decision to discontinue direct clinical services violated the federal trust responsibility to Indians, the Snyder Act, the Improvement Act, the Administrative Procedure Act, various agency regulations, and the Fifth Amendment's Due Process Clause.

II

First is the question whether it was error for the Court of Appeals to hold the substance of the Ser-

vice's decision to terminate the Program reviewable under the APA. The Act provides that "[a] person suffering legal wrong because of agency action, or adversely affected or aggrieved by agency action within the meaning of a relevant statute, is entitled to judicial review thereof," and we have read the Act as embodying a "basic presumption of judicial review." *Abbott Laboratories v. Gardner,* 387 U.S. 136. This is "just" a presumption, however, *Block v. Community Nutrition Institute,* 467 U.S. 340 (1984), and under § 701(a)(2) agency action is not subject to judicial review "to the extent that" such action "is committed to agency discretion by law." As we explained in *Heckler v. Chaney,* 470 U.S. 821 (1985), § 701(a)(2) makes it clear that "review is not to be had" in those rare circumstances where the relevant statute" is drawn so that a court would have no meaningful standard against which to judge the agency's exercise of discretion." "In such a case, the statute ('law') can be taken to have 'committed' the decisionmaking to the agency's judgment absolutely." *Heckler,* supra, at 830.

Over the years, we have read § 701(a)(2) to preclude judicial review of certain categories of administrative decisions that courts traditionally have regarded as "committed to agency discretion." . . . In *Heckler* itself, we held an agency's decision not to institute enforcement proceedings to be presumptively unreviewable under § 701(a)(2). An agency's "decision not to enforce often involves a complicated balancing of a number of factors which are peculiarly within its expertise," ibid., and for this and other good reasons, we concluded, "such a decision has traditionally been 'committed to agency discretion.'" Similarly, in *ICC v. Locomotive Engineers,* 482 U.S. 270 (1987), we held that § 701(a)(2) precludes judicial review of another type of administrative decision traditionally left to agency discretion, an agency's refusal to grant reconsideration of an action because of material error. In so holding, we emphasized "the impossibility of devising an adequate standard of review for such agency action." Ibid. Finally, . . . 701(a)(2) precludes judicial review of a decision by the Director of Central Intelligence to terminate an employee in the interests of national security, an area of executive action "in which courts have long been hesitant to intrude."

The allocation of funds from a lump-sum appropriation is another administrative decision traditionally regarded as committed to agency discretion.

After all, the very point of a lump-sum appropriation is to give an agency the capacity to adapt to changing circumstances and meet its statutory responsibilities in what it sees as the most effective or desirable way. See *International Union, United Automobile, Aerospace & Agricultural Implement Workers of America v. Donovan,* 746 F.2d 855, 861 (1984) (Scalia, J.) ("A lump-sum appropriation leaves it to the recipient agency (as a matter of law, at least) to distribute the funds among some or all of the permissible objects as it sees fit"). For this reason, a fundamental principle of appropriations law is that where "Congress merely appropriates lump-sum amounts without statutorily restricting what can be done with those funds, a clear inference arises that it does not intend to impose legally binding restrictions, and indicia in committee reports and other legislative history as to how the funds should or are expected to be spent do not establish any legal requirements on" the agency. . . . *American Hospital Assn. v. NLRB,* 111 S.Ct. 1539 (1991) (statements in committee reports do not have the force of law). Put another way, a lump-sum appropriation reflects a congressional recognition that an agency must be allowed "flexibility to shift . . . funds within a particular . . . appropriation account so that" the agency "can make necessary adjustments for 'unforeseen developments' " and " 'changing requirements.' "

[2] Like the decision against instituting enforcement proceedings, then, an agency's allocation of funds from a lump-sum appropriation requires "a complicated balancing of a number of factors which are peculiarly within its expertise": whether its "resources are best spent" on one program or another; whether it "is likely to succeed" in fulfilling its statutory mandate; whether a particular program "best fits the agency's overall policies"; and, "indeed, whether the agency has enough resources" to fund a program "at all." *Heckler,* 470 U.S., at 831. As in *Heckler,* so here, the "agency is far better equipped than the courts to deal with the many variables involved in the proper ordering of its priorities." Of course, an agency is not free simply to disregard statutory responsibilities: Congress may always circumscribe agency discretion to allocate resources by putting restrictions in the operative statutes (though not, as we have seen, just in the legislative history). And, of course, we hardly need to note that an agency's decision to ignore congressional expectations may expose it to grave political consequences. But as long as the agency allocates funds from a lump-sum appropriation to meet permissible statutory objectives, § 701(a)(2) gives the courts no leave to intrude. "[T]o [that] extent," the decision to allocate funds "is committed to agency discretion by law."

[3] The Service's decision to discontinue the Program is accordingly unreviewable under § 701(a)(2). As the Court of Appeals recognized, the appropriations Acts for the relevant period do not so much as mention the Program, and both the Snyder Act and the Improvement Act likewise speak about Indian health only in general terms. It is true that the Service repeatedly apprised Congress of the Program's continued operation, but, as we have explained, these representations do not translate through the medium of legislative history into legally binding obligations. The reallocation of agency resources to assist handicapped Indian children nationwide clearly falls within the Service's statutory mandate to provide health care to Indian people, and respondents, indeed, do not seriously contend otherwise. The decision to terminate the Program was committed to the Service's discretion. . . .

IV

The judgment of the Court of Appeals is reversed, and the case is remanded for further proceedings consistent with this opinion.

It is so ordered.

In the *Lincoln* case above, the Court finds that the agency action is unreviewable because it is committed to agency discretion by law. In the case below, the secretary of transportation argues that his decision is unreviewable, but the Court finds that it is reviewable.

CITIZENS TO PRESERVE
OVERTON PARK V. VOLPE
401 U.S. 402 (1971)

In 1968, Secretary of Transportation Volpe announced that he agreed with local Memphis officials that a six-lane federal highway would have to be routed through Overton Park. In 1969, the secretary approved the authorizations of federal highway funds for the highway through the park. Neither the announcement nor the decision was accompanied by a statement of reasons or findings of fact or an explanation.

Citizens to Preserve Overton Park sued the secretary to enjoin the release of federal monies on the basis of Section 4 of the Department of Transportation Act of 1966, 49 U.S.C. 1653, and Section 138 of the Federal-Aid Highway Act of 1968, 23 U.S.C. 138. They forbid the authorization of federal funds for highways through public parks if a "feasible and prudent" alternate route exists. If the secretary finds that no feasible and prudent alternate route exists, then the secretary may release funds only after "all possible planning to minimize harm" to the park.

Both the district and circuit courts would have dismissed the suit against Secretary of Transportation Volpe on a technicality. The Supreme Court merely said that the two lower courts were wrong to dismiss the case and sent it back for trial to the district court. In their dissent, Justices Black and Brennan argued that the secretary of transportation had abused his power and that the whole affair should be sent back to him for hearings and a new decision (they would void the secretary's decision, rather than overrule the lower courts on technical points of law).

Justice Marshall wrote the opinion, joined by Chief Justice Burger and Justices Harlan, Stewart, White, and Blackmun. Justice Black dissented, joined by Justice Brennan. Justice Douglas did not participate.

A threshold question—whether petitioners are entitled to any judicial review—is easily answered. Section 701 of the Administrative Procedure Act, 5 U.S.C. § 701, provides that the action of "each authority of the Government of the United States," which includes the Department of Transportation, is subject to judicial review except where there is a statutory prohibition on review or where "agency action is committed to agency discretion by law." In this case, there is no indication that Congress sought to prohibit judicial review and there is most certainly no "showing of 'clear and convincing evidence' of a . . . legislative intent" to restrict access to judicial review. Similarly, the Secretary's decision here does not fall within the exception for action "committed to agency discretion." This is a very narrow exception. Berger, Administrative Arbitrariness and Judicial Review, 65 *Col. L. Rev.* 55 (1965). The legislative history of the Administrative Procedure Act indicates that it is applicable in those rare instances where "statutes are drawn in such broad terms that in a given case there is no law to apply." Section 4 (f) of the Department of Transportation Act and § 138 of the Federal-Aid Highway Act are clear and specific directives. Both the Department of Transportation Act and the Federal-Aid Highway Act provide that the Secretary "shall not approve any program or project" that requires the use of any public park land "unless (1) there is no feasible and prudent alternative to the use of such land, and (2) such program includes all possible planning to minimize harm to such park. . . ." 23 U.S.C. § 138 49 U.S.C. § 1653(f). This language is a plain and explicit bar to the use of federal funds for construction of highways through parks—only the most unusual situations are exempted.

Despite the clarity of the statutory language, respondents argue that the Secretary has wide discretion. They recognize that the requirement that there be no "feasible" alternative route admits of little administrative discretion. For this exemption to apply the Secretary must find that as a matter of sound engineering it would not be feasible to build the highway along any other route. Respondents argue, however, that the requirement that there be no other "prudent" route requires the Secretary to engage in a wide-ranging balancing of competing interests. They contend that the Secretary should weigh the detriment resulting from the destruction of park land against the cost of other routes, safety considerations, and other factors, and determine on the basis of the importance that he attaches to these other factors whether, on balance, alternative feasible routes would be "prudent." But no such wide-ranging endeavor was intended. It is obvious that in most cases considerations of cost, directness of route, and community disruption will indicate that park land should be used for highway construction whenever possible. Although it may be necessary to transfer funds from one jurisdiction to another, there will always be a smaller outlay required from the public purse when park land is used since the public already owns the land and there will be no need to pay for right-of-way. And since people do not live or work in parks, if a highway is built on park land no one will have to leave his home or give up his business. Such factors are common to substantially all highway construction. Thus, if Con-

gress intended these factors to be on an equal footing with preservation of park land there would have been no need for the statutes. Congress clearly did not intend that cost and disruption of the community were to be ignored by the Secretary. But the very existence of the statutes indicates that protection of park land was to be given paramount importance. The few green havens that are public parks were not to be lost unless there were truly unusual factors present in a particular case or the cost or community disruption resulting from alternative routes reached extraordinary magnitudes. If the statutes are to have any meaning, the Secretary cannot approve the destruction of park land unless he finds that alternative routes present unique problems.

Plainly, there is "law to apply" and thus the exemption for action "committed to agency discretion" is inapplicable. But the existence of judicial review is only the start: the standard for review must also be determined.

The student should not be overly concerned that the Court's attempt to clarify the "committed to agency discretion" clause in the *Overton Park* case is of little help. What is important to grasp here is that reviewability of agency action is granted by legislation and that, generally, Congress intended to extend judicial review to most agency actions. There are two exceptions. The first exception is where Congress specifically forbids judicial review for a particular agency or a particular kind of action. The second exception is a nebulous category of actions referred to as "actions committed to agency discretion" that is hard to define and little used.

For an interesting case dealing with both standing and action committed to "agency" discretion by law, see *Dalton v. Specter,* 114 S.Ct., 1719 (1994). In this case, Senator Arlen Specter, (R) Pennsylvania, challenged the closure of the Philadelphia Naval Shipyard under the 1990 Defense Base Closure and Realignment Act. The majority of the Court found that the senator lacked standing under the APA and that President Clinton's acceptance of Closure Commission recommendations was action committed to the president and, hence, was not reviewable. A concurring opinion by four justices stated that base closure decisions statutorily precluded judicial review.

Exhaustion

If a person believes that he or she has been or is about to be injured by administrative action, that person cannot turn to the courts for help until he or she has gone through all the available channels within the agency; that is, the person must *exhaust* all legal remedies within the agency.

Every agency has published procedures for clients of the agency to follow in trying to redress an adverse agency decision or other agency action. For example, if a person believes that he or she is eligible for veterans benefits, Social Security, or a tax exemption, he or she can make application (in the case of the VA or Social Security Administration) or, in the latter case, simply claim the exemption on a tax return. If the claim is denied in any of those situations, the procedure to follow is similar for anyone wishing to challenge that denial. First, the person appeals the initial denial decision to the supervisor of the clerk who processed the application and determined that it did not qualify for the benefit (or tax exemption). Most often, the supervisor will support the position of the clerk. Next, an appeal can be made to the supervisor's supervisor, who most likely will be the director of the local office. If the person loses that appeal, he or she must appeal the decision of the local director to the regional office. If the decision from the regional office is still adverse, some agencies require (allow) an appeal to the head of the agency for a final agency decision, which can then (and only then) be challenged in the courts. That is *exhaustion,* and under normal circumstances a federal court will simply not entertain a suit by a plaintiff who has not exhausted all avenues of appeal available within the agency. Virtually all states use the concept of "exhaustion," but there are myriad differences between the states in terms of exceptions allowed by which a potential plaintiff could "short circuit" exhaustion. The purpose behind exhaustion is to provide the agency with every opportunity to correct potential errors before turning to the courts.

Primary Jurisdiction

Primary jurisdiction holds that, in those situations in which a question could be handled by either a court of law or an administrative agency, usually the courts should decline to exercise jurisdiction until the administrative agency has had the opportunity to deal with the issue first.

For example, between 1944 and 1950, the army contracted with the Bangor and Sea Board Railroad and with the Western Pacific to transport bomb casings filled with napalm. The railroads billed the army at a first-class rate for carrying "incendiary bombs," but the army paid at the lower, fifth-class rate for carrying "gasoline in steel drums." The railroads here have two choices: They can sue in a federal court of claims, or they can bring their case to the Interstate Commerce Commission (ICC).

In fact, the railroads chose the court of claims, which decided in their favor. On appeal, however, the Supreme Court said that "the question of tariff construction, as well as the reasonableness of the tariff . . . are within the exclusive primary jurisdiction of the ICC." The Court vacated the decision of the court of claims and mandated that the issue be dealt with first by the ICC.[8] Following is one of the most famous primary jurisdiction cases, in which Allegheny Airlines had the misfortune of bumping Ralph Nader from one of its flights.

NADER V. ALLEGHENY AIRLINES, INCORPORATED
426 U.S. 290 (1976)

Justice Powell delivered the opinion, joined by a unanimous court (Burger, Brennan, Stewart, White, Marshall, Blackmun, Rehnquist, and Stevens).

I

The facts are not contested. Petitioner agreed to make several appearances in Connecticut on April 28, 1972, in support of the fundraising efforts of the Connecticut Citizen Action Group (CCAG), a nonprofit public interest organization. His two principal appearances were to be at a noon rally in Hartford and a later address at the Storrs campus of the University of Connecticut. On April 25, petitioner reserved a seat on respondent's flight 864 for April 28. The flight was scheduled to leave Washington, D.C., at 10:15 a.m. and to arrive in Hartford at 11:15 a.m. Petitioner's ticket was purchased from a travel agency on the morning of the flight. It indicated, by the standard "OK" notation, that the reservation was confirmed.

Petitioner arrived at the boarding and check-in area approximately five minutes before the scheduled departure time. He was informed that all seats on the flight were occupied and that he, like several other passengers who had arrived shortly before him, could not be accommodated. Explaining that he had to arrive in Hartford in time for the noon rally, petitioner asked respondent's agent to determine whether any standby passengers had been allowed to board by mistake or whether anyone already on board would voluntarily give up his or her seat. Both requests were refused. In accordance with respondent's practice, petitioner was offered alternative transportation by air taxi to Philadelphia, where connections could be made with an Allegheny flight scheduled to arrive in Hartford at

12:15 p.m. Fearing that the Philadelphia connection, which allowed only 10 minutes between planes, was too close, petitioner rejected this offer and elected to fly to Boston, where he was met by a CCAG staff member who drove him to Storrs.

Both parties agree that petitioner's reservation was not honored because respondent had accepted more reservations for flight 864 than it could in fact accommodate. One hour prior to the flight, 107 reservations had been confirmed for the 100 seats actually available. Such overbooking is a common industry practice, designed to ensure that each flight leaves with as few empty seats as possible despite the large number of "no-shows"—reservation-holding passengers who do not appear at flight time. By the use of statistical studies of no-show patterns on specific flights, the airlines attempt to predict the appropriate number of reservations necessary to fill each flight. In this way, they attempt to ensure the most efficient use of aircraft while preserving a flexible booking system that permits passengers to cancel and change reservations without notice or penalty. At times the practice of overbooking results in oversales, which occur when more reservation-holding passengers than can be accommodated actually appear to board the flight. When this occurs, some passengers must be denied boarding ("bumped"). The chance that any particular passenger will be bumped is so negligible that few prospective passengers aware of the possibility would give it a second thought.

In April 1972, the month in which petitioner's reservation was dishonored, 6.7 confirmed passengers per 10,000 enplanements were denied boarding on domestic flights. For all domestic airlines, oversales resulted in bumping an average of 5.4

passengers per 10,000 enplanements in 1972, and 4.6 per 10,000 enplanements in 1973. In domestic operations respondent oversold 6.3 seats per 10,000 enplanements in 1972 and 4.5 seats per 10,000 enplanements in 1973. Thus, based on the 1972 experience of all domestic airlines, there was only slightly more than one chance in 2,000 that any particular passenger would be bumped on a given flight. Nevertheless, the total number of confirmed ticket holders denied seats is quite substantial, numbering over 82,000 passengers in 1972 and about 76,000 in 1973.

The only issue before us concerns the Court of Appeals' disposition on the merits of petitioner's claim of fraudulent misrepresentation. Although the court rejected respondent's argument that the existence of the Board's cease-and-desist power under § 411 of the Act eliminates all private remedies for common-law torts arising from unfair or deceptive practices by regulated carriers, it held that a determination by the Board that a practice is not deceptive within the meaning of § 411 would, as a matter of law, preclude a common-law tort action seeking damages for injuries caused by that practice. Therefore, the court held that the Board must be allowed to determine in the first instance whether the challenged practice (in this case, the alleged failure to disclose the practice of overbooking) falls within the ambit of § 411. The court took judicial notice that a rule-making proceeding concerning possible changes in reservation practices in response to the 1973-1974 fuel crisis was already underway and that a challenge to the carriers' overbooking practices had been raised by an intervenor in that proceeding. The District Court was instructed to stay further action on petitioner's misrepresentation claim pending the outcome of the rule-making proceeding. The Court of Appeals characterized its holding as "but another application of the principles of primary jurisdiction, a doctrine whose purpose is the coordination of the workings of agency and court," 512 F.2d, at 544.

The question before us, then, is whether the Board must be given an opportunity to determine whether respondent's alleged failure to disclose its practice of deliberate overbooking is a deceptive practice under § 411 before petitioner's common-law action is allowed to proceed. The decision of the Court of Appeals requires the District Court to stay the action brought by petitioner in order to give the Board an opportunity to resolve the question. If the Board were to find that there had been no

violation of § 411, respondent would be immunized from common-law liability.

The doctrine of primary jurisdiction "is concerned with promoting proper relationships between the courts and administrative agencies charged with particular regulatory duties. The doctrine has been applied, for example, when an action otherwise within the jurisdiction of the court raises a question of the validity of a rate or practice included in a tariff filed with an agency, e.g., *Danna v. Air France,* 463 F.2d 407 (CA2 1972); *Southwestern Sugar & Molasses Co. v. River Terminals Corp.,* 360 U.S. 411, 417-418 (1959), particularly when the issue involves technical questions of fact uniquely within the expertise and experience of an agency—such as matters turning on an assessment of industry conditions, e.g., *United States v. Western Pacific R. Co.,* supra, at 66-67. In this case, however, considerations of uniformity in regulation and of technical expertise do not call for prior reference to the Board.

Petitioner seeks damages for respondent's failure to disclose its overbooking practices. He makes no challenge to any provision in the tariff, and indeed there is no tariff provision or Board regulation applicable to disclosure practices. Petitioner also makes no challenge, comparable to those made in Southwestern *Sugar & Molasses Co. v. River Terminals Corp.,* supra, and *Lichten v. Eastern Airlines, Inc.,* 189 F.2d 939 (CA2 1951), to limitations on common-law damages imposed through exculpatory clauses included in a tariff. Referral of the misrepresentation issue to the Board cannot be justified by the interest in informing the court's ultimate decision with "the expert and specialized knowledge," *United States v. Western Pacific R. Co.,* supra, at 64, of the Board. The action brought by petitioner does not turn on a determination of the reasonableness of a challenged practice—a determination that could be facilitated by an informed evaluation of the economics or technology of the regulated industry. The standards to be applied in an action for fraudulent misrepresentation are within the conventional competence of the courts, and the judgment of a technically expert body is not likely to be helpful in the application of these standards to the facts of this case. . . .

III

We conclude that petitioner's tort action should not be stayed pending reference to the Board and accordingly the decision of the Court of Appeals on this issue is reversed. The Court of Appeals did not address the question whether petitioner had introduced sufficient evidence to sustain his claim. We remand the case for consideration of that question and for further proceedings consistent with this opinion.

Question

This case and previous cases make it clear that courts do not always have to defer to agencies in cases like this. Can you list the two situations that need to exist before primary jurisdiction comes into play? Try to answer this question from the case before checking the summary section at the end of the chapter.

An individual who has been adversely affected by a federal agency action or decision and who wants to sue must demonstrate that (a) the court has jurisdiction, (b) the decision is reviewable, (c) the individual has standing to challenge the administrative decision or action, (d) the individual has exhausted all administrative remedies available within the agency, and (e) primary jurisdiction problems are not involved. If all those barriers are overcome, the individual may challenge the agency action in court. The question to which we now turn our attention is this: Once a court has decided to review agency action, how closely should the court examine the agency behavior? This is the *scope of review.*

The Scope of Review

Section 706 of the APA, entitled "Scope of Review," authorized courts reviewing agency action to take two kinds of action. First, in Section 706 [1](B), courts can compel agency action if an agency has illegally refused to act (see *Heckler v. Chaney,* below) or if an agency has unreasonably delayed action (meant to provide a remedy against agency foot-dragging). Second, courts can void or reverse the following kinds of agency action: unconstitutional agency action (Sec. 706 [2](B)); agency action contrary to federal law or those beyond the jurisdiction of an agency (Sec. 706 [2](C)); agency action in violation of procedure (Sec. 706 [2](D)); agency action that is arbitrary, capricious, or an abuse of discretion (this is what you will shortly come to know as the "arbitrary or capricious" scope of review test of agency decisions, and it is located at Sec. 706 [2](A)); agency decisions not supported by substantial evidence in the record (this is what you will come to refer to as the "substantial evidence in the record (this is what you will come to refer to as the "substantial evidence test," and it is found in Sec. 706 [2](E)); and finally, courts are authorized to void agency action found to be unwarranted by the facts after a trial de novo by reviewing court (Sec. 706 [2](F)).

Court Review of Agency Foot-Dragging and Inaction

The language of Section 706 (1) makes it clear that Congress intended to authorize courts to compel agencies to act in cases of bureaucratic recalcitrance. Typically, however, courts show tremendous deference toward agency excuses for inaction. This deference is explained by the Court in the case that follows.

HECKLER V. CHANEY
470 U.S. 821 (1985)

Justice Rehnquist wrote the opinion, joined by a unanimous court (Burger, White, Blackmun, Powell, Stewart, and O'Connor). Justices Brennan and Marshall concurred.

I

Respondents have been sentenced to death by lethal injection of drugs under the laws of the States of Oklahoma and Texas. Those States, and several others, have recently adopted this method for carrying out the capital sentence. Respondents first petitioned the FDA, claiming that the drugs used by the States for this purpose, although approved by the FDA for the medical purposes stated on their labels, were not approved for use in human executions. They alleged that the drugs had not been tested for the purpose for which they were to be used, and that, given that the drugs would likely be administered by untrained personnel, it was also likely that the drugs would not induce the quick and painless death intended. They urged that use of these drugs for human execution was the "unapproved use of an approved drug" and constituted a violation of the Act's prohibitions against "misbranding." They also suggested that the FDA's requirements for approval of "new drugs" applied, since these drugs were now being used for a new purpose. Accordingly, respondents claimed that the FDA was required to approve the drugs as "safe and effective" for human execution before they could

be distributed in interstate commerce. See 21 U.S.C. § 355. They therefore requested the FDA to take various investigatory and enforcement actions to prevent these perceived violations; they requested the FDA to affix warnings to the labels of all the drugs stating that they were unapproved and unsafe for human execution, to send statements to the drug manufacturers and prison administrators stating that the drugs should not be so used, and to adopt procedures for seizing the drugs from state prisons and to recommend the prosecution of all those in the chain of distribution who knowingly distribute or purchase the drugs with intent to use them for human execution. The FDA Commissioner responded, refusing to take the requested actions. The Commissioner first detailed his disagreement with respondents' understanding of the scope of FDA jurisdiction over the unapproved use of approved drugs for human execution, concluding that FDA jurisdiction in the area was generally unclear but in any event should not be exercised to interfere with this particular aspect of state criminal justice systems. He went on to state:

"Were FDA clearly to have jurisdiction in the area, moreover, we believe we would be authorized to decline to exercise it under our inherent discretion to decline to pursue certain enforcement matters. The unapproved use of approved drugs is an area in which the case law is far from uniform. Generally, enforcement proceedings in this area are initiated only when there is a serious danger to the public health or a blatant scheme to defraud. We cannot conclude that those dangers are present under State lethal injection laws, which are duly authorized statutory enactments in furtherance of proper State functions. . . ."

I

Respondents then filed the instant suit in the United States District Court for the District of Columbia, claiming the same violations of the FDCA and asking that the FDA be required to take the same enforcement actions requested in the prior petition. Jurisdiction was grounded in the general federal-question jurisdiction statute, 28 U.S.C. § 1331, and review of the agency action was sought under the judicial review provisions of the APA, 5 U.S.C. §§ 701-706. The District Court granted summary judgment for petitioner. It began with the proposition that "decisions of executive departments and agencies to refrain from instituting investigative and enforcement proceedings are essentially unreviewable by the courts." The court then cited case law stating that nothing in the FDCA indicated an intent to circumscribe the FDA's enforcement discretion or to make it reviewable. A divided panel of the Court of Appeals for the District of Columbia Circuit reversed. The majority began by discussing the FDA's jurisdiction over the unapproved use of approved drugs for human execution, and concluded that the FDA did have jurisdiction over such a use. The court then addressed the Government's assertion of unreviewable discretion to refuse enforcement action. The APA's comprehensive provisions for judicial review of "agency actions" are contained in 5 U.S.C. §§ 701-706. Any person "adversely affected or aggrieved" by agency action, including a "failure to act," is entitled to "judicial review thereof," as long as the action is a "final agency action for which there is no other adequate remedy in a court." The standards to be applied on review are governed by the provisions of § 706. But before any review at all may be had, a party must first clear the hurdle of § 701(a). That section provides that the chapter on judicial review "applies, according to the provisions thereof, except to the extent that—(1) statutes preclude judicial review; or (2) agency action is committed to agency discretion by law." Petitioner urges that the decision of the FDA to refuse enforcement is an action "committed to agency discretion by law" under § 701(a)(2).

This Court has not had occasion to interpret this second exception in § 701(a) in any great detail. To this point our analysis does not differ significantly from that of the Court of Appeals. That court purported to apply the "no law to apply" standard of *Overton Park*. We disagree, however, with that court's insistence that the "narrow construction" of § (a)(2) required application of a presumption of reviewability even to an agency's decision not to undertake certain enforcement actions. Here we think the Court of Appeals broke with tradition, case law, and sound reasoning.

Overton Park did not involve an agency's refusal to take requested enforcement action. It involved an affirmative act of approval under a statute that set clear guidelines for determining when such approval should be given. Refusals to take enforcement steps generally involve precisely the opposite situation, and in that situation we think the presumption is that judicial review is not available. This Court has recognized on several occasions over many years that an agency's decision not to prosecute or enforce, whether through civil or criminal process, is a decision generally committed to an agency's absolute discretion. See *United States v. Batchelder*, 442 U.S. 114, 123-124 (1979); *United States v. Nixon*, 418 U.S. 683, 693 (1974); *Vaca v. Sipes*, 386 U.S. 171, 182 (1967); *Confiscation Cases*, 7 Wall. 454 (1869). This recognition of the existence of discretion is attributable in no small part to the general unsuitability for judicial review of agency decisions to refuse enforcement.

The reasons for this general unsuitability are many. First, an agency decision not to enforce often involves a complicated balancing of a number of factors which are peculiarly within its expertise. Thus, the agency must not only assess whether a violation has occurred, but whether agency resources are best spent on this violation or another, whether the agency is likely to succeed if it acts, whether the particular enforcement action requested best fits the agency's overall policies, and, indeed, whether the agency has enough resources to undertake the action at all. An agency generally cannot act against each technical violation of the statute it is charged with enforcing. The agency is far better equipped than the courts to deal with the many variables involved in the proper ordering of its priorities. Similar concerns animate the principles of administrative law that courts generally will defer to an agency's construction of the statute it is charged with implementing, and to the procedures it adopts for implementing that statute. See *Vermont Yankee Nuclear Power Corp. v. Natural Resources Defense Council, Inc.,* 435 U.S. 519, 543 (1978); *Train v. Natural Resources Defense Council, Inc.,* 421 U.S. 60, 87 (1975).

In addition to these administrative concerns, we note that when an agency refuses to act it generally does not exercise its coercive power over an individual's liberty or property rights, and thus does not infringe upon areas that courts often are called upon to protect. Similarly, when an agency does act to enforce, that action itself provides a focus for judicial review, inasmuch as the agency must have exercised its power in some manner. The action at least can be reviewed to determine whether the agency exceeded its statutory powers. See, e.g., *FTC v. Klesner,* 280 U.S. 19 (1929). Finally, we recognize that an agency's refusal to institute proceedings shares to some extent the characteristics of the decision of a prosecutor in the Executive Branch not to indict—a decision which has long been regarded as the special province of the Executive Branch, inasmuch as it is the Executive who is charged by the Constitution to "take Care that the Laws be faithfully executed." U.S. Const., Art. II, § 3.

We of course only list the above concerns to facilitate understanding of our conclusion that an agency's decision not to take enforcement action should be presumed immune from judicial review under § 701(a)(2). For good reasons, such a decision has traditionally been "committed to agency discretion," and we believe that the Congress enacting the APA did not intend to alter that tradition. In so stating, we emphasize that the decision is only presumptively unreviewable; the presumption may be rebutted where the substantive statute has provided guidelines for the agency to follow in exercising its enforcement powers. Thus, in establishing this presumption in the APA, Congress did not set agencies free to disregard legislative direction in the statutory scheme that the agency administers. Congress may limit an agency's exercise of enforcement power if it wishes, either by setting substantive priorities, or by otherwise circumscribing an agency's power to discriminate among issues or cases it will pursue. The FDA's decision not to take the enforcement actions requested by respondents is therefore not subject to judicial review under the APA. The general exception to reviewability provided by § 701(a)(2) for action "committed to agency discretion" remains a narrow one, see *Citizens to Preserve Overton Park v. Volpe,* 401 U.S. 402 (1971), but within that exception are included agency refusals to institute investigative or enforcement proceedings, unless Congress has indicated otherwise.

In so holding, we essentially leave to Congress, and not to the courts, the decision as to whether an agency's refusal to institute proceedings should be judicially reviewable. No colorable claim is made in this case that the agency's refusal to institute proceedings violated any constitutional rights of respondents, and we do not address the issue that would be raised in such a case. *Johnson v. Robison,* 415 U.S. 361, 366 (1974); *Yick Wo v. Hopkins,* 118 U.S. 356, 372-374 (1886). The fact that the drugs involved in this case are ultimately to be used in imposing the death penalty must not lead this Court or other courts to import profound differences of opinion over the meaning of the Eighth Amendment to the United States Constitution into the domain of administrative law.

The judgment of the Court of Appeals is Reversed.

The Law/Fact Distinction

As indicated in Chapter 1, agencies frequently interpret law. In making decisions or taking action, a statute is almost always involved, and usually an agency interpretation of that statute. The agency generally applies factual situations to its interpretation of the statute and makes a decision or takes some action (or refuses to act). In reviewing each agency action, courts show less deference to an agency's interpretation of the law than they do to an agency's determination of facts. This is because courts are just as well suited to interpret law as agencies are; hence, any reason such as expertise for court deference to agencies disappears.

The *law/fact distinction* addresses the notion that courts will exercise stringent judicial review of agency action on questions of laws—Does the agency action violate a provision of the Constitution or some other federal law? Is the agency's interpretation of the law consistent with congressional intent? Has the agency attempted to take some action that is beyond its jurisdiction?—but will show considerable deference to an agency's finding of fact—Were the employee's injuries work related? Does the applicant meet the requirements for a license or requested benefits? Did management engage in an unfair labor practice? Although this distinction may seem clear in the examples just presented, it is not always clear in practice. In reality, courts often do show deference to an agency's statutory interpretation, and whether a given question is one of fact or of law is not always analytically neat and clear.

The central question in the case that follows is whether newsboys are employees. The Court treats this question as one of fact, but clearly the newspapers consider it one of law.

NATIONAL LABOR RELATIONS BOARD V. HEARST PUBLICATIONS, INCORPORATED
322 U.S. 111 (1944)

Newsboys in Los Angeles decided to try to form a union and petitioned the National Labor Relations Board (NLRB) for certification as a union. The board held a hearing and determined that the newsboys were "employees" under the National Labor Relations Act and affected interstate commerce. The board ordered elections, in which a majority of the newsboys voted to unionize, and the board subsequently certified the Los Angeles Newsboys Local Industrial Union #75.

Four Los Angeles daily newspapers refused to engage in collective bargaining with the union on the theory that the newsboys were not "employees," but rather independent contractors (who are not authorized to unionize under the act). The union petitioned the NLRB to order the publishers to engage in good faith bargaining. At these hearings, the board found the newspapers to be in violation of the law, issued cease and desist orders, and ordered the newspapers to engage in bargaining with the union. In this case, the newspapers are appealing the NLRB's orders and its prior determination that the newsboys are employees.

The opinion is by Justice Rutledge, joined by Justices Stone, Black, Reed, Frankfurter, Douglas, Murphy, and Jackson. Justice Roberts dissented.

The principal question is whether the newsboys are "employees." Because Congress did not explicitly define the term, respondents say its meaning must be determined by reference to common-law standards. In their view "common-law standards" are those the courts have applied in distinguishing between "employees" and "independent contractors" when working out various problems unrelated to the Wagner Act's purposes and provisions.

The argument assumes that there is some simple, uniform and easily applicable test which the courts have used, in dealing with such problems, to determine whether persons doing work for others fall in one class or the other. Unfortunately this is not true. Only by a long and tortuous history was the simple formulation worked out which has been stated most frequently as "the test" for deciding whether one who hires another is responsible in tort for his wrongdoing. But this formula has been by no means exclusively controlling in the solution of other problems. And its simplicity has been illusory because it is more largely simplicity of formulation than of application. Few problems in the law have given greater variety of application and conflict in results than the cases arising in the borderland between what is clearly an employer-employee relationship and what is clearly one of independent, entrepreneurial dealing. This is true within the limited field of determining vicarious liability in tort. It becomes more so when the field is expanded to include all of the possible applications of the distinction.

Two possible consequences could follow. One would be to refer the decision of who are employees to local state law. The alternative would be to make it turn on a sort of pervading general essence distilled from state law. Congress obviously did not intend the former result. It would introduce variations into the statute's operation as wide as the differences the forty-eight states and other local jurisdictions make in applying the distinction for wholly different purposes. Persons who might be "employees" in one state would be "independent contractors" in another. They would be within or without the statute's protection depending not on whether their situation falls factually within the ambit Congress had in mind, but upon the accidents of the location of their work and the attitude of the particular local jurisdiction in casting doubtful cases one way or the other. Persons working across state lines might fall in one class or the other, possibly both, depending on whether the Board and the courts would be required to give effect to the law of one state or of the adjoining one, or to that of each in relation to the portion of the work done within its borders.

Both the terms and the purposes of the statute, as well as the legislative history, show that Congress had in mind no such patchwork plan for securing freedom of employees' organization and of collective bargaining. The Wagner Act is federal legislation, administered by a national agency, intended to solve a national problem on a national scale. . . . To eliminate the causes of labor disputes and industrial strife, Congress thought it necessary to create a balance of forces in certain types of economic relationships. These do not embrace simply employment associations in which controversies could be limited to disputes over proper "physical conduct in the performance of the service." On the contrary, Congress recognized those economic relationships cannot be fitted neatly into the containers designated "employee" and "employer" which an earlier law had shaped for different purposes. Its Reports on the bill disclose clearly the understanding that "employers and employees not in proximate relationship may be drawn into common controversies by economic forces," and that the very disputes sought to be avoided might involve "employees [who] are at times brought into an economic relationship with employers who are not their employers." In this light, the broad language of the Act's definitions, which in terms reject conventional limitations on such conceptions as "employee," "employer," and "labor dispute," leaves no doubt that its applicability is to be determined broadly, in doubtful situations, by underlying economic facts rather than technically and exclusively by previously established legal classifications. Cf. *Labor Board v. Blount,* supra. . . .

It is not necessary in this case to make a completely definitive limitation around the term "employee." That task has been assigned primarily to the agency created by Congress to administer the Act. Determination of "where all the conditions of the relation require protection" involves inquiries for the Board charged with this duty. Everyday experience in the administration of the statute gives it familiarity with the circumstances and backgrounds of employment relationships in various industries, with the abilities and needs of the workers for self-organization and collective action, and with the adaptability of collective bargaining for the peaceful settlement of their disputes with their employers. The experience thus acquired must be brought frequently to bear on the question who is an employee under the Act. Resolving that question, like determining whether unfair labor practices have been committed, "belongs to the usual administrative routine" of the Board.

In making that body's determinations as to the facts in these matters conclusive, if supported by evidence, Congress entrusted to it primarily the decision whether the evidence establishes the material facts. Hence in reviewing the Board's ultimate conclusions, it is not the court's function to substitute its own inferences of fact for the Board's, when the latter have support in the record. *Labor Board v. Nevada Copper Corp.,* 316 U.S. 105. Undoubtedly questions of statutory interpretation, especially when arising in the first instance in judicial proceedings, are for the courts to resolve, giving appropriate weight to the judgment of those whose special duty is to administer the questioned statute. *Norwegian Nitrogen Products Co. v. United States,* 288 U.S. 294; *United States v. American Trucking Assns.,* 310 U.S. 534. But where the question is one of specific application of a broad statutory term in a proceeding in which the agency administering the statute must determine it initially, the reviewing court's function is limited. Like the commissioner's determination under the Longshoremen's & Harbor Workers' Act, that a man is not a "member of a crew" (*South Chicago Coal & Dock Co. v. Bassett,* 309 U.S. 251) or that he was injured "in the course of employment" (*Parker v. Motor Boat Sales,* 314 U.S. 244) and the Federal Communications Commission's determination that one company is under the "control" of another (*Rochester Telephone Corp. v. United States,* 307 U.S. 125), the Board's determination that specified persons are "employees" under this Act is to be accepted if it has "warrant in the record" and a reasonable basis in law.

In this case the Board found that the designated newsboys work continuously and regularly, rely upon their earnings for the support of themselves and their families, and have their total wages influenced in large measure by the publishers, who dictate their buying and selling prices, fix their markets, and control their supply of papers. Their hours of work and their efforts on the job are supervised and to some extent prescribed by the publishers or their agents. Much of their sales equipment and advertising materials is furnished by the publishers with the intention that it be used for the publisher's benefit. Stating that "the primary consideration in the determination of the applicability of the statutory definition is whether effectuation of the declared policy and purposes of the Act comprehend securing to the individual the rights guaranteed and protection afforded by the Act," the Board concluded that the newsboys are employees. The record sustains the Board's findings and there is ample basis in the law for its conclusion.

Review of Agency Action

If a challenged agency action survives court review of the questions of law involved, review will move to scrutiny of the agency decision, rule, or action. Here, court interpretations of Section 706 of the APA have established three standards of court review. The three standards of the scope of review are (a) the arbitrary and capricious standard, (b) the substantial evidence test, and (c) de novo review. The legal term *de novo* means "completely new from the start,"[9] so de novo review of agency action would require a whole new trial on the issue or action. This type of court review of agency action is virtually nonexistent today although it is discussed in the *Overton Park* case presented later. (*Overton Park* involved two important questions: whether the secretary of transportation's decision was reviewable [presented earlier in this chapter] and, if so, what standard of review should be applied to the decision [to be presented later].)

Substantial evidence review of agency action is, by practice, limited to review of decisions, orders, or agency action that results from a quasi-judicial hearing. The *substantial evidence test* means the reviewing court should examine the full record to be satisfied that substantial evidence in the record supports the decision of the agency. This test is similar to the kind of review that appellate courts should apply when reviewing the decision of a trial court. The two interesting cases presented next are illustrative of court attempts to apply the substantial evidence test.

STATE EMPLOYEES' RETIREMENT SYSTEM V.
INDUSTRIAL ACCIDENT COMMISSION
217 P.2D 992 (1950)

The opinion is by Justice Sparks.

This is a proceeding upon writ of review of a death benefit award made by the Industrial Accident Commission in favor of the widow and three minor children of Karl Lund, deceased. Petitioner State Employees' Retirement System seeks an annulment of the award, on the grounds that respondent commission had acted without and in excess of its powers and that the evidence was insufficient to justify the findings of fact. The decedent, Karl Lund, was employed as a game warden by the Department of Natural Resources. As such officer his duties were to enforce the provisions of the Fish and Game Code, and in so doing he had no regular or prescribed hours of duty. At times he was required to go on night patrol and to station himself in isolated areas where infractions of the Fish and Game Code might occur. An automobile equipped with a two-way radio was furnished him by his employer. The car was also so equipped that it might be converted into a bed, and it was permissible for him, while on night patrol, to sleep in the car.

On June 13, 1948, the deceased went on duty at 10 o'clock in the morning. According to the entries in his diary he went on patrol to "Napa State Hospital, Soscal, thence to Cuttings Wharf, Brown's Valley to Oakville night patrol Trinity Road." At 2:58 p.m. on the 13th Lund reported by radio to the sheriff's office that he was in service. No further reports were received from him. On the 14th, Lund not having returned or checked in by radio, a search was made for him. At a point 16 or 18 miles from Napa, the car furnished Lund by the state was found. It was parked about 20 feet off a side road, facing into a hill. This side road was a slight distance from the Oakville-Trinity Mountain road. It was in "wild" country and where, according to Lund's superior officer, apprehensions were made of violators hunting deer at night with spotlights. About 12 feet to the rear of the state car there was another automobile parked. Investigation revealed that the interior of the state car had been converted into a bed, and on this bed were found the dead bodies of Karl Lund and of a woman, Chelsea Miami. The bodies were clad respectively only in shorts and panties and were partially covered by a blanket. The ignition switch, radio and heater of the car were all turned on and the gasoline tank was empty. All of the doors and windows were closed with the exception of one side wing-window which was slightly open. Lund's clothes, boots, and gun were in the back of the car and under the seat. The deaths were attributed by the coroner to carbon monoxide poisoning, the vapor of which apparently had infiltrated into the car from the running motor and been inhaled while the deceased were lying on the bed. Approximate time of death was fixed as between 1 and 3 a.m. of June 14th. Herminia Miami, the sister of Chelsea, testified that Chelsea had received a telephone call at their home from Lund shortly before 9 p.m.; that he had asked Chelsea to meet him, and within a few minutes after receiving the call Chelsea had changed to slacks and left in her own car.

There was no rule or regulation of the department by whom Lund was employed which prohibited any of the game wardens, while on duty, from having company. Upon the facts adduced at the hearing, summary of which has been given above, respondent Industrial Accident Commission made its finding that Karl Lund had sustained injury occurring in the course of and arising out of employment proximately causing his death from inhalation of carbon monoxide fumes. A petition for rehearing was granted by respondent commission, and after a further hearing respondent affirmed its findings of fact theretofore made.

Petitioner contends that these findings are irrational for the reason that the evidence shows that deceased met his death while on a personal adventure, and that in so doing he had deviated from the scope of his employment and from his duties as fish and game warden. In reviewing the evidence we are not permitted to substitute our views for those of the commission and annul an award unless there is no substantial evidence to support the findings and order. On the contrary, we are required to indulge all reasonable inferences which may be drawn legitimately from the facts in order to support the findings of the commission, and in doing so all that is required is reasonable probability; not absolute certainty. It is the duty of a reviewing court to search the record to discover whether the evidence is reasonably susceptible of the inferences drawn by the commission in support of its conclusion, and upon favorable discovery to affirm the award. Neither may the award be annulled because there are two conclusions which fairly may be drawn from the evidence, both of which are reasonable, the one sustaining and the other opposing the right to compensation. Nor may an award be rejected solely on the basis of moral or ethical considerations. Measured by these rules we note in reviewing the record the following facts and circumstances in support of respondent's findings: That Lund, as a fish and game warden, had no regular or fixed hours of employment; that frequently he did patrol duty at night for the purpose of intercepting violators of the fish and game laws; that the last entry in his diary sets forth his itinerary for the 13th and concludes, "to Oakville night patrol Trinity Road"; that his diary also discloses that he had been on night patrol on the preceding evening. His death having occurred between 1 and 3 a.m. does not therefore justify any conclusion that it happened outside of the hours of his employment. As to the place of his death, the evidence shows that he had stationed himself in a territory which was under surveillance for the illegal spotlight killing of deer. The two-way radio with which the car was equipped was turned on so that Lund could not only have received messages from headquarters, but if need be could have sent them. While on such duty he was not only permitted to, but it was contemplated that he could convert the car into a bed (for it was so equipped), and that he might retire thereon or sleep.

There was no rule that forbade his having company while on duty. The testimony of Captain Shea in this regard is as follows: "[Mr. Faulkner] Q. . . . Now, would you—is there any order or rule or regulation of the department that prohibits you, while you're sitting there in your car or stationed in your car or in bed in your car, from talking to anybody that comes along? A. Definitely not. Q. Is there any rule or regulation prohibiting that person from getting into the car and sitting down with you, having a smoke or a chat? A. No, there isn't. Q. Is there any rule or regulation of the department that

prohibits you or any of the men, any of the game wardens, from—while on duty—from talking or entertaining or enjoying the company of other people? A. No, there's no regulation to that effect. Q. No rule against it? A. No rule against it." And finally, his death was occasioned from carbon monoxide poisoning from the use of equipment furnished him by his employer. From this and other facts and circumstances in the record, we cannot say there was not substantial evidence to support the findings of the commission, or that the findings were irrational. In doing so we are well aware of the contrary inferences which might have been drawn from the same set of facts. The secluded spot in a remote area could have been selected by Lund for its advantages as a rendezvous in which to conduct an illicit love affair. The manner in which the cars were parked, the state of partial dishabille in which the bodies were found, the fact that Lund had divested himself of his uniform and placed his gun and boots underneath the seat, all are circumstances from which the trier of facts might have reasonably concluded that he had either abandoned or deviated from his duty. However, as stated above, it is not our province to resolve these facts or to substitute our own views for those of the commission. Lund, while acting in the scope of his employment, was permitted to drive to isolated spots where game violators might be found. It was a matter of discretion with him whether or not at such times he converted the car into a bed and slept. In so doing he was acting within the course of his employment. There was no rule which forbade him from having company while on duty, and the presence of a woman in the car with him does not necessarily compel a conclusion that he had thereby either abandoned his employment or deviated therefrom. There being a choice between two inferences reasonably deducible from the evidence, we cannot say that the commission acted without or in excess of its powers or that its findings of fact were unreasonable. The award is affirmed. Adams, P. J., and Peek, J., concurred.

UNITED STATES EX REL. EXARCHOU V. MURFF
265 F.2d 504 (1959)

George Exarchou entered the United States illegally in 1945. In 1949, the Immigration and Naturalization Service (INS) determined that he was deportable, but he petitioned the INS for eligibility for a discretionary grant of voluntary departure (which would allow him to reenter the United States legally at a later date). The INS found him to be qualified for a voluntary departure, but then it further recommended that his deportation be suspended. By 1953, Congress had failed to pass a resolution approving the recommended suspension of deportation, so the INS again granted him permission to voluntarily depart the United States.

Just prior to his departure, however, his case was reopened at the INS by a letter written by his estranged wife. In the letter, she charged him with infidelity and requested that her petitions of support on his behalf be withdrawn. A special inquiry officer conducted an investigation and found that, in 1954, shortly after separation from his wife, Exarchou lived with a divorcee and her two children and her mother. The inquiry officer found that Exarchou had engaged in adultery and hence was not of "good moral character" and consequently was not eligible for voluntary departure. The inquiry officer sent these findings to the INS, which then reversed its earlier position recommending voluntary departure. At a hearing in 1956, where Exarchou was again requesting voluntary departure and asking the INS to reconsider its findings, the testimony (and hence the written record) consisted of the following witnesses and their testimony:

Mr. Exarchou testified that his relationship with the divorcee was totally plutonic and not adulterous, that they occasionally went dancing but nothing else, that he paid her rent, that he slept on the living room sofa and she slept in her bedroom on the second floor with her seven-year-old son, and that the other two bedrooms were occupied by the divorcee's mother and her college-age son.

The divorced woman in question was called to the stand, but she refused to testify, based on her Fifth Amendment right against self-incrimination.

The estranged wife did not testify. In a hearing like this, the petitioner (Mr. Exarchou) has the burden of proving his good moral character. The INS found that he failed to carry that burden and ordered him deported. The decision was sustained by the district court and was appealed to the circuit court.

The pertinent part of the special inquiry officer's report is reproduced below before the Court's opinion.

"I think I can best sum up my impressions of the respondent by saying that he tells an interesting, almost fantastic, story. Certainly not one that I consider credible. In fact, I do not believe it. The

respondent would have me believe that he continued this so-called platonic relationship with this woman out of the goodness of his heart and out of his sympathy for her at a time when he was admittedly separated from his own wife. Even were it the truth, and as I say I do not believe it, it seems to me that a married man is not free to carry on such a relationship and still be considered one of good character. The mores of our times may well be most liberal but I do not think they have reached that degree of liberality as yet."

The opinion of the court is by Chief Judge Clark.

As the Service concedes, no inference may be legally drawn from the refusal of the woman at whose home Exarchou briefly resided in 1954 to testify. *United States v. Maloney,* 2 Cir., 262 F.2d 535, 537. Actually the record indicates that avoidance of embarrassment was probably a stronger factor in her refusal than fear of self-incrimination. She had remarried by the time of the hearing and stated frankly that she was annoyed at being drawn into the proceedings and had sought and obtained advice as to means—which she took—to eliminate herself from a dispute in which she had no concern or interest. Exarchou's first wife did not testify at all after a hearing in 1954, nor was her actual testimony adverse then. Her only adverse comments were contained in her rambling, accusatory letter written when domestic ties between them were strained. Even if we overlook its hearsay quality we do not believe weight should attach to a letter written under such circumstances.

Hence the Service was thrown back completely on Exarchou's own testimony as to his conduct during the period in question. Perhaps the most doubtful fact here was the amount of money he admitted to having paid the woman, more than would be a reasonable rent under the circumstances. But he seems generally to have been free with his money. Beyond this his denials of adulterous conduct were steady, persistent, and unshaken. They would appear consistent with the surrounding facts and circumstances he disclosed. It is of course true that questions of a witness' credibility must be left to the administrative fact finder. Here, however, the Special Inquiry Officer's report demonstrates an incredulity not of the witness, but of the story itself. The Officer simply did not believe it possible that a man who behaved like relator (Exarchou) could not have been committing adultery. We do not think this finding of impossibility accords with the facts of human life. Moreover, we are disturbed by the insistence in the decision upon the appearance of good moral character. The statute makes good character itself, not a reputation for it, the finding necessary to the Service's decision. Thus we cannot accept the Service's alternative conclusion that, even if Exarchou truthfully described his conduct, "a mar-

ried man is not free to carry on such a relationship and still be considered one of good character." We conclude only that Exarchou has sustained his burden of establishing good moral character under § 19(c) of the Immigration Act of 1917 and is entitled to further consideration of his application.

Question

For both preceding cases, list the evidence in the record on a sheet of paper. Do it in columns so that you can clearly see the evidence in support of a board's decision and the evidence that does not support the decision. In either case, can you conclude that the reviewing court was in error?

If de novo review does not exist in reality, and if substantial evidence applies only in those situations in which agency action resulted from a quasi-judicial hearing, then the final standard of review, the arbitrary and capricious standard, must apply to all other agency decisions and actions (and inaction, when it is reviewed). This standard of review applies to court review of agency rule promulgation or quasi-legislative decision making. It also applies to more informal agency decisions or action, such as Secretary Volpe's decision to approve federal highway funds for a highway through Overton Park. It would also apply to the decision of the secretary of health and human services (at the order of President Reagan) to remove thousands of individuals with disabilities from the disability list. Unfortunately, describing what the arbitrary and capricious standard applies to is easier than describing the standard and how it is applied. You are already familiar with the *Overton Park* case presented earlier. What follows is that part of the *Overton Park* decision relating to the scope of review of the secretary's decision.

CITIZENS TO PRESERVE
OVERTON PARK V. VOLPE
401 U.S. 402 (1971)

The facts in this case appeared earlier in this chapter.

. . . Scrutiny of the facts does not end, however, with the determination that the Secretary has acted within the scope of his statutory authority. Section

706 (2)(A) requires a finding that the actual choice made was not "arbitrary, capricious, an abuse of discretion, or otherwise not in accordance with law." 5 U.S.C. § 706(2)(A). To make this finding the court must consider whether the decision was

based on a consideration of the relevant factors and whether there has been a clear error of judgment. Although this inquiry into the facts is to be searching and careful, the ultimate standard of review is a narrow one. The court is not empowered to substitute its judgment for that of the agency. The administrative record is not, however, before us. The lower courts based their review on the litigation affidavits that were presented. These affidavits were merely "post hoc" rationalizations, *Burlington Truck Lines v. United States,* 371 U.S. 156, 168-169 (1962), which have traditionally been found to be an inadequate basis for review. And they clearly do not constitute the "whole record" compiled by the agency: the basis for review required by § 706 of the Administrative Procedure Act.

Thus it is necessary to remand this case to the District Court for plenary review of the Secretary's decision. That review is to be based on the full administrative record that was before the Secretary at the time he made his decision. But since the bare record may not disclose the factors that were considered or the Secretary's construction of the evidence it may be necessary for the District Court to require some explanation in order to determine if the Secretary acted within the scope of his authority and if the Secretary's action was justifiable under the applicable standard. The court may require the administrative officials who participated in the decision to give testimony explaining their action. Of course, such inquiry into the mental processes of administrative decisionmakers is usually to be avoided. *United States v. Morgan,* 313 U.S. 409, 422 (1941). And where there are administrative findings that were made at the same time as the decision, as was the case in *Morgan,* there must be a strong showing of bad faith or improper behavior before such inquiry may be made. But here there are no such formal findings and it may be that the only way there can be effective judicial review is by examining the decisionmakers themselves. See *Shaughnessy v. Accardi,* 349 U.S. 280 (1955).

The District Court is not, however, required to make such an inquiry. It may be that the Secretary can prepare formal findings including the information required by DOT Order 5610.1 that will provide an adequate explanation for his action. Such an explanation will, to some extent, be a "post hoc rationalization" and thus must be viewed critically. If the District Court decides that additional explanation is necessary, that court should consider which method will prove the most expeditious so that full review may be had as soon as possible.

Reversed and remanded.

Questions

1. Succinctly state the precise disposition of this case.
2. What will happen next?
3. In your opinion, was the secretary's decision arbitrary? Why?
4. Did the Supreme Court find the secretary's decision to be arbitrary?

Because of the decision in the *Overton Park* case and others like it, agency decision makers in today's world do not make decisions without at least some kind of paper trail, such as a written explanation for the decision. In informal rule making under Section 553 of the APA, a reviewing court has a record to review, and, indeed, Subsection C of 553 requires the agency to "adopt a concise general statement of their (the rules') basis and purpose." The record generated by the notice and comment hearing, however, is "indistinguishable . . . from [materials collected in] the proceedings before a legislative committee hearing on a proposed bill—letters, telegrams, and written statements from proponents and opponents, including occasional oral testimony not subject to adversary cross-examination."[10]

The point is that a court reviewing the record of an agency's decision arrived at through a 553 rule-making procedure is in exactly the same position as a court reviewing a legislative decision. The judge must be careful that he or she is not simply substituting his or her policy preferences for the preferences of the legislature (or administrative agency).

Toward that end (ensuring that administrative decisions are not arbitrary, but guarding against judicial policy making), courts have adopted what they call "reasoned decision making." Academics call it "hard look" review. It means that the reviewing court must be satisfied that the agency considered and addressed alternatives and objections to proposed agency rules or action. The case that follows is a good example of courts exercising hard look review on agency rule making.

UNITED STATES V. NOVA SCOTIA
FOOD PRODUCTS CORPORATION
568 F.2d 240 (1977)

The opinion is by Circuit Judge Gurfein.

This appeal involving a regulation of the Food and Drug Administration is not here upon a direct review of agency action. It is an appeal from a judgment of the District Court for the Eastern District of New York (Hon. John J. Dooling, Judge) enjoining the appellants, after a hearing, from processing hot smoked whitefish except in accordance with time-temperature-salinity (T-T-S) regulations contained in 21 C.F.R. Part 122 (1977). The thorough analytical opinion of the District Court is reported at 417 F.Supp. 1364 (Aug. 17, 1976). . . .

The injunction was sought and granted on the ground that smoked whitefish which has been processed in violation of the T-T-S regulation is "adulterated," Food, Drug and Cosmetics Act ("the Act") §§ 302(a) and 301(k), 21 U.S.C. § 332(a), 331(k).

Appellant Nova Scotia receives frozen or iced whitefish in interstate commerce which it processes by brining, smoking, and cooking. The fish are then sold as smoked whitefish.

The regulations cited above require that hot-process smoked fish be heated by a controlled heat process that provides a monitoring system posi-

tioned in as many strategic locations in the oven as necessary to assure a continuous temperature through each fish of not less than 180 degree F. for a minimum of 30 minutes for fish which have been brined to contain 3.5% water phase salt or at 150 degree F. for a minimum of 30 minutes if the salinity was at 5% water phase. Since each fish must meet these requirements, it is necessary to heat an entire batch of fish to even higher temperatures so that the lowest temperature for any fish will meet the minimum requirements. . . . Government inspection of appellants' plant established without question that the minimum T-T-S requirements were not being met. There is no substantial claim that the plant was processing whitefish under "insanitary conditions" in any other material respect. Appellants, on their part, do not defend on the ground that they were in compliance, but rather that the requirements could not be met if a marketable whitefish was to be produced. They defend upon the grounds that the regulation is invalid (1) because it is beyond the authority delegated by the statute; (2) because the FDA improperly relied upon undisclosed evidence in promulgating the regulation and because it is not supported by the administrative record; and (3) because there was no adequate statement setting forth the basis of the regulation. We reject the contention that the regulation is beyond the authority delegated by the statute, but we find serious inadequacies in the procedure followed in the promulgation of the regulation and hold it to be invalid as applied to the appellants herein.

1. The History of Botulism in Whitefish

The history of botulism occurrence in whitefish, as established in the trial record, which we must assume was available to the FDA in 1970, is as follows. Between 1899 and 1964 there were only eight cases of botulism reported as attributable to hot-smoked whitefish. In all eight instances, vacuum-packed whitefish was involved. All of the eight cases occurred in 1960 and 1963. The industry has abandoned vacuum-packing, and there has not been a single case of botulism associated with commercially prepared whitefish since 1963, though 2,750,000 pounds of whitefish are processed annually. Thus, in the seven-year period from 1964 through 1970, 17.25 million pounds of whitefish have been commercially processed in the United States without a single reported case of botulism. The evidence also disclosed that defendant Nova Scotia has been in business some 56 years, and that there has never been a case of botulism illness from the whitefish processed by it.

2. The Scientific Data

Interested parties were not informed of the scientific data, or at least of a selection of such data deemed important by the agency, so that comments could be addressed to the data. Appellants argue that unless the scientific data relied upon by the agency are spread upon the public records, criticism of the methodology used or the meaning to be inferred from the data is rendered impossible.

We agree with appellants in this case, for although we recognize that an agency may resort to its own expertise outside the record in an informal rulemaking procedure, we do not believe that when the pertinent research material is readily available and the agency has no special expertise on the precise parameters involved, there is any reason to conceal the scientific data relied upon from the interested parties. Here all the scientific research was collected by the agency, and none of it was disclosed to interested parties as the material upon which the proposed rule would be fashioned. Nor was an articulate effort made to connect the scientific requirements to available technology that would make commercial survival possible, though the burden of proof was on the agency. This required it to "bear a burden of adducing a reasoned presentation supporting the reliability of its methodology." Though a reviewing court will not match submission against counter-submission to decide whether the agency was correct in its conclusion on scientific matters (unless that conclusion is arbitrary), it will consider whether the agency has taken account of all "relevant factors and whether there has been a clear error of judgment." *Overton Park*, supra, 401 U.S. at 415-16. In this circuit we have said that "it is 'arbitrary or capricious' for an agency not to take into account all relevant factors in making its determination." *Hanly v. Mitchell*, 460 F.2d 640, 648 (2d Cir.).

If the failure to notify interested persons of the scientific research upon which the agency was relying actually prevented the presentation of relevant comment, the agency may be held not to have considered all "the relevant factors." We can think of no sound reasons for secrecy or reluctance to expose to public view (with an exception for trade secrets or national security) the ingredients of the deliberative process. We think that the scientific data should have been disclosed to focus on the proper interpretation of "insanitary conditions." When the basis for a proposed rule is a scientific decision, the scientific material which is believed to support the rule should be exposed to the view of interested parties for their comment. One cannot ask for comment on a scientific paper without allowing the participants to read the paper. Scientific research is sometimes rejected for diverse inadequacies of methodology; and statistical results are sometimes rebutted because of a lack of adequate gathering technique or of supportable extrapolation. Such is the stuff of scientific debate. To suppress meaningful comment by failure to disclose the basic data relied upon is akin to rejecting comment altogether. For unless there is common ground, the comments are unlikely to be of a quality that might impress a careful agency. The inadequacy of comment in turn leads in the direction of arbitrary decision-making. We do not speak of findings of fact, for such are not technically required in the informal rulemaking procedures. We speak rather of what the agency should make known so as to elicit comments that probe the fundamentals. Informal rulemaking does not lend itself to a rigid pattern. Especially, in the circumstance of our broad reading of statutory authority in support of the agency, we conclude that the failure to disclose to interested persons the scientific data upon which the FDA relied was procedurally erroneous. Moreover, the burden was upon the agency to articulate rationally why the rule should apply to a large and diverse class, with the same T-T-S parameters made applicable to all species.

C

Appellants additionally attack the "concise general statement" required by APA, 5 U.S.C. § 5531, as inadequate. We think that, in the circumstances, it was less than adequate. It is not in keeping with the rational process to leave vital questions, raised by comments which are of cogent materiality, completely unanswered. The agencies certainly have a good deal of discretion in expressing the basis of a rule, but the agencies do not have quite the preroga-

tive of obscurantism reserved to legislatures, "Congress did not purport to transfer its legislative power to the unbounded discretion of the regulatory body."

The test of adequacy of the "concise general statement" was expressed by Judge McGowan in the following terms:

"We do not expect the agency to discuss every item of fact or opinion included in the submissions made to it in informal rule making. We do expect that, if the judicial review which Congress has thought it important to provide is to be meaningful, the 'concise general statement of . . . basis and purpose' mandated by Section 4 will enable us to see what major issues of policy were ventilated by the informal proceedings and why the agency reacted to them as it did." *Automotive Parts & Accessories Ass'n v. Boyd,* 407 F.2d 330, 338 (D.C. Cir. 1968).

We hold in this enforcement proceeding, therefore, that the regulation, as it affects non-vacuum-packed hot-smoked whitefish, was promulgated in an arbitrary manner and is invalid.

Questions

1. Do you think that the agency did an adequate job of justifying its decision?
2. Do you believe that the reviewing court substituted its policy preference for that of the agency?

SUMMARY

1. *Jurisdiction.* This is the power of a court to resolve a dispute. Because federal courts have jurisdiction over any case or controversy under the laws or statutes of the United States and because all administrative actions are taken pursuant to congressional statute, federal courts have jurisdiction over conflicts arising under federal agencies.

2. *Standing.* This involves a determination of who is the proper party to challenge an administrative action. The Court has created a two-pronged test for standing to challenge an administrative decision: (a) Can the plaintiff demonstrate an identifiable injury? and (b) Is the agency action complained of arguably under the zone of interest meant to be protected by a particular statute? This test applied in those situations where agency action directly affected an individual, business, or group. The Court has recently begun applying a three-pronged test: (a) injury in fact, (b) traceability, and (c) redressability. This test is most appropriate where governmental action has "caused" an intervening party to act and the third party's action has allegedly caused injury to a plaintiff who now sues the government.

3. *Reviewability.* This is a legislative grant of authority to courts to review agency action. First, at the federal level prior to enactment of the APA (1947), there was a common law presumption that courts could not review the actions of administrative agencies unless the enabling legislation specifically provided for court review. In most states, there was also a presumption of unreviewability, which, at some levels in some states, still exists today because of a lack of legislation extending judicial review to all agency actions. Second, the intent and plain meaning of the APA is to extend court review to virtually all agency actions at the federal level with two exceptions: (a) where Congress has forbidden court review for a specific agency and (b) a nebulous category of supposedly unreviewable situations in which the agency action is "committed to agency discretion by law."

4 *Exhaustion.* Before one can sue an agency in court, one must first have exhausted all avenues of appeal within the agency.

5. *Primary jurisdiction.* Within the federal system, in those situations in which one is in conflict with an agency, one can either exhaust remedies within the agency or turn to the courts. Two situations require the courts to defer to the agency first: (a) if the conflict involves subject matter that requires one uniform national standard (e.g., ICC rates) and (b) if for resolution the subject matter requires agency expertise that courts are unlikely to possess.

6. *Scope of review.* For all practical purposes, courts apply two standards in reviewing agency activity: (a) The substantial evidence test applies to agency decisions, orders, or rulings that are made via a quasi-judicial procedure; and (b) the arbitrary and capricious test applies to all other agency activity.

END-OF-CHAPTER CASE

CITY OF LOS ANGELES V. LYONS
461 U.S. 55 (1983)

The following facts of the case are taken from Justice Marshall's dissent.

Respondent Adolph Lyons is a 24-year-old Negro male who resides in Los Angeles. According to the uncontradicted evidence in the record, at about 2 a.m. on October 6, 1976, Lyons was pulled over to the curb by two officers of the Los Angeles Police Department (LAPD) for a traffic infraction because one of his taillights was burned out. The officers greeted him with drawn revolvers as he exited from his car. Lyons was told to face his car and spread his legs. He did so. He was then ordered to clasp his hands and put them on top of his head. He again complied. After one of the officers completed a patdown search, Lyons dropped his hands, but was ordered to place them back above his head, and one of the officers grabbed Lyons' hands and slammed them onto his head. Lyons complained about the pain caused by the ring of keys he was holding in his hand. Within 5 to 10 seconds, the officer began to choke Lyons by applying a forearm against his throat. As Lyons struggled for air, the officer handcuffed him, but continued to apply the choke hold until he blacked out. When Lyons regained consciousness, he was lying face down on the ground, choking, gasping for air, and spitting up blood and dirt. He had urinated and defecated. He was issued a traffic citation and released.

The opinion is by Justice White, joined by Chief Justice Burger and Justices Powell, Rehnquist, and O'Connor. Justices Marshall, Brennan, Blackmun, and Stevens dissented.

It goes without saying that those who seek to invoke the jurisdiction of the federal courts must satisfy the threshold requirement imposed by Art. III of the Constitution by alleging an actual case or controversy. *Flast v. Cohen,* 392 U.S. 83, 94-101 (1968); *Jenkins v. McKeithen,* 395 U.S. 411, 421-425 (1969). Plaintiffs must demonstrate a "personal stake in the outcome" in order to "assure that concrete adverseness which sharpens the presentation of issues" necessary for the proper resolution of constitutional questions. *Baker v. Carr,* 369 U.S. 186, 204 (1962). Abstract injury is not enough. The plaintiff must show that he "has sustained or is immediately in danger of sustaining some direct injury" as the result of the challenged official conduct and the injury or threat of injury must be both "real and immediate," not "conjectural" or "hypothetical." See, e.g., *Golden v. Zwickler,* 394 U.S. 103, 109-110 (1969). . . .

In *O'Shea v. Littleton,* 414 U.S. 488 (1974), we dealt with a case brought by a class of plaintiffs claiming that they had been subjected to discriminatory enforcement of the criminal law. Among other things, a county magistrate and judge were accused of discriminatory conduct in various respects, such as sentencing members of plaintiff's class more harshly than other defendants. The Court of Appeals reversed the dismissal of the suit by the District Court, ruling that if the allegations were proved, an appropriate injunction could be entered.

We reversed for failure of the complaint to allege a case or controversy. Although it was claimed in that case that particular members of the plaintiff class had actually suffered from the alleged unconstitutional practices, we observed that "[p]ast exposure to illegal conduct does not in itself show a present case or controversy regarding injunctive relief . . . if unaccompanied by any continuing, present adverse effects." Past wrongs were evidence bearing on "whether there is a real and immediate threat of repeated injury." But the prospect of future injury rested "on the likelihood that [plaintiffs] will again be arrested for and charged with violations of the criminal law and will again be subjected to bond proceedings, trial, or sentencing before petitioners." The most that could be said for plaintiffs' standing was "that if [plaintiffs] proceed to violate an unchallenged law and if they are charged, held to answer, and tried in any proceedings before petitioners, they will be subjected to the discriminatory practices that petitioners are alleged to have followed." We could not find a case or controversy in those circumstances: the threat to the plaintiffs was not "sufficiently real and immediate to show an existing controversy simply because they anticipate violating lawful criminal statutes and being tried for their offenses. . . ." It was to be assumed "that [plaintiffs] will conduct their activities within the law and so avoid prosecution and conviction as well as exposure to the challenged course of conduct said to be followed by petitioners."

Another relevant decision for present purposes is *Rizzo v. Goode,* 423 U.S. 362 (1976), a case in which plaintiffs alleged widespread illegal and unconstitutional police conduct aimed at minority citizens and against city residents in general. The Court reiterated the holding in *O'Shea* that past wrongs do not in themselves amount to that real and immediate threat of injury necessary to make out a case or controversy. The claim of injury rested upon "what one of a small, unnamed minority of policemen might do to them in the future because of that unknown policeman's perception" of departmental procedures. This hypothesis was "even more attenuated than those allegations of future injury found insufficient in *O'Shea* to warrant [the] invocation of federal jurisdiction." The Court also held that plaintiffs' showing at trial of a relatively few instances of violations by individual police officers, without any showing of a deliberate policy on behalf of the named defendants, did not provide a basis for equitable relief.

No extension of *O'Shea* and *Rizzo* is necessary to hold that respondent Lyons has failed to demonstrate a case or controversy with the City that would justify the equitable relief sought. Lyons' standing to seek the injunction requested depended on whether he was likely to suffer future injury from the use of the choke holds by police officers. Count V of the complaint alleged the traffic stop and choking incident five months before. That Lyons may have been illegally choked by the police on October 6, 1976, while presumably affording Lyons standing to claim damages against the individual officers and perhaps against the City, does nothing to establish a real and immediate threat that he would again be stopped for a traffic violation, or for any other offense, by an officer or officers who would illegally choke him into unconsciousness without any provocation or resistance on his part. The additional allegation in the complaint that the police in Los Angeles routinely apply choke holds

in situations where they are not threatened by the use of deadly force falls far short of the allegations that would be necessary to establish a case or controversy between these parties.

In order to establish an actual controversy in this case, Lyons would have had not only to allege that he would have another encounter with the police but also to make the incredible assertion either, (1) that all police officers in Los Angeles always choke any citizen with whom they happen to have an encounter, whether for the purpose of arrest, issuing a citation, or for questioning, or (2) that the City ordered or authorized police officers to act in such manner. Although Count V alleged that the City authorized the use of the control holds in situations where deadly force was not threatened, it did not indicate why Lyons might be realistically threatened by police officers who acted within the strictures of the City's policy. If, for example, choke holds were authorized to be used only to counter resistance to an arrest by a suspect, or to thwart an effort to escape, any future threat to Lyons from the City's policy or from the conduct of police officers would be no more real than the possibility that he would again have an encounter with the police and that either he would illegally resist arrest or detention or the officers would disobey their instructions and again render him unconscious without any provocation.

Lyons fares no better if it be assumed that his pending damages suit affords him Art. III standing to seek an injunction as a remedy for the claim arising out of the October 1976 events. The equitable remedy is unavailable absent a showing of irreparable injury, a requirement that cannot be met where there is no showing of any real or immediate threat that the plaintiff will be wronged again—a "likelihood of substantial and immediate irreparable injury." *O'Shea v. Littleton,* 414 U.S., at 502. The speculative nature of Lyons' claim of future injury requires a finding that this prerequisite of equitable relief has not been fulfilled.

Nor will the injury that Lyons allegedly suffered in 1976 go unrecompensed; for that injury, he has an adequate remedy at law. Contrary to the view of the Court of Appeals, it is not at all "difficult" under our holding "to see how anyone can ever challenge police or similar administrative practices." 615 F.2d, at 1250. The legality of the violence to which Lyons claims he was once subjected is at issue in his suit for damages and can be determined there.

Absent a sufficient likelihood that he will again be wronged in a similar way, Lyons is no more entitled to an injunction than any other citizen of Los Angeles; and a federal court may not entertain a claim by any or all citizens who no more than assert that certain practices of law enforcement officers are unconstitutional. Cf. *Warth v. Seldin,* 422 U.S. 490 (1975); *Schlesinger v. Reservists to Stop the War,* 418 U.S. 208 (1974); *United States v. Richardson,* 418 U.S. 166 (1974). This is not to suggest that such undifferentiated claims should not be taken seriously by local authorities. Indeed, the interest of an alert and interested citizen is an essential element of an effective and fair government, whether on the local, state, or national level. A federal court, however, is not the proper forum to press such claims unless the requirements for entry and the prerequisites for injunctive relief are satisfied.

NOTES

1. Richard A. Brisbin, Jr., "The Conservatism of Antonin Scalia," *Political Science Quarterly* 105 (Spring 1990): 13.

2. *Association of Data Processing Service Organizations v. Camp,* 397 U.S. 150, 152 (1970).

3. Ibid.

4. *Decatur v. Paulding,* 39 U.S. 497, 516 (1840).

5. 5 U.S.C. 702.

6. 38 U.S.C. 211(a).

7. Anthony Lewis, *The New York Times,* 11 November 1996, A11.

8. *United States v. Western Pacific Railroad Company,* 352 U.S. 59 (1956).

9. Daniel Oran, *Oran's Dictionary of the Law* (St. Paul, MN: West, 1983), 116.

10. Ernest Gellhorn and Ronald Levin, *Administrative Law and Process: In a Nutshell* (St. Paul, MN: West, 1990), 110.

PART II

THE ADMINISTRATIVE PROCESS

CHAPTER 5

THE GOVERNMENT
AND INFORMATION

SECTION A: COLLECTING INFORMATION

CASE IN POINT:
MARSHALL V. BARLOW'S, INCORPORATED,
436 U.S. 307 (1978)

In the mid-1970s, Bill Barlow owned and operated a small plumbing and air-conditioning shop in Pocatello, Idaho. One day, an Occupational Safety and Health Administration (OSHA) inspector showed up at Barlow's shop and informed Barlow that he wanted to inspect the shop for violations of OSHA rules and regulations. Barlow asked whether OSHA had received complaints about working conditions in his shop. The inspector told Barlow that no complaints had been lodged but that Barlow's shop had simply "turned up" on the agency's list. The inspector again asked Barlow for permission to enter the back shop to conduct the inspection. As a member of the John Birch Society, Barlow believed that government, generally, and a federal administrative agency, particularly, was forbidden by the Fourth Amendment of the Constitution from entering his business without a warrant. When Barlow inquired whether the OSHA inspector had a warrant, the inspector indicated that no warrant was required because Congress had authorized warrantless inspections of businesses to enforce OSHA rules and regulations.

Barlow refused to allow the OSHA inspector into the back shop, and subsequently the secretary of labor filed suit in Idaho Federal District Court to compel Barlow to admit the inspector. The court issued the order, and when an OSHA inspector showed up again at Barlow's shop, armed with a court order but still without a warrant, Barlow again refused to allow the inspector into his shop. At this point, Barlow went to the Idaho Federal District Court to get an injunction preventing OSHA from searching his shop without a warrant. Barlow won his case at the district court, and the secretary of labor appealed.

The Fourth Amendment reads as follows:

> The right of the people to be secure in their persons, houses, papers, and effects, against unreasonable searches and seizures, shall not be violated, and no warrant shall issue, but upon probable cause, supported by oath or affirmation, and particularly describing the place to be searched, and the persons or things to be seized.

Notice that the amendment forbids unreasonable searches and seizures, but it does not define for us what an unreasonable search or seizure is. The task of deciding what constitutes an unreasonable search has fallen to the U.S. Supreme Court, and the Court has said that warrantless searches and seizures are those that are unreasonable. This is what has come to be known as the *warrant requirement:* that to meet the dictates of the Fourth Amendment, a search must be accompanied by a warrant. No sooner did the Court establish the warrant requirement than it began to create exceptions to it. Those exceptions are referred to as *exigent circumstances* and are generally created in those situations in which requiring a warrant would be impractical. For example, probable cause to stop an automobile may provide the legal authority to search the car without a warrant. Border searches, consent, plain view, and hot pursuit are some other situations in which the Court has created exceptions to the warrant requirement.

The question in *Barlow* is whether administrative searches that do not result in criminal charges are to be another exception to the warrant requirement. It would be helpful at this point to reflect on some history. One impetus for the Fourth Amendment was the hatred that businessmen of the former colonies held for the "general warrant." The general warrant was a procedure that authorized officers of the king to conduct so-called fishing expeditions; that is, the British officer would search a business (or house) without any evidence of wrongdoing just to see whether colonists were complying with certain tax measures. That is why the Fourth Amendment is so specific at the point where it says "no warrant shall issue."

The Court had decided cases on both sides of the question of whether administrative searches require a warrant. In 1967, the Court decided two cases that could support Barlow's position. In *Camara v. Municipal Court,* 387 U.S. 523 (1967), the Court said that a San Francisco public health inspector would need a warrant to inspect an apartment leased by Camara (the property was not supposed to be used as a personal dwelling, but allegedly it was). Similarly, the Court said that the Seattle Fire Department would need a warrant to conduct an inspection of a warehouse during a routine canvass of businesses for compliance with the city fire code (*See v. Seattle,* 387 U.S. 541 [1967]).

In contrast, the Court said no warrant was required to inspect a firearms business (*United States v. Biswell,* 406 U.S. 311 [1972]) or a liquor establishment (*Colonnade Catering Corporation v. United States,* 397 U.S. 72 [1970]). The Court reasoned that these were "pervasively regulated businesses" that had been subject to "close governmental supervision and inspection" for a long period of time. Furthermore, both businesses had contracted with the federal government and hence fell under a 1936 act[1] that authorizes warrantless inspections for compliance with minimum wage and hour provisions. The similarity of *Barlow* to *Biswell* and *Colonnade* is that a congressional act was authorizing OSHA's warrantless searches

---

Questions

1. Given what you know of the *Barlow* case, how do you think the Supreme Court decided? Why?

2. Barlow owned a small business and had perhaps six or seven employees. How is it that his business fell under the jurisdiction of OSHA? Is every business in the United States subject to the federal government's jurisdiction here? Where is the line drawn?

3. Barlow used to speak in my classes when I taught in Pocatello, and he indicated that it cost $60,000 in legal fees to get his case to the Supreme Court (and he got to skip the circuit court of appeals). Barlow did not have that kind of money. How do you suppose "little people" like Barlow get their cases to the Supreme Court?

GOVERNMENT'S NEED FOR INFORMATION

Toward the end of Chapter 3, the point was made that as the United States began to reject the ideology of negative freedom, limited government, and laissez-faire economics and to embrace a newer ideology of positive freedom, positive government, and Keynesian economics, the government became increasingly more involved in distributive, redistributive, and regulatory policy. *Distributive policies* attempt to encourage private activity, often using subsidies or tax incentives or both.[2] In the area of distributive policies, cozy triangles occur most frequently. Both the triangle that provides subsidies to tobacco growers and the triangle that provides research funds to fight cancer are examples of distributive policies. The federal tax deductions for interest on a home mortgage and for property tax are also examples of distributive policy.

As the name implies, *redistributive policies* attempt to "manipulate the allocation of wealth, property, rights, or some other value, among social classes or racial groups in society."[3] A reduction in the rate at which capital gains are taxed would be redistributive from the bottom to the top, whereas programs such as Aid to Families With Dependent Children (AFDC), legal aid, food stamps, and affirmative action are examples of redistributive policies in the other direction.

Regulatory policies can attempt to regulate competition, primarily because of scarce resources (the licensing of businesses that use airwaves and interstate common carriers), or they can regulate in the interest of protecting the public (consumer and environmental laws).

Whether a specific policy involves an agricultural subsidy, a tax incentive, regulation of an industry, protection of the environment, or provision of an entitlement program, you can see that Congress needs to rely on the expertise of agencies. Those agencies need to collect and use information. The agencies need information to make the rules necessary to implement the policy. They may need information to assess the execution of the policy or to ensure compliance with the policy. Gellhorn and Levin stated the problem simply: "Good decisions require good data."[4]

Primarily, federal agencies (state and local agencies as well) acquire information in three ways: Agencies can (a) require regulated parties to maintain records, to make the records available for agency inspection, and even to submit periodic reports; (b) subpoena information from businesses, individuals, or other parties; and (c) conduct physical inspections of businesses or property (as in the *Barlow* case).

Requiring Regulated Parties to Keep Records

Agencies acquire the power to compel information from private parties in two ways. First, occasionally Congress will specify that power in legislation. The Fair Labor Standards Act (FLSA), the federal minimum wage and hour law, requires those businesses that fall under the act's jurisdiction to keep records relating to hourly pay and overtime. The act further authorizes the secretary of labor (or designate) to enforce provisions of the act by examining those records. Second, if a statute does not specifically require private parties to maintain records for agency inspection, that power can be inferred from the delegation of power. In that case, the agency will generally go through the public notice and comment procedure (see Chapter 7) to notify regulated parties that it will require certain information to be kept.

What constitutional problem do you think of in a situation in which government says to you, "We want you to keep records about X, and an agency will look at your records. If we find that you are not in compliance with X, we will fine you." During World War II, the Price Control Act established price controls on many crucial commodities. It required retailers to maintain sales records for inspection by the price control administrator. As suggested in the case that follows, Shapiro was suspected of selling goods at prices above the set level. The Price Control Administration requested his sales receipts, and he refused.

SHAPIRO V. UNITED STATES
335 U.S. 1 (1948)

Chief Justice Vinson delivered the opinion of the Court, joined by Justices Black, Reed, Douglas, and Burton. Justices Frankfurter, Jackson, Rutledge, and Murphy dissented.

Petitioner was tried on charges of having made tie-in sales in violation of regulations under the Emergency Price Control. A plea in bar, claiming immunity from prosecution based on § 202(g) of the Act, was overruled by the trial judge; judgment of conviction followed and was affirmed on appeal, 159 F.2d 890. A contrary conclusion was reached by the district judge in *United States v. Hoffman,* 335 U.S. 77. Because this conflict involves an important question of statutory construction, these cases were brought here and heard together. Additional minor considerations involved in the *Hoffman* case are dealt with in a separate opinion. . . .

The petitioner, a wholesaler of fruit and produce, on September 29, 1944, was served with a subpoena duces tecum and adtestificandum issued, by the Price Administrator, under authority of the Emergency Price Control Act. The subpoena directed petitioner to appear before designated enforcement attorneys of the Office of Price Administration and to produce "all duplicate sales invoices, sales books, ledgers, inventory records, contracts and records relating to the sale of all commodities from September 1st, 1944, to September 28, 1944." In compliance with the subpoena, petitioner appeared and, after being sworn, was requested to turn over the subpoenaed records. Petitioner's counsel inquired whether petitioner was being granted immunity "as to any and all matters for information obtained as a result of the investigation and examination of these records." The presiding official stated that the "witness is entitled to whatever immunity which flows as a matter of law from the production of these books and records which are required to be kept." Petitioner thereupon produced the records, but claimed constitutional privilege. . . . The plea in bar alleged that the name of the purchaser in the transactions involved in the information appeared in the subpoenaed sales invoices and other similar documents. And it was alleged that the Office of Price Administration had used the name and other unspecified leads obtained from these documents to search out evidence of the violations, which had occurred in the preceding year.

The Circuit Court of Appeals ruled that the records which petitioner was compelled to produce were records required to be kept by a valid regulation under the Price Control Act; that thereby they became public documents, as to which no constitutional privilege against self-incrimination attaches; that accordingly the immunity of § 202(g) did not extend to the production of these records and the plea in bar was properly overruled by the trial court.

It should be observed at the outset that the decision in the instant case turns on the construction of a compulsory testimony-immunity provision which incorporates by reference the Compulsory Testimony Act of 1893. This provision, in conjunction with broad record-keeping requirements, has been included not merely in a temporary wartime measure, but also, in substantially the same terms, in virtually all of the major regulatory enactments of the Federal Government. . . .

In adopting the language used in the earlier act, Congress "must be considered to have adopted also the construction given by this Court to such language, and made it a part of the enactment." That judicial construction is made up of the doctrines enunciated by this Court in spelling out the non-privileged status of records validly required by law to be kept, in *Wilson v. United States,* 221 U.S. 361, and the inapplicability of immunity provisions to non-privileged documents, in *Heike v. United States,* 227 U.S. 131. . . .

In view of the clear rationale in *Wilson,* taken together with the ruling in *Heike* as to how statutory immunity provisos should be construed, the conclusion seems inevitable that Congress must have intended the immunity proviso in the Price Control Act to be coterminous with what would otherwise

have been the constitutional privilege of petitioner in the case at bar. Since he could assert no valid privilege as to the required records here in question, he was entitled to no immunity under the statute thus viewed. . . .

It may be assumed at the outset that there are limits which the government cannot constitutionally exceed in requiring the keeping of records which may be inspected by an administrative agency and may be used in prosecuting statutory violations committed by the record-keeper himself. But no serious misgiving that those bounds have been overstepped would appear to be evoked when there is a sufficient relation between the activity sought to be regulated and the public concern so that the government can constitutionally regulate or forbid the basic activity concerned, and can constitutionally require the keeping of particular records, subject to inspection by the Administrator.

It is not questioned here that Congress has constitutional authority to prescribe commodity prices as a war emergency measure, and that the licensing and record-keeping requirements of the Price Control Act represent a legitimate exercise of that power. Accordingly, the principle enunciated in the *Wilson* case, and reaffirmed as recently as the *Davis* case, is clearly applicable here: namely, that the privilege which exists as to private papers cannot be maintained in relation to "records required by law to be kept in order that there may be suitable information of transactions which are the appropriate subjects of governmental regulation, and the enforcement of restrictions validly established." Even the dissenting Justices in the *Davis* case conceded that "there is an important difference in the constitutional protection afforded their possessors between papers exclusively private and documents having public aspects," a difference whose essence is that the latter papers, "once they have been legally obtained, are available as evidence." In the case at bar, it cannot be doubted that the sales record which petitioner was required to keep as a licensee under the Price Control Act has "public aspects." Nor can there be any doubt that when it was obtained by the Administrator through the use of subpoena, as authorized specifically by § 202(b) of the statute, it was "legally obtained" and hence "available as evidence." The record involved in the case at bar was a sales record required to be maintained under an appropriate regulation, its relevance to the lawful purpose of the Administrator is unquestioned, and the transaction which it recorded was one in which the petitioner could lawfully engage solely by virtue of the license granted to him under the statute.

In the view that we have taken of the case, we find it unnecessary to consider the additional contention by the government that, in any event, no immunity attaches to the production of the books by the petitioner because the connection between the books and the evidence produced at the trial was too tenuous to justify the claim.

For the foregoing reasons, the judgment of the Circuit Court of Appeals is affirmed.

Affirmed.

Question

The Court often resolves difficult issues by what is called a "balancing test"; that is, the Court will balance the interest of the parties to see which interest outweighs the other. That is what the Court did in this case. Can you articulate the two interests? Which interest won? Why?

The Court has decided many cases in the area of the Fifth Amendment's self-incrimination clause since 1948 although relatively few of them have involved administrative law. The Court has restricted the concept of "self-incrimination" so that it applies only to individuals and not to businesses. It applies only in cases in which criminal charges could result and hence does not apply in civil actions such as administrative law. Finally, self-incrimination applies only to oral testimony. It does not apply to physical evidence, such as records or test results. Therefore, the Court today rarely has occasion to apply the self-incrimination clause in this area of administrative law.

You will probably notice as you read administrative law cases a propensity on behalf of the courts to show deference toward agency expertise. That deference is apparent in cases involving agency acquisition of information. If the courts do not interfere with congressional attempts to acquire information, why should the courts be any more prone to interfere with Congress's expert delegate (bureaucracy)? See, for example, *Superior Oil Company v. Federal Energy Regulatory Commission,* 563 F.2d. 191 (1977), and the *Line of Business Report* case at the end of this chapter.

Subpoenaing Information

Sometimes agencies need information that is readily available, sometimes they require specific types of information to be made available (as in the preceding cases), and sometimes they need additional information that a private party may be unwilling to surrender. In these latter situations, agencies have the power to subpoena the desired information. A *subpoena* is a court's order for a person to appear in court and to testify or perhaps bring documents. It differs from a warrant in that a subpoena can be challenged prior to execution, whereas a warrant can be challenged only after the fact. For example, if a court issued a subpoena to a physician, then his or her lawyer might be able to challenge the subpoena on the grounds of privileged information (physician-client privilege) and perhaps get the subpoena quashed. In the public administration context, a subpoena is an order by an agency to appear before the agency or, more typically, to bring certain documents to the agency. Another difference between a warrant and a subpoena is that the Fourth Amendment specifies a warrant can be issued only on the basis of probable cause. But what if an administrative agency wants to go on a "fishing expedition" with a subpoena? The two cases that follow address the question of the Fourth Amendment and administrative subpoenas. They are also interesting in that they represent the two different ideologies discussed in Chapter 1.

FEDERAL TRADE COMMISSION V. AMERICAN TOBACCO COMPANY
264 U.S. 298 (1924)

Justice Holmes delivered the opinion for a unanimous Court.

[1] These are two petitions for writs of mandamus to the respective corporations respondent, manufacturers and sellers of tobacco, brought by the Federal Trade Commission under the Act of September 26, 1914, and in alleged pursuance of a resolution of the Senate passed on August 9, 1921. The purpose of the petitions is to require production of records, contracts, memoranda and correspondence for inspection and making copies. They were denied by the District Court. 283 Fed. 999. The resolution directs the Commission to investigate the tobacco situation as to domestic and export trade with particular reference to market price to producers, etc. The act directs the Commission to prevent the use of unfair methods of competition in commerce and provides for a complaint by the Commission, a hearing and a report, with an order to desist if it deems the use of a prohibited method proved. The Commission and the party concerned are both given a resort to the Circuit Court of Appeals. By section 6 the Commission shall have power (a) to gather information concerning, and to investigate the business, conduct, practices, and management of any corporation engaged in commerce, except banks and common carriers, and its relation to other corporations and individuals; (b) to require reports and answers under oath to specific questions furnishing the Commission such information as it may require on the above subjects . . . (d) upon the direction of the President or either House of Congress to investigate and report the facts as to alleged violation of the Anti-Trust Acts. By section 9 for the purposes of this act the Commission shall at all reasonable times have access to, for the purposes of examination, and the right to copy any documentary evidence of any corporation being investigated or proceeded against and shall have power to require by subpoena the attendance and testimony of witnesses and the production of all such documentary evidence relating to any matter under investigation. In case of disobedience an order may be obtained from a District Court. Upon application of the Attorney General the District Courts are given jurisdiction to issue writs of man-

damus to require compliance with the act or any order of the commission made in pursuance thereof. The petitions are filed under this clause and the question is whether orders of the Commission to allow inspection and copies of the documents and correspondence referred to were authorized by the act.

The petitions allege that complaints have been filed with the Commission charging the respondents severally with unfair competition by regulating the prices at which their commodities should be resold. . . . There are the necessary formal allegations and a prayer that unless the accounts, books, records, documents, memoranda, contracts, papers, and correspondence of the respondents are immediately submitted for inspection and examination and for the purpose of making copies thereof, a mandamus issue requiring, in the case of the American Tobacco Company, the exhibition during business hours when the Commission's agent requests it, of all letters and telegrams received by the Company from or sent by it to all of its jobber customers, between January 1, 1921, to December 31, 1921, inclusive. In the case of the P. Lorillard Company the same requirement is made and also all letters, telegrams, or reports from or to its salesmen, or from or to all tobacco jobbers' or wholesale grocers' associations, all contracts or arrangements with such associations, and correspondence and agreements with a list of corporations named.

The mere facts of carrying on a commerce not confined within State lines and of being organized as a corporation do not make men's affairs public, as those of a railroad company now may be. *Smith v. Interstate Commerce Commission,* 245 U.S. 33. Anyone who respects the spirit as well as the letter of the Fourth Amendment would be loath to believe that Congress intended to authorize one of its subordinate agencies to sweep all our traditions into the fire . . . and to direct fishing expeditions into private papers on the possibility that they may disclose evidence of crime. We do not discuss the question whether it could do so if it tried, as nothing short of the most explicit language would induce us to attribute to Congress that intent. The interruption of business, the possible revelation of trade secrets, and the expense that compliance with the Commission's wholesale demand would cause are the least considerations. It is contrary to the first principles of justice to allow a search through all the respondents' records, relevant or irrelevant, in the hope that something will turn up. The unwillingness of this Court to sustain such a claim is shown in *Harriman v. Interstate Commerce Commission,* 211 U.S. 407, and as to correspondence, even in the case of a common carrier, in *United States v. Louisville & Nashville R. R. Co.,* 236 U.S. 318. The question is a different one where the State granting the charter gives its Commission power to inspect. . . .

[3] The right of access given by the statute is to documentary evidence—not to all documents, but to such documents as are evidence. The analogies of the law do not allow the party wanting evidence to call for all documents in order to see if they do not contain it. Some ground must be shown for supposing that the documents called for do contain it. Formerly in equity the ground must be found in admissions in the answer. We assume that the rule to be applied here is more liberal but still a ground must be laid and the ground and the demand must be reasonable. A general subpoena in the form of these petitions would be bad. Some evidence of the materiality of the papers demanded must be produced. . . . We assume for present purposes that even some part of the presumably large mass of papers relating only to intrastate business may be so connected with charges of unfair competition in interstate matters as to be relevant, but that possibility does not warrant a demand for the whole. For all that appears the corporations would have been willing to produce such papers as they conceived to be relevant to the matter in hand. If their judgment upon that matter was not final, at least some evidence must be offered to show that it was wrong. No such evidence is shown.

We have considered this case on the general claim of authority put forward by the Commission. The argument for the Government attaches some force to the investigations and proceedings upon which the Commission had entered. The investigations and complaints seem to have been only on hearsay or suspicion—but even if they were induced by substantial evidence under oath the rudimentary principles of justice that we have laid down would apply. We cannot attribute to Congress an intent to defy the Fourth Amendment or even to come so near to doing so as to raise a serious question of constitutional law.

Judgment affirmed.

OKLAHOMA PRESS PUBLISHING COMPANY V. WALLING
327 U.S. 186 (1946)

Justice Rutledge delivered the opinion of the Court. Justice Murphy dissented, and Justice Jackson did not participate.

These cases bring for decision important questions concerning the Administrator's right to judicial enforcement of subpoenas duces tecum issued by him in the course of investigations conducted pursuant to § 11(a) of the Fair Labor Standards Act. . . . The subpoenas sought the production of specified records to determine whether petitioners were violating the Fair Labor Standards Act, including records relating to coverage. Petitioners, newspaper publishing corporations, maintain that the Act is not applicable to them, for constitutional and other reasons, and insist that the question of coverage must be adjudicated before the subpoenas may be enforced.

I

Coloring almost all of petitioners' position, as we understand them, is a primary misconception that the First Amendment knocks out any possible application of the Fair Labor Standards Act to the business of publishing and distributing newspapers. The argument has two prongs.

The broadside assertion that petitioners "could not be covered by the Act," for the reason that "application of this Act to its newspaper publishing business would violate its rights as guaranteed by the First Amendment," is without merit. . . . If Congress can remove obstructions to commerce by requiring publishers to bargain collectively with employees and refrain from interfering with their rights of self-organization, matters closely related to eliminating low wages and long hours, Congress likewise may strike directly at those evils when they adversely affect commerce.

II

Other questions pertain to whether enforcement of the subpoenas as directed by the Circuit Courts of Appeals will violate any of petitioners' rights secured by the Fourth Amendment and related issues concerning Congress' intent. It is claimed that enforcement would permit the Administrator to conduct general fishing expeditions into petitioners' books, records, and papers, in order to secure evidence that they have violated the Act, without a prior charge or complaint and simply to secure information upon which to base one, all allegedly in violation of the Amendment's search and seizure provisions. Supporting this is an argument that Congress did not intend such use to be made of the delegated power, which rests in part upon asserted constitutional implications, but primarily upon the reports of legislative committees, particularly in the House of Representatives, made in passing upon appropriations for years subsequent to the Act's effective date. . . . The short answer to the Fourth Amendment objections is that the records in these cases present no question of actual search and seizure, but raise only the question whether orders of court for the production of specified records have been validly made; and no sufficient showing appears to justify setting them aside. No officer or other person has sought to enter petitioners' premises against their will, to search them, or to seize or examine their books, records, or papers without their assent, otherwise than pursuant to orders of court authorized by law and made after adequate opportunity to present objections, which in fact were made. Nor has any objection been taken to the breadth of the subpoenas or to any other specific defect which would invalidate them. . . . What petitioners seek is not to prevent an unlawful search and seizure. It is rather a total immunity to the Act's provisions, applicable to all others similarly situated, requiring them to submit their pertinent records for the Administrator's inspection under every judicial safeguard, after and only after an order of court made pursuant to and in exact compliance with authority granted by Congress. This broad claim of immunity no doubt is induced by petitioners' First Amendment contentions. But beyond them it is rested also upon conceptions of the Fourth Amendment equally lacking in merit.

Petitioners' plea that the Fourth Amendment places them so far above the law that they are beyond the reach of congressional and judicial power as those powers have been exerted here only raises the ghost of controversy long since settled adversely to their claim.

Section 11(a) expressly authorizes the Administrator to "enter and inspect such places and such records (and make such transcriptions thereof), question such employees, and investigate such facts, conditions, practices, or matters as he may deem appropriate to determine whether any person has violated any provision of this Act, or which may aid in the enforcement of the provisions of this Act." The subpoena power conferred by § 9 . . . is given in aid of this investigation and, in case of disobedience, the District Courts are called upon to enforce the subpoena through their contempt powers, without express condition requiring showing of coverage. . . . In view of these provisions, with which the Administrator's action was in exact compliance, this case presents an instance of "the most explicit language" which leaves no room for questioning Congress' intent. The very purpose of the subpoena and of the order, as of the authorized investigation, is to discover and procure evidence, not to prove a pending charge or complaint, but upon which to make one if, in the Administrator's judgment, the facts thus discovered should justify doing so. . . .

III

Whatever limits there may be to congressional power to provide for the production of corporate or other business records, therefore, they are not to be found, in view of the course of prior decisions, in any such absolute or universal immunity as petitioners seek. . . . Without attempt to summarize or accurately distinguish all of the cases, the fair distillation, in so far as they apply merely to the production of corporate records and papers in response to a subpoena or order authorized by law and safeguarded by judicial sanction, seems to be that the Fifth Amendment affords no protection by virtue of the self-incrimination provision, whether for the corporation or for its officers; and the Fourth, if applicable, at the most guards against abuse only by way of too much indefiniteness or breadth in the things required to be "particularly described," if also the inquiry is one the demanding agency is authorized by law to make and the materials specified are relevant. The gist of the protection is in the requirement, expressed in terms, that the disclosure sought shall not be unreasonable.

As this has taken form in the decisions, the following specific results have been worked out. It is not necessary, as in the case of a warrant, that a specific charge or complaint of violation of law be pending or that the order be made pursuant to one. It is enough that the investigation be for a lawfully authorized purpose, within the power of Congress to command. . . . The requirement of "probable cause, supported by oath or affirmation" literally applicable in the case of a warrant is satisfied, in that of an order for production, by the court's determination that the investigation is authorized by Congress, is for a purpose Congress can order, and the documents sought are relevant to the inquiry. Beyond this the requirement of reasonableness, including particularity in "describing the place to be searched, and the persons or things to be seized," also literally applicable to warrants, comes down to specification of the documents to be produced adequate, but not excessive, for the purposes of the relevant inquiry. . . .

When these principles are applied to the facts of the present cases, it is impossible to conceive how a violation of petitioners' rights could have been involved. Both were corporations. The only records or documents sought were corporate ones. No possible element of self-incrimination was therefore presented or in fact claimed. All the records sought were relevant to the authorized inquiry, the purpose of which was to determine two issues, whether petitioners were subject to the Act and, if so, whether they were violating it. These were subjects of investigation authorized by § 11(a), the latter expressly, the former by necessary implication. It is not to be doubted that Congress could authorize investigation of these matters. In all these respects, the specifications more than meet the requirements long established by many precedents. The Administrator is authorized to enter and inspect, but the Act makes his right to do so subject in all cases to judicial supervision. Persons from whom he seeks relevant information are not required to submit to his demand, if in any respect it is unreasonable or overreaches the authority Congress has given. To it they may make "appropriate defense" surrounded by every safeguard of judicial restraint.

Nor is there room for intimation that the Administrator has proceeded in these cases in any manner contrary to petitioners' fundamental rights or otherwise than strictly according to law. It is to be remembered that petitioners' are not the only rights which may be involved or threatened with possible infringement. Their employees' rights and the public interest under the declared policy of Congress also would be affected if petitioners should enjoy the practically complete immunity they seek.

No sufficient reason was set forth in the returns or the accompanying affidavits for not enforcing the subpoenas, a burden petitioners were required to assume in order to make "appropriate defense."

Accordingly the judgments in both causes, No. 61 and No. 63, are affirmed.

Affirmed.

Justice Murphy, dissenting.

It is not without difficulty that I dissent from a procedure the constitutionality of which has been established for many years. But I am unable to approve the use of non-judicial subpoenas issued by administrative agents.

Administrative law has increased greatly in the past few years and seems destined to be augmented even further in the future. But attending this growth should be a new and broader sense of responsibility on the part of administrative agencies and officials. Excessive use or abuse of authority can not only destroy man's instinct for liberty but will eventually undo the administrative processes themselves. Our history is not without a precedent of a successful revolt against a ruler who "sent hither swarms of officers to harass our people."

Perhaps we are too far removed from the experiences of the past to appreciate fully the consequences that may result from an irresponsible though well-meaning use of the subpoena power. To allow a non-judicial officer, unarmed with judicial process, to demand the books and papers of an individual is an open invitation to abuse of that power. It is no answer that the individual may refuse to produce the material demanded. Many persons have yielded solely because of the air of authority with which the demand is made, a demand that cannot be enforced without subsequent judicial aid. Many invasions of private rights thus occur without the restraining hand of the judiciary ever intervening.

Only by confining the subpoena power exclusively to the judiciary can there be any insurance against this corrosion of liberty. Statutory enforcement would not thereby be made impossible.

Indeed, it would be made easier. A people's desire to cooperate with the enforcement of a statute is in direct proportion to the respect for individual rights shown in the enforcement process. Liberty is too priceless to be forfeited through the zeal of an administrative agent.

Questions

1. What is your answer to the question whether administrative agencies may go on "fishing expeditions" with a subpoena?
2. Would the administrative state exist without this investigative tool? Is that good or bad? Why?

According to Gellhorn, Byse, and Strauss, the test that the courts apply now when a party challenges an administrative subpoena is "whether the topic to which the inquiry pertains is a topic the official has been empowered to investigate."[5] In other words, the Court will ask whether the subject matter of the subpoena is subject matter the agency has the power to investigate. In the *Oklahoma Press* case, for example, the subject matter of the subpoena was employee records, and the secretary of labor is empowered under the FLSA to investigate violations of wage and hour provisions; hence, the Court will enforce the subpoena. Provided that a subpoena seeks information in an area the agency is empowered to investigate, that it does not request privileged information, and that it is sufficiently specific, the courts will generally enforce agency subpoenas.

The fact that an agency has issued a subpoena does not necessarily mean that requested documents will be immediately forthcoming. That is because, unlike court-issued subpoenas, administrative agencies rarely have any enforcement mechanism. If an individual ignored a court-issued subpoena and failed to appear before the court at the proper time, a bench warrant would likely be issued for the subject's arrest, and contempt of court proceedings would follow. Congress has made it a federal misdemeanor to fail to comply with a subpoena issued by the Securities and Exchange Commission (SEC), but that is the exception, rather than the rule. More typically, if an agency issues a subpoena and the party refuses to comply, then the agency must go to federal court to obtain a court order to comply with the subpoena. At such hearings, the courts will apply the test cited earlier, "whether the topic to which the inquiry pertains is a topic the official has been empowered to investigate." Frequently, a court will issue the order for compliance with the subpoena, and if the party still refuses to comply, then the agency must go back to court and instigate contempt proceedings. The problem is that a court's decision to issue a judicial order requiring compliance with an agency subpoena is an appealable decision and can be appealed to the circuit court of appeals. It could be appealed further to the U.S. Supreme Court, as the *American Tobacco* and *Oklahoma Press* cases were. The point is that, given a good enough legal division, a business or corporation could tie up compliance with an agency subpoena for years, if it so chooses.

Conducting Physical Inspections

Physical inspection is an indispensable tool in an agency's arsenal for implementing laws and policies. There are fire inspections, housing code inspections, meat inspections, nuclear plant inspections, mine safety inspections, plant effluent inspections, defense plant inspections, AFDC inspections, bank inspections—the list is almost endless. To this point, we know that the Fifth Amendment's self-incrimination clause is not involved in those situations in which agencies require businesses to maintain certain records and, as a consequence of inspecting those records, may impose fines. We also know that the Fourth Amendment is rarely involved where agencies issue subpoenas. The question that opened this chapter, and to which we now turn, is whether the Fourth Amendment is involved in administrative searches or physical inspections.

MARSHALL V. BARLOW'S, INCORPORATED
436 U.S. 307 (1978)

Justice White delivered the opinion of the Court, joined by Chief Justice Burger and Justices Brennan, Stewart, Marshall, and Powell. Justice Stevens dissented, joined by Justices Blackmun and Rehnquist.

Section 8(a) of the Occupational Safety and Health Act of 1970 (OSHA or Act) empowers agents of the Secretary of Labor (Secretary) to search the work area of any employment facility within the Act's jurisdiction. The purpose of the search is to inspect for safety hazards and violations of OSHA regulations. No search warrant or other process is expressly required under the Act. . . . On the morning of September 11, 1975, an OSHA inspector entered the customer service area of Barlow's, Inc., an electrical and plumbing installation business located in Pocatello, Idaho. The president and general manager, Ferrol G. "Bill" Barlow, was on hand; and the OSHA inspector, after showing his credentials, informed Mr. Barlow that he wished to conduct a search of the working areas of the business. Mr. Barlow inquired whether any complaint had been received about his company. The inspector answered no, but that Barlow's, Inc., had simply turned up in the agency's selection process. The inspector again asked to enter the nonpublic area of the business; Mr. Barlow's response was to inquire whether the inspector had a search warrant. The inspector had none. Thereupon, Mr. Barlow refused the inspector admission to the employee area of his business. He said he was relying on his rights as guaranteed by the Fourth Amendment of the United States Constitution. . . . Three months later, the Secretary petitioned the United States District Court for the District of Idaho to issue an order compelling Mr. Barlow to admit the inspector. The requested order was issued on December 30, 1975, and was presented to Mr. Barlow on January 5, 1976. Mr. Barlow again refused admission, and he sought his own injunctive relief against the warrantless searches assertedly permitted by OSHA. A three-judge court was convened. On December 30, 1976, it ruled in Mr. Barlow's favor. 424 F.Supp. 437. Concluding that *Camara v. Municipal Court,* 387 U.S. 523 (1967), and *See v. City of Seattle,* 387 U.S. 541 (1967), controlled this case, the court held that the Fourth Amendment required a warrant for the type of search involved here and that the statutory authorization for warrantless inspections was unconstitutional. An injunction against searches or inspections pursuant to § 8(a) was entered. The Secretary appealed, challenging the judgment, and we noted probable jurisdiction. . . .

[1] The Warrant Clause of the Fourth Amendment protects commercial buildings as well as private homes. To hold otherwise would belie the origin of that Amendment, and the American colonial experience. An important forerunner of the first 10 Amendments to the United States Constitution, the Virginia Bill of Rights, specifically opposed "general warrants, whereby an officer or messenger may be commanded to search suspected places without evidence of a fact committed." The general warrant was a recurring point of contention in the Colonies immediately preceding the Revolution. The particular offensiveness it engendered was acutely felt by the merchants and businessmen whose premises and products were inspected for compliance with the several parliamentary revenue measures that most irritated the colonists. "[T]he Fourth Amendment's commands grew in large measure out of the colonists' experience with the writs of assistance . . . [that] granted sweeping power to customs officials and other agents of the King to search at large for smuggled goods."

Against this background, it is untenable that the ban on warrantless searches was not intended to shield places of business as well as of residence. . . . This Court has already held that warrantless searches are generally unreasonable, and that this rule applies to commercial premises as well as homes. In *Camara v. Municipal Court,* supra, 387 U.S., we held: "[E]xcept in certain carefully defined classes of cases, a search of private property without proper consent is 'unreasonable' unless it has been authorized by a valid search warrant." On the same day, we also ruled: "As we explained in *Camara,* a search of private houses is presumptively unreasonable if conducted without a warrant. The businessman, like the occupant of a residence, has a constitutional right to go about his business free from unreasonable official entries upon his private commercial property. The businessman, too, has that right placed in jeopardy if the decision to enter and inspect for violation of regulatory laws can be made and enforced by the inspector in the field without official authority evidenced by a warrant." These same cases also held that the Fourth Amendment prohibition against unreasonable searches protects against warrantless intrusions during civil as well as criminal investigations. The reason is found in the "basic purpose of this Amendment . . . [which] is to safeguard the privacy and security of individuals against arbitrary invasions by governmental officials." If the government intrudes on a person's property, the privacy interest suffers whether the government's motivation is to investigate violations of criminal laws or breaches of other statutory or regulatory standards. It therefore appears that unless some recognized exception to the warrant requirement applies, *See v. City of Seattle* would require a warrant to conduct the inspection sought in this case.

The clear import of our cases is that the closely regulated industry of the type involved in *Colonnade* and *Biswell* is the exception. The Secretary would make it the rule. Invoking the Walsh-Healey Act of 1936, 41 U.S.C. § 35 et seq., the Secretary attempts to support a conclusion that all businesses involved in interstate commerce have long been subjected to close supervision of employee safety and health conditions. But the degree of federal involvement in employee working circumstances has never been of the order of specificity and pervasiveness that OSHA mandates. It is quite unconvincing to argue that the imposition of minimum wages and maximum hours on employers who contracted with the Government under the Walsh-Healey Act prepared the entirety of American interstate commerce for regulation of working conditions to the minutest detail. Nor can any but the most fictional sense of voluntary consent to later searches be found in the single fact that one conducts a business affecting interstate commerce; under current practice and law, few businesses can be conducted without having some effect on interstate commerce. . . .

Whether the Secretary proceeds to secure a warrant or other process, with or without prior notice, his entitlement to inspect will not depend on his demonstrating probable cause to believe that conditions in violation of OSHA exist on the premises. Probable cause in the criminal law sense is not required. For purposes of an administrative search such as this, probable cause justifying the issuance of a warrant may be based not only on specific evidence of an existing violation but also on a showing that "reasonable legislative or administrative standards for conducting an . . . inspection are

satisfied with respect to a particular [establishment]." *Camara v. Municipal Court,* 387 U.S., at 538. A warrant showing that a specific business has been chosen for an OSHA search on the basis of a general administrative plan for the enforcement of the Act derived from neutral sources such as, for example, dispersion of employees in various types of industries across a given area, and the desired frequency of searches in any of the lesser divisions of the area, would protect an employer's Fourth Amendment rights. We doubt that the consumption of enforcement energies in the obtaining of such warrants will exceed manageable proportions. . . . Nor do we agree that the incremental protections afforded the employer's privacy by a warrant are so marginal that they fail to justify the administrative burdens that may be entailed. The authority to make warrantless searches devolves almost unbridled discretion upon executive and administrative officers, particularly those in the field, as to when to search and whom to search. A warrant, by contrast, would provide assurances from a neutral officer that the inspection is reasonable under the Constitution, is authorized by statute, and is pursuant to an administrative plan containing specific neutral criteria. Also, a warrant would then and there advise the owner of the scope and objects of the search, beyond which limits the inspector is not expected to proceed. These are important functions for a warrant to perform, functions which underlie the Court's prior decisions that the Warrant Clause applies to inspections for compliance with regulatory statutes. We conclude that the concerns expressed by the Secretary do not suffice to justify warrantless inspections under OSHA or vitiate the general constitutional requirement that for a search to be reasonable a warrant must be obtained.

III

We hold that Barlow was entitled to a declaratory judgment, that the Act is unconstitutional insofar as it purports to authorize inspections without warrant or its equivalent and to an injunction enjoining the Act's enforcement to that extent. The judgment of the District Court is therefore affirmed. So ordered.

Justice Stevens, dissenting.

Justice Stevens was joined by Justices Blackmun and Rehnquist.

I

The warrant requirement is linked "textually . . . to the probable-cause concept" in the Warrant Clause. The routine OSHA inspections are, by definition, not based on cause to believe there is a violation on the premises to be inspected. Hence, if the inspections were measured against the requirements of the Warrant Clause, they would be automatically and unequivocally unreasonable.

Because of the acknowledged importance and reasonableness of routine inspections in the enforcement of federal regulatory statutes such as OSHA, the Court recognizes that requiring full compliance with the Warrant Clause would invalidate all such inspection programs. Yet, rather than simply analyzing such programs under the "Reasonableness" Clause of the Fourth Amendment, the Court holds the OSHA program invalid under the Warrant Clause and then avoids a blanket prohibition on all routine regulatory inspections by relying on the notion that the "probable cause" requirement in the Warrant Clause may be relaxed whenever the Court believes that the governmental need to conduct a category of "searches" outweighs the intrusion on interests protected by the Fourth Amendment.

The Court's approach disregards the plain language of the Warrant Clause and is unfaithful to the balance struck by the Framers of the Fourth Amendment. . . . "[O]ur constitutional fathers were not concerned about warrantless searches, but about overreaching warrants. It is perhaps too much to say that they feared the warrant more than the search, but it is plain enough that the warrant was the prime object of their concern. Far from looking at the warrant as a protection against unreasonable searches, they saw it as an authority for unreasonable and oppressive searches. . . ."

Since the general warrant, not the warrantless search, was the immediate evil at which the Fourth Amendment was directed, it is not surprising that the Framers placed precise limits on its issuance. The requirement that a warrant only issue on a showing of particularized probable cause was the means adopted to circumscribe the warrant power. While the subsequent course of Fourth Amendment jurisprudence in this Court emphasizes the dangers posed by warrantless searches conducted without probable cause, it is the general reasonableness standard in the first Clause, not the Warrant Clause,

that the Framers adopted to limit this category of searches. It is, of course, true that the existence of a valid warrant normally satisfies the reasonableness requirement under the Fourth Amendment. But we should not dilute the requirements of the Warrant Clause in an effort to force every kind of governmental intrusion which satisfies the Fourth Amendment definition of a "search" into a judicially developed, warrant-preference scheme.

Fidelity to the original understanding of the Fourth Amendment, therefore, leads to the conclusion that the Warrant Clause has no application to routine, regulatory inspections of commercial premises. If such inspections are valid, it is because they comport with the ultimate reasonableness standard of the Fourth Amendment. If the Court were correct in its view that such inspections, if undertaken without a warrant, are unreasonable in the constitutional sense, the issuance of a "newfangled warrant"—to use Mr. Justice Clark's characteristically expressive term—without any true showing of particularized probable cause would not be sufficient to validate them. . . .

Even if a warrant requirement does not "frustrate" the legislative purpose, the Court has no authority to impose an additional burden on the Secretary unless that burden is required to protect the employer's Fourth Amendment interests. The essential function of the traditional warrant requirement is the interposition of a neutral magistrate between the citizen and the presumably zealous law enforcement officer so that there might be an objective determination of probable cause. But this purpose is not served by the newfangled inspection warrant.

What purposes, then, are served by the administrative warrant procedure? The inspection warrant purports to serve three functions: to inform the employer that the inspection is authorized by the statute, to advise him of the lawful limits of the inspection, and to assure him that the person demanding entry is an authorized inspector. An examination of these functions in the OSHA context reveals that the inspection warrant adds little to the protections already afforded by the statute and pertinent regulations, and the slight additional benefit it might provide is insufficient to identify a constitutional violation or to justify overriding Congress' judgment that the power to conduct warrantless inspections is essential. . . .

The pertinent inquiry is not whether the inspection program is authorized by a regulatory statute directed at a single industry, but whether Congress has limited the exercise of the inspection power to those commercial premises where the evils at which the statute is directed are to be found. Thus, in *Biswell,* if Congress had authorized inspections of all commercial premises as a means of restricting the illegal traffic in firearms, the Court would have found the inspection program unreasonable; the power to inspect was upheld because it was tailored to the subject matter of Congress' proper exercise of regulatory power. Similarly, OSHA is directed at health and safety hazards in the workplace, and the inspection power granted the Secretary extends only to those areas where such hazards are likely to be found. Here, as well as in *Biswell,* businesses are required to be aware of and comply with regulations governing their business activities. In both situations, the validity of the regulations depends not upon the consent of those regulated, but on the existence of a federal statute embodying a congressional determination that the public interest in the health of the Nation's work force or the limitation of illegal firearms traffic outweighs the businessman's interest in preventing a Government inspector from viewing those areas of his premises which relate to the subject matter of the regulation.

The case before us involves an attempt to conduct a warrantless search of the working area of an electrical and plumbing contractor. The statute authorizes such an inspection during reasonable hours. The inspection is limited to those areas over which Congress has exercised its proper legislative authority. The area is also one to which employees have regular access without any suggestion that the work performed or the equipment used has any special claim to confidentiality. Congress has determined that industrial safety is an urgent federal interest requiring regulation and supervision, and further, that warrantless inspections are necessary to accomplish the safety goals of the legislation. While one may question the wisdom of pervasive governmental oversight of industrial life, I decline to question Congress' judgment that the inspection power is a necessary enforcement device in achieving the goals of a valid exercise of regulatory power. . . . I respectfully dissent.

Questions

1. The state of the law prior to *Barlow* was that businesses were generally protected by the Fourth Amendment and that a warrant would be required to inspect a business unless that business was in a "pervasively regulated industry." Did the decision in *Barlow* change the state of the law?
2. Do administrative search warrants require probable cause?
3. What good does it do to require a warrant and then allow one to be issued without probable cause?

Although *Marshall v. Barlow's* is a famous administrative law case, it really set no new precedent and, in fact, followed the reasoning established in *See v. Seattle* and *Camara v. Municipal Court.* What makes the *Barlow* case unusual is the presence of a federal law authorizing warrantless searches and the fact that the Court declared that particular part of the law unconstitutional. Often, we assume that because judicial review exists, the Court frequently uses it to declare acts of Congress unconstitutional. The Court has declared only approximately one hundred acts of Congress to be unconstitutional, however, although the Court has shown less deference to state legislatures.

As stated in the first question following the *Barlow* case, the state of the law, both before and after *Barlow,* was that warrantless administrative searches were unconstitutional except in heavily regulated (and licensed) industries. The problem is that not all situations will fit neatly into that dichotomy. For example, can a fire marshall search the scene of a burned business for evidence of arson without a warrant (*Michigan v. Tyler,* 436 U.S. 399 [1978])? Can a pollution control inspector enter business property—but not the building—and take an air sample to determine whether the business is in compliance with standards without a warrant (*Air Pollution Variance Board v. Western Alfalfa Corporation,* 416 U.S. 861 [1974])? Can a high school vice principal search a student's purse without a warrant (*New Jersey v. T.L.O.,* 469 U.S. 325 [1985])? Can the Environmental Protection Agency (EPA) fly over a business and use aerial photographs as a means of physical inspection without a warrant (*Dow Chemical Company v. United States,* 476 U.S. 227 [1986])? Can the Immigration and Naturalization Service (INS) conduct a "factory survey" (in a factory survey, INS agents block the exits of a business and walk through the plant, systematically asking questions of workers of Mexican descent about their presence in the United States and arresting those whom the agents suspect of being illegal immigrants) without the warrant being specific (*INS v. Delgado,* 466 U.S. 210 [1984])? Does the Constitution require the exclusion of admittedly illegally seized evidence by the INS at a deportation hearing (*INS v. Lopez-Mendoza,* 468 U.S. 1032 [1984])? The *Tyler, Dow Chemical,* and *Delgado* cases appear at the end of this chapter.

The questions posed in the preceding cases do not readily fit into the "heavily regulated industry versus other businesses" dichotomy suggested by the Court's decisions. In the criminal area, one crucial variable regarding whether a warrant is required is the notion of an expectation of privacy. The more likely it is that the individual (or business) has a legitimate expectation of privacy, the more likely it is that a warrant will be required. The automobile is an exception to the warrant requirement because the Court has said that individuals have less of an expectation of privacy in an automobile than they do in their homes and businesses. The reason pervasively regulated industries are exceptions to the warrant requirement is that "certain industries have such a history of governmental oversight that *no reasonable expectation of privacy* [italics added] . . . could exist for a proprietor over the stock of such an enterprise. Liquor (*Colonnade*) and firearms (*Biswell*) are industries of this type."[6]

OSHA must obtain a warrant prior to inspecting Barlow's business because, once past the public areas of Barlow's business, Barlow has a reasonable expectation of privacy in his back shop. The Court has said that an individual has a reasonable expectation of privacy in a public telephone booth (*Katz v. United States,* 389 U.S. 347 [1967]) and in a footlocker (*United States v. Chadwick,* 433 U.S. 1 [1977]). Given that, do you think Dow Chemical has a reasonable expectation of privacy from aerial inspections by the EPA? Do you believe that the student, T.L.O., had a reasonable expectation of privacy in her purse? The case that follows presents the interesting question of whether a welfare recipient has a reasonable expectation of privacy in her own home.

WYMAN V. JAMES
400 U.S. 309 (1971)

Justice Blackmun delivered the opinion of the Court, joined by Chief Justice Burger and Justices Black, Harlan, and Stewart. Justice White concurred in part, and dissents were filed by Justices Douglas and Marshall, joined by Brennan.

This appeal presents the issue of whether a beneficiary of the program for Aid to Families with Dependent Children (AFDC) may refuse a home visit by the caseworker without risking the termination of benefits. . . . The District Court majority held that a mother receiving AFDC relief may refuse, without forfeiting her right to that relief, the periodic home visit which the cited New York statutes and regulations prescribe as a condition for the continuance of assistance under the program. The beneficiary's thesis, and that of the District Court majority, is that home visitation is a search and, when not consented to or when not supported by a warrant based on probable cause, violates the beneficiary's Fourth and Fourteenth Amendment rights. . . . Plaintiff Barbara James is the mother of a son, Maurice, who was born in May 1967. They reside in New York City. Mrs. James first applied for AFDC assistance shortly before Maurice's birth. A caseworker made a visit to her apartment at that time without objection. The assistance was authorized.

Two years later, on May 8, 1969, a caseworker wrote Mrs. James that she would visit her home on May 14. Upon receipt of this advice, Mrs. James telephoned the worker that, although she was willing to supply information "reasonable and relevant" to her need for public assistance, any discussion was not to take place at her home. The worker told Mrs. James that she was required by law to visit in her home and that refusal to permit the visit would result in the termination of assistance. Permission was still denied.

On May 13 the City Department of Social Services sent Mrs. James a notice of intent to discontinue assistance because of the visitation refusal. The notice advised the beneficiary of her right to a hearing before a review officer. The hearing was requested and was held on May 27. Mrs. James appeared with an attorney at that hearing. They continued to refuse permission for a worker to visit the James home, but again expressed willingness to cooperate and to permit visits elsewhere. The review officer ruled that the refusal was a proper ground for the termination of assistance. . . .

III

When a case involves a home and some type of official intrusion into that home, as this case appears to do, an immediate and natural reaction is one of concern about Fourth Amendment rights and the protection which that Amendment is intended to afford. Its emphasis indeed is upon one of the most precious aspects of personal security in the home: "The right of the people to be secure in their persons, houses, papers, and effects * * *." This Court has characterized that right as "basic to a free society." *Wolf v. Colorado,* 338 U.S. 25 (1949);

Camara v. Municipal Court, 387 U.S. 523 (1967). And over the years the Court consistently has been most protective of the privacy of the dwelling. In *Camara* Mr. Justice White . . . went on to observe, "Nevertheless, one governing principle, justified by history and by current experience, has consistently been followed: except in certain carefully defined classes of cases, a search of private property without proper consent is 'unreasonable' unless it has been authorized by a valid search warrant." He pointed out, too, that one's Fourth Amendment protection subsists apart from his being suspected of criminal behavior.

IV

This natural and quite proper protective attitude, however, is not a factor in this case, for the seemingly obvious and simple reason that we are not concerned here with any search by the New York social service agency in the Fourth Amendment meaning of that term. It is true that the governing statute and regulations appear to make mandatory the initial home visit and the subsequent periodic "contacts" (which may include home visits) for the inception and continuance of aid. It is also true that the caseworker's posture in the home visit is perhaps, in a sense, both rehabilitative and investigative. But this latter aspect, we think, is given too broad a character and far more emphasis than it deserves if it is equated with a search in the traditional criminal law context. We note, too, that the visitation in itself is not forced or compelled, and that the beneficiary's denial of permission is not a criminal act. If consent to the visitation is withheld, no visitation takes place. The aid then never begins or merely ceases, as the case may be. There is no entry of the home and there is no search.

V

If, however, we were to assume that a caseworker's home visit, before or subsequent to the beneficiary's initial qualification for benefits, somehow (perhaps because the average beneficiary might feel she is in no position to refuse consent to the visit), and despite its interview nature, does possess some of the characteristics of a search in the traditional sense, we nevertheless conclude that the visit does not fall within the Fourth Amendment's proscription. This is because it does not descend to the level of unreasonableness.

There are a number of factors that compel us to conclude that the home visit proposed for Mrs. James is not unreasonable:

1. The public's interest in this particular segment of the area of assistance to the unfortunate is protection and aid for the dependent child whose family requires such aid for that child. The focus is on the child and, further, it is on the child who is dependent.

2. The agency, with tax funds provided from federal as well as from state sources, is fulfilling a public trust. The State, working through its qualified welfare agency, has appropriate and paramount interest and concern in seeing and assuring that the intended and proper objects of that tax-produced assistance are the ones who benefit from the aid it dispenses. Surely it is not unreasonable, in the Fourth Amendment sense or in any other sense of that term, that the State have at its command a gentle means, of limited extent and of practical and considerate application, of achieving that assurance.

3. One who dispenses purely private charity naturally has an interest in and expects to know how his charitable funds are utilized and put to work. The public, when it is the provider, rightly expects the same.

4. The home visit, it is true, is not required by federal statute or regulation. But it has been noted that the visit is "the heart of welfare administration"; that it affords "a personal, rehabilitative orientation, unlike that of most federal programs"; and that the "more pronounced service orientation" effected by Congress with the 1956 amendments to the Social Security Act "gave redoubled importance to the practice of home visiting." Mrs. James, in fact, on this record presents no specific complaint of any unreasonable intrusion of her home and nothing that supports an inference that the desired home visit had as its purpose the obtaining of information as to criminal activity. She complains of no proposed visitation at an awkward or retirement hour. She suggests no forcible entry. She refers to no snooping. She describes no impolite or reprehensible conduct of any kind. She alleges only, in general and nonspecific terms, that on previous visits and, on information and belief, on visitation at the home of other aid recipients, "questions concerning personal relationships, beliefs and behavior are raised and pressed which are unnecessary for a determination of continuing eligibility." Paradoxically, this same complaint could be made

of a conference held elsewhere than in the home, and yet this is what is sought by Mrs. James. The same complaint could be made of the census taker's questions. What Mrs. James appears to want from the agency that provides her and her infant son with the necessities for life is the right to receive those necessities upon her own informational terms, to utilize the Fourth Amendment as a wedge for imposing those terms, and to avoid questions of any kind. We are not persuaded, as Mrs. James would have us be, that all information pertinent to the issue of eligibility can be obtained by the agency through an interview at a place other than the home, or, as the District Court majority suggested, by examining a lease or a birth certificate, or by periodic medical examinations, or by interviews with school personnel. Although these secondary sources might be helpful, they would not always assure verification of actual residence or of actual physical presence in the home, which are requisites for AFDC benefits, or of impending medical needs. And, of course, little children, such as Maurice James, are not yet registered in school. The visit is not one by police or uniformed authority. It is made by a caseworker of some training whose primary objective is, or should be, the welfare, not the prosecution, of the aid recipient for whom the worker has profound responsibility. It seems to us that the situation is akin to that where an Internal Revenue Service agent, in making a routine civil audit of a taxpayer's income tax return, asks that the taxpayer produce for the agent's review some proof of a deduction the taxpayer has asserted to his benefit in the computation of his tax. If the taxpayer refuses, there is, absent fraud, only a disallowance of the claimed deduction and a consequent additional tax. The taxpayer is fully within his "rights" in refusing to produce the proof, but in maintaining and asserting those rights a tax detriment results and it is a detriment of the taxpayer's own making. So here Mrs. James has the "right" to refuse the home visit, but a consequence in the form of cessation of aid, similar to the taxpayer's resultant additional tax, flows from that refusal. The choice is entirely hers, and nothing of constitutional magnitude is involved.

Camara v. Municipal Court, 387 U.S. 523 (1967), and its companion case, *See v. City of Seattle,* 387 U.S. 541 (1967), both by a divided Court, are not inconsistent with our result here. Those cases concerned, respectively, a refusal of entry to city housing inspectors checking for a violation of a building's occupancy permit, and a refusal of entry to a fire department representative interested in compliance with a city's fire code.

In each case a majority of this Court held that the Fourth Amendment barred prosecution for refusal to permit the desired warrantless inspection. *Frank v. Maryland,* 359 U.S. 360, 79 S.Ct. 804, 3 L.Ed.2d 877 (1959), a case that reached an opposing result and that concerned a request by a health officer for entry in order to check the source of a rat infestation, was pro tanto overruled. Both *Frank* and *Camara* involved dwelling quarters. *See* had to do with a commercial warehouse.

But the facts of the three cases are significantly different from those before us. Each concerned a true search for violations. *Frank* was a criminal prosecution for the owner's refusal to permit entry. So, too, was *See. Camara* had to do with a writ of prohibition sought to prevent an already pending criminal prosecution. The community welfare aspects, of course, were highly important, but each case arose in a criminal context where a genuine search was denied and prosecution followed.

In contrast, Mrs. James is not being prosecuted for her refusal to permit the home visit and is not about to be so prosecuted. . . .

VII

Our holding today does not mean, of course, that a termination of benefits upon refusal of a home visit is to be upheld against constitutional challenge under all conceivable circumstances. The early morning mass raid upon homes of welfare recipients is not unknown. See *Parrish v. Civil Service Comm.,* 425 P.2d 223 (1967); *Reich, Midnight Welfare Searches and the Social Security Act,* 72 Yale L. J. 1347 (1963). But that is not this case. Facts of that kind present another case for another day.

We therefore conclude that the home visitation as structured by the New York statutes and regulations is a reasonable administrative tool; that it serves a valid and proper administrative purpose for the dispensation of the AFDC program; that it is not an unwarranted invasion of personal privacy; and that it violates no right guaranteed by the Fourth Amendment. Reversed and remanded with directions to enter a judgment of dismissal.

It is so ordered.

Reversed and remanded with directions.

Questions

1. Do you believe that Mrs. James had a reasonable expectation of privacy?
2. Do you believe that, by accepting "welfare," one should forfeit his or her expectation of privacy?
3. Does James's expectation of privacy have anything to do with the disposition of this case? Why?

The Court has several options open to it when it hears a case involving administrative searches and physical inspections. The Court can find that no warrant is required because a heavily regulated industry is involved, as in *Donovan v. Dewey,* 452 U.S. 594 (1981), which upheld the warrantless inspection of a stone quarry, and *New York v. Burger,* 482 U.S. 691 (1987), which upheld the warrantless search of a junkyard. The Court can find, as it did in the *Wyman* case, that the inspection is not a search, or, if it is, that it is a reasonable search. This is the result reached in the *Dow Chemical* case, the student search case, and the case of the pollution control inspector who sampled the air on the property of the alfalfa company. This is also what the Court said about factory surveys by the INS.

Finally, the Court can find a reasonable expectation of privacy and require a warrant as it did in the *Barlow* case. Most of the Court's recent physical inspection cases, however, allow warrantless searches, rather than follow the *Barlow* precedent. That allowance is somewhat unexpected, given the Nixon-Reagan-Bush appointees' (Rehnquist, O'Connor, Scalia, Kennedy, Souter) proclivity in favor of business. The most recent physical inspection case, however, is the *Dow Chemical* case in 1986, and Kennedy, Souter, Thomas, and Breyer were not on the Court at that time. It would be difficult, though not inconceivable, for the Court to restrict the Fourth Amendment rights of those accused of crime, while expanding search and seizure protection for businesses at the same time.

Before the discussion moves to what government does with the information after obtaining it, the student should be aware that agencies are not necessarily limited to the three methods discussed earlier (requiring the regulated to keep certain records, subpoena, and physical inspection). For example, you may have read in the newspaper that the California Department of Consumer Affairs caught Sears Roebuck bilking auto repair customers. This information was obtained through a "sting" operation, in which the agency took cars in top mechanical condition to Sears Auto Centers, where investigators were overcharged an average of $223 per car.[7]

SECTION B: AGENCIES AS
REPOSITORIES OF INFORMATION

"The way we think about information [has] changed during the past 20 years. Government information in the 1980s has become a tangible commodity with a dollar value. 'Information Management' is being defined as a multi-faceted process involving the collection, processing, storage, transmission and use of information."[8] As an undergraduate student in the early 1960s, I was continually frustrated because government conducted its business in secret and the citizens knew only what government wanted them to know. For the most part, that has changed. It has changed because of the Freedom of Information Act (FOIA, 1966), the Privacy Act (1974), and the Open Meeting Act (1976). The FOIA[9] requires agencies to release information in their possession if another party has requested such information, unless the information is protected by an exemption under the act. The Privacy Act,[10] better known as the Buckley Amendment, provides for an individual to access his or her records that are in an agency's possession. It allows the citizen to correct such records, and it provides the individual with a remedy of money damages in the event of unauthorized release of such information by an agency. In the Sunshine Act or Open Meetings Act,[11] the government requires those agencies headed by a "collegial body" to notify the public and to conduct "official agency business" in public. Again, there are exceptions.

By now, most states have similar legislation, so anyone who works for a governmental agency at any level should be familiar with administrative law regarding information. At the federal level, neither the Privacy Act nor the Sunshine Act has spawned much litigation (for an example, see *Common Cause v. NRC,* 674 F.2d 921 [D.C. Cir. 1982]), but the FOIA has been litigated a lot.

THE FREEDOM OF INFORMATION ACT

The FOIA is presented in the appendix of this book (sec. 552 of the APA), and you should read it now. According to Professor Latte E. Feinberg, "the FOIA uneasily rests on four broad, often incompatible premises." It is based on the belief that "an informed electorate is essential to safeguard democracy; publicity is one of the best protections against the potential for official misconduct; privacy is a fundamental right and corresponds with a need to restrict government's intrusions into people's lives; and secrecy is endemic to bureaucracy and perhaps facilitates organizational efficiency."[12] In her study of the government's processing of FOIA requests, Feinberg documented that specific agencies processed the following FOIA requests in 1985: Department of Defense 83,173; Department of Health and Human Services 105,687; Department of the Treasury 23,217; and Department of Energy 5,723.[13] The FBI occasionally must call agents in from the field to help meet statutory deadlines in processing FOIA requests.

The key to understanding the litigation surrounding FOIA requests is to understand the exemptions. Although there are nine exemptions under the FOIA, this discussion concentrates on those most difficult to understand and that have spawned considerable litigation. Those exemptions are Number 4, the trade secrets and commercial information exemption; Number 5, the evidentiary privilege exemption; and Number 6, the invasion of privacy exemption.

You will notice from your reading of the FOIA that the language favors release of information by the agency. The requester need only reasonably describe the material, and the agency is given only ten days to identify the material and make an initial decision to either release or withhold (although an extension for an additional ten days is possible). If the agency decision is to withhold, then the requester must be informed of the reason and of the right to appeal the withholding decision to the head of the agency. The agency must identify by name the bureaucrat who made the decision to withhold. If the requester appeals to the head of the agency, that official must make a decision within twenty days. If the requester decides to appeal the agency head's decision to the federal courts, such suits are to be placed in the federal courts' expedited calendar, and the government has only thirty days to answer the requester's complaint. Attorney fees are possible for requesters who "substantially prevail" in the courts. If the agency does provide the requested material, the agency may not charge a fee that exceeds the direct costs of search and duplication. Finally, when an agency determines that some portions of a document are exempt and not releasable, the act requires that the agency block out the exempt material and release the rest.[14] Most of the language in the FOIA, exacting agency action within specific time frames, was added by amendments in 1974 and 1976 because Congress found "foot dragging by the federal bureaucracy and difficulties in convincing the 'secrecy minded bureaucrat that public records are public property.' "[15]

Section b, Number 4, of the FOIA reads as follows: "(b) This section does not apply to matters that are . . . (4) trade secrets and commercial or financial information obtained from a person and privileged or confidential." This means that if an agency possesses information that an individual has requested and if the information constitutes a trade secret, then the agency can—if it chooses—withhold the information. If it is not a trade secret but is commercial or financial information obtained from an individual or a business or corporation (not obtained from another governmental agency) and if the information is either privileged (attorney-client) or confidential, then the agency can withhold. Most of this is not difficult to recognize. We can recognize a trade secret (usually). We do recognize commercial or financial information, and we know whether it has come from a business, individual, or corporation. The business, individual, or corporation will inform us if the information is clothed with a legally recognized privilege. The question of whether the information sought is confidential is the problem, and the case you are about to read defines the term *confidential.*

NATIONAL PARKS AND CONSERVATION ASSOCIATION V. MORTON
498 F.2d 765 (1974)

The opinion is by Circuit Judge Tamm.

Appellant brought this action under the Freedom of Information Act, 5 U.S.C. 552 (1970), seeking to enjoin officials of the Department of the Interior from refusing to permit inspection and copying of certain agency records concerning concessions operated in the national parks. The district court granted summary judgment for the defendant on the ground that the information sought is exempt from disclosure under section 552(b)(4) of the Act which states: (b) This section does not apply to matters that are . . . (4) trade secrets and commercial or financial information obtained from a person and privileged or confidential. . . . In order to bring a matter (other than a trade secret) within this exemption, it must be shown that the information is (a) commercial or financial, (b) obtained from a person, and (c) privileged or confidential. Since the parties agree that the matter in question is financial information obtained from a person and that it is not privileged, the only issue on appeal is whether the information is "confidential" within the meaning of the exemption.

I

Unfortunately, the statute contains no definition of the word "confidential." In the past, our decisions concerning this exemption have been guided by the following passage from the Senate Report. . . . This exception is necessary to protect the confidentiality of information which is obtained by the Government through questionnaires or other inquiries, but which would customarily not be released to the public by the person from whom it was obtained. . . . Whether particular information would customarily be disclosed to the public by the person from whom it was obtained is not the only relevant inquiry in determining whether that information is "confidential" for purposes of section 552(b)(4). A court must also be satisfied that non-disclosure is justified by the legislative purpose which underlies the exemption. Our first task, therefore, is to ascertain the ends which Congress sought to attain in enacting the exemption for "commercial or financial" information. In general, the various exemptions included in the statute serve two interests—that of the Government in efficient operation and that of persons supplying certain kinds of information in maintaining its secrecy. The Senate Report acknowledges both of these legislative goals: . . .

The "financial information" exemption recognizes the need of government policymakers to have access to commercial and financial data. Unless persons having necessary information can be assured that it will remain confidential, they may decline to cooperate with officials and the ability of the Government to make intelligent, well informed decisions will be impaired. This concern finds expression in the legislative history as well as the case law. . . . Apart from encouraging cooperation with the Government by persons having information useful to officials, section 552(b)(4) serves another distinct but equally important purpose. It protects persons who submit financial or commercial data to government agencies from the competitive disadvantages which would result from its publication. The need for such protection was raised several times during hearings. . . .

In each of these instances it was suggested that an exemption for "trade secrets" would avert the danger that valuable business information would be made public by agencies which had obtained it pursuant to statute or regulation. A representative of the Department of Justice endorsed this idea at length: A second problem area lies in the large body of the Government's information involving private business data and trade secrets, the disclosure of which could severely damage individual enterprise and cause widespread disruption of the channels of commerce. Much of this information is volunteered by employers, merchants, manufacturers, carriers, exporters, and other businessmen and professional people for purposes of market news services, labor and wage statistics, commercial reports, and other Government services which are considered useful to the cooperating reporters, the public, and the agencies. Perhaps the greater part of such information is exacted, by statute, in the course of necessary regulatory or other governmental functions. Again, not only as a matter of fairness, but as a matter of right, and as a matter basic to our free enterprise system, private business information should be afforded appropriate protection, at least from competitors.

A particularly significant aspect of the latter statement is its recognition of a twofold justification for the exemption of commercial material: (1) encouraging cooperation by those who are not obliged to provide information to the government and (2) protecting the rights of those who must.

II

The financial information sought by appellant consists of audits conducted upon the books of companies operating concessions in national parks, annual financial statements filed by the concessionaires with the National Park Service, and other financial information. The district court concluded that this information was of the kind "that would not generally be made available for public perusal." While we discern no error in this finding, we do not think that, by itself, it supports application of the financial information exemption. The district court must also inquire into the possibility that disclosure will harm legitimate private or governmental interests in secrecy.

On the record before us the Government has no apparent interest in preventing disclosure of the matter in question. Some, if not all, of the information is supplied to the Park Service pursuant to statute. Whether supplied pursuant to statute, regulation, or some less formal mandate, however, it is clear that disclosure of this material to the Park Service is a mandatory condition of the concessionaires' right to operate in national parks. Since the concessionaires are required to provide this financial information to the government, there is presumably no danger that public disclosure will impair the ability of the Government to obtain this information in the future.

As we have already explained, however, section 552(b)(4) may be applicable even though the Government itself has no interest in keeping the information secret. The exemption may be invoked for the benefit of the person who has provided commercial or financial information if it can be shown that public disclosure is likely to cause substantial harm to his competitive position. Appellant argues that such a showing cannot be made in this case because the concessionaires are monopolists, protected from competition during the term of their contracts and enjoying a statutory preference over other bidders at renewal time. In other words, appellant argues that disclosure cannot impair the concessionaires' competitive position because they have no competition. While this argument is very compelling, we are reluctant to accept it without first providing appellee the opportunity to develop a fuller record in the district court. It might be shown, for example, that disclosure of information about concession activities will injure the concessioner's competitive position in a nonconcession enterprise. In that case disclosure would be improper. This matter is therefore remanded to the district court for the purpose of determining whether public disclosure of the information in question poses the likelihood of substantial harm to the competitive positions of the parties from whom it has been obtained. If the district court finds in the affirmative, then the information is "confidential" within the meaning of section 552(b)(4) and exempt from disclosure. If only some parts of the information are confidential, the district court may prevent inappropriate disclosures by excising from otherwise disclosable documents any matters which are confidential in the sense that the word has been construed in this opinion.

The judgment of the district court is reversed and this matter is remanded for further proceedings consistent with this opinion.

So ordered.

Question

The Court provides a two-pronged test for the confidentiality of requested material. First, material is confidential when the person (or business) from whom it was obtained would not ordinarily release it to the public. Second, withholding of information must fit the legislative purpose for the exemption. In the preceding case, the Court lists two legislative purposes for Exemption 4. Can you identify them?

Table 5.1. Decision Tree: FOIA Exemption 4

1. Is the material a trade secret?

   YES = withhold

   NO = Go to #2

2. Is the material financial or commercial information?

   YES = Go to #3

   NO = It is not covered by this exemption and release unless covered by another exemption.

3. Was the material obtained from an individual or business?

   YES = Go to #4

   NO = If it was obtained from another agency, look to Exemption 5, but it is releasable under Exemption 4.

4. Is it privileged information (attorney-client)?

   YES = withhold

   NO = go to #5

5. Is the material confidential?

   A. Is it the kind of information that the person who gave it to the agency would not want released to the public?

      YES = potentially confidential, proceed to B

      NO = not confidential—release

   B. If the information were withheld, would that be consistent with the legislative purpose behind the exemption?

      B-1. Would release impair the government's ability to obtain information in the future?

         YES = probably confidential, withhold

         NO = Do not release the information yet; proceed to B-2.

      B-2. Would release of the information harm the competitive position of the individual or business that provided it?

         YES = confidential, withhold

         NO = Even if the material is not the kind that the provider would release to the public, if both B-1 and B-2 are negative, then the material is releasable because to withhold would not be consistent with the reasons why Congress created the exemption.

As you are confronted with situations in which commercial or financial information or both are sought and an agency must decide whether to release or withhold, it may help you to follow the decision tree in Table 5.1.

The case you are about to read next, *Chrysler v. Brown,* addresses the question of what happens when an agency possesses information that it clearly could withhold under Exemption 4 but chooses to release anyway. This is a difficult and confusing case, but you will understand it better if you follow the decision tree and try to answer the following questions: (a) Why does the agency want to release exemptible information? The agency argues that it has to, but by what authority? (b) The Trade Secrets Act[16] makes it a crime for bureaucrats to release certain information that comes to them during the course of employment. Why cannot Chrysler use this law to stop the agency in this case from releasing information?

CHRYSLER V. BROWN
441 U.S. 281 (1979)

Justice Rehnquist delivered the opinion for a unanimous Court, with Justice Marshall concurring.

The expanding range of federal regulatory activity and growth in the Government sector of the economy have increased federal agencies' demands for information about the activities of private individuals and corporations. These developments have paralleled a related concern about secrecy in Government and abuse of power.

The Freedom of Information Act (hereinafter FOIA) was a response to this concern, but it has also had a largely unforeseen tendency to exacerbate the uneasiness of those who comply with governmental demands for information. For under the FOIA third parties have been able to obtain Government files containing information submitted by corporations and individuals who thought that the information would be held in confidence.

This case belongs to a class that has been popularly denominated "reverse-FOIA" suits. The Chrysler Corp. (hereinafter Chrysler) seeks to enjoin agency disclosure on the grounds that it is inconsistent with the FOIA and 18 U.S.C. § 1905, a criminal statute with origins in the 19th century that proscribes disclosure of certain classes of business and personal information. We agree with the Court of Appeals for the Third Circuit that the FOIA is purely a disclosure statute and affords

Chrysler no private right of action to enjoin agency disclosure. But we cannot agree with that court's conclusion that this disclosure is "authorized by law" within the meaning of § 1905. Therefore, we vacate the Court of Appeals' judgment and remand so that it can consider whether the documents at issue in this case fall within the terms of § 1905.

I

As a party to numerous Government contracts, Chrysler is required to comply with Executive Orders 11246 and 11375, which charge the Secretary of Labor with ensuring that corporations that benefit from Government contracts provide equal employment opportunity regardless of race or sex. The United States Department of Labor's Office of Federal Contract Compliance Programs (OFCCP) has promulgated regulations which require Government contractors to furnish reports and other information about their affirmative-action programs and the general composition of their work forces. . . .

Regulations promulgated by the Secretary of Labor provide for public disclosure of information from records of the OFCCP and its compliance agencies. Those regulations state that notwithstanding exemption from mandatory disclosure under the FOIA, 5 U.S.C. § 552, "records obtained or generated pursuant to Executive Order 11246 (as amended) . . . shall be made available for inspection and copying . . . if it is determined that the requested inspection or copying furthers the public interest and does not impede any of the functions of the OFCC or the Compliance Agencies except in the case of records disclosure of which is prohibited by law." . . .

It is the voluntary disclosure contemplated by this regulation, over and above that mandated by the FOIA, which is the gravamen of Chrysler's complaint in this case.

This controversy began on May 14, 1975, when the DLA [Defense Logistics Agency] informed Chrysler that third parties had made an FOIA request for disclosure of the 1974 AAP [affirmative action program] for Chrysler's Newark, Del., assembly plant and an October 1974 CIR [complaint investigation report] for the same facility. Nine days later, Chrysler objected to release of the requested information, relying on OFCCP's disclosure regulations and on exemptions to the FOIA. Chrysler also requested a copy of the CIR, since it had never seen it. DLA responded the following week that it had determined that the requested material was subject to disclosure under the FOIA and the OFCCP disclosure rules, and that both documents would be released five days later.

On the day the documents were to be released Chrysler filed a complaint in the United States District Court for Delaware seeking to enjoin release of the Newark documents. The District Court granted a temporary restraining order barring disclosure of the Newark documents and requiring that DLA give five days' notice to Chrysler before releasing any similar documents. Pursuant to this order, Chrysler was informed on July 1, 1975, that DLA had received a similar request for information about Chrysler's Hamtramck, Mich., plant. Chrysler amended its complaint and obtained a restraining order with regard to the Hamtramck disclosure as well.

Chrysler made three arguments in support of its prayer for an injunction: that disclosure was barred by the FOIA; that it was inconsistent with 18 U.S.C. § 1905, 42 U.S.C. § 2000e-8(e), and 44 U.S.C. § 3508, which for ease of reference will be referred to as the "confidentiality statutes"; and finally that disclosure was an abuse of agency discretion insofar as it conflicted with OFCCP rules. The District Court held that it had jurisdiction to subject the disclosure decision to review under the Administrative Procedure Act (APA). It conducted a trial de novo on all of Chrysler's claims; both sides presented extensive expert testimony during August 1975.

On April 20, 1976, the District Court issued its opinion. It held that certain of the requested information, the "manning" tables, fell within Exemption 4 of the FOIA. The District Court reasoned from this holding that the tables may or must be withheld, depending on applicable agency regulations, and that here a governing regulation required that the information be withheld. Pursuant to 5 U.S.C. § 301, the enabling statute which gives federal department heads control over department records, the Secretary of Labor has promulgated a regulation, 29 C.F.R. § 70.21(a) (1978), stating that no officer or employee of the Department is to violate 18 U.S.C. § 1905. That section imposes criminal sanctions on Government employees who make unauthorized disclosure of certain classes of information submitted to a Government agency, including trade secrets and confidential statistical data. In essence, the District Court read § 1905 as not merely a prohibition of unauthorized disclosure of sensitive information by Government employees, but as a restriction on official agency actions taken pursuant to promulgated regulations. Both sides appealed, and the Court of Appeals for the Third Circuit vacated the District Court's judgment. Because of a conflict in the Circuits and the general importance of these "reverse-FOIA" cases, we granted certiorari, and now vacate the judgment of the Third Circuit and remand for further proceedings.

II

[1] We have decided a number of FOIA cases in the last few years. Although we have not had to face squarely the question whether the FOIA ex proprio vigore forbids governmental agencies from disclosing certain classes of information to the public, we have in the course of at least one opinion intimated an answer. We have, moreover, consistently recognized that the basic objective of the Act is disclosure. In contending that the FOIA bars disclosure of the requested equal employment opportunity information, Chrysler relies on the Act's nine exemptions and argues that they require an agency to withhold exempted material. In this case it relies specifically on Exemption 4: "(b) [FOIA] does not apply to matters that are . . . (4) trade

secrets and commercial or financial information obtained from a person and privileged or confidential. . . ." Chrysler contends that the nine exemptions in general, and Exemption 4 in particular, reflect a sensitivity to the privacy interests of private individuals and nongovernmental entities. That contention may be conceded without inexorably requiring the conclusion that the exemptions impose affirmative duties on an agency to withhold information sought. In fact, that conclusion is not supported by the language, logic, or history of the Act. The organization of the Act is straightforward. Subsection (a), 5 U.S.C. § 552(a), places a general obligation on the agency to make information available to the public and sets out specific modes of disclosure for certain classes of information.

Subsection (b), which lists the exemptions, simply states that the specified material is not subject to the disclosure obligations set out in subsection (a). By its terms, subsection (b) demarcates the agency's obligation to disclose; it does not foreclose disclosure.

. . . We simply hold here that Congress did not design the FOIA exemptions to be mandatory bars to disclosure. We therefore conclude that Congress did not limit an agency's discretion to disclose information when it enacted the FOIA. It necessarily follows that the Act does not afford Chrysler any right to enjoin agency disclosure.

III

Chrysler contends, however, that even if its suit for injunctive relief cannot be based on the FOIA, such an action can be premised on the Trade Secrets Act, 18 U.S.C. § 1905. The Act provides: "Whoever, being an officer or employee of the United States or of any department or agency thereof, publishes, divulges, discloses, or makes known in any manner or to any extent not authorized by law any information coming to him in the course of his employment or official duties or by reason of any examination or investigation made by, or return, report or record made to or filed with, such department or agency or officer or employee thereof, which information concerns or relates to the trade secrets, processes, operations, style of work, or apparatus, or to the identity, confidential statistical data, amount or source of any income, profits, losses, or expenditures of any person, firm, partnership, corporation, or association; or permits any income return or copy thereof or any book contain-

ing any abstract or particulars thereof to be seen or examined by any person except as provided by law; shall be fined not more than $1,000, or imprisoned not more than one year, or both; and shall be removed from office or employment." There are necessarily two parts to Chrysler's argument: that § 1905 is applicable to the type of disclosure threatened in this case, and that it affords Chrysler a private right of action to obtain injunctive relief.

A

The Court of Appeals held that § 1905 was not applicable to the agency disclosure at issue here because such disclosure was "authorized by law" within the meaning of the Act. The court found the source of that authorization to be the OFCCP regulations that DLA relied on in deciding to disclose information on the Hamtramck and Newark plants. Chrysler contends here that these agency regulations are not "law" within the meaning of § 1905. . . .

In order for a regulation to have the "force and effect of law," it must have certain substantive characteristics and be the product of certain procedural requisites. The central distinction among agency regulations found in the APA is that between "substantive rules" on the one hand and "interpretative rules, general statements of policy, or rules of agency organization, procedure, or practice" on the other. A "substantive rule" is not defined in the APA, and other authoritative sources essentially offer definitions by negative inference. But in *Morton v. Ruiz,* 415 U.S. 199 (1974), we noted a characteristic inherent in the concept of a "substantive rule." We described a substantive rule—or a "legislative-type rule,"—as one "affecting individual rights and obligations." This characteristic is an important touchstone for distinguishing those rules that may be "binding" or have the "force of law." That an agency regulation is "substantive," however, does not by itself give it the "force and effect of law." The legislative power of the United States is vested in the Congress, and the exercise of quasi-legislative authority by governmental departments and agencies must be rooted in a grant of such power by the Congress and subject to limitations which that body imposes. . . . Likewise the promulgation of these regulations must conform with any procedural requirements imposed by Congress. For agency discretion is limited not only by substantive, statutory grants of authority, but also by the procedural requirements which "assure fairness and mature consideration of rules of general application." The pertinent procedural limitations in this case are those found in the APA.

The regulations relied on by the respondents in this case as providing "authoriz[ation] by law" within the meaning of § 1905 certainly affect individual rights and obligations; they govern the public's right to information in records obtained under Executive Order 11246 and the confidentiality rights of those who submit information to OFCCP and its compliance agencies. It is a much closer question, however, whether they are the product of a congressional grant of legislative authority.

But in order for such regulations to have the "force and effect of law," it is necessary to establish a nexus between the regulations and some delegation of the requisite legislative authority by Congress. For purposes of this case, it is not necessary to decide whether Executive Order 11246 as amended is authorized by the Federal Property and Administrative Services Act of 1949, Titles VI and VII of the Civil Rights Act of 1964, the Equal Employment Opportunity Act of 1972, or some more general notion that the Executive can impose reasonable contractual requirements in the exercise of its procurement authority.

The pertinent inquiry is whether under any of the arguable statutory grants of authority the OFCCP disclosure regulations relied on by the respondents are reasonably within the contemplation of that grant of authority. We think that it is clear that when it enacted these statutes, Congress was not concerned with public disclosure of trade secrets or confidential business information, and, unless we were to hold that any federal statute that implies some authority to collect information must grant legislative authority to disclose that information to the public, it is simply not possible to find in these statutes a delegation of the disclosure authority asserted by the respondents here. There is also a procedural defect in the OFCCP disclosure regulations which precludes courts from affording them the force and effect of law. That defect is a lack of strict compliance with the APA. Section 4 of the APA, 5 U.S.C. § 553, specifies that an agency shall afford interested persons general notice of proposed rule-making and an opportunity to comment before a substantive rule is promulgated. When the Secretary of Labor published the regulations pertinent in this case, he stated: "As the changes made

by this document relate solely to interpretive rules, general statements of policy, and to rules of agency procedure and practice, neither notice of proposed rule making nor public participation therein is required by 5 U.S.C. 553. We need not decide whether these regulations are properly characterized as " 'interpretative rules.' "

It is enough that such regulations are not properly promulgated as substantive rules, and therefore not the product of procedures which Congress prescribed as necessary prerequisites to giving a regulation the binding effect of law. An interpretative regulation or general statement of agency policy cannot be the "authoriz[ation] by law" required by § 1905. We reject, however, Chrysler's contention that the Trade Secrets Act affords a private right of action to enjoin disclosure in violation of the statute. In *Cort v. Ash,* 422 U.S. 66 (1975), we noted that this Court has rarely implied a private right of action under a criminal statute, and where it has done so "there was at least a statutory basis for inferring that a civil cause of action of some sort lay in favor of someone." Nothing in § 1905 prompts such an inference. Nor are other pertinent circumstances outlined in *Cort* present here. As our review of the legislative history of § 1905—or lack of same—might suggest, there is no indication of legislative intent to create a private right of action. Most importantly, a private right of action under § 1905 is not "necessary to make effective the congressional purpose," for we find that review of DLA's decision to disclose Chrysler's employment data is available under the APA. . . .

IV

Therefore, we conclude that DLA's decision to disclose the Chrysler reports is reviewable agency action and Chrysler is a person "adversely affected or aggrieved" within the meaning of § 10(a). . . . For the reasons previously stated, we believe any disclosure that violates § 1905 is "not in accordance with law" within the meaning of 5 U.S.C. § 706(2)(A). De novo review by the District Court is ordinarily not necessary to decide whether a contemplated disclosure runs afoul of § 1905. The District Court in this case concluded that disclosure of some of Chrysler's documents was barred by § 1905, but the Court of Appeals did not reach the issue. We shall therefore vacate the Court of Appeals' judgment and remand for further proceedings consistent with this opinion in order that the

Court of Appeals may consider whether the contemplated disclosures would violate the prohibition of § 1905.

Since the decision regarding this substantive issue—the scope of § 1905—will necessarily have some effect on the proper form of judicial review pursuant to § 706(2), we think it unnecessary, and therefore unwise, at the present stage of this case for us to express any additional views on that issue. Vacated and remanded.

Question

What did the Court decide about whether an agency may release otherwise exempt information?

Two events took place in 1987 that modify the Court's decision in *Chrysler v. Brown*. First, a D.C. Circuit Court interpreted the Trade Secrets Act to require agencies to withhold material that qualifies for a Number 4 exemption.[17] Second, President Reagan issued an executive order that requires agencies to notify a provider when an agency is considering a request to release material that qualifies for exemption. It requires the agency to permit the provider to present arguments to the agency.

Exemption 5 states: "(5) inter-agency or intra-agency memorandums or letters which would not be available by law to a party other than an agency in litigation with the agency." This means that those materials that a party suing the agency would not be able to obtain through the discovery process are exempt. The *discovery process* is simply an "exchange of information between sides in a lawsuit."[18] This process can be formal, controlled by an administrative law judge, or it can be less formal communication between attorneys. In any case, not all information requested by the other side in a lawsuit need be released. For example, some information is protected as privileged (attorney-client), and a prosecutor is not obligated to turn over to the defense any information that is not material to the case (information that could influence the outcome). In terms of the FOIA, Congress apparently intended to exempt under Number 5 two kinds of privileged material: (a) Attorney-client work product is exempted, and (b) those materials clothed with executive privilege may be withheld.

The notion of executive privilege is addressed in two other FOIA exemptions, Number 1 and Number 7. Exemption 1 exempts classified material, especially in the area of defense or foreign policy. Exemption 7 is referred to as the "law enforcement exemption" and could be used, for example, to protect the identity of an informant. The executive privilege contemplated in Exemption 5 is what I call "decisional executive privilege," in that it is meant to preserve the integrity of the decision-making process. The concept is addressed in the case that you are about to read, but it is aimed at ensuring that a decision maker is presented with all options and full information before a decision is made. More accurately, executive privilege in this context means to ensure that an option, piece of advice, or information is not withheld from the decision maker's consideration out of fear that the advice will be held up to public ridicule at a later date.

NATIONAL LABOR RELATIONS BOARD V. SEARS, ROEBUCK & COMPANY
421 U.S. 132 (1975)

Justice White delivered the opinion for a unanimous Court, with Chief Justice Burger concurring and Justice Powell not participating.

The National Labor Relations Board (the Board) and its General Counsel seek to set aside an order of the United States District Court directing disclosure to respondent, Sears, Roebuck & Co. (Sears), pursuant to the Freedom of Information Act, of certain memoranda, known as "Advice Memoranda" and "Appeals Memoranda," and related documents generated by the Office of the General Counsel in the course of deciding whether or not to permit the filing with the Board of unfair labor practice complaints.

The Act's background and its principal objectives are described in *EPA v. Mink,* 410 U.S. 73 (1973), and will not be repeated here. It is sufficient to note for present purposes that the Act seeks "to establish a general philosophy of full agency disclosure unless information is exempted under clearly delineated statutory language." As the Act is structured, virtually every document generated by an agency is available to the public in one form or another, unless it falls within one of the Act's nine exemptions.... The Act expressly states, however, that the disclosure obligation "does not apply" to those documents described in the nine enumerated exempt categories listed in § 552(b)....

Sears claims, and the courts below ruled, that the memoranda sought are expressions of legal and policy decisions already adopted by the agency and constitute "final opinions" and "instructions to staff that affect a member of the public," both categories being expressly disclosable under § 552(a)(2) of the Act, pursuant to its purposes to prevent the creation of "secret law." In any event, Sears claims, the memoranda are nonexempt "identifiable records" which must be disclosed under § 552(a)(3). The General Counsel, on the other hand, claims that the memoranda sought here are not final opinions under § 552(a)(2) and that even if they are "identifiable records" otherwise disclosable under § 552(a)(3), they are exempt under § 552(b), principally as "intra-agency" communications under § 552(b)(5) (Exemption 5), made in the course of formulating agency decisions on legal and policy matters.

II

This case arose in the following context. By letter dated July 14, 1971, Sears requested that the General Counsel disclose to it pursuant to the Act all Advice and Appeals Memoranda issued within the previous five years on the subjects of "the propriety of withdrawals by employers or unions from multi-employer bargaining, disputes as to commencement date of negotiations, or conflicting interpretations in any other context of the Board's Retail Associates rule." The letter also sought the subject-matter index or digest of Advice and Appeals Memoranda. The letter urged disclosure on the theory that the Advice and Appeals Memoranda are the only source of agency "law" on some issues. By letter dated July 23, 1971, the General Counsel declined Sears' disclosure request in full. The letter stated that Advice Memoranda are simply "guides for a Regional Director" and are not final; that they are exempt from disclosure under 5 U.S.C. § 552(b)(5) as "intra-agency memoranda" which reflect the thought processes of the General Counsel's staff; and that they are exempt pursuant to 5 U.S.C. § 552(b)(7) as part of the "investigative process." The letter said that Appeals Memoranda were not indexed by subject matter and, therefore, the General Counsel was "unable" to comply with Sears' request. In further explanation of his decision, with respect to Appeals Memoranda, the General Counsel wrote to Sears on August 4, 1971, and stated that Appeals Memoranda which ordered the filing of a complaint were not "final opinions." The letter further stated that those Appeals Memoranda which were "final opinions, i.e., those in which an appeal was denied" and which directed that no complaint be filed, numbered several thousand, and that in the General Counsel's view they had no precedential significance. Accordingly, if disclosable at all, they were disclosable under 5 U.S.C. § 552(a)(3) relating to "identifiable records." The General Counsel then said that Sears had failed adequately to identify the material sought and that he could not justify the expenditure of time necessary for the agency to identify them.

. . . On August 4, 1971, Sears filed a complaint pursuant to the Act seeking a declaration that the General Counsel's refusal to disclose the Advice and Appeals Memoranda and indices thereof requested by Sears violated the Act, and an injunction enjoining continued violations of the Act. On August 24, 1971, the current General Counsel took office. In order to give him time to develop his own disclosure policy, the filing of his answer was postponed until February 3, 1972. The answer denied that the Act required disclosure of any of the documents sought but referred to a letter of the same date in which the General Counsel informed Sears that he would make available the index to Advice Memoranda and also all Advice and Appeals Memoranda in cases which had been closed—either because litigation before the Board had been completed or because a decision not to file a complaint had become final. He stated, however, that he would not disclose the memoranda in open cases; that he would, in any event, delete names of witnesses and "security sensitive" matter from the memoranda he did disclose; and that he did not consider the General Counsel's Office bound to pursue this new policy "in all instances" in the future.

Not wholly satisfied with the voluntary disclosures offered and made by the General Counsel, Sears moved for summary judgement and the General Counsel did likewise. Sears thus continued to seek memoranda in open cases. Moreover, Sears objected to the deletions in the memoranda in closed cases and asserted that many Appeals Memoranda were unintelligible because they incorporated by reference documents which were not themselves disclosed and also referred to "the circumstances of the case" which were not set out and about which Sears was ignorant. The General Counsel contended that all of the documents were exempt from disclosure as "intra-agency" memoranda within the coverage of 5 U.S.C. § 552(b)(5); and that the documents incorporated by reference were exempt from disclosure as "investigatory files" pursuant to 5 U.S.C. § 552(b)(7). The parties also did not agree as to the function of an Advice Memorandum. Sears claimed that Advice Memoranda are binding on Regional Directors. The General Counsel claimed that they are not, noting the fact that the Regional Director himself has the delegated power to issue a complaint. The District Court granted Sears' motion for summary judgment and denied that of the General Counsel. . . .

III

It is clear, and the General Counsel concedes, that Appeals and Advice Memoranda are at the least "identifiable records" which must be disclosed on demand, unless they fall within one of the Act's exempt categories. It is also clear that, if the memoranda do fall within one of the Act's exempt categories, our inquiry is at an end, for the Act "does not apply" to such documents. Thus our inquiry, strictly speaking, must be into the scope of the exemptions which the General Counsel claims to be applicable—principally Exemption 5 relating to "intra-agency memorandums." The General Counsel also concedes, however, and we hold for the reasons set forth below, that Exemption 5 does not apply to any document which falls within the meaning of the phrase "final opinion . . . made in the adjudication of cases." The General Counsel argues, therefore, as he must, that no Advice or Appeals Memorandum is a final opinion made in the adjudication of a case and that all are "intra-agency" memoranda within the coverage of Exemption 5. He bases this argument in large measure on what he claims to be his lack of adjudicative authority. It is true that the General Counsel lacks any authority finally to adjudicate an unfair labor practice claim in favor of the claimant; but he does possess the authority to adjudicate such a claim against the claimant through his power to decline to file a complaint with the Board. We hold for reasons more fully set forth below that those Advice and Appeals Memoranda which explain decisions by the General Counsel not to file a complaint are "final opinions" made in the adjudication of a case and fall outside the scope of Exemption 5; but that those Advice and Appeals Memoranda which explain decisions by the General Counsel to file a complaint and commence litigation before the Board are not "final opinions" made in the adjudication of a case and do fall within the scope of Exemption 5. . . .

A

The parties are in apparent agreement that Exemption 5 withholds from a member of the public documents which a private party could not discover in litigation with the agency. Since virtually any document not privileged may be discovered by the appropriate litigant, if it is relevant to his litigation, and since the Act clearly intended to give any member of the public as much right to disclosure as one with a special interest therein, it is reasonable to construe Exemption 5 to exempt those documents, and only those documents, normally privileged in the civil discovery context. The privileges claimed by petitioners to be relevant to this case are (i) the "generally . . . recognized" privilege for "confidential intra-agency advisory opinions . . . ," disclosure of which "would be injurious to the consultative functions of government . . ." (sometimes referred to as "executive privilege"), and (ii) the attorney-client and attorney work-product privileges generally available to all litigants. . . .

(i)

That Congress had the Government's executive privilege specifically in mind in adopting Exemption 5 is clear. The precise contours of the privilege in the context of this case are less clear, but may be gleaned from expressions of legislative purpose and the prior case law. The cases uniformly rest the privilege on the policy of protecting the "decision making processes of government agencies," and focus on documents "reflecting advisory opinions, recommendations and deliberations comprising part of a process by which governmental decisions and policies are formulated." The point, plainly made in the Senate Report, is that the "frank discussion of legal or policy matters" in writing might

be inhibited if the discussion were made public; and that the "decisions" and "policies formulated" would be the poorer as a result. As a lower court has pointed out, "there are enough incentives as it is for playing it safe and listing with the wind," and as we have said in an analogous context, "[h]uman experience teaches that those who expect public dissemination of their remarks may well temper candor with a concern for appearances . . . to the detriment of the decision-making process." *United States v. Nixon,* 418 U.S. 683 (1974).

Manifestly, the ultimate purpose of this long-recognized privilege is to prevent injury to the quality of agency decisions. The quality of a particular agency decision will clearly be affected by the communications received by the decision-maker on the subject of the decision prior to the time the decision is made. However, it is difficult to see how the quality of a decision will be affected by communications with respect to the decision occurring after the decision is finally reached; and therefore equally difficult to see how the quality of the decision will be affected by forced disclosure of such communications, as long as prior communications and the ingredients of the decision-making process are not disclosed. Accordingly, the lower courts have uniformly drawn a distinction between predecisional communications, which are privileged, and communications made after the decision and designed to explain it, which are not. This distinction is supported not only by the lesser injury to the decision-making process flowing from disclosure of post-decisional communications, but also, in the case of those communications which explain the decision, by the increased public interest in knowing the basis for agency policy already adopted. The public is only marginally concerned with reasons supporting a policy which an agency has rejected, or with reasons which might have supplied, but did not supply, the basis for a policy which was actually adopted on a different ground. In contrast, the public is vitally concerned with the reasons which did supply the basis for an agency policy actually adopted. These reasons, if expressed within the agency, constitute the "working law" of the agency and have been held by the lower courts to be outside the protection of Exemption 5. . . . Exemption 5, properly construed, calls for "disclosure of all 'opinions and interpretations' which embody the agency's effective law and policy, and the withholding of all papers which reflect the agency's group thinking in the process of working out its policy and determining what its law shall be."

(ii)

It is equally clear that Congress had the attorney's work-product privilege specifically in mind when it adopted Exemption 5 and that such a privilege had been recognized in the civil discovery context by the prior case law. The Senate Report states that Exemption 5 "would include the working papers of the agency attorney and documents which would come within the attorney-client privilege if applied to private parties," and the case law clearly makes the attorney's work-product rule of *Hickman v. Taylor,* 329 U.S. 495, applicable to Government attorneys in litigation. Whatever the outer boundaries of the attorney's work-product rule are, the rule clearly applies to memoranda prepared by an attorney in contemplation of litigation which set forth the attorney's theory of the case and his litigation strategy.

B

Applying these principles to the memoranda sought by Sears, it becomes clear that Exemption 5 does not apply to those Appeals and Advice Memoranda which conclude that no complaint should be filed and which have the effect of finally denying relief to the charging party; but that Exemption 5 does protect from disclosure those Appeals and Advice Memoranda which direct the filing of a complaint and the commencement of litigation before the Board.

(i)

Under the procedures employed by the General Counsel, Advice and Appeals Memoranda are communicated to the Regional Director after the General Counsel, through his Advice and Appeals Branches, has decided whether or not to issue a complaint; and represent an explanation to the Regional Director of a legal or policy decision already adopted by the General Counsel. In the case of decisions not to file a complaint, the memoranda effect as "final" a "disposition," as an administrative decision can—representing, as it does, an unreviewable rejection of the charge filed by the private party. Disclosure of these memoranda would not intrude on predecisional processes, and protecting them would not improve the quality of agency decisions, since when the memoranda are communicated to the Regional Director, the General Counsel has already reached his decision and the Regional Director who receives them has no decision to make—he is bound to dismiss the charge. Moreover, the General Counsel's decisions not to file complaints together with the Advice and Appeals Memoranda explaining them, are precisely the kind of agency law in which the public is so vitally interested and which Congress sought to prevent the agency from keeping secret.

(ii)

Advice and Appeals Memoranda which direct the filing of a complaint, on the other hand, fall within the coverage of Exemption 5. The filing of a complaint does not finally dispose even of the General Counsel's responsibility with respect to the case. The case will be litigated before and decided by the Board; and the General Counsel will have the responsibility of advocating the position of the charging party before the Board. The Memoranda will inexorably contain the General Counsel's theory of the case and may communicate to the Regional Director some litigation strategy or settlement advice. Since the Memoranda will also have been prepared in contemplation of the upcoming litigation, they fall squarely within Exemption 5's protection of an attorney's work product. At the same time, the public's interest in disclosure is substantially reduced by the fact, as pointed out by the ABA [American Bar Association] Committee, see supra, at 1519, that the basis for the General Counsel's legal decision will come out in the course of litigation before the Board; and that the "law" with respect to these cases will ultimately be made not by the General Counsel but by the Board or the courts.

We recognize that an Advice or Appeals Memorandum directing the filing of a complaint—although representing only a decision that a legal issue is sufficiently in doubt to warrant determination by another body—has many of the characteristics of the documents described in 5 U.S.C. § 552(a)(2). Although not a "final opinion" in the "adjudication" of a "case" because it does not effect a "final disposition," the memorandum does explain a decision already reached by the General Counsel which has real operative effect—it permits litigation before the Board; and we have indicated a reluctance to construe Exemption 5 to protect such documents. We do so in this case only because the decision-maker—the General Counsel—must become a litigating party to the case with respect to which he has made his decision. The attorney's work-product policies which Congress clearly incorporated into Exemption 5 thus come into play and lead us to hold that the Advice and Appeals Memoranda directing the filing of a complaint are exempt whether or not they are, as the District Court held, "instructions to staff that affect a member of the public." The probability that an agency employee will be inhibited from freely advising a decision-maker for fear that his advice, if adopted, will become public is slight. First, when adopted, the reasoning becomes that of the agency and becomes its responsibility to defend. Second, agency employees will generally be encouraged rather than discouraged by public knowledge that their policy suggestions have been adopted by the agency. Moreover, the public interest in knowing the reasons for a policy actually adopted by an agency supports the District Court's decision below.

Thus, we hold that, if an agency chooses expressly to adopt or incorporate by reference an intra-agency memorandum previously covered by Exemption 5 in what would otherwise be a final opinion, that memorandum may be withheld only on the ground that it falls within the coverage of some exemption other than Exemption 5.

Questions

1. The purpose of the FOIA was to benefit the public. What was the purpose of Sears's FOIA request? Should the FOIA be used by lawyers as a supplement or substitute for normal discovery tools in suits with an agency?

2. It is clear from this case that not all attorney-client, interagency, or intraagency communications will fall under Exemption 5. Can you describe which are exempt and which are not? Can you explain why?

Students often find the question of whether material is exempt as privileged under Exemption 5 to be confusing. If you bear in mind that the exemption was meant to maintain decisional integrity, then the notion that no postdecisional material can be withheld is not surprising. You may find Table 5.2 helpful in interpreting Exemption 5 questions.

Finally, Exemption 6 is somewhat self-explanatory. It provides for exemptions of "personnel and medical files and similar files the disclosure of which would constitute a clearly unwarranted invasion of personal privacy." Obvi-

Table 5.2 FOIA Exemption 5 Dichotomy: Does the Information Predate the Decision? Was It Relied On to Make the Decision?

	Predecisional	Postdecisional
Relied on to Make Decision	Release (public has a right to know)	Not privileged, release
Not Relied on to Make Decision	Privileged (exempt under Number 5)	Not privileged, release

ously, this exemption was meant to protect against the release of personal information that an agency might possess. The problem is that the language specifies that "clearly unwarranted" invasions of privacy are covered by the exemption and that presumably it does not protect against incidental invasions of privacy. The following case, having to do with the honor code of the Air Force Academy, is the classic case involving Exemption 6.

DEPARTMENT OF THE AIR FORCE V. ROSE
425 U.S. 352 (1976)

Justice Brennan delivered the opinion of the Court, joined by Justices Stewart, White, Marshall, Powell, and Stevens. Chief Justice Burger and Justices Blackmun and Rehnquist dissented.

Respondents, student editors, or former student editors of the *New York University Law Review* researching disciplinary systems and procedures at the military service academies for an article for the *Law Review* were denied access by petitioners to case summaries of honor and ethics hearings, with personal references or other identifying information deleted, maintained in the United States Air Force Academy's Honor and Ethics Code reading files, although Academy practice is to post copies of such summaries on 40 squadron bulletin boards throughout the Academy and to distribute copies to Academy faculty and administration officials. Thereupon respondents brought this action under the Freedom of Information Act, in the District Court for the Southern District of New York against petitioners, the Department of the Air Force, and Air Force officers who supervise cadets at the United States Air Force Academy (hereinafter collectively the Agency).

II

Our discussion may conveniently begin by again emphasizing the basic thrust of the Freedom of Information Act. Congress therefore structured a revision whose basic purpose reflected "a general philosophy of full agency disclosure unless information is exempted under clearly delineated statutory language." To make crystal clear the congressional objective in the words of the Court of Appeals, "to pierce the veil of administrative secrecy and to open agency action to the light of public scrutiny," 495 F.2d, at 263. Congress provided in § 552(c) that

nothing in the Act should be read to "authorize withholding of information or limit the availability of records to the public, except as specifically stated. . . ." Consistently with that objective, the Act repeatedly states "that official information shall be made available 'to the public,' 'for public inspection.' " There are, however, exemptions from compelled disclosure. They are nine in Number and are set forth in § 552(b). But these limited exemptions do not obscure the basic policy that disclosure, not secrecy, is the dominant objective of the Act.

Mindful of the congressional purpose, we then turn to consider whether mandatory disclosure of the case summaries is exempted by either of the exemptions involved here, discussing, First, Exemption 2, and, Second, Exemption 6.

III

The phrasing of Exemption 2 is traceable to congressional dissatisfaction with the exemption from disclosure under former § 3 of the Administrative Procedure Act of "any matter relating solely to the internal management of an agency." The sweep of that wording led to withholding by agencies from disclosure of matter "rang(ing) from the important to the insignificant."

. . . The general thrust of the exemption is simply to relieve agencies of the burden of assembling and maintaining for public inspection matter in which the public could not reasonably be expected to have an interest. The case summaries plainly do not fit that description. They are not matter with merely internal significance. They do not concern only routine matters. Their disclosure entails no particular administrative burden. We therefore agree with the Court of Appeals that, given the Senate interpretation, "the Agency's withholding of the case summaries (as edited to preserve anonymity) cannot be upheld by reliance on the second exemption." . . .

IV

Additional questions are involved in the determination whether Exemption 6 exempts the case summaries from mandatory disclosure as "personnel and medical files and similar files the disclosure of which would constitute a clearly unwarranted invasion of personal privacy."

We agree with these views, for we find nothing in the wording of Exemption 6 or its legislative history to support the Agency's claim that Congress created a blanket exemption for personnel files. Judicial interpretation has uniformly reflected the view that no reason would exist for nondisclosure in the absence of a showing of a clearly unwarranted invasion of privacy, whether the documents are filed in "personnel" or "similar" files. *Vaughn v. Rosen.* Congressional concern for the protection of the kind of confidential personal data usually included in a personnel file is abundantly clear. But Congress also made clear that nonconfidential matter was not to be insulated from disclosure merely because it was stored by an agency in its "personnel" files. Rather, Congress sought to construct an exemption that would require a balancing of the individual's right of privacy against the preservation of the basic purpose of the Freedom of Information Act "to open agency action to the light of public scrutiny." The device adopted to achieve that balance was the limited exemption, where privacy was threatened, for "clearly unwarranted" invasions of personal privacy. Congress' recent action in amending the Freedom of Information Act to make explicit its agreement with judicial decisions requiring the disclosure of nonexempt portions of otherwise exempt files is consistent with this conclusion. Thus, now provides that "[a]ny reasonably segregable portion of a record shall be provided to any person requesting such record after deletion of the portions which are exempt under this subsection." And § 552(a)(4)(B) was added explicitly to authorize In Camera inspection of matter claimed to be exempt "to determine whether such records or any part thereof shall be withheld." The Senate Report accompanying this legislation explains, without distinguishing "personnel and medical files" from "similar files," that its effect is to require courts . . . "to look beneath the label on a file or record when the withholding of information is challenged." . . .

(W)here files are involved (courts will) have to examine the records themselves and require disclosure of portions to which the purposes of the exemption under which they are withheld does not apply. . . .

The Agency argues secondly that, even taking the case summaries as files to which the "clearly unwarranted invasion of personal privacy" qualification applies, the Court of Appeals nevertheless improperly ordered the Agency to produce the case summaries in the District Court for In Camera examination to eliminate information that could result in identifying cadets involved in Honor or Ethics Code violations. The argument is, in substance, that the recognition by the Court of Appeals of "the harm that might result to the cadets from disclosure" itself demonstrates "[t]he ineffectiveness of excision of names and other identifying facts as a means of maintaining the confidentiality of persons named in government reports. . . ."

This contention has no merit. First, the argument implies that Congress barred disclosure in any case in which the conclusion could not be guaranteed that disclosure would not trigger recollection of identity in any person whatever. But this ignores Congress' limitation of the exemption to cases of "clearly unwarranted" invasions of personal privacy. Second, Congress vested the courts with the responsibility ultimately to determine "de novo" any dispute as to whether the exemption was properly invoked in order to constrain agencies from withholding nonexempt matters. No court has yet seen the case histories, and the Court of Appeals was therefore correct in holding that the function of examination must be discharged in the first instance by the District Court. . . .

In striking the balance whether to order disclosure of all or part of the case summaries, the District Court, in determining whether disclosure will entail a "clearly unwarranted" invasion of personal privacy, may properly discount its probability in light of Academy tradition to keep identities confidential within the Academy. Respondents sought only such disclosure as was consistent with this tradition. Their request for access to summaries "with personal references or other identifying information deleted," respected the confidentiality interests embodied in Exemption 6. As the Court of Appeals recognized, however, what constitutes identifying information regarding a subject cadet must be weighed not only from the viewpoint of the public, but also from the vantage of those who would have been familiar, as fellow cadets or Academy staff, with other aspects of his career at the Academy. Despite the summaries' distribution within the Academy, many of this group with earlier access to summaries may never have identified a particular cadet, or may have wholly forgotten his encounter with Academy discipline. And the risk to the privacy interests of a former cadet, particularly one who has remained in the military, posed by his identification by otherwise unknowing former colleagues or instructors cannot be rejected as trivial.

We nevertheless conclude that consideration of the policies underlying the Freedom of Information Act, to open public business to public view when no "clearly unwarranted" invasion of privacy will result, requires affirmance of the holding of the Court of Appeals, that although "no one can guarantee that all those who are 'in the know' will hold their tongues, particularly years later when time may have eroded the fabric of cadet loyalty," it sufficed to protect privacy at this stage in these proceedings by enjoining the District Court, Id., at 268, that if in its opinion deletion of personal references and other identifying information "is not sufficient to safeguard privacy, then the summaries should not be disclosed to (respondents)." We hold, therefore, in agreement with the Court of Appeals, "that the in camera procedure (ordered) will further the statutory goal of Exemption Six: a workable compromise between individual rights 'and the preservation of public rights to Government information.' " . . .

Affirmed.

I have mentioned elsewhere the concept of "unintended or second-order consequences." The FOIA has spawned not only considerable litigation but unintended consequences as well. For example, it can be argued that the foot-dragging in compliance with FOIA requests referred to earlier was not so much evidence of recalcitrance on the part of bureaucrats refusing to comply with the law as it was reflective of a bureaucracy inundated by requests and without the personnel to process them.[19] Estimates are that the federal government receives more than 300,000 FOIA requests each year, that more than 90 percent are granted by the agencies, and that the cost of compliance is upwards of $250 million annually.[20] The most common type of request comes from a business attempting to gain an edge on its competition.[21] Further, evidence suggests that whereas regulated businesses and parties once turned over information to agencies on request without reservation, those same businesses now resist subpoenas out of fear that the information in agency possession will be turned over to FOIA requesters.[22] Indeed, it appears as though the SEC has found a way around this information problem. SEC staff, rather than requesting information of regulated parties to be sent to the agency, are traveling to the regulated businesses to examine information.[23] This way, the information is never in the possession of the agency. Justice Scalia argues that the costs of compliance with the strict deadlines of the FOIA do not outweigh the benefits to society.[24]

This is one of those difficult democratic questions. There appears to be little argument that the American polity is more open now than it was before the FOIA. There also appears to be general agreement that the demands placed on the bureaucracy by the FOIA far exceed early estimates. Compliance is costly.

SUMMARY

Acquisition of Information

1. Generally, there is no violation of the Fifth Amendment's self-incrimination clause whereby an agency requires a regulated business to maintain certain records, inspects those records, and as a result, imposes sanctions on the regulated business.

2. Agencies do not need probable cause to issue subpoenas for information. Indeed, the courts will allow a "fishing expedition" via the administrative subpoena.

3. When the sufficiency of an agency subpoena is challenged in court, the test is simply whether the topic under inquiry is a topic that the agency is empowered to investigate.

4. Cases involving physical inspections or searches by agencies fall into two broad categories: those that require a warrant and those that do not. The following administrative searches require a warrant:

   a. city health inspector, to enter living quarters
   b. city fire inspector, to enter a business
   c. OSHA inspector, to enter a business
   d. fire marshall, to continue to look for evidence of arson after the coals of the fire are cold

These administrative searches do not require a warrant:

   a. heavily regulated industries, such as alcohol, firearms, and mining
   b. those inspections that are not searches within the meaning of the Fourth Amendment or, if they are, are reasonable (exceptions to the warrant requirement)

Cases in the last category involve AFDC home visits, aerial inspection of a plant by the EPA, a sample of air taken on plant property for evidence of violation of pollution standards, a vice principal's search of a student's purse, and INS factory surveys.

Agency Release of Information Under the Freedom of Information Act

1. The language of the FOIA compels release of information under normal circumstances. In nine situations, an agency may withhold information.

2. Although it was not always the case, today, if an agency can withhold information (especially commercial or financial information), it should.

3. Exemption 4 allows the following kind of information to be withheld:

    a. trade secrets
    b. commercial or financial information if (a) it was obtained from a person or business, (b) it is privileged (attorney-client), or (c) it is confidential

4. Commercial or financial information is confidential under the following circumstances:

    a. This information would not normally be released to the public by the individual or business that provided it.
    b. To withhold this information would be consistent with the legislative purposes of the exemption if (a) release would impair the government's ability to obtain such information in the future and (b) release of the information would harm the competitive edge of the provider.

5. Exemption 5 protects privileged information such as attorney-client and executive privilege. To qualify for a Number 5 exemption, the material sought must predate the decision, and it must not have been relied on to make the decision.

6. Exemption 6 protects citizens from release of information an agency might possess that would constitute a clearly unwarranted invasion of privacy.

END-OF-CHAPTER CASES

IN RE FEDERAL TRADE COMMISSION LINE OF BUSINESS REPORT LITIGATION
595 F.2d 685 (D.C. Cir. 1978)

Opinion per curiam.

We review the decisions of the District Court granting summary judgment to the Federal Trade Commission (Commission or FTC) and enforcing the Commission's orders requiring appellant corporations to file financial performance reports as part of the Line of Business (LB) and Corporate Patterns Report (CPR) surveys. These two broad-based statistical surveys are conducted by the FTC pursuant to its authority under Section 6(b) of the Federal Trade Commission Act, which empowers the Commission to require corporations to file informational reports regarding the company's "organization, business, conduct, practices, management, and relation to other corporations." . . .

I. THE FTC SURVEYS

A. The Line of Business Program.

In August 1975, as part of the Line of Business survey, the Commission ordered 450 of the nation's largest domestic manufacturing concerns to file reports disclosing certain indicia of financial performance for 1974. The 1974 LB form sent to each corporate respondent consists of four schedules. Schedule I seeks information identifying the company and its subsidiaries. Schedule II elicits a description of the company's lines of business. Schedule III, the heart of the form, exacts specific financial and statistical data including revenues, costs, profits and assets for each of the company's lines of business. Schedule IV requires reconciliation with other parts of the form and with the company's published financial data. The key feature of the survey is its requirement that each company present its financial performance statistics in terms of a uniform set of market categories. The Commission proposes to aggregate the LB statistics within each market category in order to identify areas of the economy in which profits are relatively high or low and to assess relationships between market structure and performance, and to use this information to target particular markets for industry-wide investigations into potential antitrust violations or unfair trade practices.

Since corporate financial performance data otherwise available to the Commission are not reported in terms of uniform market categories, the LB survey is expected to provide the only performance statistics susceptible to comparison on an industry-by-industry basis. Aside from internal use of the LB data, the Commission has indicated an interest in publishing the aggregate market statistics to facilitate efforts by investors, managers, and scholars to further the effectiveness of the competitive system. . . . The Commission began developing the Line of Business form in 1970. After extended consideration and extensive revisions, a limited survey was conducted to collect 1973 data. Revisions were made as a result of the Commission's experience with the 1973 survey, and in April 1975 the Commission published the proposed 1974 LB form in the *Federal Register* and solicited comments. In addition, the FTC distributed copies of the proposed form and the Commission's supporting statement to numerous interested parties, inviting their responses. On May 20, 1975, the full Commission conducted a hearing at which testimony was elicited from twenty witnesses regarding the proposed LB program. After considering the nearly 100 comments received and the testimony presented, the FTC revised the LB form and submitted it to the General Accounting Office (GAO) for clearance under the Federal Reports Act. Notice was published again in the *Federal Register* and comments were solicited by the GAO. Upon consideration of the comments received, the GAO approved the LB form for use by the FTC in a letter detailing its deliberations. The Line of Business orders were subsequently served on approximately 450 corporations. Motions to quash the LB orders were made by 180 companies and denied by the Commission in a statement responding to the objections advanced by the corporations.

B. The Corporate Patterns Report Program.

The Corporate Patterns Report survey requires over 1100 major domestic corporations to report the value of shipments from their domestic manufacturing establishments in 1972, in terms of product classifications developed by the Census Bureau for use in the Quinquennial Census of Manufactures. The CPR survey also solicits 1972 data regarding, Inter alia, consolidated net manufacturing activities and major acquisitions and disposals since 1972. As with the LB program, the FTC proposes to use the CPR survey to create a data bank on market structures for use by the Commission in antitrust enforcement, economic analysis and policy planning. The value of shipments data will be used in conjunction with aggregate data published by the Census Bureau based on similar information contained in the 1972 Census of Manufactures. The Corporate Patterns Report survey was considered initially by the Commission in 1972. After testing the proposed form on a small number of companies and effecting some modifications, the FTC submitted the CPR form to the General Accounting Office for clearance as required under the

Federal Reports Act. The GAO published notice of the proposed survey in the *Federal Register* and solicited comments. The comments received were duly considered, and the GAO approved the CPR form in a letter to the FTC detailing the substance of these comments. In addition to entertaining the comments supplied by the GAO, the FTC conferred with representatives from the Census Bureau and the Office of Management and Budget in a public meeting in June 1975 and less formally on other occasions. In July 1975 the Commission adopted a resolution authorizing the use of compulsory process, and the Corporate Patterns Report orders were served on 1100 companies. In response, motions to quash were filed by 390 companies raising numerous factual and legal objections. In an effort to accommodate corporate claims, the Commission deleted an unduly burdensome requirement that each company rank itself as to each product category and responded to each of the corporations' objections in a letter denying the motions to quash.

II. DISCUSSION

Enforcement actions were commenced in the District Court against the companies that had refused to comply with the Commission's orders. Dissatisfied in several respects with the disposition rendered by the trial court, the corporations perfected this appeal. Appellants contend first that the orders in both the LB and CPR surveys were issued in violation of the rule-making requirements of the Administrative Procedure Act (APA). Second, appellants urge that the CPR survey is invalid because it violates the confidentiality provisions of the Census Act. Third, appellants assert both substantive and procedural errors by the District Court in the enforcement proceeding. Finally, appellants submit that the LB orders are infirm because of the alleged failure of the Comptroller General to review the LB forms in accordance with the requirements of the Federal Reports Act. We address each of these contentions in turn. The Federal Trade Commission Act (FTC Act) provides a clear basis of authority for the Commission to issue orders requiring corporations to submit informational reports to the FTC. Section 6(b) of the Act states that the Commission shall have the power . . . "[t]o require by general or special orders, persons, partnerships, and corporations, engaged in or whose business affects commerce, excepting banks and common carriers subject to the Act to regulate commerce or any class of them or any of them, respectively, to file with the Commission in such form as the Commission may prescribe annual or special, or both annual and special, reports or answers in writing to specific questions, furnishing to the Commission such information as it may require as to the organization, business, conduct, practices, management, and relation to other corporations, partnerships, and individuals of the respective persons, partnerships, and corporations filing such reports or answers in writing. . . ."

Appellants claim that the Commission's exercise of this authority, which they do not challenge, in the development and implementation of the Line of Business and Corporate Patterns Report surveys was procedurally improper because the Commission failed to comply with the rule-making requirements of the Administrative Procedure Act. Our first inquiry is whether the Federal Trade Commission Act obligates the Commission to observe APA rule-making procedures when exercising its authority to require informational reporting pursuant to Section 6(b) of the FTC Act. We conclude that neither Section 6(b) nor any other section of the FTC Act requires adherence to the APA's rule-making procedures nor does any section of the Act prescribe other procedural prerequisites to the exercise of the Commission's authority to require reporting.

In this case, the enabling statutory provision is Section 6(b) of the FTC Act, which, as we demonstrated above, does not impose rule-making upon the FTC. Accordingly, the Commission is not obligated under the Administrative Procedure Act to pursue rule-making proceedings prior to implementation of the LB and CPR programs. . . . Our view comports with the Commission's interpretation of the procedural requirements of the Federal Trade Commission Act and the Administrative Procedure Act. The Commission has stated: "It has been the Commission's long-standing interpretation of the interrelationship of the APA and the FTC Act that the Commission is not required to follow the APA procedures for rule-making when the Commission decides to use its powers under Section 6, 15 U.S.C. § 46, or other provisions of the FTC Act, to gather information or to investigate."

The only power that is involved here is the power to get information from those who best can give it and who are most interested in not doing so. Because judicial power is reluctant if not unable to summon evidence until it is shown to be relevant to issues in litigation, it does not follow that an administrative agency charged with seeing that the laws are enforced may not have and exercise powers of original inquiry. It has a power of inquisition, if one chooses to call it that, which is not derived from the judicial function. It is more analogous to the Grand Jury, which does not depend on a case or controversy for power to get evidence but can investigate merely on suspicion that the law is being violated, or even just because it wants assurance that it is not.

III. CONCLUSION

The judgment of the District Court is affirmed. The corporate parties shall comply with the Line of Business and Corporate Patterns Report orders as issued by the Federal Trade Commission within 30 days of the date of this opinion.

So ordered.

MICHIGAN V. TYLER
436 U.S. 499 (1978)

Justice Stewart delivered the opinion of the Court, joined by Chief Justice Burger and Justices Brennan and Powell. Justices Stevens and Blackmun concurred in part. Justices White and Marshall concurred in part and dissented in part. Justice Rehnquist dissented.

The respondents, Loren Tyler and Robert Tompkins, were convicted in a Michigan trial court of conspiracy to burn real property in violation of Mich. Laws. Various pieces of physical evidence and testimony based on personal observation, all obtained through unconsented and warrantless entries by police and fire officials onto the burned premises, were admitted into evidence at the respondents' trial. On appeal, the Michigan Supreme Court reversed the convictions, holding that "the warrantless searches were unconstitutional and that the evidence obtained was therefore inadmissible." 250 N.W.2d 467, 477 (1977). We granted certiorari to consider the applicability of the Fourth and Fourteenth Amendments to official entries onto fire-damaged premises.

I

Shortly before midnight on January 21, 1970, a fire broke out at Tyler's Auction, a furniture store in Oakland County, Mich. The building was leased to respondent Loren Tyler, who conducted the business in association with respondent Robert Tompkins.

According to the trial testimony of various witnesses, the fire department responded to the fire and was "just watering down smoldering embers" when Fire Chief See arrived on the scene around 2 a.m. It was Chief See's responsibility "to determine the cause and make out all reports." Chief See was met by Lt. Lawson, who informed him that two plastic containers of flammable liquid had been found in the building. Using portable lights, they entered the gutted store, which was filled with smoke and steam, to examine the containers. Concluding that the fire "could possibly have been an arson," Chief See called Police Detective Webb, who arrived around 3:30 a.m. Detective Webb took several pictures of the containers and of the interior of the store, but finally abandoned his efforts because of the smoke and steam. Chief See briefly "[l]ooked throughout the rest of the building to see if there was any further evidence, to determine what the cause of the fire was." By 4 a.m. the fire had been extinguished and the firefighters departed. See and Webb took the two containers to the fire station, where they were turned over to Webb for safekeeping. There was neither consent nor a warrant for any of these entries into the building, nor for the removal of the containers. The respondents challenged the introduction of these containers at trial, but abandoned their objection in the State Supreme Court.

Four hours after he had left Tyler's Auction, Chief See returned with Assistant Chief Somerville, whose job was to determine the "origin of all fires that occur within the Township." The fire had been extinguished and the building was empty. After a cursory examination they left, and Somerville returned with Detective Webb around 9 a.m. In Webb's words, they discovered suspicious "burn marks in the carpet, which [Webb] could not see earlier that morning, because of the heat, steam, and the darkness." They also found "pieces of tape, with burn marks, on the stairway." After leaving the building to obtain tools, they returned and removed pieces of the carpet and sections of the stairs to preserve these bits of evidence suggestive of a fuse trail. Somerville also searched through the rubble "looking for any other signs or evidence that showed how this fire was caused." Again, there was neither consent nor a warrant for these entries and seizures. Both at trial and on appeal, the respondents objected to the introduction of evidence thereby obtained.

On February 16, Sergeant Hoffman of the Michigan State Police Arson Section returned to Tyler's Auction to take photographs. During this visit or during another at about the same time, he checked the circuit breakers, had someone inspect the furnace, and had a television repairman examine the remains of several television sets found in the ashes. He also found a piece of fuse. Over the course of his several visits, Hoffman secured physical evidence and formed opinions that played a substantial role at trial in establishing arson as the cause of the fire and in refuting the respondents' testimony about what furniture had been lost. His entries into the building were without warrants or Tyler's consent, and were for the sole purpose "of making an investigation and seizing evidence." At the trial, respondents' attorney objected to the admission of physical evidence obtained during these visits, and also moved to strike all of Hoffman's testimony "because it was got in an illegal manner."

II

The decisions of this Court firmly establish that the Fourth Amendment extends beyond the paradigmatic entry into a private dwelling by a law enforcement officer in search of the fruits or instrumentalities of crime. As this Court stated in *Camara v. Municipal Court,* 387 U.S. 523, 528, the "basic purpose of this Amendment . . . is to safeguard the privacy and security of individuals against arbitrary invasions by governmental officials." The officials may be health, fire, or building inspectors. Their purpose may be to locate and abate a suspected public nuisance, or simply to perform a routine periodic inspection. The privacy that is invaded may be sheltered by the walls of a warehouse or other commercial establishment not open to the public. These deviations from the typical police search are thus clearly within the protection of the Fourth Amendment.

The petitioner argues, however, that an entry to investigate the cause of a recent fire is outside that protection because no individual privacy interests are threatened. If the occupant of the premises set the blaze, then, in the words of the petitioner's brief, his "actions show that he has no expectation of privacy" because "he has abandoned those premises within the meaning of the Fourth Amendment." And if the fire had other causes, "the occupants of the premises are treated as victims by police and fire officials." In the petitioner's view, "[t]he likelihood that they will be aggrieved by a possible intrusion into what little remains of their privacy in badly burned premises is negligible."

This argument is not persuasive. For even if the petitioner's contention that arson establishes abandonment be accepted, its second proposition—that innocent fire victims inevitably have no protectable expectations of privacy in whatever remains of their property—is contrary to common experience. People may go on living in their homes or working in their offices after a fire. Even when that is impossible, private effects often remain on the fire-damaged premises. The petitioner may be correct in the view that most innocent fire victims are treated courteously and welcome inspections of their property to ascertain the origin of the blaze, but "even if true, [this contention] is irrelevant to the question whether the . . . inspection is reasonable within the meaning of the Fourth Amendment." Once it is recognized that innocent fire victims retain the protection of the Fourth Amendment, the rest of the petitioner's argument unravels. For it is, of course, impossible to justify a warrantless search on the ground of abandonment by arson when that arson has not yet been proved, and a conviction cannot be used ex post facto to validate the introduction of evidence used to secure that same conviction.

Thus, there is no diminution in a person's reasonable expectation of privacy nor in the protection of the Fourth Amendment simply because the official conducting the search wears the uniform of a firefighter rather than a policeman, or because his purpose is to ascertain the cause of a fire rather than to look for evidence of a crime, or because the fire might have been started deliberately. Searches for administrative purposes, like searches for evidence of crime, are encompassed by the Fourth Amendment. And under that Amendment, "one governing principle, justified by history and by current experience, has consistently been followed: except in certain carefully defined classes of cases, a search of private property without proper consent is 'unreasonable' unless it has been authorized by a valid search warrant." The showing of probable cause necessary to secure a warrant may vary with the object and intrusiveness of the search, but the necessity for the warrant persists.

III

Our decisions have recognized that a warrantless entry by criminal law enforcement officials may be legal when there is compelling need for official action and no time to secure a warrant. . . . A burning building clearly presents an exigency of sufficient proportions to render a warrantless entry "reasonable." Indeed, it would defy reason to suppose that firemen must secure a warrant or consent before entering a burning structure to put out the blaze. And once in a building for this purpose, firefighters may seize evidence of arson that is in plain view. . . . Fire officials are charged not only with extinguishing fires, but with finding their causes. Prompt determination of the fire's origin may be necessary to prevent its recurrence, as through the detection of continuing dangers such as faulty wiring or a defective furnace. Immediate investigation may also be necessary to preserve evidence from intentional or accidental destruction. And, of course, the sooner the officials complete their duties, the less will be their subsequent interference with the privacy and the recovery efforts of the victims. For these reasons, officials need no warrant to remain in a building for a reasonable time to investigate the cause of a blaze after it has been extinguished. And if the warrantless entry to put out the fire and determine its cause is constitutional, the warrantless seizure of evidence while inspecting the premises for these purposes also is constitutional. . . .

In summation, we hold that an entry to fight a fire requires no warrant, and that once in the building, officials may remain there for a reasonable time to investigate the cause of the blaze. Thereafter, additional entries to investigate the cause of the fire must be made pursuant to the warrant procedures governing administrative searches. Evidence of arson discovered in the course of such investigations is admissible at trial, but if the investigating officials find probable cause to believe that arson has occurred and require further access to gather evidence for a possible prosecution, they may obtain a warrant only upon a traditional showing of probable cause applicable to searches for evidence of crime.

These principles require that we affirm the judgment of the Michigan Supreme Court ordering a new trial.

DOW CHEMICAL COMPANY V. UNITED STATES
476 U.S. 227 (1986)

Chief Justice Burger delivered the opinion of the Court, in which Justices White, Rehnquist, Stevens, and O'Connor joined, and in Part III of which Justices Brennan, Marshall, Blackmun, and Powell joined. Justice Powell filed an opinion concurring in part and dissenting in part, in which Justices Brennan, Marshall, and Blackmun joined.

We granted certiorari to review the holding of the Court of Appeals (a) that the Environmental Protection Agency's aerial observation of petitioner's plant complex did not exceed EPA's statutory investigatory authority, and (b) that EPA's aerial photography of petitioner's 2,000-acre plant complex without a warrant was not a search under the Fourth Amendment.

I

Petitioner Dow Chemical Co. operates a 2,000-acre facility manufacturing chemicals at Midland, Michigan. The facility consists of numerous covered buildings, with manufacturing equipment and piping conduits located between the various buildings exposed to visual observation from the air. At all times, Dow has maintained elaborate security around the perimeter of the complex barring ground-level public views of these areas. It also investigates any low-level flights by aircraft over the facility. Dow has not undertaken, however, to conceal all manufacturing equipment within the complex from aerial views. Dow maintains that the cost of covering its exposed equipment would be prohibitive.

In early 1978, enforcement officials of EPA, with Dow's consent, made an on-site inspection of two powerplants in this complex. A subsequent EPA request for a second inspection, however, was denied, and EPA did not thereafter seek an administrative search warrant. Instead, EPA employed a commercial aerial photographer, using a standard floor-mounted, precision aerial mapping camera, to take photographs of the facility from altitudes of 12,000, 3,000, and 1,200 feet. At all times the aircraft was lawfully within navigable airspace. EPA did not inform Dow of this aerial photography, but when Dow became aware of it, Dow brought suit in the District Court alleging that EPA's action violated the Fourth Amendment and was beyond EPA's statutory investigative authority. The District Court granted Dow's motion for summary judgment on the ground that EPA had no authority to take aerial photographs and that doing so was a search violating the Fourth Amendment. EPA was permanently enjoined from taking aerial photographs of Dow's premises and from disseminating, releasing, or copying the photographs already taken. The Court of Appeals then held that EPA clearly acted within its statutory powers even absent express authorization for aerial surveillance, concluding that the delegation of general investigative authority to EPA, similar to that of other law enforcement agencies, was sufficient to support the use of aerial photography. Dow claims first that EPA has no authority to use aerial photography to implement its statutory authority for "site inspection" under § 114(a) of the Clean Air Act, 42 U.S.C. § 7414(a); second, Dow claims EPA's use of aerial photography was a "search" of an area that, notwithstanding the large size of the plant, was within an "industrial curtilage" rather than an "open field," and that it had a reasonable expectation of privacy from such photography protected by the Fourth Amendment. . . .

III

Congress has vested in EPA certain investigatory and enforcement authority, without spelling out precisely how this authority was to be exercised in all the myriad circumstances that might arise in monitoring matters relating to clean air and water standards. When Congress invests an agency with enforcement and investigatory authority, it is not necessary to identify explicitly each and every technique that may be used in the course of executing the statutory mission. Aerial observation authority, for example, is not usually expressly extended to police for traffic control, but it could hardly be thought necessary for a legislative body to tell police that aerial observation could be employed for traffic control of a metropolitan area, or to expressly authorize police to send messages to ground highway patrols that a particular over-the-road truck was traveling in excess of 55 miles per hour. Common sense and ordinary human experience teach that traffic violators are apprehended by observation.

[3] Regulatory or enforcement authority generally carries with it all the modes of inquiry and investigation traditionally employed or useful to execute the authority granted. Environmental standards such as clean air and clean water cannot be enforced only in libraries and laboratories, helpful as those institutions may be. . . . We hold that the use of aerial observation and photography is within EPA's statutory authority. . . . We turn now to Dow's contention that taking aerial photographs constituted a search without a warrant, thereby violating Dow's rights under the Fourth Amendment. In making this contention, however, Dow concedes that a simple flyover with naked-eye observation, or the taking of a photograph from a nearby hillside overlooking such a facility, would give rise to no Fourth Amendment problem. We pointed out in *Donovan v. Dewey,* 452 U.S. 594 (1981), that the Government has "greater latitude to conduct warrantless inspections of commercial property" because "the expectation of privacy that the owner of commercial property enjoys in such property differs significantly from the sanctity accorded an individual's home." We emphasized that unlike a homeowner's interest in his dwelling, "[t]he interest of the owner of commercial property is not one in being free from any inspections." And with regard to regulatory inspections, we have held that "[w]hat is observable by the public is observable without a warrant, by the Government inspector as well." *Marshall v. Barlow's, Inc.,* 436 U.S., at 315.

Oliver recognized that in the open field context, "the public and police lawfully may survey lands from the air." 466 U.S., at 179. Here, EPA was not employing some unique sensory device that, for example, could penetrate the walls of buildings and record conversations in Dow's plants, offices, or laboratories, but rather a conventional, albeit precise, commercial camera commonly used in map-making. The Government asserts it has not yet enlarged the photographs to any significant degree, but Dow points out that simple magnification permits identification of objects such as wires as small as ½-inch in diameter.

It may well be, as the Government concedes, that surveillance of private property by using highly sophisticated surveillance equipment not generally available to the public, such as satellite technology, might be constitutionally proscribed absent a warrant. But the photographs here are not so revealing of intimate details as to raise constitutional concerns. Although they undoubtedly give EPA more detailed information than naked-eye views, they remain limited to an outline of the facility's buildings and equipment. The mere fact that human vision is enhanced somewhat, at least to the degree here, does not give rise to constitutional problems. An electronic device to penetrate walls or windows so as to hear and record confidential discussions of chemical formulae or other trade secrets would raise very different and far more serious questions; other protections such as trade secret laws are available to protect commercial activities from private surveillance by competitors. . . .

[6] We conclude that the open areas of an industrial plant complex with numerous plant structures spread over an area of 2,000 acres are not analogous to the "curtilage" of a dwelling for purposes of aerial surveillance; such an industrial complex is more comparable to an open field and as such it is open to the view and observation of persons in aircraft lawfully in the public airspace immediately above or sufficiently near the area for the reach of cameras. We hold that the taking of aerial photographs of an industrial plant complex from navigable airspace is not a search prohibited by the Fourth Amendment.

Affirmed.

IMMIGRATION AND NATURALIZATION SERVICE V. DELGADO
466 U.S. 210 (1984)

Justice Rehnquist delivered the opinion of the Court, joined by Chief Justice Burger and Justices White, Blackmun, and O'Connor. Justices Stevens and Powell concurred. Justices Brennan and Marshall concurred in part and dissented in part.

In the course of enforcing the immigration laws, petitioner Immigration and Naturalization Service (INS) enters employers' worksites to determine whether any illegal aliens may be present as employees. The Court of Appeals for the Ninth Circuit held that the "factory surveys" involved in this case amounted to a seizure of the entire work forces and further held that the INS could not question individual employees during any of these surveys unless its agents had a reasonable suspicion that the employee to be questioned was an illegal alien. *Garment Workers v. Sureck*, 681 F.2d 624 (9th Cir. 1982). We conclude that these factory surveys did not result in the seizure of the entire work forces, and that the individual questioning of the respondents in this case by INS agents concerning their citizenship did not amount to a detention or seizure under the Fourth Amendment. Accordingly, we reverse the judgment of the Court of Appeals.

Acting pursuant to two warrants, in January and September, 1977, the INS conducted a survey of the work force at Southern California Davis Pleating Company (Davis Pleating) in search of illegal aliens. The warrants were issued on a showing of probable cause by the INS that numerous illegal aliens were employed at Davis Pleating, although neither of the search warrants identified any particular illegal aliens by name. A third factory survey was conducted with the employer's consent in October, 1977, at Mr. Pleat, another garment factory. At the beginning of the surveys several agents positioned themselves near the buildings' exits, while other agents dispersed throughout the factory to question most, but not all, employees at their work stations. The agents displayed badges, carried walkie-talkies, and were armed, although at no point during any of the surveys was a weapon ever drawn. Moving systematically through the factory, the agents approached employees and, after identifying themselves, asked them from one to three questions relating to their citizenship. If the employee gave a credible reply that he was a United States citizen, the questioning ended, and the agent moved on to another employee. If the employee gave an unsatisfactory response or admitted that he was an alien, the employee was asked to produce his immigration papers. During the survey, employees continued with their work and were free to walk around within the factory. Respondents are four employees questioned in one of the three surveys (Delgado is a U.S. citizen). In 1978 respondents and their union representative, the International Ladies Garment Workers' Union, filed two actions, later consolidated, in United States District Court for the Central District of California challenging the constitutionality of INS factory surveys and seeking declaratory and injunctive relief. Respondents argued that the factory surveys violated their Fourth Amendment right to be free from unreasonable searches or seizures and the equal protection component of the Due Process Clause of the Fifth Amendment.

Given the diversity of encounters between police officers and citizens, however, the Court has been cautious in defining the limits imposed by the Fourth Amendment on encounters between the police and citizens. As we have noted elsewhere, "Obviously, not all personal intercourse between policemen and citizens involves 'seizures' of persons. Only when the officer, by means of physical force or show of authority, has restrained the liberty of a citizen may we conclude that a 'seizure' has occurred." *Terry v. Ohio,* 392 U.S. 1 (1968). While applying such a test is relatively straightforward in a situation resembling a traditional arrest, see *Dunaway v. New York,* 442 U.S. 200 (1979), the protection against unreasonable seizures also extends to "seizures that involve only a brief detention short of traditional arrest." *United States v. Brignoni-Ponce,* 422 U.S. 873 (1975). What has evolved from our cases is a determination that an initially consensual encounter between a police officer and a citizen can be transformed into a seizure or detention within the meaning of the Fourth Amendment, "if, in view of all the circumstances surrounding the incident, a reasonable person would have believed that he was not free to leave." . . .

Although we have yet to rule directly on whether mere questioning of an individual by a police official, without more, can amount to a seizure under the Fourth Amendment, our recent decision in *Royer,* supra, plainly implies that interrogation relating to one's identity or a request for identification by the police does not, by itself, constitute a Fourth Amendment seizure. In *Royer,* when DEA [Drug Enforcement Agency] agents found that the respondent matched a drug courier profile, the agents approached the defendant and asked him for his airplane ticket and driver's license, which the agents then examined. A majority of the Court believed that the request and examination of the documents was "permissible in themselves." In contrast, a much different situation prevailed in *Brown v. Texas,* 443 U.S. 47 (1979), when two policemen physically detained the defendant to determine his identity, after the defendant refused the officers' request to identify himself. The Court held that absent some reasonable suspicion of misconduct, the detention of the defendant to determine his identity violated the defendant's Fourth Amendment right to be free from an unreasonable seizure. . . .

What is apparent from *Royer* and *Brown* is that police questioning, by itself, is unlikely to result in a Fourth Amendment violation. While most citizens will respond to a police request, the fact that people do so, and do so without being told they are free not to respond, hardly eliminates the consensual nature of the response. Unless the circumstances of the encounter are so intimidating as to demonstrate that a reasonable person would have believed he was not free to leave if he had not responded, one cannot say that the questioning resulted in a detention under the Fourth Amendment. But if the person refuses to answer and the police take additional steps—such as those taken in *Brown*—to obtain an answer, then the Fourth Amendment imposes some minimal level of objective justification to validate the detention or seizure. . . .

The Court of Appeals held that "the manner in which the factory surveys were conducted in this case constituted a seizure of the workforce" under the Fourth Amendment. 681 F.2d, at 634. While the element of surprise and the systematic questioning of individual workers by several INS agents contributed to the court's holding, the pivotal factor in its decision was the stationing of INS agents near the exits of the factory buildings.

According to the Court of Appeals, the stationing of agents near the doors meant that "departures were not to be contemplated," and thus, workers were "not free to leave." Id. In support of the decision below, respondents argue that the INS created an intimidating psychological environment when it intruded unexpectedly into the workplace with such a show of officers. Besides the stationing of agents near the exits, respondents add that the length of the survey and the failure to inform workers they were free to leave resulted in a Fourth Amendment seizure of the entire work force.

We reject the claim that the entire work forces of the two factories were seized for the duration of the surveys when the INS placed agents near the exits of the factory sites. Ordinarily, when people are at work their freedom to move about has been meaningfully restricted, not by the actions of law enforcement officials, but by the workers' voluntary obligations to their employers. The record indicates that when these surveys were initiated, the employees were about their ordinary business, operating machinery and performing other job assignments. While the surveys did cause some disruption, including the efforts of some workers to hide, the record also indicates that workers were not prevented by the agents from moving about the factories. Respondents argue, however, that the stationing of agents near the factory doors showed the INS's intent to prevent people from leaving. But there is nothing in the record indicating that this is what the agents at the doors actually did. The obvious purpose of the agents' presence at the factory doors was to insure that all persons in the factories were questioned. The record indicates that the INS agents' conduct in this case consisted simply of questioning employees and arresting those they had probable cause to believe were unlawfully present in the factory. This conduct should have given respondents no reason to believe that they would be detained if they gave truthful answers to the questions put to them or if they simply refused to answer. If mere questioning does not constitute a seizure when it occurs inside the factory, it is no more a seizure when it occurs at the exits.

A similar conclusion holds true for all other citizens or aliens lawfully present inside the factory buildings during the surveys. The presence of agents by the exits posed no reasonable threat of detention to these workers while they walked throughout the factories on job assignments. Likewise, the mere possibility that they would be questioned if they sought to leave the buildings should not have resulted in any reasonable apprehension by any of them that they would be seized or detained in any meaningful way. Since most workers could have had no reasonable fear that they would be detained upon leaving, we conclude that the work forces as a whole were not seized.

The Court of Appeals also held that "detentive questioning" of individuals could be conducted only if INS agents could articulate "objective facts providing investigators with a reasonable suspicion that each questioned person, so detained, is an alien illegally in the country." 681 F.2d, at 638. Under our analysis, however, since there was no seizure of the work forces by virtue of the method of conducting the factory surveys, the only way the issue of individual questioning could be presented would be if one of the named respondents had in fact been seized or detained. Reviewing the deposition testimony of respondents, we conclude that none were.

The questioning of each respondent by INS agents seems to have been nothing more than a brief encounter. None of the three Davis Pleating employees were questioned during the January survey. During the September survey at Davis Pleating, respondent Delgado was discussing the survey with another employee when two INS agents approached him and asked him where he was from and from what city. When Delgado informed them that he came from Mayaguez, Puerto Rico, the agent made an innocuous observation to his partner and left. Respondent Correa's experience in the September survey was similar. Walking from one part of the factory to another, Correa was stopped by an INS agent and asked where she was born. When she replied "Huntington Park [California]," the agent walked away and Correa continued about her business. Respondent Labonte, the third Davis Pleating employee, was tapped on the shoulder and asked in Spanish, "Where are your papers?" Labonte responded that she had her papers and without any further request from the INS agents, showed the papers to the agents, who then left. Finally, respondent Miramontes, the sole Mr. Pleat employee involved in this case, encountered an agent en route from an office to her worksite. Questioned concerning her citizenship, Miramontes replied that she was a resident alien and, on the agent's request, produced her work permit. The agent then left.

Respondents argue that the manner in which the surveys were conducted and the attendant disruption caused by the surveys created a psychological environment which made them reasonably afraid they were not free to leave. Consequently, when respondents were approached by INS agents and questioned concerning their citizenship and right to work, they were effectively detained under the Fourth Amendment, since they reasonably feared that refusing to answer would have resulted in their arrest. But it was obvious from the beginning of the surveys that the INS agents were only questioning people. Persons such as respondents who simply went about their business in the workplace were not detained in any way; nothing more occurred than that a question was put to them. While persons who attempted to flee or evade the agents may eventually have been detained for questioning, respondents did not do so and were not in fact detained. The manner in which respondents were questioned,

given its obvious purpose, could hardly result in a reasonable fear that respondents were not free to continue working or to move about the factory.

Respondents may only litigate what happened to them, and our review of their description of the encounters with the INS agents satisfies us that the encounters were classic consensual encounters rather than Fourth Amendment seizures.

Accordingly, the judgment of the Court of Appeals is Reversed.

NOTES

1. Walsh-Healey Act of 1936, 41 U.S.C. 35.

2. The material on types of policies comes from Randall Ripley and Grace Franklin, *Congress, the Bureaucracy, and Public Policy,* 4th ed. (Chicago: Dorsey Press, 1987), 21-28.

3. Ibid., 25.

4. Ernest Gellhorn and Ronald M. Levin, *Administrative Law and Process: In a Nutshell,* 3d ed. (St. Paul, MN: West, 1990), 124.

5. Walter Gellhorn, Clark Byse, and Peter Strauss, *Administrative Law: Cases and Comments,* 7th ed. (Mineola, NY: Foundation Press, 1979), 556.

6. *Marshall v. Barlow's, Incorporated,* 436 U.S. 307, 313 (1978).

7. Denise Gellene, "Sears Auto Shops Come Under Fire," *Topeka Capital-Journal,* 6 November 1992, 3A.

8. Latte E. Feinberg, "Managing the Freedom of Information Act and Federal Information Policy," *Public Administration Review* 46 (1986): 615.

9. 5 U.S.C. 551-59.

10. 5 U.S.C. 552a.

11. 5 U.S.C. 552b.

12. Feinberg, "Managing the Freedom of Information Act," 615.

13. Ibid.

14. The procedure described is contained in the act, but the condensed description comes from Gellhorn, Byse, and Strauss, *Administrative Law,* 583-84.

15. Ibid., 582.

16. 18 U.S.C. § 1905.

17. Gellhorn and Levin, *Administrative Law and Process,* 156.

18. Daniel Oran, *Oran's Dictionary of the Law* (St. Paul, MN: West, 1983), 133.

19. Gellhorn, Byse, and Strauss, *Administrative Law,* 582-83. See also Robert L. Saloschin, "The FOIA—A Government Perspective," *Public Administration Review* 35 (1975): 10.

20. Arthur E. Bonfield and Michael Asimow, *State and Federal Administrative Law* (St. Paul, MN: West, 1989), 538.

21. Ibid.

22. Gellhorn, Byse, and Strauss, *Administrative Law,* 585.

23. Ibid.

24. Antonin Scalia, "The Freedom of Information Act Has No Clothes," *Regulation,* March/April 1982, 14.

CHAPTER 6

INFORMAL
AGENCY ACTIVITY

Although the Administrative Procedure Act (APA) was intended to standardize and regulate the procedure of agency decision making, it addresses agency decisions in only two contexts. Section 553 regulates quasi-legislative activity or agency rule making through the notice and comment procedure. Sections 554, 556, and 557 regulate quasi-judicial activity, such as disability termination hearings held before an administrative law judge (ALJ). In fact, much, if not most, of what agencies do falls outside the activities covered by those sections of the act.

CASE IN POINT:
THE SOCIAL SECURITY ADMINISTRATION—
NOT CURRENTLY DISABLED[1]

The federal Disability Insurance (DI) Program was started in 1954 by amending the Social Security Act of 1935. It was initially intended to be a small program with very strict eligibility requirements.[2] To be eligible, a potential claimant cannot be currently employed and must be able to document a medical impairment so severe that the claimant is precluded from holding any meaningful job in the national economy.[3] In 1960, 14.8 million Americans were receiving Social Security benefits, but fewer than a million of those were on disability (687,451), or 4.6 percent.[4] By 1975, the DI rolls had grown to 4.3 million, which constituted 13.6 percent of all Social Security beneficiaries.[5]

By the late 1970s, Congress was concerned with a mounting deficit in the area of some $70 billion and was looking for ways to cut spending. Aided by rumors of inefficiency within the Social Security Administration (SSA), Congress began to shape new legislation for the disability program, which culminated in the Social Security Disability Amendments of 1980.[6] The amendments contained measures to encourage those on the disability rolls to move off and adjusted the benefits to ensure that one could not earn more income on DI than one could in the workforce.[7] Because it is possible for a claimant to meet the eligibility standards temporarily, Congress also encouraged the SSA to review periodically the cases of those DI beneficiaries whose impairments were not permanent.

After finding a claimant eligible for disability, the SSA places him or her into one of three categories: permanently disabled, less severely disabled, or nonpermanently disabled. Before 1981, only those with certain preselected, targeted impairments (those in which improvement could be expected through either time or surgery) were usually slated to have their cases reviewed.[8] On that basis, the SSA typically reviewed only 130,000 or so DI cases per year.[9] Of the cases the SSA reviewed, not many were actually terminated. Other than those cases in which income records indicated a return to work or the claimant notified the SSA of a return to work, the SSA had to document a medical improvement before it could terminate disability benefits. That was referred to as the "medical improvement standard," but the SSA switched from the medical improvement standard to the current medical evidence standard in 1976.[10]

Remember that part of the definition of disability is that one cannot find meaningful employment in the economy. Hence, it is possible for either technology or the economy to have changed so that, without medical improvement, it might be possible for a DI beneficiary to be found not currently disabled and to have benefits terminated.

The procedure for termination of disability benefits is initiated by a review of a beneficiary's file at the Disability Determination Service (DDS), a state agency under contract to the SSA. The beneficiary is notified of pending review and given time to submit documentation of continuing eligibility. The actual determination of continuing eligibility, then, is simply a review of paperwork in the beneficiary's file. If the decision is made to terminate, the beneficiary is notified and informed that he or she can apply for reconsideration before the DDS. If a beneficiary goes through reconsideration (also a paper review process) and the decision to terminate is not reversed (and most are not), then he or she can appeal to the SSA, where a quasi-judicial hearing will take place before an ALJ. This hearing looks like a trial but is "nonadversarial" in the sense that there are few, if any, rules of procedure or evidence, the judge asks a lot of questions, and the agency is not represented by an attorney. The ex-beneficiary may be represented by an attorney if finances allow. This hearing is the first time the ex-beneficiary has actually had a face-to-face meeting with anyone involved in the case. This procedure was standard prior to 1984 legislation, but the episode with Bruce Merli, which will be described in a moment, occurred between 1981 and 1984. At that time, DI benefits stopped immediately after the initial finding that beneficiaries were no longer disabled. There was no opportunity for a face-to-face meeting with anyone in the agency until the claimant saw the ALJ, and in many cases it took well over a year to get to the ALJ.[11]

The ALJ is to make a finding of fact based on testimony and evidence and to make a determination that the individual is either disabled or not. That determination, however, is really a recommendation to the SSA Appeals Council (AC), which is free to accept or reject the ALJ's findings. The AC's decision is final and becomes the decision of the secretary of Health and Human Services (HHS). The ex-beneficiary can appeal the secretary's decision to a U.S. district court and may be able to appeal to the circuit court of appeals, but appeal to the Supreme Court is unlikely because the cases rarely involve constitutional issues (see *Mathews v. Eldridge,* in Chapter 9).

The Reagan administration began in mid-January 1981 and, operating on the assumptions that (a) massive fraud existed in the disability program and (b) substantial deficit reduction savings could be found in that program,[12] began a massive assault on disability beneficiaries.

Taking advantage of the congressional authorization of periodic review of DI beneficiaries and the SSA's current medical evidence standard, President Reagan's Secretary of Health and Human Services, Margaret Heckler, began an intensive review of DI beneficiaries in March 1981. This was done through a process called *profiling*; that is, DI recipients were targeted for review on the basis of a profile. If the recipient was young, recently awarded benefits, or receiving benefits at a high level (DI benefits levels are determined by prior employment history), he or she was selected for potential review.[13] At that point, those with permanent disabilities were eliminated from the list for potential review.[14] Earlier agency studies had suggested that increased review of DI recipients would produce a termination rate of 20 percent of cases reviewed, but it turned out to be 50 percent.[15]

The SSA scheduled 180,000 cases for the DDS to review in 1981 (fiscal year), 500,000 for 1982, and 850,000 for 1983.[16] Although the 1983 goal was not met, more than a million cases were reviewed between March 1981 and November 1983.[17] The million cases reviewed produced more than 470,000 terminations.[18] Bear in mind that these terminations were accomplished through a paper review process in which the primary question asked by the agency was "whether the DI recipient was currently disabled as defined by the Law" (unable "to do substantial gainful economic activity"), and the fact that the recipient had been declared disabled at an earlier date was considered to be irrelevant.[19]

This procedure produced a plethora of anecdotal stories of "bedridden and incoherent"[20] ex-beneficiaries showing up at the hearings with ALJs. For example, Bruce Merli had been shot in the head in Vietnam and discharged with a 100 percent veterans disability. He qualified for SSA disability in 1968 with severe brain damage, which caused "an inability to understand and use language and defective vision,"[21] but his benefits were terminated in the 1981 review process.[22] The ALJs overturned 60 percent of all the disability termination cases appealed to them,[23] a fact not lost on DI recipients forced through this process. As this procedure began in March 1981, 70 percent of those whose benefits were terminated appealed to the ALJ, but by the end of 1983, 90 percent appealed.[24] In the meantime, federal courts were either reversing or remanding termination decisions appealed to them at a rate of 49 percent.[25] The SSA was so upset at the ALJ reversal rate that it put pressure on ALJs with high reversal rates to modify their decision making, and the agency also pressured all ALJs to increase their productivity so that more termination cases could be processed.[26]

Secretary Heckler was so unhappy with federal court decisions in DI termination cases that she adopted a policy of nonacquiescence. The Ninth Circuit Court of Appeals made two decisions in 1981 and 1982 that imposed, as a matter of law in the ninth circuit, that the SSA could not terminate a DI recipient without a showing (supported by substantial evidence) of medical improvement in the recipient's condition.[27] Other circuits soon followed. When an agency adopts a nonacquiescence policy, the agency applies the Court's holding to the affected litigant (e.g., Bruce Merli) but refuses to apply it as precedent to all other termination cases. In short, it does as ordered by the Court with respect to the immediate case but refuses to apply the law in all other cases.[28]

A class action lawsuit was filed to challenge the secretary's nonacquiescence policy, and the federal judge issuing an injunction against the secretary's policy scolded her with the following words:

Regarding the plaintiffs' motions for class certification and for a preliminary injunction, the issues raised are inextricably intertwined with each other and with the merits of the plaintiffs' constitutional challenge. Our Court of Appeals has stated that to obtain a preliminary injunction the moving party must demonstrate "either a combination of probable success on the merits and the possibility of irreparable injury, or that serious questions are raised and the balance of hardships tips sharply in the moving party's favor." The plaintiffs have fulfilled both tests.

As to the first test, they have demonstrated probable success on the merits by making a strong argument that agencies are bound by the laws of the circuit. "It is emphatically the province and duty of the judicial department to say what the law is. Those who apply the rule to particular cases must of necessity expound and interpret that rule." This principle was laid down many years ago by Chief Justice Marshall in the landmark case of *Marbury v. Madison,* 5 U.S. (1 Cranch) 137, 177 (1803). It has generally been accepted and acclaimed ever since, and it is the cornerstone of the doctrine of Separation of Powers that has served our country so well. Thus, governmental agencies, like all individuals and other entities, are obliged to follow and apply the law as it is interpreted by the courts. The courts of appeals in other circuits categorically have denied the authority of a federal executive body to nonacquiesce in the law enunciated by our courts of appeals. In announcing the policy of nonacquiescence that is challenged here, the Secretary commented that in "many" instances the evidence on which disability was originally allowed "may not be available, or may not even exist." Such a circumstance would, indeed, make it very difficult, perhaps impossible, fully to apply the rule announced by the Court of Appeals in *Patti* and *Finnegan.* If such problems arise, as they occasionally may do, the obligation of the administrative body is to do the best that it can to proceed in harmony with the rule, and infer only such exception as is made necessary by the facts in the particular case. But for the Secretary to make the general assertion that a decision of the Court of Appeals is not to be followed because she disagrees with it is to operate outside the law.

The policy of nonacquiescence announced by the Secretary creates two standards governing claimants whose disability benefits are terminated as a result of such nonacquiescence. If such a claimant has the determination and the financial and physical strength and lives long enough to make it through the administrative process, he can turn to the courts and ultimately expect them to apply the law as announced in *Patti* and *Finnegan.* If exhaustion overtakes him and he falls somewhere along the road leading to such ultimate relief, the nonacquiescence and the resulting termination stand. Particularly with respect to the types of individuals here concerned, whose resources, health and prospective longevity are, by definition, relatively limited, such a dual system of law is prejudicial and unfair.

The plaintiffs have fulfilled the second requirement of the first test for preliminary injunction by showing that delay for the litigants creates a strong possibility of irreparable injury. The record shows that some who have unexpectedly lost benefits have already suffered deprivation of life's necessities, further illness, or even death from the very disabilities that the Secretary deemed them not to have. Retroactive relief would be inadequate, and perhaps too late, to ensure that the purpose of Social Security disability bene-fits, i.e., provision of a minimum standard of living for the poor and disabled, will be served. As to the second test for preliminary injunction, the plaintiffs' claim that the Secretary's failure to abide by federal appellate precedents de-nies them due process of law certainly raises serious legal questions. Because many plaintiffs have their sole means of support at stake, the balance of hard-ships tips sharply in their favor. Thus, under both alternative tests for prelimi-nary injunction, the plaintiffs have demonstrated their right to provisional relief pending the final disposition of this case.[29]

Questions

1. Do you believe that it would have been more efficient if the agency had purged those in the permanently disabled category prior to the profile?
2. In your opinion, is this an example of (a) a bureaucracy out of control or (b) an administration carrying out its electoral mandate? Why?

Secretary Heckler appealed the case and ultimately won a stay of the injunction from Chief Justice Rehnquist that was eventually upheld by the Supreme Court.[30] In the face of heavy criticism by federal judges, SSA ALJs, the press, governors, and both Republican and Democratic members of Congress, the Reagan administration stopped the accelerated review of DI recipients and began to soften its rhetoric on nonacquiescence.[31] It took an act of Congress, however, to finally end the disability affair. The Disability Reform Act of 1984 restored the medical improvement standard for disability termination, allowed for a face-to-face appearance by the terminated recipient at the reconsideration stage in the process at the DDS, and continued benefits to those terminated through their appeal process.[32] The act passed the House by a vote of 410 to 1[33] and the Senate by 96 to 0.[34]

INFORMAL ACTIVITY

In the disability scenario above, the agency's decision to switch from the medical improvement standard to the current medical evidence standard was an unregulated decision, as was the secretary's decision to adopt a nonacqui-escence policy. Neither decision was covered by the APA, and although in 1980 the SSA published in the *Federal Register* the fact that it had changed standards four years earlier, no notice was published prior to the decision, nor was public input sought.[35] Indeed, many of the decisions you are familiar with from the cases you have read so far are "informal" decisions in that they were not covered by the APA and are examples of unregulated discretion. The following is a list of such decisions:

- the secretary of transportation's various decisions to reopen automobile safety standard hearings in the *State Farm* case
- the collector of customs' decision to raise the duty on barium dioxide in the *Hampton* case
- the Internal Revenue Service's (IRS) decision not to enforce its policy regarding charitable contributions and private academies in *Allen v. Wright et al.*
- the Food and Drug Administration's (FDA) decision not to test the drug used in lethal injections involving capital punishment (*Heckler v. Chaney*)
- the secretary of transportation's decision to run a six-lane highway through a city park in *Overton Park*
- the police officer's use of a choke hold in *Los Angeles v. Lyons* (most likely, the chief's policy of allowing the unrestrained and unregulated use of choke holds also falls into this category)
- the agency's demand for receipts in *Shapiro*
- the agencies' decisions to issue subpoenas for information in *American Tobacco* and *Oklahoma Press*
- all decisions by any agency not to release (or to release) requested information under the Freedom of Information Act (FOIA) and any agency's decision to conduct an inspection of (or not to inspect) certain businesses

Other obvious agency activity falls into this category. For example, in the processing of applications for nearly any governmental program, the initial decision on the application is just such an informal decision. Applications for Social Security, food stamps, veterans benefits, a small business loan, or a federal research grant are examples.

Kenneth Culp Davis has argued that 90 percent of what agencies do is informal activity and, further, that rarely are such activities challenged in court.[36] Because it could lead to confusion in subsequent chapters, we should take time to be precise about what the terms *formal rule making, informal rule making,* and *informal activity* mean. In the next chapter, you will discover that under the APA are two processes for rule making by agencies: formal and informal. Formal rule making is what I refer to throughout the rest of this book as a "554 hearing," or "quasi-judicial." Such hearings are used in several contexts—for example, in the appeals process for DI terminations—but sometimes Congress requires agencies to go through this quasi-judicial procedure to make policy. In Chapter 3, we discussed the fact that the Federal Trade

Commission had to go through this process to force peanut butter manufacturers to increase the amount of peanuts in their product by 2 percent. The result of such a process is called an *order,* and it constitutes the 10 percent of formal agency activity to which Davis refers. Informal rule making, in public administration jargon, is what we have called "rule promulgation," "notice and comment process," or a "quasi-legislative hearing"; all are the same thing, and all are guided by Section 553 of the APA but are nevertheless considered by Davis to be informal activity because they are not guided by trial-type hearings. Hence, there is formal rule making, informal rule making, and, simply, unregulated decisions. The latter category I call "informal agency activity" and is addressed in this chapter.

Gellhorn and Levin have listed nine areas in which considerable informal agency activity takes place: (a) agency settlement, negotiation, and alternative disputes resolution (an agency's decision to settle a potential legal conflict, such as breach of contract, or to enter a consent decree is all at the absolute unregulated discretion of the agency); (b) processing of applications and claims (this was touched on earlier, but according to Gellhorn and Levin, "In a single year . . . the SSA disburses about two hundred billion dollars and makes over four million determinations in administering the Old-Age, Survivors, Disability and Health Insurance programs")[37]; (c) tests and inspections (Chapter 5); (d) suspensions, seizures, and recalls (if a product is considered by an agency to pose a serious immediate threat to public health or safety—for instance, contaminated food—then the summary decision to seize the product or suspend a license is made without a hearing although one may be required after the fact); (e) agency supervision (e.g., nearly constant supervision of banks); (f) agency use of publicity (e.g., the decision to leak a story to the media; we can probably assume that a good deal of the bad publicity that President Reagan and Secretary Heckler received during the disability affair was leaked by bureaucrats within the DDS who disagreed with agency policy); (g) agency advice (e.g., when you call the IRS toll-free number for help in filling out your income tax return—a subject to which we will turn our attention momentarily); (h) contracts and grants (the federal government is certainly the biggest contractor in the United States, and each decision to enter a contract is absolutely at the discretion of an agency; the same is true of grants although there are general guidelines); and (i) agency management (the Bureau of Land Management, Forest Service, and the National Park Service all manage tremendous natural resources and make decisions such as who will get a concession in a national park, who can cut timber and how and where they can cut, and who can graze cattle on public land, practically free).

Although all of these areas have generated some litigation, certainly the most litigation has been generated in the area in which a government employee gives advice to a citizen. More particularly, suits are generated when the citizen relies on the government's advice but the advice turns out to be wrong and the citizen ends up in trouble or suffering an economic loss.

Estoppel

What happens when a taxpayer calls the toll-free number and gets advice on a deduction from the IRS employee; takes the deduction, which flags an audit; and then finds that the IRS wants not only the missing tax money but also interest and penalties? Does the taxpayer have to pay the interest and penalties? The real-world answer is that it depends. Factors that go into the resolution are the amount of money involved, how assertive the taxpayer is and how far he or she is willing to fight the IRS through the process, how good the taxpayer's attorney is, and even the mood of the IRS decision maker on the day the taxpayer's case hits his or her desk.[38] The safe, and theoretically correct, answer, however, is that, yes, the taxpayer is liable for fines and interest accrued as a result of relying on the IRS advice. Why do you suppose this is the case?

In spring 1945, Idaho farmers, the Merrill brothers, applied to the County Agricultural Conservation Committee for federal crop insurance. The Merrills informed the committee that they planned to plant 460 acres of spring wheat but that 400 of those acres would be reseeded on winter wheat. The committee, acting as the agent for the Federal Crop Insurance Agency within the Department of Agriculture, informed the Merrills that the entire crop would be covered. The committee further recommended to the regional office that the corporation accept the Merrills' application for insurance (although the application itself made no mention of reseeded wheat). The Federal Crop Insurance Corporation accepted the Merrills' application. By July, most of the Merrills' crop was wiped out by drought (a calamity normally covered by insurance).[39] After the corporation discovered that the destroyed acreage had been reseeded, it refused to cover the loss. The case follows.

FEDERAL CROP INSURANCE CORPORATION V. MERRILL
332 U.S. 380 (1947)

Justice Frankfurter delivered the opinion of the Court, joined by Chief Justice Vinson and Justices Reed, Murphy, and Burton. Justices Jackson, Black, Douglas, and Rutledge dissented.

The trial court rejected the Corporation's contention, presented by a demurrer to the complaint, that the Wheat Crop Insurance Regulations barred recovery as a matter of law. Evidence was thereupon permitted to go to the jury to the effect that the respondents had no actual knowledge of the Regulations, insofar as they precluded insurance for reseeded wheat, and that they had in fact been misled by petitioner's agent into believing that spring wheat reseeded on winter wheat acreage was insurable by the Corporation. The jury returned a verdict for the loss on all the 460 acres and the Supreme Court of Idaho affirmed the resulting judgment. 174 P.2d 834. That court in effect adopted the theory of the trial judge, that since the knowledge of the agent of a private insurance company, under the circumstances of this case, would be attributed to, and thereby bind, a private insurance company, the Corporation is equally bound.

The case no doubt presents phases of hardship. We take for granted that, on the basis of what they were told by the Corporation's local agent, the respondents reasonably believed that their entire crop was covered by petitioner's insurance. And so we assume that recovery could be had against a private insurance company. But the Corporation is not a private insurance company. It is too late in the day to urge that the Government is just another private litigant, for purposes of charging it with liability, whenever it takes over a business theretofore conducted by private enterprise or engages in competition with private ventures. Government is not partly public or partly private, depending upon the governmental pedigree of the type of a particular activity or the manner in which the Government conducts it. The Government may carry on its operations through conventional executive agencies or through corporate forms especially created for defined ends. Whatever the form in which the Government functions, anyone entering into an arrangement with the Government takes the risk of having accurately ascertained that he who purports to act for the Government stays within the bounds of his authority. The scope of this authority may be explicitly defined by Congress or be limited by delegated legislation, properly exercised through the rule-making power. And this is so even though, as here, the agent himself may have been unaware of the limitations upon his authority. If the Federal Crop Insurance Act had by explicit language prohibited the insurance of spring wheat which is reseeded on winter wheat acreage, the ignorance of

such a restriction, either by the respondents or the Corporation's agent, would be immaterial and recovery could not be had against the Corporation for loss of such reseeded wheat. Congress could hardly define the multitudinous details appropriate for the business of crop insurance when the Government entered it. Inevitably "the terms and conditions" upon which valid governmental insurance can be had must be defined by the agency acting for the Government. And so Congress has legislated in this instance, as in modern regulatory enactments it so often does by conferring the rule-making power upon the agency created for carrying out its policy. . . . Just as everyone is charged with knowledge of the United States Statutes at Large, Congress has provided that the appearance of rules and regulations in the *Federal Register* gives legal notice of their contents.

Accordingly, the Wheat Crop Insurance Regulations were binding on all who sought to come within the Federal Crop Insurance Act, regardless of actual knowledge of what is in the Regulations or of the hardship resulting from innocent ignorance. The oft-quoted observation in *Rock Island, Arkansas & Louisiana R. Co. v. United States,* 254 U.S. 141, that "Men must turn square corners when they deal with the Government," does not reflect a callous outlook. It merely expresses the duty of all courts to observe the conditions defined by Congress for charging the public treasury. The "terms and conditions" defined by the Corporation, under authority of Congress, for creating liability on the part of the Government preclude recovery for the loss of the reseeded wheat no matter with what good reason the respondents thought they had obtained insurance from the Government. Indeed, not only do the Wheat Regulations limit the liability of the Government as if they had been enacted by Congress directly, but they were in fact incorporated by reference in the application, as specifically required by the Regulations. We have thus far assumed, as did the parties here and the courts below, that the controlling regulation in fact precluded insurance coverage for spring wheat reseeded on winter wheat acreage. It explicitly states that the term "wheat crop shall not include * * * winter wheat in the 1945 crop year, and spring wheat which has been reseeded on winter wheat acreage in the 1945 crop year." . . . Wheat Crop Insurance Regulations, 10 F.R. 1591. The circumstances of this case tempt one to read the regulation, since it is for us to read it, with charitable laxity. But not even the temptations of a hard case can elude the clear meaning of the regulation. It precludes recovery for "spring wheat which has been reseeded on winter wheat acreage in the 1945 crop year." Concerning the validity of the regulation, as "not inconsistent with the provisions" of the Federal Crop Insurance Act, no question has been raised.

The judgment is reversed and the case remanded for further proceedings not inconsistent with this opinion.

Reversed.

Mr. Justice Black, and Mr. Justice Rutledge, dissent.

Justice Jackson, dissenting.

I would affirm the decision of the court below. If crop insurance contracts made by agencies of the United States Government are to be judged by the law of the State in which they are written, I find no error in the court below. If, however, we are to hold them subject only to federal law and to declare what that law is, I can see no reason why we should not adopt a rule which recognizes the practicalities of the business.

It was early discovered that fair dealing in the insurance business required that the entire contract between the policyholder and the insurance company be embodied in the writings which passed between the parties, namely the written application, if any, and the policy issued. It may be well enough to make some types of contracts with the Government subject to long and involved regulations published in the *Federal Register.* To my mind, it is an absurdity to hold that every farmer who insures his crops knows what the *Federal Register* contains or even knows that there is such a publication. If he were to peruse this voluminous and dull publication as it is issued from time to time in order to make sure whether anything has been promulgated that affects his rights, he would never need crop insurance, for he would never get time to plant any crops. Nor am I convinced that a reading of technically worded regulations would enlighten him much in any event.

In this case, the Government entered a field which required the issuance of large numbers of insurance policies to people engaged in agriculture. It could not expect them to be lawyers, except in rare instances, and one should not be expected to have to employ a lawyer to see whether his own Government is issuing him a policy which in case of loss would turn out to be no policy at all. There was no fraud or concealment, and those who represented the Government in taking on the risk apparently no more suspected the existence of a hidden regulation that would render the contract void than did the policyholder. It is very well to say that those who deal with the Government should turn square corners. But there is no reason why the square corners should constitute a one-way street.

The Government asks us to lift its policies out of the control of the States and to find or fashion a federal rule to govern them. I should respond to that request by laying down a federal rule that would hold these agencies to the same fundamental principles of fair dealing that have been found essential in progressive states to prevent insurance from being an investment in disappointment. Mr. Justice Douglas joins in this opinion.

Question

The *Merrill* case is famous because it established a doctrine for dealing with cases like it. The Court was asked to "fashion a federal law," which it did. Can you articulate what that doctrine is?

The *Merrill* case raises questions of estoppel (see *estoppel, collateral,* and *equitable estoppel* in your law dictionary). *Estoppel* is a legal term that means one is stopped from taking some legal action by prior action or activity. In the

Merrill case, the question is whether the government is estopped from denying the Merrills' insurance claims because the government's agent gave them bad advice.

Using the *Merrill* case as a guide, how would you resolve the following cases?

In *Schweiker v. Hansen,* 450 U.S. 785 (1981), Ms. Hansen asked an SSA field representative whether she was eligible for her mother's insurance benefits. (She was.) The field representative, however, erroneously told her that she was not. Further, the SSA claims manual instructs field representatives to advise claimants to fill out an application regardless of the advice given, but the representative failed to advise Hansen to fill out the application. When Hansen found out she was, in fact, eligible for the benefits, she sued for the year's worth of benefits she had lost. The SSA's position was that she was not deserving of the benefits for that year because the SSA has a rule requiring a written application (just like the crop insurance rule against reseeded wheat). The legal issue is whether the SSA should be estopped from applying the rule to Hansen because of the erroneous advice given and the failure to inform her by the SSA's field agent. How would you resolve this issue and why?

An old law called the Rivers and Harbors Act forbids the discharge of any "refuse matter" into navigable waterways in the United States. The act delegates to the Army Corps of Engineers the power to enforce it. The Army Corps enforces the law through a permit system, and, historically, permits were issued for dumping into navigable waterways matter that would not impede navigation, but permits were consistently denied for dumping any refuse that would impede navigation. In the early 1970s, there was no Clean Water Act, but environmental groups had raised awareness that our lakes and rivers were dangerously polluted. Environmental lawyers had some success urging government to use the Rivers and Harbors Act to get at companies dumping effluent into rivers. The Pennsylvania Industrial Chemical Corporation, relying on the past behavior of the Army Corps to deny permits only to those who would dump matter that would impede navigation, failed to secure the appropriate permit prior to dumping a chemical into the Monongahela River. The Army Corps brought criminal charges against the chemical company. This case (*United States v. Pennsylvania Industrial Chemical Corporation,* 411 U.S. 655 [1973]) presented a narrow procedural issue of whether the company could present evidence of the Army Corps's past enforcement behavior at trial. Although, technically, this is not an estoppel case, think of the issue in this way: Can the government be estopped from bringing criminal charges because its past enforcement behavior misled the company into believing its actions were not criminal? How would you resolve this issue, and why?

If you resolved both the *Hansen* and *Chemical Corporation* cases in the same way, you were wrong. Indeed, the SSA was not estopped from applying the "written application rule" to Hansen, but the government was prohibited from pressing criminal charges against the chemical company.

You will see from *Heckler v. Community Health Services* at the end of this chapter that the Court has articulated a two-pronged test for when a private citizen attempts to estop the government. First, the party claiming estoppel must show that reliance on the government's advice or conduct resulted in a change of position for the worse. The Merrills were going to plant the reseeded wheat in any case. Hansen might have been able to meet this prong of the test, but the test was not created until 1984. Second, the party claiming estoppel cannot have acted out of ignorance, "and that reliance must have been reasonable in that the party claiming estoppel did not know nor should have known that its adversary's conduct was misleading."[40]

The concept in the second prong of the test is common to all the cases discussed except the *Chemical Corporation* case. It is a taxpayer's duty to know (or find out) the regulations. It was the Merrills' duty to read the *Federal Register* to find out about reseeded wheat, and it was Hansen's duty to read the Social Security regulations and make appropriate application.

Chief Justice Rehnquist points out that the Court has decided seven estoppel cases and that in five of them the Court did not estop the government.[41] The two cases in which the government was estopped were unique. The *Chemical Corporation* case, for example, was a criminal case in which the company got into trouble, not out of ignorance, but precisely because it relied on governmental behavior and therefore had no appropriate warnings of the kind of conduct the government considered illegal.[42]

We have discussed examples of informal agency activity and the exercise of discretion. Let us move to a consideration of how or whether to control such discretion.

CONTROLLING INFORMAL ACTIVITY

It is perhaps not a good state of affairs in a democratic country to allow (encourage?) law enforcement officers to apply a choke hold that can injure, cripple, or kill a citizen over a minor traffic violation. Neither is it a good indicator of the health of a democracy when an administrative agency literally declares war on a half million of its disabled citizens to purge them from an entitlement program to which they have already documented entitlement.

Because the legislative branch cannot be expected to consider every contingency, to foresee every nuance, or to control for every variable, the administrative state presumes the exercise of discretion by administrative agencies. The question, then, is not whether agencies should exercise discretion but, rather, to what degree that discretion should be controlled.

The Founding Fathers attempted to control the discretion of those in power through a written constitution and the concept of "separation of power." These do not apply much to modern agencies in the administrative state. Legislative delegations of power, which should serve the channeling purposes of the Constitution, are written so loosely and vaguely as to impose almost no constraints at all on agency behavior, and there is no separation of power within agencies. Agencies may, however, be checked by other branches, as in judicial review. Although the lower federal courts seemed consistently to check agency discretion in the disability cases, the Supreme Court overruled a lower-court decision enjoining the SSA's nonacquiescence policy. Although a lower-court decision awarded Lyons money for his injuries, the Supreme Court refused to enjoin the limitless use of choke holds by police. According to Kenneth Culp Davis, "Judicial review is sometimes available, but much informal action is not even theoretically reviewable and more than ninety-nine percent of what is reviewable is not in fact reviewed."[43]

Davis, who is perhaps the foremost authority on the problem of discretion, argues that much discretion is unnecessary and should be eliminated and that the remaining necessary discretion should be "structured" by rules.[44] For example, prosecutors exercise tremendous discretion in deciding whether to charge, what to charge with, and what to recommend regarding bail (whether a defendant is free on bail at the time of trial is related to findings of guilt or innocence). This is probably necessary discretion, but successful attempts have been made to control it. For example, a point system that determines what the prosecutor must recommend in terms of bail reduces the possibility that other factors, such as race, can enter the discretionary decision.

There is no escape from the fact that law enforcement officers must exercise discretion "on the street." That is not to say that we must accept and live with officers' decisions to apply a choke hold to citizens who pose no threat to the officers or other citizens. If the Los Angeles Police Department had adopted an internal procedural rule limiting the application of choke holds to those situations in which an officer perceives a threat either to him- or herself or to other citizens, fewer incidents of "official violence" would occur.

Davis's solution of limiting discretion through written rules does not always work, however. There was a written and duly promulgated rule in the *Merrill* case, and apparently the government agent, on whom citizens rely to know the rules, was ignorant of the rule, to the Merrills' detriment. The same can be said in the *Hansen* case.

Most of the material in a text such as this deals with challenges to agency activity covered by the APA or the enabling legislation. The student should be aware that this constitutes only a small part of agencies' activity. A good deal of agency activity is what I have labeled *informal activity.* This activity affects citizens, but a good deal of it never gets reviewed by the courts. It raises serious democratic issues of accountability, but experts are undecided on a solution to the questions it raises.

SUMMARY

The two-pronged test from *Heckler v. Community Health Services* consists of the following considerations: (a) The party claiming estoppel must show that reliance on governmental advice or conduct resulted in a change in his or her position for the worse, and (b) the party claiming estoppel cannot have acted out of ignorance of the law or agency rule.

END-OF-CHAPTER CASES

HECKLER V. COMMUNITY HEALTH SERVICES
467 U.S. 51 (1984)

Justice Stevens delivered the opinion for a unanimous Court, with Chief Justice Burger and Justice Rehnquist concurring.

Under what is recognized for present purposes as an incorrect interpretation of rather complex federal regulations, during 1975, 1976, and 1977 respondent received and expended $71,480 in federal funds to provide health care services to Medicare beneficiaries to which it was not entitled. The question presented is whether the Government is estopped from recovering those funds because respondent relied on the express authorization of a responsible government agent in making the expenditures.

I

Under the Medicare program, Title XVIII of the Social Security Act, providers of health care services are reimbursed for the reasonable cost of services rendered to Medicare beneficiaries as determined by petitioner, the Secretary of Health and Human Services. Providers receive interim payments at least monthly covering the cost of services they have rendered. Congress recognized, however, that these interim payments would not always correctly reflect the amount of reimbursable costs, and accordingly instructed petitioner to develop mechanisms for making appropriate retroactive adjustments when reimbursement is found to be inadequate or excessive. Pursuant to this statutory mandate, petitioner requires providers to submit annual cost reports which are then audited to determine actual costs. Petitioner may reopen any reimbursement determination within a three-year period and make appropriate adjustments. The Act also permits a provider to elect to receive reimbursement through a "fiscal intermediary." If the intermediary the provider has nominated meets her requirements, petitioner then enters into an agreement with the intermediary to have it perform those administrative responsibilities she assigns it. These duties include receipt, disbursement and accounting for funds used in making Medicare payments, auditing the records of providers in order to ensure payments have been proper, resolving disputes over cost reimbursement, reviewing and reconsidering payments to providers, and recovering overpayments to providers. The fiscal intermediary must also "serve as a center for, and communicate to providers, any information or instructions furnished to it by the Secretary, and serve as a channel of communication from providers to the Secretary."

Respondent Community Health Services of Crawford County, Inc., is a nonprofit corporation. In 1966 it entered into a contract with petitioner's predecessor, the Secretary of Health, Education and Welfare, to provide home health care services to individuals eligible for benefits under Part A of the Medicare program. Under the contract, respondent received reimbursement through a fiscal intermediary, the Travelers Insurance Companies (Travelers).

In 1973 Congress enacted the Comprehensive Employment and Training Act (CETA), now codified as amended at 29 U.S.C. §§ 801-999 authorizing the use of federal funds to provide training and job opportunities for economically disadvantaged persons. In 1975 respondent began participating in the program, which reimbursed it for the salaries and fringe benefits paid to certain of its employees. CETA funds made it possible for respondent to take on additional personnel and to provide additional home health care services.

To prevent what would be in effect double-reimbursement of providers' costs, one of the regulations concerning reasonable costs reimbursable under the Medicare program indicates that grants received by a provider in order to pay specific operating costs must be subtracted from the reasonable costs for which the provider may receive reimbursement. After obtaining a CETA grant, re-

spondent's administrator contacted Travelers to ask whether the salaries of its CETA-funded employees who provided services to patients eligible for Medicare benefits were reimbursable as reasonable costs under Medicare. Travelers' Medicare manager orally advised respondent that the CETA funds were "seed money" within the meaning of the Provider Reimbursement Manual, which is defined as "[g]rants designated for the development of new health care agencies or for expansion of services of established agencies," and therefore, even though the CETA employees' salaries constituted specific operating costs paid by a federal grant, they were reimbursable under the Medicare program. Relying on Travelers' advice, respondent included costs for which it was receiving CETA reimbursement in its cost reports, and received reimbursement for those sums amounting to $7,694, $32,460, and $31,326 in fiscal 1975, 1976, and 1977, respectively. On several occasions during this period, respondent requested and received from Travelers oral verification of the propriety of this treatment. With these additional funds, respondent expanded its annual number of home health care visits from approximately 4,000 in 1974 to over 81,000 in the next three years. Its annual budget increased during that period from about $53,000 to about $900,000. It is undisputed that correct administrative practice required Travelers to refer respondent's inquiry to the Department of Health and Human Services for a definitive answer. However, Travelers did not do this until August 7, 1977, when a written request for instructions was finally submitted to the Philadelphia office of the Department's Bureau of Health Insurance. Travelers was then formally advised that the CETA funds were not seed money and therefore had to be subtracted from respondent's Medicare reimbursement. On October 7, 1977, Travelers formally notified respondent of this determination. Travelers then reopened respondent's cost reports for the preceding three years and recomputed respondent's reimbursable costs, determining that respondent had been overpaid a total of $71,480.

Estoppel is an equitable doctrine invoked to avoid injustice in particular cases. While a hallmark of the doctrine is its flexible application, certain principles are tolerably clear: "If one person makes a definite misrepresentation of fact to another person having reason to believe that the other will rely upon it and the other in reasonable reliance upon it does an act . . . the first person is not entitled . . .

(b) to regain property or its value that the other acquired by the act, if the other in reliance upon the misrepresentation and before discovery of the truth has so changed his position that it would be unjust to deprive him of that which he thus acquired." Restatement (Second) of Torts. Thus, the party claiming the estoppel must have relied on its adversary's conduct "in such a manner as to change his position for the worse." And that reliance must have been reasonable in that the party claiming the estoppel did not know nor should it have known that its adversary's conduct was misleading.

When the Government is unable to enforce the law because the conduct of its agents has given rise to an estoppel, the interest of the citizenry as a whole in obedience to the rule of law is undermined. It is for this reason that it is well-settled that the Government may not be estopped on the same terms as any other litigant. Petitioner urges us to expand this principle into a flat rule that estoppel may not in any circumstances run against the Government. We have left the issue open in the past, and do so again today. Though the arguments the Government advances for the rule are substantial, we are hesitant, when it is unnecessary to decide this case, to say that there are no cases in which the public interest in ensuring that the Government can enforce the law free from estoppel might be outweighed by the countervailing interest of citizens in some minimum standard of decency, honor, and reliability in their dealings with their Government. But however heavy the burden might be when an estoppel is asserted against the Government, the private party surely cannot prevail without at least demonstrating that the traditional elements of an estoppel are present. We are unpersuaded that that has been done in this case with respect to either respondent's change in position or its reliance on Travelers' advice. . . .

III

To analyze the nature of a private party's detrimental change in position, we must identify the manner in which reliance on the Government's misconduct has caused the private citizen to change his position for the worse. In this case the consequences of the Government's misconduct were not entirely adverse. Respondent did receive an immediate benefit as a result of the double reimbursement. Its detriment is the inability to retain money that it should never have received in the first place. Thus, this is not a case in which the respondent has lost any legal right, either vested or contingent, or suffered any adverse change in its status. When a private party is deprived of something to which it was entitled of right, it has surely suffered a detrimental change in its position. Here respondent lost no rights but merely was induced to something which could be corrected at a later time. . . .

IV

Justice Holmes wrote: "Men must turn square corners when they deal with the Government." This observation has its greatest force when a private party seeks to spend the Government's money. Protection of the public fisc requires that those who seek public funds act with scrupulous regard for the requirements of law; respondent could expect no less than to be held to the most demanding standards in its quest for public funds. This is consistent with the general rule that those who deal with the Government are expected to know the law and may not rely on the conduct of government agents contrary to law.

As a participant in the Medicare program, respondent had a duty to familiarize itself with the legal requirements for cost reimbursement. Since it also had elected to receive reimbursement through Travelers, it also was acquainted with the nature of and limitations on the role of a fiscal intermediary. When the question arose concerning respondent's CETA funds, respondent's own action in consulting Travelers demonstrates the necessity for it to have obtained an interpretation of the applicable regulations; respondent indisputably knew that this was a doubtful question not clearly covered by existing policy statements. The fact that Travelers' advice was erroneous is, in itself, insufficient to raise an estoppel, as is the fact that petitioner had not anticipated this problem and made a clear resolution available to respondent. There is simply no requirement that the Government anticipate every problem that may arise in the administration of a complex program such as Medicare, neither can it be expected to ensure that every bit of informal advice given by its agents in the course of such a program will be sufficiently reliable to justify expenditure of sums of money as substantial as those spent by respondent. Nor was the advice given under circumstances that should have induced respondent's reliance. As a recipient of public funds well-acquainted with the role of a fiscal intermediary, respondent knew Travelers only acted as a conduit; it could not resolve policy questions. The relevant statute, regulations, and reimbursement manual, with which respondent should have been and was acquainted, made that perfectly clear. Yet respondent made no attempt to have the question resolved by petitioner; it was satisfied with the policy judgment of a mere conduit.

The appropriateness of respondent's reliance is further undermined because the advice it received from Travelers was oral. It is not merely the possibility of fraud that undermines our confidence in the reliability of official action that is not confirmed or evidenced by a written instrument. Written advice, like a written judicial opinion, requires its author to reflect about the nature of the advice that is given to the citizen, and subjects that advice to the possibility of review, criticism and reexamination. The necessity for ensuring that governmental agents stay within the lawful scope of their authority, and that those who seek public funds act with scrupulous exactitude, argues strongly for the conclusion that an estoppel cannot be erected on the basis of the oral advice that underlay respondent's cost reports. That is especially true when a complex program such as Medi-care is involved, in which the need for written records is manifest.

In sum, the regulations governing the cost reimbursement provisions of Medicare should and did put respondent on ample notice of the care with which its cost reports must be prepared, and the care which would be taken to review them within the relevant three-year period. Yet respondent prepared those reports on the basis of an oral policy judgment by an official who, it should have known, was not in the business of making policy. That is not the kind of reasonable reliance that would even give rise to an estoppel against a private party. It therefore cannot estop the Government.

Thus, assuming estoppel can ever be appropriately applied against the Government, it cannot be said that the detriment respondent faces is so severe or has been imposed in such an unfair way that petitioner ought to be estopped from enforcing the law in this case. Accordingly, the judgment of the Court of Appeals is reversed and the case is remanded to that court for further proceedings consistent with this opinion.

It is so ordered.

WISCONSIN V. CITY OF NEW YORK
116 S.Ct. 109 (1996)

Chief Justice Rehnquist delivered the opinion for a unanimous Court.

In conducting the 1990 United States Census, the Secretary of Commerce decided not to use a particular statistical adjustment that had been designed to correct an undercount in the initial enumeration. The Court of Appeals for the Second Circuit held that the Secretary's decision was subject to heightened scrutiny because of its effect on the right of individual respondents to have their vote counted equally. We hold that the Secretary's decision was not subject to heightened scrutiny, and that it conformed to applicable constitutional and statutory provisions.

I

The Constitution requires an "actual Enumeration" of the population every 10 years and vests Congress with the authority to conduct that census "in such Manner as they shall by Law direct." Art. I, § 2, cl. 3. Through the Census Act, 13 U.S.C.

Congress has delegated to the Secretary of the Department of Commerce the responsibility to take "a decennial census of the population . . . in such form and content as he may determine. . . ." The Secretary is assisted in the performance of that responsibility by the Bureau of the Census and its head, the Director of the Census. ("[The] Director shall perform such duties as may be imposed upon him by law, regulations, or orders of the Secretary"). . . .

The Constitution provides that the results of the census shall be used to apportion the Members of the House of Representatives among the States. . . . Today, census data also have important consequences not delineated in the Constitution: The Federal Government considers census data in dispensing funds through federal programs to the States, and the States use the results in drawing intrastate political districts.

There have been 20 decennial censuses in the history of the United States. Although each was designed with the goal of accomplishing an "actual Enumeration" of the population, no census is recognized as having been wholly successful in achieving that goal (recognizing that "census data are not perfect," and that "population counts for particular localities are outdated long before they are completed"); *Gaffney v. Cummings,* 412 U.S. 735, 745 (census data "are inherently less than absolutely accurate"). Despite consistent efforts to improve the quality of the count, errors persist. Persons who should have been counted are not counted at all or are counted at the wrong location; persons who should not have been counted (whether because they died before or were born after the decennial census date, because they were not a citizen of the country, or because they did not exist) are counted; and persons who should have been counted only once are counted twice. It is thought that these errors have resulted in a net "undercount" of the actual American population in every decennial census. In 1970, for instance, the Census Bureau concluded that the census results were 2.7% lower than the actual population.

The undercount is not thought to be spread consistently across the population: Some segments of the population are "undercounted" to a greater degree than are others, resulting in a phenomenon termed the "differential undercount." Since at least 1940, the Census Bureau has thought that the undercount affects some racial and ethnic minority groups to a greater extent than it does whites. In 1940, for example, when the undercount for the entire population was 5.4%, the undercount for blacks was estimated at 8.4% (and the undercount for whites at 5.0%). The problem of the differential undercount has persisted even as the census has come to provide a more numerically accurate count of the population. In the 1980 census, for example, the overall undercount was estimated at 1.2%, and the undercount of blacks was estimated at 4.9%.

The Census Bureau has recognized the undercount and the differential undercount as significant problems, and in the past has devoted substantial effort toward achieving their reduction. Most recently, in its preparations for the 1990 census, the Bureau initiated an extensive inquiry into various means of overcoming the impact of the undercount and the differential undercount. As part of this effort, the Bureau created two task forces: the Undercount Steering Committee (USC), responsible for planning undercount research and policy develop-

ment; and the Undercount Research Staff (URS), which conducted research into various methods of improving the accuracy of the census. In addition, the Bureau consulted with state and local governments and various outside experts and organizations.

Largely as a result of these efforts, the Bureau adopted a wide variety of measures designed to reduce the rate of error in the 1990 enumeration, including an extensive advertising campaign, a more easily completed census questionnaire, and increased use of automation, which among other things facilitated the development of accurate maps and geographic files for the 1990 census. The Bureau also implemented a number of improvements specifically targeted at eliminating the differential undercount; these included advertising campaigns developed by and directed at traditionally undercounted populations and expanded questionnaire assistance operations for non-English speaking residents.

In preparing for the 1990 census, the Bureau and the task forces also looked into the possibility of using large-scale statistical adjustment to compensate for the undercount and differential undercount. Although the Bureau had previously considered that possibility (most recently in 1980), it always had decided instead to rely upon more traditional methodology and the results of the enumeration. See *Cuomo v. Baldrige,* 674 F.Supp. 1089 (S.D. N.Y. 1987) (noting that Bureau rejected large-scale statistical adjustment of 1980 census). In 1985, preliminary investigations by the URS suggested that the most promising method of statistical adjustment was the "capture-recapture" or "dual system estimation" approach.

The particular variations of the "dual system estimation" considered by the Bureau are not important for purposes of this opinion, but an example may serve to make the "dual system estimation" more understandable. Imagine that one wanted to use DSE in order to determine the number of pumpkins in a large pumpkin patch. First, one would choose a particular section of the patch as the representative subset to which the "recapture" phase will be applied. Let us assume here that it is a section exactly 1/10 the size of the entire patch that is selected. Then, at the next step—the "capture" stage—one would conduct a fairly quick count of the entire patch, making sure to record both the number of pumpkins counted in the entire patch and the number of pumpkins counted in the selected section.

Let us imagine that this stage results in a count of 10,000 pumpkins for the entire patch and 1,000 pumpkins for the selected section. Next, at the "recapture" stage, one would perform an exacting count of the number of pumpkins in the selected section. Let us assume that we now count 1,100 pumpkins in that section. By comparing the results of the "capture" phase and the results of the "recapture" phase for the selected section, it is possible to estimate that approximately 100 pumpkins actually in the patch were missed for every 1,000 counted at the "capture" phase. Extrapolating this data to the count for the entire patch, one would conclude that the actual number of pumpkins in the patch is 11,000.

In the context of the census, the initial enumeration of the entire population (the "capture") would be followed by the post-enumeration survey (PES) (the "recapture") of certain representative geographical areas. The Bureau would then compare the results of the PES to the results of the initial enumeration for those areas targeted by the PES, in order to determine a rate of error in those areas for the initial enumeration (i.e., the rate at which the initial enumeration undercounted people in those areas). That rate of error would be extrapolated to the entire population, and thus would be used to statistically adjust the results of the initial enumeration.

The URS thought that the PES also held some promise for correcting the differential undercount. The PES would be conducted through the use of a system called post-stratification. Thus, each person counted through the PES would be placed into one, and only one, of over 1,000 post-strata defined by five categories: geography; age; sex; status of housing unit (rent v. own); and race (including Hispanic versus non-Hispanic origin). By comparing the post-stratified PES data to the results of the initial enumeration, the Bureau would be able to estimate not only an overall undercount rate, but also an undercount rate for each post-strata. Hence, the statistical adjustment of the census could reflect differences in the undercount rate for each post-strata. . . .

Through the mid-1980s, the Bureau conducted a series of field tests and statistical studies designed to measure the utility of the PES as a tool for adjusting the census. The Director of the Bureau decided to adopt a PES-based adjustment, and in June 1987, he informed his superiors in the Department of Commerce of that decision. The Secretary of Commerce disagreed with the Director's deci-

sion to adjust, however, and in October 1987, the Department of Commerce announced that the 1990 Census would not be statistically adjusted. . . .

In July 1991, the Secretary issued his decision not to use the PES to adjust the 1990 census. The Secretary began by noting that large-scale statistical adjustment of the census through the PES would "abandon a two hundred year tradition of how we actually count people." Before taking a "step of that magnitude," he held, it was necessary to be "certain that it would make the census better and the distribution of the population more accurate." Emphasizing that the primary purpose of the census was to apportion political representation among the States, the Secretary concluded that "the primary criterion for accuracy should be distributive accuracy—that is, getting most nearly correct the proportions of people in different areas." . . .

II

In recent years, we have twice considered constitutional challenges to the conduct of the census. In *Department of Commerce v. Montana,* 503 U.S. 442 (1992), the State of Montana, several state officials, and Montana's Members of Congress brought suit against the Federal Government, challenging as unconstitutional the method used to determine the number of Representatives to which each State is entitled. . . .

In conclusion, we recognized the historical pedigree of the challenged method of apportionment, and reemphasized that Congress' "good-faith choice of a method of apportionment of Representatives among the several States 'according to their respective Numbers' commands far more deference than a state districting decision that is capable of being reviewed under a relatively rigid mathematical standard." *Montana,* supra, at 464.

In *Franklin v. Massachusetts*, 505 U.S. (1992), we reiterated our conclusion that the Constitution vests Congress with wide discretion over apportionment decisions and the conduct of the census. In *Franklin,* the State of Massachusetts and two of its registered voters sued the Federal Government, arguing that the method used by the Secretary to count federal employees serving overseas was (among other things) unconstitutional. Restating the standard of review established by *Montana,* we examined the Secretary's decision in order to determine whether it was "consistent with the constitutional language and the constitutional goal of equal representation." . . . Concluding that the Secretary's decision reflected a "judgment, consonant with, though not dictated by, the text and history of the Constitution . . .," we held the Secretary's decision to be well within the constitutional limits on his discretion.

[1] We think that the Court of Appeals erred in holding the "one person-one vote" standard of *Wesberry* and its progeny applicable to the case at hand. For several reasons, the "good-faith effort to achieve population equality" required of a State conducting intrastate redistricting does not translate into a requirement that the Federal Government conduct a census that is as accurate as possible. First, we think that the Court of Appeals understated the significance of the two differences that it recognized between state redistricting cases and the instant case. The court failed to recognize that the Secretary's decision was made pursuant to Congress' direct delegation of its broad authority over the census. See Art. I, § 2, cl. 3 (Congress may conduct the census "in such Manner as they shall by Law direct.") The court also undervalued the significance of the fact that the Constitution makes it impossible to achieve population equality among interstate districts. As we have noted before, the Constitution provides that "[t]he number of Representatives shall not exceed one for every 30,000 persons; each State shall have at least one Representative; and district boundaries may not cross state lines." *Montana,* 503 U.S., at 447-448.

While a court can easily determine whether a State has made the requisite "good-faith effort" toward population equality through the application of a simple mathematical formula, we see no way in which a court can apply the *Wesberry* standard to the Federal Government's decisions regarding the conduct of the census. The Court of Appeals found that *Wesberry* required the Secretary to conduct a census that "would achieve population equality," which it understood to mean a census that was as accurate as possible. But in so doing, the court implicitly found that the Constitution prohibited the Secretary from preferring distributive accuracy to numerical accuracy, and that numerical accuracy—which the court found to be improved by a PES-based adjustment—was constitutionally preferable to distributive accuracy. (". . . the Secretary did not make the required effort to achieve numerical accuracy as nearly as practicable, . . . the burden thus shifted to the Secretary to

justify his decision not to adjust. . . .") As in *Montana,* where we could see no constitutional basis upon which to choose between absolute equality and relative equality, so here can we see no ground for preferring numerical accuracy to distributive accuracy, or for preferring gross accuracy to some particular measure of accuracy. The Constitution itself provides no real instruction on this point, and extrapolation from our intrastate districting cases is equally unhelpful. Quite simply, "[t]he polestar of equal representation does not provide sufficient guidance to allow us to discern a single constitutionally permissible course." *Montana,* supra, at 463. . . .

[4] Rather than the standard adopted by the Court of Appeals, we think that it is the standard established by this Court in *Montana* and *Franklin* that applies to the Secretary's decision not to adjust. The text of the Constitution vests Congress with virtually unlimited discretion in conducting the decennial "actual Enumeration," see Art. I, 2, cl. 3, and notwithstanding the plethora of lawsuits that inevitably accompany each decennial census, there is no basis for thinking that Congress' discretion is more limited than the text of the Constitution provides. See also *Baldrige v. Shapiro,* 455 U.S. 345, 361 (1982) (noting broad scope of Congress' discretion over census). Through the Census Act, Congress has delegated its broad authority over the census to the Secretary. See 13 U.S.C. § 141(a) (Secretary shall take "a decennial census of [the] population . . . in such form and content as he may determine. . . .") Hence, so long as the Secretary's conduct of the census is "consistent with the constitutional language and the constitutional goal of equal representation," *Franklin,* 505 U.S., at 804, it is within the limits of the Constitution. In light of the Constitution's broad grant of authority to Congress, the Secretary's decision not to adjust need bear only a reasonable relationship to the accomplishment of an actual enumeration of the population, keeping in mind the constitutional purpose of the census. . . .

In 1990, the Census Bureau made an extraordinary effort to conduct an accurate enumeration, and was successful in counting 98.4% of the population. See 58 Fed.Reg. 70 (1993). The Secretary then had to consider whether to adjust the census using statistical data derived from the PES. He based his decision not to adjust the census upon three determinations. First, he held that in light of the constitutional purpose of the census, its distributive accuracy was more important than its numerical accuracy. Second, he determined that the unadjusted census data would be considered the most distributively accurate absent a showing to the contrary. And finally, after reviewing the results of the PES in light of extensive research and the recommendations of his advisors, the Secretary found that the PES-based adjustment would not improve distributive accuracy. Each of these three determinations is well within the bounds of the Secretary's constitutional discretion.

[5] As we have already seen the Secretary's decision to focus on distributive accuracy is not inconsistent with the Constitution. Indeed, a preference for distributive accuracy (even at the expense of some numerical accuracy) would seem to follow from the constitutional purpose of the census, viz., to determine the apportionment of the Representatives among the States. Respondents do not dispute this point. Rather, they challenge the Secretary's first determination by arguing that he improperly "regarded evidence of superior numeric accuracy as 'not relevant' to the determination of distributive accuracy." Id., at 39 (quoting Pet.App. 201a) In support of this argument, respondents note that an enumeration that results in increased numerical accuracy will also result in increased distributive accuracy.

We think that respondents rest too much upon the statement by the Secretary to which they refer. When quoted in full, the statement reads: "[w]hile the preponderance of the evidence leads me to believe that the total population at the national level falls between the census counts and the adjusted figures, that conclusion is not relevant to the determination of distributive accuracy." In his decision, the Secretary found numerical accuracy (in addition to distributive accuracy) to be relevant to his decision whether to adjust. Even if the Secretary had chosen to subordinate numerical accuracy, we are not sure why the fact that distributive and numerical accuracy correlate closely in an improved enumeration would require the Secretary to conclude that they correlate also for a PES-based statistical adjustment. . . .

Nevertheless, respondents challenge the Secretary's second determination by arguing that his understanding of historical practice is flawed. According to respondents, the Secretary assumed that the census traditionally was conducted via a simple "headcount," thereby ignoring the fact that statistical adjustment had been used in both the 1970 and 1980 census. We need not tarry long with this argument. The Secretary reasonably recognized that a PES-based statistical adjustment would be a significant change from the traditional method of conducting the census. The statistical adjustments in 1970 and 1980 to which respondents refer were of an entirely different type than the adjustment considered here, and they took place on a dramatically smaller scale. See *Cuomo v. Baldrige,* 674 F.Supp., at 1107 (rejecting argument that Secretary had to conduct PES-like statistical adjustment of 1980 census and finding that "none of [the] adjustments in 1970 were even remotely similar to the types of wholesale adjustments presently suggested. . . .") . . .

[8] Turning finally to review the Secretary's conclusion that the PES adjustment would not improve distributive accuracy, we need note only that the Secretary's conclusion is supported by the reasoning of some of his advisors, and was therefore a reasonable choice in an area where technical experts disagree. . . .

III

The Constitution confers upon Congress the responsibility to conduct an "actual Enumeration" of the American public every 10 years, with the primary purpose of providing a basis for apportioning political representation among the States. Here, the Secretary of Commerce, to whom Congress has delegated its constitutional authority over the census, determined that in light of the constitutional purpose of the census, an "actual Enumeration" would best be achieved without the PES-based statistical adjustment of the results of the initial enumeration. We find that conclusion entirely reasonable. Therefore we hold that the Secretary's decision was well within the constitutional bounds of discretion over the conduct of the census provided to the Federal Government. The judgment of the Court of Appeals is
    Reversed.

NOTES

1. The title "Not Currently Disabled" is language that the Social Security Administration uses, but the idea and material on the disability issue come from Susan Gluck Mezey, *No Longer Disabled: The Federal Courts and the Politics of Social Security Disability* (New York: Greenwood Press, 1988) and from *The New York Times*.

2. Mezey, *No Longer Disabled,* 28.

3. Ibid., 44, n. 47.

4. Ibid., 32.

5. Ibid.

6. Ibid., 71, 76.

7. Ibid., 76.

8. Ibid., 73.

9. Ibid.

10. Ibid., 74.

11. "Court Voids Deadline for U.S. in Disability Claims Reviews," *The New York Times,* 23 May 1984, D27, national edition.

12. Mezey, *No Longer Disabled,* 86.

13. Ibid., 81.

14. Ibid.

15. Ibid., 82.

16. Ibid.

17. Ibid.

18. "House Votes to Ease Review of Disability Benefits," *The New York Times,* 28 March 1984, A18, national edition.

19. Mezey, *No Longer Disabled,* 75.

20. "Sunshine at Last for the Disabled," *The New York Times,* 19 April 1984, A18.

21. Alfonso Narvaez, "Judge Criticizes U.S. Agency on Denial of Benefits," *The New York Times,* 8 June 1984, B5, national edition.

22. Ibid.

23. Robert Pear, "Reagan Suspends Benefits Cutoff," *The New York Times,* 14 April 1984, A1, national edition.

24. Mezey, *No Longer Disabled,* 82.

25. Narvaez, "Judge Criticizes U.S. Agency."

26. Mezey, *No Longer Disabled,* 49-65.

27. See *Patti v. Schweiker,* 669 F.2d 582 (9th Cir. 1982); *Finnegan v. Matthews,* 641 F.2d 1340 (9th Cir. 1981); see also *Lopez v. Heckler,* 572 F.Supp. 26 (C.D. Cal. 1983).

28. See editorials on nonacquiescence by Paul Bator (deputy solicitor general in 1984), "Disability: No 'Lawless' Government Stance . . . ," *The New York Times,* 28 June 1984, A19; Robert Abrams (New York attorney general in 1984), "How to Put a Stop to Arbitrary Removal From Benefit Rolls," *The New York Times,* 28 June 1984, A19; and Anthony Lewis, "A Profound Contempt," *The New York Times,* 21 May 1984, A17.

29. *Lopez v. Heckler,* 572 F.Supp. 26, 29-30 (C.D. Cal. 1983).

30. *Heckler v. Lopez,* 464 U.S. 879 (1983).

31. Mezey, *No Longer Disabled,* 147-68; Pear, "Reagan Suspends Benefits Cutoff."

32. Mezey, *No Longer Disabled,* 147-68.

33. "House Votes to Ease Review of Disability Benefits."

34. "Court Voids Deadline."

35. Mezey, *No Longer Disabled,* 75.

36. Kenneth Culp Davis, *Administrative Law Treatise,* 2d ed., vol. 1 (San Diego, CA: K. C. Davis, 1978), 14.

37. Ernest Gellhorn and Ronald Levin, *Administrative Law and Process: In a Nutshell* (St. Paul, MN: West, 1990), 167.

38. In my own case, when I appealed to the regional director's office, the official I spoke with told me he believed that I was using the IRS as a case study in my Ph.D. dissertation (I was not), and he absolutely refused to budge even though I had three district court cases in my favor. When I filed my suit, the IRS offered to settle for half. I took the offer.

39. The facts are contained in the opinion; see *Federal Crop Insurance Corporation v. Merrill,* 332 U.S. 380, 381 (1947).

40. 467 U.S. 51, 59 (1984).

41. 467 U.S. 51, 68 (1984) (Chief Justice Rehnquist concurring).

42. Ibid.

43. Kenneth Culp Davis, *Administrative Law: Cases—Text—Problems,* 6th ed. (St. Paul, MN: West, 1977), 443.

44. Ibid., 444.

CHAPTER 7

RULE MAKING AND ADJUDICATION

CASE IN POINT:
SECURITIES AND EXCHANGE COMMISSION
V. CHENERY CORPORATION, 332 U.S. 194 (1947)

To the degree that corporate reorganizations and holding companies are understandable to people like us, the facts of this case are fairly simple. The holding of this case affects administrative law today.

The Securities and Exchange Commission (SEC) is empowered to approve the reorganization of public utility holding companies, provided that the reorganization is "fair and equitable to the persons affected thereby."[1] A *holding company* is simply a company that owns (holds) stock in other companies.

The Federal Water Service Corporation was a public utilities holding company, and its officers submitted a reorganization plan to the SEC. While the SEC was considering the plan, the officers of the corporation purchased approximately 7 percent of the corporation's preferred stock. (*Preferred stock* earns a fixed rate of return and pays dividends before other stocks can pay out. Because shareholders fail to attend shareholder meetings and fail to exercise their proxies, it is possible to own a controlling share of a company's stock by owning 7 to 10 percent of the shares.)

By their own admission, Federal's officers were attempting to ensure their controlling interest in the reorganized company, as well as a nice profit for themselves. At the time they attempted this reorganization, no law, administrative rule, or order indicated that corporate officers could not profit from reorganization. Their purchase of the stock was reported to the SEC and became an amendment to the reorganization plan.

Ultimately, a quasi-judicial hearing was held at the SEC, and the commission ruled that the corporate officers of Federal were a fiduciary and that the purchase of the stock violated an implied trust. The commission denied the reorganization plan. A *fiduciary* is one who "manages money or property for another person and in whom that person has a right to place great trust."[2] The SEC denied the reorganization plan because it believed that the corporation's officers had failed in that fiduciary trust. The company officers appealed, and when the case got to the Supreme Court, the Court said that whatever the corporate officers were, they were not legally a fiduciary and the SEC could not base its decision on a misapplication of the law.[3] The Court remanded the case to the SEC for further consideration.

This case was decided in 1943 and is referred to as *Chenery I.* It is important to note here that this was a four-to-three decision. Justice Frankfurter wrote the opinion for Chief Justice Stone and Justices Roberts and Jackson. Justices Black, Reed, and Murphy dissented. Justice Byrnes had resigned, and his seat had not yet been filled by Rutledge; Justice Douglas, a former SEC commissioner, did not participate in the case.

The officers of Federal submitted a new amendment to the reorganization plan in which their preferred stock would convert to common stock after reorganization. Again, the SEC held a quasi-judicial hearing, and this time it decided that the purchase of the stock and its conversion to common stock would not be "fair and equitable to the persons affected thereby."[4] The SEC ordered the officers to surrender the stock to the corporation at cost plus 4 percent interest.

The officers again appealed, and the circuit court of appeals reversed the SEC, saying the decision of the SEC was barred by the holding in *Chenery I.* The SEC appealed to the Supreme Court, and this case became known as *Chenery II. Chenery II* was decided in 1947, and by that time two of the majority of four in *Chenery I* were no longer on the Court. Chief Justice Stone had been replaced by Vinson, who did not participate in *Chenery II,* and Roberts had been replaced by Burton, who concurred with the new majority in *Chenery II.* This time, the Supreme Court voted five to two to sustain the SEC's order. Justice Murphy wrote the opinion for Justices Black, Reed, and Rutledge, with Justice Burton concurring. Justice Jackson wrote a stinging dissent, which was joined by Justice Frankfurter. Justice Douglas still did not participate.

The position of the officers of Federal (Chenery Corp.) was that there was no law against doing what they did at the time they did it. If the SEC had wanted to make such activity (what we now call *insider trading*) illegal, the way to do it would have been to promulgate a rule that said "Beginning on such and such a date, it will no longer be acceptable. . . ." For the SEC to hold a hearing and make a decision on the question of corporate officers' profiting on reorganization and then to apply that decision retroactively to those officers was the civil counterpart to an ex post facto law. Further, it amounted to the taking of property without just compensation (everyone admits that the cost plus 4 percent was well below the value of the stock).

The Court's position, however, was that the SEC had applied its expertise to the question of whether it was "fair and equitable" to the persons affected by a corporate reorganization to allow officers of the former corporation to profit by the reorganization. In its expert judgment, supported by substantial evidence in the record, the SEC had found such behavior not to be "fair and equitable," and once a reviewing court is satisfied that an agency order is supported by substantial evidence, court review is at an end.[5]

In response to objections from the Chenery Corporation about the method used by the agency to reach that decision, the Court said:

> In other words, problems may arise in a case which the administrative agency could not reasonably foresee, problems which must be solved despite the absence of a relevant general rule. . . . In those situations, the agency must retain power to deal with the problems on a case-by-case basis if the administrative process is to be effective. There is thus a very definite place for the case-by-case evolution of statutory standards. *And the choice made between proceeding by general rule or by individual, ad hoc litigation is one that lies primarily in the informed discretion of the administrative agency.*[6]

The doctrine from this case is that when an agency is faced with a problem to deal with (whether management can capitalize on corporate reorganization), the choice of whether to deal with it by promulgating a general rule applicable to all in the future or to adjudicate each case separately is a choice left to the agency. But as Justice Jackson pointed out in his dissent in *Chenery II,* if an agency chooses the second route of adjudication, it is left to that agency to decide issues without having to apply law. For example, would you expect that, given both the SEC and the Supreme Court decisions in *Chenery II,* future attempts by management to profit from reorganization would result in similar decisions by the SEC? If that is what you assumed, you are wrong. The Supreme Court's decision in *Chenery II* was announced in June 1947, but in October of that year, the SEC held two more adjudicatory hearings involving the same issue involved in *Chenery,* but with different companies, and reached the opposite decision.[7] We will return to this notion of choice between rule making and adjudication toward the end of this chapter.

Questions

1. Should the courts have forced the SEC to adopt a rule applicable to all future situations? Why?
2. In the 1960s, Jackson, Mississippi, was found to be in violation of the equal protection clause of the Constitution for operating segregated municipal facilities (e.g., zoo, library). The city agreed to desegregate all city facilities except the swimming pool, which it chose to close rather than desegregate. The city said its reasons for taking that action were public safety and fiscal responsibility. Most of us who lived during that period of time do not believe that the city's motives were so innocent. Black plaintiffs challenging Jackson's decision to close its pool asked the courts to look beyond the stated reasons for the decision. The courts refused (see *Palmer v. Thompson,* 403 U.S. 217 [1971]). There is some similarity in the *Chenery* case because Federal's corporate managers did not believe the SEC's stated reasons in *Chenery II.* Should courts attempt to look beyond stated reasons for a decision by an agency? Why?

THE NEED FOR RULE MAKING

In 1899, the Denver Board of Public Works recommended to the city council that certain streets be paved.[8] The council accepted the recommendation, the mayor ordered the work to be done, and a special assessment district to pay for it was created. After completion of the work, the board ascertained the total cost of the work and apportioned a special assessment tax on each piece of property according to the extent that each tract benefited from the improvements. The city clerk then published in the newspaper the total cost of the work and each lot's assessment. The notice in the newspaper further notified affected property owners that they had thirty days to file written complaints with the city council. The city council received complaints, read them into the record, and then voted to accept the board's apportioned assessments.

The plaintiff property owners sued on the basis of the due process clause of the Fourteenth Amendment, which forbids the state from taking life, liberty, or property without due process of law (*Londoner v. City of Denver,* 210 U.S. 373 [1908]).

The basic elements of due process are (a) a notice that government is about to take some action that may affect your life, liberty, or property and (b) an opportunity for those affected to be heard (a hearing). The plaintiffs challenged both the sufficiency of the notice (they thought they should have been notified about the work, not just the assessments) and the sufficiency of the hearing. The Court said that the notice was sufficient but that the procedure was not. The Court noted that the Constitution places few restrictions on a state legislature's power to tax (also true of Congress); that is, a legislature is not required to notify citizens and provide them with an opportunity to speak before it imposes a tax. However, when a legislature delegates the power to lower units of government to decide "whether, in what amount, and upon whom"[9] to levy a tax, lower units of government are required to provide notice and a hearing. At a minimum, that hearing should consist of an opportunity to make arguments and submit proof.[10] Although the Court spoke only of a state legislature's delegation to lower units of government, we can assume that the same logic applies to legislative or congressional delegations to agencies.

Justice Holmes dissented in the *Londoner* case. Seven years later, the Court was presented with the issue again, and this time Justice Holmes wrote the opinion for the majority.

BI-METALLIC INVESTMENT COMPANY V. STATE BOARD OF EQUALIZATION
239 U.S. 441 (1915)

Justice Holmes delivered the opinion for a unanimous Court.

This is a suit to enjoin the State Board of Equalization and the Colorado Tax Commission from putting in force and the defendant Pitcher, as assessor of Denver, from obeying, an order of the boards, increasing the valuation of all taxable property in Denver 40 per cent. The order was sustained and the suit directed to be dismissed by the supreme court of the state. The plaintiff is the owner of real estate in Denver, and brings the case here on the ground that it was given no opportunity to be heard, and that therefore its property will be taken without due process of law, contrary to the 14th Amendment of the Constitution of the United States. That is the only question with which we have to deal. For the purposes of decision we assume that the constitutional question is presented in the baldest way,—that neither the plaintiff nor the assessor of Denver, who presents a brief on the plaintiff's side, nor any representative of the city and county, was given an opportunity to be heard, other than such as they may have had by reason of the fact that the time of meeting of the boards is fixed by law. On this assumption it is obvious that injustice may be suffered if some property in the county already has been valued at its full worth. But if certain property has been valued at a rate different from that generally prevailing in the county, the owner has had his opportunity to protest and appeal as usual in our system of taxation so that it must be assumed that the property owners in the county all stand alike. The question, then, is whether all individuals have a constitutional right to be heard before a matter can be decided in which all are equally concerned,—here, for instance, before a superior board decides that the local taxing officers have adopted a system of undervaluation throughout a county, as notoriously often has been the case. The answer of this court in the *State R. Tax Cases,* 92 U.S. 575, at least, as to any further notice, was that it was hard to believe that the proposition was seriously made.

Where a rule of conduct applies to more than a few people, it is impracticable that everyone should have a direct voice in its adoption. The Constitution does not require all public acts to be done in town meeting or an assembly of the whole. General stat-utes within the state power are passed that affect the person or property of individuals, sometimes to the point of ruin, without giving them a chance to be heard. Their rights are protected in the only way that they can be in a complex society, by their power, immediate or remote, over those who make the rule. If the result in this case had been reached, as it might have been by the state's doubling the rate of taxation, no one would suggest that the 14th Amendment was violated unless every person affected had been allowed an opportunity to raise his voice against it before the body intrusted by the state Constitution with the power. In considering this case in this court we must assume that the proper state machinery has been used, and the question is whether, if the state Constitution had declared that Denver had been undervalued as compared with the rest of the state, and had decreed that for the current year the valuation should be 40 per cent higher, the objection now urged could prevail. It appears to us that to put the question is to answer it. There must be a limit to individual argument in such matters if government is to go on. In *Londoner v. Denver,* 210 U.S. 373, a local board had to determine "whether, in what amount, and upon whom" a tax for paving a street should be levied for special benefits. A relatively small number of persons was concerned, who were exceptionally affected, in each case upon individual grounds, and it was held that they had a right to a hearing. But that decision is far from reaching a general determination dealing only with the principle upon which all the assessments in a county had been laid.

Judgment affirmed.

The state of the law after 1915 was that where a small number of people each individually and exceptionally are affected, a hearing is required (*Londoner*). Where governmental action applies to more than a few people and it is impractical to hold a hearing, none is required by due process (*Bi-Metallic*). Just so the student does not assume that these ancient cases have no practical application today, let me provide an example: Kansas adopted an Administrative Procedure Act in 1985, and that act imposes on all state agencies what I have elsewhere called "notice and comment procedures." It does not, however, impose those procedural requirements on lower units of government. Even into the twenty-first century, cities and counties and other units of government and their agencies in Kansas looked to *Londoner* and *Bi-Metallic* to determine whether they were required to provide notice and a hearing prior to taking action.[11]

Administrative Procedure Act Rule Making

Federal administrative agencies avoid the *Londoner/Bi-Metallic* question by compliance with the Administrative Procedure Act (APA). Section 551 of the APA defines a *rule* as "the whole of a part of an agency statement of general or particular applicability and future effect designed to implement, interpret or prescribe law or policy or describing the organization, procedure or practice requirements of an agency."[12] Section 553 of the APA requires agencies (with a few exceptions) to publish notice of proposed rule making in the *Federal Register.* It requires that the notice state the time, date, place, and nature of the public hearing on the proposed rule ("nature of the public hearing" refers to whether the agency will allow oral testimony or whether it will simply accept written input). The procedure requires the agency to cite the legal authority for the rule and to provide the gist of the proposed rule. It then requires the agency to consider the input on the proposed rule, to write the rule and include a "concise general statement of [the rule's] basis and purpose," and to publish the rule in the *Federal Register* again, thirty days after which it becomes effective and has the force and effect of law. In cases in which courts have attempted to require more elaborate procedures than those just described, the Supreme Court has reversed those decisions. See the *Vermont Yankee Nuclear Power Corporation* case at the end of this chapter.

TYPES OF RULES

This rule-making procedure has several names, which we discussed in Chapter 6. It is called "informal rule making," "rule promulgation," and "notice and comment." It is also referred to as "553 procedure." In defining a rule, Section 553 of the APA establishes three types of rules: (a) *interpretive rules,* when an agency issues a rule interpreting a statute the agency must apply or work with; (b) *procedural rules,* which are simply rules stating the agency's procedure for dealing with a situation; and (c) *substantive rules,* which have the force and effect of law and are the basic way most agencies implement congressional delegations of power. To have the force and effect of law, substantive rules must go through the appropriate 553 procedure. Procedural and interpretive rules do not need to go through the 553 or any other procedure, although once adopted, they must be published in the *Federal Register* so that those dealing with an agency will be apprised of the agency's interpretation of the law and of its internal procedures.

Interpretive Rules

It is not always easy to tell a substantive rule from the other two types of rules. The easiest way to tell is to simply look at the process. If the agency employed the 553 procedure, then it is a substantive rule. If it sounds like a substantive rule but no 553 procedure was applied, then it is probably an interpretive rule.

NATIONAL MUFFLER DEALERS ASSOCIATION, INC., V. UNITED STATES
440 U.S. 472 (1979)

Justice Blackmun delivered the opinion of the Court, joined by Chief Justice Berger and Justices Brennan, White, Marshall, and Powell. Justice Stewart's dissent was joined by Justices Rehnquist and Stevens.

Petitioner, National Muffler Dealers Association, Inc. (Association), as its name indicates, is a trade organization for muffler dealers. The issue in this case is whether the Association, which has confined its membership to dealers franchised by Midas International Corporation (Midas), and its activities to the Midas muffler business, and thus is not "industrywide," is a "business league" entitled to the exemption from federal income tax provided by § 501(c)(6) of the Internal Revenue Code of 1954.

I

In 1971, during a contest for control of Midas, Midas muffler franchisees organized the Association under the New York Not-for-Profit Corporation Law. The Association's purpose was to establish a group to negotiate unitedly with Midas management. Its principal activity has been to serve as a bargaining agent for its members in dealing with Midas. It has enrolled most Midas franchisees as members. The Association was successful in negotiating a new form of franchise agreement which prevents termination during its 20-year life except for cause. It also persuaded Midas to eliminate its requirement that a customer pay a service charge when a guaranteed Midas muffler is replaced. And the Association sponsors group insurance programs, holds an annual convention, and publishes a newsletter for members.

The Association sought the exemption from federal income tax which § 501(c)(6) provides for a "business league." Treasury Regulation § 1.501(c)(6)-1, 26 C.F.R. § 1.501(c)(6)-1 (1978), states that the activities of a tax exempt business league "should be directed to the improvement of business conditions of one or more lines of business." In view of that requirement, the Internal Revenue Service initially rejected the Association's exemption application, stating that § 501(c)(6) "would not apply to an organization that is not industry wide."

The Association then (in October 1972) amended its bylaws and eliminated the requirement that its members be Midas franchisees. Despite that amendment, and despite the Association's announced purpose to promote the interests of individuals "engaged in business as muffler dealers," it neither recruited nor acquired a member who was not a Midas franchisee.

In 1974, after the Internal Revenue Service had issued a final rejection of the Association's exemption application, the Association filed income tax returns for its fiscal years 1971, 1972, and 1973, and, thereafter, claims for refund of the taxes paid with those returns. The 1972 claim was formally denied. . . . Subsequent to that denial, the Association brought this suit in the United States District Court for the Southern District of New York asserting its entitlement to a refund for the income taxes paid for the three fiscal years. . . .

II

[1] The statute's term "business league" has no well-defined meaning or common usage outside the perimeters of § 501(c)(6). It is a term "so general

. . . as to render an interpretive regulation appropriate." *Helvering v. Reynolds Co.,* 306 U.S. 110, 114 (1939). In such a situation, this Court customarily defers to the regulation, which, "if found to 'implement the congressional mandate in some reasonable manner,' must be upheld." *United States v. Cartwright,* 411 U.S. 546, 550 (1973).

We do this because "Congress has delegated to the [Secretary of the Treasury and his delegate, the] Commissioner [of Internal Revenue], not to the courts, the task of prescribing 'all needful rules and regulations for the enforcement' of the Internal Revenue Code. 26 U.S.C. § 7805(a)." *United States v. Correll,* 389 U.S., at 307. That delegation helps ensure that in "this area of limitless factual variations," ibid., like cases will be treated alike. It also helps guarantee that the rules will be written by "masters of the subject," who will be responsible for putting the rules into effect.

In determining whether a particular regulation carries out the congressional mandate in a proper manner, we look to see whether the regulation harmonizes with the plain language of the statute, its origin, and its purpose. A regulation may have particular force if it is a substantially contemporaneous construction of the statute by those presumed to have been aware of congressional intent. If the regulation dates from a later period, the manner in which it evolved merits inquiry. Other relevant considerations are the length of time the regulation has been in effect, the reliance placed on it, the consistency of the Commissioner's interpretation, and the degree of scrutiny Congress has devoted to the regulation during subsequent re-enactments of the statute. See *Commissioner v. South Texas Lumber Co.,* 333 U.S. 496 (1948).

III

A

[2][3] The history of Treas. Reg. § 1.501(c)(6)-1 and its "line of business" requirement provides much that supports the Government's view that the Association, which is not tied to a particular community and is not industrywide, should not be exempt. The exemption for "business leagues" from federal income tax had its genesis at the inception of the modern income tax system with the enactment of the Tariff Act of October 3, 1913. . . .

Ultimately the Congress, provided that the tax would not apply to "business leagues, nor to chambers of commerce or boards of trade, not organized for profit or no part of the net income of which inures to the benefit of the private stockholder or individual." Tariff Act of Oct. 3, 1913, § II G(a), 38 Stat. 172.

Congress has preserved this language, with few modifications, in each succeeding Revenue Act.

The Commissioner of Internal Revenue had little difficulty determining which organizations were "chambers of commerce" or "boards of trade" within the meaning of the statute. Those terms had commonly understood meanings before the statute was enacted. "Business league," however, had no common usage, and in 1919 the Commissioner undertook to define its meaning by regulation. The initial definition was the following:

"A business league is an association of persons having some common business interest, which limits its activities to work for such common interest and does not engage in a regular business of a kind ordinarily carried on for profit. Its work need not be similar to that of a chamber of commerce or board of trade."

This language, however, proved too expansive to identify with precision the class of organizations Congress intended to exempt. . . .

In 1927, the Board of Tax Appeals, in a reviewed decision *with* some dissents, applied the principle of *noscitur a sociis* and denied a claimed "business league" exemption to a corporation organized by associations of insurance companies to provide printing services for member companies. *Uniform Printing & Supply Co. v. Commissioner,* 33 F.2d 445(CA7). . . .

In 1929, the Commissioner incorporated the principle of *noscitur a sociis* into the regulation itself. The sentence, "Its work need not be similar to that of a chamber of commerce or board of trade," was dropped and was replaced with the following qualification:

"It is an organization of the same general class as a chamber of commerce or board of trade. Thus, its activities should be directed to the improvement of business conditions or to the promotion of the general objects of one or more lines of business as distinguished from the performance of particular services for individual persons."

This language has stood almost without change for half a century through several re-enactments and one amendment of the statute.

During that period, the Commissioner and the courts have been called upon to define "line of business" as that phrase is employed in the regulation. True to the representation made by the Chamber of Commerce, in its statement to the Senate in 1913, that benefits would be received "in common with all other members of their communities or of their industries," supra, at 1308, the term "line of business" has been interpreted to mean either an entire industry, see, e.g., *American Plywood Assn. v. United States,* 267 F.Supp. 830 (WD Wash. 1967); or all components of an industry within a geographic area, see, e.g., *Commissioner v. Chicago Graphic Arts Federation, Inc.,* 128 F.2d 424 (CA7 1942).

Most trade associations fall within one of these two categories. The Commissioner consistently has denied exemption to business groups whose membership and purposes are narrower. Those who have failed to meet the "line of business" test, in the view of the Commissioner, include groups composed of businesses that market a single brand of automobile, or have licenses to a single patented product, or bottle one type of soft drink. The Commissioner has reasoned that these groups are not designed to better conditions in an entire industrial "line," but, instead, are devoted to the promotion of a particular product at the expense of others in the industry.

In short, while the Commissioner's interpretation of reading of § 501(c)(6) perhaps is not the only possible one, it does bear a fair relationship to the language of the statute, it reflects the views of those who sought its enactment, and it matches the purpose they articulated. It evolved as the Commissioner administered the statute and attempted to give to a new phrase a content that would reflect congressional design. The regulation has stood for 50 years, and the Commissioner infrequently but consistently has interpreted it to exclude an organization like the Association that is not industrywide. The Commissioner's view therefore merits serious deference.

In sum, the "line of business" limitation is well grounded in the origin of § 501(c)(6) and in its enforcement over a long period of time. The distinction drawn here, that a tax exemption is not available to aid one group in competition with another within an industry, is but a particular manifestation of an established principle of tax administration. Because the Association has not shown that either the regulation or the Commissioner's interpretation of it fails to "implement the congressional mandate in some reasonable manner," *United States v. Correll,* 389 U.S., at 307, 88 S.Ct. at 450, the Association's claim for a § 501(c)(6) exemption must be denied.

The judgment of the Court of Appeals is affirmed.

It is so ordered.

Question

The Court lists about seven variables that courts should examine when reviewing an agency's interpretation of a statute. How many of the variables does the Court apply to the IRS's interpretation of the term *business league*?

Although interpretive and substantive rules may look alike, it is not just the procedure that differentiates them. A substantive rule has the force and effect of law, whereas an interpretive rule does not. If an agency has adopted a rule through the 553 procedure, then it may legally enforce that rule, perhaps through agency adjudication. Those adversely affected by the rule, who may wish to challenge the substance of the rule in court, are not likely to succeed. That is because, as you know from Chapter 4, the scope of review for a substantive rule is whether the rule is arbitrary and/or capricious. In very few cases has a court found an agency rule to be arbitrary if it has gone through the proper 553 procedure.

An agency is not necessarily free, however, to begin to enforce an interpretive rule. In the *National Muffler* case, the IRS adopted an interpretation of the statutory term *business league.* That interpretation, however, was not self-executing. The IRS used its interpretation in denying the application for a business league exemption for the National Muffler Dealers Association. Then, the association paid its taxes in protest and proceeded through a series of hearings within the IRS, challenging the IRS's interpretation at every turn. Finally, the question of the reasonableness of the agency's interpretation was settled in litigation ultimately by the U.S. Supreme Court.

Further, court review of interpretive rules is much broader than court review of substantive rules. That is the case because although courts should show some deference toward agency expertise in interpreting congressional intent, courts are just as capable of determining congressional intent as agencies are. To simply state that interpretive rules do not have the force and effect of law is to oversimplify their effect.

When an agency announces that it plans to proceed in a certain way, that is exactly what it plans to do whether it has gone through a 553 procedure or not, and this can adversely affect those who deal with the agency. Turn back now to Chapter 5 and reread *Chrysler v. Brown.* There, the agency announced a rule that said even though material requested under the Freedom of Information Act (FOIA) may be exempt from release, the agency would release it anyway. By the agency's admission, this rule was an interpretive one, but the agency intended to implement it, to Chrysler's detriment, anyway. Chrysler was forced to spend considerable resources, legal and otherwise, to stop the agency from enforcing a rule that did not have the "force and effect" of law.

What if you owned a new business and had secured a contract with a natural gas pipeline company to deliver gas to your plant? Suppose natural gas is in short supply, so you feel fortunate because of your contract. The federal agency that regulates natural gas, however, has just published an interpretive rule dealing with curtailment of natural gas deliveries because of shortages. The rule says the agency will curtail according to prior use rather than current contract and that all low-volume uses will be completely curtailed before high-volume uses will be curtailed at all. Because this is not a substantive rule and does not have the force and effect of law, do you need to worry about your plant's staying in production? Of course you do. In the actual case challenging the rule, *Pacific Gas and Electric v. Federal Power Commission (FPC),*[13] the Court did not invalidate the rule because no curtailments would actually occur on the basis of the rule alone. Only pursuant to a quasi-judicial hearing within the agency first would curtailment occur. So although the rule informed buyers of how the agency intended to proceed, it did not have the force and effect of law, and smaller users could make their case in hearings. Because it is possible for an agency to affect citizens or businesses through interpretive rules without citizen input, there is much discussion involving whether some procedure should be required prior to the adoption of such rules.[14] In the *Chevron* case, which follows, the Court adopted a doctrine for dealing with interpretive rules when there is little suggestion of legislative intent.

CHEVRON U.S.A., INCORPORATED V. NATURAL RESOURCES DEFENSE COUNCIL
467 U.S. 837 (1984)

Justice Stevens delivered the opinion for a unanimous Court of six. Justices Marshall and O'Connor and Chief Justice Burger did not participate in the decision.

In the Clean Air Act Amendments of 1977, Pub.L. 95-95, 91 Stat. 685, Congress enacted certain requirements applicable to States that had not achieved the national air quality standards established by the Environmental Protection Agency (EPA) pursuant to earlier legislation. The amended Clean Air Act required these "nonattainment" States to establish a permit program regulating "new or modified major stationary sources" of air pollution. Generally, a permit may not be issued for a new or modified major stationary source unless several stringent conditions are met. The EPA regulation promulgated to implement this permit requirement allows a State to adopt a statewide definition of the term "stationary source." Under this definition, an existing plant that contains several pollution-emitting devices may install or modify one piece of equipment without meeting the permit conditions if the alteration will not increase the total emissions from the plant. The question presented by this case is whether EPA's decision to allow States to treat all of the pollution-emitting devices within the same industrial grouping as though they were encased within a single "bubble" is based on a reasonable construction of the statutory term "stationary source."

I

The EPA regulations containing the plantwide definition of the term *stationary source* were promulgated on October 14, 1981. 46 Fed.Reg. 50766.

Respondents filed a timely petition for review in the United States Court of Appeals for the District of Columbia Circuit. The Court of Appeals set aside the regulations. *National Resources Defense Council, Inc. v. Gorsuch,* 685 F.2d 718 (1982).

The court observed that the relevant part of the amended Clean Air Act "does not explicitly define what Congress envisioned as a 'stationary source,' to which the permit program . . . should apply," and further stated that the precise issue was not "squarely addressed in the legislative history." In light of its conclusion that the legislative history bearing on the question was "at best contradictory," it reasoned that "the purposes of the nonattainment program should guide our decision here." Based on two of its precedents concerning the applicability of the bubble concept to certain Clean Air Act programs, the court stated that the bubble concept was "mandatory" in programs designed merely to maintain existing air quality, but held that it was "inappropriate" in programs enacted to improve air quality. Since the purpose of the permit program— its "raison d'etre," in the court's view—was to improve air quality, the court held that the bubble concept was inapplicable in this case under its prior precedents. It therefore set aside the regulations embodying the bubble concept as contrary to law. We granted certiorari to review that judgment, and we now reverse.

II

When a court reviews an agency's construction of the statute which it administers, it is confronted with two questions. First, always, is the question whether Congress has directly spoken to the precise question at issue. If the intent of Congress is clear, that is the end of the matter; for the court, as well as the agency, must give effect to the unambiguously expressed intent of Congress. If, however, the court determines Congress has not directly addressed the precise question at issue, the court does not simply impose its own construction on the statute, as would be necessary in the absence of an administrative interpretation. Rather, if the statute is silent or ambiguous with respect to the specific issue, the question for the court is whether the agency's answer is based on a permissible construction of the statute.

"The power of an administrative agency to administer a congressionally created . . . program necessarily requires the formulation of policy and the making of rules to fill any gap left, implicitly or explicitly, by Congress." If Congress has explicitly left a gap for the agency to fill, there is an express delegation of authority to the agency to elucidate a specific provision of the statute by regulation. Such legislative regulations are given controlling weight unless they are arbitrary, capricious, or manifestly contrary to the statute. Sometimes the legislative delegation to an agency on a particular question is implicit rather than explicit. In such a case, a court may not substitute its own construction of a statutory provision for a reasonable interpretation made by the administrator of an agency.

We have long recognized that considerable weight should be accorded to an executive department's construction of a statutory scheme it is entrusted to administer, and the principle of deference to administrative interpretations . . . "has been consistently followed by this Court whenever decision as to the meaning or reach of a statute has involved reconciling conflicting policies, and a full understanding of the force of the statutory policy in the given situation has depended upon more than ordinary knowledge respecting the matters subjected to agency regulations. . . ."

In light of these well-settled principles it is clear that the Court of Appeals misconceived the nature of its role in reviewing the regulations at issue. Once it determined, after its own examination of the legislation, that Congress did not actually have an intent regarding the applicability of the bubble concept to the permit program, the question before it was not whether in its view the concept is "inappropriate" in the general context of a program designed to improve air quality, but whether the

Administrator's view that it is appropriate in the context of this particular program is a reasonable one. Based on the examination of the legislation and its history which follows, we agree with the Court of Appeals that Congress did not have a specific intention on the applicability of the bubble concept in these cases, and conclude that the EPA's use of that concept here is a reasonable policy choice for the agency to make. The legislative history of the portion of the 1977 Amendments dealing with nonattainment areas does not contain any specific comment on the "bubble concept" or the question whether a plantwide definition of a stationary source is permissible under the permit program. It does, however, plainly disclose that in the permit program Congress sought to accommodate the conflict between the economic interest in permitting capital improvements to continue and the environmental interest in improving air quality. We are not persuaded that parsing of general terms in the text of the statute will reveal an actual intent of Congress. We know full well that this language is not dispositive; the terms are overlapping and the language is not precisely directed to the question of the applicability of a given term in the context of a larger operation. To the extent any congressional "intent" can be discerned from this language, it would appear that the listing of overlapping, illustrative terms was intended to enlarge, rather than to confine, the scope of the agency's power to regulate particular sources in order to effectuate the policies of the Act.

Our review of the EPA's varying interpretations of the word "source"—both before and after the 1977 Amendments—convinces us that the agency primarily responsible for administering this important legislation has consistently interpreted it flexibly—not in a sterile textual vacuum, but in the context of implementing policy decisions in a technical and complex arena. The fact that the agency has from time to time changed its interpretation of the term "source" does not, as respondents argue, lead us to conclude that no deference should be accorded the agency's interpretation of the statute. An initial agency interpretation is not instantly carved in stone. On the contrary, the agency, to engage in informed rulemaking, must consider varying interpretations and the wisdom of its policy on a continuing basis. Moreover, the fact that the agency has adopted different definitions in different contexts adds force to the argument that the definition itself is flexible, particularly since Congress has never indicated any disapproval of a flexible reading of the statute.

In this case, the Administrator's interpretation represents a reasonable accommodation of manifestly competing interests and is entitled to deference: the regulatory scheme is technical and complex, the agency considered the matter in a detailed and reasoned fashion, and the decision involves reconciling conflicting policies. Congress intended to accommodate both interests, but did not do so itself on the level of specificity presented by this case. Perhaps that body consciously desired the Administrator to strike the balance at this level, thinking that those with great expertise and charged with responsibility for administering the provision would be in a better position to do so; perhaps it simply did not consider the question at this level; and perhaps Congress was unable to forge a coalition on either side of the question, and those on each side decided to take their chances with the scheme devised by the agency. For judicial purposes, it matters not which of these things occurred.

Judges are not experts in the field, and are not part of either political branch of the Government. Courts must, in some cases, reconcile competing political interests, but not on the basis of the judges' personal policy preferences. In contrast, an agency to which Congress has delegated policymaking responsibilities may, within the limits of that delegation, properly rely upon the incumbent administration's views of wise policy to inform its judgments. While agencies are not directly accountable to the people, the Chief Executive is, and it is entirely appropriate for this political branch of the Government to make such policy choices—resolving the competing interests which Congress itself either inadvertently did not resolve, or intentionally left to be resolved by the agency charged with the administration of the statute in light of everyday realities.

When a challenge to an agency construction of a statutory provision, fairly conceptualized, really centers on the wisdom of the agency's policy, rather than whether it is a reasonable choice within a gap left open by Congress, the challenge must fail. In such a case, federal judges—who have no constituency—have a duty to respect legitimate policy choices made by those who do. The responsibilities for assessing the wisdom of such policy choices and resolving the struggle between competing views of the public interest are not judicial ones: "Our Constitution vests such responsibilities in the political branches."

We hold that the EPA's definition of the term "source" is a permissible construction of the statute which seeks to accommodate progress in reducing air pollution with economic growth. "The Regulations which the Administrator has adopted provide what the agency could allowably view as . . . [an] effective reconciliation of these twofold ends. . . ."

The judgment of the Court of Appeals is reversed.

It is so ordered.

Questions

1. What is the first thing a reviewing court should do when an agency's interpretation of a statute is challenged?
2. If the plain meaning of the statute cannot be gleaned, what must the reviewing court analyze next?
3. If Congress chooses to obfuscate the issue of clean air by using language such as "new or modified major stationary source," is it constitutionally acceptable for the agency to consider the view of the current occupant of the White House in formulating its interpretation of that language? If so, is it acceptable for that interpretation to change every four to eight years? See *Chamber of Commerce v. Occupational Safety and Health Administration*, 636 F.2d 464 (D.C. Cir. 1980).

Procedural Rules

Procedural rules, like interpretive rules, are exempted from the requirements of Section 553 of the APA. It may not always be easy to differentiate procedural rules from the other types of rules, but generally they specify an internal agency procedure, and so they are often referred to as *internal procedural agency rules*. It is perhaps not so important to be able to distinguish between an interpretive rule and a procedural rule. What is important is to be aware of two notions: First, neither can be a substantive rule without going through the notice and comment procedure. Second, both interpretive and procedural rules can affect citizens without any citizen input. In the case that follows, the Bureau of Indian Affairs (BIA) adopted a procedural rule that required the agency to publish eligibility requirements in the *Federal Register.* Although Congress authorized BIA benefits to be paid to Indians who lived on or near reservations, because of funding insufficient to provide benefits to all such Indians, the BIA adopted an interpretive rule. The interpretive rule restricted benefits to Indians who lived on a reservation, but the rule was not published in the *Federal Register.* The doctrine from the case is that agencies must adhere to their internal procedural rules.

MORTON V. RUIZ
415 U.S. 199 (1974)

Justice Blackmun delivered the opinion for a unanimous Court.

This case presents a narrow but important issue in the administration of the federal general assistance program for needy Indians: Are general assistance benefits available only to those Indians living on reservations in the United States (or in areas regulated by the Bureau of Indian Affairs in Alaska and Oklahoma), and are they thus unavailable to Indians (outside Alaska and Oklahoma) living off, although near, a reservation? The United States District Court for the District of Arizona answered this question favorably to petitioner, the Secretary of the Interior, when, without opinion and on cross-motions for summary judgment, it dismissed the respondents' complaint. The Court of Appeals, one judge dissenting, reversed. 462 F.2d 818 (CA9 1972). We granted certiorari because of the significance of the issue and because of the vigorous assertion that the judgment of the Court of Appeals was inconsistent with long-established policy of the Secretary and of the Bureau.

I

The pertinent facts are agreed upon, although, as to some, the petitioner Secretary denies knowledge but does not dispute them. The respondents, Ramon Ruiz and his wife, Anita, are Papago Indians and United States citizens. In 1940 they left the Papago Reservation in Arizona to seek employment 15 miles away at the Phelps-Dodge copper mines at Ajo. Mr. Ruiz found work there, and they settled in a community at Ajo called the "Indian Village" and populated almost entirely by Papagos. Practically all the land and most of the homes in the Village are owned or rented by Phelps-Dodge. The Ruizes have lived in Ajo continuously since 1940 and have been in their present residence since 1947. A minor daughter lives with them. They speak and understand the Papago language but only limited English. Apart from Mr. Ruiz' employment with Phelps-Dodge, they have not been assimilated into the dominant culture, and they appear to have maintained a close tie with the nearby reservation. . . .

In July 1967, 27 years after the Ruizes moved to Ajo, the mine where he worked was shut down by a strike. It remained closed until the following March. While the strike was in progress, Mr. Ruiz' sole income was a $15 per week striker's benefit paid by the union. He sought welfare assistance from the State of Arizona but this was denied because of the State's apparent policy that striking workers are not eligible for general assistance or emergency relief. . . . On December 11, 1967, Mr. Ruiz applied for general assistance benefits from the Bureau of Indian Affairs (BIA). He was immediately notified by letter that he was ineligible for general assistance because of the provisions (in effect since 1952) in 66 *Indian Affairs Manual* 3.1.4 (1965) that eligibility is limited to Indians living "on reservations" and in jurisdictions under the BIA in Alaska and Oklahoma. An appeal to the Superintendent of the Papago Indian Agency was unsuccessful. A further appeal to the Phoenix Area Director of the BIA led to a hearing, but this, too, proved unsuccessful. The sole ground for the denial of general assistance benefits was that the Ruizes resided outside the boundaries of the Papago Reservation.

II

The Snyder Act, 25 U.S.C. § 13, approved November 2, 1921, provides the underlying congressional authority for most BIA activities including, in particular and importantly, the general assistance program. Prior to the Act, there was no such general authorization. As a result, appropriation requests made by the House Committee on Indian Affairs were frequently stricken on the House floor by point-of-order objections. The Snyder Act was designed to remedy this situation. It is comprehensively worded for the apparent purpose of avoiding these point-of-order motions to strike. Since the passage of the Act, the BIA has presented its budget requests without further interruption of that kind and Congress has enacted appropriation bills annually in response to the requests. . . .

The appropriation legislation at issue here, Department of Interior and Related Agencies Appropriation Act, 1968, Pub.L. 90—28, 81 Stat. 59, 60 (1967), recited: "Bureau of Indian Affairs Education and Welfare Services. For expenses necessary to provide education and welfare services for Indians, either directly or in cooperation with States and other organizations, including payment (in advance or from date of admission), of care, tuition, assistance, and other expenses of Indians in boarding homes, institutions, or schools; grants and other assistance to needy Indians; maintenance of law and order, and payment of rewards for information or evidence concerning violations of law on Indian reservations or lands; and operation of Indian arts and crafts shops; $126,478,000." This wording, except for the amount, is identical to that employed in similar legislation for prior fiscal years and, indeed, for subsequent ones. It is to be that neither the language of the Snyder Act nor that of the Appropriations Act imposes any geographical limitation on the availability of general assistance benefits and does not prescribe eligibility requirements or the details of any program. Instead, the Snyder Act states that the BIA (under the supervision of the Secretary) "shall direct, supervise, and expend . . . for the benefit, care, and assistance of the Indians throughout the United States" for the stated purposes including, as the two purposes first described, "[g]eneral support" and "relief of distress." This is broadly phrased material and obviously is intended to include all BIA activities.

The general assistance program is designed by the BIA to provide direct financial aid to needy Indians where other channels of relief, federal, state, and tribal, are not available. Benefits generally are paid on a scale equivalent to the State's welfare payments. Any Indian, whether living on a reservation or elsewhere, may be eligible for benefits under the various social security programs in which his State participates and no limitation may be placed on social security benefits because of an Indian claimant's residence on a reservation.

III

We are confronted, therefore, with the issues whether the geographical limitation placed on general assistance eligibility by the BIA is consistent with congressional intent and the meaning of the applicable statutes, or, to phrase it somewhat differently, whether the congressional appropriations are properly limited by the BIA's restrictions, and, if so, whether the limitation withstands constitutional analysis. On the initial question, the Secretary argues, first, that the Snyder Act is merely an enabling act with no definition of the scope of the general assistance program, that the Appropriation

Act did not provide for off-reservation Indian welfare (other than in Oklahoma and Alaska), and that Congress did not intend to expand the program beyond that presented to it by the BIA request. Secondly, he points to the "on reservations" limitation in the *Manual* and suggests that Congress was well acquainted with that limitation, and that, by legislating in the light of the *Manual's* limiting provision, its appropriation amounted to a ratification of the BIA's definitive practice. He notes that, in recent years, Congress has twice rejected proposals that clearly would have provided off-reservation general assistance for Indians. Thus, it is said, Congress has appropriated no funds for general assistance for off-reservation Indians and, as a practical matter, the Secretary is unable to provide such a program.

Wholly aside from this appropriation subcommittee legislative history, the Secretary suggests that Congress, each year since 1952, appropriated only in accord with the "on reservations" limitation contained in the *BIA Manual*. By legislating annually "in the light of (this) clear provision," the Secretary argues, Congress implicitly ratified the BIA policy. This argument, also, is not convincing. The limitation has not been published in the *Federal Register* or in the *Code of Federal Regulations,* and there is nothing in the legislative history to show that the *Manual's* provision was brought to the subcommittees' attention, let alone to the entire Congress. To assume that Congress was aware of this provision, contained only in an internally circulated BIA document, would be most strained. But, even assuming that Congress was fully cognizant of the *Manual's* limitation when the 1958 appropriation was made, the language of geographic restriction in the *Manual* must be considered in conjunction with the representations consistently made. There is no reason to assume that Congress did not equate the "on reservations" language with the "on or near" category that continuously was described as the service area. In the light of the Manual's particular inclusion of Oklahoma and Alaska off-reservation Indians, it would seem that this interpretation of the provision would have been the logical one for anyone in Congress, who in fact was aware of it, to accept.

V

A. Having found that the congressional appropriation was intended to cover welfare services at least to those Indians residing "on or near" the reservation, it does not necessarily follow that the Secretary is without power to create reasonable classifications and eligibility requirements in order to allocate the limited funds available to him for this purpose. Thus, if there were only enough funds appropriated to provide meaningfully for 10,000 needy Indian beneficiaries and the entire class of eligible beneficiaries numbered 20,000, it would be incumbent upon the BIA to develop an eligibility standard to deal with this problem, and the standard, if rational and proper, might leave some of the class otherwise encompassed by the appropriation without benefits. But in such a case the agency must, at a minimum, let the standard be generally known so as to assure that it is being applied consistently and so as to avoid both the reality and the appearance of arbitrary denial of benefits to potential beneficiaries.

The Administrative Procedure Act was adopted to provide, inter alia, that administrative policies affecting individual rights and obligations be promulgated pursuant to certain stated procedures so as to avoid the inherently arbitrary nature of unpublished ad hoc determinations. See generally S.Rep.No. 752, 79th Cong., 1st Sess., 12—13 (1945); H.R.Rep.No. 1980, 79th Cong., 2d Sess., 21—23 (1946). That Act states in pertinent part: "Each Agency shall separately state and currently publish in the *Federal Register* for the guidance of the public—(D) substantive rules of general applicability adopted as authorized by law, and statements of general policy or interpretations of general applicability formulated and adopted by the agency." 5 U.S.C. § 552(a)(1). The sanction added in 1967 by Pub.L. 90—23, 81 Stat. 54, provides: "Except to the extent that a person has actual and timely notice of the terms thereof, a person may not in any manner be required to resort to, or be adversely affected by, a matter required to be published in the *Federal Register* and not so published."

In the instant case the BIA itself has recognized the necessity of formally publishing its substantive policies and has placed itself under the structure of the APA procedures. The 1968 introduction to the *Manual* reads: *"Code of Federal Regulations:* Directives which relate to the public, including Indians, are published in the *Federal Register* and codified in 25 *Code of Federal Regulations* (25 C.F.R.). These directives inform the public of privileges and benefits available; eligibility qualifications, requirements, and procedures; and of appeal rights and procedures. They are published in accordance with rules and regulations issued by the Director of the *Federal Register* and the Administrative Procedure Act as amended. . . .

"*Bureau of Indian Affairs Manual:* Policies, procedures, and instructions which do not relate to the public but are required to govern the operations of the Bureau are published in the *Bureau of Indian Affairs Manual.*"

Unlike numerous other programs authorized by the Snyder Act and funded by the annual appropriations, the BIA has chosen not to publish its eligibility requirements for general assistance in the *Federal Register* or in the C.F.R. This continues to the present time. The only official manifestation of this alleged policy of restricting general assistance to those directly on the reservations is the material in the *Manual* which is, by BIA's own admission, solely an internal-operations brochure intended to cover policies that "do not relate to the public." Indeed, at oral argument the Government conceded that for this to be a "real legislative rule," itself endowed with the force of law, it should be published in the *Federal Register.* Where the rights of individuals are affected, it is incumbent upon agencies to follow their own procedures. This is so even where the internal procedures are possibly more rigorous than otherwise would be required. The BIA, by its *Manual,* has declared that all directives that "inform the public of privileges and benefits available" and of "eligibility requirements" are among those to be published. The requirement that, in order to receive general assistance, an Indian must reside directly "on" a reservation is clearly an important substantive policy that fits within this class of directives. Before the BIA may extinguish the entitlement of these otherwise eligible beneficiaries, it must comply, at a minimum, with its own internal procedures. The Secretary has presented no reason why the requirements of the Administrative Procedure Act could not or should not have been met. The BIA itself has not attempted to defend its rule as a valid exercise of its "legislative power," but rather depends on the argument that Congress itself has not appropriated funds for Indians not directly on the reservations. The conscious choice of the Secretary not to treat this extremely significant eligibility requirement, affecting rights of needy Indians, as a legislative-type rule, renders it ineffective so far as extinguishing rights of those otherwise within the class of beneficiaries contemplated by Congress is concerned.

. . . Before benefits may be denied to these otherwise entitled Indians, the BIA must first promulgate eligibility requirements according to established procedures.

The judgment of the Court of Appeals is affirmed and the case is remanded for further proceedings consistent with this opinion.

It is so ordered.

Affirmed and remanded.

Substantive Rules

Substantive rules can be distinguished from (a) those that do not have the force and effect of law (interpretive and procedural rules) and (b) orders that result from a quasi-judicial hearing but also have the force and effect of law. Refer again to *Chrysler v. Brown*. In that case, Justice Rehnquist defined a substantive rule as opposed to either interpretive or procedural rules. He said that a substantive rule has three properties: (a) It affects individual rights and obligations; (b) its source of authority is a legitimate congressional delegation of power; and (c) it must have been adopted pursuant to the proper procedures as outlined in Section 553 of the APA.

You may remember that the Office of Federal Contract Compliance Programs (OFCCP) had issued a rule indicating its intent to release exemptible material under the FOIA, and the OFCCP was about to do just that when Chrysler obtained a temporary restraining order. Ultimately, the case narrowed to the nature and character of the rule. That is because Chrysler's first two lines of attack were not successful. The Court rejected Chrysler's first argument that material qualifying for an FOIA exemption *must* be withheld. The Court also rejected Chrysler's second argument that the Trade Secrets Act provides Chrysler with a legal basis to prohibit the release of the information. Here, the Court reasoned there was no indication that Congress intended for a private party to use a criminal statute to block the distribution of information. Therefore, if the OFCCP rule is one "authorized by law," Chrysler is out of luck. The question now comes down to whether the OFCCP rule is a substantive rule "authorized by law." Justice Rehnquist tells us it is not a substantive rule with the force and effect of law because although it meets the first criterion (it does affect individual rights and obligations), it does not meet the last two criteria. This is the case because the source of authority for the rule was an executive order, not a congressional delegation of power, and the agency did not observe the 553 procedure in adopting the rule.

Another Justice Rehnquist opinion distinguished when substantive rules are required, as opposed to when agency orders are appropriate. The Interstate Commerce Act authorizes the Interstate Commerce Commission (ICC) to take certain actions "after a hearing."[15] The ICC notified railroads that it was going to look into the question of adopting incentives that would address the boxcar shortage. Later, the ICC required railroads to gather and submit data on boxcar supply and demand. When several railroads complained, the ICC staff met with railroad representatives and left them with the impression that hearings would be held on the question. Further hearings were never held, however. On the basis of the data provided by the railroads at the agency's request, the ICC promulgated a rule adopting a per diem charge on any boxcar on a railroad's line if the boxcar did not belong to that railroad. The purpose of the rule was to provide an incentive to return another railroad's boxcar quickly or to make it financially attractive for railroads to purchase more boxcars. After notice in the *Federal Register* that the ICC intended to adopt the per diem rate, several railroad companies objected and requested an oral hearing based on those objections. The ICC modified its proposed rate somewhat but denied all oral hearings.

Railroad companies hurt by the new per diem rate sued, alleging that a quasi-judicial hearing should have been required (*United States v. Florida East Coast Railway Company,* 410 U.S. 224 [1973]). This case presents the issue of when substantive rule making is appropriate, as opposed to when a quasi-judicial order is appropriate. Justice Rehnquist first indicated that the simple reference to the term *hearing* in the act does not necessarily connote a quasi-judicial hearing. Indeed, only when the enabling legislation uses the language "hearing on the record" is a quasi-judicial hearing required. Beyond that, the nature of the subject matter suggests which type of hearing is appropriate.

Drawing on the *Londoner/Bi-Metallic* distinction, Justice Rehnquist differentiated between those situations dealing with general applicability requiring legislative-type decision and those involving "a small number of persons, exceptionally affected," and individual grounds that are appropriate for quasi-judicial decision making.

In reality, there are two ways to distinguish legislative-type decision-making situations from those in which quasi-judicial decisions are more appropriate. Justice Rehnquist discussed the general/specific dichotomy, but the APA distinguishes between future effect and past effect. A 553 procedure is appropriate for questions of a more general nature that will apply to future situations. A quasi-judicial (554) procedure is more appropriate in dealing with particularized, individual situations or events that have already occurred.

Although the distinction is worth attention, the *Chenery* case should signal caution in this area. First, the question in the *Chenery* case was whether stocks acquired by management in corporate reorganization should be treated the same as stocks owned by others. If we apply the dichotomies just mentioned, it would appear that the issue is one of a general nature that begs future application. The officers of Federal already having purchased the stock and a decision from the SEC apparently necessary, however, the issue becomes a particular and individual one involving a past event. Because of the question's having been decided once in *Chenery* (every time a court decides a novel issue, there will be some retroactive application), there is a real issue about whether the SEC should have been allowed to continue to treat the issue in a series of case-by-case quasi-judicial hearings. We know, however, that the doctrine from *Chenery* was that the choice of how an agency handles such problems is a question left to the agency. In *Florida East Coast Railroad,* Justice Rehnquist decided that the issue of per diem fees on railroad cars was one of general application even though only a few railroads were severely adversely affected by the rate.

So that the reader can get a better grasp of federal substantive rule-making activity, what follows is a list of areas involving federal rule making, most of which appeared on front pages of *The New York Times:*

definition of AIDS (Social Security Administration and Centers for Disease Control and Prevention [CDC])[16]

breast implants (Food and Drug Administration [FDA])[17]

labeling on consumer products (FDA)[18]

regulation of the market in government securities (Treasury, SEC, and Federal Reserve)[19]

acid rain (EPA)[20]

access to information about trading in huge blocks of stocks (SEC)[21]

bank examining (Treasury)[22]

modification of state/federal funding for Medicare (Health and Human Services [HHS])[23]

landfill pollution (EPA)[24]

elimination of a farm pesticide (EPA)[25]

access to Bell telephone system (Federal Communication Commission [FCC])[26]

early morning trading of stocks (SEC)[27]

air traffic control signs and procedure (National Transportation Safety Board [NTSB])[28]

municipal liability for toxic dump sites (EPA)[29]

television station ownership (FCC)[30]

management of wetlands (EPA and Army Corps of Engineers)[31]

regulation of day care centers that receive federal funds (HHS)[32]

regulation of AIDS-infected health care workers (CDC)[33]

reporting of management trading in corporate stocks (SEC)[34]

television manufacturers and retailers putting pressure on the FCC to make a rule about the date to begin broadcasting in the new digital programming to coincide with the Christmas shopping season[35]

Despite the depth and breadth of the preceding list, bear in mind that although rule making is important, it constitutes relatively little of what agencies do. Agencies produce procedural and interpretive rules far more often than substantive rules, and from the previous chapter you learned that informal activity constitutes about 90 percent of what agencies do. Although we have not dealt with state agencies, except by way of occasional example, the reader should be aware that the real growth in bureaucratic activity in the past twenty years or so has been at the state and local levels. California's pollution control agency, for example, promulgated rules to regulate some polluting ingredients in household adhesives, laundry starch, perfumes and colognes, and dusting aids.[36]

Finally, although the 553 procedure specified in the APA is the procedure of choice, Congress has modified the APA to allow for a process called *reg-neg,* which stands for "regulation by negotiation."[37] This is a process by which all interested and potentially affected parties submit proposed regulations and then negotiate the proposals, with the agency acting as a referee. Recently, environmental interest groups and oil company representatives attempted to negotiate regulations implementing the new Clean Air Act.[38] This process is thought to enhance compliance with agency rules because those who must live by the rules helped write them. Actually, that is often the case under normal 553 procedures as well. In the boxcar case cited earlier, the ICC said it wanted to place a per diem fee on boxcars, but the railroads determined what the rate would be. To help you appreciate the role of expertise in agency rule making, I note here a few of the questions being hammered out in the Clean Air reg-negs: (a) how much volatility gasoline may have (*volatility* is the rate at which it evaporates) and (b) what statistical formula should be used for calculating minimum levels of oxygenates (oxygen-carrying molecules in gasoline).[39] No wonder courts defer to agency expertise in court review of agency rule making! If you refer back to Chapter 3, in the discussion of delegation of power, a famous case is mentioned: *Schechter Poultry Corporation v. United States* (the "Sick Chicken Case"). It is worth noting that the procedure the court declared unconstitutional in that case is almost exactly the neg-reg procedure.

ADJUDICATION

From the earlier discussion, you learned that when the enabling legislation says the agency shall engage in rule making after a "hearing on the record," that language requires the agency to go through a quasi-judicial hearing. Sometimes Congress requires this procedure to engage in rule making of a general nature with future applications (as was the case with the FTC, in which the question was, Should peanut butter manufacturers be required to increase the peanuts in peanut butter by 2 percent?). Sometimes it is required to decide factual matters (the National Labor Relations Board [NLRB] is required to conduct a hearing on the record in a case alleging an unfair labor practice). Sometimes Congress requires this procedure just to make decisions (the FCC is required to conduct a hearing on the record to decide whether to grant or renew a license).

When the adjudicative procedure is used for rule making, it is referred to as "formal rule making," "rule making on the record," or a "554 procedure" (see the APA, secs. 554, 556, and 557). You are already familiar with some of its components from the discussion of the disability issue in the preceding chapter.

Basically, the procedure looks like a trial. The affected parties must receive a formal notice. Pleadings (which assert the facts that may be in dispute) and a discovery process are involved, but they are all less formal than in a real trial. Direct and cross-examination of witnesses occurs, but because of the nature of the subject matter, direct examination often involves the submission of a written statement rather than the witness's being led through a direct examination by an attorney.[40] The purpose of a judicial trial is to discover facts (did *X* kill *Y*?). In an administrative adjudication, the question may be, Should the percentage of peanuts in peanut butter be increased by 2 percent? Agencies are free to adopt procedures, within limits, and some have adopted an "interval hearing" system in which the government presents its case and the hearing may be recessed for months so that the other parties can prepare their case.[41] The proponent of a rule or order has the burden of proof, which is by a "preponderance of the evidence."[42] Rules of evidence apply, but again, because of the nature of the questions involved, the rules of evidence are not as strict as in a court of law. At the close of the adjudication, the parties are provided with an opportunity to submit findings of fact and conclusions of law to the administrative law judge (ALJ), similar to the submission of jury instructions by attorneys to the judge in a trial. The ALJ then issues a written decision, which must include the ALJ's findings of fact and conclusions of law and reasons for accepting certain findings of fact and conclusions of law on "all material issues of fact, law or discretion presented on the record."[43]

Adjudicatory hearings constitute a small amount of agency activity. Although their statistics include the period of time the Reagan administration was processing numerous disability cases, however, Gellhorn and Levin document that, in 1983, 400,000 new cases were referred to ALJs.[44] Only 275,000 cases were filed in U.S. district courts for the same year.[45]

AGENCY DISCRETION IN THE USE
OF RULE MAKING AND ADJUDICATION

To summarize, when the enabling legislation uses language that requires a hearing on the record, presumably the agency must use a quasi-judicial, 554-type hearing. Otherwise, the enabling legislation will specify a 553 hearing, will simply use the term *hearing,* or will say nothing, and in all three cases the 553 procedure should guide agency rule making.

We know from *Chenery,* however, that the law is not really black and white. Lest the reader believe the *Chenery* case to be an aberration, consider the case of *National Labor Relations Board v. Wyman-Gordon Company,* 394 U.S. 759

(1969) (see also *National Labor Relations Board v. Bell Aerospace Company,* at the end of this chapter). The issue in the *Wyman-Gordon* case is whether management must provide a list of all employees to a labor union prior to an election on the question of whether to unionize. That is a question of general application that should apply to all future unionization elections. Further, the National Labor Relations Act (NLRA) requires the NLRB to use the APA 553 procedure for the adoption of "such rules and regulations as may be necessary to carry out the provisions of this act."[46] Three years before this case, in 1966, the NLRB decided on this issue for the first time in an adjudicatory hearing, and its decision was to require management to turn over such lists to the union. In its order, the board did not make its decision apply to the company involved in the adjudication, but issued an order applicable to all future union elections. In the *Wyman-Gordon* case,[47] relying on its earlier order, the board ordered Wyman-Gordon to produce the list and present it to the union. The company refused, the election was held, and the unions lost. The unions appealed to the board, and the board invalidated the election because of the company's failure to produce the list. The board ordered new elections and again ordered the company to produce the list. The company again refused. The board issued a subpoena for the names and addresses of the employees, which the company ignored, so the board went to court to enforce the subpoena. The district court issued an order to enforce the subpoena, but the court of appeals reversed on the basis of the board's failure to promulgate a rule in accordance with the enabling legislation and the APA.

When the case came to the Supreme Court, Justice Fortas wrote an opinion that agreed with everything the court of appeals said, except the resulting decision. Fortas's opinion said there could not be a rule of general application and future effect with the force and effect of law until the agency had gone through the proper 553 procedure. Still, Fortas continued, the case is properly before the NLRB on an adjudicating hearing, and the board does have the authority to order the company to produce the list, so the court of appeals, though right, was overruled and the district court's order to the company to comply with the subpoena was affirmed.

The principle, reaffirmed again in 1974 (the *Bell Aerospace Case,* at the end of this chapter), seems to be that despite the nature of the subject matter and enabling legislation that would seem to suggest that an agency proceed by rule promulgation, the courts will not interfere with the agency's choice to proceed by adjudication.

The flip side of this principle is called the *Storer Doctrine,* and it comes from the next case (see also *Heckler v. Campbell,* at the end of this chapter).

UNITED STATES V. STORER BROADCASTING COMPANY
351 U.S. 192 (1956)

Justice Reed delivered the opinion of the Court, joined by Chief Justice Warren and Justices Black, Douglas, Burton, Clark, and Brennan. Justices Frankfurter and Harlan dissented.

The Federal Communications Commission issued, on August 19, 1948, a notice of proposed rule making under the authority of (Communications Act of 1934, as amended, 47 U.S.C. § 301 et seq.) It was proposed, so far as is pertinent to this case, to amend Rules 3.35, 3.240, and 3.636 relating to Multiple Ownership of standard, FM, and television broadcast stations. Those rules provide that licenses for broadcasting stations will not be granted if the applicant, directly or indirectly, has an interest in other stations beyond a limited number. The purpose of the limitations is to avoid overconcentration of broadcasting facilities.

As required, the notice permitted "interested" parties to file statements or briefs. Such parties might also intervene in appeals. Respondent, licensee of a number of radio and television stations, filed a statement objecting to the proposed changes, as did other interested broadcasters. Respondent based its objections largely on the fact that the proposed rules did not allow one person to hold as many FM and television stations as standard stations. Storer argued that such limitations might cause irreparable financial damage to owners of standard stations if an obsolescent standard station could not be augmented by FM and television facilities. In November 1953 the Commission entered an order amending the Rules in question without significant changes from the proposed forms. A review was sought in due course by respondent in the Court of Appeals for the District of Columbia Circuit. Respondent alleged it owned or controlled, within the meaning of the Multiple Ownership Rules, seven standard radio, five FM radio, and five television broadcast stations. It asserted that the Rules complained of were in conflict with the statutory mandates that applicants should be granted licenses if the public interest would be served and that applicants must have a hearing before denial of an application.

Respondent also claimed: . . . "The Rules, in considering the ownership of one (1%) per cent or more of the voting stock of a broadcast licensee corporation as equivalent to ownership, operation or control of the station, are unreasonable and bear no rational relationship to the national Anti-Trust policy." This latter claim was important to respondent because allegedly 20% of its voting stock was in scattered ownership and was traded in by licensed dealers. This stock was thus beyond its control. . . .

On the day the amendments to the Rules were adopted, a pending application of Storer for an additional television station at Miami was dismissed on the basis of the Rules. . . . The Commission asserts that its power to make regulations gives it the authority to limit concentration of stations under a single control. It argues that rules may go beyond the technical aspects of radio, that rules may validly give concreteness to a standard of public interest, and that the right to a hearing does not exist where an applicant admittedly does not meet those standards as there would be no facts to ascertain. The Commission shows that its regulations permit applicants to seek amendments and waivers of or exceptions to its Rules. "This does not mean, of course, that the mere filing of an application for a waiver . . . would necessarily require the holding of a hearing, for if that were the case a rule would no longer be a rule. It means only that it might be an abuse of discretion to fail to hear a request for a waiver which showed, on its face, the existence of circumstances making application of the rule inappropriate."

Respondent defends the position of the Court of Appeals. It urges that an application cannot be rejected under 47 U.S.C. § 309, without a "full hearing" to applicant. We agree that a "full hearing" under § 309 means that every party shall have the right to present his case or defense by oral or documentary evidence, to submit rebuttal evidence, and to conduct such cross-examination as may be required for a full and true disclosure of the facts. Such a hearing is essential for wise and just application of the authority of administrative boards and agencies.

We do not read the hearing requirement, however, as withdrawing from the power of the Commission the rulemaking authority necessary for the orderly conduct of its business. As conceded by

Storer, "Section 309(b) does not require the Commission to hold a hearing before denying a license to operate a station in ways contrary to those that the Congress has determined are in the public interest." The challenged Rules contain limitations against licensing not specifically authorized by statute. But that is not the limit of the Commission's rulemaking authority. 47 U.S.C. § 154(i) and § 303(r) grant general rulemaking power not inconsistent with the Act or law. . . .

This Commission, like other agencies, deals with the public interest. Its authority covers new and rapidly developing fields. Congress sought to create regulation for public protection with careful provision to assure fair opportunity for open competition in the use of broadcasting facilities. Accordingly, we cannot interpret § 309(b) as barring rules that declare a present intent to limit the number of stations consistent with a permissible "concentration of control." It is but a rule that announces the Commission's attitude on public protection against such concentration. The Communications Act must be read as a whole and with appreciation of the responsibilities of the body charged with its fair and efficient operation. The growing complexity of our economy induced the Congress to place regulation of businesses like communication in specialized agencies with broad powers. Courts are slow to interfere with their conclusions when reconcilable with statutory directions. We think the Multiple Ownership Rules, as adopted, are reconcilable with the Communications Act as a whole. An applicant files his application with knowledge of the Commission's attitude toward concentration of control. . . .

Point III of the National Broadcasting Company brief argued the matter under this heading, "The Commission Cannot Escape Its Duty to Evaluate and Decide Each License Application on Its Own Facts." At that time § 309(a) had the hearing pro-

vision. It read: "Sec. 309. (a) If upon examination of any application for a station license or for the renewal or modification of a station license the Commission shall determine that public interest, convenience, or necessity would be served by the granting thereof, it shall authorize the issuance, renewal, or modification thereof in accordance with said finding. In the event the Commission upon examination of any such application does not reach such decision with respect thereto, it shall notify the applicant thereof, shall fix and give notice of a time and place for hearing thereon, and shall afford such applicant an opportunity to be heard under such rules and regulations as it may prescribe." 48 Stat. 1085. Change to the present form was merely for more certainty and clarification to avoid the possibility of arbitrary Commission action. . . .

We read the Act and Regulations as providing a "full hearing" for applicants who have reached the existing limit of stations, upon their presentation of applications conforming to Rules 1.361(c) and 1.702, that set out adequate reasons why the Rules should be waived or amended. The Act, considered as a whole, requires no more. We agree with the contention of the Commission that a full hearing, such as is required by § 309(b), would not be necessary on all such applications. As the Commission has promulgated its Rules after extensive administrative hearings, it is necessary for the accompanying papers to set forth reasons, sufficient if true, to justify a change or waiver of the Rules. We do not think Congress intended the Commission to waste time on applications that do not state a valid basis for a hearing. If any applicant is aggrieved by a refusal, the way for review is open.

We reverse the judgment of the Court of Appeals and remand the case to that court so that it may consider respondent's other objections to the Multiple Ownership Rules.

Reversed and remanded

Justice Reed's opinion in the *Storer* case was perhaps not as clear as it might have been. Section 309(A) and (B) of the Federal Communications Act (FCA) requires the FCC to hold an adjudicatory hearing in each case of a license denial or revocation. The FCC promulgated a rule, however, that limited the number of FM and television stations a company could own to five. Further, the FCC announced its intentions to deny a license to any company that owned five or more stations and also to deny any such company the adjudicatory hearing required under Section 309 of the FCA. The same principle is applied to disability applicants in *Heckler v. Campbell*, at the end of this chapter.

The problem in this area of administrative law lies not so much in the lack of agency hearings, but rather in trying to channel discretion by encouraging agencies to go through the proper procedure in making decisions that affect people's lives. Generally, statutory requirements command agencies to go through a specified APA procedure to make either a rule or an order. Further, supplemental case law suggests when rule making is appropriate (general and future application) and when an order is more appropriate (specific/past event). Also, somewhat contradictory case law says that (a) where a statute requires rule promulgation (553) but the agency chooses to proceed on a case-by-case adjudicatory basis, the courts will not interfere (*Chenery, Wyman-Gordon,* and *Bell Aerospace*) and (b) where a statute requires a hearing on the record (adjudication), the agency is not precluded (by the courts) from promulgating a rule and denying the adjudicatory hearing to those who do not meet the dictates of the rule (*Storer* and *Campbell;* see also *American Airlines v. Civil Aeronautics Board* [CAB], 359 F.2d 624 [1966]).

Questions

1. Can you describe the Storer Doctrine?
2. Do the results reached in the *Chenery, Wyman-Gordon,* and *Storer* cases seem fair to you? Are they democratic? What do these cases portend for control of agencies by elected (or judicial) branches?

SUMMARY

1. The student should be familiar with the doctrines from the *Londoner* and *Bi-Metallic* cases because they relate to both due process (next two chapters) and rule making:

   a. Although a state legislature need not provide each citizen with a hearing before affecting his or her property or liberty, when the legislature delegates that power, the delegate is required to hold a hearing. The hearing presumes oral presentation (*Londoner*).

    b. When government action applies to more than a few people (in terms of liberty or property) and it is impractical to hold a hearing, then none is required by the due process clause of the Fourteenth Amendment (*Bi-Metallic*).

    c. At the federal level and in most states, the *Londoner/Bi-Metallic* jurisprudence has been replaced by legislation requiring agencies to hold hearings (APA).

    2. The student should be familiar with the three types of rules: interpretive, substantive, and procedural. You should have a grasp of the procedural requirements in Sections 553, 554, 556, and 557 of the APA:

    a. Courts cannot impose procedural requirements above those required in the APA (*Vermont Yankee*).

    b. When reviewing an agency's interpretation of a statute, a court should look first to whether Congress has clearly addressed the issue. If it has, that is the end of it, and agency interpretation must be consistent with congressional intent. Second, if congressional intent and meaning are obscure, then the court must determine whether the agency's interpretation is a reasonable one (*Chevron*).

    c. Where an agency has adopted internal procedural rules for it to follow, failure to follow those rules will invalidate subsequent agency action (*Ruiz*).

    3. Where a statute requires an agency to proceed by Section 553 of the APA but an agency chooses instead to deal with an issue on a case-by-case basis via adjudication, the courts will not interfere with the agency's choice (*Chenery*).

    4. Where an agency is required by statute to provide a hearing on the record but chooses instead to promulgate a general rule and deny the required hearing to whoever fails to meet the terms of the rule, the courts will not interfere with the agency's choice (*Storer*).

    5. The last two doctrines (Numbers 3 and 4) are contemplated in the following quote from *Chenery II:* "The choice . . . between proceeding by general rule or by individual, ad hoc litigation is one that lies primarily in the informed discretion of the administrative agency" (332 U.S. 194, 202-03).

END-OF-CHAPTER CASES

RUST V. SULLIVAN
500 U.S. 173 (1991)

Chief Justice Rehnquist delivered the opinion of the Court, joined by Justices White, Scalia, Kennedy, and Souter. Justices Marshall, Blackmun, Stevens, and O'Connor dissented.

These cases concern a facial challenge to Department of Health and Human Services (HHS) regulations which limit the ability of Title X fund recipients to engage in abortion-related activities. . . .

In 1970, Congress enacted Title X of the Public Health Service Act (Act), as amended, which provides federal funding for family-planning services. The Act authorizes the Secretary to "make grants to and enter into contracts with public or nonprofit private entities to assist in the establishment and operation of voluntary family planning projects which shall offer a broad range of acceptable and effective family planning methods and services." Grants and contracts under Title X must "be made in accordance with such regulations as the Secretary may promulgate." Section 1008 of the Act, however, provides that "[n]one of the funds appropriated under this subchapter shall be used in programs where abortion is a method of family planning." . . .

In 1988, the Secretary promulgated new regulations designed to provide " 'clear and operational guidance' to grantees about how to preserve the distinction between Title X programs and abortion as a method of family planning." 53 Fed.Reg. 2923-2924 (1988). The regulations clarify, through the definition of the term "family planning," that Congress intended Title X funds "to be used only to support preventive family planning services." Accordingly, Title X services are limited to "preconceptional counseling, education, and general reproductive health care," and expressly exclude "pregnancy care (including obstetric or prenatal care)." The regulations "focus the emphasis of the Title X program on its traditional mission: The provision of preventive family planning services specifically designed to enable individuals to determine the number and spacing of their children, while clarifying that pregnant women must be referred to appropriate prenatal care services."

The regulations attach three principal conditions on the grant of federal funds for Title X projects. First, the regulations specify that a "Title X project may not provide counseling concerning the use of abortion as a method of family planning or provide referral for abortion as a method of family planning." . . .

Second, the regulations broadly prohibit a Title X project from engaging in activities that "encourage, promote or advocate abortion as a method of family planning." . . .

Third, the regulations require that Title X projects be organized so that they are "physically and financially separate" from prohibited abortion activities. . . .

B

Petitioners are Title X grantees and doctors who supervise Title X funds suing on behalf of themselves and their patients. Respondent is the Secretary of HHS. . . .

II

We begin by pointing out the posture of the cases before us. Petitioners are challenging the facial validity of the regulations. Thus, we are concerned only with the question whether, on their face, the regulations are both authorized by the Act and can be construed in such a manner that they can be applied to a set of individuals without infringing upon constitutionally protected rights. . . .

We turn first to petitioners' contention that the regulations exceed the Secretary's authority under Title X and are arbitrary and capricious. We begin with an examination of the regulations concerning abortion counseling, referral, and advocacy, which every Court of Appeals has found to be authorized by the statute, and then turn to the "program integrity requirement," with respect to which the courts below have adopted conflicting positions. We then address petitioner's claim that the regulations must be struck down because they raise a substantial constitutional question.

A

[1] We need not dwell on the plain language of the statute because we agree with every court to have addressed the issue that the language is ambiguous. The language of § 1008—that "[n]one of the funds appropriated under this subchapter shall be used in programs where abortion is a method of family planning"—does not speak directly to the issues of counseling, referral, advocacy, or program integrity. If a statute is "silent or ambiguous with respect to the specific issue, the question for the court is whether the agency's answer is based on a permissible construction of the statute." *Chevron,* 467 U.S., at 842-843.

The Secretary's construction of Title X may not be disturbed as an abuse of discretion if it reflects a plausible construction of the plain language of the statute and does not otherwise conflict with Congress' expressed intent. Ibid. In determining whether a construction is permissible, "[t]he court need not conclude that the agency construction was the only one it permissibly could have adopted . . .

or even the reading the court would have reached if the question initially had arisen in a judicial proceeding." Id., at 843. Rather, substantial deference is accorded to the interpretation of the authorizing statute by the agency authorized with administering it.

[2] The broad language of Title X plainly allows the Secretary's construction of the statute. By its own terms, § 1008 prohibits the use of Title X funds "in programs where abortion is a method of family planning." Title X does not define the term "method of family planning," nor does it enumerate what types of medical and counseling services are entitled to Title X funding. Based on the broad directives provided by Congress in Title X in general and § 1008 in particular, we are unable to say that the Secretary's construction of the prohibition in § 1008 to require a ban on counseling, referral, and advocacy within the Title X project is impermissible.

The District Courts and Courts of Appeals that have examined the legislative history have all found, at least with regard to the Act's counseling, referral, and advocacy provisions, that the legislative history is ambiguous with respect to Congress' intent in enacting Title X and the prohibition of § 1008. ("Congress has not addressed specifically the question of the scope of the abortion prohibition. The language of the statute and the legislative history can support either of the litigants' positions"); *Planned Parenthood Federation of America v. Sullivan,* 913 F.2d 1492 (CA10 1990) ("[T]he contemporaneous legislative history does not address whether clinics receiving Title X funds can engage in nondirective counseling including the abortion option and referrals"); 889 F.2d, at 407 (case below) ("Nothing in the legislative history of Title X detracts" from the Secretary's construction of § 1008). We join these courts in holding that the legislative history is ambiguous and fails to shed light on relevant congressional intent. At no time did Congress directly address the issues of abortion counseling, referral, or advocacy. The parties' attempts to characterize highly generalized, conflicting statements in the legislative history into accurate revelations of congressional intent are unavailing.

When we find, as we do here, that the legislative history is ambiguous and unenlightening on the matters with respect to which the regulations deal, we customarily defer to the expertise of the agency. Petitioners argue, however, that the regulations are entitled to little or no deference because they "reverse a longstanding agency policy that permitted nondirective counseling and referral for abortion," Brief for Petitioners in No. 89-1392, p. 20, and thus represent a sharp break from the Secretary's prior construction of the statute. Petitioners argue that the agency's prior consistent interpretation of § 1008 to permit nondirective counseling and to encourage coordination with local and state family planning services is entitled to substantial weight.

[3] This Court has rejected the argument that an agency's interpretation "is not entitled to deference because it represents a sharp break with prior interpretations" of the statute in question. *Chevron,* 467 U.S., at 862. In *Chevron,* we held that a revised interpretation deserves deference because "[a]n initial agency interpretation is not instantly carved in stone" and "the agency, to engage in informed rulemaking, must consider varying interpretations and the wisdom of its policy on a continuing basis." Id., at 863-864. An agency is not required to " 'establish rules of conduct to last forever,' " *Motor Vehicle Mfrs. Assn. of United States, Inc. v. State Farm Mut. Automobile Ins. Co.,* 463 U.S. 29 (1983), quoting but rather "must be given ample latitude to 'adapt [its] rules and policies to the demands of changing circumstances.' " *Motor Vehicle Mfrs.,* supra, 463 U.S., at 42.

[4] We find that the Secretary amply justified his change of interpretation with a "reasoned analysis." *Motor Vehicle Mfrs.,* supra, 463 U.S., at 42, 103 S.Ct., at 2866. The Secretary explained that the regulations are a result of his determination, in the wake of the critical reports of the General Accounting Office (GAO) and the Office of the Inspector General (OIG), that prior policy failed to implement properly the statute and that it was necessary to provide " 'clear and operational guidance' to grantees about how to preserve the distinction between Title X programs and abortion as a method of family planning." 53 Fed.Reg. 2923-2924 (1988). He also determined that the new regulations are more in keeping with the original intent of the statute, are justified by client experience under the prior policy, and are supported by a shift in attitude against the "elimination of unborn children by abortion." We believe that these justifications are sufficient to support the Secretary's revised approach. Having concluded that the plain language and legislative history are ambiguous as to Congress' intent in enacting Title X, we must defer to the Secretary's permissible construction of the statute.

B

[5] We turn next to the "program integrity" requirements embodied at § 59.9 of the regulations, mandating separate facilities, personnel, and records. These requirements are not inconsistent with the plain language of Title X. Petitioners contend, however, that they are based on an impermissible construction of the statute because they frustrate the clearly expressed intent of Congress that Title X programs be an integral part of a broader, comprehensive, health-care system. They argue that this integration is impermissibly burdened because the efficient use of non-Title X funds by Title X grantees will be adversely affected by the regulations.

The Secretary defends the separation requirements of § 59.9 on the grounds that they are necessary to assure that Title X grantees apply federal funds only to federally authorized purposes and that grantees avoid creating the appearance that the Government is supporting abortion-related activities. The program integrity regulations were promulgated in direct response to the observations in the GAO and OIG reports that "[b]ecause the distinction between the recipients' Title X and other activities may not be easily recognized, the public can get the impression that Federal funds are being improperly used for abortion activities." . . .

We agree that the program integrity requirements are based on a permissible construction of the statute and are not inconsistent with congressional intent. As noted, the legislative history is clear about very little, and program integrity is no exception. The statements relied upon by petitioners to infer such an intent are highly generalized and do not directly address the scope of § 1008.

While petitioners' interpretation of the legislative history may be a permissible one, it is by no means the only one, and it is certainly not the one found by the Secretary. It is well established that legislative history which does not demonstrate a clear and certain congressional intent cannot form the basis for enjoining regulations. See *Motor Vehicle Mfrs.*, 463 U.S., at 42. The Secretary based the need for the separation requirements "squarely on the congressional intent that abortion not be a part of a Title X funded program." 52 Fed.Reg. 33212 (1987). Indeed, if one thing is clear from the legislative history, it is that Congress intended that Title X funds be kept separate and distinct from abortion-related activities. It is undisputed that Title X was intended to provide primarily prepregnancy preventive services. Certainly the Secretary's interpretation of the statute that separate facilities are necessary, especially in light of the express prohibition of § 1008, cannot be judged unreasonable. Accordingly, we defer to the Secretary's reasoned determination that the program integrity requirements are necessary to implement the prohibition.

The Secretary's regulations are a permissible construction of Title X and do not violate either the First or Fifth Amendments to the Constitution. Accordingly, the judgment of the Court of Appeals is
  Affirmed.

NATIONAL LABOR RELATIONS BOARD V. BELL AEROSPACE COMPANY
461 U.S. 267 (1974)

Justice Powell delivered the opinion of the Court, joined by Chief Justice Burger and Justices Douglas, Blackmun, and Rehnquist. Justice White dissented in part and was joined by Justices Brennan, Stewart, and Marshall.

This case presents two questions: first, whether the National Labor Relations Board properly determined that all "managerial employees," except those whose participation in a labor organization would create a conflict of interest with their job responsibilities, are covered by the National Labor Relations Act; and second, whether the Board must proceed by rulemaking rather than by adjudication in determining whether certain buyers are "managerial employees." We answer both questions in the negative. . . .

I

Respondent Bell Aerospace Co., Division of Textron, Inc. (company), operates a plant in Wheatfield, New York, where it is engaged in research and development in the design and fabrication of aerospace products. On July 30, 1970, Amalgamated Local No. 1286 of the United Automobile, Aerospace and Agricultural Implement Workers of America (union) petitioned the National Labor Relations Board (Board) for a representation election to determine whether the union would be certified as the bargaining representative of the 25 buyers in the purchasing and procurement department at the company's plant. The company opposed the petition on the ground that the buyers were "managerial employees" and thus were not covered by the Act.

Absent specific instructions to the contrary, buyers have full discretion, without any dollar limit, to select prospective vendors, draft invitations to bid, evaluate submitted bids, negotiate price and terms, and prepare purchase orders. Buyers execute all purchase orders up to $50,000. They may place or cancel orders of less than $5,000 on their own signature. On commitments in excess of $5,000, buyers must obtain the approval of a superior, with higher levels of approval required as the purchase cost increases. For the Minute Man missile project, which represents 70% of the company's sales, purchase decisions are made by a team of personnel from the engineering, quality assurance, finance, and manufacturing departments. The buyer serves as team chairman and signs the purchase order, but a representative from the pricing and negotiation department participates in working out the terms.

After the representation hearing, the Regional Director transferred the case to the Board. On May 20, 1971, the Board issued its decision holding that the company's buyers constituted an appropriate unit for purposes of collective bargaining and directing an election. 190 N.L.R.B. 431. Relying on its recent decision in *North Arkansas Electric Cooperative, Inc.,* 185 N.L.R.B. 550 (1970), the Board first stated that even though the company's buyers might be "managerial employees," they were nevertheless covered by the Act and entitled to its protections. The Board then rejected the company's alternative contention that representation should be denied because the buyers' authority to commit the company's credit, select vendors, and negotiate purchase prices would create a potential conflict of interest between the buyers as union members and the company. In essence, the company argued that buyers would be more receptive to bids from union contractors and would also influence "make or buy" decisions in favor of "make," thus creating additional work for sister unions in the plant. The Board thought, however,

that any possible conflict was "unsupported conjecture" since the buyers' "discretion and latitude for independent action must take place within the confines of the general directions which the Employer has established" and that "any possible temptation to allow sympathy for sister unions to influence such decisions could effectively be controlled by the Employer." . . .

On June 16, 1971, a representation election was conducted in which 15 of the buyers voted for the union and nine against. On August 12, the Board certified the union as the exclusive bargaining representative for the company's buyers. That same day, however, the Court of Appeals for the Eighth Circuit denied enforcement of another Board order in *NLRB v. North Arkansas Electric Cooperative, Inc.,* 446 F.2d 602, and held that "managerial employees" were not covered by the Act and were therefore not entitled to its protections. . . .

Encouraged by the Eighth Circuit's decision, the company moved the Board for reconsideration of its earlier order. The Board denied the motion, 196 N.L.R.B. 827 (1972), stating that it disagreed with the Eighth Circuit and would adhere to its own decision in North Arkansas. In the Board's view, Congress intended to exclude from the Act only those "managerial employees" associated with the "formulation and implementation of labor relations policies." In each case, the "fundamental touchstone" was "whether the duties and responsibilities of any managerial employee or group of managerial employees do or do not include determinations which should be made free of any conflict of interest which could arise if the person involved was a participating member of a labor organization." Turning to the present case, the Board reiterated its prior finding that the company had not shown that union organization of its buyers would create a conflict of interest in labor relations.

The company stood by its contention that the buyers, as "managerial employees," were not covered by the Act and refused to bargain with the union. An unfair labor practice complaint resulted in a Board finding that the company had violated §§ 8(a)(5) and (1) of the Act, 29 U.S.C. and an order compelling the company to bargain with the union. 197 N.L.R.B. 209 (1972). Subsequently, the company petitioned the United States Court of Appeals for the Second Circuit for review of the order and the Board cross-petitioned for enforcement.

II

We begin with the question whether all "managerial employees," rather than just those in positions susceptible to conflicts of interest in labor relations, are excluded from the protections of the Act. The Board's early decisions, the legislative history of the Taft-Hartley Act of 1947, and subsequent Board and court decisions provide the necessary guidance for our inquiry. In examining these authorities, we draw on several established principles of statutory construction. In addition to the importance of legislative history, a court may accord great weight to the longstanding interpretation placed on a statute by an agency charged with its administration. This is especially so where Congress has re-enacted the statute without pertinent change. In these circumstances, congressional failure to revise or repeal the agency's interpretation is persuasive evidence that the interpretation is the one intended by Congress. We have also recognized that subsequent legislation declaring the intent of an earlier statute is entitled to significant weight. Application of these principles leads us to conclude, as did the Court of Appeals, that Congress intended to exclude from the protections of the Act all employees properly classified as "managerial."

. . .

D

In sum, the Board's early decisions, the purpose and legislative history of the Taft-Hartley Act of 1947, the Board's subsequent and consistent construction of the Act for more than two decades, and the decisions of the courts of appeals all point unmistakably to the conclusion that "managerial employees" are not covered by the Act. We agree with the Court of Appeals below that the Board "is not now free" to read a new and more restrictive meaning into the Act. . . .

III

The Court of Appeals also held that, although the Board was not precluded from determining that buyers or some types of buyers were not "managerial employees," it could do so only by invoking its rulemaking procedures under § 6 of the Act, 29 U.S.C. § 156. We disagree. At the outset, the precise nature of the present issue must be noted. The question is not whether the Board should have resorted to rulemaking, or in fact improperly promulgated a "rule," when in the context of the prior representation proceeding it held that the Act covers all "managerial employees" except those meeting the new "conflict of interest in labor relations" touchstone. Our conclusion that the Board applied the wrong legal standard makes consideration of that issue unnecessary. Rather, the present question is whether on remand the Board must invoke its rulemaking procedures if it determines, in light of our opinion, that these buyers are not "managerial employees" under the Act. The Court of Appeals thought that rulemaking was required because any Board finding that the company's buyers are not "managerial" would be contrary to its prior decisions and would presumably be in the nature of a general rule designed "to fit all cases at all times."

. . .

A similar issue was presented to this Court in its second decision in *SEC v. Chenery Corp.,* 332 U.S. 194 (1947) (*Chenery II*). There, the respondent corporation argued that in an adjudicative proceeding the Commission could not apply a general standard that it had formulated for the first time in that proceeding. Rather, the Commission was required to resort instead to its rulemaking procedures if it desired to promulgate a new standard that would govern future conduct. In rejecting this contention, the Court first noted that the Commission had a statutory duty to decide the issue at hand in light of the proper standards and that this duty remained "regardless of whether those standards previously had been spelled out in a general rule or regulation." The Court continued: . . . "The function of filling in the interstices of the (Securities) Act should be performed, as much as possible, through this quasi-legislative promulgation of rules to be applied in the future. But any rigid requirement to that effect would make the administrative process inflexible and incapable of dealing with many of the specialized problems which arise. . . .

Not every principle essential to the effective administration of a statute can or should be cast immediately into the mold of a general rule. Some principles must await their own development, while others must be adjusted to meet particular, unforeseeable situations. In performing its important functions in these respects, therefore, an administrative agency must be equipped to act either by general rule or by individual order. To insist upon one form of action to the exclusion of the other is to exalt form over necessity. "In other words, problems may arise in a case which the administrative agency could not reasonably foresee, problems which must be solved despite the absence of a relevant general rule. Or the agency may not have had sufficient experience with a particular problem to warrant rigidifying its tentative judgment into a hard and fast rule. Or the problem may be so specialized and varying in nature as to be impossible of capture within the boundaries of a general rule. In those situations, the agency must retain power to deal with the problems on a case-to-case basis if the administrative process is to be effective. There is thus a very definite place for the case-by-case evolution of statutory standards." The Court concluded that "the choice made between proceeding by general rule or by individual, ad hoc litigation is one that lies primarily in the informed discretion of the administrative agency."

And in *NLRB v. Wyman-Gordon Co.*, 394 U.S. 759, 89 S.Ct. 1426, 22 L.Ed.2d 709 (1969), the Court upheld a Board order enforcing an election list requirement first promulgated in an earlier adjudicative proceeding in *Excelsior Underwear Inc.*, 156 N.L.R.B. 1236 (1966). The plurality opinion of Mr. Justice Fortas, joined by the Chief Justice, Mr. Justice Stewart, and Mr. Justice White, recognized that "[a]djudicated cases may and do . . . serve as vehicles for the formulation of agency policies, which are applied and announced therein," and that such cases "generally provide a guide to action that the agency may be expected to take in future cases." *NLRB v. Wyman-Gordon Co.*, supra, at 765—766, 89 S.Ct., at 1429. The concurring opinion of Mr. Justice Black, joined by Mr. Justice Brennan and Mr. Justice Marshall, also noted that the Board had both adjudicative and rule-making powers and that the choice between the two was "within its informed discretion."

The views expressed in *Chenery II* and *Wyman-Gordon* make plain that the Board is not precluded

from announcing new principles in an adjudicative proceeding and that the choice between rulemaking and adjudication lies in the first instance within the Board's discretion. Although there may be situations where the Board's reliance on adjudication would amount to an abuse of discretion or a violation of the Act, nothing in the present case would justify such a conclusion. Indeed, there is ample indication that adjudication is especially appropriate in the instant context. As the Court of Appeals noted, "[t]here must be tens of thousands of manufacturing, wholesale and retail units which employ buyers, and hundreds of thousands of the latter." Moreover, duties of buyers vary widely depending on the company or industry. It is doubtful whether any generalized standard could be framed which would have more than marginal utility. The Board thus has reason to proceed with caution, developing its standards in a case-by-case manner with attention to the specific character of the buyers' authority and duties in each company. The Board's judgment that adjudication best serves this purpose is entitled to great weight. It is true, of course, that rulemaking would provide the Board with a forum for soliciting the informed views of those affected in industry and labor before embarking on a new course. But surely the Board has discretion to decide that the adjudicative procedures in this case may also produce the relevant information necessary to mature and fair consideration of the issues. Those most immediately affected, the buyers and the company in the particular case, are accorded a full opportunity to be heard before the Board makes its determination.

The judgment of the Court of Appeals is therefore affirmed in part and reversed in part, and the cause remanded to that court with directions to remand to the Board for further proceedings in conformity with this opinion.

Judgment of the Court of Appeals affirmed in part and reversed in part, and cause remanded.

It is so ordered.

HECKLER V. CAMPBELL
461 U.S. 458 (1983)

Justice Powell delivered the opinion for seven members of the Court. Justice Brennan concurred, and Justice Marshall concurred in part and dissented in part. The issue is whether the secretary of Health and Human Services may rely on published medical-vocational guidelines to deter-

mine a claimant's right to Social Security disability benefits.

I

The Social Security Act defines "disability" in terms of the effect a physical or mental impairment has on a person's ability to function in the work place. It provides disability benefits only to persons who are unable "to engage in any substantial gainful activity by reason of any medically determinable physical or mental impairment." 42 U.S.C. § 423(d)(1)(A). And it specifies that a person must "not only [be] unable to do his previous work but [must be unable], considering his age, education, and work experience, [to] engage in any other kind of substantial gainful work which exists in the national economy, regardless of whether such work exists in the immediate area in which he lives, or whether a specific job vacancy exists for him, or whether he would be hired if he applied for work."

In 1978, the Secretary of Health and Human Services promulgated regulations implementing this definition. See 43 Fed.Reg. 55349 (1978). The regulations recognize that certain impairments are so severe that they prevent a person from pursuing any gainful work. A claimant who establishes that he suffers from one of these impairments will be considered disabled without further inquiry. If a claimant suffers from a less severe impairment, the Secretary must determine whether the claimant retains the ability to perform either his former work or some less demanding employment. If a claimant can pursue his former occupation, he is not entitled to disability benefits. If he cannot, the Secretary must determine whether the claimant retains the capacity to pursue less demanding work.

The regulations divide this last inquiry into two stages. First, the Secretary must assess each claimant's present job qualifications. The regulations direct the Secretary to consider the factors Congress has identified as relevant: physical ability, age, education, and work experience. Second, she must consider whether jobs exist in the national economy. . . .

Prior to 1978, the Secretary relied on vocational experts to establish the existence of suitable jobs in the national economy. After a claimant's limitations and abilities had been determined at a hearing, a vocational expert ordinarily would testify whether work existed that the claimant could perform. Although this testimony often was based on standardized guides, vocational experts frequently were criticized for their inconsistent treatment of similarly situated claimants. See *Santise v. Schweiker,* 676 F.2d 925 (1982). To improve both the uniformity and efficiency of this determination, the Secretary promulgated medical-vocational guidelines as part of the 1978 regulations. . . . These guidelines relieve the Secretary of the need to rely on vocational experts by establishing through rulemaking the types and numbers of jobs that exist in the national economy. They consist of a matrix of the four factors identified by Congress—physical ability, age, education, and work experience—and set forth rules that identify whether jobs requiring specific combinations of these factors exist in significant numbers in the national economy. Where a claimant's qualifications correspond to the job requirements identified by a rule, the guidelines direct a conclusion as to whether work exists that the claimant could perform. If such work exists, the claimant is not considered disabled. . . .

II

In 1979, Carmen Campbell applied for disability benefits because a back condition and hypertension prevented her from continuing her work as a hotel maid. After her application was denied, she requested a hearing de novo before an Administrative Law Judge. He determined that her back problem was not severe enough to find her disabled without further inquiry, and accordingly considered whether she retained the ability to perform either her past work or some less strenuous job. He concluded that even though Campbell's back condition prevented her from returning to her work as a maid, she retained the physical capacity to do light work. In accordance with the regulations, he found that Campbell was 52 years old, that her previous employment consisted of unskilled jobs and that she had a limited education. He noted that Campbell, who had been born in Panama, experienced difficulty in speaking and writing English. She was able, however, to understand and read English fairly well. Relying on the medical-vocational guidelines, the Administrative Law Judge found that a significant number of jobs existed that a person of Campbell's qualifications could perform. Accordingly, he concluded that she was not disabled.

This determination was upheld by both the Social Security Appeals Council and the District Court for the Eastern District of New York. The

Court of Appeals for the Second Circuit reversed. *Campbell v. Secretary of HHS,* 665 F.2d 48 (CA2 1982). It accepted the Administrative Law Judge's determination that Campbell retained the ability to do light work. And it did not suggest that he had classified Campbell's age, education, or work experience incorrectly. The court noted, however, that it "has consistently required that 'the Secretary identify specific alternative occupations available in the national economy that would be suitable for the claimant' and that 'these jobs be supported by "a job description clarifying the nature of the job, [and] demonstrating that the job does not require" exertion or skills not possessed by the claimant.' " (quoting *Decker v. Harris,* 647 F.2d 291, 298 (CA2 1981)). The court found that the medical-vocational guidelines did not provide the specific evidence that it previously had required. It explained that in the absence of such a showing, "the claimant is deprived of any real chance to present evidence showing that she cannot in fact perform the types of jobs that are administratively noticed by the guidelines." The court concluded that because the Secretary had failed to introduce evidence that specific alternative jobs existed, the determination that Campbell was not disabled was not supported by substantial evidence. We granted certiorari to resolve a conflict among the Courts of Appeals. We now reverse.

[1] The Social Security Act directs the Secretary to "adopt reasonable and proper rules and regulations to regulate and provide for the nature and extent of the proofs and evidence and the method of taking and furnishing the same" in disability cases. As we previously have recognized, Congress has "conferred on the Secretary exceptionally broad authority to prescribe standards for applying certain sections of the [Social Security] Act." *Schweiker v. Gray Panthers,* 453 U.S. 34 (1981). Where, as here, the statute expressly entrusts the Secretary with the responsibility for implementing a provision by regulation, our review is limited to determining whether the regulations promulgated exceeded the Secretary's statutory authority and whether they are arbitrary and capricious. . . .

[2] We do not think that the Secretary's reliance on medical-vocational guidelines is inconsistent with the Social Security Act. It is true that the statutory scheme contemplates that disability hearings will be individualized determinations based on evidence adduced at a hearing. See 42 U.S.C. § 423(d)(2)(A) (specifying consideration of each individual's condition); 42 U.S.C. § 405(b) (disability determination to be based on evidence adduced at hearing). But this does not bar the Secretary from relying on rulemaking to resolve certain classes of issues. The Court has recognized that even where an agency's enabling statute expressly requires it to hold a hearing, the agency may rely on its rulemaking authority to determine issues that do not require case-by-case consideration. *United States v. Storer Broadcasting Co.,* 351 U.S. 192, 205 (1956). A contrary holding would require the agency continually to relitigate issues that may be established fairly and efficiently in a single rulemaking proceeding.

The Secretary's decision to rely on medical-vocational guidelines is consistent with *Texaco* and *Storer.* As noted above, in determining whether a claimant can perform less strenuous work, the Secretary must make two determinations. She must assess each claimant's individual abilities and then determine whether jobs exist that a person having the claimant's qualifications could perform. The first inquiry involves a determination of historic facts, and the regulations properly require the Secretary to make these findings on the basis of evidence adduced at a hearing. We note that the regulations afford claimants ample opportunity both to present evidence relating to their own abilities and to offer evidence that the guidelines do not apply to them. The second inquiry requires the Secretary to determine an issue that is not unique to each claimant—the types and numbers of jobs that exist in the national economy. This type of general factual issue may be resolved as fairly through rulemaking as by introducing the testimony of vocational experts at each disability hearing. See *American Airlines, Inc. v. CAB* [Civil Aeronautics Board], 123 U.S.App.D.C. 310 (1966) (en banc). . . .

IV

The Court of Appeals' decision would require the Secretary to introduce evidence of specific available jobs that respondent could perform. It would limit severely her ability to rely on the medical-vocational guidelines. We think the Secretary reasonably could choose to rely on these guidelines in appropriate cases rather than on the testimony of a vocational expert in each case. Accordingly, the judgment of the Court of Appeals is Reversed.

VERMONT YANKEE NUCLEAR POWER CORPORATION V.
NATURAL RESOURCES DEFENSE COUNCIL
435 U.S. 519 (1978)

Justice Rehnquist delivered the opinion of the Court of seven Justices. Justices Blackmun and Powell did not participate.

In 1946, Congress enacted the Administrative Procedure Act, which as we have noted elsewhere was not only "a new, basic and comprehensive regulation of procedures in many agencies," but was also a legislative enactment which settled "long-continued and hard-fought contentions, and enacts a formula upon which opposing social and political forces have come to rest." Section 4 of the Act, 5 U.S.C. § 553 dealing with rulemaking, requires in subsection (b) that "notice of proposed rule making shall be published in the *Federal Register* . . . ," describes the contents of that notice, and goes on to require in subsection (c) that after the notice the agency "shall give interested persons an opportunity to participate in the rule making through submission of written data, views, or arguments with or without opportunity for oral presentation. After consideration of the relevant matter presented, the agency shall incorporate in the rules adopted a concise general statement of their basis and purpose." Interpreting this provision of the Act in *United States v. Allegheny-Ludlum Steel Corp.,* 406 U.S. 742 (1972), and *United States v. Florida East Coast R. Co.,* 410 U.S. 224 (1973), we held that generally speaking this section of the Act established the maximum procedural requirements which Congress was willing to have the courts impose upon agencies in conducting rulemaking procedures. Agencies are free to grant additional procedural rights in the exercise of their discretion, but reviewing courts are generally not free to impose them if the agencies have not chosen to grant them. This is not to say necessarily that there are no circumstances which would ever justify a court in overturning agency action because of a failure to employ procedures beyond those required by the statute. But such circumstances, if they exist, are extremely rare.

Even apart from the Administrative Procedure Act this Court has for more than four decades emphasized that the formulation of procedures was basically to be left within the discretion of the agencies to which Congress had confided the responsibility for substantive judgments. The Court explicated this principle, describing it as "an outgrowth of the congressional determination that administrative agencies and administrators will be familiar with the industries which they regulate and will be in a better position than federal courts or Congress itself to design procedural rules adapted to the peculiarities of the industry and the tasks of the agency involved." It is in the light of this background of statutory and decisional law that we granted certiorari to review two judgments of the Court of Appeals for the District of Columbia Circuit because of our concern that they had seriously misread or misapplied this statutory and decisional law cautioning reviewing courts against engrafting their own notions of proper procedures upon agencies entrusted with substantive functions by Congress. We conclude that the Court of Appeals has done just that in these cases, and we therefore remand them to it for further proceedings. We also find it necessary to examine the Court of Appeals' decision with respect to agency action taken after full adjudicatory hearings. We again conclude that the court improperly intruded into the agency's decisionmaking process, making it necessary for us to reverse and remand with respect to this part of the case also.

I

A

Under the Atomic Energy Act of 1954, 42 U.S.C. § 2011 et seq., the Atomic Energy Commission is given broad regulatory authority over the development of nuclear energy. Under the terms of the Act, a utility seeking to construct and operate a nuclear power plant must obtain a separate permit or license at both the construction and the operation stage of the project. In order to obtain the construction permit, the utility must file a preliminary safety analysis report, an environmental report, and certain information regarding the antitrust implications of the proposed project. This application then undergoes exhaustive review by the Commission's staff and by the Advisory Committee on Reactor Safeguards (ACRS), a group of distinguished experts in the field of atomic energy. Both groups submit to the Commission their own evaluations, which then become part of the record of the utility's application. The Commission staff also undertakes the review required by the National Environmental Policy Act of 1969 (NEPA), 42 U.S.C. § 4321 et seq., and prepares a draft environmental impact statement, which, after being circulated for comment, is revised and becomes a final environmental impact statement.

Thereupon a three-member Atomic Safety and Licensing Board conducts a public adjudicatory hearing, and reaches a decision which can be appealed to the Atomic Safety and Licensing Appeal Board, and currently, in the Commission's discretion, to the Commission itself. The final agency decision may be appealed to the courts of appeals. The same sort of process occurs when the utility applies for a license to operate the plant, except that a hearing need only be held in contested cases and may be limited to the matters in controversy.

These cases arise from two separate decisions of the Court of Appeals for the District of Columbia Circuit. In the first, the court remanded a decision of the Commission to grant a license to petitioner Vermont Yankee Nuclear Power Corp. to operate a nuclear power plant. *Natural Resources Defense Council v. NRC* [Nuclear Regulatory Commission], 547 F.2d 633 (1976). In the second, the court remanded a decision of that same agency to grant a permit to petitioner Consumers Power Co. to construct two pressurized water nuclear reactors to generate electricity and steam. *Aeschliman v. NRC,* 547 F.2d 622.

B

In December 1967, after the mandatory adjudicatory hearing and necessary review, the Commission granted petitioner Vermont Yankee a permit to build a nuclear power plant in Vernon, Vt. See 4 A.E.C. 36 (1967). Thereafter, Vermont Yankee applied for an operating license. Respondent Natural Resources Defense Council (NRDC) objected to the granting of a license, however, and therefore a hearing on the application commenced on August 10, 1971. Excluded from consideration at the hearings, over NRDC's objection, was the issue of the environmental effects of operations to reprocess fuel or dispose of wastes resulting from the reprocessing operations. This ruling was affirmed by the Appeal Board in June 1972. . . . In November 1972, however, the Commission, making specific refer-

ence to the Appeal Board's decision with respect to the Vermont Yankee license, instituted rulemaking proceedings "that would specifically deal with the question of consideration of environmental effects associated with the uranium fuel cycle in the individual cost-benefit analyses for light water cooled nuclear power reactors." The notice of proposed rulemaking offered two alternatives, both predicated on a report prepared by the Commission's staff entitled Environmental Survey of the Nuclear Fuel Cycle. The first would have required no quantitative evaluation of the environmental hazards of fuel reprocessing or disposal because the Environmental Survey had found them to be slight. The second would have specified numerical values for the environmental impact of this part of the fuel cycle, which values would then be incorporated into a table, along with the other relevant factors, to determine the overall cost-benefit balance for each operating license.

Much of the controversy in this case revolves around the procedures used in the rulemaking hearing which commenced in February 1973. In a supplemental notice of hearing the Commission indicated that while discovery or cross-examination would not be utilized, the Environmental Survey would be available to the public before the hearing along with the extensive background documents cited therein. All participants would be given a reasonable opportunity to present their position and could be represented by counsel if they so desired. Written and, time permitting, oral statements would be received and incorporated into the record. All persons giving oral statements would be subject to questioning by the Commission. At the conclusion of the hearing, a transcript would be made available to the public and the record would remain open for 30 days to allow the filing of supplemental written statements. More than 40 individuals and organizations representing a wide variety of interests submitted written comments. On January 17, 1973, the Licensing Board held a planning session to schedule the appearance of witnesses and to discuss methods for compiling a record. The hearing was held on February 1 and 2, with participation by a number of groups, including the Commission's staff, the United States Environmental Protection Agency, a manufacturer of reactor equipment, a trade association from the nuclear industry, a group of electric utility companies, and a group called Consolidated National Intervenors which represented 79 groups and individuals including respondent NRDC.

After the hearing, the Commission's staff filed a supplemental document for the purpose of clarifying and revising the Environmental Survey. Then the Licensing Board forwarded its report to the Commission without rendering any decision. The Licensing Board identified as the principal procedural question the propriety of declining to use full formal adjudicatory procedures. The major substantive issue was the technical adequacy of the Environmental Survey. In April 1974, the Commission issued a rule which adopted the second of the two proposed alternatives described above. The Commission also approved the procedures used at the hearing, and indicated that the record, including the Environmental Survey, provided an "adequate data base for the regulation adopted." Finally, the Commission ruled that to the extent the rule differed from the Appeal Board decisions in Vermont Yankee "those decisions have no further precedential significance," but that since "the environmental effects of the uranium fuel cycle have been shown to be relatively insignificant, . . . it is unnecessary to apply the amendment to applicant's environmental reports submitted prior to its effective date or to Final Environmental Statements for which Draft Environmental Statements have been circulated for comment prior to the effective date."

[5] But this much is absolutely clear. Absent constitutional constraints or extremely compelling circumstances the "administrative agencies 'should be free to fashion their own rules of procedure and to pursue methods of inquiry capable of permitting them to discharge their multitudinous duties.'" Indeed, our cases could hardly be more explicit in this regard. The Court has, as we noted in *FCC v. Schreiber,* upheld this principle in a variety of applications, including that case where the District Court, instead of inquiring into the validity of the Federal Communications Commission's exercise of its rulemaking authority, devised procedures to be followed by the agency on the basis of its conception of how the public and private interest involved could best be served.

We have continually repeated this theme through the years, most recently in *FPC v. Transcontinental Gas Pipe Line Corp.,* 423 U.S. 326 (1976), decided just two Terms ago. In that case, in determining the proper scope of judicial review of agency action under the Natural Gas Act, we held that while a court may have occasion to remand an agency decision because of the inadequacy of the record, the agency should normally be allowed to "exercise its

administrative discretion in deciding how, in light of internal organization considerations, it may best proceed to develop the needed evidence and how its prior decision should be modified in light of such evidence as develops." We went on to emphasize: "At least in the absence of substantial justification for doing otherwise, a reviewing court may not, after determining that additional evidence is requisite for adequate review, proceed by dictating to the agency the methods, procedures, and time dimension of the needed inquiry and ordering the results to be reported to the court without opportunity for further consideration on the basis of the new evidence by the agency."

Such a procedure clearly runs the risk of "propel[ling] the court into the domain which Congress has set aside exclusively for the administrative agency." *SEC v. Chenery Corp.,* 332 U.S. 194 (1947). Secondly, it is obvious that the court in these cases reviewed the agency's choice of procedures on the basis of the record actually produced at the hearing, and not on the basis of the information available to the agency when it made the decision to structure the proceedings in a certain way. This sort of Monday morning quarterbacking not only encourages but almost compels the agency to conduct all rulemaking proceedings with the full panoply of procedural devices normally associated only with adjudicatory hearings.

Finally, and perhaps most importantly, this sort of review fundamentally misconceives the nature of the standard for judicial review of an agency rule. The court below uncritically assumed that additional procedures will automatically result in a more adequate record because it will give interested parties more of an opportunity to participate in and contribute to the proceedings. But informal rulemaking need not be based solely on the transcript of a hearing held before an agency. Indeed, the agency need not even hold a formal hearing. See 5 U.S.C. § 553(c). Thus, the adequacy of the "record" in this type of proceeding is not correlated directly to the type of procedural devices employed, but rather turns on whether the agency has followed the statutory mandate of the Administrative Procedure Act or other relevant statutes. If the agency is compelled to support the rule which it ultimately adopts with the type of record produced only after a full adjudicatory hearing, it simply will have no choice but to conduct a full adjudicatory hearing prior to promulgating every rule. In sum, this sort of unwarranted judicial examination of perceived procedural shortcomings of a rulemaking proceeding can do nothing but seriously interfere with that process prescribed by Congress. Thus, it is clear NEPA cannot serve as the basis for a substantial revision of the carefully constructed procedural specifications of the APA.

In short, nothing in the APA, NEPA, the circumstances of this case, the nature of the issues being considered, past agency practice, or the statutory mandate under which the Commission operates permitted the court to review and overturn the rulemaking proceeding on the basis of the procedural devices employed (or not employed) by the Commission so long as the Commission employed at least the statutory minima, a matter about which there is no doubt in this case.

MOTOR VEHICLE MANUFACTURERS ASSOCIATION OF THE UNITED STATES V. STATE FARM MUTUAL AUTOMOBILE INSURANCE COMPANY
463 U.S. 29 (1983)

Justice White delivered the opinion, joined by Justices Brennan, Marshall, Blackmun, and Stevens. Justices Burger, Powell, Rehnquist, and O'Connor dissented in part.

Facts: The development of the automobile gave Americans unprecedented freedom to travel, but exacted a high price for enhanced mobility. Since 1929, motor vehicles have been the leading cause of accidental deaths and injuries in the United States. In 1982, 46,300 Americans died in motor vehicle accidents and hundreds of thousands more were maimed and injured. While a consensus exists that the current loss of life on our highways is unacceptably high, improving safety does not admit to easy solution. In 1966, Congress decided that at least part of the answer lies in improving the design and safety features of the vehicle itself. But much of the technology for building safer cars was undeveloped or untested. Before changes in automobile design could be mandated, the effectiveness of these changes had to be studied, their costs examined, and public acceptance considered. This task called for considerable expertise and Congress responded by enacting the National Traffic and Motor Vehicle Safety Act of 1966 (Act), 15 U.S.C. § 1381 et seq. The Act, created for the purpose of "reduc[ing] traffic accidents and deaths and injuries to persons resulting from traffic accidents," directs the Secretary of Transportation or his delegate to issue motor vehicle safety standards that "shall be practicable, shall meet the need for motor vehicle safety, and shall be stated in objective terms." In issuing these standards, the Secretary is directed to consider "relevant available motor vehicle safety data," whether the proposed standard "is reasonable, practicable and appropriate" for the particular type of motor vehicle, and the "extent to which such standards will contribute to carrying out the purposes" of the Act. The Act also authorizes judicial review under the provisions of the Administrative Procedure Act (APA), 5 U.S.C. § 706, of all "orders establishing, amending, or revoking a Federal motor vehicle safety standard." Under this authority, we review today whether NHTSA [National Highway Traffic Safety Administration] acted arbitrarily and capriciously in revoking the requirement in Motor Vehicle Safety Standard 208 that new motor vehicles produced after September 1982 be equipped with passive restraints to protect the safety of the occupants of the vehicle in the event of a collision. Briefly summarized, we hold that the agency failed to present an adequate basis and explanation for rescinding the passive restraint requirement and that the agency must either consider the matter further or adhere to or amend Standard 208 along lines which its analysis supports.

I

The regulation whose rescission is at issue bears a complex and convoluted history. Over the course of approximately 60 rulemaking notices, the requirement has been imposed, amended, rescinded, reimposed, and now rescinded again.

As originally issued by the Department of Transportation in 1967, Standard 208 simply required the installation of seatbelts in all automobiles. 32 Fed. Reg. 2415. It soon became apparent that the level of seatbelt use was too low to reduce traffic injuries to an acceptable level. The Department therefore began consideration of "passive occupant restraint systems"—devices that do not depend for their effectiveness upon any action taken by the occupant except that necessary to operate the vehicle. Two types of automatic crash protection emerged: automatic seatbelts and air bags. The automatic seatbelt is a traditional safety belt, which when fastened to the interior of the door remains attached without impeding entry or exit from the vehicle, and deploys automatically without any action on the part of the passenger. The air bag is an inflatable device concealed in the dashboard and steering column. It automatically inflates when a sensor indicates that deceleration forces from an accident have exceeded a preset minimum, then rapidly deflates to dissipate those forces. The life-saving potential of these devices was immediately recognized, and in 1977, after substantial on-the-road experience with both devices, it was estimated by NHTSA that passive restraints could prevent approximately 12,000 deaths and over 100,000 serious injuries annually. 42 Fed. Reg. 34298.

In 1969, the Department formally proposed a standard requiring the installation of passive restraints, 34 Fed. Reg. 11148, thereby commencing a lengthy series of proceedings. In 1970, the agency revised Standard 208 to include passive protection requirements, 35 Fed. Reg. 16927, and in 1972, the agency amended the Standard to require full passive protection for all front seat occupants of vehicles manufactured after August 15, 1975. 37 Fed. Reg. 3911. In the interim, vehicles built between August 1973 and August 1975 were to carry either passive restraints or lap and shoulder belts coupled with an "ignition interlock" that would prevent starting the vehicle if the belts were not connected. On review, the agency's decision to require passive restraints was found to be supported by "substantial evidence" and upheld. *Chrysler Corp. v. Department of Transportation,* 472 F.2d 659 (CA6 1972). In preparing for the upcoming model year, most car makers chose the "ignition interlock" option, a decision which was highly unpopular, and led Congress to amend the Act to prohibit a motor vehicle safety standard from requiring or permitting compliance by means of an ignition interlock or a continuous buzzer designed to indicate that safety belts were not in use. The 1974 Amendments also provided that any safety standard that could be satisfied by a system other than seatbelts would have to be submitted to Congress where it could be vetoed by concurrent resolution of both Houses. 15 U.S.C. § 1410b(b)(2). The effective date for mandatory passive restraint systems was extended for a year until August 31, 1976. But in June 1976,

Secretary of Transportation William T. Coleman, Jr., initiated a new rulemaking on the issue. After hearing testimony and reviewing written comments, Coleman extended the optional alternatives indefinitely and suspended the passive restraint requirements. Although he found passive restraints technologically and economically feasible, the Secretary based his decision on the expectation that there would be widespread public resistance to the new systems. He instead proposed a demonstration project involving up to 500,000 cars installed with passive restraints, in order to smooth the way for public acceptance of mandatory passive restraints at a later date.

Coleman's successor as Secretary of Transportation disagreed. Within months of assuming office, Secretary Brock Adams decided that the demonstration project was unnecessary. He issued a new mandatory passive restraint regulation, known as Modified Standard 208. 42 Fed. Reg. 34289 (1977). The Modified Standard mandated the phasing in of passive restraints beginning with large cars in model year 1982 and extending to all cars by model year 1984. The two principal systems that would satisfy the Standard were air bags and passive belts; the choice of which system to install was left to the manufacturers. In *Pacific Legal Foundation v. Department of Transportation,* 593 F.2d 1338, the Court of Appeals upheld Modified Standard 208 as a rational, nonarbitrary regulation consistent with the agency's mandate under the Act. The Standard also survived scrutiny by Congress, which did not exercise its authority under the legislative veto provision of the 1974 Amendments. Over the next several years, the automobile industry geared up to comply with Modified Standard 208. As late as July 1980, NHTSA reported:

"On the road experience in thousands of vehicles equipped with air bags and automatic safety belts has confirmed agency estimates of the life-saving and injury-preventing benefits of such systems. When all cars are equipped with automatic crash protection systems, each year an estimated 9,000 more lives will be saved, and tens of thousands of serious injuries will be prevented." In February 1981, however, Secretary of Transportation Andrew Lewis reopened the rulemaking due to changed economic circumstances and, in particular, the difficulties of the automobile industry. 46 Fed. Reg. 12033. Two months later, the agency ordered a one-year delay in the application of the Standard to large cars, extending the deadline to September 1982, and at the same time, proposed the possible rescission of the entire Standard. After receiving written comments and holding public hearings, NHTSA issued a final rule (Notice 25) that rescinded the passive restraint requirement contained in Modified Standard 208.

II

In a statement explaining the rescission, NHTSA maintained that it was no longer able to find, as it had in 1977, that the automatic restraint requirement would produce significant safety benefits. This judgment reflected not a change of opinion on the effectiveness of the technology, but a change in plans by the automobile industry. In 1977, the agency had assumed that air bags would be installed in 60% of all new cars and automatic seatbelts in 40%. By 1981 it became apparent that automobile manufacturers planned to install the automatic seatbelts in approximately 99% of the new cars. For this reason, the lifesaving potential of air bags would not be realized. Moreover, it now appeared that the overwhelming majority of passive belts planned to be installed by manufacturers could be detached easily and left that way permanently. Passive belts, once detached, then required "the same type of affirmative action that is the stumbling block to obtaining high usage levels of manual belts." For this reason, the agency concluded that there was no longer a basis for reliably predicting that the Standard would lead to any significant increased usage of restraints at all.

In view of the possible minimal safety benefits, the automatic restraint requirement no longer was reasonable or practicable in the agency's view. The requirement would require approximately $1 billion to implement and the agency did not believe it would be reasonable to impose such substantial costs on manufacturers and consumers without more adequate assurance that sufficient safety benefits would accrue. In addition, NHTSA concluded that automatic restraints might have an adverse effect on the public's attitude toward safety. Given the high expense and limited benefits of detachable belts, NHTSA feared that many consumers would regard the Standard as an instance of ineffective regulation, adversely affecting the public's view of safety regulation and, in particular, "poisoning . . . popular sentiment toward efforts to improve occupant restraint systems in the future."

The ultimate question before us is whether NHTSA's rescission of the passive restraint requirement of Standard 208 was arbitrary and capricious. We conclude, as did the Court of Appeals, that it was. We also conclude, but for somewhat different reasons, that further consideration of the issue by the agency is therefore required. We deal separately with the rescission as it applies to air bags and as it applies to seatbelts.

A

The first and most obvious reason for finding the rescission arbitrary and capricious is that NHTSA apparently gave no consideration whatever to modifying the Standard to require that air bag technology be utilized. . . .

Given the effectiveness ascribed to air bag technology by the agency, the mandate of the Act to achieve traffic safety would suggest that the logical response to the faults of detachable seatbelts would be to require the installation of air bags. At the very least this alternative way of achieving the objectives of the Act should have been addressed and adequate reasons given for its abandonment. But the agency not only did not require compliance through air bags, it also did not even consider the possibility in its 1981 rulemaking. Not one sentence of its rulemaking statement discusses the air bags-only option. Because, as the Court of Appeals stated, "NHTSA's . . . analysis of air bags was nonexistent," what we said in *Burlington Truck Lines, Inc. v. United States,* 371 U.S., at 167, is apropos here: "There are no findings and no analysis here to justify the choice made, no indication of the basis on which the [agency] exercised its expert discretion. We are not prepared to and the Administrative Procedure Act will not permit us to accept such . . . practice. . . . Expert discretion is the lifeblood of the administrative process, but 'unless we make the requirements for administrative action strict and demanding, expertise, the strength of modern government, can become a monster which rules with no practical limits on its discretion.' *New York v. United States,* 342 U.S. 882, 884 (dissenting opinion)" [footnote omitted].

B

Although the issue is closer, we also find that the agency was too quick to dismiss the safety benefits of automatic seatbelts. NHTSA's critical finding was that, in light of the industry's plans to install readily detachable passive belts, it could not reliably predict "even a 5 percentage point increase as the minimum level of expected usage increase." The Court of Appeals rejected this finding because there is "not one iota" of evidence that Modified Standard 208 will fail to increase nationwide seatbelt use by at least 13 percentage points, the level of increased usage necessary for the Standard to justify its cost. Given the lack of probative evidence, the court held that "only a well justified refusal to seek more evidence could render rescission non-arbitrary." In these cases, the agency's explanation for rescission of the passive restraint requirement is not sufficient to enable us to conclude that the rescission was the product of reasoned decisionmaking. To reach this conclusion, we do not upset the agency's view of the facts, but we do appreciate the limitations of this record in supporting the agency's decision.

"The Committee intends that safety shall be the overriding consideration in the issuance of standards under this bill. The Committee recognizes . . . that the Secretary will necessarily consider reasonableness of cost, feasibility and adequate leadtime." The agency also failed to articulate a basis for not requiring nondetachable belts under Standard 208. By failing to analyze the continuous seatbelts option in its own right, the agency has failed to offer the rational connection between facts and judgment required to pass muster under the arbitrary-and-capricious standard. The agency also failed to offer any explanation why a continuous passive belt would engender the same adverse public reaction as the ignition interlock, and, as the Court of Appeals concluded, "every indication in the record points the other way."

"An agency's view of what is in the public interest may change, either with or without a change in circumstances. But an agency changing its course must supply a reasoned analysis. . . ." *Greater Boston Television Corp. v. FCC,* 444 F.2d 841, 852 (1970). We do not accept all of the reasoning of the Court of Appeals but we do conclude that the agency has failed to supply the requisite "reasoned analysis" in this case. Accordingly, we vacate the judgment of the Court of Appeals and remand the cases to that court with directions to remand the matter to the NHTSA for further consideration consistent with this opinion.

NOTES

1. *Securities and Exchange Commission v. Chenery Corporation,* 332 U.S. 194, 204 (1947).

2. Daniel Oran, *Oran's Dictionary of the Law* (St. Paul, MN: West, 1983), 171

3. *Securities and Exchange Commission v. Chenery Corporation,* 381 U.S. 80, 94 (1943). The case is referred to as *Chenery I.*

4. 332 U.S. 194, 204 (1947).

5. Ibid., 207.

6. Ibid., 202-03.

7. Kenneth Culp Davis, *Administrative Law: Cases—Text—Problems,* 6th ed. (St. Paul, MN: West, 1977), 552.

8. *Londoner v. City of Denver,* 210 U.S. 373 (1908).

9. Ibid., 385.

10. Ibid., 386.

11. David Ryan, *Kansas Administrative Law With Federal References* (Topeka: Kansas Bar Association, 1985), 87.

12. 5 U.S.C. 551 (4).

13. 506 F.2d. 33 (D.C. Cir. 1974).

14. See Michael Asimow, "Public Participation in the Adoption of Interpretive Rules and Policy Statements," *Michigan Law Review,* 75 (1977): 521; Michael Asimow, "Nonlegislative Rulemaking and Regulatory Reform," *Duke Law Journal,* Part I (1985): 381.

15. See *United States v. Florida East Coast Railway Company,* 410 U.S. 224 (1973).

16. Mireya Navarro, "Agency Slowed in Effort to Widen Definition of AIDS," *The New York Times,* 10 February 1992, A1, A12, national edition.

17. Philip J. Hilts, "FDA Seeks Halt in Breast Implants Made of Silicone," *The New York Times,* 7 January 1992, A1, B6, national edition.

18. Marian Burros, "Less Strict Rules on Labels Offered," *The New York Times,* 11 February 1992, C18, national edition.

19. Jonathan Fuerbringer, "Tough Regulation of Treasury Sales Announced by U.S.,"

The New York Times, 23 January 1992, A1, C5, national edition.

20. John H. Cushman, Jr., "U.S. Proposes Regulations to Decrease Acid Rain," *The New York Times,* 30 October 1991, A11, national edition.

21. "S.E.C. Plans New Rules," *The New York Times,* 13 August 1991, C17, national edition.

22. Leslie Wayne, "Easier Rules for Banks Are Issued," *The New York Times,* 8 November 1991, A1, C5, national edition.

23. Robert Pear, "U.S. Moves to Curb Medicaid Payments for Many States," *The New York Times,* 11 September 1991, A1, A16, national edition.

24. Keith Schneider, "Rules Force Towns to Pick Big New Dumps or Big Costs," *The New York Times,* 12 September 1991, A1, A8, national edition.

25. Robert Reinhold, "U.S. Moving to End Use of Deadly Farm Pesticide," *The New York Times,* 6 September 1991, A11, national edition.

26. Edmund L. Andrews, "F.C.C. Backs Rivals to Regional Bells," *The New York Times,* 10 May 1991, A1, A12, national edition.

27. Steven Labaton, "S.E.C. Backs Early Stock Trading to Compete With British Brokers," *The New York Times,* 11 October 1991, A1, C5, national edition.

28. John H. Cushman, Jr., "F.A.A. Seeks to Address Rise in Near Jet Collisions," *The New York Times,* 18 October 1991, A11, national edition.

29. Keith Schneider, "Industries Battle Cities on Funds for Toxic Waste," *The New York Times,* 19 July 1991, A1, A9, national edition.

30. "F.C.C. to Review Its Rules on TV Station Ownership," *The New York Times,* 12 July 1991, E5, national edition.

31. Keith Schneider, "Developers Leery of Wetlands Plan," *The New York Times,* 22 July 1991, A7, national edition.

32. Robert Pear, "New Proposals by U.S. on Child Care Lead to Dispute Over States' Role," *The New York Times,* 2 July 1991, 1, 8, national edition.

33. Laurence K. Altman, "Rules for AIDS-Infected Workers Are Resisted by Medical Groups," *The New York Times,* 30 August 1991, A1, A13, national edition.

34. Bloomsburg Business News, "More Insiders Must Report Trades They Make in Their Company Stock to the S.E.C.," *The New York Times,* 25 June 1991, C6, national edition.

35. Joel Brinkley, "F.C.C. Is Ready to Ease Timing on Digital TV," *The New York Times,* 3 April 1997, A1.

36. Mathew Wald, "California Air Agency Limits Personal Goods" *The New York Times,* 10 January 1992, A8, national edition.

37. 104 Stat 4969, P.L. 101-648, 1990.

38. Mathew Wald, "Environmental Negotiators Flesh Out Bare-Bones Law," *The New York Times,* 24 June 1991, C2, national edition.

39. Ibid.

40. Ernest Gellhorn and Ronald Levin, *Administrative Law and Process: In a Nutshell,* 3d ed. (St. Paul, MN: West, 1990), 559-60.

41. Ibid., 246.

42. 5 U.S.C. 556 (d).

43. 5 U.S.C. 557 (c).

44. Gellhorn and Levin, *Administrative Law and Process,* 244.

45. U.S. Bureau of the Census, *Statistical Abstract of the United States 1991,* 111th ed. (Washington, DC: U.S. Government Printing Office, 1991), 189.

46. 29 U.S.C. 156.

47. The facts are found at 394 U.S. 759, 761-62 (1969).

PART III

SUBSTANTIVE ISSUES IN ADMINISTRATIVE LAW

CHAPTER 8

THE LAW OF PUBLIC EMPLOYMENT

Certain basic principles in the law of public employment apply to anyone who works for government at nearly any level. Those principles could be demonstrated by any line of cases, but because the reader is currently in college and consequently familiar with some of the terminology, we begin by examining cases in the field of education.

Recall from the material in Chapter 2 dealing with executive control over agencies through the power of appointment and removal that in only a limited number of policy-making and advisory-level positions does the employee serve at the pleasure of the executive. The discussion that follows focuses instead on civil service employees and those who usually do not make policy. Merit, rather than political party considerations, is supposed to guide personnel decisions regarding the employees discussed in the section that follows. Although general principles of the law of public employment are elucidated, remember, too, that these may be modified from jurisdiction to jurisdiction by labor union contracts and statutes.

CASE IN POINT:
HALE V. WALSH, 747 P.2D 1288 (1987)

Dr. Thomas Hale gave up his tenured teaching position at a state university in Louisiana in 1977 to become the untenured chairman of the Department of History at Idaho State University. As part of his teaching load, he was assigned the history seminar that all seniors majoring in history had to take. One student who had transferred to Idaho State University got to the spring semester of his senior year and still had not enrolled in the senior seminar. That spring semester, he was scheduled to student teach, which conflicted with the seminar, and after receiving his degree he was to begin a teaching position at a local high school. After much negotiation, Hale agreed to allow this student to complete the senior seminar credits by writing a research paper. When Hale received the paper near the end of the semester, he suspected that the paper was plagiarized. After a relatively easy library search, Hale documented the plagiarism and failed the student. The student would not graduate or get the job. The student was the son-in-law of a former dean, however, and the former dean was the best friend of the academic vice president (provost at some universities). The vice president put pressure on Hale's dean to put pressure on Hale to change the student's grade. Ultimately, the dean's attempts at persuasion failed, so the vice president ordered the dean to threaten Hale with termination unless the professor changed the grade. Hale refused to compromise academic standards and refused to change the grade. Because of his experience with the Louisiana University system, which is unionized, Hale understood enough of the law of public employment to appreciate his precarious legal position and that the university would issue him a terminal contract (one more year of teaching at this university); despite the apparent unfairness of the situation, he would not be able to get any court to hear his case.

Short of caving in on the academic standard question, Hale could not stop the fact that he would lose his job, but he could manipulate the situation so that he could get a court to hear his case. Capitalizing on his previous limited experience with faculty unions in Louisiana, Hale became very active in a union that was trying to become the bargaining agent for the Idaho State faculty (the American Federation of Teachers). Indeed, within months, he became the chapter president of the union. In that capacity, he made a speech critical of the university president on the steps of the administration building and invited the local media, which gave the event appropriate coverage. Shortly thereafter, Hale received a terminal contract, and a year later he was out of a job.

Questions

1. It is obvious from the preceding scenario that Hale believed that the union activity and the speech would help his legal situation. Do you believe he was right? Why? If so, does that make sense to you?
2. Why, do you suppose, was Hale's legal situation hopeless without the union activity and the public speech?

Usually, public employees who are allegedly wrongly fired must sue under the Fifth Amendment due process clause (if they work for the federal government) or the Fourteenth Amendment due process clause (if they work for state or local governments). Both due process clauses prohibit government from taking an individual's life, liberty, or property without due process of law. Hence, to establish a lawsuit under a due process clause, one must show that governmental action is about to take one's life or inhibit the exercise of one's liberty or the use of one's property.

When a government allegedly wrongly fires an employee, has it not taken away that employee's property by taking his or her paycheck? No, not necessarily. The first principle of public employment law is that *the employee must establish either a property interest or a liberty interest to challenge an employment termination in court.* Indeed, one must establish a liberty or property interest to establish a due process suit of any kind.

PROPERTY INTEREST

Almost all employees, whether they work for government or in the private sector, serve a probationary period of employment when they first start a job. Usually, the probationary period of employment is specified—say, six months; at the end of that period, a supervisor provides some type of formal evaluation of the probationary employee's work (this process is also typically specified in an employee handbook). A decision is made to either retain or terminate the employee as a result of that formal review process.

If the decision is made to retain the employee, then the employee has what the courts refer to as a "continuing expectation of employment." That is what establishes a property interest in the law of public employment under the due process clause. If the decision is made not to retain the employee, then there is no continuing expectation of employment and therefore no property interest and the employee cannot sue. Employees who lack the requisite property interest can never challenge their employment termination in court (unless they can demonstrate a liberty interest).

In education, the way one establishes a continuing expectation of employment and hence a property interest is by obtaining tenure. In the secondary schools, the probationary employment period is about three years; in universities, it is five years but can approach eight or even ten years. The usual probationary period for most other public employees is six months to a year.

BOARD OF REGENTS V. ROTH
408 U.S. 564 (1972)

The opinion is by Justice Stewart, joined by Justices Burger, White, Blackmun, and Rehnquist. Justices Brennan, Douglas, and Marshall dissented. Justice Powell took no part in the decision.

Respondent (Roth), hired for a fixed term of one academic year to teach at a state university, was informed without explanation that he would not be rehired for the ensuing year. A statute provided that all state university teachers would be employed initially on probation and that only after four years' continuous service would teachers achieve permanent employment "during efficiency and good behavior," with procedural protection against separation. University rules gave an untenured teacher "dismissed" before the end of the year some opportunity for review of the "dismissal" but provided that no reason need be given for nonretention of an untenured teacher, and no standards were specified for reemployment. Respondent brought this action claiming deprivation of his Fourteenth Amendment rights, alleging infringement of (1) his free speech right because the true reason for his non-retention was his criticism of the university administration, and (2) his procedural due process right because of the university's failure to advise him of the reason for its decision. The District Court granted sum-mary judgment for the respondent on the procedural issue. The Court of Appeals affirmed.

II

"While this Court has not attempted to define with exactness the liberty . . . guaranteed [by the Fourteenth Amendment], the term has received much consideration and some of the included things have been definitely stated. Without doubt, it denotes not merely freedom from bodily restraint but also the right of the individual to contract, to engage in any of the common occupations of life, to acquire useful knowledge, to marry, establish a home and bring up children, to worship God according to the dictates of his own conscience, and generally to enjoy those privileges long recognized . . . as essential to the orderly pursuit of happiness by free men." *Meyer v. Nebraska,* 262 U.S. 390, 399. In a Constitution for a free people, there can be no doubt that the meaning of "liberty" must be broad indeed. See, e.g., *Bolling v. Sharpe,* 347 U.S. 497, 499-500; *Stanley v. Illinois,* 405 U.S. 645.

There might be cases in which a State refused to reemploy a person under such circumstances that interests in liberty would be implicated. But this is not such a case.

The State, in declining to rehire the respondent, did not make any charge against him that might seriously damage his standing and associations in his community. It did not base the nonrenewal of his contract on a charge, for example, that he had been guilty of dishonesty, or immorality. Had it done so, this would be a different case. For "[w]here a person's good name, reputation, honor, or integrity is at stake because of what the government is doing to him, notice and an opportunity to be heard are essential." *Wisconsin v. Constantineau,* 400 U.S. 433, 437 *Wieman v. Updegraff,* 344 U.S. 183, 191; *Joint Anti-Fascist Refugee Committee v. McGrath,* 341 U.S. 123; *United States v. Lovett,* 328 U.S. 303, 316-317; *Peters v. Hobby,* 349 U.S. 331, 352 (Douglas, J., concurring). See *Cafeteria Workers v. McElroy,* 367 U.S. 886, 898. In such a case, due process would accord an opportunity to refute the charge before University officials. In the present case, however, there is no suggestion whatever that the respondent's "good name, reputation, honor, or integrity" is at stake.

Similarly, there is no suggestion that the State, in declining to re-employ the respondent, imposed on him a stigma or other disability that foreclosed his freedom to take advantage of other employment opportunities. The State, for example, did not invoke any regulations to bar the respondent from all other public employment in state universities. Had it done so, this, again, would be a different case. For "[t]o be deprived not only of present government employment but of future opportunity for it certainly is no small injury. . . ." *Joint Anti-Fascist Refugee Committee v. McGrath* (Jackson, J., concurring). See *Truax v. Raich,* 239 U.S. 33, 41. The Court has held, for example, that a State, in regulating eligibility for a type of professional employment, cannot foreclose a range of opportunities "in a manner . . . that contravene[s] . . . Due Process," *Schware v. Board of Bar Examiners,* 353 U.S. 232, 238, and, specifically, in a manner that denies the right to a full prior hearing. *Willner v. Committee on Character,* 373 U.S. 96, 103. See *Cafeteria Workers v. McElroy,* supra, at 898. In the present case, however, this principle does not come into play.

To be sure, the respondent has alleged that the non-renewal of his contract was based on his exercise of his right to freedom of speech. But this allegation is not now before us. The District Court stayed proceedings on this issue, and the respon-

dent has yet to prove that the decision not to rehire him was, in fact, based on his free speech activities.

Hence, on the record before us, all that clearly appears is that the respondent was not rehired for one year at one university. It stretches the concept too far to suggest that a person is deprived of "liberty" when he simply is not rehired in one job but remains as free as before to seek another. *Cafeteria Workers v. McElroy,* supra, at 895-896.

III

The Fourteenth Amendment's procedural protection of property is a safeguard of the security of interests that a person has already acquired in specific benefits. These interests—property interests—may take many forms.

Thus, the Court has held that a person receiving welfare benefits under statutory and administrative standards defining eligibility for them has an interest in continued receipt of those benefits that is safeguarded by procedural due process. *Goldberg v. Kelly,* 397 U.S. 254. See *Flemming v. Nestor,* 363 U.S. 603, 611. Similarly, in the area of public employment, the Court has held that a public college professor dismissed from an office held under tenure provisions, *Slochower v. Board of Education,* 350 U.S. 551, and college professors and staff members dismissed during the terms of their contracts, *Wieman v. Updegraff,* 344 U.S. 183, have interests in continued employment that are safeguarded by due process. Only last year, the Court held that this principle "proscribing summary dismissal from public employment without hearing or inquiry required by due process" also applied to a teacher recently hired without tenure or a formal contract, but nonetheless with a clearly implied promise of continued employment. *Connell v. Higginbotham,* 403 U.S. 207, 208.

Certain attributes of "property" interests protected by procedural due process emerge from these decisions. To have a property interest in a benefit, a person clearly must have more than an abstract need or desire for it. He must have more than a unilateral expectation of it. He must, instead, have a legitimate claim of entitlement to it. It is a purpose of the ancient institution of property to protect those claims upon which people rely in their daily lives, reliance that must not be arbitrarily undermined. It is a purpose of the constitutional right to a hearing to provide an opportunity for a person to vindicate those claims.

Property interests, of course, are not created by the Constitution. Rather, they are created and their dimensions are defined by existing rules or understandings that stem from an independent source such as state law—rules or understandings that secure certain benefits and that support claims of entitlement to those benefits. Thus, the welfare recipients in *Goldberg v. Kelly,* supra, had a claim of entitlement to welfare payments that was grounded in the statute defining eligibility for them. The recipients had not yet shown that they were, in fact, within the statutory terms of eligibility. But we held that they had a right to a hearing at which they might attempt to do so.

Just as the welfare recipients' "property" interest in welfare payments was created and defined by statutory terms, so the respondent's "property" interest in employment at Wisconsin State University—Oshkosh was created and defined by the terms of his appointment. Those terms secured his interest in employment up to June 30, 1969. But the important fact in this case is that they specifically provided that the respondent's employment was to terminate on June 30. They did not provide for contract renewal absent "sufficient cause." Indeed, they made no provision for renewal whatsoever.

Thus, the terms of the respondent's appointment secured absolutely no interest in re-employment for the next year. They supported absolutely no possible claim of entitlement to re-employment. Nor, significantly, was there any state statute or University rule or policy that secured his interest in re-employment or that created any legitimate claim to it. In these circumstances, the respondent surely had an abstract concern in being rehired, but he did not have a property interest sufficient to require the University authorities to give him a hearing when they declined to renew his contract of employment.

IV

Our analysis of the respondent's constitutional rights in this case in no way indicates a view that an opportunity for a hearing or a statement of reasons for nonretention would, or would not, be appropriate or wise in public colleges and universities. For it is a written Constitution that we apply. Our role is confined to interpretation of that Constitution. We must conclude that the summary judgment for the respondent should not have been granted, since the respondent has not shown that he was deprived of liberty or property protected by the Fourteenth Amendment. The judgment of the Court of Appeals, accordingly, is reversed and the case is remanded for further proceedings consistent with this opinion.

It is so ordered.

Questions

1. The Court says that "property interests are not created by the Constitution." What does create a property interest?
2. Roth lost this case. Can you explain why?
3. At this point, you should be able to articulate why Hale's legal position was hopeless prior to his union activity and speech. Can you do that?

We return now to *Hale v. Walsh,* at the beginning of this chapter: The problem for Hale was that because he lacked tenure, he had no continuing expectation of employment and so could not demonstrate to a court a property interest.

LIBERTY INTEREST

An employee can establish a liberty interest if, as a result of termination, the former employee's reputation is damaged or his or her ability to seek employment is inhibited. Usually, a simple decision not to retain an employee does not sufficiently damage either reputation or employability enough to establish a liberty interest. If, however, a teacher's contract was not renewed and if the former teacher asked why and was publicly told "because you are incompetent and a terrible teacher," then that would establish a liberty interest.

For that reason, one canon of personnel management in public administration is that probationary employees who are terminated from employment should never be told why. The logic goes like this: Because they are probationary employees, they lack a property interest. To discuss with them the reasons for the termination may provide the grounds to establish a liberty interest. Silence means that the affected employee will have difficulty getting into court because he or she cannot show a property interest, and the silence has ensured the lack of ability to demonstrate a liberty interest. Within the university community, an almost cabalistic silence surrounds the decision to deny a faculty member tenure or, as in the Hale case, not to renew a contract.[1]

A terminated public employee may establish a liberty interest in one more way. Because it is unconstitutional for government to punish an individual as a result of the exercise of a constitutionally protected right (e.g., freedom of speech, freedom of association [e.g., to join a union; to be free from discrimination based on race, gender, age]), it follows that government usually cannot fire an employee for having exercised a constitutional right. Hence, in some cases in which a probationary public employee can demonstrate that the *primary reason* behind a decision to terminate was that the employee exercised a constitutionally protected right, that will establish a liberty interest under the due process clause.

The case presented next, *Pickering v. Board of Education* (1968), is a classic case that discusses the First Amendment protection of public employees. Marvin Pickering, a high school teacher, was fired for writing a letter to the editor in the local newspaper. The letter is reproduced next, and the case follows.

Dear Editor:

I enjoyed reading the back issues of your paper which you loaned to me. Perhaps others would enjoy reading them in order to see just how far the two new high schools have deviated from the original promises by the Board of Education. First, let me state that I am referring to the February through November, 1961 issues of your paper, so that it can be checked.

One statement in your paper declared that swimming pools, athletic fields, and auditoriums had been left out of the program. They may have been left out but they got put back in very quickly because Lockport West has both an auditorium and athletic field. In fact, Lockport West has a better athletic field than Lockport Central. It has a track that isn't quite regulation distance even though the board spent a few thousand dollars on it. Whose fault is that? Oh, I forgot, it wasn't supposed to be there in the first place. It must have fallen out of the sky. Such responsibility has been touched on in other letters but it seems one just can't help noticing it. I am not saying the school shouldn't have these facilities, because I think they should, but promises are promises, or are they?

Since there seems to be a problem getting all the facts to the voter on the twice defeated bond issue, many letters have been written to this paper and probably more will follow, I feel I must say something about the letters and their writers. Many of these letters did not give the whole story. Letters by your Board and Administration have stated that teachers' salaries total $1,297,746 for one year. Now that must have been the total payroll, otherwise the teachers would be getting $10,000 a year. I teach at the high school and I know this just isn't the case. However, this shows their "stop at nothing" attitude. To illustrate further, do you know that the superintendent told the teachers, and I quote, "Any teacher that opposes the referendum should be prepared for the consequences." I think this gets at the reason we have problems passing bond issues. Threats take something away; these are insults to voters in a free society. We should try to sell a program on its merits, if it has any.

Remember those letters entitled "District 205 Teachers Speak," I think the voters should know that those letters have been written and agreed to by only five or six teachers, not 98% of the teachers in the high school. In fact, many teachers didn't even know who was writing them. Did you know that those letters had to have the approval of the superintendent before they could be put in the paper? That's the kind of totalitarianism teachers live in at the high school, and your children go to school in.

In last week's paper, the letter written by a few uninformed teachers threatened to close the school cafeteria and fire its personnel. This is ridiculous and insults the intelligence of the voter because properly managed school cafeterias do not cost the school district any money. If the cafeteria is losing money, then the board should not be packing free lunches for athletes on days of athletic contests. Whatever the case, the taxpayer's child should only have to pay about 30 cents for his lunch instead of 35 cents to pay for free lunches for the athletes. In a reply to this letter your Board of Administration will probably state that these lunches are paid for from receipts from the games. But $20,000 in receipts doesn't pay for the $200,000 a year they have been spending on varsity sports while neglecting the wants of teachers. You see we don't need an increase in the transportation tax unless the voters want to keep paying $50,000 or more a year to transport athletes home after practice and to away games, etc. Rest of the $200,000 is made up in coaches' salaries, athletic directors' salaries, baseball pitching machines, sodded football fields, and thousands of dollars for other sports equipment.

These things are all right, provided we have enough money for them. To sod football fields on borrowed money and then not be able to pay teachers' salaries is getting the cart before the horse. If these things aren't enough for you, look at East High. No doors on many of the classrooms, a plant room without any sunlight, no water in a first aid treatment room, are just a few of many things. The taxpayers were really taken to the cleaners. A part of the sidewalk in front of the building has already collapsed. Maybe Mr. Hess would be interested to know that we need blinds on the windows in that building also.

Once again, the board must have forgotten they were going to spend $3,200,000 on the West building and $2,300,000 on the East building.

As I see it, the bond issue is a fight between the Board of Education that is trying to push tax-supported athletics down our throats with education, and a public that has mixed emotions about both of these items because they feel they are already paying enough taxes, and simply don't know whom to trust with any more tax money. I must sign this letter as a citizen, taxpayer and voter, not as a teacher, since that freedom has been taken from the teachers by the administration. Do you really know what goes on behind those stone walls at the high school?

Respectfully,

Marvin L. Pickering

PICKERING V. BOARD OF EDUCATION
391 U.S. 563 (1968)

In 1961, the Board of Education for District 205 of Will County, Illinois, submitted two bond issues to the voters; the first was defeated, but the second passed ($5,500,000). Again in 1964, the board submitted two bond issues to the voters, who rejected both. In response to these elections, many letters to the editor were printed in the local newspaper. Marvin Pickering, a teacher in one of the local high schools, wrote a letter to the editor that was printed after the elections were over. The school board determined that portions of Pickering's letter were false and that the letter was "detrimental to the efficient operation and administration of the schools" and fired Pickering. Pickering argued that his letter was protected speech under the First

Amendment. A state trial court reviewing the board's decision only to determine whether there was substantial evidence in the record to support the decision sustained the board's decision. The decision was also affirmed by the Illinois Supreme Court, so Pickering appealed to the U.S. Supreme Court.

Justice Marshall wrote the opinion for a unanimous Court.

II

To the extent that the Illinois Supreme Court's opinion may be read to suggest that teachers may constitutionally be compelled to relinquish the First Amendment rights they would otherwise enjoy as citizens to comment on matters of public interest in connection with the operation of the public schools in which they work, it proceeds on a premise that has been unequivocally rejected in numerous prior decisions of this Court. E.g., *Wieman v. Updegraff,* 344 U.S. 183 (1952); *Shelton v. Tucker,* 364 U.S. 479 (1960); *Keyishian v. Board of Regents,* 385 U.S. 589 (1967). "[The] theory that public employment which may be denied altogether may be subjected to any conditions, regardless of how unreasonable, has been uniformly rejected." *Keyishian v. Board of Regents,* supra, at 605-606. At the same time it cannot be gainsaid that the State has interests as an employer in regulating the speech of its employees that differ significantly from those it possesses in connection with regulation of the speech of the citizenry in general. The problem in any case is to arrive at a balance between the interests of the teacher, as a citizen, in commenting upon matters of public concern and the interest of the State, as an employer, in promoting the efficiency of the public services it performs through its employees.

III

The Board contends that "the teacher by virtue of his public employment has a duty of loyalty to support his superiors in attaining the generally accepted goals of education and that, if he must speak out publicly, he should do so factually and accurately, commensurate with his education and experience." Appellant, on the other hand, argues that the test applicable to defamatory statements directed against public officials by persons having no occupational relationship with them, namely, that statements to be legally actionable must be made "with knowledge that [they were] . . . false or with reckless disregard of whether [they were] . . . false or not," *New York Times Co. v. Sullivan,* 376 U.S. 254, 280 (1964), should also be applied to public statements made by teachers. Because of the enormous variety of fact situations in which critical statements by teachers and other public employees may be thought by their superiors, against whom the statements are directed, to furnish grounds for dismissal, we do not deem it either appropriate or feasible to attempt to lay down a general standard against which all such statements may be judged. However, in the course of evaluating the conflicting claims of First Amendment protection and the need for orderly school administration in the context of this case, we shall indicate some of the general lines along which an analysis of the controlling interests should run.

An examination of the statements in appellant's letter objected to by the Board reveals that they, like the letter as a whole, consist essentially of criticism of the Board's allocation of school funds between educational and athletic programs, and of both the Board's and the superintendent's methods of informing, or preventing the informing of, the district's taxpayers of the real reasons why additional tax revenues were being sought for the schools. The statements are in no way directed towards any person with whom appellant would normally be in contact in the course of his daily work as a teacher. Thus no question of maintaining either discipline by immediate superiors or harmony among coworkers is presented here. Appellant's employment relationships with the Board and, to a somewhat lesser extent, with the superintendent are not the kind of close working relationships for which it can persuasively be claimed that personal loyalty and confidence are necessary to their proper functioning. Accordingly, to the extent that the Board's position here can be taken to suggest that even comments on matters of public concern that are substantially correct, such as statements (1)-(4) of appellant's letter, may furnish grounds for dismissal if they are sufficiently critical in tone, we unequivocally reject it.

We next consider the statements in appellant's letter which we agree to be false. The Board's original charges included allegations that the publication of the letter damaged the professional reputations of the Board and the superintendent and would foment controversy and conflict among the Board, teachers, administrators, and the residents of the district. However, no evidence to support these allegations was introduced at the hearing. So far as the record reveals, Pickering's letter was greeted by everyone but its main target, the Board, with massive apathy and total disbelief. The Board must, therefore, have decided, perhaps by analogy with the law of libel, that the statements were per se harmful to the operation of the schools.

However, the only way in which the Board could conclude, absent any evidence of the actual effect of the letter, that the statements contained therein were per se detrimental to the interest of the schools was to equate the Board members' own interests with that of the schools. Certainly an accusation that too much money is being spent on athletics by the administrators of the school system (which is precisely the import of that portion of appellant's letter containing the statements that we have found to be false, see Appendix, infra) cannot reasonably be regarded as per se detrimental to the district's schools. Such an accusation reflects rather a difference of opinion between Pickering and the Board as to the preferable manner of operating the school system, a difference of opinion that clearly concerns an issue of general public interest. In addition, the fact that particular illustrations of the Board's claimed undesirable emphasis on athletic programs are false would not normally have any necessary impact on the actual operation of the schools, beyond its tendency to anger the Board. For example, Pickering's letter was written after the defeat at the polls of the second proposed tax increase. It could, therefore, have had no effect on the ability of the school district to raise necessary revenue, since there was no showing that there was any proposal to increase taxes pending when the letter was written.

More importantly, the question whether a school system requires additional funds is a matter of legitimate public concern on which the judgment of the school administration, including the School Board, cannot, in a society that leaves such questions to popular vote, be taken as conclusive. On such a question free and open debate is vital to informed decision-making by the electorate. Teachers are, as a class, the members of a community most likely to have informed and definite opinions as to how funds allotted to the operation of the schools should be spent. Accordingly, it is essential that they be able to speak out freely on such questions without fear of retaliatory dismissal.

What we do have before us is a case in which a teacher has made erroneous public statements upon issues then currently the subject of public attention, which are critical of his ultimate employer but which are neither shown nor can be presumed to have in any way either impeded the teacher's proper performance of his daily duties in the classroom or to have interfered with the regular operation of the schools generally. In these circumstances we conclude that the interest of the school administration in limiting teachers' opportunities to contribute to public debate is not significantly greater than its interest in limiting a similar contribution by any member of the general public.

In sum, we hold that, in a case such as this, absent proof of false statements knowingly or recklessly made by him, a teacher's exercise of his right to speak on issues of public importance may not furnish the basis for his dismissal from public employment. Since no such showing has been made in this case regarding appellant's letter, his dismissal for writing it cannot be upheld and the judgment of the Illinois Supreme Court must, accordingly, be reversed and the case remanded for further proceedings not inconsistent with this opinion.

It is so ordered.

Questions

1. It is clear that Pickering made some factual representations in his letter that turned out to be wrong. Do false statements receive constitutional protection?

2. It is also clear that Pickering's letter fell on deaf ears and that it was not effective. The Court said, "Pickering's letter was greeted with massive apathy and total disbelief." Do you think a different result would have been reached in this case if Pickering had written prior to the election and the letter was a substantial factor for the defeat of the bond issues? Does the Constitution protect only speech that has no "detrimental" effect?

3. In cases involving a liberty interest, courts will nearly always do a balancing test. Courts will balance the right of the employee (citizen) against the interests of the state (employer). Describe the interests on both sides of the scale.

4. Can you explain now why Professor Hale felt compelled to engage in union activity and give the public speech?

In what other kinds of activities could employees engage that would be constitutionally protected but would upset administrators to the point that they would fire an employee? Professor Aumiller, a homosexual and faculty adviser to the gay rights student organization, gave an interview to the student newspaper. The university president, fearing a loss of alumni contributions if the alumni sensed that the administration encouraged or tolerated homosexuality, fired Aumiller; the school did not renew his next contract and, of course, refused to say why (*Aumiller v. University of Delaware* [1973]).[2] Professor Duke was fired for teaching Marxism in a Texas state university (*Duke v. North Texas State University* [1973]).[3] Teachers have been fired for criticizing discriminatory conditions in schools (*Givhan v. Western Line Consolidated School District* [1979][4] and *Bernasconi v. Tempe Elementary School District* [1977]).[5] Teachers have even been fired for too effectively representing the teachers' union in negotiations with the school board (*Simard v. Board of Education* [1973]).[6] Usually, these cases involve some kind of speech (as in the *Pickering* case earlier) or union activity (freedom of association is a constitutionally protected right).

The reader will notice from the discussion in the *Pickering* case that not all speech is protected. Some forms of expression have been determined by the Supreme Court to be beyond the Constitution's protection. Obscenity is not protected expression. Libel is not protected, nor are "fighting words," but even though an employee's speech may not fall into one of those categories, it may nevertheless be unprotected speech. If a public employee says something critical about a supervisor or the higher administration, such criticism will be protected only under the following conditions: (a) Ordinarily, it must be a public statement, (b) it must pertain to an issue of public importance, and (c) the expression cannot destroy the working relationship between the employee/employees and administration (for teachers, it cannot disrupt discipline or the orderly educational process).

Absent a property interest, then, a probationary public employee can challenge employment termination in a court of law only under the following two conditions: (a) An administrator has publicly discussed the reason for the termination, and that has damaged the former employee's reputation and, consequently, his or her ability to find another job in the field; and (b) the administrator has refused to say why employment was terminated, but the employee suspects the primary reason was that he or she may have said something publicly critical of the agency (as in the case of Pickering).

In the latter types of cases, the plaintiff (terminated employee) must present some evidence to the judge (jury) that some form of constitutionally protected behavior was engaged in and the exercise of that protected behavior was the primary reason for the termination. Once sufficient evidence is presented to that effect, the burden of proof switches to the administration, which has three courses of action open. First, it can try to prove that the exercise of protected behavior was not the primary reason to terminate. Second, and closely related to the first, is the "same decision anyway" defense, which essentially argues that although the exercise of a protected right may have been part of the decision to terminate, the administration would have reached the decision to terminate on other grounds anyway (say, incompetence or insubordination). Finally, the administration can attempt to argue that the speech is not the kind of speech that is protected under the Constitution (perhaps the speech does not relate to issues of public importance).

So, how did Professor Hale establish a liberty interest sufficient to get his case to court? First, it is important to understand what did not create a liberty interest. Even though the ultimate issue here was the academic integrity of a university, that was not a sufficient enough public issue to clothe it with constitutional protection, even if Hale had gone to the press (the courts consider such issues to be internal squabbling and traditionally defer to the expertise of the administration).

One can only imagine the conversations that must have taken place between Professor Hale and the dean, but whatever was said, it was not protected speech either. That is because it was not public (although, in some cases, speech between two people has been protected), and ultimately it did not relate to matters of sufficient public interest.

Hale created a liberty interest by becoming active in union politics and convincing the court that that activity was the primary reason for his nonretention. It was primarily that public speech, clothed in official union activity, that created the liberty interest.

The Court recently applied the same jurisprudence to the termination of public contracts that applies to the termination of public employees. In the case of *Board of County Commissioners, Wabaunsee County v. Umbehr* (at the end of this chapter), a small businessman who had a contract with the county to haul trash sued the commissioners successfully when they canceled his contract because he had publicly criticized the commission.

TERMINATION OF PUBLIC EMPLOYEES WHO POSSESS A PROPERTY INTEREST

Apparently, it is fashionable these days for students to refer to tenure as "a job for life." Actually, that is not quite accurate. Once a public employee acquires a property interest, he or she has a continuing expectation of employment. That expectation of employment can be interrupted in two ways. First, a public employee with a property interest can be fired for cause. Second, his or her employment with a public agency can be terminated for financial reasons (*financial exigency*).

Termination for Cause

Usually, both public and private employers will provide an employee's handbook covering all aspects of employment. This handbook includes the specific period of probationary employment, the process of evaluation at the end of probationary employment, the criteria to be considered in the evaluation process, and the specific reasons for which employees can be terminated once they have passed beyond probationary employment. This employee handbook should also describe the procedure the public employer must go through to terminate an employee for cause. What constitutes a for-cause termination varies from agency to agency and from state to state, but usually they are such things as incompetence, insubordination, malfeasance, immoral conduct, and dishonesty. Even with a property interest, one can be (and many have been) fired for cause.

Remember that the combination of the due process clauses of the Fifth and Fourteenth Amendments forbids government from taking your life, liberty, or property without due process. This due process notion applies only to government, not to private employers, although labor unions have forced some degree of due process on private business through collective bargaining agreements. And it is not that government cannot take your liberty or property; it is just that it must go through due process first.

What is *due process*? It is a procedure that government must follow to avoid the arbitrary, capricious, or mistaken taking of an individual's liberty or property (or, obviously, life as well). Basically, due process consists of a notice (that government is about to take some action that may affect your liberty or property) and a hearing. How intricate that hearing must be is a matter of confusion and the cause of considerable litigation. Due process ranges from a notice from the vice principal (or dean of students) that one is about to be suspended from school for a particular reason and a very simple hearing before that same vice principal or dean on the one hand, to the myriad kinds of protection afforded those accused of capital offenses on the other hand. So, the amount of process due depends on the nature of the liberty or property about to be affected.

There is no typical due process hearing to describe in terms of public employment. Usually, strict rules of evidence do not apply, and attorneys may

Table 8.1. Disposition of Termination Cases for Litigants With Tenure

Winner	For Cause	Financial Exigency	Other	Total
Plaintiff/teacher	43% (84)	38% (22)	57% (12)	118
Defendant/board	57% (111)	62% (36)	43% (9)	156
Total	195	58	21	$N = 274$

SOURCE: Steven Cann, "A Virus in the Ivory Tower," *Educational Considerations* 18 (1991): 43-44.

be present but are not required. If allowed to be present, attorneys often may not have input during the hearing. Generally, reviewing courts look at the procedure first, to be satisfied that it is fair.

The reader is already aware from the material in Chapter 4 that courts reviewing quasi-judicial decisions (which due process hearings are) will apply the substantial evidence test on review. To successfully terminate a public employee for cause, administrators must first be certain that the procedure (notice and the hearing) is fair and that sufficient evidence supports the specific charge. If all of that is done, then a reviewing court will simply examine the procedure and, should it find no procedural flaws, apply the substantial evidence test and most often sustain the decision.

In a study of 500 teacher termination cases, 274, or 55 percent, involved tenured teachers. Contrary to the popular perception of "a job for life," tenured teachers lost in 57 percent of their appeals to the courts[7] (see Table 8.1).

Tenured teachers lost 57 percent of dismissals for cause and 62 percent of cases involving either financial exigency or forced retirement. That is only to be expected because the administration or employer is forced by the due process hearing to build a reasonably sound case. Indeed, this research shows that the most frequent reason for a plaintiff/teacher to win a challenged for-cause termination is that the administration failed to provide adequate procedures. Once a reviewing court is satisfied with the procedure, however, the most common disposition of these cases is for the reviewing court to find substantial evidence to support the termination (67 percent of cases).

Termination for Financial Reasons

Suppose that your state loses millions of dollars in revenue because of a recession. Sales tax receipts fall by several million dollars, and corporate tax revenues drop off by an equal percentage. Suppose, further, that the federal government decides to reduce grants and other federal monies that used to be turned back to the states. The state legislature will have only two courses of action open to it: raise taxes or reduce spending (many states are forbidden to deficit spend). Most states facing exactly these choices in the late 1980s and early 1990s chose to reduce state spending. When governmental units are forced to reduce spending, a common way to go about that is to reduce personnel. Because personnel account for more than 75 percent of agency budgets, that is a logical place for administrators to begin looking to cut costs. Basically, personnel may be reduced (the public administration term is *RIF,* which stands for "reduction in force") in three ways: "last hired, first fired"; attrition; and program review. Two of these options—last hired, first fired and attrition—are perhaps the "easier" options for administrators and do not generally involve administrative law or litigation.

The *last hired, first fired* option means that probationary employees are not offered a contract at the end of the probationary period. *Attrition* simply means that as employees die, retire, or transfer, they are not replaced (President Clinton reduced the size of the civilian federal workforce [the bureaucracy] by 100,000 from 1993 to 1996 through the attrition method). Both of these options are easier for administrators than the third option in that no due process hearings are required, they generally do not lead to litigation, and they are the least disruptive way to accomplish this unpleasant task within the agency. However, these two methods are not good options from a planning perspective. To RIF under either of these options could, for example, leave an English department without faculty to teach, say, creative writing, a business school without someone to teach marketing or finance, a history department without someone to teach early American history, or worse yet, a department could be left without a secretary!

The third option is to conduct a program review, ascertain which programs are not cost-efficient, and eliminate those programs (and their personnel) that have been found to be inefficient and not necessary or fundamental to the agency or institution. If the decision is made to RIF an entire program, the likelihood is that employees who possess a property interest will be terminated. That means the institution must provide a due process hearing first.

Usually, reviewing courts will not interfere with administrative decisions relating to financial exigency so long as objective criteria are applied to determine who will be terminated and a due process hearing is available to those who possess a property interest (*Levitt v. Board of Trustees,* 376 F.Supp. 950 [1974]). This assessment of court deference to administrators' RIF decisions is supported by the data in Table 8.1.

CONSEQUENCES OF THE COURT'S JURISPRUDENCE IN PUBLIC EMPLOYMENT LAW

The second-order consequences of the Court's decisions in *Roth* and its progeny have been (a) to create a dual legal subsystem in public employment law, (b) to encourage poor personnel decisions, (c) to encourage disruption (the only way for Professor Hale to get a court to look at his case was to join a union and give a critical speech on the front steps of the administration building), and (d) to cause unnecessary litigation.

The dual legal system in public employment law exists because the Court has created two classes of litigants: those with a property interest who get administrative law applied to their suits, and those without a property interest who get constitutional law applied to their cases. Regardless of the reason for the termination, a plaintiff with a property interest has a right to a due process hearing. *A fortiori,* the public employer must make an attempt to provide adequate procedures and supply reasons and evidence at a hearing to support the decision. Because this is a quasi-judicial hearing, the only questions for a reviewing court to answer are (a) whether the procedure is adequate to meet the dictates of due process and (b) whether the record contains substantial evidence to sustain the decision (classic administrative law, which public employers win nearly 60 percent of the time). The plaintiff who does not possess a property interest, however, cannot get his or her case into court without establishing a liberty interest. These frequently involve questions under the First Amendment or the equal protection clause. That being the case, there is no reason to expect a reviewing court to show deference to agency expertise or to concentrate on procedural issues (because no procedure is involved), and there will be no substantial evidence test (because there is no hearing, there is no record). The court will have to determine whether the alleged protected activity was a primary reason in the decision to terminate and whether the activity falls under the Constitution's protection (classic constitutional law, which the plaintiffs win nearly 60 percent of the time).

Poor personnel decisions fall into two categories. The first category are those situations in which employees with a property interest are retained when they should be let go. They are retained out of fear of the inevitable lawsuit. Public administrators need to appreciate the fact that the hearing protects both the employee and the employer. If the procedure is fair and the record contains substantial evidence to sustain the decision, then it is unlikely that a reviewing court would interfere with the decision. The second category are those situations in which employees without a property interest are terminated for reasons not related to job performance.

That this jurisprudence encourages disruption should be evident from the *Hale* case. The lesson is simple: A public employee without a property interest who fears termination has only one course of action open if he or she wants protection from the courts: Turn the issue into a liberty interest by public criticism of the employer.

Finally, three situations would probably not get litigated if probationary public employees were entitled to an internal due process hearing. The first category of situations are those cases like Pickering's and Hale's. The mere existence of an internal hearing in cases like these (116 in my sample of 500, or nearly one fourth) would modify the administration's behavior in a more constitutional direction. Fewer employees in situations such as these would be terminated; hence, fewer suits. The second category of situations are those in which employers present a successful "same decision anyway" defense; that is, at trial they are able to satisfy the Court that sufficient evidence exists to sustain a specific charge (e.g., incompetence, insubordination). A hearing before a board of peers at which such evidence is presented would limit employees' propensity to sue. The third category of situations are those I call "frivolous," in which the plaintiff can establish neither a property nor a liberty interest and that, generally, are dismissed at an early stage. Such a case would probably be screened out of the courts by an internal hearing. These three categories of cases constituted 35 percent of suits by untenured litigants.[8]

SUMMARY OF DISCRIMINATION IN PUBLIC EMPLOYMENT

In 1865, a sufficient number of states in the union ratified the proposed Thirteenth Amendment (outlawing slavery) so that it became the law of the land. The Fourteenth Amendment (1868) and the Fifteenth Amendment (1870) soon followed. Collectively referred to as the *Civil War Amendments,* they were meant to end legally the system of slavery and apartheid in this country. The Fifteenth Amendment prohibits the states from denying the right to vote on the basis of race. It is primarily the Fourteenth Amendment, forbidding the states from denying citizens equal protection of the laws, on which this discussion focuses. The final section of all three amendments gives Congress the power to pass laws to enforce the amendments. Generally, Congress does this in the form of civil rights acts (or voting rights acts, in the case of the Fifteenth Amendment).

During the past 125 years, Congress has passed several civil rights acts, including the Civil Rights Act of 1875, which made it a federal crime for owners of public accommodations (hotels, churches, amusement places, theaters, and common carriers) to discriminate on the basis of race. When the federal government pressed charges against individuals and a railroad that had discriminated against blacks, the Supreme Court said that Congress did not have the power to pass such laws regulating private discrimination. The Court reasoned that because the Fourteenth Amendment says "no state shall deny equal protection," the power of Congress to enforce that amendment should be limited to instances of official state discrimination (*Civil Rights Cases,* 109 U.S. 3 [1883]). That precedent, set in 1883, is still valid law today.

Indeed, because of the ruling in the *Civil Rights Cases,* when Congress passed the Civil Rights Act of 1964, it based that act on the commerce clause (banning discrimination in interstate commerce), rather than on the Fourteenth Amendment. Because the federal government's reach is so broad and extensive under the commerce clause (e.g., Occupational Safety and Health Administration [OSHA], minimum wage), that is how the federal government attacks private discrimination today.

Generally, administrative law involves governmental discrimination, rather than private discrimination. The aspiring public administrator ought to have some familiarity with equal protection law generally and as it relates to racial discrimination particularly. That is because, as you will discover in Chapter 10, if you (as an administrator) illegally discriminate against someone, you can, and most likely will, be sued personally. A court will simply look to see whether you knew or should have known that your actions violated someone's rights. The law presumes that midlevel managers and those above them "know or should know" when actions will violate another's constitutional rights.

Although there is no consensus among the nine members of the Supreme Court on the continued use of it, the Court currently applies a three-tiered analysis to equal protection cases. The first and lowest tier is referred to as the *simple rationality test.* It applies only to state regulation of business and assumes that the state's law is constitutional; the party challenging the law has the burden to prove it unconstitutional. Although there is a lack of consensus regarding the precise legislative intent behind the language "equal protection of the laws," it has come to be interpreted by the Supreme Court as follows: (a) It does not forbid the states from creating categories and treating people differently among the categories; and (b) in the exercise of their police powers, the states are free to create categories so long as the categories are *reasonable and not arbitrary.*[9]

The simple rationality test, then, merely looks to see whether the state had a reason for the category. New York City apparently concluded that advertising on the sides of vehicles led to an increase in accidents, so it passed an ordinance banning advertisement on vehicles but then exempted business advertising on certain business vehicles.[10] Oklahoma passed several measures aimed at putting opticians out of business but then exempted the ready-to-wear glasses industry from the regulations.[11] More recently, New Orleans passed an ordinance banning pushcart vendors in the French Quarter but then exempted any vendor who had been in business prior to January 1, 1972.[12]

In these and similar business regulation cases, the Court simply takes the stated reason for the category and then looks to see whether the legislative body could reasonably have believed, at the time it passed it, that the legislation would accomplish the goal (e.g., reduce traffic accidents in New York City, protect the eyesight of Oklahoma residents, preserve the aesthetic character of the French Quarter). This standard of review is so lax because the Supreme Court is extremely sensitive to charges of substituting its economic preferences for those of a legislative body in the area of business regulation. This is exactly what the Supreme Court did between 1932 and 1937, which is what caused President Franklin Roosevelt to propose his "court packing plan." This plan caused Chief Justice Hughes to switch his vote, and that created a majority on the Court willing to accept the expanded role of the federal government discussed in Chapter 1.

The middle-tier equal protection analysis is also a reasonableness test, but here the Court conducts in-depth analysis to determine whether the reason for the category will, in fact, accomplish the desired results. The Court applies this middle-tier analysis to social and economic discrimination that does not fit into either of the other two tiers. Gender discrimination cases are common here, as are cases involving age discrimination (for a recent case, see *O'Connor v. Consolidated Coin Caterers Corp.,* 116 S.Ct. 1307 [1996]), discrimination based on whether one was born in or out of wedlock, and whether one is a U.S. citizen.

The Court found that it was unreasonable for Idaho to give a statutory preference to the male if both a male and a female were equally qualified to administer an estate. The Court found that Idaho's reason (administrative efficiency) was irrational because it was based on outmoded stereotypes.[13] It was also unreasonable for the military to provide a family allowance to any male who got married, whereas a female had to prove that she supplied more than half of the family income before she could qualify for the family allowance.[14] The Court found a Florida scheme that provided a property tax break for widows but not for widowers to be a rational classification. The Court agreed with the Florida legislature that women suffer disproportionately when a spouse dies.[15] The Oklahoma Legislature, citing statistics that tended to show drunk driving by young males was a leading cause of accidents, passed a law that banned males from purchasing 3.2 percent beer until the age of twenty-one but allowed females to purchase such beer at the age of eighteen. The Supreme Court said that was an irrational and unreasonable classification.[16] Finally, the Court has said that it is reasonable for a state to require state police to retire at age fifty regardless of physical condition[17] and to limit the teaching profession to U.S. citizens[18] (but it is unreasonable to require notary publics to be U.S. citizens).[19]

The third and highest tier of equal protection analysis is called *strict scrutiny,* or the *compelling interest test.* The Court applies this level of analysis to state discrimination involving a suspect class (race) or a fundamental right (e.g., to vote, to travel).

Here, the assumptions are just the opposite of the first tier. Any state classification based on race is assumed to be unconstitutional, and the state would have to show a compelling reason to discriminate on such a basis to save it. Only rarely can a government meet the compelling-interest standard. The federal government was able to demonstrate a compelling interest in its minority business set-aside program, which required that 10 percent of funds for public works projects go to minority contractors.[20] The Court allowed this discrimination because the program was experimental and closely supervised, it was intended to remedy past discrimination, and Congress has more constitutional power to do this sort of thing than the states do. No state has ever been able to meet the compelling-interest test.

In 1995, the Supreme Court reversed itself on the issue of minority business set-asides (see *Adarand v. Pena,* 115 S.Ct. 2097 [1995]). Subsequently, the Clinton administration began reviewing all federal contracts to ensure compliance with the *Adarand* decision (no federal contract can be awarded solely on the basis of race, absent verifiable evidence of past racial discrimination).

Instances involving official state discrimination against blacks are rare these days, but a recent case is *Palmore v. Sidoti.*[21] The case was a custody suit in which the divorced father sued for custody of his daughter because his white ex-wife was cohabiting with a man (who happened to be black). By the time of the trial, the ex-wife and the man had married and the Court found both parents to be fit, so the case turned on the welfare of the child. The trial court found that, despite racial gains in this century, children of racially mixed marriages are subjected to social pressures that children of uniracial marriages are not, and the judge awarded custody to the father. The Supreme Court reversed that decision because it was a decision based solely on race (had the former Mrs. Sidoti married a similarly respectable white man, the result would have been different) and because the state's reason was not compelling. Speculation about the effects of private racial prejudice on children of interracial marriages is not a compelling reason.

Today, most discrimination against racial minorities is what is called *de facto discrimination*—that is, discrimination in fact but not mandated by law. Such cases involve discrimination in education (all-black and all-white schools within a school district or jurisdiction) or in the workplace (less than 1 percent of skilled labor jobs are held by blacks where blacks constitute 30 percent to 50 percent of the labor force or where less than 1 percent of contractors in a city are owned by blacks where blacks constitute 50 percent of the population).

The Court has dealt with this type of racial discrimination by requiring a finding that this discrimination be purposeful discrimination before it violates the Constitution.[22] For example, in Topeka, Kansas, nearly 50 years after the famous desegregation decision (*Brown v. Board of Education*),[23] the school district still contains schools that are more than 70 percent black and other schools that are 100 percent white. Because the situation is not mandated by law, it is defacto segregation, and before it can be found to be unconstitutional, the plaintiffs have to prove that the segregation exists by design of policymakers; if the racial pattern is the result of forces such as migration and housing patterns, such segregation is not unconstitutional.[24]

The most common purposeful discrimination in which state and local governments engage today is affirmative action. The Court has been badly divided on the question of affirmative action. Its decisions in this area have been unpredictable and make little or no jurisprudential sense. The first Supreme Court case to address the merits of an affirmative action program was *Regents of the University of California v. Bakke,* 438 U.S. 265, 1978. That case involved a special admissions program for admission to medical school at the University of California at Davis. The program was aimed at economically disadvantaged applicants who, by virtue of exposure to less sophisticated educational programs, could not be expected to perform on the Medical Career Aptitude Test (MCAT) at the same level as those whose socioeconomic level had afforded them private prep schools or public education in the suburbs. Although race was not a written factor in the special admissions process, only blacks had benefited from the affirmative action process. Allan Bakke, a white man who was refused admission twice, had both science and overall grade point averages and MCAT scores in excess of many who were admitted under the special program, and he claimed discrimination on the basis of race. The Court noted that although UC Davis proffered laudable reasons for such discrimination (reducing the deficit of minorities in medical school and the medical profession, countering societal discrimination, increasing the number of physicians who will practice in areas currently underserved, and achieving a diverse student body), those reasons (for the most part) were not compelling reasons to discriminate on the basis of race. The Court said that affirmative action programs may be constitutional so long as race is not the sole criterion. Race may be one among other criteria in affirmative action programs.

The Court seems to have moved to a point in two recent cases where it allows race-conscious remedies to be valid only in those cases in which such discrimination is used to eradicate the effects of specifically identifiable past discrimination.[25]

To the degree that administrative law deals with discrimination of any kind, it is always public or governmental discrimination. Private discrimination is a matter of constitutional law under the 1964 Civil Rights Act and, to a lesser degree, the Thirteenth Amendment. Some of you are probably wondering, What about "quota bills" and constitutional amendments banning affirmative action? Although this is not a matter of administrative law, it is important enough to take the time to clear confusion.

First, it should be obvious to you from the preceding discussion and the *Bakke* case that no state government or state governmental agency can have a "quota" system. It cannot have an affirmative action program in which race is the sole criterion, although race can be a factor. To the degree that a state's medical school or law school has a set-aside program, race cannot be the sole criterion.

Although it has become popular to refer to it as "reverse discrimination," the more appropriate descriptive term is *affirmative action*. There are affirmative action programs of all kinds. Harvard University (and most Ivy League universities as well) gives "bonus" affirmative action points in its application point system to applicants who attended public schools in such states as Kansas, Iowa, Texas, Oklahoma, and Georgia. The theory for this is simple: Students who are the product of such schools cannot compete on the SAT exam with students who are the product of the Eastern private academies. If Harvard did not do something to "level the playing field," it would still be a homogeneous elitist university filled only with the children of the rich who could afford private academies (where the curriculum is geared to producing high SAT scores). Because a diverse student body is seen as essential to a well-rounded education, affirmative programs of all kinds are appropriate for universities. Indeed, the Supreme Court has said that a diverse student body constitutes a "compelling state interest."

Quotas, however, to the degree that they exist anywhere (they are few and far between), are found almost exclusively in the private sector. Generally, they are created by an agreement between management and a union, and their purpose is to remedy empirically verifiable past discrimination. For example, the United Steelworkers Union forced an employer to accept a program that ensured that 50 percent of all trainees in an in-plant craft training program be black. This quota was to remain in effect until the number of skilled craft workers in the plant matched the proportion of blacks in the local workforce.[26] A federal district court found racial discrimination in a union's admission practices and imposed a goal of 29 percent nonwhite membership in the union by a set date (the 29 percent matched the nonwhite percentage in the local labor pool).[27] This is how we get quotas. Although the 1964 Civil Rights Act bans discrimination in interstate commerce, the Supreme Court has noted that the act's purpose was to promote the employment of blacks who had previously been excluded from participating in the national economy. So, private, benign discrimination (to make up for past discrimination) is constitutional under the 1964 Civil Rights Act.[28] Benign racial discrimination by a government is not constitutional under the equal protection clause.

The final area that involves what sounds like quotas is the area of preemployment criteria. A height criterion of, say, five feet eight inches, together with a weight requirement of 160 pounds as criteria before one can apply for a job with a state correctional agency, excludes without reason 75 percent of the female population. A specific score on a preemployment examination may disproportionately discriminate against blacks. In the early 1970s, the Court said that preemployment criteria that (a) have a disproportionate impact on a clearly identifiable minority and (b) are not related to job performance will be unconstitutional.[29] The Court soon overruled that case and began to employ a purposeful discrimination analysis to preemployment criteria cases; that is, preemployment criteria with a clearly identifiable disproportionate impact on a minority were not unconstitutional unless they could be shown to be part of purposeful discrimination. In 1989, the Court decided another case that made it easier for business to justify such criteria.[30] The Civil Rights Act of 1991 (often referred to as a "quota bill") was meant to reverse Rehnquist Court decisions in this area.[31]

Although the Civil Rights Act of 1991 does not impose or even mention quotas, it restores the Court's original two-pronged test (disproportionate impact and unrelated to job performance) and forbids the application of purposeful discrimination to these kinds of cases. Some have argued that this Civil Rights Act will cause businesses to "voluntarily" impose "quotas" on themselves to avoid a "disproportionate impact."

There has been movement in the states to abolish affirmative action. Two observations should be made about that. First, no state is permitted to have a law that conflicts with federal law (the supremacy clause of the Constitution). Second, and connected to the first, under federal jurisprudence (the *Bakke* case and its progeny) decisions based solely on race are unconstitutional.

Finally, a growing area in discrimination cases is the question of sexual harassment in the workplace. Recent cases in this area of the law involve sexual harassment in private industry, so the cases fall under the 1964 Civil Rights Act and are not administrative law. There is no reason to assume, however, that the Court would not apply the holdings to government employment as well.

In one case, the Court said that a plaintiff does not have to show a loss of any tangible or economic benefit to sue successfully for sexual harassment; that is, the fact of sexual harassment alone will substantiate such a suit. The plaintiff in this case had advanced from bank teller to assistant manager but was eventually fired for abuse of a sick leave policy.[32] In another case, the Court addressed what is required to establish the creation of an "abusive" or "hostile" work environment. The Court adopted a "totality of the circumstances" approach, saying that relevant criteria are (a) the frequency and severity of offensive behavior, (b) whether the behavior was physically threatening or emotionally humiliating, and (c) whether the behavior may have interfered with the employee's ability to perform her work.[33]

SUMMARY

1. Public employees can be categorized as either probationary or permanent employees. Only permanent employees have a property interest in their jobs.

2. The right to a pretermination hearing is contingent on the ability to demonstrate either a property interest or a liberty interest.

3. Because probationary employees lack a property interest, they must rely on the establishment of a liberty interest.

4. Liberty interests are established in one of two ways: (a) if publicly stated reasons for termination cause damage to one's reputation or ability to seek employment in the field or both and (b) if the primary reason behind the decision to terminate an employee was the employee's exercise of a constitutionally protected right.

5. The range of constitutionally protected expression is narrower for public employees than it is for all other citizens (expression that hampers the working relationship between an employee and an administrator is not protected).

6. Employees with a property interest can be terminated for cause (or financial exigency), but a pretermination hearing is required.

END-OF-CHAPTER CASES

BISHOP V. WOOD
426 U.S. 341 (1976)

The facts are contained in the opinion written by Justice Stevens, joined by Justices Burger, Stewart, Powell, and Rehnquist. Justices White, Brennan, Marshall, and Blackmun dissented.

The questions for us to decide are (1) whether petitioner's employment status was a property interest protected by the Due Process Clause of the Fourteenth Amendment, and (2) assuming that the explanation for his discharge was false, whether that false explanation deprived him of an interest in liberty protected by that Clause.

I

Petitioner was employed by the city of Marion as a probationary policeman on June 9, 1969. After six months he became a permanent employee. He was dismissed on March 31, 1972. He claims that he had either an express or an implied right to continued employment. A city ordinance provides that a permanent employee may be discharged if he fails to perform work up to the standard of his classification, or if he is negligent, inefficient, or unfit to perform his duties. Petitioner first contends that even though the ordinance does not expressly so provide, it should be read to prohibit discharge for any other reason, and therefore to confer tenure on all permanent employees. In addition, he contends that his period of service, together with his "permanent" classification, gave him a sufficient expectancy of continued employment to constitute a protected property interest. A property interest in

employment can, of course, be created by ordinance, or by an implied contract. In either case, however, the sufficiency of the claim of entitlement must be decided by reference to state law. The North Carolina Supreme Court has held that an enforceable expectation of continued public employment in that State can exist only if the employer, by statute or contract, has actually granted some form of guarantee. *Still v. Lance,* 279 N.C. 254, 182 S.E.2d 403 (1971). Whether such a guarantee has been given can be determined only by an examination of the particular statute or ordinance in question. On its face the ordinance on which petitioner relies may fairly be read as conferring such a guarantee. However, such a reading is not the only possible interpretation; the ordinance may also be construed as granting no right to continued employment but merely conditioning an employee's removal on compliance with certain specified procedures.

We do not have any authoritative interpretation of this ordinance by a North Carolina state court. We do, however, have the opinion of the United States District Judge who, of course, sits in North Carolina and practiced law there for many years. Based on his understanding of state law, he concluded that petitioner "held his position at the will and pleasure of the city." This construction of North Carolina law was upheld by the Court of Appeals for the Fourth Circuit, albeit by an equally divided court. In comparable circumstances, this

Court has accepted the interpretation of state law in which the District Court and the Court of Appeals have concurred even if an examination of the state-law issue without such guidance might have justified a different conclusion. In this case, as the District Court construed the ordinance, the City Manager's determination of the adequacy of the grounds for discharge is not subject to judicial review; the employee is merely given certain procedural rights which the District Court found not to have been violated in this case. The District Court's reading of the ordinance is tenable; it derives some support from a decision of the North Carolina Supreme Court, *Still v. Lance,* supra; and it was accepted by the Court of Appeals for the Fourth Circuit. These reasons are sufficient to foreclose our independent examination of the state-law issue.

Under that view of the law, petitioner's discharge did not deprive him of a property interest protected by the Fourteenth Amendment.

II

Petitioner's claim that he has been deprived of liberty has two components. He contends that the reasons given for his discharge are so serious as to constitute a stigma that may severely damage his reputation in the community; in addition, he claims that those reasons were false.

In our appraisal of petitioner's claim we must accept his version of the facts since the District Court granted summary judgment against him. His evidence established that he was a competent police officer; that he was respected by his peers; that he made more arrests than any other officer on the force; that although he had been criticized for engaging in high-speed pursuits, he had promptly heeded such criticism; and that he had a reasonable explanation for his imperfect attendance at police training sessions. We must therefore assume that his discharge was a mistake and based on incorrect information. In *Board of Regents v. Roth,* 408 U.S. 564, we recognized that the nonretention of an untenured college teacher might make him somewhat less attractive to other employers, but nevertheless concluded that it would stretch the concept too far "to suggest that a person is deprived of 'liberty' when he simply is not rehired in one job but remains as free as before to seek another." Id., at 575. This same conclusion applies to the discharge of a public employee whose position is terminable at the will of the employer when there

is no public disclosure of the reasons for the discharge.

In this case the asserted reasons for the City Manager's decision were communicated orally to the petitioner in private and also were stated in writing in answer to interrogatories after this litigation commenced. Since the former communication was not made public, it cannot properly form the basis for a claim that petitioner's interest in his "good name, reputation, honor, or integrity" was thereby impaired. And since the latter communication was made in the course of a judicial proceeding which did not commence until after petitioner had suffered the injury for which he seeks redress, it surely cannot provide retroactive support for his claim. A contrary evaluation of either explanation would penalize forthright and truthful communication between employer and employee in the former instance, and between litigants in the latter. Petitioner argues, however, that the reasons given for his discharge were false. Even so, the reasons stated to him in private had no different impact on his reputation than if they had been true. And the answers to his interrogatories, whether true or false, did not cause the discharge. The truth or falsity of the City Manager's statement determines whether or not his decision to discharge the petitioner was correct or prudent, but neither enhances nor diminishes petitioner's claim that his constitutionally protected interest in liberty has been impaired. A contrary evaluation of his contention would enable every discharged employee to assert a constitutional claim merely by alleging that his former supervisor made a mistake. The federal court is not the appropriate forum in which to review the multitude of personnel decisions that are made daily by public agencies. We must accept the harsh fact that numerous individual mistakes are inevitable in the day-to-day administration of our affairs. The United States Constitution cannot feasibly be construed to require federal judicial review for every such error. In the absence of any claim that the public employer was motivated by a desire to curtail or to penalize the exercise of an employee's constitutionally protected rights, we must presume that official action was regular and, if erroneous, can best be corrected in other ways. The Due Process Clause of the Fourteenth Amendment is not a guarantee against incorrect or ill-advised personnel decisions. The judgment is affirmed.

So ordered.

WATERS V. CHURCHILL
511 U.S. 661 (1994)

The opinion is by Justice O'Connor, joined by the Chief Justice and Justice Ginsburg. Justice Souter filed a concurring opinion, as did Justice Scalia, joined by Justices Kennedy and Thomas. Justice Stevens dissented, joined by Justice Blackmun.

In *Connick v. Myers,* 461 U.S. 138 (1983), we set forth a test for determining whether speech by a government employee may, consistently with the First Amendment, serve as a basis for disciplining or discharging that employee. In this case, we decide whether the *Connick* test should be applied to what the government employer thought was said, or to what the trier of fact ultimately determines to have been said.

I

This case arises out of a conversation that respondent Cheryl Churchill had on January 16, 1987, with Melanie Perkins-Graham. Both Churchill and Perkins-Graham were nurses working at McDonough District Hospital; Churchill was in the obstetrics department, and Perkins-Graham was considering transferring to that department. The conversation took place at work during a dinner break. Petitioners heard about it, and fired Churchill, allegedly because of it. There is, however, a dispute about what Churchill actually said, and therefore about whether petitioners were constitutionally permitted to fire Churchill for her statements.

The conversation was overheard in part by two other nurses, Mary Lou Ballew and Jean Welty, and by Dr. Thomas Koch, the clinical head of obstetrics. A few days later, Ballew told Cynthia Waters, Churchill's supervisor, about the incident. According to Ballew, Churchill took "the cross trainee into the kitchen for . . . at least 20 minutes to talk about [Waters] and how bad things are in [obstetrics] in general." Ballew said that Churchill's statements led Perkins-Graham to no longer be interested in switching to the department.

Shortly after this, Waters met with Ballew a second time for confirmation of Ballew's initial report. Ballew said that Churchill "was knocking the department" and that "in general [Churchill] was saying what a bad place [obstetrics] is to work." Ballew said she heard Churchill say Waters "was trying to find reasons to fire her." Ballew also said Churchill described a patient

complaint for which Waters had supposedly wrongly blamed Churchill.

Waters, together with petitioner Kathleen Davis, the hospital's vice president of nursing, also met with Perkins-Graham, who told them that Churchill "had indeed said unkind and inappropriate negative things about [Waters]." Also, according to Perkins-Graham, Churchill mentioned a negative evaluation that Waters had given Churchill, which arose out of an incident in which Waters had cited Churchill for an insubordinate remark. The evaluation stated that Churchill "promotes an unpleasant atmosphere and hinders constructive communication and cooperation," and "exhibits negative behavior towards [Waters] and [Waters'] leadership through her actions and body language"; the evaluation said Churchill's work was otherwise satisfactory. Churchill allegedly told Perkins-Graham that she and Waters had discussed the evaluation, and that Waters "wanted to wipe the slate clean . . . but [Churchill thought] this wasn't possible." Churchill also allegedly told Perkins-Graham "that just in general things were not good in OB and hospital administration was responsible." Churchill specifically mentioned Davis, saying Davis "was ruining MDH." Perkins-Graham told Waters that she knew Waters and Davis "could not tolerate that kind of negativism."

Churchill's version of the conversation is different. For several months, Churchill had been concerned about the hospital's "cross-training" policy, under which nurses from one department could work in another when their usual location was overstaffed. Churchill believed this policy threatened patient care because it was designed not to train nurses but to cover staff shortages, and she had complained about this to Davis and Waters. According to Churchill, the conversation with Perkins-Graham primarily concerned the cross-training policy. Churchill denies that she said some of what Ballew and Perkins-Graham allege she said. She does admit she criticized Kathy Davis, saying her staffing policies threatened to "ruin" the hospital because they "seemed to be impeding nursing care." She claims she actually defended Waters and encouraged Perkins-Graham to transfer to obstetrics.

Koch's and Welty's recollections of the conversation match Churchill's. Davis and Waters, however, never talked to Koch or Welty about this, and they did not talk to Churchill until the time they told her she was fired. Moreover, Churchill claims, Ballew was biased against Churchill because of an incident in which Ballew apparently made an error and Churchill had to cover for her.

After she was discharged, Churchill filed an internal grievance. The president of the hospital, petitioner Stephen Hopper, met with Churchill in regard to this and heard her side of the story. He then reviewed Waters' and Davis' written reports of their conversations with Ballew and Perkins-Graham, and had Bernice Magin, the hospital's vice president of human resources, interview Ballew one more time. After considering all this, Hopper rejected Churchill's grievance.

Churchill then sued under Rev.Stat. § 1979, 42 U.S.C. § 1983, claiming that the firing violated her First Amendment rights because her speech was protected under *Connick v. Myers,* 461 U.S. 138 (1983). In May 1991, the United States District Court for the Central District of Illinois granted summary judgment to petitioners. The Court held that neither version of the conversation was protected under *Connick.* . . . Therefore, the court held, management could fire Churchill for the conversation with impunity.

The United States Court of Appeals for the Seventh Circuit reversed. 977 F.2d 1114 (1992). The court held that Churchill's speech, viewed in the light most favorable to her, was protected speech under the *Connick* test: It was on a matter of public concern—"the hospital's [alleged] violation of state nursing regulations as well as the quality and level of nursing care it provides its patients," and it was not disruptive.

The court also concluded that the inquiry must turn on what the speech actually was, not on what the employer thought it was.

II

A

[1] There is no dispute in this case about when speech by a government employee is protected by the First Amendment.

The dispute is over how the factual basis for applying the test—what the speech was, in what tone it was delivered, what the listener's reactions were, is to be determined. Should the court apply the *Connick* test to the speech as the government employer found it to be, or should it ask the jury to

determine the facts for itself? The Court of Appeals held that the employer's factual conclusions were irrelevant, and that the jury should engage in its own factfinding. Petitioners argue that the employer's factual conclusions should be dispositive. Respondents take a middle course: They suggest that the court should accept the employer's factual conclusions, but only if those conclusions were arrived at reasonably, something they say did not happen here.

We agree that it is important to ensure not only that the substantive First Amendment standards are sound, but also that they are applied through reliable procedures. This is why we have often held some procedures—a particular allocation of the burden of proof, a particular quantum of proof, a particular type of appellate review, and so on—to be constitutionally required in proceedings that may penalize protected speech. See *Freedman v. Maryland,* 380 U.S. 51 (1965) (government must bear burden of proving that speech is unprotected); *Philadelphia Newspapers, Inc. v. Hepps,* 475 U.S. 767 (1986) (libel plaintiff must bear burden of proving that speech is false); *Masson v. New Yorker Magazine, Inc.,* 501 U.S. 496 (1991) (actual malice must be proved by clear and convincing evidence); *Bose Corp. v. Consumers Union of United States, Inc.,* 466 U.S. 485 (1984) (appellate court must make independent judgment about presence of actual malice).

[2] These cases establish a basic First Amendment principle: Government action based on protected speech may under some circumstances violate the First Amendment even if the government actor honestly believes the speech is unprotected. . . .

Nonetheless, not every procedure that may safeguard protected speech is constitutionally mandated. True, the procedure adopted by the Court of Appeals may lower the chance of protected speech being erroneously punished. A speaker is more protected if she has two opportunities to be vindicated—first by the employer's investigation and then by the jury—than just one. But each procedure involves a different mix of administrative burden, risk of erroneous punishment of protected speech, and risk of erroneous exculpation of unprotected speech. Though the First Amendment creates a strong presumption against punishing protected speech even inadvertently, the balance need not always be struck in that direction. We have never, for instance, required proof beyond a reasonable doubt in civil cases where First Amendment interests are at stake, though such a requirement would protect speech more than the alternative standards would. . . .

We have never set forth a general test to determine when a procedural safeguard is required by the First Amendment—just as we have never set forth a general test to determine what constitutes a compelling state interest, see *Boos v. Barry,* 485 U.S. 312 (1988), or what categories of speech are so lacking in value that they fall outside the protection of the First Amendment, *New York v. Ferber,* 458 U.S. 747 (1982), or many other matters—and we do not purport to do so now. But though we agree with Justice SCALIA that the lack of such a test is inconvenient, this does not relieve us of our responsibility to decide the case that is before us today. Both Justice SCALIA and we agree that some procedural requirements are mandated by the First Amendment and some are not. None of us have discovered a general principle to determine where the line is to be drawn. We must therefore reconcile ourselves to answering the question on a case-by-case basis, at least until some workable general rule emerges.

[3] Accordingly, all we say today is that the propriety of a proposed procedure must turn on the particular context in which the question arises—on the cost of the procedure and the relative magnitude and constitutional significance of the risks it would decrease and increase. And to evaluate these factors here we have to return to the issue we dealt with in *Connick* and in the cases that came before it: What is it about the government's role as employer that gives it a freer hand in regulating the speech of its employees than it has in regulating the speech of the public at large?

B

[4] We have never explicitly answered this question, though we have always assumed that its premise is correct—that the government as employer indeed has far broader powers than does the government as sovereign. See *Pickering,* supra, at 568 (1973); *Connick,* 461 U.S., at 147. This assumption is amply borne out by considering the practical realities of government employment, and the many situations in which, we believe, most observers would agree that the government must be able to restrict its employees' speech.

To begin with, even many of the most fundamental maxims of our First Amendment jurisprudence cannot reasonably be applied to speech by government employees. The First Amendment demands a tolerance of "verbal tumult, discord, and even offensive utterance," as "necessary side effects of . . . the process of open debate," *Cohen v. California,* 403 U.S. 15 (1971). But we have never expressed doubt that a government employer may bar its employees from using Mr. Cohen's offensive utterance to members of the public, or to the people with whom they work. "Under the First Amendment there is no such thing as a false idea," *Gertz,* supra, at 339, the "fitting remedy for evil counsels is good ones," *Whitney v. California,* 274 U.S. 357, d(1927) (BRANDEIS, J., concurring). But when an employee counsels her coworkers to do their job in a way with which the public employer disagrees, her managers may tell her to stop, rather than relying on counter-speech. The First Amendment reflects the "profound national commitment to the principle that debate on public issues should be uninhibited, robust, and wide-open." *New York Times Co. v. Sullivan,* 376 U.S. 254 (1964). But though a private person is perfectly free to uninhibitedly and robustly criticize a state governor's legislative program, we have never suggested that the Constitution bars the governor from firing a high-ranking deputy for doing the same thing. Cf. *Branti v. Finkel,* 445 U.S. 507 (1980). Even something as close to the core of the First Amendment as participation in political campaigns may be prohibited to government employees. *Broadrick v. Oklahoma,* 413 U.S. 601 (1973); *Public Workers v. Mitchell,* 330 U.S. 75 (1947).

[5] Government employee speech must be treated differently with regard to procedural requirements as well. For example, speech restrictions must generally precisely define the speech they target. *Baggett v. Bullitt,* 377 U.S. 360, 367-368, 84 S.Ct. 1316, 1320-1321, 12 L.Ed.2d 377 (1964); *Hustler Magazine, Inc. v. Falwell,* 485 U.S. 46, 55, 108 S.Ct. 876, 881, 99 L.Ed.2d 41 (1988). Yet surely a public employer may, consistently with the First Amendment, prohibit its employees from being "rude to customers," a standard almost certainly too vague when applied to the public at large. Cf. *Arnett v. Kennedy,* 416 U.S. 134, 158-162, 94 S.Ct. 1633, 1646-1648, 40 L.Ed.2d 15 (1974) (plurality opinion) (upholding a regulation that allowed discharges for speech which hindered the "efficiency of the service"); id., at 164, 94 S.Ct., at 1649 (Powell, J., concurring in part and concurring in result in part) (agreeing on this point).

Likewise, we have consistently given greater deference to government predictions of harm used to justify restriction of employee speech than to predictions of harm used to justify restrictions on the speech of the public at large. Few of the examples we have discussed involve tangible, present interference with the agency's operation. The danger in them is mostly speculative. One could make a respectable argument that political activity by government employees is generally not harmful, see *Public Workers v. Mitchell,* supra, 330 U.S. at 99, 67 S.Ct., at 569, or that high officials should allow more public dissent by their subordinates, see *Connick,* supra, 461 U.S., at 168-169, 103 S.Ct., at 1701-1702 (BRENNAN, J., dissenting); Whistleblower Protection Act of 1989, 103 Stat. 16, or that even in a government workplace the free market of ideas is superior to a command economy. But we have given substantial weight to government employers' reasonable predictions of disruption, even when the speech involved is on a matter of public concern, and even though when the government is acting as sovereign our review of legislative predictions of harm is considerably less deferential. Compare, e.g., *Connick,* supra, at 151-152, 103 S.Ct., at 1692-1693; *Letter Carriers,* supra, 413 U.S., at 566-567, 93 S.Ct., at 2890-2891, with *Sable Communications of Cal., Inc. v. FCC,* 492 U.S. 115, 129, 109 S.Ct. 2829, 2838, 106 L.Ed.2d 93 (1989); *Texas v. Johnson,* 491 U.S. 397, 409, 109 S.Ct. 2533, 2542, 105 L.Ed.2d 342 (1989). Similarly, we have refrained from intervening in government employer decisions that are based on speech that is of entirely private concern. Doubtless some such speech is sometimes nondisruptive; doubtless it is sometimes of value to the speakers and the listeners. But we have declined to question government employers' decisions on such matters. *Connick,* supra, 461 U.S., at 146-149, 103 S.Ct., at 1689-1691.

[6] This does not, of course, show that the First Amendment should play no role in government employment decisions. Government employees are often in the best position to know what ails the agencies for which they work; public debate may gain much from their informed opinions, *Pickering v. Board of Ed. of Township High School Dist.,* 391 U.S., at 572, 88 S.Ct., at 1736. And a government employee, like any citizen, may have a strong, legitimate interest in speaking out on public matters. In many such situations the government may have to make a substantial showing that the speech is, in fact, likely to be disruptive before it may be punished. See, e.g., *Rankin v. McPherson,* 483 U.S. 378, 388, 107 S.Ct. 2891, 2899, 97 L.Ed.2d 315 (1987); *Connick,* 461 U.S., at 152, 103 S.Ct., at 1692; *Pickering,* supra, 391 U.S., at 569-571, 88 S.Ct., at 1735-1736. Moreover, the government may certainly choose to give additional protections to its employees beyond what is mandated by the First Amendment, out of respect for the values underlying the First Amendment, values central to our social order as well as our legal system. See, e.g., Whistleblower Protection Act of 1989, supra.

[7] But the above examples do show that constitutional review of government employment decisions must rest on different principles than review of speech restraints imposed by the government as sovereign. The restrictions discussed above are allowed not just because the speech interferes with the government's operation. Speech by private people can do the same, but this does not allow the government to suppress it.

Rather, the extra power the government has in this area comes from the nature of the government's mission as employer. Government agencies are charged by law with doing particular tasks. Agencies hire employees to help do those tasks as effectively and efficiently as possible. When someone who is paid a salary so that she will contribute to an agency's effective operation begins to do or say things that detract from the agency's effective operation, the government employer must have some power to restrain her. The reason the governor may, in the example given above, fire the deputy is not that this dismissal would somehow be narrowly tailored to a compelling government interest. It is that the governor and the governor's staff have a job to do, and the governor justifiably feels that a quieter subordinate would allow them to do this job more effectively.

[8] The key to First Amendment analysis of government employment decisions, then, is this: The government's interest in achieving its goals as effectively and efficiently as possible is elevated from a relatively subordinate interest when it acts as sovereign to a significant one when it acts as employer. The government cannot restrict the speech of the public at large just in the name of efficiency. But where the government is employing someone for the very purpose of effectively achieving its goals, such restrictions may well be appropriate.

C

1

The problem with the Court of Appeals' approach—under which the facts to which the *Connick* test is applied are determined by the judicial factfinder—is that it would force the government employer to come to its factual conclusions through procedures that substantially mirror the evidentiary rules used in court. The government manager would have to ask not what conclusions she, as an experienced professional, can draw from the circumstances, but rather what conclusions a jury would later draw. If she relies on hearsay, or on what she knows about the accused employee's character, she must be aware that this evidence might not be usable in court. If she knows one party is, in her personal experience, more credible than another, she must realize that the jury will not share that personal experience. If she thinks the alleged offense is so egregious that it is proper to discipline the accused employee even though the evidence is ambiguous, she must consider that a jury might decide the other way.

[9] But employers, public and private, often do rely on hearsay, on past similar conduct, on their personal knowledge of people's credibility, and on other factors that the judicial process ignores. Such reliance may sometimes be the most effective way for the employer to avoid future recurrences of improper and disruptive conduct. What works best in a judicial proceeding may not be appropriate in the employment context. If one employee accuses another of misconduct, it is reasonable for a government manager to credit the allegation more if it is consistent with what the manager knows of the character of the accused. Likewise, a manager may legitimately want to discipline an employee based on complaints by patrons that the employee has been rude, even though these complaints are hearsay.

[10] On the other hand, we do not believe that the court must apply the *Connick* test only to the facts as the employer thought them to be, without considering the reasonableness of the employer's conclusions. Even in situations where courts have recognized the special expertise and special needs of certain decisionmakers, the deference to their conclusions has never been complete. Cf. *New Jersey v. T.L.O.,* 469 U.S. 325, 342-343, 105 S.Ct. 733, 743-744, 83 L.Ed.2d 720 (1985); *United States v. Leon,* 468 U.S. 897, 914, 104 S.Ct. 3405, 3416, 82 L.Ed.2d 677 (1984); *Universal Camera Corp. v. NLRB,* 340 U.S. 474, 490-491, 71 S.Ct. 456, 465-466, 95 L.Ed. 456 (1951). It is necessary that the decisionmaker reach its conclusion about what was said in good faith, rather than as a pretext; but it does not follow that good faith is sufficient. Justice SCALIA is right in saying that we have often held various laws to require only an inquiry into the decisionmaker's intent, but, as discussed supra in Part II-A, this has not been our view of the First Amendment.

We think employer decisionmaking will not be unduly burdened by having courts look to the facts as the employer reasonably found them to be. It may be unreasonable, for example, for the employer to come to a conclusion based on no evidence at all. Likewise, it may be unreasonable for an employer to act based on extremely weak evidence when strong evidence is clearly available—if, for instance, an employee is accused of writing an improper letter to the editor, and instead of just reading the letter, the employer decides what it said based on unreliable hearsay.

[11] If an employment action is based on what an employee supposedly said, and a reasonable supervisor would recognize that there is a substantial likelihood that what was actually said was protected, the manager must tread with a certain amount of care. This need not be the care with which trials, with their rules of evidence and procedure, are conducted. It should, however, be the care that a reasonable manager would use before making an employment decision—discharge, suspension, reprimand, or whatever else—of the sort involved in the particular case. Justice SCALIA correctly points out that such care is normally not constitutionally required unless the employee has a protected property interest in her job, post, at 1894; see also *Board of Regents of State Colleges v. Roth,* 408 U.S. 564, 576-578, 92 S.Ct. 2701, 2708-2710, 33 L.Ed.2d 548 (1972); but we believe that the possibility of inadvertently punishing someone for exercising her First Amendment rights makes such care necessary.

Of course, there will often be situations in which reasonable employers would disagree about who is to be believed, or how much investigation needs to be done, or how much evidence is needed to come to a particular conclusion. In those situations, many different courses of action will necessarily be reasonable. Only procedures outside the range of what a reasonable manager would use may be condemned as unreasonable.

III

[13] Applying the foregoing to this case, it is clear that if petitioners really did believe Perkins-Graham's and Ballew's story, and fired Churchill because of it, they must win. Their belief, based on the investigation they conducted, would have been entirely reasonable. After getting the initial report from Ballew, who overheard the conversation, Waters and Davis approached and interviewed Perkins-Graham, and then interviewed Ballew again for confirmation. In response to Churchill's grievance, Hopper met directly with Churchill to hear her side of the story, and instructed Magin to interview Ballew one more time. Management can spend only so much of their time on any one employment decision. By the end of the termination process, Hopper, who made the final decision, had the word of two trusted employees, the endorsement of those employees' reliability by three hospital managers, and the benefit of a face-to-face meeting with the employee he fired. With that in hand, a reasonable manager could have concluded that no further time needed to be taken. As respondents themselves point out, "if the belief an employer forms supporting its adverse personnel action is 'reasonable,' an employer has no need to investigate further." Brief for Respondents 39.

[14] And under the *Connick* test, Churchill's speech as reported by Perkins-Graham and Ballew was unprotected. Even if Churchill's criticism of cross-training reported by Perkins-Graham and Ballew was speech on a matter of public concern—something we need not decide—the potential disruptiveness of the speech as reported was enough to outweigh whatever First Amendment value it might have had. According to Ballew, Churchill's speech may have substantially dampened Perkins-Graham's interest in working in obstetrics. Discouraging people from coming to work for a department certainly qualifies as disruption. Moreover, Perkins-Graham perceived Churchill's statements about Waters to be "unkind and inappropriate," and told management that she knew they could not continue to "tolerate that kind of negativism" from Churchill. This is strong evidence that Churchill's complaining, if not dealt with, threatened to undermine management's authority in Perkins-Graham's eyes. And finally, Churchill's statement, as reported by Perkins-Graham, that it "wasn't possible" to "wipe the slate clean" between her and Waters could certainly make management doubt

Churchill's future effectiveness. As a matter of law, this potential disruptiveness was enough to outweigh whatever First Amendment value the speech might have had.

[15] This is so even if, as Churchill suggests, Davis and Waters were "[d]eliberately [i]ndifferent," Brief for Respondents 31, to the possibility that much of the rest of the conversation was solely about cross-training. So long as Davis and Waters discharged Churchill only for the part of the speech that was either not on a matter of public concern, or on a matter of public concern but disruptive, it is irrelevant whether the rest of the speech was, unbeknownst to them, both on a matter of public concern and nondisruptive. The *Connick* test is to be applied to the speech for which Churchill was fired. Cf. *Connick,* supra, 461 U.S., at 149, 103 S.Ct., at 1691 (evaluating the disruptiveness of part of plaintiff's speech because that part was "upon a matter of public concern and contributed to [plaintiff's] discharge" (emphasis added)); *Mt. Healthy,* supra, 429 U.S., at 286-287, 97 S.Ct., at 575-576. An employee who makes an unprotected statement is not immunized from discipline by the fact that this statement is surrounded by protected statements.

Nonetheless, we agree with the Court of Appeals that the District Court erred in granting summary judgment in petitioners' favor. Though Davis and Waters would have been justified in firing Churchill for the statements outlined above, there remains the question whether Churchill was actually fired because of those statements, or because of something else. See *Mt. Healthy,* supra, at 286-287, 97 S.Ct., at 575-576.

Rather, we vacate the judgment of the Court of Appeals and remand the case for further proceedings consistent with this opinion.

So ordered.

Justice STEVENS, with whom Justice BLACKMUN joins, dissenting.

This is a free country. Every American has the right to express an opinion on issues of public significance. In the private sector, of course, the exercise of that right may entail unpleasant consequences. Absent some contractual or statutory provision limiting its prerogatives, a private-sector employer may discipline or fire employees for speaking their minds. The First Amendment, however, demands that the Government respect its em-

ployees' freedom to express their opinions on issues of public importance. As long as that expression is not unduly disruptive, it simply may not
provide the basis for discipline or termination. The
critical issues in a case of this kind are (1) whether
the speech is protected, and (2) whether it was the
basis for the sanction imposed on the employee.

Applying these standards to the case before us is
quite straightforward. Everyone agrees that respondent Cheryl Churchill was fired because of what
she said in a conversation with co-workers during
a dinner break. Given the posture in which this case
comes to us, we must assume that Churchill's statements were fully protected by the First Amendment. [FN1] Nevertheless, the plurality concludes
that a dismissal for speech is valid as a matter of
law as long as the public employer reasonably
believed that the employee's speech was unprotected. See ante, at 1888-1890. This conclusion is
erroneous because it provides less protection for a
fundamental constitutional right than the law ordinarily provides for less exalted rights, including
contractual and statutory rights applicable in the
private sector.

If, for example, a hospital employee had a contract providing that she could retain her job for a
year if she followed the employer's rules and did
competent work, that employee could not be fired
because her supervisor reasonably but mistakenly
believed she had been late to work or given a patient
the wrong medicine. Ordinarily, when someone
acts to another person's detriment based upon a
factual judgment, the actor assumes the risk that an
impartial adjudicator may come to a different conclusion. [FN2] Our legal system generally delegates the determination of facts upon which important
rights depend to neutral factfinders, notwithstanding the attendant risks of error and overdeterrence.

Federal constitutional rights merit at least the
normal degree of protection. Doubts concerning
the ability of juries to find the truth, an ability for
which we usually have high regard, should be resolved in favor of, not against, the protection of
First Amendment rights. See, e.g., *New York Times
Co. v. Sullivan,* 376 U.S. 254, 279-280, 84 S.Ct.
710, 725-726, 11 L.Ed.2d 686 (1964). Unfortunately, the plurality underestimates the importance
of freedom of speech for the more than 18 million
civilian employees of this country's Federal, State,
and local Governments, [FN3] and subordinates
that freedom to an abstract interest in bureaucratic

efficiency. The need for governmental efficiency
that so concerns the plurality is amply protected by
the substantive limits on public employees' rights
of expression. See generally *Connick v. Myers,* 461
U.S. 138, 103 S.Ct. 1684, 75 L.Ed.2d 708 (1983);
*Pickering v. Board of Ed. of Township High School
Dist.,* 391 U.S. 563, 88 S.Ct. 1731, 20 L.Ed.2d 811
(1968). Efficiency does not demand an additional
layer of deference to employers' "reasonable" factual errors. Today's ruling will surely deter speech
that would be fully protected under *Pickering* and
Connick.

The plurality correctly points out that we have
never decided whether the governing version of the
facts in public employment free speech cases is
"what the government employer thought was said,
or . . . what the trier of fact ultimately determines
to have been said." Ante, at 1882. [FN4] To me it
is clear that the latter must be controlling. The First
Amendment assures public employees that they
may express their views on issues of public concern
without fear of discipline or termination as long as
they do so in an appropriate manner and at an
appropriate time and place. A violation occurs
when a public employee is fired for uttering speech
on a matter of public concern that is not unduly
disruptive of the operations of the relevant agency.
The violation does not vanish merely because the
firing was based upon a reasonable mistake about
what the employee said. [FN5] A First Amendment
claimant need not allege bad faith; the controlling
question is not the regularity of the agency's investigative procedures, or the purity of its motives, but
whether the employee's freedom of speech has
been "abridged."

The risk that a jury may ultimately view the facts
differently from even a conscientious employer, is
not, as the plurality would have it, a needless fetter
on public employers' ability to discharge their duties. It is the normal means by which our legal
system protects legal rights and encourages those
in authority to act with care. Here, for example,
attention to "conclusions a jury would later draw,"
ante, at 1888, about the content of Churchill's
speech might have caused petitioners to talk to
Churchill about what she said before deciding to
fire her. There is nothing unfair or onerous about
putting the risk of error on an employer in these
circumstances.

Government agencies are often the site of sharp
differences over a wide range of important public

issues. In offices where the First Amendment commands respect for candid deliberation and individual opinion, such disagreements are both inevitable and desirable. When those who work together disagree, reports of speech are often skewed, and supervisors are apt to misconstrue even accurate reports. The plurality, observing that managers "can spend only so much of their time on any one employment decision," ante, at 1890, adopts a rule that invites discipline, rather than further discussion,

when such disputes arise. That rule is unwise, for deliberation within the government, like deliberation about it, is an essential part of our "profound national commitment" to the freedom of speech. Cf. *New York Times,* 376 U.S., at 270, 84 S.Ct., at 721. A proper regard for that principle requires that, before firing a public employee for her speech, management get its facts straight.

I would affirm the judgment of the Court of Appeals.

CLEVELAND BOARD OF EDUCATION V. LOUDERMILL
470 U.S. 532 (1985)

Justice White delivered the opinion of the Court, joined by Chief Justice Burger and Justices Blackmun, Powell, Stevens, and O'Connor. Justice Marshall concurred, Justice Brennan concurred in part and dissented in part, and Justice Rehnquist dissented.

In these cases we consider what pretermination process must be accorded a public employee who can be discharged only for cause.

I

In 1979 the Cleveland Board of Education, petitioner in No. 83-1362, hired respondent James Loudermill as a security guard. On his job application, Loudermill stated that he had never been convicted of a felony. Eleven months later, as part of a routine examination of his employment records, the Board discovered that in fact Loudermill had been convicted of grand larceny in 1968. By letter dated November 3, 1980, the Board's Business Manager informed Loudermill that he had been dismissed because of his dishonesty in filling out the employment application. Loudermill was not afforded an opportunity to respond to the charge of dishonesty or to challenge his dismissal. On November 13, the Board adopted a resolution officially approving the discharge. Under Ohio law, Loudermill was a "classified civil servant." Such employees can be terminated only for cause, and may obtain administrative review if discharged. Pursuant to this provision, Loudermill filed an appeal with the Cleveland Civil Service Commission on November 12. The Commission appointed a referee, who held a hearing on January 29, 1981. Loudermill argued that he had thought that his 1968

larceny conviction was for a misdemeanor rather than a felony. The referee recommended reinstatement. On July 20, 1981, the full Commission heard argument and orally announced that it would uphold the dismissal. Proposed findings of fact and conclusions of law followed on August 10, and Loudermill's attorneys were advised of the result by mail on August 21.

Although the Commission's decision was subject to judicial review in the state courts, Loudermill instead brought the present suit in the Federal District Court for the Northern District of Ohio. The complaint alleged that § 124.34 was unconstitutional on its face because it did not provide the employee an opportunity to respond to the charges against him prior to removal. As a result, discharged employees were deprived of liberty and property without due process. The complaint also alleged that the provision was unconstitutional as applied because discharged employees were not given sufficiently prompt postremoval hearings.
. . .

The Due Process Clause provides that certain substantive rights—life, liberty, and property—cannot be deprived except pursuant to constitutionally adequate procedures. The categories of substance and procedure are distinct. Were the rule otherwise, the Clause would be reduced to a mere tautology. "Property" cannot be defined by the procedures provided for its deprivation any more than can life or liberty. The right to due process "is conferred, not by legislative grace, but by constitutional guarantee. While the legislature may elect not to confer a property interest in [public] employment, it may not constitutionally authorize the deprivation of such an interest, once conferred, without appropriate procedural safeguards."

In short, once it is determined that the Due Process Clause applies, "the question remains what process is due." *Morrissey v. Brewer*, 408 U.S. 471, 481 (1972). The answer to that question is not to be found in the Ohio statute. . . .

III

[4, 5] An essential principle of due process is that a deprivation of life, liberty, or property "be preceded by notice and opportunity for hearing appropriate to the nature of the case." *Mullane v. Central Hanover Bank & Trust Co.,* 339 U.S. 306 (1950). We have described "the root requirement" of the Due Process Clause as being "that an individual be given an opportunity for a hearing before he is deprived of any significant property interest." *Boddie v. Connecticut,* 401 U.S. 371 (1971). This principle requires "some kind of a hearing" prior to the discharge of an employee who has a constitutionally protected property interest in his employment. . . .

The need for some form of pretermination hearing, recognized in these cases, is evident from a balancing of the competing interests at stake. These are the private interests in retaining employment, the governmental interest in the expeditious removal of unsatisfactory employees and the avoidance of administrative burdens, and the risk of an erroneous termination. See *Mathews v. Eldridge,* 424 U.S. 319, 335 (1976).

First, the significance of the private interest in retaining employment cannot be gainsaid. We have frequently recognized the severity of depriving a person of the means of livelihood. While a fired worker may find employment elsewhere, doing so will take some time and is likely to be burdened by the questionable circumstances under which he left his previous job.

Second, some opportunity for the employee to present his side of the case is recurringly of obvious value in reaching an accurate decision. Dismissals for cause will often involve factual disputes. Even where the facts are clear, the appropriateness or necessity of the discharge may not be; in such cases, the only meaningful opportunity to invoke the discretion of the decisionmaker is likely to be before the termination takes effect. See *Goss v. Lopez,* 419 U.S., at 583-584. . . .

[6] The cases before us illustrate these considerations. Both respondents had plausible arguments to make that might have prevented their discharge. The fact that the Commission saw fit to reinstate Donnelly suggests that an error might have been avoided had he been provided an opportunity to make his case to the Board. As for Loudermill, given the Commission's ruling we cannot say that the discharge was mistaken. Nonetheless, in light of the referee's recommendation, neither can we say that a fully informed decisionmaker might not have exercised its discretion and decided not to dismiss him, notwithstanding its authority to do so. In any event, the termination involved arguable issues, and the right to a hearing does not depend on a demonstration of certain success.

Loudermill's dismissal turned not on the objective fact that he was an ex-felon or the inaccuracy of his statement to the contrary, but on the subjective question whether he had lied on his application form. His explanation for the false statement is plausible in light of the fact that he received only a suspended 6-month sentence and a fine on the grand larceny conviction.

The governmental interest in immediate termination does not outweigh these interests. As we shall explain, affording the employee an opportunity to respond prior to termination would impose neither a significant administrative burden nor intolerable delays. Furthermore, the employer shares the employee's interest in avoiding disruption and erroneous decisions; and until the matter is settled, the employer would continue to receive the benefit of the employee's labors. It is preferable to keep a qualified employee on than to train a new one. A governmental employer also has an interest in keeping citizens usefully employed rather than taking the possibly erroneous and counterproductive step of forcing its employees onto the welfare rolls. Finally, in those situations where the employer perceives a significant hazard in keeping the employee on the job, it can avoid the problem by suspending with pay. . . .

IV

[7] The foregoing considerations indicate that the pretermination "hearing," though necessary, need not be elaborate. We have pointed out that "[t]he formality and procedural requisites for the hearing can vary, depending upon the importance of the interests involved and the nature of the subsequent proceedings." In general, "something less" than a full evidentiary hearing is sufficient prior to adverse administrative action. *Mathews v. Eldridge,*

424 U.S., at 343. Under state law, respondents were later entitled to a full administrative hearing and judicial review. The only question is what steps were required before the termination took effect.

In only one case, *Goldberg v. Kelly,* 397 U.S. 254 (1970), has the Court required a full adversarial evidentiary hearing prior to adverse governmental action. However, as the Goldberg Court itself pointed out, that case presented significantly different considerations than are present in the context of public employment. Here, the pretermination hearing need not definitively resolve the propriety of the discharge. It should be an initial check against mistaken decisions—essentially, a determination of whether there are reasonable grounds to believe that the charges against the employee are true and support the proposed action. See *Bell v. Burson,* 402 U.S., at 540.

The essential requirements of due process, and all that respondents seek or the Court of Appeals required, are notice and an opportunity to respond. The opportunity to present reasons, either in person or in writing, why proposed action should not be taken is a fundamental due process requirement. See Friendly, "Some Kind of Hearing," 123 U.Pa.L.Rev. 1267, 1281 (1975). The tenured public employee is entitled to oral or written notice of the charges against him, an explanation of the employer's evidence, and an opportunity to present his side of the story. To require more than this prior to termination would intrude to an unwarranted extent on the government's interest in quickly removing an unsatisfactory employee. . . .

VI

We conclude that all the process that is due is provided by a pretermination opportunity to respond, coupled with post-administrative procedures as provided by the Ohio statute. Because respondents allege in their complaints that they had no chance to respond, the District Court erred in dismissing for failure to state a claim. The judgment of the Court of Appeals is affirmed, and the case is remanded for further proceedings consistent with this opinion.

BOARD OF COUNTY COMMISSIONERS, WABAUNSEE COUNTY V. UMBEHR
115 S.Ct. 2342 (1995)

Justice O'Connor delivered the opinion of the Court, joined by Chief Justice Rehnquist (except for a small part of the opinion that he disagreed with) and Justices Stevens, Kennedy, Souter, Ginsburg, and Breyer. Justice Scalia's dissent was joined by Justice Thomas.

This case requires us to decide whether, and to what extent, the First Amendment protects independent contractors from the termination of at-will government contracts in retaliation for their exercise of the freedom of speech.

I

Under state law, Wabaunsee County, Kansas (County) is obliged to provide for the disposal of solid waste generated within its borders. In 1981, and, after renegotiation, in 1985, the County contracted with respondent Umbehr for him to be the exclusive hauler of trash for cities in the county at a rate specified in the contract. Each city was free to reject or, on 90 days' notice, to opt out of, the contract. By its terms, the contract between Umbehr and the County was automatically renewed annually unless either party terminated it by giving notice at least 60 days before the end of the year or a renegotiation was instituted on 90 days' notice. Pursuant to the contract, Umbehr hauled trash for six of the County's seven cities from 1985 to 1991 on an exclusive and uninterrupted basis.

During the term of his contract, Umbehr was an outspoken critic of petitioner, the Board of County Commissioners of Wabaunsee County (Board), the three-member governing body of the County. Umbehr spoke at the Board's meetings, and wrote critical letters and editorials in local newspapers regarding the County's landfill user rates, the cost of obtaining official documents from the County, alleged violations by the Board of the Kansas Open Meetings Act, the County's alleged mismanagement of taxpayers' money, and other topics. His allegations of violation of the Kansas Open Meetings Act were vindicated in a consent decree signed by the Board's members. Umbehr also ran unsuccessfully for election to the Board.

The Board's members allegedly took Umbehr's criticism badly, threatening the official county newspaper with censorship for publishing his writings. In 1990, they voted, 2 to 1, to terminate (or prevent the automatic renewal of) Umbehr's contract with the County. That attempt at termination failed because of a technical defect, but in 1991, the Board succeeded in terminating Umbehr's contract, again by a 2 to 1 vote. Umbehr subsequently negotiated new contracts with five of the six cities that he had previously served.

In 1992, Umbehr brought this suit against the two majority Board members in their individual and official capacities under 42 U.S.C. § 1983, alleging that they had terminated his government contract in retaliation for his criticism of the County and the Board. The Board members moved for summary judgment. The District Court . . . held that . . . as an independent contractor, Umbehr was not entitled to the First Amendment protection afforded to public employees. *Umbehr v. McClure,* 840 F.Supp. 837, 839 (D.Kan. 1993).

The United States Court of Appeals for the Tenth Circuit reversed, holding that "an independent contractor is protected under the First Amendment from retaliatory governmental action, just as an employee would be."

We agree with the Tenth Circuit that independent contractors are protected, and that the Pickering balancing test, adjusted to weigh the government's interests as contractor rather than as employer, determines the extent of their protection. We therefore affirm.

II

A

[1] This Court has not previously considered whether and to what extent the First Amendment restricts the freedom of federal, state, or local governments to terminate their relationships with independent contractors because of the contractors' speech. We have, however, considered the same issue in the context of government employees' rights on several occasions. The similarities between government employees and government contractors with respect to this issue are obvious. The government needs to be free to terminate both employees and contractors for poor performance, to improve the efficiency, efficacy and responsiveness of ser-

vice to the public, and to prevent the appearance of corruption. And, absent contractual, statutory or constitutional restriction, the government is entitled to terminate them for no reason at all. But either type of relationship provides a valuable financial benefit, the threat of the loss of which in retaliation for speech may chill speech on matters of public concern by those who, because of their dealings with the government, "are often in the best position to know what ails the agencies for which they work," *Waters v. Churchill,* 114 S.Ct. 1878. Because of these similarities, we turn initially to our government employment precedents for guidance.

[2] Those precedents have long since rejected Justice Holmes' famous dictum, that a policeman "may have a constitutional right to talk politics, but he has no constitutional right to be a policeman," *McAuliffe v. Mayor of New Bedford,* 29 N.E. 517 (1892). Recognizing that "constitutional violations may arise from the deterrent, or 'chilling,' effect of governmental [efforts] that fall short of a direct prohibition against the exercise of First Amendment rights," *Laird v. Tatum,* 408 U.S. 1 (1972), our modern "unconstitutional conditions" doctrine holds that the government "may not deny a benefit to a person on a basis that infringes his constitutionally protected . . . freedom of speech" even if he has no entitlement to that benefit, *Perry v. Sindermann,* 408 U.S. 593 (1972). We have held that government workers are constitutionally protected from dismissal for refusing to take an oath regarding their political affiliation, *Wieman v. Updegraff,* 344 U.S. 183 (1952); *Keyishian v. Board of Regents of Univ. of State of N.Y.,* 385 U.S. 589 (1967), for publicly or privately criticizing their employer's policies, see *Perry,* supra; for expressing hostility to prominent political figures, see *Rankin v. McPherson,* 483 U.S. 378 (1987), or, except where political affiliation may reasonably be considered an appropriate job qualification, for supporting or affiliating with a particular political party, see, *Branti v. Finkel,* 445 U.S. 507 (1980). See also *United States v. Treasury Employees,* 115 S.Ct. 1310 (1995) (government employees are protected from undue burdens on their expressive activities created by a prohibition against accepting honoraria); *Abood v. Detroit Bd. of Ed.,* 431 U.S. 209 (1977) (government employment cannot be conditioned on making or not making financial contributions to particular political causes).

While protecting First Amendment freedoms, we have, however, acknowledged that the First

Amendment does not create property or tenure rights, and does not guarantee absolute freedom of speech. The First Amendment's guarantee of freedom of speech protects government employees from termination because of their speech on matters of public concern. See *Connick v. Myers,* 461 U.S. 138 (1983) (speech on merely private employment matters is unprotected). To prevail, an employee must prove that the conduct at issue was constitutionally protected, and that it was a substantial or motivating factor in the termination. If the employee discharges that burden, the government can escape liability by showing that it would have taken the same action even in the absence of the protected conduct. See *Mt. Healthy,* supra. And even termination because of protected speech may be justified when legitimate countervailing government interests are sufficiently strong. Government employees' First Amendment rights depend on the "balance between the interests of the [employee], as a citizen, in commenting upon matters of public concern and the interest of the State, as an employer, in promoting the efficiency of the public services it performs through its employees." *Pickering,* 391 U.S., at 568. In striking that balance, we have concluded that "[t]he government's interest in achieving its goals as effectively and efficiently as possible is elevated from a relatively subordinate interest when it acts as sovereign to a significant one when it acts as employer." *Waters,* 114 S.Ct., at 1888 (plurality opinion). We have, therefore, "consistently given greater deference to government predictions of harm used to justify restriction of employee speech than to predictions of harm used to justify restrictions on the speech of the public at large." Id., at 114 S.Ct., at 1887 . . .;

Both parties observe that independent contractors in general, and Umbehr in particular, work at a greater remove from government officials than do most government employees. In the Board's view, the key feature of an independent contractor's contract is that it does not give the government the right to supervise and control the details of how work is done. The Board argues that the lack of day-to-day control accentuates the government's need to have the work done by someone it trusts, and to resort to the sanction of termination for unsatisfactory performance. Umbehr, on the other hand, argues that the government interests in maintaining harmonious working environments and relationships recognized in our government employee cases are attenuated where the contractor does not work at

the government's workplace and does not interact daily with government officers and employees. He also points out that to the extent that he is publicly perceived as an independent contractor, any government concern that his political statements will be confused with the government's political positions is mitigated. The Board and the dissent, retort that the cost of fending off litigation, and the potential for government contracting practices to ossify into prophylactic rules to avoid potential litigation and liability, outweigh the interests of independent contractors, who are typically less financially dependent on their government contracts than are government employees.

Each of these arguments for and against the imposition of liability has some force. But all of them can be accommodated by applying our existing framework for government employee cases to independent contractors. *Mt. Healthy* assures the government's ability to terminate contracts so long as it does not do so in retaliation for protected First Amendment activity. *Pickering* requires a fact-sensitive and deferential weighing of the government's legitimate interests. The dangers of burdensome litigation and the de facto imposition of rigid contracting rules necessitate attentive application of the *Mt. Healthy* requirement of proof of causation and substantial deference, as mandated by *Pickering, Connick* and *Waters,* to the government's reasonable view of its legitimate interests, but not a per se denial of liability. Nor can the Board's and the dissent's generalization that independent contractors may be less dependent on the government than government employees, justify denial of all First Amendment protection to contractors. The tests that we have established in our government employment cases must be judicially administered with sensitivity to governmental needs, but First Amendment rights must not be neglected. . . .

We therefore see no reason to believe that proper application of the *Pickering* balancing test cannot accommodate the differences between employees and independent contractors.

In sum, neither the Board nor Umbehr have persuaded us that there is a "difference of constitutional magnitude," 414 U.S., at 83, between independent contractors and employees in this context. Independent government contractors are similar in most relevant respects to government employees, although both the speaker's and the government's interests are typically—though not always—somewhat less strong in the independent contractor case.

We therefore conclude that the same form of balancing analysis should apply to each. . . .

III

Finally, we emphasize the limited nature of our decision today. Because Umbehr's suit concerns the termination of a pre-existing commercial relationship with the government, we need not address the possibility of suits by bidders or applicants for new government contracts who cannot rely on such a relationship.

Subject to these limitations and caveats, however, we recognize the right of independent government contractors not to be terminated for exercising their First Amendment rights. The judgment of the Court of Appeals is, therefore, affirmed, and the case is remanded for proceedings consistent with this opinion.

It is so ordered.

NATIONAL TREASURY EMPLOYEES UNION V. VON RAAB
489 U.S. 656 (1989)

Justice Kennedy delivered the opinion of the Court, joined by Chief Justice Rehnquist and Justices White, Blackmun, and O'Connor. Justice Marshall filed a dissent, joined by Justice Brennan, and Justice Scalia dissented with Justice Stevens.

We granted certiorari to decide whether it violates the Fourth Amendment for the United States Customs Service to require a urinalysis test from employees who seek transfer or promotion to certain positions.

I

A

The United States Customs Service, a bureau of the Department of the Treasury, is the federal agency responsible for processing persons, carriers, cargo, and mail into the United States, collecting revenue from imports, and enforcing customs and related laws. An important responsibility of the Service is the interdiction and seizure of contraband, including illegal drugs. Ibid. In 1987 alone, Customs agents seized drugs with a retail value of nearly $9 billion. In the routine discharge of their duties, many Customs employees have direct contact with those who traffic in drugs for profit. Drug import operations, often directed by sophisticated criminal syndicates, may be effected by violence or its threat. As a necessary response, many Customs operatives carry and use firearms in connection with their official duties.

In December 1985, respondent, the Commissioner of Customs, established a Drug Screening Task Force to explore the possibility of implementing a drug-screening program within the Service. After extensive research and consultation with experts in the field, the task force concluded "that drug screening through urinalysis is technologically reliable, valid and accurate." Citing this conclusion, the Commissioner announced his intention to require drug tests of employees who applied for, or occupied, certain positions within the Service. The Commissioner stated his belief that "Customs is largely drug-free," but noted also that "unfortunately no segment of society is immune from the threat of illegal drug use." Drug interdiction has become the agency's primary enforcement mission, and the Commissioner stressed that "there is no room in the Customs Service for those who break the laws prohibiting the possession and use of illegal drugs." In May 1986, the Commissioner announced implementation of the drug-testing program. Drug tests were made a condition of placement or employment for positions that meet one or more of three criteria. The first is direct involvement in drug interdiction or enforcement of related laws, an activity the Commissioner deemed fraught with obvious dangers to the mission of the agency and the lives of customs agents. The second criterion is a requirement that the incumbent carry firearms, as the Commissioner concluded that "[p]ublic safety demands that employees who carry deadly arms and are prepared to make instant life or death decisions be drug free."

The third criterion is a requirement for the incumbent to handle "classified" material, which the Commissioner determined might fall into the hands of smugglers if accessible to employees who, by reason of their own illegal drug use, are susceptible to bribery or blackmail. After an employee qualifies for a position covered by the Customs testing program, the Service advises him by letter that his final selection is contingent upon successful completion of drug screening. An independent contractor contacts the employee to fix the time and place for collecting the sample. On reporting for the test, the employee must produce photographic identification and remove any outer garments, such as a coat or a jacket, and personal belongings. The employee may produce the sample behind a partition, or in the privacy of a bathroom stall if he so chooses. To ensure against adulteration of the specimen, or substitution of a sample from another person, a monitor of the same sex as the employee remains close at hand to listen for the normal sounds of urination. Dye is added to the toilet water to prevent the employee from using the water to adulterate the sample.

Upon receiving the specimen, the monitor inspects it to ensure its proper temperature and color, places a tamper-proof custody seal over the container, and affixes an identification label indicating the date and the individual's specimen number. The employee signs a chain-of-custody form, which is initialed by the monitor, and the urine sample is placed in a plastic bag, sealed, and submitted to a laboratory. . . .

Customs employees who test positive for drugs and who can offer no satisfactory explanation are subject to dismissal from the Service. Test results may not, however, be turned over to any other agency, including criminal prosecutors, without the employee's written consent.

B

Petitioners, a union of federal employees and a union official, commenced this suit in the United States District Court for the Eastern District of Louisiana on behalf of current Customs Service employees who seek covered positions. Petitioners alleged that the Custom Service drug-testing program violated, inter alia, the Fourth Amendment. The District Court agreed. 649 F.Supp. 380 (1986). The court acknowledged "the legitimate governmental interest in a drug-free work place and work force," but concluded that "the drug testing plan constitutes an overly intrusive policy of searches and seizures without probable cause or reasonable

suspicion, in violation of legitimate expectations of privacy." The court enjoined the drug-testing program, and ordered the Customs Service not to require drug tests of any applicants for covered positions.

A divided panel of the United States Court of Appeals for the Fifth Circuit vacated the injunction. 816 F.2d 170 (1987). We now affirm so much of the judgment of the Court of Appeals as upheld the testing of employees directly involved in drug interdiction or required to carry firearms. We vacate the judgment to the extent it upheld the testing of applicants for positions requiring the incumbent to handle classified materials, and remand for further proceedings.

It is clear that the Customs Service's drug-testing program is not designed to serve the ordinary needs of law enforcement. Test results may not be used in a criminal prosecution of the employee without the employee's consent. The purposes of the program are to deter drug use among those eligible for promotion to sensitive positions within the Service and to prevent the promotion of drug users to those positions. These substantial interests, no less than the Government's concern for safe rail transportation at issue in *Railway Labor Executives,* present a special need that may justify departure from the ordinary warrant and probable-cause requirements.

Furthermore, a warrant would provide little or nothing in the way of additional protection of personal privacy. A warrant serves primarily to advise the citizen that an intrusion is authorized by law and limited in its permissible scope and to interpose a neutral magistrate between the citizen and the law enforcement officer "engaged in the often competitive enterprise of ferreting out crime." But in the present context, "the circumstances justifying toxicological testing and the permissible limits of such intrusions are defined narrowly and specifically . . . , and doubtless are well known to covered employees." Under the Customs program, every employee who seeks a transfer to a covered position knows that he must take a drug test, and is likewise aware of the procedures the Service must follow in administering the test. A covered employee is simply not subject "to the discretion of the official in the field." The process becomes automatic when the employee elects to apply for, and thereafter pursue, a covered position. Because the Service does not make a discretionary determination to search based on a judgment that certain conditions are present, there are simply "no special facts for a neutral magistrate to evaluate."

C

We think the Government's need to conduct the suspicionless searches required by the Customs program outweighs the privacy interests of employees engaged directly in drug interdiction, and of those who otherwise are required to carry firearms.

Employees of the United States Mint, for example, should expect to be subject to certain routine personal searches when they leave the workplace every day. Similarly, those who join our military or intelligence services may not only be required to give what in other contexts might be viewed as extraordinary assurances of trustworthiness and probity, but also may expect intrusive inquiries into their physical fitness for those special positions.

We think Customs employees who are directly involved in the interdiction of illegal drugs or who are required to carry firearms in the line of duty likewise have a diminished expectation of privacy in respect to the intrusions occasioned by a urine test. Unlike most private citizens or government employees in general, employees involved in drug interdiction reasonably should expect effective inquiry into their fitness and probity. Much the same is true of employees who are required to carry firearms. Because successful performance of their duties depends uniquely on their judgment and dexterity, these employees cannot reasonably expect to keep from the Service personal information that bears directly on their fitness. While reasonable tests designed to elicit this information doubtless infringe some privacy expectations, we do not believe these expectations outweigh the Government's compelling interests in safety and in the integrity of our borders. . . .

III

Where the Government requires its employees to produce urine samples to be analyzed for evidence of illegal drug use, the collection and subsequent chemical analysis of such samples are searches that must meet the reasonableness requirement of the Fourth Amendment. Because the testing program adopted by the Customs Service is not designed to serve the ordinary needs of law enforcement, we have balanced the public interest in the Service's testing program against the privacy concerns implicated by the tests, without reference to our usual presumption in favor of the procedures specified in the Warrant Clause, to assess whether the tests required by Customs are reasonable.

We hold that the suspicionless testing of employees who apply for promotion to positions directly involving the interdiction of illegal drugs, or to positions that require the incumbent to carry a firearm, is reasonable. The Government's compelling interests in preventing the promotion of drug users to positions where they might endanger the integrity of our Nation's borders or the life of the citizenry outweigh the privacy interests of those who seek promotion to these positions, who enjoy a diminished expectation of privacy by virtue of the special, and obvious, physical and ethical demands of those positions. We do not decide whether testing those who apply for promotion to positions where they would handle "classified" information is reasonable because we find the record inadequate for this purpose.

The judgment of the Court of Appeals for the Fifth Circuit is affirmed in part and vacated in part, and the case is remanded for further proceedings consistent with this opinion.

It is so ordered.

Justice Scalia, dissenting.

Justice Stevens joined with Justice Scalia in dissenting.

The issue in this case is not whether Customs Service employees can constitutionally be denied promotion, or even dismissed, for a single instance of unlawful drug use, at home or at work. They assuredly can. The issue here is what steps can constitutionally be taken to detect such drug use. The Government asserts it can demand that employees perform "an excretory function traditionally shielded by great privacy," *Skinner v. Railway Labor Executives' Assn.,* 489 U.S., at 626, while "a monitor of the same sex . . . remains close at hand to listen for the normal sounds," and that the excretion thus produced be turned over to the Government for chemical analysis. The Court agrees that this constitutes a search for purposes of the Fourth Amendment—and I think it obvious that it is a type of search particularly destructive of privacy and offensive to personal dignity. Until today this Court had upheld a bodily search separate from arrest and without individualized suspicion of wrongdoing only with respect to prison inmates, relying upon the uniquely dangerous nature of that environment. See *Bell v. Wolfish,* 441 U.S. 520, 558-560 (1979). Today, in *Skinner,* we allow a less intrusive bodily search of railroad employees involved in train accidents. I joined the Court's opinion there because the demonstrated frequency of drug and alcohol use by the targeted class of employees, and the demonstrated connection between such use and grave harm, rendered the search a reasonable means of protecting society. I decline to join the Court's opinion in the present case because neither frequency of use nor connection to harm is demonstrated or even likely. In my view the Customs Service rules are a kind of immolation of privacy and human dignity in symbolic opposition to drug use.

The Fourth Amendment protects the "right of the people to be secure in their persons, houses, papers, and effects, against unreasonable searches and seizures." While there are some absolutes in Fourth Amendment law, as soon as those have been left behind and the question comes down to whether a particular search has been "reasonable," the answer depends largely upon the social necessity that prompts the search. What is absent in the Government's justifications—notably absent, revealingly absent, and as far as I am concerned dispositively absent—is the recitation of even a single instance in which any of the speculated horribles actually occurred: an instance, that is, in which the cause of bribe-taking, or of poor aim, or of unsympathetic law enforcement, or of compromise of classified information, was drug use. Although the Court points out that several employees have in the past been removed from the Service for accepting bribes and other integrity violations, and that at least nine officers have died in the line of duty since 1974, there is no indication whatever that these incidents were related to drug use by Service employees. Perhaps concrete evidence of the severity of a problem is unnecessary when it is so well known that courts can almost take judicial notice of it; but that is surely not the case here. The Commissioner of Customs himself has stated that he "believe[s] that Customs is largely drug-free," that "[t]he extent of illegal drug use by Customs employees was not the reason for establishing this program," and that he "hope[s] and expect[s] to receive reports of very few positive findings through drug screening." The test results have fulfilled those hopes and expectations. According to the Service's counsel, out of 3,600 employees tested, no more than 5 tested positive for drugs.

The Court's response to this lack of evidence is that "[t]here is little reason to believe that American workplaces are immune from [the] pervasive social problem" of drug abuse. Perhaps such a generalization would suffice if the workplace at issue could produce such catastrophic social harm that no risk whatever is tolerable—the secured areas of a nuclear power plant, for example, see *Rushton v. Nebraska Public Power District,* 844 F.2d 562 (CA8 1988). But if such a generalization suffices to justify demeaning bodily searches, without particularized suspicion, to guard against the bribing or blackmailing of a law enforcement agent, or the careless use of a firearm, then the Fourth Amendment has become frail protection indeed. In *Skinner, Bell, T.L.O.,* and *Martinez-Fuerte,* we took pains to establish the existence of special need for the search or seizure—a need based not upon the existence of a "pervasive social problem" combined with speculation as to the effect of that problem in the field at issue, but rather upon well known or well demonstrated evils in that field, with well known or well demonstrated consequences.

There is irony in the Government's citation, in support of its position, of Justice Brandeis' statement in *Olmstead v. United States,* 277 U.S. 438, 485 (1928) that "[f]or good or for ill, [our Government] teaches the whole people by its example." Brandeis was there dissenting from the Court's admission of evidence obtained through an unlawful Government wiretap. He was not praising the Government's example of vigor and enthusiasm in combatting crime, but condemning its example that "the end justifies the means," 277 U.S., at 485. An even more apt quotation from that famous Brandeis dissent would have been the following: "[I]t is . . . immaterial that the intrusion was in aid of law enforcement. Experience should teach us to be most on our guard to protect liberty when the Government's purposes are beneficent. Men born to freedom are naturally alert to repel invasion of their liberty by evil-minded rulers. The greatest dangers to liberty lurk in insidious encroachment by men of zeal, well-meaning but without understanding." Those who lose because of the lack of understanding that begot the present exercise in symbolism are not just the Customs Service employees, whose dignity is thus offended, but all of us—who suffer a coarsening of our national manners that ultimately give the Fourth Amendment its content, and who become subject to the administration of federal officials whose respect for our privacy can hardly be greater than the small respect they have been taught to have for their own.

NOTES

1. Because it takes, say, five years to get tenure, employment consists of five one-year contracts until the tenure decision.

2. 434 F.Supp. 1273 (D. Del. 1977).

3. 469 F.2d 829 (5th Cir. 1972).

4. 439 U.S. 410 (1979).

5. 548 F.2d 857 (9th Cir. 1977).

6. 473 F.2d 988 (2d Cir. 1973).

7. Steven Cann, "A Virus in the Ivory Tower," *Educational Considerations* 18 (1991): 43.

8. Ibid., 44.

9. For an early interpretation that the Court has continued to sustain, see *Lindsley v. Natural Carbonic Gas Company,* 220 U.S. 61, 78 (1911).

10. *Railway Express Agency v. New York,* 336 U.S. 106 (1949).

11. *Williamson v. Lee Optical Company,* 348 U.S. 483 (1955).

12. *New Orleans v. Dukes,* 427 U.S. 297 (1976).

13. *Reed v. Reed,* 404 U.S. 71 (1971).

14. *Frantinero v. Richardson,* 411 U.S. 677 (1973).

15. *Kahn v. Shevin,* 416 U.S. 351 (1974).

16. *Craig v. Borne,* 429 U.S. 190 (1976).

17. *Massachusetts Board of Retirement v. Murgia,* 427 U.S. 307 (1976).

18. *Ambach v. Norwick,* 441 U.S. 68 (1979).

19. *Bernal v. Fainter,* 467 U.S. 216 (1984).

20. *Fullilove v. Klutznick,* 448 U.S. 448 (1980).

21. 466 U.S. 429 (1984).

22. *Washington v. Davis,* 426 U.S. 229 (1976).

23. 347 U.S. 483 (1954).

24. *Brown v. Board of Education* has been in litigation almost constantly since 1954. The Supreme Court, in a 1955 implementation decision, said desegregation had to be implemented "with all deliberate speed" (*Brown II,* 349 U.S. 294 [1955]). There was a *Brown III* in the 1970s (892 F.2d 851 [1979]), and recently the situation is being relitigated (*Brown IV,* 892 F.2d 851 [10th Cir. 1989]). In *Brown IV,* the district court found no purposeful discrimination, but the circuit court did. The Supreme Court sent the case back to the circuit court, *Brown v. Board of Education,* 112 S.Ct. 1657 (1992), in the light of its recent decision in *Board of Education of Oklahoma City Public Schools v. Dowell,* 111 S.Ct. 630 (1991). On October 28, 1992, the Tenth Circuit Court of Appeals, after reconsidering *Brown IV,* once again found the requisite purposeful discrimination. The Topeka School Board decided not to litigate further and adopted a magnet school plan for the primary schools. There are still racially identifiable high schools in Topeka. The case is still titled *Brown v. Board of Education* because Linda Brown, a child plaintiff in the original case, now has two children who are plaintiffs.

25. *Shaw v. Reno,* 509 U.S. 630 (1993); *Miller v. Johnson,* 115 S.Ct. 2475 (1995).

26. *United Steelworkers of America v. Weber,* 443 U.S. 193 (1979).

27. *Local 28 Sheet Metal Workers Union v. Equal Employment Opportunity Commission,* 478 U.S. 421 (1986).

28. *United Steelworkers v. Weber,* 443 U.S. 193 (1979).

29. *Griggs v. Duke Power Company,* 401 U.S. 424 (1971).

30. *Wards Cove Packing v. Atonio,* 490 U.S. 642 (1989).

31. Adam Clymer, "White House and Senate Republicans Reach Agreement on Civil Rights Bill," *The New York Times,* 25 October 1991, A10, national edition; Adam Clymer, "Senate Approves Rights Bill, Ending Bitter Job-Bias Rift," *The New York Times,* 31 October 1991, A10, national edition; Adam Clymer, "Civil Rights Bill Is Passed by House," *The New York Times,* 18 November 1991, A10, national edition.

32. *Meritor Savings Bank v. Vinson,* 477 U.S. 57 (1986).

33. *Harris v. Forklift Systems, Inc.,* 113 S.Ct. 367 (1993).

CHAPTER 9

DUE PROCESS OF LAW
IN OTHER CONTEXTS

CASE IN POINT:
MATHEWS V. ELDRIDGE
424 U.S. 319 (1976)[1]

The Tammany Hall machine had a somewhat notorious ward boss named George Washington Plunkett. In response to reporters' questions about Plunkett's enriching himself through Tammany Hall graft and corruption, Plunkett would simply reply, "I seen my opportunities and I took 'em."

In the case of *Mathews v. Eldridge,* the Supreme Court "seen its opportunity" and took it. The four Nixon appointees (Burger, Blackmun, Powell, and Rehnquist) coalesced with Justices White and Stewart to restrict what had become known as the "due process revolution."

The due process revolution started with the landmark case *Goldberg v. Kelly.*[2] In that case, New York welfare officials sent a termination of benefits notice to a recipient of Aid to Families With Dependent Children (AFDC). The procedure required the notice and allowed for an internal paper review; if the beneficiary lost at that stage, then benefits would cease, but a posttermination adjudicatory hearing was possible. The issue in *Goldberg* was whether the due process clause of the Fourteenth Amendment requires a pretermination hearing under these circumstances (prior to termination of benefits). The Court answered in the affirmative.

Despite the specific language of the due process clause, in several situations government can take property without a due process hearing first. Those situations include the summary seizure of mislabeled vitamins,[3] the seizure of food inventory suspected of being spoiled,[4] the freezing of rents during and after World War II,[5] the destruction of an imported ornamental tree,[6] the disqualification of a contractor doing business with the federal government,[7] and employment as a cook for a concession in a defense contractor's plant.[8] Most of these summary takings of property are justified as threats to the public health or safety or are emergency situations, and the Court has said that a postdeprivation hearing or a "just compensation" lawsuit satisfies the due process clause.

After the *Goldberg* decision in 1970, however, the Court decided a series of cases, all of which required a predeprivation hearing and constituted the due process revolution. Those cases involved the revocation of parole,[9] probation,[10] good time credit for inmates,[11] suspension of a driver's license,[12] and suspension from high school.[13] The Court also required a due process hearing before the state of Wisconsin could publicly post the names of people deemed unfit to consume alcohol[14] and before a state could evict persons from a public housing project.[15] Hearings were required before the state could play a role in the repossession of property[16] or the garnishment of wages,[17] and the Court said that a state violated the due process clause if it disallowed a student to establish residency for tuition purposes while attending college (this created the unconstitutional, irrebuttable presumption that once a noncitizen, always a noncitizen).[18]

Against this background of expanding due process protections for citizens against potentially adverse governmental action, *Mathews v. Eldridge* was decided.

George Eldridge dropped out of school in the fifth grade and went to work as a laborer for a railroad until he was drafted into the military.[19] While in the military, he was involved in an accident in a military Jeep. After his military discharge, Eldridge went back to work for the railroad. By this time (early 1950s), George had been diagnosed with spinal arthritis, but lacking enough education to find less strenuous work and with the financial pressures of providing for his family, Eldridge saw no choice but to keep working hard.[20] Eventually, he did quit the railroad and took a job as a deliveryman for Royal

Crown Cola. He worked for R.C. for about eight years, until one day when he got down from his truck and was unable to move his legs.[21] He was hospitalized for more than a month and eventually developed diabetes as well.[22] Eldridge applied for disability benefits in 1967. His application was originally denied, a decision that was upheld in the internal paper reconsideration process (see Chapter 6). Eldridge asked for and received a hearing before an administrative law judge (ALJ), whose decision reversed the denial of benefits, and in June 1968, Eldridge was placed on disability benefits.[23] Approximately one year later, George received a notice from the disability office, asking him to submit evidence that he was still disabled. This he did.[24] In early 1970, he was notified that he was no longer disabled and that his benefits would cease in February. By this time, George owed a mortgage on a house, had six children, and his wife had developed cancer.[25] George immediately started the reconsideration and appeals process, but he knew from his first experience with the agency that it would take at least a year to get to the ALJ. From his perspective, he had proved that he was totally disabled; he knew he could not work and that nothing had changed. He thought he should have a right to make his case to someone before the government shut off his income, so while continuing the appeals process, he went to see a lawyer.[26] Eldridge's lawyer filed suit in federal district court, arguing that disability beneficiaries have a constitutional right to a due process hearing prior to the termination of benefits.

In June 1970, the trial judge ordered the Social Security Administration (SSA) to continue benefits to Eldridge until the case was decided.[27] From February to June 1970, the Eldridge family survived on George's $136-a-month disability check from the Veterans Administration (VA).[28] Mrs. Eldridge died of cancer in June of that year.[29] As the lawsuit moved through the courts, so the appeals process moved through the SSA. In March 1971, George finally got his second hearing before an ALJ, albeit a different one from the 1968 hearing, who also declared George to be totally disabled, ordered the benefits to continue, and ordered back pay.[30] As a result of this decision, the district court judge declared George's case to be moot and dismissed the suit.

In May 1972, George received another letter from the SSA, asking him to submit proof of his continuing disability.[31] Once again, George filled out the papers, included the names of treating physicians, and sent along a rather calm letter, given the circumstances. In his letter, George reminded the SSA that he had documented his total disability twice in the past four years and that nothing had changed in that regard.[32] He also clarified that the ailment he suffered from was arthritis of the spine, rather than the "strained back" the SSA had claimed, and he admonished them to check their own records on that score.[33]

Nevertheless, in June 1972, the SSA informed George that his benefits were to be terminated because he was no longer disabled. This time, rather than go through the internal review process, Eldridge just went to court.[34] The issue was the same as it had been in the first suit: whether the Constitution required an oral hearing before disability benefits could be terminated.

In April 1973, the district court judge entered a decision in Eldridge's favor, based on the Supreme Court's decision in *Goldberg* and its progeny.[35] The SSA appealed to the Fourth Circuit Court of Appeals, which, in April 1974, upheld the district court decision in favor of Eldridge.[36] The SSA appealed to the U.S. Supreme Court, which handed down a decision in spring 1976.

Justice Powell's decision applied a balancing test that involved three con siderations: The first consideration is the need to analyze the private interest involved. In this case, the private interest was George's property interest in continued disability benefits. According to Powell, although this indeed involved a property interest under the due process clause, it was not the same kind of property interest that was involved in *Goldberg*. *Goldberg* involved benefits that a recipient had to show poverty to receive. Almost by definition, the termination of those benefits would leave one destitute. Because disability benefits do not depend on income or need, it does not necessarily follow that the termination of disability benefits would leave one without a means of support.

The second consideration is what Powell termed "the risk of an erroneous decision." Here, the Court reasoned that the risk of error was high in AFDC termination cases but was very low in disability termination cases. That is because of the nature of the evidence. Evidence that an AFDC beneficiary may no longer be eligible might be based on hearsay and is very subjective, whereas evidence of a disability is scientific and not likely to produce erroneous decisions.

The third consideration is the balance between all of the preceding and the government's (people's?) interest. Here, things to take into account include administrative efficiency and the cost to the taxpayers of requiring a pretermination hearing, given the benefits of such a hearing.

Weighing all these factors in Eldridge's case, the Court concluded that (a) the property interest of disability claimants, as a class, was not as acute as the property interest of AFDC beneficiaries; (b) the risk of making an erroneous decision in disability termination cases was minimal and would not be reduced by adding more procedural requirements; and (c) the government's interests were substantial enough that a posttermination hearing in disability cases would satisfy the due process requirements.

With the announcement of the Court's decision in George's case, he initiated the internal appeals process again to see whether he could get his benefits restored. His case was reconsidered within the agency a year and a half after he requested it, and that decision, again, upheld his termination.[37] In March 1978, two years after the Court's decision, George received his third hearing before an ALJ. The ALJ again declared George to be totally disabled and ordered restoration of benefits with back pay.[38] During his fight with the SSA over his disability, the mortgage holder foreclosed on Eldridge's home. He and his six children moved into a trailer, but the furniture was repossessed, so they all had to sleep in one bed.[39]

Questions

1. Given that the rate of reversals in disability termination cases at the ALJ stage was 50 percent, how do you suppose the Court could argue that the risk of an erroneous decision was unlikely?

2. In your opinion, is this case an example of judicial activism or a case of judicial self-restraint? Why?

3. At the time, Solicitor General Robert Bork told the Court in his brief that if Eldridge won and the government had to continue to pay benefits to those terminated until after they had a hearing, it would cost the taxpayers an additional $25 million annually to comply. Assuming that Bork's figures are correct and given the suffering of George Eldridge (and hundreds like him), is it cost-efficient to provide the pretermination hearing? Why or why not?

DUE PROCESS AND
YOUR POTENTIAL FUTURE

If you are reading this book, you are probably in a political science, public administration, or prelaw class of some kind. Given that the average liberal arts college graduate changes careers (not just jobs) three times, even if you are not thinking about public service right now, you may end up at some point working for the government. You will discover in the next chapter that, as a government employee, you may be sued as a consequence of decisions you make. One constitutional test involving whether a government employee has incurred liability is whether the employee knew or should have known that his or her actions would violate the constitutional rights of another. This test presumes that the employee knows and understands the Constitution and constitutional rights.

The constitutional right most frequently involved in such suits is the due process clause. That is why this book spends two chapters on it. It would be nice to be able to assure you that, after mastery of a few principles, you will understand due process, but the concept is too slippery for that. Actually, it is not that the concept itself is so difficult but that changes of personnel on the Supreme Court have led to inconsistent decisions and confusing opinions. With the presidency of Bill Clinton and his subsequent judicial appointments, due process is certain to change again.

Due process analysis is fairly straightforward. First, it requires governmental action. Second, it comes into play only after the finding that a liberty interest or property interest is affected. The third and final part of the analysis is, How much process is due?

STATE ACTION

Generally, it is easy to tell whether government or a private entity is taking the action. Recently, however, several cases have turned on just that issue. Is the local power company "private," given that it would not exist but for a government-granted monopoly?[40] Are heavily regulated industries, such as establishments that sell liquor, "private," given the necessity of a liquor license?[41] Is a nursing home a private business, given that it would not be in business but for state subsidies?[42] Are entities like the U.S. Olympic Committee and the National Collegiate Athletic Association (NCAA) private?[43] Although these cases are about equal protection rather than due process, the concept is the same because both clauses are under the Fourteenth Amendment, which states, "No state shall deny equal protection." The Court found each of the preceding entities to be private and beyond the reach of the Fourteenth Amendment, but because the Court seems to deal with the issue on a case-by-case basis, the question of state action is not resolved yet.

LIBERTY OR PROPERTY INTEREST

You are already familiar with the notion of liberty interest and property interest from the previous chapter. Novel questions of this nature are constantly presented to the Court. Three cases at the end of this chapter present questions about the interest involved. In *Collins v. City of Harker Heights,* a city sanitation worker died of asphyxiation after entering a manhole to unplug a sewer line. His widow sued the city, claiming that the city's failure to properly train its employees was a violation of due process. What is the interest claimed?

In *Walters v. National Association of Radiation Survivors,* several veterans and their survivors challenged the "ten-dollar rule." The ten-dollar rule is a statutory maximum fee of $10 that can be paid to an attorney or anyone else who represents a veteran before the VA who is seeking benefits for a service-connected death or disability. The ten-dollar limit is challenged as a violation of due process of law. What is the interest?

In *Pacific Mutual Life Insurance Company v. Haslip,* the plaintiff (Haslip) filed suit after she had paid into the city's group health insurance plan but ended up with a hospital bill because she was not covered. She was not covered because the insurance agent to whom the city paid the premiums absconded with the money, and the insurance company (Pacific Mutual) failed to properly advise the city and the insured workers that premiums had not been received. A jury awarded Haslip compensatory damages plus punitive damages of more than a million dollars. The insurance company appealed the award of punitive damages as a violation of due process of law. What is the interest claimed?

Although it is not a case presented in this book, when a city police department adopted a rule regulating the length of officers' hair, one officer challenged the rule as a violation of due process.[44] What is the interest? Even when the interest involved is recognizable, the Court's treatment of the interest varies from case to case. The Court's decisions in the following two cases parallel the decisions in *Goldberg* and *Eldridge.*

WISCONSIN V. CONSTANTINEAU
400 U.S. 433 (1971)

Justice Douglas delivered the opinion of the Court, joined by Justices Brennan, Stewart, White, and Marshall. Chief Justice Burger dissented, joined by Justices Blackmun and Black.

Appellee is an adult resident of Hartford, Wis. She brought suit in a federal district court in Wisconsin to have a Wisconsin statute declared unconstitutional. A three-judge court was convened. That court, by a divided vote, held the Act unconstitutional, 302 F.Supp. 861, and we noted probable jurisdiction. . . .

The Act, Wis.Stat. § 176.26 (1967), provides that designated persons may in writing forbid the sale or gift of intoxicating liquors to one who "by excessive drinking" produces described conditions or exhibits specified traits, such as exposing himself or family "to want" or becoming "dangerous to the peace" of the community. . . . The chief of police of Hartford, without notice or hearing to appellee, caused to be posted a notice in all retail liquor outlets in Hartford that sales or gifts of liquors to appellee were forbidden for one year. Thereupon this suit was brought against the chief of police claiming damages and asking for injunctive relief. The State of Wisconsin intervened as a defendant on the injunctive phase of the case and that was the only issue tried and decided, the three-judge court holding the Act unconstitutional on its face and enjoining its enforcement. The court said: "In 'posting' an individual, the particular city official or spouse is doing more than denying him the ability to purchase alcoholic beverages within the city limits. In essence, he is giving notice to the public that he has found the particular individual's behavior to fall within one of the categories enumerated in the statutes. It would be naive not to recognize that such 'posting' or characterization of an individual will expose him to public embarrassment and ridicule, and it is our opinion that procedural due process requires that before one acting pursuant to State statute can make such a quasi-judicial determination, the individual involved must be given notice of the intent to post and an opportunity to present his side of the matter."

We have no doubt as to the power of a State to deal with the evils described in the Act. The police power of the States over intoxicating liquors was extremely broad even prior to the Twenty-First Amendment. The only issue present here is whether the label or characterization given a person by "posting," though a mark of serious illness to some, is to others such a stigma or badge of disgrace that procedural due process requires notice and an opportunity to be heard. We agree with the District Court that the private interest is such that those requirements of procedural due process must be met.

It is significant that most of the provisions of the Bill of Rights are procedural, for it is procedure that marks much of the difference between rule by law and rule by fiat.

We reviewed in *Cafeteria and Restaurant Workers Union, Local 473, A.F.L.-C.I.O. v. McElroy,* 367 U.S. 886, the nature of the various "private interest(s)" that have fallen on one side or the other of the line. See also *Sniadach v. Family Finance Corp.,* 395 U.S. 337. Generalizations are hazardous as some state and federal administrative procedures are summary by reason of necessity or history. Yet certainly where the State attaches "a badge of infamy" to the citizen, due process comes into play. *Wieman v. Updegraff,* 344 U.S. 183. "[T]he right to be heard before being condemned to suffer grievous loss of any kind, even though it may not involve

the stigma and hardships of a criminal conviction, is a principle basic to our society." *Joint Anti-Fascist Refugee Committee v. McGrath,* 341 U.S. 123.

Where a person's good name, reputation, honor, or integrity is at stake because of what the government is doing to him, notice and an opportunity to be heard are essential. "Posting" under the Wisconsin Act may to some be merely the mark of illness, to others it is a stigma, an official branding of a person. The label is a degrading one. Under the Wisconsin Act, a resident of Hartford is given no process at all. This appellee was not afforded a chance to defend herself. She may have been the victim of an official's caprice. Only when the whole proceedings leading to the pinning of an unsavory label on a person are aired can oppressive results be prevented.

It is suggested that the three-judge court should have stayed its hand while the aggrieved person repaired to the state courts to obtain a construction of the Act or relief from it. The fact that Wisconsin does not raise the point does not, of course, mean that it lacks merit. Yet the suggestion is not in keeping with the precedents.

Congress could, of course, have routed all federal constitutional questions through the state court systems, saving to this Court the final say when it came to review of the state court judgments. But our First Congress resolved differently and created the federal court system and in time granted the federal courts various heads of jurisdiction, which today involve most federal constitutional rights. Once that jurisdiction was granted, the federal courts resolved those questions even when they were enmeshed with state law questions.

In the present case the Wisconsin Act does not contain any provision whatsoever for notice and hearing. There is no ambiguity in the state statute. There are no provisions which could fairly be taken to mean that notice and hearing might be given under some circumstances or under some construction but not under others. The Act on its face gives the chief of police the power to do what he did to the appellee. Hence the naked question, uncomplicated by an unresolved state law, is whether that Act on its face is unconstitutional. As we said in *Zwickler v. Koota,* 389 U.S. 241, abstention should not be ordered merely to await an attempt to vindicate the claim in a state court. Where there is no ambiguity in the state statute, the federal court should not abstain but should proceed to decide the federal constitutional claim. We would negate the history of the enlargement of the jurisdiction of the federal district courts, if we held the federal court

should stay its hand and not decide the question before the state courts decided it.

Affirmed.

PAUL V. DAVIS
424 U.S. 693 (1976)

Justice Rehnquist delivered the opinion of the Court, joined by Chief Justice Burger and Justices Stewart, Blackmun, Powell, and Stevens. Justices Brennan, Marshall, and White dissented.

We granted certiorari, in this case to consider whether respondent's charge that petitioners' defamation of him, standing alone and apart from any other governmental action with respect to him, stated a claim for relief under 42 U.S.C. § 1983 and the Fourteenth Amendment. For the reasons hereinafter stated, we conclude that it does not.

Petitioner Paul is the Chief of Police of the Louisville, Ky., Division of Police, while petitioner McDaniel occupies the same position in the Jefferson County, Ky., Division of Police. In late 1972 they agreed to combine their efforts for the purpose of alerting local area merchants to possible shoplifters who might be operating during the Christmas season. In early December petitioners distributed to approximately 800 merchants in the Louisville metropolitan area a "flyer," which began as follows: "TO: BUSINESS MEN IN THE METROPOLITAN AREA. The Chiefs of the Jefferson County and City of Louisville Police Departments, in an effort to keep their officers advised on shoplifting activity, have approved the attached alphabetically arranged flyer of subjects known to be active in this criminal field. This flyer is being distributed to you, the business man, so that you may inform your security personnel to watch for these subjects. These persons have been arrested during 1971 and 1972 or have been active in various criminal fields in high density shopping areas. Only the photograph and name of the subject is shown on this flyer. If additional information is desired, please forward a request in writing. . . ."

The flyer consisted of five pages of "mug shot" photos, arranged alphabetically. Each page was headed:

"NOVEMBER 1972
CITY OF LOUISVILLE

JEFFERSON COUNTY
POLICE DEPARTMENTS
ACTIVE SHOPLIFTERS"

In approximately the center of page 2 there appeared photos and the name of the respondent, Edward Charles Davis III.

Respondent appeared on the flyer because on June 14, 1971, he had been arrested in Louisville on a charge of shoplifting. He had been arraigned on this charge in September 1971, and, upon his plea of not guilty, the charge had been "filed away with leave (to reinstate)," a disposition which left the charge outstanding. Thus, at the time petitioners caused the flyer to be prepared and circulated respondent had been charged with shoplifting but his guilt or innocence of that offense had never been resolved. Shortly after circulation of the flyer the charge against respondent was finally dismissed by a judge of the Louisville Police Court.

At the time the flyer was circulated respondent was employed as a photographer by the *Louisville Courier-Journal* and *Times*. The flyer, and respondent's inclusion therein, soon came to the attention of respondent's supervisor, the executive director of photography for the two newspapers. This individual called respondent in to hear his version of the events leading to his appearing in the flyer. Following this discussion, the supervisor informed respondent that although he would not be fired, he "had best not find himself in a similar situation" in the future.

Respondent thereupon brought this § 1983 action in the District Court for the Western District of Kentucky, seeking redress for the alleged violation of rights guaranteed to him by the Constitution of the United States. Claiming jurisdiction under 28 U.S.C. § 1343(3), respondent sought damages as well as declaratory and injunctive relief. Petitioners moved to dismiss this complaint. The District Court granted this motion, ruling that "[t]he facts alleged in this case do not establish that plaintiff has been deprived of any right secured to him by the Constitution of the United States."

Respondent appealed to the Court of Appeals for the Sixth Circuit which recognized that, under our decisions, for respondent to establish a claim cognizable under § 1983 he had to show that petitioners had deprived him of a right secured by the Constitution of the United States, and that any such deprivation was achieved under color of law. *Adickes v. Kress & Co.*, 398 U.S. 144 (1970). The Court of Appeals concluded that respondent had set forth a § 1983 claim "in that he has alleged facts that constitute a denial of due process of law." 505 F.2d 1180 (1974). In its view our decision in *Wisconsin v. Constantineau*, 400 U.S. 433 (1971), mandated reversal of the District Court. . . .

I

Respondent's due process claim is grounded upon his assertion that the flyer, and in particular the phrase "Active Shoplifters" appearing at the head of the page upon which his name and photograph appear, impermissibly deprived him of some "liberty" protected by the Fourteenth Amendment. His complaint asserted that the "active shoplifter" designation would inhibit him from entering business establishments for fear of being suspected of shoplifting and possibly apprehended, and would seriously impair his future employment opportunities. Accepting that such consequences may flow from the flyer in question, respondent's complaint would appear to state a classical claim for defamation actionable in the courts of virtually every State. Imputing criminal behavior to an individual is generally considered defamatory per se, and actionable without proof of special damages.

Respondent brought his action, however, not in the state courts of Kentucky, but in a United States District Court for that State. He asserted not a claim for defamation under the laws of Kentucky, but a claim that he had been deprived of rights secured to him by the Fourteenth Amendment of the United States Constitution. Concededly if the same allegations had been made about respondent by a private individual, he would have nothing more than a claim for defamation under state law. But, he contends, since petitioners are respectively an official of city and of county government, his action is thereby transmuted into one for deprivation by the State of rights secured under the Fourteenth Amendment.

II

The result reached by the Court of Appeals, which respondent seeks to sustain here, must be bottomed on one of two premises. The first is that the Due Process Clause of the Fourteenth Amendment and § 1983 make actionable many wrongs inflicted by government employees which had heretofore been thought to give rise only to state-law tort claims. The second premise is that the infliction by state officials of a "stigma" to one's reputation is somehow different in kind from the infliction by the same official of harm or injury to other interests protected by state law, so that an injury to reputation is actionable under § 1983 and the Fourteenth Amendment even if other such harms are not. We examine each of these premises in turn.

B

The second premise upon which the result reached by the Court of Appeals could be rested that the infliction by state officials of a "stigma" to one's reputation is somehow different in kind from infliction by a state official of harm to other interests protected by state law is equally untenable. The words "liberty" and "property" as used in the Fourteenth Amendment do not in terms single out reputation as a candidate for special protection over and above other interests that may be protected by state law. While we have in a number of our prior cases pointed out the frequently drastic effect of the "stigma" which may result from defamation by the government in a variety of contexts, this line of cases does not establish the proposition that reputation alone, apart from some more tangible interests such as employment, is either "liberty" or "property" by itself sufficient to invoke the procedural protection of the Due Process Clause. As we have said, the Court of Appeals, in reaching a contrary conclusion, relied primarily upon *Wisconsin v. Constantineau*, 400 U.S. 433 (1971). We think the correct import of that decision, however, must be derived from an examination of the precedents upon which it relied, as well as consideration of the other decisions by this Court, before and after Constantineau, which bear upon the relationship between governmental defamation and the guarantees of the Constitution. While not uniform in their treatment of the subject, we think that the weight of our decisions establishes no constitutional doctrine converting every defamation by a public official into a deprivation of liberty within the meaning of the Due Process Clause of the Fifth or Fourteenth Amendment. . . .

III

[3] It is apparent from our decisions that there exists a variety of interests which are difficult of definition but are nevertheless comprehended within the meaning of either "liberty" or "property" as meant in the Due Process Clause. These interests attain this constitutional status by virtue of the fact that they have been initially recognized and protected by state law, and we have repeatedly ruled that the procedural guarantees of the Fourteenth Amendment apply whenever the State seeks to remove or significantly alter that protected status. In *Bell v. Burson,* 402 U.S. 535 (1971), for example, the State by issuing drivers' licenses recognized in its citizens a right to operate a vehicle on the highways of the State. The Court held that the State could not withdraw this right without giving petitioner due process. In *Morrissey v. Brewer,* 408 U.S. 471 (1972), the State afforded parolees the right to remain at liberty as long as the conditions of their parole were not violated. Before the State could alter the status of a parolee because of alleged violations of these conditions, we held that the Fourteenth Amendment's guarantee of due process of law required certain procedural safeguards. Kentucky law does not extend to respondent any legal guarantee of present enjoyment of reputation which has been altered as a result of petitioners' actions. Rather his interest in reputation is simply one of a number which the State may protect against injury by virtue of its tort law, providing a forum for vindication of those interests by means of damages actions. And any harm or injury to that interest, even where as here inflicted by an officer of the State, does not result in a deprivation of any "liberty" or "property" recognized by state or federal law, nor has it worked any change of respondent's status as theretofore recognized under the State's laws. For these reasons we hold that the interest in reputation asserted in this case is neither "liberty" nor "property" guaranteed against state deprivation without due process of law.

Respondent in this case cannot assert denial of any right vouchsafed to him by the State and thereby protected under the Fourteenth Amendment. That being the case, petitioners' defamatory publications, however seriously they may have harmed respondent's reputation, did not deprive him of any "liberty" or "property" interests protected by the Due Process Clause. The judgment of the Court of Appeals holding otherwise is Reversed.

Questions

1. What was the interest in *Constantineau*?
2. What was the interest in *Paul v. Davis*?
3. Can you explain why one's interest in a good name and reputation deserves more protection than when a good name and reputation have been slandered?

Suffice it to say that, generally, one can recognize a property or liberty interest and that public administrators need to exercise caution in decision making that affects those interests.

HOW MUCH PROCESS IS DUE?

Having established that a governmental entity or agent took action that affected the property or liberty interest of another, the final question is, What kind of procedure should be required? The short answer is that it depends on the nature of the affected interest.

Suppose the administration of your university accused you of taking part in a demonstration that resulted in the destruction of property and wanted to expel you. Is there a liberty or property interest? What is it? What kinds of procedures would the university have to provide? Suppose the university was going to suspend you for academic reasons. Would the situation be any different?

To a degree, the *Goldberg* and *Eldridge* cases you are already somewhat familiar with represent the extremes in the notion of how elaborate a hearing must be (and at what point it is required). The *Goldberg* case, which follows, requires what have been labeled the "ten *Goldberg* requirements" at a predeprivation hearing.

GOLDBERG V. KELLY
397 U.S. 254 (1970)

Justice Brennan delivered the opinion of the Court, joined by Justices Douglas, Harlan, White, Marshall, and Blackmun. Chief Justice Burger and Justice Black dissented. Justice Stewart dissented in the companion case, 397 U.S. 282, 285.

The question for decision is whether a State that terminates public assistance payments to a particular recipient without affording him the opportunity for an evidentiary hearing prior to termination denies the recipient procedural due process in violation of the Due Process Clause of the Fourteenth Amendment.

This action was brought in the District Court for the Southern District of New York by residents of New York City receiving financial aid under the federally assisted program of Aid to Families with Dependent Children (AFDC) or under New York State's general Home Relief program. Their complaint alleged that the New York State and New York City officials administering those programs terminated, or were about to terminate, such aid without prior notice and hearing, thereby denying them due process of law. At the time the suits were filed there was no requirement of prior notice or hearing of any kind before termination of financial aid. However, the State and city adopted procedures for notice and hearing after the suits were brought, and the plaintiffs, appellees here, then challenged the constitutional adequacy of those procedures.

The State Commissioner of Social Services amended the State Department of Social Services' Official Regulations to require that local social services officials proposing to discontinue or suspend a recipient's financial aid do so according to a procedure that conforms to either subdivision (a) or subdivision (b) of § 351.26 of the regulations as amended. The City of New York elected to promulgate a local procedure according to subdivision (b). That subdivision, so far as here pertinent, provides that the local procedure must include the giving of notice to the recipient of the reasons for a proposed discontinuance or suspension at least seven days prior to its effective date, with notice also that upon request the recipient may have the proposal reviewed by a local welfare official holding a position superior to that of the supervisor who approved the proposed discontinuance or suspension, and, further, that the recipient may submit, for purposes of the review, a written statement to demonstrate why his grant should not be discontinued or suspended. The decision by the reviewing official whether to discontinue or suspend aid must be made expeditiously, with written notice of the decision to the recipient.

The section further expressly provides that "[a]ssistance shall not be discontinued or suspended prior to the date such notice of decision is sent to the recipient and his representative, if any, or prior to the proposed effective date of discontinuance or suspension, whichever occurs later." This case presents no issue of the validity or construction of the federal regulations. It is only subdivision (b) of § 351.26 of the New York State regulations and implementing procedure 68–18 of New York City that pose the constitutional question before us. Even assuming that the constitutional question might be avoided in the context of AFDC by construction of the Social Security Act or of the present federal regulations thereunder, or by waiting for the new regulations to become effective, the question must be faced and decided in the context of New York's Home Relief program, to which the procedures also apply.

Pursuant to subdivision (b), the New York City Department of Social Services promulgated Procedure No. 68–18. A caseworker who has doubts about the recipient's continued eligibility must first discuss them with the recipient. If the caseworker concludes that the recipient is no longer eligible, he recommends termination of aid to a unit supervisor. If the latter concurs, he sends the recipient a letter stating the reasons for proposing to terminate aid and notifying him that within seven days he may request that a higher official review the record, and may support the request with a written statement prepared personally or with the aid of an attorney or other person. If the reviewing official affirms the

determination of ineligibility, aid is stopped immediately and the recipient is informed by letter of the reasons for the action. Appellees' challenge to this procedure emphasizes the absence of any provisions for the personal appearance of the recipient before the reviewing official, for oral presentation of evidence, and for confrontation and cross-examination of adverse witnesses. However, the letter does inform the recipient that he may request a post-termination "fair hearing." This is a proceeding before an independent state hearing officer at which the recipient may appear personally, offer oral evidence, confront and cross-examine the witnesses against him, and have a record made of the hearing. If the recipient prevails at the "fair hearing" he is paid all funds erroneously withheld. A recipient whose aid is not restored by a "fair hearing" decision may have judicial review. The recipient is so notified.

I

The constitutional issue to be decided, therefore, is the narrow one whether the Due Process Clause requires that the recipient be afforded an evidentiary hearing before the termination of benefits. . . . Under all the circumstances, we hold that due process requires an adequate hearing before termination of welfare benefits, and the fact that there is a later constitutionally fair proceeding does not alter the result. Although state officials were party defendants in the action, only the Commissioner of Social Services of the City of New York appealed. We noted probable jurisdiction, to decide important issues that have been the subject of disagreement in principle between the three-judge court in the present case and that convened in *Wheeler v. Montgomery,* 397 U.S. 280. We affirm. . . .

"Consideration of what procedures due process may require under any given set of circumstances must begin with a determination of the precise nature of the governmental function involved as well as of the private interest that has been affected by governmental action." See also *Hannah v. Larche,* 363 U.S. 420, 1307 (1960).

[5][6] It is true, of course, that some governmental benefits may be administratively terminated without affording the recipient a pre-termination evidentiary hearing. But we agree with the District Court that when welfare is discontinued, only a pre-termination evidentiary hearing provides the recipient with procedural due process. Cf. *Sniadach v. Family Finance Corp.,* 395 U.S. 337 (1969). For

qualified recipients, welfare provides the means to obtain essential food, clothing, housing, and medical care. Thus the crucial factor in this context—a factor not present in the case of the blacklisted government contractor, the discharged government employee, the taxpayer denied a tax exemption, or virtually anyone else whose governmental entitlements are ended—is that termination of aid pending resolution of a controversy over eligibility may deprive an eligible recipient of the very means by which to live while he waits. Since he lacks independent resources, his situation becomes immediately desperate. His need to concentrate upon finding the means for daily subsistence, in turn, adversely affects his ability to seek redress from the welfare bureaucracy. . . . Moreover, important governmental interests are promoted by affording recipients a pre-termination evidentiary hearing. From its founding the Nation's basic commitment has been to foster the dignity and well-being of all persons within its borders. We have come to recognize that forces not within the control of the poor contribute to their poverty. This perception, against the background of our traditions, has significantly influenced the development of the contemporary public assistance system. Welfare, by meeting the basic demands of subsistence, can help bring within the reach of the poor the same opportunities that are available to others to participate meaningfully in the life of the community. At the same time, welfare guards against the societal malaise that may flow from a widespread sense of unjustified frustration and insecurity. Public assistance, then, is not mere charity, but a means to "promote the general Welfare, and secure the Blessings of Liberty to ourselves and our Posterity." The same governmental interests that counsel the provision of welfare, counsel as well its uninterrupted provision to those eligible to receive it; pre-termination evidentiary hearings are indispensable to that end. . . .

II

[8][9][10] We also agree with the District Court, however, that the pre-termination hearing need not take the form of a judicial or quasi-judicial trial. We bear in mind that the statutory "fair hearing" will provide the recipient with a full administrative review. Accordingly, the pre-termination hearing has one function only: to produce an initial determination of the validity of the welfare department's grounds for discontinuance of payments in order to protect a recipient against an erroneous termination

of his benefits. Thus, a complete record and a comprehensive opinion, which would serve primarily to facilitate judicial review and to guide future decisions, need not be provided at the pre-termination stage. We recognize, too, that both welfare authorities and recipients have an interest in relatively speedy resolution of questions of eligibility, that they are used to dealing with one another informally, and that some welfare departments have very burdensome caseloads. These considerations justify the limitation of the pre-termination hearing to minimum procedural safeguards, adapted to the particular characteristics of welfare recipients, and to the limited nature of the controversies to be resolved. We wish to add that we, no less than the dissenters, recognize the importance of not imposing upon the States or the Federal Government in this developing field of law any procedural requirements beyond those demanded by rudimentary due process.

[11][12] "The fundamental requisite of due process of law is the opportunity to be heard." The hearing must be "at a meaningful time and in a meaningful manner." In the present context these principles require that a recipient have timely and adequate notice detailing the reasons for a proposed termination, and an effective opportunity to defend by confronting any adverse witnesses and by presenting his own arguments and evidence orally. These rights are important in cases such as those before us, where recipients have challenged proposed terminations as resting on incorrect or misleading factual premises or on misapplication of rules or policies to the facts of particular cases.

[15] The city's procedures presently do not permit recipients to appear personally with or without counsel before the official who finally determines continued eligibility. Thus a recipient is not permitted to present evidence to that official orally, or to confront or cross-examine adverse witnesses. These omissions are fatal to the constitutional adequacy of the procedures.

[16][17][18][19] The opportunity to be heard must be tailored to the capacities and circumstances of those who are to be heard. It is not enough that a welfare recipient may present his position to the decision maker in writing or secondhand through his caseworker. . . . Therefore a recipient must be allowed to state his position orally. Informal procedures will suffice; in this context due process does not require a particular order of proof or mode of offering evidence. . . .

[20][21][22] In almost every setting where important decisions turn on questions of fact, due process requires an opportunity to confront and cross-examine adverse witnesses. What we said in *Greene v. McElroy,* 360 U.S. 474 (1959), is particularly pertinent here: "Certain principles have remained relatively immutable in our jurisprudence. One of these is that where governmental action seriously injures an individual, and the reasonableness of the action depends on fact findings, the evidence used to prove the Government's case must be disclosed to the individual so that he has an opportunity to show that it is untrue. While this is important in the case of documentary evidence, it is even more important where the evidence consists of the testimony of individuals whose memory might be faulty or who, in fact, might be perjurers or persons motivated by malice, vindictiveness, intolerance, prejudice, or jealousy. We have formalized these protections in the requirements of confrontation and cross-examination. They have ancient roots. They find expression in the Sixth Amendment * * *.

[23] "The right to be heard would be, in many cases, of little avail if it did not comprehend the right to be heard by counsel." *Powell v. Alabama,* 287 U.S. 45 (1932). We do not say that counsel must be provided at the pre-termination hearing, but only that the recipient must be allowed to retain an attorney if he so desires. Counsel can help delineate the issues, present the factual contentions in an orderly manner, conduct cross-examination, and generally safeguard the interests of the recipient. We do not anticipate that this assistance will unduly prolong or otherwise encumber the hearing. Evidently HEW has reached the same conclusion.

[24][25] Finally, the decision maker's conclusion as to a recipient's eligibility must rest solely on the legal rules and evidence adduced at the hearing. To demonstrate compliance with this elementary requirement, the decision maker should state the reasons for his determination and indicate the evidence he relied on, cf. *Wichita R. & Light Co. v. PUC,* 260 U.S. 48 (1922) though his statement need not amount to a full opinion or even formal findings of fact and conclusions of law. And, of course, an impartial decision maker is essential. We agree with the District Court that prior involvement in some aspects of a case will not necessarily bar a welfare official from acting as a decision maker. He should not, however, have participated in making the determination under review.

Affirmed.

Questions

1. What is the affected interest?
2. Can you list the ten requirements of the hearing?

MATHEWS V. ELDRIDGE
424 U.S. 319 (1976)

Justice Powell delivered the opinion of the Court, joined by Chief Justice Burger and Justices White, Stewart, Blackmun, and Rehnquist. Justices Brennan and Marshall dissented. Justice Stevens did not participate.

The issue in this case is whether the Due Process Clause of the Fifth Amendment requires that prior to the termination of Social Security disability benefit payments the recipient be afforded an opportunity for an evidentiary hearing.

I

Cash benefits are provided to workers during periods in which they are completely disabled under the disability insurance benefits program created by the 1956 amendments to Title II of the

Social Security Act. 42 U.S.C. § 423. Respondent Eldridge was first awarded benefits in June 1968. In March 1972, he received a questionnaire from the state agency charged with monitoring his medical condition. Eldridge completed the questionnaire, indicating that his condition had not improved and identifying the medical sources, including physicians, from whom he had received treatment recently. The state agency then obtained reports from his physician and a psychiatric consultant. After considering these reports and other information in his file the agency informed Eldridge by letter that it had made a tentative determination that his disability had ceased in May 1972. The letter included a statement of reasons for the proposed termination of benefits, and advised Eldridge that he might request reasonable time in which to obtain and submit additional information pertaining to his condition. . . . In his written response, Eldridge disputed one characterization of his medical condition and indicated that the agency already had enough evidence to establish his disability. The state agency then made its final determination that he had ceased to be disabled in May 1972. This determination was accepted by the Social Security Administration (SSA), which notified Eldridge in July that his benefits would terminate after that month. The notification also advised him of his right to seek reconsideration by the state agency of this initial determination within six months. . . .

Instead of requesting reconsideration Eldridge commenced this action challenging the constitutional validity of the administrative procedures established by the Secretary of Health, Education, and Welfare for assessing whether there exists a continuing disability. He sought an immediate reinstatement of benefits pending a hearing on the issue of his disability. 361 F.Supp. 520 (W.D.Va. 1973). The Secretary moved to dismiss on the grounds that Eldridge's benefits had been terminated in accordance with valid administrative regulations and procedures and that he had failed to exhaust available remedies. In support of his contention that due process requires a pretermination hearing, Eldridge relied exclusively upon this Court's decision in *Goldberg v. Kelly,* 397 U.S. 254 (1970), which established a right to an "evidentiary hearing" prior to termination of welfare benefits. The Secretary contended that *Goldberg* was not controlling since eligibility for disability benefits, unlike eligibility for welfare benefits, is not based on financial need and since issues of credibility and

veracity do not play a significant role in the disability entitlement decision, which turns primarily on medical evidence. . . .

The District Court concluded that the administrative procedures pursuant to which the Secretary had terminated Eldridge's benefits abridged his right to procedural due process. The court viewed the interest of the disability recipient in uninterrupted benefits as indistinguishable from that of the welfare recipient in *Goldberg.* It further noted that decisions subsequent to *Goldberg* demonstrated that the due process requirement of pretermination hearings is not limited to situations involving the deprivation of vital necessities. See *Fuentes v. Shevin,* 407 U.S. 67, 88-89 (1972); *Bell v. Burson,* 402 U.S. 535 (1971). Reasoning that disability determinations may involve subjective judgments based on conflicting medical and nonmedical evidence, the District Court held that prior to termination of benefits Eldridge had to be afforded an evidentiary hearing of the type required for welfare beneficiaries under Title IV of the Social Security Act. 361 F.Supp., at 528. Relying entirely upon the District Court's opinion, the Court of Appeals for the Fourth Circuit affirmed the injunction barring termination of Eldridge's benefits prior to an evidentiary hearing. 493 F.2d 1230 (1974). We reverse. . . .

III

A

[3] Procedural due process imposes constraints on governmental decisions which deprive individuals of "liberty" or "property" interests within the meaning of the Due Process Clause of the Fifth or Fourteenth Amendment. The Secretary does not contend that procedural due process is inapplicable to terminations of Social Security disability benefits. He recognizes, as has been implicit in our prior decisions, that the interest of an individual in continued receipt of these benefits is a statutorily created "property" interest protected by the Fifth Amendment. Rather, the Secretary contends that the existing administrative procedures, detailed below, provide all the process that is constitutionally due before a recipient can be deprived of that interest.

[4] This Court consistently has held that some form of hearing is required before an individual is finally deprived of a property interest. *Wolff v. McDonnell,* 418 U.S. 539 (1974). See, e.g., *Phillips v. Commissioner of Internal Revenue,* 283 U.S. 589

(1931). See also *Dent v. West Virginia,* 129 U.S. 114 (1889). The "right to be heard before being condemned to suffer grievous loss of any kind, even though it may not involve the stigma and hardships of a criminal conviction, is a principle basic to our society." *Joint Anti-Fascist Comm. v. McGrath,* 341 U.S. 123 (1951) (Frankfurter, J., concurring). The fundamental requirement of due process is the opportunity to be heard "at a meaningful time and in a meaningful manner." Eldridge agrees that the review procedures available to a claimant before the initial determination of ineligibility becomes final would be adequate if disability benefits were not terminated until after the evidentiary hearing stage of the administrative process. The dispute centers upon what process is due prior to the initial termination of benefits, pending review.

[5][6] These decisions underscore the truism that "[d]ue process," unlike some legal rules, is not a technical conception with a fixed content unrelated to time, place and circumstances." "[D]ue process is flexible and calls for such procedural protections as the particular situation demands." Accordingly, resolution of the issue whether the administrative procedures provided here are constitutionally sufficient requires analysis of the governmental and private interests that are affected. More precisely, our prior decisions indicate that identification of the specific dictates of due process generally requires consideration of three distinct factors: First, the private interest that will be affected by the official action; second, the risk of an erroneous deprivation of such interest through the procedures used, and the probable value, if any, of additional or substitute procedural safeguards; and finally, the Government's interest, including the function involved and the fiscal and administrative burdens that the additional or substitute procedural requirement would entail. . . .

C

[7] Despite the elaborate character of the administrative procedures provided by the Secretary, the courts below held them to be constitutionally inadequate, concluding that due process requires an evidentiary hearing prior to termination. In light of the private and governmental interests at stake here and the nature of the existing procedures, we think this was error.

Since a recipient whose benefits are terminated is awarded full retroactive relief if he ultimately

prevails, his sole interest is in the uninterrupted receipt of this source of income pending final administrative decision on his claim. His potential injury is thus similar in nature to that of the welfare recipient in *Goldberg,* the nonprobationary federal employee in *Arnett,* see 416 U.S., at 146, and the wage earner in *Sniadach.*

Only in *Goldberg* has the Court held that due process requires an evidentiary hearing prior to a temporary deprivation. It was emphasized there that welfare assistance is given to persons on the very margin of subsistence: "The crucial factor in this context a factor not present in the case of . . . virtually anyone else whose governmental entitlements are ended is that termination of aid pending resolution of a controversy over eligibility may deprive an eligible recipient of the very means by which to live while he waits." Eligibility for disability benefits, in contrast, is not based upon financial need. Indeed, it is wholly unrelated to the worker's income or support from many other sources, such as earnings of other family members, workmen's compensation awards, tort claims awards, savings, private insurance, public or private pensions, veterans' benefits, food stamps, public assistance, or the "many other important programs, both public and private, which contain provisions for disability payments affecting a substantial portion of the work force. . . ."

In view of the torpidity of this administrative review process, and the typically modest resources of the family unit of the physically disabled worker, the hardship imposed upon the erroneously terminated disability recipient may be significant. Still, the disabled worker's need is likely to be less than that of a welfare recipient. In addition to the possibility of access to private resources, other forms of government assistance will become available where the termination of disability benefits places a worker or his family below the subsistence level. In view of these potential sources of temporary income, there is less reason here than in *Goldberg* to depart from the ordinary principle, established by our decisions, that something less than an evidentiary hearing is sufficient prior to adverse administrative action.

D

An additional factor to be considered here is the fairness and reliability of the existing pretermination procedures, and the probable value, if any, of additional procedural safeguards. Central to the evaluation of any administrative process is the nature of the relevant inquiry. See Friendly, Some Kind of Hearing, 123 *U.Pa.L.Rev.* 1267, 1281 (1975). In order to remain eligible for benefits the disabled worker must demonstrate by means of "medically acceptable clinical and laboratory diagnostic techniques," that he is unable "to engage in any substantial gainful activity by reason of any medically determinable physical or mental impairment. . . ." In short, a medical assessment of the worker's physical or mental condition is required. This is a more sharply focused and easily documented decision than the typical determination of welfare entitlement. In the latter case, a wide variety of information may be deemed relevant, and issues of witness credibility and veracity often are critical to the decisionmaking process. *Goldberg* noted that in such circumstances "written submissions are a wholly unsatisfactory basis for decision."

By contrast, the decision whether to discontinue disability benefits will turn, in most cases, upon "routine, standard, and unbiased medical reports by physician specialists," concerning a subject whom they have personally examined. . . .

In striking the appropriate due process balance the final factor to be assessed is the public interest. This includes the administrative burden and other societal costs that would be associated with requiring, as a matter of constitutional right, an evidentiary hearing upon demand in all cases prior to the termination of disability benefits. The most visible burden would be the incremental cost resulting from the increased number of hearings and the expense of providing benefits to ineligible recipients pending decision. No one can predict the extent of the increase, but the fact that full benefits would continue until after such hearings would assure the exhaustion in most cases of this attractive option. Nor would the theoretical right of the Secretary to recover undeserved benefits result, as a practical matter, in any substantial offset to the added outlay of public funds. The parties submit widely varying estimates of the probable additional financial cost. We only need say that experience with the constitutionalizing of government procedures suggests that the ultimate additional cost in terms of money and administrative burden would not be insubstantial.

Financial cost alone is not a controlling weight in determining whether due process requires a particular procedural safeguard prior to some administrative decision. But the Government's interest, and hence that of the public, in conserving scarce fiscal and administrative resources is a factor that must be weighed. At some point the benefit of an additional safeguard to the individual affected by the administrative action and to society in terms of increased assurance that the action is just, may be outweighed by the cost. Significantly, the cost of protecting those whom the preliminary administrative process has identified as likely to be found undeserving may in the end come out of the pockets of the deserving since resources available for any particular program of social welfare are not unlimited.

But more is implicated in cases of this type than ad hoc weighing of fiscal and administrative burdens against the interests of a particular category of claimants. The ultimate balance involves a determination as to when, under our constitutional system, judicial-type procedures must be imposed upon administrative action to assure fairness. We reiterate the wise admonishment of Mr. Justice Frankfurter that differences in the origin and function of administrative agencies "preclude wholesale transplantation of the rules of procedure, trial and review which have evolved from the history and experience of courts." *FCC v. Pottsville Broadcasting Co.,* 309 U.S. 134, 143 (1940). The judicial model of an evidentiary hearing is neither a required, nor even the most effective, method of decisionmaking in all circumstances. The essence of due process is the requirement that "a person in jeopardy of serious loss (be given) notice of the case against him and opportunity to meet it." All that is necessary is that the procedures be tailored, in light of the decision to be made, to "the capacities and circumstances of those who are to be heard," to insure that they are given a meaningful opportunity to present their case. This is especially so where, as here, the prescribed procedures not only provide the claimant with an effective process for asserting his claim prior to any administrative action, but also assure a right to an evidentiary hearing, as well as to subsequent judicial review, before the denial of his claim becomes final.

We conclude that an evidentiary hearing is not required prior to the termination of disability benefits and that the present administrative procedures fully comport with due process.

The judgment of the Court of Appeals is Reversed.

Justice Brennan, dissenting.

Justice Marshall concurred with Justice Brennan's dissent.

For the reasons stated in my dissenting opinion in *Richardson v. Wright,* 405 U.S. 208, 212 (1972), I agree with the District Court and the Court of Appeals that, prior to termination of benefits, Eldridge must be afforded an evidentiary hearing of the type required for welfare beneficiaries under Title IV of the Social Security Act, 42 U.S.C. § 601 et seq. See *Goldberg v. Kelly,* 397 U.S. 254 (1970). I would add that the Court's consideration that a discontinuance of disability benefits may cause the recipient to suffer only a limited deprivation is no argument. It is speculative. Moreover, the very legislative determination to provide disability benefits, without any prerequisite determination of need in fact, presumes a need by the recipient which is not this Court's function to denigrate. Indeed, in the present case, it is indicated that because disability benefits were terminated there was a foreclosure upon the Eldridge home and the family's furniture was repossessed, forcing Eldridge, his wife, and their children to sleep in one bed. Finally, it is also no argument that a worker, who has been placed in the untenable position of having been denied disability benefits, may still seek other forms of public assistance.

Questions

1. Why, do you suppose, did the Court's statement of the facts not mention that Eldridge had already been through the termination process twice before?
2. Can you articulate what has become known as the due process test from *Mathews v. Eldridge*? For a modern application of this test, see *Walters v. National Association of Radiation Survivors* at the end of this chapter.

The case you are about to read next, *Goss v. Lopez,* requires a due process hearing prior to a ten-day suspension from high school (the Court said "preferably prior to . . ."). This case was decided just one year before the decisions in *Paul v. Davis* and *Eldridge.*

GOSS V. LOPEZ
419 U.S. 565 (1975)

Justice White delivered the opinion of the Court, joined by Justices Brennan, Stewart, Marshall, and Stevens. Justice Powell filed a dissent, joined by Chief Justice Burger and Justices Blackmun and Rehnquist.

This appeal by various administrators of the Columbus, Ohio, Public School System (CPSS) challenges the judgment of a three-judge federal court, declaring that appellees—various high school students in the CPSS—were denied due process of law contrary to the command of the Fourteenth Amendment in that they were temporarily suspended from their high schools without a hearing either prior to suspension or within a reasonable time thereafter, and enjoining the administrators to remove all references to such suspensions from the students' records.

I

Ohio law, Rev.Code Ann. § 3313.64 (1972), provides for free education to all children between the ages of six and 21. Section 3313.66 of the Code empowers the principal of an Ohio public school to suspend a pupil for misconduct for up to 10 days or to expel him. In either case, he must notify the student's parents within 24 hours and state the reasons for his action. A pupil who is expelled, or his parents, may appeal the decision to the Board of Education and in connection therewith shall be permitted to be heard at the board meeting. The Board may reinstate the pupil following the hearing. No similar procedure is provided in § 3313.66 or any other provision of state law for a suspended student. Aside from a regulation tracking the statute, at the time of the imposition of the suspensions in this case the CPSS itself had not issued any written procedure applicable to suspensions. Nor, so far as the record reflects, had any of the individual high schools involved in this case. Each, however, had formally or informally described the conduct for which suspension could be imposed. The nine named appellees, each of whom alleged that he or she had been suspended from public high school in Columbus for up to 10 days without a hearing pursuant to § 3313.66, filed an action under 42 U.S.C. § 1983 against the Columbus Board of Education and various administrators of the CPSS. The complaint sought a declaration that § 3313.66 was unconstitutional in that it permitted public school administrators to deprive plaintiffs of their rights to an education without a hearing of any kind, in violation of the procedural due process component of the Fourteenth Amendment. It also sought to enjoin the public school officials from issuing future suspensions pursuant to § 3313.66 and to require them to remove references to the past suspensions from the records of the students in question. . . .

The proof below established that the suspensions arose out of a period of widespread student unrest in the CPSS during February and March 1971. Six of the named plaintiffs, Rudolph Sutton, Tyrone Washington, Susan Cooper, Deborah Fox, Clarence Byars, and Bruce Harris, were students at the Marion-Franklin High School and were each suspended for 10 days on account of disruptive or disobedient conduct committed in the presence of the school administrator who ordered the suspension. One of these, Tyrone Washington, was among a group of students demonstrating in the school auditorium while a class was being conducted there. He was ordered by the school principal to leave, refused to do so, and was suspended. Rudolph Sutton, in the presence of the principal, physically attacked a police officer who was attempting to

remove Tyrone Washington from the auditorium. He was immediately suspended. The other four Marion-Franklin students were suspended for similar conduct. None was given a hearing to determine the operative facts underlying the suspension, but each, together with his or her parents, was offered the opportunity to attend a conference, subsequent to the effective date of the suspension, to discuss the student's future. Two named plaintiffs, Dwight Lopez and Betty Crome, were students at the Central High School and McGuffey Junior High School, respectively. The former was suspended in connection with a disturbance in the lunchroom which involved some physical damage to school property. Lopez testified that at least 75 other students were suspended from his school on the same day. He also testified below that he was not a party to the destructive conduct but was instead an innocent bystander. Because no one from the school testified with regard to this incident, there is no evidence in the record indicating the official basis for concluding otherwise. Lopez never had a hearing. Betty Crome was present at a demonstration at a high school other than the one she was attending. There she was arrested together with others, taken to the police station, and released without being formally charged. Before she went to school on the following day, she was notified that she had been suspended for a 10-day period. Because no one from the school testified with respect to this incident, the record does not disclose how the McGuffey Junior High School principal went about making the decision to suspend Crome, nor does it disclose on what information the decision was based. It is clear from the record that no hearing was ever held.

There was no testimony with respect to the suspension of the ninth named plaintiff, Carl Smith. The school files were also silent as to his suspension, although as to some, but not all, of the other named plaintiffs the files contained either direct references to their suspensions or copies of letters sent to their parents advising them of the suspension.

On the basis of this evidence, the three-judge court declared that plaintiffs were denied due process of law because they were "suspended without hearing prior to suspension or within a reasonable time thereafter," and that Ohio Rev.Code Ann. § 3313.66 (1972) and regulations issued pursuant thereto were unconstitutional in permitting such suspensions. It was ordered that all references to plaintiffs' suspensions be removed from school files.

II

At the outset, appellants contend that because there is no constitutional right to an education at public expense, the Due Process Clause does not protect against expulsions from the public school system. This position misconceives the nature of the issue and is refuted by prior decisions. The Fourteenth Amendment forbids the State to deprive any person of life, liberty, or property without due process of law. Protected interests in property are normally "not created by the Constitution. Rather, they are created and their dimensions are defined" by an independent source such as state statutes or rules entitling the citizen to certain benefits. *Board of Regents v. Roth,* 408 U.S. 564 (1972).

Here, on the basis of state law, appellees plainly had legitimate claims of entitlement to a public education. Ohio Rev.Code Ann. §§ 3313.48 and 3313.64 (1972 and Supp.1973) direct local authorities to provide a free education to all residents between five and 21 years of age, and a compulsory-attendance law requires attendance for a school year of not less than 32 weeks. It is true that § 3313.66 of the Code permits school principals to suspend students for up to 10 days; but suspensions may not be imposed without any grounds whatsoever. All of the schools had their own rules specifying the grounds for expulsion or suspension. Having chosen to extend the right to an education to people of appellees' class generally, Ohio may not withdraw that right on grounds of misconduct absent fundamentally fair procedures to determine whether the misconduct has occurred.

Among other things, the State is constrained to recognize a student's legitimate entitlement to a public education as a property interest which is protected by the Due Process Clause and which may not be taken away for misconduct without adherence to the minimum procedures required by that Clause.

The Due Process Clause also forbids arbitrary deprivations of liberty. "Where a person's good name, reputation, honor, or integrity is at stake because of what the government is doing to him," the minimal requirements of the Clause must be satisfied. *Wisconsin v. Constantineau,* 400 U.S. 433 (1971); *Board of Regents v. Roth,* supra, 408 U.S.

at 573. School authorities here suspended appellees from school for periods of up to 10 days based on charges of misconduct. If sustained and recorded, those charges could seriously damage the students' standing with their fellow pupils and their teachers as well as interfere with later opportunities for higher education and employment. It is apparent that the claimed right of the State to determine unilaterally and without process whether that misconduct has occurred immediately collides with the requirements of the Constitution. . . .

III

"Once it is determined that due process applies, the question remains what process is due." We turn to that question, fully realizing as our cases regularly do that the interpretation and application of the Due Process Clause are intensely practical matters and that "[t]he very nature of due process negates any concept of inflexible procedures universally applicable to every imaginable situation.". . .

Students facing temporary suspension have interests qualifying for protection of the Due Process Clause, and due process requires, in connection with a suspension of 10 days or less, that the student be given oral or written notice of the charges against him and, if he denies them, an explanation of the evidence the authorities have and an opportunity to present his side of the story. The Clause requires at least these rudimentary precautions against unfair or mistaken findings of misconduct and arbitrary exclusion from school. There need be no delay between the time notice is given and the time of the hearing. In the great majority of cases the disciplinarian may informally discuss the alleged misconduct with the student minutes after it has occurred. We hold only that, in being given an opportunity to explain his version of the facts at this discussion, the student first be told what he is accused of doing and what the basis of the accusation is. . . .

Since the hearing may occur almost immediately following the misconduct, it follows that as a general rule notice and hearing should precede removal of the student from school. We agree with the District Court, however, that there are recurring situations in which prior notice and hearing cannot be insisted upon. Students whose presence poses a continuing danger to persons or property or an ongoing threat of disrupting the academic process may be immediately removed from school. In such cases, the necessary notice and rudimentary hear-ing should follow as soon as practicable, as the District Court indicated.

Affirmed.

Questions

1. What is the interest involved?
2. What procedure is required?
3. Must the procedure be administered predeprivation?

The Court says in *Goss* that what is required is that the student be notified of the charges, be provided with an explanation of the evidence the school officials have, and be given an opportunity to explain his or her side of the facts. In this case, Dwight Lopez said that he was a bystander in a disturbance in the school cafeteria, that he took no part in activities that led to destruction of property, and that he was suspended along with seventy-five other students. Betty Crome, a junior high school student, was present at a demonstration at a high school, where she was rounded up with students, taken to the police station, and then released without being charged. In both cases, the students would be going before the very vice principal who wanted to suspend them for their "hearing." How much protection against a "wrongful suspension" do you think the process provides?

The next case involves the issue of academic suspensions. Compare the result in *Horowitz* with the decision in *Goss.*

BOARD OF CURATORS OF THE UNIVERSITY OF MISSOURI V. HOROWITZ
435 U.S. 78 (1978)

Justice Rehnquist delivered the opinion of the Court.

Respondent, a student at the University of Missouri-Kansas City Medical School, was dismissed by petitioner officials of the school during her final year of study for failure to meet academic standards. Respondent sued petitioners under 42 U.S.C. § 1983 in the United States District Court for the Western District of Missouri alleging, among other constitutional violations, that petitioners had not accorded her procedural due process prior to her dismissal. The District Court, after conducting a full trial, concluded that respondent had been afforded all of the rights guaranteed her by the Fourteenth Amendment to the United States Constitution and dismissed her complaint. The Court of Appeals for the Eighth Circuit reversed, 538 F.2d 1317 (1976), and a petition for rehearing en banc was denied by a divided court. We granted certiorari, to consider what procedures must be accorded to a student at a state educational institution whose dismissal may constitute a deprivation of "liberty" or "property" within the meaning of the Fourteenth Amendment. We reverse the judgment of the Court of Appeals.

I

Respondent was admitted with advanced standing to the Medical School in the fall of 1971. During the final years of a student's education at the school, the student is required to pursue in "rotational units" academic and clinical studies pertaining to various medical disciplines such as obstetrics-gynecology, pediatrics, and surgery. Each student's academic performance at the school is evaluated on a periodic basis by the Council on Evaluation, a body composed of both faculty and students, which can recommend various actions including probation and dismissal. The recommendations of the Council are reviewed by the Coordinating Committee, a body composed solely of faculty members, and must ultimately be approved by the Dean. Students are not typically allowed to appear before either the Council or the Coordinating Committee on the occasion of their review of the student's academic performance.

In the spring of respondent's first year of study, several faculty members expressed dissatisfaction with her clinical performance during a pediatrics rotation. The faculty members noted that respondent's "performance was below that of her peers in all clinical patient-oriented settings," that she was erratic in her attendance at clinical sessions, and that she lacked a critical concern for personal hygiene. Upon the recommendation of the Council on Evaluation, respondent was advanced to her second and final year on a probationary basis.

Faculty dissatisfaction with respondent's clinical performance continued during the following year. For example, respondent's docent, or faculty adviser, rated her clinical skills as "unsatisfactory." In the middle of the year, the Council again reviewed respondent's academic progress and concluded that respondent should not be considered for graduation in June of that year; furthermore, the Council recommended that, absent "radical improvement," respondent be dropped from the school.

Respondent was permitted to take a set of oral and practical examinations as an "appeal" of the decision not to permit her to graduate. Pursuant to this "appeal," respondent spent a substantial portion of time with seven practicing physicians in the area who enjoyed a good reputation among their peers. The physicians were asked to recommend whether respondent should be allowed to graduate on schedule and, if not, whether she should be dropped immediately or allowed to remain on probation. Only two of the doctors recommended that respondent be graduated on schedule. Of the other five, two recommended that she be immediately dropped from the school. The remaining three recommended that she not be allowed to graduate in June and be continued on probation pending further reports on her clinical progress. Upon receipt of these recommendations, the Council on Evaluation reaffirmed its prior position.

The Council met again in mid-May to consider whether respondent should be allowed to remain in school beyond June of that year. Noting that the report on respondent's recent surgery rotation rated her performance as "low-satisfactory," the Council unanimously recommended that "barring receipt of any reports that Miss Horowitz has improved radically, [she] not be allowed to re-enroll in the . . . School of Medicine." The Council delayed making its recommendation official until receiving reports on other rotations; when a report on respondent's emergency rotation also turned out to be negative, the Council unanimously reaffirmed its recommendation that respondent be dropped from the school. The Coordinating Committee and the Dean approved the recommendation and notified respondent, who appealed the decision in writing to the University's Provost for Health Sciences. The Provost sustained the school's actions after reviewing the record compiled during the earlier proceedings.

II

A

To be entitled to the procedural protections of the Fourteenth Amendment, respondent must in a case such as this demonstrate that her dismissal from the school deprived her of either a "liberty" or a "property" interest. Respondent has never alleged that she was deprived of a property interest. Because property interests are creatures of state law, respondent would have been required to show at trial that her seat at the Medical School was a "property" interest recognized by Missouri state law. Instead, respondent argued that her dismissal deprived her of "liberty" by substantially impairing her opportunities to continue her medical education or to return to employment in a medically related field.

The Court of Appeals agreed, citing this Court's opinion in *Board of Regents v. Roth,* 408 U.S. 564 (1972). . . .

B

[1] We need not decide, however, whether respondent's dismissal deprived her of a liberty interest in pursuing a medical career. Nor need we decide whether respondent's dismissal infringed any other interest constitutionally protected against deprivation without procedural due process. Assuming the existence of a liberty or property interest, respondent has been awarded at least as much due process as the Fourteenth Amendment requires. The school fully informed respondent of the faculty's dissatisfaction with her clinical progress and the danger that this posed to timely graduation and continued enrollment. The ultimate decision to dismiss respondent was careful and deliberate. These procedures were sufficient under the Due Process Clause of the Fourteenth Amendment. We agree with the District Court that respondent "was afforded full procedural due process by the [school]. In fact, the Court is of the opinion, and so finds, that the school went beyond [constitutionally required] procedural due process by affording [respondent] the opportunity to be examined by seven independent physicians in order to be absolutely certain that their grading of the [respondent] in her medical skills was correct." . . .

Since the issue first arose 50 years ago, state and lower federal courts have recognized that there are distinct differences between decisions to suspend or dismiss a student for disciplinary purposes and similar actions taken for academic reasons which

may call for hearings in connection with the former but not the latter. These prior decisions of state and federal courts, over a period of 60 years, unanimously holding that formal hearings before decisionmaking bodies need not be held in the case of academic dismissals, cannot be rejected lightly. . . . Academic evaluations of a student, in contrast to disciplinary determinations, bear little resemblance to the judicial and administrative fact-finding proceedings to which we have traditionally attached a full-hearing requirement. In *Goss,* the school's decision to suspend the students rested on factual conclusions that the individual students had participated in demonstrations that had disrupted classes, attacked a police officer, or caused physical damage to school property. The requirement of a hearing, where the student could present his side of the factual issue, could under such circumstances "provide a meaningful hedge against erroneous action." The decision to dismiss respondent, by comparison, rested on the academic judgment of school officials that she did not have the necessary clinical ability to perform adequately as a medical doctor and was making insufficient progress toward that goal. Such a judgment is by its nature more subjective and evaluative than the typical factual questions presented in the average disciplinary decision. Like the decision of an individual professor as to the proper grade for a student in his course, the determination whether to dismiss a student for academic reasons requires an expert evaluation of cumulative information and is not readily adapted to the procedural tools of judicial or administrative decisionmaking.

The Judgment of the Court of Appeals is therefore Reversed.

Questions

1. How much process is due in academic suspensions?
2. Do you think it makes a difference that this involved a graduate program?
3. What role does court deference to expertise play in this case?

If a hearing (of some kind) is necessary prior to termination of AFDC benefits, disciplinary suspensions from both high school and college, state cooperation in garnishment and repossession of personal property, suspension of a driver's license, and posting of a name to inhibit the individual's ability to purchase alcohol, then what kind of a hearing, do you suppose, is required before a public school administrator can administer corporal punishment to a student?

INGRAHAM V. WRIGHT
438 U.S. 651 (1977)

Justice Powell delivered the opinion of the Court, joined by Chief Justice Burger and Justices Stewart, Blackmun, and Rehnquist. Justices White, Brennan, Marshall, and Stevens dissented.

This case presents questions concerning the use of corporal punishment in public schools: First, whether the paddling of students as a means of maintaining school discipline constitutes cruel and unusual punishment in violation of the Eighth Amendment; and, second, to the extent that paddling is constitutionally permissible, whether the Due Process Clause of the Fourteenth Amendment requires prior notice and an opportunity to be heard.

I

Petitioners James Ingraham and Roosevelt Andrews filed the complaint in this case on January 7, 1971, in the United States District Court for the Southern District of Florida. At the time both were enrolled in the Charles R. Drew Junior High School in Dade County, Fla., Ingraham in the eighth grade and Andrews in the ninth. The complaint contained three counts, each alleging a separate cause of action for deprivation of constitutional rights, under 42 U.S.C. §§ 1981-1988. Counts one and two were individual actions for damages by Ingraham and Andrews based on paddling incidents that allegedly occurred in October 1970 at Drew Junior High School. Count three was a class action for declaratory and injunctive relief filed on behalf of all students in the Dade County schools. Named as defendants in all counts were respondents Willie J. Wright (principal at Drew Junior High School), Lemmie Deliford (an assistant principal), Solomon Barnes (an assistant to the principal), and Edward L. Whigham (superintendent of the Dade County School System).

Petitioners' evidence may be summarized briefly. In the 1970-1971 school year many of the 237 schools in Dade County used corporal punishment as a means of maintaining discipline pursuant to Florida legislation and a local School Board regulation. The statute then in effect authorized limited corporal punishment by negative inference, proscribing punishment which was "degrading or unduly severe" or which was inflicted without prior consultation with the principal or the teacher in charge of the school. Fla.Stat.Ann. § 232.27 (1961). The regulation, Dade County School Board Policy 5144, contained explicit directions and limitations. The authorized punishment consisted of paddling the recalcitrant student on the buttocks with a flat wooden paddle measuring less than two feet long, three to four inches wide, and about one-half inch thick. The normal punishment was limited to one to five "licks" or blows with the paddle and resulted in no apparent physical injury to the student. School authorities viewed corporal punishment as a less drastic means of discipline than suspension or expulsion. Contrary to the procedural requirements of the statute and regulation, teachers often paddled students on their own authority without first consulting the principal. . . .

Petitioners focused on Drew Junior High School, the school in which both Ingraham and Andrews were enrolled in the fall of 1970. In an apparent reference to Drew, the District Court found that "[t]he instances of punishment which could be characterized as severe, accepting the students' testimony as credible, took place in one junior high school." The evidence, consisting mainly of the testimony of 16 students, suggests that the regime at Drew was exceptionally harsh. The testimony of Ingraham and Andrews, in support of their individual claims for damages, is illustrative. Because he was slow to respond to his teacher's instructions, Ingraham was subjected to more than 20 licks with a paddle while being held over a table in the principal's office. The paddling was so severe that he suffered a hematoma requiring medical attention and keeping him out of school for several days. Andrews was paddled several times for minor infractions. On two occasions he was struck on his arms, once depriving him of the full use of his arm for a week. . . .

(1) The Eighth Amendment provides: "Excessive bail shall not be required, nor excessive fines imposed, nor cruel and unusual punishments inflicted." Bail, fines, and punishment traditionally have been associated with the criminal process, and by subjecting the three to parallel limitations the text of the Amendment suggests an intention to limit the power of those entrusted with the criminal-law function of government. An examination of the history of the Amendment and the decisions of this Court construing the proscription against cruel and unusual punishment confirms that it was designed to protect those convicted of crimes. We adhere to this longstanding limitation and hold that the Eighth Amendment does not apply to the paddling of children as a means of maintaining discipline in public schools. . . .

IV

The Fourteenth Amendment prohibits any state deprivation of life, liberty, or property without due process of law. Application of this prohibition requires the familiar two-stage analysis: We must first ask whether the asserted individual interests are encompassed within the Fourteenth Amendment's protection of "life, liberty or property"; if protected interests are implicated, we then must decide what procedures constitute "due process of law." Following that analysis here, we find that corporal punishment in public schools implicates a constitutionally protected liberty interest, but we hold that the traditional common-law remedies are fully adequate to afford due process.

While the contours of this historic liberty interest in the context of our federal system of government have not been defined precisely, they always have been thought to encompass freedom from bodily restraint and punishment. It is fundamental that the state cannot hold and physically punish an individual except in accordance with due process of law. . . .

[5] This constitutionally protected liberty interest is at stake in this case. There is, of course a de minimis level of imposition with which the Constitution is not concerned. But at least where school authorities, acting under color of state law, deliberately decide to punish a child for misconduct by restraining the child and inflicting appreciable physical pain, we hold that Fourteenth Amendment liberty interests are implicated. . . .

B

[6] "[T]he question remains what process is due." Were it not for the common-law privilege permitting teachers, to inflict reasonable corporal punishment on children in their care, and the availability of the traditional remedies for abuse, the case for requiring advance procedural safeguards would be strong indeed. But here we deal with a punishment paddling within that tradition, and the question is whether the common-law remedies are adequate to afford due process. . . ."

"[D]ue process," unlike some legal rules, is not a technical conception with a fixed content unrelated to time, place and circumstances. . . . Representing a profound attitude of fairness . . . "due process" is compounded of history, reason, the past course of decisions, and stout confidence in the strength of the democratic faith which we profess. . . . Whether in this case the common-law remedies for excessive corporal punishment constitute due process of law must turn on an analysis of the competing interests at stake, viewed against the background of "history, reason, (and) the past course of decisions." The analysis requires consideration of three distinct factors: "First, the private interest that will be affected . . . ; second, the risk of an erroneous deprivation of such interest . . . and the probable value, if any, of additional or substitute procedural safeguards; and, finally, the (state) interest, including the function involved and the fiscal and administrative burdens that the additional or substitute procedural requirement would entail."

1

Because it is rooted in history, the child's liberty interest in avoiding corporal punishment while in the care of public school authorities is subject to historical limitations. Under the common law, an invasion of personal security gave rise to a right to recover damages in a subsequent judicial proceeding. But the right of recovery was qualified by the concept of justification. Thus, there could be no recovery against a teacher who gave only "moderate correction" to a child. To the extent that the force used was reasonable in light of its purpose, it was not wrongful, but rather "justifiable or lawful." The concept that reasonable corporal punishment in school is justifiable continues to be recognized in the laws of most States. . . .

2

[7] Florida has continued to recognize, and indeed has strengthened by statute, the common-law right of a child not to be subjected to excessive corporal punishment in school. Under Florida law the teacher and principal of the school decide in the first instance whether corporal punishment is reasonably necessary under the circumstances in order to discipline a child who has misbehaved. But they must exercise prudence and restraint. For Florida has preserved the traditional judicial proceedings for determining whether the punishment was justified. If the punishment inflicted is later found to have been excessive, not reasonably believed at the time to be necessary for the child's discipline or training the school authorities inflicting it may be held liable in damages to the child and, if malice is shown, they may be subject to criminal penalties. . . .

Although students have testified in this case to specific instances of abuse, there is every reason to believe that such mistreatment is an aberration. The uncontradicted evidence suggests that corporal punishment in the Dade County schools was, "[w]ith the exception of a few cases, . . . unremarkable in physical severity." Moreover, because paddlings are usually inflicted in response to conduct directly observed by teachers in their presence, the risk that a child will be paddled without cause is typically insignificant. In the ordinary case, a disciplinary paddling neither threatens seriously to violate any

substantive rights nor condemns the child "to suffer grievous loss of any kind."

3

But even if the need for advance procedural safeguards were clear, the question would remain whether the incremental benefit could justify the cost. Acceptance of petitioners' claims would work a transformation in the law governing corporal punishment in Florida and most other States. Given the impracticability of formulating a rule of procedural due process that varies with the severity of the particular imposition, the prior hearing petitioners seek would have to precede any paddling, however moderate or trivial. . . .

Such a universal constitutional requirement would significantly burden the use of corporal punishment as a disciplinary measure. . . .

Elimination or curtailment of corporal punishment would be welcomed by many as a societal advance. But when such a policy choice may result from this Court's determination of an asserted right to due process, rather than from the normal processes of community debate and legislative action, the societal costs cannot be dismissed as insubstantial.

V

Petitioners cannot prevail on either of the theories before us in this case. The Eighth Amendment's prohibition against cruel and unusual punishment is inapplicable to school paddlings, and the Fourteenth Amendment's requirement of procedural due process is satisfied by Florida's preservation of common-law constraints and remedies. We therefore agree with the Court of Appeals that petitioners' evidence affords no basis for injunctive relief, and that petitioners cannot recover damages on the basis of any Eighth Amendment or procedural due process violation.

Affirmed.

Question

Aside from the awkwardness of a due process hearing prior to the administration of corporal punishment, the Court provides another legal reason why due process might not be necessary. Can you explain that reason?

One area of administrative law that has been touched on only tangentially is licensing. When the federal government requires a license, frequently that touches on a property interest, and therefore the quasi-judicial procedure of Section 554 of the Administrative Procedure Act is required. The states license not only drivers but a whole host of occupations, including physicians, lawyers, plumbers, electricians, and barbers. Walter Gellhorn had this to say about occupational licensing in the states:

> Possibly the founding fathers knew of restrictions in some of the new American states on the practices of law and medicine. They would, however, have been aghast to learn that in many parts of this country today aspiring bee keepers, embalmers, lightening rod salesmen, septic tank cleaners, taxidermists, and tree surgeons must obtain official approval before seeking the public's patronage. After examining the roster of those who must receive official permission to function, a cynic might conclude that virtually the only people who remain unlicensed in at least one of the United States are clergymen and university professors, presumably because they are nowhere taken seriously.[45]

The reader should have passing familiarity with this area because the decisions and procedures of licensing boards can have serious property implications. The Kansas Board of Medical Examiners revoked a physician's license because the physician claimed publicly to have had contact with extraterrestrial beings. In some cases, those who sit on licensing boards have used their power to enrich themselves at the expense of those without access to the board.[46] In Georgia, the liquor license procedure called for the board to consider patronage as well as statutory requirements, which led a federal court to declare a license denial based on the patronage criterion to be a violation of due process.[47]

To this point, you have been exposed to the seminal cases in administrative law due process. As a result, you know that (a) a fairly elaborate pretermination hearing is required prior to termination of AFDC benefits; (b) a posttermination hearing before an ALJ is sufficient due process in a disability termination case (remember, however, from the material in Chapter 6 that Congress amended the process to allow a face-to-face "hearing" in which the claimant can present his or her case at the reconsideration stage); (c) notice and an opportunity to refute is required before a state may "post" the name of an individual forbidden to purchase alcohol, but none is required to post the name of a cleared "shoplifter"; and (d) notice and an opportunity to refute are required before suspension from a public school for disciplinary reasons, but no due process is necessary for suspension from school for academic reasons or for the imposition of corporal punishment. Can you detect a pattern in these decisions?

It is difficult to summarize due process because the Court has not been consistent in recognizing property interest or liberty interest and in determining what procedures are due at what point. We can identify some common notions about due process in administrative law. First, so long as minimal due process protections exist, courts are likely to show deference to administrative agencies. Second, so long as the potential deprivation is not a severe deprivation of liberty or property, minimal acceptable due process appears to consist of notice, some kind of opportunity to explain and refute, and an impartial decision maker. Administrative agencies get into trouble in terms of due process and judicial review when they fail to provide any hearing at all or when the procedure is not fair. The disability scenario in Chapter 6 and the *Eldridge* case aside, the purpose of due process in public administration is to avoid the likelihood of error in the taking of citizens' property or in limiting the exercise of their liberties. Generally, where minimal due process procedures are in place, that risk of error is reduced enough to satisfy reviewing courts.

SUMMARY

1. Due process litigation requires governmental or state action.

2. Liberty interests and property interests are created by state law or authority (not by the U.S. Constitution).

3. *Goldberg* is the only case in which the Court has required full due process protection in a predeprivation administrative context. Presumably, that is because the deprivation means certain destitution for the parent and children.

4. For cases in which the deprivation is not as severe as in *Goldberg,* minimal due process will usually suffice.

5. Minimal due process appears to be (a) notice, (b) appraisal of evidence against, (c) some form of opportunity to refute and explain, and (d) generally, a neutral decision maker.

6. Whether a pre- or a postdeprivation hearing will suffice is sometimes determined by applying the three-pronged balancing test from *Mathews v. Eldridge*: (a) What is the private interest? (b) What is the risk of an erroneous decision? What would the value be in requiring additional procedures? and (c) What is the government's interest?

END-OF-CHAPTER CASES

COLLINS V. CITY OF HARKER HEIGHTS
112 S.CT. 1061 (1992)

Justice Stevens delivered the opinion for a unanimous Court.

The question presented is whether § 1 of the Civil Rights Act of 1871, 42 U.S.C. § 1983, provides a remedy for a municipal employee who is fatally injured in the course of his employment because the city customarily failed to train or warn its employees about known hazards in the workplace. Even though the city's conduct may be actionable under state law, we hold that § 1983 does not apply because such conduct does not violate the Due Process Clause.

On October 21, 1988, Larry Michael Collins, an employee in the sanitation department of the city of Harker Heights, Texas, died of asphyxia after entering a manhole to unstop a sewer line. Petitioner, his widow, brought this action alleging that Collins "had a constitutional right to be free from unreasonable risks of harm to his body, mind and emotions and a constitutional right to be protected from the city of Harker Heights' custom and policy of deliberate indifference toward the safety of its employees." Her complaint alleged that the city violated that right by following a custom and policy of not training its employees about the dangers of working in sewer lines and manholes, not providing safety equipment at job sites, and not providing safety warnings. The complaint also alleged that a prior incident had given the city notice of the risks of entering the sewer lines and that the city had systematically and intentionally failed to provide the equipment and training required by a Texas statute. The District Court dismissed the complaint on the ground that a constitutional violation had not been alleged. The Court of Appeals for the Fifth Circuit affirmed on a different theory. 916 F.2d 284 (CA5 1990). It did not reach the question whether the city had violated Collins' constitutional rights because it denied recovery on the ground that there had been no "abuse of governmental power," which the Fifth Circuit had found to be a necessary element of a § 1983 action. . . .

The First Amendment, the Equal Protection and Due Process Clauses of the Fourteenth Amendment, and other provisions of the Federal Constitution afford protection to employees who serve the government as well as to those who are served by them, and § 1983 provides a cause of action for all citizens injured by an abridgement of those protections. Neither the fact that petitioner's decedent was a government employee nor the characterization of the city's deliberate indifference to his safety as something other than an "abuse of governmental power" is a sufficient reason for refusing to entertain petitioner's federal claim under § 1983. . . .

II

Section 1983 provides a remedy against "any person" who, under color of state law, deprives another of rights protected by the Constitution. In *Monell,* the Court held that Congress intended municipalities and other local government entities to be included among those persons to whom § 1983 applies. 436 U.S., at 690. At the same time, the Court made it clear that municipalities may not be held liable "unless action pursuant to official municipal policy of some nature caused a constitutional tort."

III

[7] Petitioner's constitutional claim rests entirely on the Due Process Clause of the Fourteenth Amendment. The most familiar office of that Clause is to provide a guarantee of fair procedure in connection with any deprivation of life, liberty, or property by a State. Petitioner, however, does not advance a procedural due process claim in this case. Instead, she relies on the substantive component of the Clause that protects individual liberty against "certain government actions regardless of the fairness of the procedures used to implement them." *Daniels v. Williams,* 474 U.S. 327, 331 (1986). . . .

As a general matter, the Court has always been reluctant to expand the concept of substantive due process because guideposts for responsible decisionmaking in this unchartered area are scarce and open-ended. The doctrine of judicial self-restraint requires us to exercise the utmost care whenever we are asked to break new ground in this field. It is important, therefore, to focus on the allegations in the complaint to determine how petitioner describes the constitutional right at stake and what the city allegedly did to deprive her husband of that right.

A fair reading of petitioner's complaint does not charge the city with a willful violation of Collins' rights. Petitioner does not claim that the city or any of its agents deliberately harmed her husband. In fact, she does not even allege that his supervisor instructed him to go into the sewer when the supervisor knew or should have known that there was a significant risk that he would be injured. Instead, she makes the more general allegation that the city deprived him of life and liberty by failing to provide a reasonably safe work environment. Fairly analyzed, her claim advances two theories: that the Federal Constitution imposes a duty on the city to provide its employees with minimal levels of safety and security in the workplace, or that the city's "deliberate indifference" to Collins' safety was arbitrary Government action that must "shock the conscience" of federal judges. Cf. *Rochin v. California,* 342 U.S. 165 (1952). . . .

[8][9] Neither the text nor the history of the Due Process Clause supports petitioner's claim that the governmental employer's duty to provide its employees with a safe working environment is a substantive component of the Due Process Clause. "[T]he Due Process Clause of the Fourteenth Amendment was intended to prevent government 'from abusing [its] power, or employing it as an instrument of oppression.' " *DeShaney v. Winnebago County Department of Social Services,* 489 U.S., at 196. As we recognized in *DeShaney,* "The Clause is phrased as a limitation on the State's power to act, not as a guarantee of certain minimal levels of safety and security. It forbids the State itself to deprive individuals of life, liberty, or property without 'due process of law,' but its language cannot fairly be extended to impose an affirmative obligation on the State to ensure that those interests do not come to harm through other means. Nor does history support such an expansive reading of the constitutional text." . . .

[10] Petitioner's submission that the city violated a federal constitutional obligation to provide its employees with certain minimal levels of safety and security is unprecedented. It is quite different from the constitutional claim advanced by plaintiffs in several of our prior cases who argued that the State owes a duty to take care of those who have already been deprived of their liberty. We have held, for example, that apart from the protection against cruel and unusual punishment provided by the Eighth Amendment, the Due Process Clause of its own force requires that conditions of confinement satisfy certain minimal standards for pretrial detainees, see *Bell v. Wolfish,* 441 U.S. 520, 535 (1979), for persons in mental institutions, *Youngberg v. Romeo,* 457 U.S. 307 (1982), for convicted felons, *Turner v. Safley,* 482 U.S. 78 (1987), and for persons under arrest, see *Revere v. Massachusetts General Hospital,* 463 U.S. 239 (1983). The "process" that the Constitution guarantees in connection with any deprivation of liberty thus includes a continuing obligation to satisfy certain minimal custodial standards. See *DeShaney,* 489 U.S., at 200. Petitioner cannot maintain, however, that the city deprived Collins of his liberty when it made, and he voluntarily accepted, an offer of employment.

[11][12] We also are not persuaded that the city's alleged failure to train its employees, or to warn them about known risks of harm, was an omission that can properly be characterized as arbitrary, or conscience-shocking, in a constitutional sense. Petitioner's claim is analogous to a fairly typical state law tort claim: The city breached its duty of care to her husband by failing to provide a safe work environment. Because the Due Process Clause "does not purport to supplant traditional tort law in laying down rules of conduct to regulate liability for injuries that attend living together in society," we have previously rejected claims that the Due Process Clause should be interpreted to impose federal duties that are analogous to those traditionally imposed by state tort law. The reasoning in those cases applies with special force to claims asserted against public employers because state law, rather than the Federal Constitution, generally governs the substance of the employment relationship. See, e.g., *Bishop v. Wood,* 426 U.S. 341, 350 (1976); *Board of Regents of State Colleges v. Roth,* 408 U.S. 564 (1972).

[13][14] Our refusal to characterize the city's alleged omission in this case as arbitrary in a con-

stitutional sense rests on the presumption that the administration of Government programs is based on a rational decisionmaking process that takes account of competing social, political, and economic forces. Decisions concerning the allocation of resources to individual programs, such as sewer maintenance, and to particular aspects of those programs, such as the training and compensation of employees, involve a host of policy choices that must be made by locally elected representatives, rather than by federal judges interpreting the basic charter of Government for the entire country. The Due Process Clause "is not a guarantee against incorrect or ill-advised personnel decisions." *Bishop v. Wood,* 426 U.S., at 350. Nor does it guarantee municipal employees a workplace that is free of unreasonable risks of harm.

The judgment of the Court of Appeals is therefore affirmed.

It is so ordered.

WALTERS V. NATIONAL ASSOCIATION OF RADIATION SURVIVORS
473 U.S. 305 (1985)

Justice Rehnquist delivered the opinion of the Court, joined by Justices White, Powell, and Scalia. Justices O'Connor and Blackmun concurred. Justices Brennan, Marshall, and Stevens dissented.

Title 38 U.S.C. § 3404(c) limits to $10 the fee that may be paid an attorney or agent who represents a veteran seeking benefits for service-connected death or disability. The United States District Court for the Northern District of California held that this limit violates the Due Process Clause of the Fifth Amendment, and the First Amendment, because it denies veterans or their survivors the opportunity to retain counsel of their choice in pursuing their claims. We noted probable jurisdiction of the Government's appeal, and we now reverse.

I

Congress has by statute established an administrative system for granting service-connected death or disability benefits to veterans. See 38 U.S.C. § 301 et seq. The amount of the benefit award is not based upon need, but upon service connection—that is, whether the disability is causally related to an injury sustained in the service—and the degree of incapacity caused by the disability. A detailed system has been established by statute and Veterans' Administration (VA) regulation for determining a veteran's entitlement, with final authority resting with an administrative body known as the Board of Veterans' Appeals (BVA). Judicial review of VA decisions is precluded by statute. 38 U.S.C. § 211(a); *Johnson v. Robison,* 415 U.S. 361 (1974). The controversy in this case centers on the opportunity for a benefit applicant or recipient to obtain legal counsel to aid in the presentation of his claim to the VA. Section 3404(c) of Title 38 provides: "The Administrator shall determine and pay fees to agents or attorneys recognized under this section in allowed claims for monetary benefits under laws administered by the Veterans' Administration. Such fees . . . (2) shall not exceed $10 with respect to any one claim. . . ." Section 3405 provides criminal penalties for any person who charges fees in excess of the limitation of § 3404. . . .

Congress began providing veterans pensions in early 1789, and after every conflict in which the nation has been involved Congress has, in the words of Abraham Lincoln, "provided for him who has borne the battle, and his widow and his orphan." The VA was created by Congress in 1930, and since that time has been responsible for administering the congressional program for veterans' benefits. In 1978, the year covered by the report of the Legal Services Corporation to Congress that was introduced into evidence in the District Court, approximately 800,000 claims for service-connected disability or death and pensions were decided by the 58 regional offices of the VA. Slightly more than half of these were claims for service-connected disability or death, and the remainder were pension claims. Of the 800,000 total claims in 1978, more than 400,000 were allowed, and some 379,000 were denied. Sixty-six thousand of these denials were contested at the regional level; about a quarter of these contests were dropped, 15% prevailed on reconsideration at the local level, and the remaining 36,000 were appealed to the BVA. At that level some 4,500, or 12%, prevailed, and another 13% won a remand for further proceedings. Although these figures are from 1978, the statistics in evidence indicate that the figures remain fairly constant from year to year.

As might be expected in a system which processes such a large number of claims each year, the process prescribed by Congress for obtaining disability benefits does not contemplate the adversary mode of dispute resolution utilized by courts in this country. A claimant is "entitled to a hearing at any time on any issue involved in a claim. . . ." Proceedings in front of the rating board "are ex parte in nature," no Government official appears in opposition. The principal issues are the extent of the claimant's disability and whether it is service connected. The board is required by regulation "to assist a claimant in developing the facts pertinent to his claim," and to consider any evidence offered by the claimant. In deciding the claim the board generally will request the applicant's Armed Service and medical records, and will order a medical examination by a VA hospital. Moreover, the board is directed by regulation to resolve all reasonable doubts in favor of the claimant. . . .

After reviewing the evidence the board renders a decision either denying the claim or assigning a disability "rating" pursuant to detailed regulations developed for assessing various disabilities. Money benefits are calculated based on the rating. The claimant is notified of the board's decision and its reasons, and the claimant may then initiate an appeal by filing a "notice of disagreement" with the local agency. If the local agency adheres to its original decision it must then provide the claimant with a "statement of the case"—a written description of the facts and applicable law upon which the board based its determination—so that the claimant may adequately present his appeal to the BVA. Hearings in front of the BVA are subject to the same rules as local agency hearings—they are ex parte, there is no formal questioning or cross-examination, and no formal rules of evidence apply. The BVA's decision is not subject to judicial review. . . .

In reaching its conclusions the court relied heavily on the problems presented by what it described as "complex cases"—a class of cases also focused on in the depositions. Though never expressly defined by the District Court, these cases apparently include those in which a disability is slow developing and therefore difficult to find service connected, such as the claims associated with exposure to radiation or harmful chemicals, as well as other cases identified by the deponents as involving difficult matters of medical judgment. Nowhere in the opinion of the District Court is there any estimate of what percentage of the annual VA caseload of 800,000 these cases comprise, nor is there any more precise description of the class. There is no question but what the 3 named plaintiffs and the plaintiff veteran's widow asserted such claims, and in addition there are declarations in the record from 12 other claimants who were asserting such claims. The evidence contained in the record, however, suggests that the sum total of such claims is extremely small; in 1982, for example, roughly 2% of the BVA caseload consisted of "agent orange" or "radiation" claims, and what evidence there is suggests that the percentage of such claims in the regional offices was even less—perhaps as little as 3 in 1,000.

With respect to the service representatives, the court again found the representation unsatisfactory. Although admitting that this was not due to any "lack of dedication," the court found that a heavy caseload and the lack of legal training combined to prevent service representatives from adequately researching a claim. Facts are not developed, and "it is standard practice for service organization representatives to submit merely a one to two page handwritten brief."

Based on the inability of the VA and service organizations to provide the full range of services that a retained attorney might, the court concluded that appellees had demonstrated a "high risk of erroneous deprivation" from the process as administered. Ibid. The court then found that the Government had "failed to demonstrate that it would suffer any harm if the statutory fee limitation . . . were lifted." The only Government interest suggested was the "paternalistic" assertion that the fee limitation is necessary to ensure that claimants do not turn substantial portions of their benefits over to unscrupulous lawyers. The court suggested that there were "less drastic means" to confront this problem. . . .

In the face of this congressional commitment to the fee limitation for more than a century, the District Court had only this to say with respect to the governmental interest: "The government has neither argued nor shown that lifting the fee limit would harm the government in any way, except as the paternalistic protector of claimants' supposed best interests. To the extent the paternalistic role is valid, there are less drastic means available to ensure that attorneys' fees do not deplete veterans' death or disability benefits." 589 F.Supp., at 1323.

It is not for the District Court or any other federal court to invalidate a federal statute by so cavalierly dismissing a long-asserted congressional purpose. If "paternalism" is an insignificant Government interest, then Congress first went astray in 1792, when by its Act of March 23 of that year it prohibited the "sale, transfer or mortgage . . . of the pension . . . [of a] soldier . . . before the same shall become due." Acts of Congress long on the books, such as the Fair Labor Standards Act, might similarly be described as "paternalistic"; indeed, this Court once opined that "[s]tatutes of the nature of that under review, limiting the hours in which grown and intelligent men may labor to earn their living, are mere meddlesome interferences with the rights of the individual. . . ." *Lochner v. New York,* 198 U.S. 45, 61 (1905). That day is fortunately long gone, and with it the condemnation of rational paternalism as a legitimate legislative goal.

There can be little doubt that invalidation of the fee limitation would seriously frustrate the oft-repeated congressional purpose for enacting it. Attorneys would be freely employable by claimants to veterans' benefits, and the claimant would as a result end up paying part of the award, or its equivalent, to an attorney.

The flexibility of our approach in due process cases is intended in part to allow room for other forms of dispute resolution; with respect to the individual interests at stake here, legislatures are to be allowed considerable leeway to formulate such processes without being forced to conform to a rigid constitutional code of procedural necessities. It would take an extraordinarily strong showing of probability of error under the present system—and the probability that the presence of attorneys would sharply diminish that possibility—to warrant a holding that the fee limitation denies claimants due process of law. We have no hesitation in deciding that no such showing was made out on the record before the District Court.

[7] Thus none of our cases dealing with constitutionally required representation by counsel requires the conclusion reached by the District Court. Especially in light of the Government interests at stake, the evidence adduced before the District Court as to success rates in claims handled with or without lawyers shows no such great disparity as to warrant the inference that the congressional fee limitation under consideration here violates the Due Process Clause of the Fifth Amendment. What evidence we have been pointed to in the record regarding complex cases falls far short of the kind which would warrant upsetting Congress' judgment that this is the manner in which it wishes claims for veterans' benefits adjudicated. The District Court abused its discretion in holding otherwise.

PACIFIC MUTUAL LIFE INSURANCE COMPANY V. HASLIP
111 S.CT. 1032 (1991)

Justice Blackmun delivered the opinion of the Court, joined by Chief Justice Rehnquist and Justices White, Marshall, and Stevens. Justices Scalia and Kennedy filed opinions concurring in the judgment. Justice O'Connor filed a dissenting opinion, and Justice Souter took no part in the consideration or decision of the case.

This case is yet another that presents a challenge to a punitive damages award.

I

In 1981, Lemmie L. Ruffin, Jr., was an Alabama-licensed agent for petitioner Pacific Mutual Life

Insurance Company. He also was a licensed agent for Union Fidelity Life Insurance Company. Pacific Mutual and Union are distinct and nonaffiliated entities. Union wrote group health insurance for municipalities. Pacific Mutual did not.

Respondents Cleopatra Haslip, Cynthia Craig, Alma M. Calhoun, and Eddie Hargrove were employees of Roosevelt City, an Alabama municipality. Ruffin, presenting himself as an agent of Pacific Mutual, solicited the city for both health and life insurance for its employees. The city was interested. Ruffin gave the city a single proposal for both coverages. The city approved and, in August

1981, Ruffin prepared separate applications for the city and its employees for group health with Union and for individual life policies with Pacific Mutual. This packaging of health insurance with life insurance, although from different and unrelated insurers, was not unusual. Indeed, it tended to boost life insurance sales by minimizing the loss of customers who wished to have both health and life protection. The initial premium payments were taken by Ruffin and submitted to the insurers with the applications. Thus far, nothing is claimed to have been out of line. Respondents were among those with the health coverage.

An arrangement was made for Union to send its billings for health premiums to Ruffin at Pacific Mutual's Birmingham office. Premium payments were to be effected through payroll deductions. The city clerk each month issued a check for those premiums. The check was sent to Ruffin or picked up by him. He, however, did not remit to Union the premium payments received from the city; instead, he misappropriated most of them. In late 1981, when Union did not receive payment, it sent notices of lapsed health coverage to respondents in care of Ruffin and Patrick Lupia, Pacific Mutual's agent-in-charge of its Birmingham office. Those notices were not forwarded to respondents. Although there is some evidence to the contrary, the trial court found, that respondents did not know that their health policies had been canceled.

II

Respondent Haslip was hospitalized on January 23, 1982. She incurred hospital and physician's charges. Because the hospital could not confirm health coverage, it required Haslip, upon her discharge, to make a payment upon her bill. Her physician, when he was not paid, placed her account with a collection agency. The agency obtained a judgment against Haslip and her credit was adversely affected.

In May 1982, respondents filed this suit, naming as defendants Pacific Mutual (but not Union) and Ruffin, individually and as a proprietorship, in the Circuit Court for Jefferson County, Ala. It was alleged that Ruffin collected premiums but failed to remit them to the insurers so that respondents' respective health insurance policies lapsed without their knowledge. Damages for fraud were claimed. The case against Pacific Mutual was submitted to the jury under a theory of *respondeat superior.*

Following the trial court's charge on liability, the jury was instructed that if it determined there was

liability for fraud, it could award punitive damages. That part of the instructions is set forth in the margin. Pacific Mutual made no objection on the ground of lack of specificity in the instructions and it did not propose a more particularized charge. No evidence was introduced as to Pacific Mutual's financial worth. The jury returned general verdicts for respondents against Pacific Mutual and Ruffin in the following amounts: Haslip: $1,040,000; Calhoun: 15,290. . . .

Judgments were entered accordingly.

On Pacific Mutual's appeal, the Supreme Court of Alabama, by a divided vote, affirmed. 553 So.2d 537 (1989). In addition to issues not now before us, the court ruled that, while punitive damages are not recoverable in Alabama for misrepresentation made innocently or by mistake, they are recoverable for deceit or willful fraud, and that on the evidence in this case a jury could not have concluded that Ruffin's misrepresentations were made either innocently or mistakenly. The majority then specifically upheld the punitive damages award. . . . Pacific Mutual, but not Ruffin, then brought the case here. It challenged punitive damages in Alabama as the product of unbridled jury discretion and as violative of its due process rights. We stayed enforcement of the Haslip judgment, to review the punitive damages procedures and award in the light of the long-enduring debate about their propriety. . . .

III

This Court and individual Justices thereof on a number of occasions in recent years have expressed doubts about the constitutionality of certain punitive damages awards. . . . There is some authority in our opinions for the view that the Due Process Clause places outer limits on the size of a civil damages award made pursuant to a statutory scheme . . . but we have never addressed the precise question presented here: whether due process acts as a check on undue jury discretion to award punitive damages in the absence of any express statutory limit. . . . That inquiry must await another day. . . .

[5] So far as we have been able to determine, every state and federal court that has considered the question has ruled that the common-law method for assessing punitive damages does not in itself violate due process. In view of this consistent history, we cannot say that the common-law method for assessing punitive damages is so inherently unfair as to deny due process and be per se unconstitutional. . . .

[6] This, however, is not the end of the matter. It would be just as inappropriate to say that, because punitive damages have been recognized for so long, their imposition is never unconstitutional. ("[N]either the antiquity of a practice nor the fact of steadfast legislative and judicial adherence to it through the centuries insulates it from constitutional attack. . . .") We note once again our concern about punitive damages that "run wild." Having said that, we conclude that our task today is to determine whether the Due Process Clause renders the punitive damages award in this case constitutionally unacceptable. . . .

VI

[7] One must concede that unlimited jury discretion—or unlimited judicial discretion for that matter—in the fixing of punitive damages may invite extreme results that jar one's constitutional sensibilities. We need not, and indeed we cannot, draw a mathematical bright line between the constitutionally acceptable and the constitutionally unacceptable that would fit every case. We can say, however, that general concerns of reasonableness and adequate guidance from the court when the case is tried to a jury properly enter into the constitutional calculus. With these concerns in mind, we review the constitutionality of the punitive damages awarded in this case. . . .

[8] We conclude that the punitive damages assessed by the jury against Pacific Mutual were not violative of the Due Process Clause of the Fourteenth Amendment.

[9] 1. We have carefully reviewed the instructions to the jury. By these instructions, see n. 1, supra, the trial court expressly described for the jury the purpose of punitive damages, namely, "not to compensate the plaintiff for any injury" but "to punish the defendant" and "for the added purpose of protecting the public by [deterring] the defendant and others from doing such wrong in the future." . . .

These instructions, we believe, reasonably accommodated Pacific Mutual's interest in rational decisionmaking and Alabama's interest in meaningful individualized assessment of appropriate deterrence and retribution.

[14] We are aware that the punitive damages award in this case is more than 4 times the amount of compensatory damages, is more than 200 times the out-of-pocket expenses of respondent Haslip, and, of course, is much in excess of the fine that could be imposed for insurance fraud under Ala.Code §§ 13A-5-11 and 13A-5-12(a) (1982).

Imprisonment, however, could also be required of an individual in the criminal context. While the monetary comparisons are wide and, indeed, may be close to the line, the award here did not lack objective criteria. We conclude, after careful consideration, that in this case it does not cross the line into the area of constitutional impropriety. Accordingly, Pacific Mutual's due process challenge must be, and is, rejected. The judgment of the Supreme Court of Alabama is affirmed.

It is so ordered.

Justice O'Connor, dissenting.

Punitive damages are a powerful weapon. Imposed wisely and with restraint, they have the potential to advance legitimate state interests. Imposed indiscriminately, however, they have a devastating potential for harm. Regrettably, common-law procedures for awarding punitive damages fall into the latter category. States routinely authorize civil juries to impose punitive damages without providing them any meaningful instructions on how to do so. Rarely is a jury told anything more specific than "do what you think best." See *Browning-Ferris Industries v. Kelco Disposal, Inc.,* 492 U.S. 257, 109 S.Ct. 2909, 2923, 106 L.Ed.2d 219 (1989) (Brennan, J., concurring).

In my view, such instructions are so fraught with uncertainty that they defy rational implementation. Instead, they encourage inconsistent and unpredictable results by inviting juries to rely on private beliefs and personal predilections. Juries are permitted to target unpopular defendants, penalize unorthodox or controversial views, and redistribute wealth. Multimillion dollar losses are inflicted on a whim. While I do not question the general legitimacy of punitive damages, I see a strong need to provide juries with standards to constrain their discretion so that they may exercise their power wisely, not capriciously or maliciously. The Constitution requires as much. . . .

III

" 'The touchstone of due process is protection of the individual against arbitrary action of government.' " *Daniels v. Williams,* 474 U.S. 327, 331 (1986). Alabama's common-law scheme for awarding punitive damages provides a jury with "such skeletal guidance," *Browning-Ferris,* supra, 492 U.S. at —— (Brennan, J., concurring), that it invites—even requires—arbitrary results. It gives free reign to the biases and prejudices of individual jurors, allowing them to target unpopular defendants and punish selectively. In short, it is the antithesis of due process. It does not matter that the system has been around for a long time, or that the result in this particular case may not seem glaringly unfair. The common-law scheme yields unfair and inconsistent results "in so many instances that it should be held violative of due process in every case."

For more than 20 years, this Court has criticized common-law punitive damages procedures, see supra, at 1062-1063, but has shied away from its duty to step in, hoping that the problems would go away. It is now clear that the problems are getting worse, and that the time has come to address them squarely. The Court does address them today. In my view, however, it offers an incorrect answer.

You may have noticed that the majority opinion in the *Haslip* case said it was a close call but that, given the facts, the punitive damage award did not violate due process. Justice O'Connor's dissent said that whenever juries are sent off to consider punitive damages without instructions, it causes arbitrary jury decisions and hence a violation of due process. In 1996, a badly divided Court finally found a case in which a jury award of punitive damages did violate due process. The case is *BMW of North America v. Gore,* 116 S.Ct. 1589 (1996). Dr. Gore purchased a $40,000 BMW and drove it about for nine months without notice of problems. When he took it to an auto body shop, the auto body worker told him it had been repainted as if it had been in an accident. BMW admitted that the car had suffered damage and had been repainted but said that the company adopted a rule in 1983 that it would not inform its dealers (and hence its customers) of prior damage to its cars if the damage was less than 3 percent of the total cost of the car. The jury awarded compensatory damages of $4,000 and punitive damages of $2,000,000. The Supreme Court reversed, saying that the award violated BMW's due process.

The case is important because it established three criteria for when a jury award of punitive damages is so grossly excessive that it violates due process. The three criteria are (a) the reprehensibility of the defendant's conduct, (b) the disparity between the compensatory damage award and the punitive damage award, and (c) whether the punitive award is comparable to other similar cases.

FOUCHA V. LOUISIANA
112 S.CT. 1780 (1992)

Justice White announced the judgment of the Court and delivered the opinion of the Court with respect to Parts I and II, in which Justices Blackmun, Stevens, O'Connor, and Souter joined, and an opinion with respect to Part III, in which Justices Blackmun, Stevens, and Souter joined. Justice O'Connor filed an opinion concurring in part and

concurring in the judgment. Justice Kennedy filed a dissenting opinion, joined by Chief Justice Rehnquist. Justice Thomas filed a dissenting opinion, joined by Chief Justice Rehnquist and Justice Scalia.

When a defendant in a criminal case pending in Louisiana is found not guilty by reason of insanity, he is committed to a psychiatric hospital unless he proves that he is not dangerous. This is so whether or not he is then insane. After commitment, if the acquittee or the superintendent begins release proceedings, a review panel at the hospital makes a written report on the patient's mental condition and whether he can be released without danger to himself or others. If release is recommended, the court must hold a hearing to determine dangerousness; the acquittee has the burden of proving that he is not dangerous. If found to be dangerous, the acquittee may be returned to the mental institution whether or not he is then mentally ill. Petitioner contends that this scheme denies him due process and equal protection because it allows a person acquitted by reason of insanity to be committed to a mental institution until he is able to demonstrate that he is not dangerous to himself and others, even though he does not suffer from any mental illness.

I

Petitioner Terry Foucha was charged by Louisiana authorities with aggravated burglary and illegal discharge of a firearm. Two medical doctors were appointed to conduct a pretrial examination of Foucha. The doctors initially reported, and the trial court initially found, that Foucha lacked mental capacity to proceed, but four months later the trial court found Foucha competent to stand trial. The doctors reported that Foucha was unable to distinguish right from wrong and was insane at the time of the offense. On October 12, 1984, the trial court ruled that Foucha was not guilty by reason of insanity, finding that he "is unable to appreciate the usual, natural and probable consequences of his acts; that he is unable to distinguish right from wrong; that he is a menace to himself and others; and that he was insane at the time of the commission of the above crimes and that he is presently insane." He was committed to the East Feliciana Forensic Facility until such time as doctors recommend that he be released, and until further order of the court.

In 1988, the superintendent of Feliciana recommended that Foucha be discharged or released. A three-member panel was convened at the institution to determine Foucha's current condition and whether he could be released or placed on probation without being a danger to others or himself. On March 21, 1988, the panel reported that there had been no evidence of mental illness since admission

and recommended that Foucha be conditionally discharged. The trial judge appointed a two-member sanity commission made up of the same two doctors who had conducted the pretrial examination. Their written report stated that Foucha "is presently in remission from mental illness [but] [w]e cannot certify that he would not constitute a menace to himself or others if released." One of the doctors testified at a hearing that upon commitment Foucha probably suffered from a drug induced psychosis but that he had recovered from that temporary condition; that he evidenced no signs of psychosis or neurosis and was in "good shape" mentally; that he has, however, an antisocial personality, a condition that is not a mental disease and that is untreatable. The doctor also testified that Foucha had been involved in several altercations at Feliciana and that he, the doctor, would not "feel comfortable in certifying that [Foucha] would not be a danger to himself or to other people." . . .

After it was stipulated that the other doctor, if he were present, would give essentially the same testimony, the court ruled that Foucha was dangerous to himself and others and ordered him returned to the mental institution. The Court of Appeals refused supervisory writs, and the State Supreme Court affirmed, holding that Foucha had not carried the burden placed upon him by statute to prove that he was not dangerous, that our decision in *Jones v. United States,* 463 U.S. 354 (1983), did not require Foucha's release, and that neither the Due Process Clause nor the Equal Protection Clause was violated by the statutory provision permitting confinement of an insanity acquittee based on dangerousness alone.

Because the case presents an important issue and was decided by the court below in a manner arguably at odds with prior decisions of this Court, we granted certiorari.

II

Addington v. Texas, 441 U.S. 418 (1979), held that to commit an individual to a mental institution in a civil proceeding, the State is required by the Due Process Clause to prove by clear and convincing evidence the two statutory preconditions to commitment: that the person sought to be committed is mentally ill and that he requires hospitalization for his own welfare and protection of others. Proof beyond reasonable doubt was not required, but proof by preponderance of the evidence fell short of satisfying due process. . . .

When a person charged with having committed a crime is found not guilty by reason of insanity, however, a State may commit that person without satisfying the *Addington* burden with respect to mental illness and dangerousness. *Jones v. United States,* supra. Such a verdict, we observed in *Jones,* "establishes two facts: (i) the defendant committed an act that constitutes a criminal offense, and (ii) he committed the act because of mental illness," an illness that the defendant adequately proved in this context by a preponderance of the evidence. From these two facts, it could be properly inferred that at the time of the verdict, the defendant was still mentally ill and dangerous and hence could be committed. . . .

[1] We held, however, that "[t]he committed acquittee is entitled to release when he has recovered his sanity or is no longer dangerous," i.e., the acquittee may be held as long as he is both mentally ill and dangerous, but no longer. We relied on *O'Connor v. Donaldson,* 422 U.S. 563 (1975), which held as a matter of due process that it was unconstitutional for a State to continue to confine a harmless, mentally ill person. . . . In this case, Louisiana does not contend that Foucha was mentally ill at the time of the trial court's hearing. Thus, the basis for holding Foucha in a psychiatric facility as an insanity acquittee has disappeared, and the State is no longer entitled to hold him on that basis. . . .

The State, however, seeks to perpetuate Foucha's confinement at Feliciana on the basis of his antisocial personality which, as evidenced by his conduct at the facility, the court found rendered him a danger to himself or others. There are at least three difficulties with this position. First, even if his continued confinement were constitutionally permissible, keeping Foucha against his will in a mental institution is improper absent a determination in civil commitment proceedings of current mental illness and dangerousness. Due process requires that the nature of commitment bear some reasonable relation to the purpose for which the individual is committed. Here, according to the testimony given at the hearing in the trial court, Foucha is not suffering from a mental disease or illness. If he is to be held, he should not be held as a mentally ill person.

Second, if Foucha can no longer be held as an insanity acquittee in a mental hospital, he is entitled to constitutionally adequate procedures to establish the grounds for his confinement.

Third, "the Due Process Clause contains a substantive component that bars certain arbitrary, wrongful government actions 'regardless of the fairness of the procedures used to implement them.' " *Zinermon v. Burch,* 494 U.S. 113 (1990). Freedom from bodily restraint has always been at the core of the liberty protected by the Due Process Clause from arbitrary governmental action. *Youngberg v. Romeo,* 457 U.S. 307, 316 (1982). "It is clear that commitment for any purpose constitutes a significant deprivation of liberty that requires due process protection" (internal quotation marks omitted). We have always been careful not to "minimize the importance and fundamental nature" of the individual's right to liberty.

A State, pursuant to its police power, may of course imprison convicted criminals for the purposes of deterrence and retribution. But there are constitutional limitations on the conduct that a State may criminalize. See, e.g., *Brandenburg v. Ohio,* 395 U.S. 444 (1969); *Robinson v. California,* 370 U.S. 660 (1962). Here, the State has no such punitive interest. As Foucha was not convicted, he may not be punished. Here, Louisiana has by reason of his acquittal exempted Foucha from criminal responsibility as La.Rev.Stat.Ann. § 14:14 (West 1986) requires.

[2] The State may also confine a mentally ill person if it shows "by clear and convincing evidence that the individual is mentally ill and dangerous." Here, the State has not carried that burden; indeed, the State does not claim that Foucha is now mentally ill. . . . "In our society liberty is the norm, and detention prior to trial or without trial is the carefully limited exception." *United States v. Salerno,* supra, 481 U.S., at 755. The narrowly focused pretrial detention of arrestees permitted by the Bail Reform Act was found to be one of those carefully limited exceptions permitted by the Due Process Clause. We decline to take a similar view of a law like Louisiana's, which permits the indefinite detention of insanity acquittees who are not mentally ill but who do not prove they would not be dangerous to others. . . . For the foregoing reasons the judgment of the Louisiana Supreme Court is reversed.

So ordered.

NOTES

1. Because the Court's treatment of the facts in this case was, to be generous, antiseptic, additional factual information in this scenario comes from Phillip J. Cooper, *Public Law and Public Administration,* 2d ed. (Upper Saddle River, NJ: Prentice Hall, 1988), 403-52.

2. 397 U.S. 254 (1970).

3. *Ewing v. Mytinger and Casselberry, Incorporated,* 339 U.S. 594 (1950).

4. *North American Cold Storage Company v. Chicago,* 211 U.S. 306 (1908).

5. *Yakus v. United States,* 321 U.S. 414 (1944).

6. *Miller v. Schoene,* 276 U.S. 272 (1928).

7. *Gonzalez v. Freeman,* 334 F.2d. 570 (D.C. Cir. 1964).

8. *Cafeteria and Restaurant Workers Union v. McElroy,* 367 U.S. 886 (1961).

9. *Morrissey v. Brewer,* 408 U.S. 471 (1972).

10. *Gagnon v. Scarpelli,* 411 U.S. 778 (1973).

11. *Wolff v. McDonnell,* 418 U.S. 539 (1974).

12. *Bell v. Burson,* 402 U.S. 535 (1971).

13. *Goss v. Lopez,* 419 U.S. 565 (1975).

14. *Wisconsin v. Constantineau,* 400 U.S. 208 (1971).

15. *Caulker v. Durham,* 433 F.2d 998 (4th Cir. 1970), Cert. denied 401 U.S. 1003 (1971).

16. *Fuentes v. Shevin,* 407 U.S. 67 (1972).

17. *Sniadach v. Family Finance Corporation,* 395 U.S. 337 (1969).

18. *Vlandis v. Kline,* 412 U.S. 441 (1973).

19. Cooper, *Public Law and Public Administration,* 404-05.

20. Ibid., 405.

21. Ibid.

22. Ibid.

23. Ibid.

24. Ibid.

25. Ibid., 407.

26. Ibid.

27. Ibid., 408.

28. Ibid.

29. Ibid.

30. Ibid.

31. Ibid.

32. Ibid., 409.

33. Ibid.

34. Ibid., 409-10.

35. *Eldridge v. Weinberger,* 651 F.Supp. 520 (1973).

36. 493 F.2d. 1230 (4th Cir. 1974).

37. Cooper, *Public Law and Public Administration,* 447.

38. Ibid.

39. Ibid., 404.

40. *Jackson v. Metropolitan Edison Company,* 419 U.S. 345 (1974).

41. *Moose Lodge #107 v. Irvis,* 407 U.S. 163 (1972).

42. *Blum v. Yaretsky,* 457 U.S. 991 (1982).

43. *San Francisco Arts and Athletic Inc. v. U.S. Olympic Committee,* 483 U.S. 522 (1987) and *National Collegiate Athletic Association v. Tarkanian,* 108 S.Ct. 454 (1988).

44. *Kelly v. Johnson,* 425 U.S. 238 (1976).

45. Walter Gellhorn, "The Abuse of Occupational Licensing," *University of Chicago Law Review* 44 (1976): 6.

46. See, for example, *Gibson v. Berryhill,* 411 U.S. 564 (1973).

47. *Hornsby v. Allen,* 326 F.2d. 605 (5th Cir. 1964).

CHAPTER 10

SUING THE GOVERNMENT

CASE IN POINT:
DALEHITE V. UNITED STATES,
346 U.S. 15 (1953)

At the end of World War II, a good deal of Europe lay in ruins. To help preserve the peace and the stability of European governments, the United States embarked on a policy of helping Europe feed itself. It was not possible for the United States to send enough food, so part of the policy adopted was to send fertilizer to help Europe grow plentiful crops as soon as possible. The fertilizer chosen was "fertilizer grade ammonium nitrate" (FGAN). Ammonium nitrate is a component that was then found in explosives. Indeed, it is the explosive the government says was used to blow up the Murrah Federal Building in Oklahoma City. The government reopened munitions plants that had been closed after the war and produced the ammonium nitrate. The nitrate was sent to private companies (DuPont and Hercules Powder Company), which contracted with the government to produce FGAN. An army ordinance officer was assigned to each plant that produced FGAN to oversee its production.

The government of France purchased 2,800 tons of FGAN and stored it in a warehouse for three weeks in Texas City, Texas, while waiting for ships to transport the fertilizer to France. On June 15, 1947, 1,850 tons of FGAN were loaded into a hold on a French ship, the *Grandcamp,* and the other 1,000 tons were loaded into the *High Flyer,* which also held 2,000 tons of sulfur. The *Grandcamp* also held substantial additional explosives on board. On June 16, at 8:15 a.m., smoke in the hold where the FGAN was stored led to the discovery of a fire in that hold aboard the *Grandcamp.* All hatches were closed, and steam was introduced into the hold, but it did not retard the fire. The captain ordered the ship to be vacated, and less than an hour after the smoke was first detected, the FGAN in the hold exploded, causing the FGAN in the other holds to explode, which then caused the other explosives aboard the *Grandcamp* to explode. Fire was thrown to the dock area of the city and to the *High Flyer,* which was docked at the next pier. Efforts to contain the blaze aboard the *High Flyer* were unsuccessful, as was an attempt to tow it out to sea. At 1 a.m. on June 17, the sulfur and FGAN aboard the *High Flyer* exploded with a blast that leveled what was left of the burning dock area of the city. The explosions and fire claimed the lives of 560 people, injured 3,000,[1] and caused property damage in the neighborhood of $200 million.[2]

The survivors of Henry G. Dalehite were among three hundred parties who sued the government for negligence. The plaintiffs claimed in this case,[3] and the trial judge found as a matter of fact, that the controlling negligence law is that of the place where the negligent act (or omission) occurred. The FGAN involved in the Texas City incident was manufactured in Iowa and Nebraska, so their negligence laws were controlling. The Erie Doctrine[4] requires that, in a federal court action in which no federal law applies (Congress does not pass tort or negligence laws because they are the sole province of the states), the federal courts must apply appropriate state law. The negligence laws of both Nebraska and Iowa hold that a manufacturer is liable for defects in its product that could have been avoided by the exercise of reasonable care (sometimes called "due care"). The plaintiffs also claimed, and the trial judge found, that the government failed to exercise reasonable care by (a) discontinuing the testing of FGAN when tests at that point indicated "suspected but unverified dangers," (b) packaging the FGAN at temperatures that were too high and packaging it in paper bags, (c) ignoring a history of unexplained fires and explosions involving ammonium nitrate, and (d) failing to warn (by labeling the sacks of FGAN as "fertilizer" instead of warning of the explosive nature of the product).

This last finding, failure to warn, is important because the cause of the fire was either spontaneous combustion or a smoldering cigarette left by a longshoreman.

If it was the latter, then the failure to warn becomes almost dispositive of the case. The Dalehite plaintiffs were awarded $75,000 by the trial judge.[5]

The plaintiffs in this case sued the federal government under an act of Congress called the Federal Tort Claims Act (FTCA),[6] which was passed in 1946 and waived sovereign immunity for the federal government. *Sovereign immunity* is the notion that a sovereign (the people in the United States) cannot be sued without the sovereign's consent. The FTCA is the vehicle through which the federal government consented to allow itself to be held liable for its torts (negligence).

Prior to the passage of the FTCA, when citizens were injured as a result of government's (or a government employee's) negligence, they simply could not sue the government to recover damages. The only process available was to have their representative submit a private bill in Congress. In the 70th Congress (1927-29), 2,268 private bills claiming damages from government wrongs were introduced.[7] These bills sought more than $100 million collectively, and Congress passed 336 of them for a total of $2,830,000. During the next eight Congresses (up to 1945), 2,118 such private bills were introduced per session. Only 408 (19 percent) passed, calling for $1.5 million per Congress (the figures are averages).

Because the government has the power to decide whether it can be sued, it can also decide under what conditions it will allow itself to be sued; hence, the FTCA has certain exemptions or situations under which the government will not be liable. The exemption involved in this case is called the *discretionary exemption*. It is found in Section 2680 of the act and reads as follows:

> The provisions of this chapter . . . shall not apply to . . . (a) any claim based upon an act or omission of an employee of the government, exercising due care, in the execution of a statute or regulation, whether or not the statute or regulation be valid [this part of the exemption is meant to bar citizens from using tort suits to challenge the legality of acts of Congress or regulations] or based upon the exercise or performance or the failure to exercise or perform a discretionary function or duty on the part of a federal agency or an employee of the government, whether or not the discretion involved be abused.

The second part is the discretionary exemption, and its purpose is to make acts of discretion immune from negligence suits so that those in government will not hesitate to make a decision out of fear of a lawsuit.

When the government lost in the *Dalehite* case at the trial court, it appealed to the circuit court, which overturned the trial judge. On review by the Supreme Court, the question narrowed to an interpretation of the discretionary exemption clause (whether the decisions to stop testing FGAN, to bag it at high temperatures, to put it into paper bags rather than something more stable, and to label it as "fertilizer" were acts of discretion within the meaning of the exemption). In a four-to-three decision (two justices did not participate), the Court said the exemption was meant to make immune acts of discretion in the exercise of governmental functions. Whether negligence exists or not, the act meant to protect, for example, flood control, irrigation, activities of the Federal Trade Commission, the Securities and Exchange Commission, and other regulatory agencies. Indeed, the Court said the only negligence that could be liable under the act was the "common law torts of employees of agencies," such as negligence in driving an automobile. Therefore, all the above-mentioned decisions claimed by the plaintiff to constitute negligence, whether they were negligent or not, are exempted under Section 2680 of the Act. The Dalehite plaintiffs (and all the rest of them as well) lost their suit, and Justice Jackson wrote a strong dissent:

> Many acts of government officials deal only with the housekeeping side of federal activities. The Government, as landowner, as manufacturer, as shipper, as warehouseman, as shipowner and operator, is carrying on activities indistinguishable from those performed by private persons. In this area, there is no good reason to stretch the legislative text to immunize the Government or its officers from responsibility for their acts, if done without appropriate care for the safety of others. Many official decisions even in this area may involve a nice balancing of various considerations, but this is the same kind of balancing which citizens do at their peril and we think it is not within the exception of the statute.
>
> The Government's negligence here was not in policy decisions of a regulatory or governmental nature, but involved actions akin to those of a private manufacturer, contractor, or shipper. Reading the discretionary exception as we do, in a way both workable and faithful to legislative intent, we would hold that the Government was liable under these circumstances. Surely a statute so long debated was meant to embrace more than traffic accidents. If not, the ancient and discredited doctrine that "The King can do no wrong" has not been uprooted; it has merely been amended to read, "The King can do only little wrongs." (346 U.S. 15, 60)

Questions

1. What was the legal situation of the affected citizens of Texas City after the Court's ruling? Did they have a remedy left at all, or were they simply out of luck (and money)?[8]
2. Does this decision seem to you to be a democratically acceptable one? Why or why not?

THE FEDERAL TORT CLAIMS ACT

As a good deal of U.S. law does, the concept of "sovereign immunity" dates from medieval England. It means, as Justice Jackson said in dissent in the *Dalehite* case, that the king (or sovereign) can do no wrong and therefore cannot be sued. Lest you believe that sovereign immunity has no practical consequences in the twenty-first century, the 1996 case of *Lane v. Pena* (116 S.Ct. 2092) should be instructive.

Lane entered the U.S. Merchant Marine Academy in 1991 after passing a defense department physical examination. During his freshman year, however, he was diagnosed with diabetes by a private physician. Lane informed the academy medical staff, and a hearing was held to determine whether his condition would prohibit service in the merchant marine or in the navy. The hearing found that insulin-dependent diabetes was a "disqualifying condition," and Lane was involuntarily separated from the academy. The problem is that a federal statute called the Rehabilitation Act of 1973 forbids any activity receiving federal funds or any programs run by the federal executive branch from discriminating against a person solely on the basis of a disability. All parties to the suit agreed that the academy violated the Rehabilitation Act in its treatment of Lane, and he was awarded reinstatement back into the academy. The question in the lawsuit that went all the way to the Supreme Court was whether the academy could be sued by Lane or whether it was clothed with sovereign immunity. The answer to that issue is not easy. First, what the academy did to Lane is not a tort, so Lane could not sue under the Tort Claims Act. That means the only way Lane could sue is if Congress waived its sovereign immunity in the Rehabilitation Act. Here is what Congress said: "The remedies, procedures, and rights set forth in Title VI of the Civil Rights Act of 1964 shall be available to any person aggrieved by any act or failure to act by any recipient of federal assistance." Because the 1964 Civil Rights Act authorizes suits for money damages, Lane assumed he could sue the academy because he was a "person aggrieved" according to the Rehabilitation Act. The U.S. Supreme Court, however, disagreed.

The Court said that the Rehabilitation Act is clear to distinguish between activities that receive federal funds and programs of the executive branch. Further, Congress can only waive sovereign immunity in "clear and unequivocal" language. Because Congress did not "clearly and unequivocally" include the language containing executive branch programs in its reference to the 1964

Civil Rights Act remedies, that means Congress did not relinquish sovereign immunity in this case (the U.S. Merchant Marine Academy is run by the Department of Transportation–an executive branch agency).

Hence, sovereign immunity is alive and well. Indeed, a few state legislatures still have not waived their respective sovereign immunities. The point that you should understand is that citizens cannot sue government unless government consents to be sued. As we move through the chapter, you will find that sometimes some government employees cannot be sued either. That is called a *qualified immunity.*

Whether state or federal, a tort claims act is necessary if citizens are to be able to sue government for its acts of negligence. Anytime a lawsuit is filed, it contains identifiable components. A suit is started by the filing of a complaint. The complaint will state the name and address of the plaintiff (to help establish jurisdiction), allege that the defendant (name and address) did certain acts that resulted in injury to the plaintiff, and ask the court for certain relief—known in U.S. jurisprudence as a *remedy.* U.S. remedies fall into two categories: common-law remedies and equitable remedies. *Common-law remedies* involve money damages; *equitable remedies* are allowed only where a common-law remedy is not adequate to take care of the plaintiff's situation. There are several equitable remedies, but perhaps the most common (and the ones you are already familiar with) are injunctions and declaratory judgments. An *injunction* is a court order stopping certain action; a *declaratory judgment* is a judgment by which a court declares a law or agency activity to be unconstitutional or otherwise unlawful. Of the cases that began each chapter, only two have involved common-law remedies: the *Dalehite* case in this chapter, and *Hale v. Walsh* in Chapter 8, in which Professor Hale asked the Court for both types of remedies (compensatory damages for lost wages and retraining expenses incurred, and reinstatement to his position as professor of history—an equity remedy).

So long as a government refuses to waive its sovereign immunity, theoretically neither type of action—common-law or equity—can be maintained against the government. The federal legislation permitting suits in equity against the government is found in Section 702 of the Administrative Procedure Act (APA), although the language permitting equity actions was not added until 1976. Some case law involving declaratory judgments and injunctions instituted against the government prior to amending Section 702 of the APA is inconsistent.

At least one type of suit at common law was permitted with the passage of the FTCA in 1946—torts. A *tort* is a "legal wrong done to another person."[9]

Before one can prevail in a tort suit, one needs to establish the existence of a legal duty and the breach of that duty, which is the proximate cause of harm to the plaintiff's person or property. There are two categories of torts: intentional and unintentional. You are probably familiar with at least the names of *intentional torts*—for example, invasion of privacy, defamation of character (libel and slander), assault, battery, false imprisonment, and malicious prosecution. Negligence is the *unintentional tort*. Because most intentional torts are exempted under the FTCA, our discussion focuses on negligence.

Just as criminal law presumes that all adults know and understand the law and are possessed of free will to choose right from wrong, so negligence law imposes a legal duty on all adults to take reasonable care (due care) that their actions (or failures to act) do not cause harm to others. Because the latter is legal duty, negligence suits often narrow to whether the defendant took reasonable care. Such was the essence of the *Dalehite* case at the trial court, and the trial judge found as a matter of fact that the government had breached its duty to exercise reasonable care.

How would one know whether another had failed to take reasonable care? When Domino's Pizza began to advertise nationally that customers would get their pizza free if it had not been delivered within a half hour, the survivors of a Domino's delivery boy sued the company when the boy was killed in an automobile accident caused by his speeding to meet the deadline. Has the company breached its duty to take reasonable care through its scheme to capture a larger share of the pizza delivery market? Yes, because the average reasonable person would have foreseen that the scheme and the way it was implemented (the free pizza came out of the delivery person's pocket, not company profits) could lead to injury. Hence, the test for whether a breach of a duty to exercise reasonable care had occurred is whether the average reasonable person would have foreseen that the actions taken by the defendant could cause harm. Foreseeability does not have to be specific; that is, the average reasonable person would not have had to foresee a delivery boy's speeding and getting killed or two ships blowing up and leveling a city along with its citizens. One only need foresee that some general harm might result from the defendant's actions, and that is a question of fact often submitted to a jury (except that juries are forbidden under the FTCA).

Aside from the question of how much money in damages should be awarded, a successful negligence action requires that the plaintiff prove that the failure to exercise reasonable care was the proximate cause of the injuries to the plaintiff. Although first-year law students spend six months or so with proximate cause, you need only be exposed to it here to appreciate a tort claims act suit. Kimble's survivors sued a company when its roof fell in and killed Kimble. The negligence alleged was that the roof was in disrepair and the defendant had failed to repair it; hence, the failure to exercise reasonable care was the proximate cause of Kimble's death. In defense, the company admitted that the roof was in need of repair but claimed it fell in because of a violent storm; hence, the proximate cause of Kimble's death was an act of God and not the company's negligence.[10] These questions are often resolved by applying the "but-for" test. But for the negligence of the defendant, would the plaintiff have been injured? This, too, is a question of fact to be determined by the trier of fact (judge or jury). In the *Kimble* case, if the plaintiff's attorney could establish that no other roofs fell in during the storm, that would probably satisfy the but-for test.

In a usual negligence action, then, the plaintiff must prove that (a) a failure to exercise reasonable care occurred, (b) the failure was the proximate cause of the injury, and (c) the failure to exercise reasonable care resulted in a specific dollar amount of injury. In an FTCA case, the plaintiff has another hurdle or so to clear because the government can say, "Yes, we were negligent and our negligence was the proximate cause of injury, but the negligence arose out of an act of discretion; therefore, we are not liable." Indeed, in the *Dalehite* case, nearly all these elements were in dispute. The government's attorneys claimed that the acts complained of (stopping the test, bagging at high temperatures and in paper, and labeling) did not amount to a failure to exercise reasonable care because there was a rational scientific explanation for each. The cause of the fire was in dispute, and the amount of damages was also disputed, as was whether the alleged acts of negligence were covered by the discretionary exemption.

Over the years, the Court's interpretation of the discretionary function has not remained quite so restrictive. It is not simply "the common law torts of employees" that fall within the exemption. Today, the courts distinguish between acts of discretion with policy implications and acts of discretion simply implementing policy (or planning vs. operational acts of discretion). The former are covered by the discretionary exemption, but the latter are not. Actually, the planning/operational dichotomy was recognized in *Dalehite,* with the trial judge finding the acts complained of to be operational but the Supreme Court finding them to be planning in nature.[11] Unfortunately, the distinction between the two types of discretionary acts has not been clarified by the Court to the point where we can predict with accuracy which is which. The *Varig Airlines* case, which follows, is a recent case in which the Court attempted to clarify the distinction for lower courts.

UNITED STATES V. VARIG AIRLINES
467 U.S. 797 (1984)

Chief Justice Burger delivered the unanimous opinion of the Court.

We granted certiorari in these two cases to determine whether the United States may be held liable under the Federal Tort Claims Act, 28 U.S.C. § 2671 for the negligence of the Federal Aviation Administration in certifying certain aircraft for use in commercial aviation.

I

A. No. 82-1349

On July 11, 1973, a commercial jet aircraft owned by respondent S.A. Empresa De Viacao Aerea Rio Grandense (Varig Airlines) was flying from Rio de Janeiro to Paris when a fire broke out in one of the aft lavatories. The fire produced a thick black smoke, which quickly filled the cabin and cockpit. Despite the pilots' successful effort to land the plane, 124 of the 135 persons on board died from asphyxiation or the effects of toxic gases produced by the fire. Most of the plane's fuselage was consumed by a postimpact fire.

The aircraft involved in this accident was a Boeing 707, a product of the Boeing Co. In 1958 the Civil Aeronautics Agency, a predecessor of the FAA, had issued a type certificate for the Boeing 707, certifying that its designs, plans, specifications, and performance data had been shown to be in conformity with minimum safety standards. Seaboard Airlines originally purchased this particular plane for domestic use; in 1969 Seaboard sold the plane to respondent Varig Airlines, a Brazilian air carrier, which used the plane commercially from 1969 to 1973.

After the accident, respondent, Varig Airlines, brought an action against the United States under the Federal Tort Claims Act seeking damages for the destroyed aircraft. The families and personal representatives of many of the passengers, also respondents here, brought a separate suit under the Act pressing claims for wrongful death. The two actions were consolidated in the United States District Court for the Central District of California.

Respondents asserted that the fire originated in the towel disposal area located below the sink unit in one of the lavatories and alleged that the towel disposal area was not capable of containing fire. In support of their argument, respondents pointed to an air safety regulation requiring that waste receptacles be made of fire-resistant materials and incorporate covers or other provisions for containing possible fires. 14 C.F.R. § 4b.381(d) (1956). Respondents claimed that the CAA had been negligent when it inspected the Boeing 707 and issued a type certificate to an aircraft that did not comply with CAA fire protection standards. The District Court granted summary judgment for the United States on the ground that California law does not recognize an actionable tort duty for inspection and certification activities. The District Court also found that, even if respondents had stated a cause of action in tort, recovery against the United States was barred by two exceptions to the Act: the discretionary function exception, 28 U.S.C. § 2680(a), and the misrepresentation exception.

B. No. 82-1350

On October 8, 1968, a DeHavilland Dove aircraft owned by respondent John Dowdle and used in the operation of an air taxi service caught fire in midair, crashed, and burned near Las Vegas, Nev. The pilot, copilot, and two passengers were killed. The cause of the crash was an in-flight fire in the forward baggage compartment of the aircraft.

The DeHavilland Dove airplane was manufactured in the United Kingdom in 1951 and then purchased by Air Wisconsin, another air taxi operator. In 1965 Air Wisconsin contracted with Aerodyne Engineering Corp. to install a gasoline-burning cabin heater in the airplane. Aerodyne applied for, and was granted, a supplemental type certificate [FN4] from the FAA authorizing the installation of the heater. Aerodyne then installed the heater pursuant to its contract with Air Wisconsin. In 1966, relying in part upon the supplemental type certificate as an indication of the airplane's airworthiness, respondent Dowdle purchased the DeHavilland Dove from Air Wisconsin.

In the aftermath of the crash, respondent Dowdle filed this action for property damage against the United States under the Federal Tort Claims Act. . . .

We granted certiorari, and we now reverse.

II

In the Federal Aviation Act of 1958, 49 U.S.C. § 1421(a)(1), Congress directed the Secretary of Transportation to promote the safety of flight of civil aircraft in air commerce by establishing minimum standards for aircraft design, materials, workmanship, construction, and performance. Congress also granted the Secretary the discretion to prescribe reasonable rules and regulations governing the inspection of aircraft, including the manner in which such inspections should be made. Congress emphasized, however, that air carriers themselves retained certain responsibilities to promote the public interest in air safety: the duty to perform their services with the highest possible degree of safety, the duty to make or cause to be made every inspection required by the Secretary, and the duty to observe and comply with all other administrative requirements established by the Secretary.

Congress also established a multistep certification process to monitor the aviation industry's compliance with the requirements developed by the Secretary. Acting as the Secretary's designee, the FAA has promulgated a comprehensive set of regulations delineating the minimum safety standards with which the designers and manufacturers of aircraft must comply before marketing their products. At each step in the certification process, FAA employees or their representatives evaluate materials submitted by aircraft manufacturers to determine whether the manufacturer has satisfied these regulatory requirements. Upon a showing by the manufacturer that the prescribed safety standards have been met, the FAA issues an appropriate certificate permitting the manufacturer to continue with production and marketing.

The first stage of the FAA compliance review is type certification. A manufacturer wishing to introduce a new type of aircraft must first obtain FAA approval of the plane's basic design in the form of a type certificate. After receiving an application for a type certificate, the Secretary must "make, or require the applicant to make, such tests during manufacture and upon completion as the Secretary . . . deems reasonably necessary in the interest of safety. . . ." By regulation, the FAA has made the applicant itself responsible for conducting all inspections and tests necessary to determine that the aircraft comports with FAA airworthiness requirements. The applicant submits to the FAA the designs, drawings, test reports, and computations

necessary to show that the aircraft sought to be certificated satisfies FAA regulations. In the course of the type certification process, the manufacturer produces a prototype of the new aircraft and conducts both ground and flight tests. FAA employees or their representatives then review the data submitted by the applicant and make such inspections or tests as they deem necessary to ascertain compliance with the regulations. If the FAA finds that the proposed aircraft design comports with minimum safety standards, it signifies its approval by issuing a type certificate.

Production may not begin, however, until a production certificate authorizing the manufacture of duplicates of the prototype is issued. 49 U.S.C. To obtain a production certificate, the manufacturer must prove to the FAA that it has established and can maintain a quality control system to assure that each aircraft will meet the design provisions of the type certificate. When it is satisfied that duplicate aircraft will conform to the approved type design, the FAA issues a production certificate, and the manufacturer may begin mass production of the approved aircraft.

Before any aircraft may be placed into service, however, its owner must obtain from the FAA an airworthiness certificate, which denotes that the particular aircraft in question conforms to the type certificate and is in condition for safe operation. It is unlawful for any person to operate an aircraft in air commerce without a valid airworthiness certificate.

An additional certificate is required when an aircraft is altered by the introduction of a major change in its type design. To obtain this supplemental type certificate, the applicant must show the FAA that the altered aircraft meets all applicable airworthiness requirements. The applicant is responsible for conducting the inspections and tests necessary to demonstrate that each change in the type design complies with the regulations. The methods used by FAA employees or their representatives to determine an applicant's compliance with minimum safety standards are generally the same as those employed for basic type certification.

With fewer than 400 engineers, the FAA obviously cannot complete this elaborate compliance review process alone. Accordingly, 49 U.S.C. § 1355 authorizes the Secretary to delegate certain inspection and certification responsibilities to properly qualified private persons. By regulation, the Secretary has provided for the appointment of private individuals to serve as designated engineering representatives to assist in the FAA certification process. These representatives are typically employees of aircraft manufacturers who possess detailed knowledge of an aircraft's design based upon their day-to-day involvement in its development. The representatives act as surrogates of the FAA in examining, inspecting, and testing aircraft for purposes of certification. In determining whether an aircraft complies with FAA regulations, they are guided by the same requirements, instructions, and procedures as FAA employees. FAA employees may briefly review the reports and other data submitted by representatives before certificating a subject aircraft.

The nature and scope of § 2680(a) were carefully examined in *Dalehite v. United States,* supra. *Dalehite* involved vast claims for damages against the United States arising out of a disastrous explosion of ammonium nitrate fertilizer, which had been produced and distributed under the direction of the United States for export to devastated areas occupied by the Allied Armed Forces after World War II. Numerous acts of the Government were charged as negligent: the cabinet-level decision to institute the fertilizer export program, the failure to experiment with the fertilizer to determine the possibility of explosion, the drafting of the basic plan of manufacture, and the failure properly to police the storage and loading of the fertilizer.

The Court concluded that these allegedly negligent acts were governmental duties protected by the discretionary function exception and held the action barred by § 2680(a). Describing the discretion protected by § 2680(a) as "the discretion of the executive or the administrator to act according to one's judgment of the best course," id., at 34. . . .

Respondents here insist that the view of § 2680(a) expressed in *Dalehite* has been eroded, if not overruled, by subsequent cases construing the Act, particularly *Indian Towing Co. v. United States,* 350 U.S. 61 (1955), and *Eastern Air Lines, Inc. v. Union Trust Co.,* 221 F.2d 62, *United States v. Union Trust Co.,* 350 U.S. 907 (1955). While the Court's reading of the Act admittedly has not followed a straight line, we do not accept the supposition that *Dalehite* no longer represents a valid interpretation of the discretionary function exception.

Indian Towing Co. v. United States, supra, involved a claim under the Act for damages to cargo aboard a vessel that ran aground, allegedly owing to the failure of the light in a lighthouse operated by the Coast Guard. The plaintiffs contended that the Coast Guard had been negligent in inspecting, maintaining, and repairing the light. Significantly, the Government conceded that the discretionary function exception was not implicated in *Indian Towing,* arguing instead that the Act contained an implied exception from liability for "uniquely governmental functions." Id., 350 U.S., at 64. The Court rejected the Government's assertion, reasoning that it would "push the courts into the 'non-governmental'-'governmental' quagmire that has long plagued the law of municipal corporations." Id., at 65.

[1][2] As in *Dalehite,* it is unnecessary—and indeed impossible—to define with precision every contour of the discretionary function exception. From the legislative and judicial materials, however, it is possible to isolate several factors useful in determining when the acts of a Government employee are protected from liability by § 2680(a). First, it is the nature of the conduct, rather than the status of the actor, that governs whether the discretionary function exception applies in a given case. As the Court pointed out in *Dalehite,* the exception covers "[n]ot only agencies of government . . . but all employees exercising discretion." 346 U.S., at 33. Thus, the basic inquiry concerning the application of the discretionary function exception is whether the challenged acts of a Government employee—whatever his or her rank—are of the nature and quality that Congress intended to shield from tort liability.

[3] Second, whatever else the discretionary function exception may include, it plainly was intended to encompass the discretionary acts of the Government acting in its role as a regulator of the conduct of private individuals. Time and again the legislative history refers to the acts of regulatory agencies as examples of those covered by the exception, and it is significant that the early tort claims bills considered by Congress specifically exempted two major regulatory agencies by name. This emphasis upon protection for regulatory activities suggests an underlying basis for the inclusion of an exception for discretionary functions in the Act: Congress wished to prevent judicial "second-guessing" of legislative and administrative decisions grounded in social, economic, and political policy through the medium of an action in tort. By fashioning an exception for discretionary governmental functions, including regulatory activities, Congress took "steps to protect the Government from liability that would

seriously handicap efficient government operations." *United States v. Muniz,* 374 U.S. 150, 163. . . .

IV

[4] We now consider whether the discretionary function exception immunizes from tort liability the FAA certification process involved in these cases. Respondents in No. 82-1349 argue that the CAA was negligent in issuing a type certificate for the Boeing 707 aircraft in 1958 because the lavatory trash receptacle did not satisfy applicable safety regulations. Similarly, respondents in No. 82-1350 claim negligence in the FAA's issuance of a supplemental type certificate in 1965 for the De-Havilland Dove aircraft; they assert that the installation of the fuel line leading to the cabin heater violated FAA airworthiness standards. From the records in these cases there is no indication that either the Boeing 707 trash receptacle or the De-Havilland Dove cabin heater was actually inspected or reviewed by an FAA inspector or representative. Respondents thus argue in effect that the negligent failure of the FAA to inspect certain aspects of aircraft type design in the process of certification gives rise to a cause of action against the United States under the Act.

The Government, on the other hand, urges that the basic responsibility for satisfying FAA air safety standards rests with the manufacturer, not with the FAA. The role of the FAA, the Government says, is merely to police the conduct of private individuals by monitoring their compliance with FAA regulations. According to the Government, the FAA accomplishes its monitoring function by means of a "spot-check" program designed to encourage manufacturers and operators to comply fully with minimum safety requirements. Such regulatory activity, the Government argues, is the sort of governmental conduct protected by the discretionary function exception to the Act. We agree that the discretionary function exception precludes a tort action based upon the conduct of the FAA in certificating these aircraft for use in commercial aviation.

As noted, the Secretary of Transportation has the duty to promote safety in air transportation by promulgating reasonable rules and regulations governing the inspection, servicing, and overhaul of civil aircraft. 49 U.S.C. In her discretion, the Secretary may also prescribe "the periods for, and the manner in, which such inspection, servicing, and overhaul shall be made, including provision for

examinations and reports by properly qualified private persons whose examinations or reports the Secretary of Transportation may accept in lieu of those made by its officers and employees." § 1421(a)(3)(C).

Thus, Congress specifically empowered the Secretary to establish and implement a mechanism for enforcing compliance with minimum safety standards according to her "judgment of the best course." *Dalehite v. United States,* 346 U.S., at 34.

In the exercise of this discretion, the FAA, as the Secretary's designee, has devised a system of compliance review that involves certification of aircraft design and manufacture at several stages of production. The FAA certification process is founded upon a relatively simple notion: the duty to ensure that an aircraft conforms to FAA safety regulations lies with the manufacturer and operator, while the FAA retains the responsibility for policing compliance. Thus, the manufacturer is required to develop the plans and specifications and perform the inspections and tests necessary to establish that an aircraft design comports with the applicable regulations; the FAA then reviews the data for conformity purposes by conducting a "spot-check" of the manufacturer's work.

The operation of this "spot-check" system is outlined in detail in the handbooks and manuals developed by the CAA and FAA for the use of their employees. . . .

The FAA's implementation of a mechanism for compliance review is plainly discretionary activity of the "nature and quality" protected by § 2680(a). When an agency determines the extent to which it will supervise the safety procedures of private individuals, it is exercising discretionary regulatory authority of the most basic kind. Decisions as to the manner of enforcing regulations directly affect the feasibility and practicality of the Government's regulatory program; such decisions require the agency to establish priorities for the accomplishment of its policy objectives by balancing the objectives sought to be obtained against such practical considerations as staffing and funding. Here, the FAA has determined that a program of "spot-checking" manufacturers' compliance with minimum safety standards best accommodates the goal of air transportation safety and the reality of finite agency resources. Judicial intervention in such decision-making through private tort suits would require the courts to "second-guess" the political, social, and economic judgments of an agency exercising its regulatory function. It was precisely this sort of judicial intervention in policymaking that the discretionary function exception was designed to prevent.

It follows that the acts of FAA employees in executing the "spot-check" program in accordance with agency directives are protected by the discretionary function exception as well. See *Dalehite v. United States,* 346 U.S., at 36. The FAA employees who conducted compliance reviews of the aircraft involved in this case were specifically empowered to make policy judgments regarding the degree of confidence that might reasonably be placed in a given manufacturer, the need to maximize compliance with FAA regulations, and the efficient allocation of agency resources. In administering the "spot-check" program, these FAA engineers and inspectors necessarily took certain calculated risks, but those risks were encountered for the advancement of a governmental purpose and pursuant to the specific grant of authority in the regulations and operating manuals. Under such circumstances, the FAA's alleged negligence in failing to check certain specific items in the course of certificating a particular aircraft falls squarely within the discretionary function exception of § 2680(a).

V

In rendering the United States amenable to some suits in tort, Congress could not have intended to impose liability for the regulatory enforcement activities of the FAA challenged in this case. The FAA has a statutory duty to promote safety in air transportation, not to insure it. We hold that these actions against the FAA for its alleged negligence in certificating aircraft for use in commercial aviation are barred by the discretionary function exception of the Federal Tort Claims Act. Accordingly, the judgments of the United States Court of Appeals for the Ninth Circuit are reversed.

It is so ordered.

Judge Jenkins, a federal district court judge in Utah, created an analogy that might be useful in dealing with planning and operational acts of discretion. The case is *Allen v. United States,* an FTCA case alleging that the Atomic Energy Commission (AEC; today, it would be the Nuclear Regulatory Commission [NRC]) negligently caused cancer and leukemia in citizens in southern Utah because it failed to warn the citizens downwind of nuclear tests about the tests and the dangers of fallout. The judge found for the plaintiffs but was overruled at the Circuit Court:

> The United States seems to argue that because a choice has been made, a discretionary choice at the highest levels of government, that all subsequent operational choices and actions executing the original policy choice are to be regarded as identical with the original policy choice, and insulated as the original choice is insulated from the reach of the Tort Claims Act. The United States misperceives the intent of the act. For example, we choose the objective: Rome. We choose the road: the Appian Way. Discretionary choices both. We make such choices as a matter of power and as a matter of right.
>
> The manner in which we drive from our location to Rome, carelessly or carefully, is also a matter of choice. But, it is not a matter of discretion as used in the Tort Claims Act. It is not a matter of discretion because such a choice is subject to a standard, a limitation. It is subject to a limitation imposed by a civilized society as to appropriate conduct.
>
> It is not a matter of discretion because while we have a power to choose, we have no right to breach the standard and without responsibility choose to

drive carelessly. If we do, we are answerable for exercising power without right.

In 1951, in response to international pressures, the United States chose the objective—to try to stabilize the restless balance of world power. It chose the road—open air atomic testing. Discretionary choices both. Both choices were made as a matter of power and as a matter of right.

The manner in which the tests were conducted, carefully or carelessly, was also a matter of choice but was not a matter of discretion because such operational conduct was subject to a standard, a limitation. That limiting standard of conduct, due care, reasonable care under the circumstances, is called a duty.[12]

INTENTIONAL TORTS

The other exclusion in the FTCA is intentional torts. *Assault* (putting one in fear or apprehension) and *battery* (an unauthorized touching) are two intentional torts with which you are probably familiar. *Defamation of character* (slander and libel) is another. As originally passed, the FTCA maintained sovereign immunity for the government in the event that one of its employees committed an intentional tort. As this chapter moves to the notion of official immunity, you will be introduced to the case of *Barr v. Matteo,* in which federal employees who had been libeled by their boss sued him individually for the tort of libel. In a case similar to the *Dalehite* case, the jury found that the employer had libeled the employees, but the Supreme Court said the boss was clothed with (a different kind of) immunity.

In the early 1970s, many events caused policymakers to question the wisdom of continuing the intentional tort exemption.[13] There were, for example, the wholesale arrests of thousands who demonstrated in Washington, D.C., on May Day in 1971 (they were held in a football stadium). There was a Supreme Court decision in a case called *Bivens v. Six Unknown Named Agents of the Federal Bureau of Narcotics* (which you will read shortly), which was handed down in June 1971. There were the shootings at Kent State University and Jackson State University in May 1970. But it was the cumulation of several events in and around St. Louis in 1973 that caused Congress to amend the intentional tort exception to the FTCA in March 1974.

A former federal program called Drug Abuse Law Enforcement (DALE) was a special effort by state and local law enforcement agents and Bureau of Narcotics and Dangerous Drugs officers to get at drug trafficking in the United States. One regional DALE office was in St. Louis. DALE officers frequently worked undercover and were described by several citizens who had contact with them as "shabbily dressed and with long hair."[14]

Herbert and Evelyn Giglotto lived in Collinsville, Illinois, and were awakened at 9:30 p.m. on April 23, 1973, by the sound of someone breaking down their front door. According to Boger, Gitenstein, and Verkuil, who studied the case, Mr. Giglotto was met in the hallway outside the bedroom by five shabbily dressed men who grabbed him and dragged him back to the bedroom, threw him on the bed, tied his hands behind his back, put a gun to his head, and told him that if he moved they would kill him. The men shouted abuse at Mr. Giglotto, then grabbed his wife (who was wearing only a negligee), threw her on the bed, and gave her the same treatment her husband had received. The men identified themselves as federal agents, and eventually fifteen or so of them entered and left the bedroom. After about fifteen minutes, one of the agents came into the bedroom with Giglotto's checkbook and other documents and announced, "Well, we have the wrong people." The couple were untied and allowed to sit on the bed but were not allowed to get dressed. The agents left without explanation, "leaving behind a smashed television, a broken camera, scattered books, scratched furniture and a shattered antique vase,"[15] not to mention the lack of a front door. DALE agents would later arrest a man who lived next door to the Giglottos.

A half hour later, across town, shabbily dressed men broke into the home of the Askews, who were accosted at the dinner table. Mr. Askew would eventually testify that, from the appearance of the men and the weapons they brandished (sawed-off shotguns), he first thought his son had been in a fight with a motorcycle gang member and now the gang had come to his house to kill the boy.[16] After Mrs. Askew, who had fainted, was revived, the DALE agents were able to convince the Askews that they were federal agents. The Askews were not treated with the abuse, verbal or physical, the Giglottos had received, but the house was searched while they were held at gunpoint. Eventually, one agent said it must have been a "bad tip," and they left. Different and more pleasant agents appeared at both houses the next day, with assurances that the property damage would be paid for, but no apology was forthcoming, and no offer was made to pay for the trauma that DALE agents had caused the two families.

The actions of the DALE agents constitute the torts of assault, battery, and false imprisonment, but because of the intentional tort exclusion in the FTCA, the Giglottos and the Askews were without a legal remedy.

It turned out that several of the agents involved in the April 23 raids had been involved in two similar incidents during the preceding year. A special assistant attorney general said that he had suspended the four agents. One of the "suspended" agents, however, was caught by the press at another raid shortly after the "suspension." It turned out that the four agents had simply been reassigned to planning and coordinating the raids.

The incidents received nationwide coverage in the press. The administrative reaction was to create a new agency, the Drug Enforcement Agency (DEA); severely restrict the use of "no-knock" entries; stress the importance of obtaining a warrant (it appears there was no warrant in either case); and finally to see to it that federal agents wear identifying clothing in raids and searches. The Giglottos and the Askews went to Washington, D.C., to testify, and as a result of the publicity surrounding this incident, Congress amended the FTCA to remove sovereign immunity for intentional torts such as assault, battery, and false imprisonment when committed by a federal law enforcement officer.

OFFICIAL IMMUNITY

One thing the FTCA does is to absolve the individual federal employee of liability and spread the financial burden to the taxpayers. In the case you are about to read next, Federal Bureau of Narcotics agents entered (they broke in) a man's apartment, searched him and the apartment, and arrested him for alleged narcotics violations—all without a warrant. Except to the extent that it may involve a battery or false imprisonment (which at the time—1971—were intentional torts exempted under the FTCA), this is not an action for a tort. The man, Mr. Bivens, was suing the narcotics agents individually (not the agency or the federal government) for violating his Fourth Amendment rights. If Congress has never authorized such suits, can they be maintained?

BIVENS V. SIX UNKNOWN NAMED AGENTS
OF THE FEDERAL BUREAU OF NARCOTICS
403 U.S. 388 (1971)

Justice Brennan delivered the opinion of the Court, joined by Justices Douglas, Stewart, White, and Marshall. Justice Harlan concurred, and Chief Justice Burger and Justices Black and Blackmun filed dissents.

The Fourth Amendment provides that: "The right of the people to be secure in their persons, houses, papers, and effects, against unreasonable searches and seizures, shall not be violated. * * *"

In *Bell v. Hood*, 327 U.S. 678 (1946), we reserved the question whether violation of that command by a federal agent acting under color of his authority gives rise to a cause of action for damages consequent upon his unconstitutional conduct. Today we hold that it does.

This case has its origin in an arrest and search carried out on the morning of November 26, 1965. Petitioner's complaint alleged that on that day respondents, agents of the Federal Bureau of Narcotics acting under claim of federal authority, entered his apartment and arrested him for alleged narcotics violations. The agents manacled petitioner in front of his wife and children, and threatened to arrest the entire family. They searched the apartment from stem to stern. Thereafter, petitioner was taken to the federal courthouse in Brooklyn, where he was interrogated, booked, and subjected to a visual strip search.

On July 7, 1967, petitioner brought suit in Federal District Court. In addition to the allegations above, his complaint asserted that the arrest and search were effected without a warrant, and that unreasonable force was employed in making the arrest; fairly read, it alleges as well that the arrest was made without probable cause. Petitioner claimed to have suffered great humiliation, embarrassment, and mental suffering as a result of the agents' unlawful conduct, and sought $15,000 damages from each of them. The District Court, on respondents' motion, dismissed the complaint on the ground, inter alia, that it failed to state a cause of action. 276 F.Supp. 12 1967. The Court of Appeals, one judge concurring specially, affirmed on that basis. 409 F.2d 718 (CA2 1969). We granted certiorari. We reverse. . . .

I

Respondents do not argue that petitioner should be entirely without remedy for an unconstitutional invasion of his rights by federal agents. In respondents' view, however, the rights that petitioner asserts—primarily rights of privacy—are creations of state and not of federal law. Accordingly, they argue, petitioner may obtain money damages to redress invasion of these rights only by an action in tort, under state law, in the state courts. In this scheme the Fourth Amendment would serve merely to limit the extent to which the agents could defend the state law tort suit by asserting that their actions were a valid exercise of federal power: if the agents were shown to have violated the Fourth Amendment, such a defense would be lost to them and they would stand before the state law merely as private individuals. Candidly admitting that it is the policy of the Department of Justice to remove all such suits from the state to the federal courts for decision, respondents nevertheless urge that we uphold dismissal of petitioner's complaint in federal court, and remit him to filing an action in the state courts in order that the case may properly be removed to the federal court for decision on the basis of state law. We think that respondents' thesis rests upon an unduly restrictive view of the Fourth Amendment's protection against unreasonable searches and seizures by federal agents, a view that has consistently been rejected by this Court. Respondents seek to treat the relationship between a citizen and a federal agent unconstitutionally exercising his authority as no different from the relationship between two private citizens. In so doing, they ignore the fact that power, once granted, does not disappear like a magic gift when it is wrongfully used. An agent acting—albeit unconstitutionally—in the name of the United States possesses a far greater capacity for harm than an individual trespasser exercising no authority other than his own.

Accordingly, as our cases make clear, the Fourth Amendment operates as a limitation upon the exercise of federal power regardless of whether the State in whose jurisdiction that power is exercised would prohibit or penalize the identical act if engaged in by a private citizen. It guarantees to citizens of the United States the absolute right to be free from unreasonable searches and seizures carried out by virtue of federal authority. And "where federally protected rights have been invaded, it has been the rule from the beginning that courts will be alert to adjust their remedies so as to grant the necessary relief." . . .

Second. The interests protected by state laws regulating trespass and the invasion of privacy, and those protected by the Fourth Amendment's guarantee against unreasonable searches and seizures, may be inconsistent or even hostile. Thus, we may bar the door against an unwelcome private intruder, or call the police if he persists in seeking entrance. The availability of such alternative means for the protection of privacy may lead the State to restrict imposition of liability for any consequent trespass. A private citizen, asserting no authority other than his own, will not normally be liable in trespass if he demands, and is granted, admission to another's house. But one who demands admission under a claim of federal authority stands in a far different position. The mere invocation of federal power by a federal law enforcement official will normally render futile any attempt to resist an unlawful entry or arrest by resort to the local police; and a claim of authority to enter is likely to unlock the door as well. . . .

Third. That damages may be obtained for injuries consequent upon a violation of the Fourth

Amendment by federal officials should hardly seem a surprising proposition. Historically, damages have been regarded as the ordinary remedy for an invasion of personal interests in liberty. . . .

Of course, the Fourth Amendment does not in so many words provide for its enforcement by an award of money damages for the consequences of its violation. But "it is * * * well settled that where legal rights have been invaded, and a federal statute provides for a general right to sue for such invasion, federal courts may use any available remedy to make good the wrong done." The question is merely whether petitioner, if he can demonstrate an injury consequent upon the violation by federal agents of his Fourth Amendment rights, is entitled to redress his injury through a particular remedial mechanism normally available in the federal courts. "The very essence of civil liberty certainly consists in the right of every individual to claim the protection of the laws, whenever he receives an injury." *Marbury v. Madison,* 1 Cranch 137, 163, 2 L.Ed. 60 (1803). Having concluded that petitioner's complaint states a cause of action under the Fourth Amendment, we hold that petitioner is entitled to recover money damages for any injuries he has suffered as a result of the agents' violation of the Amendment.

II

In addition to holding that petitioner's complaint had failed to state facts making out a cause of action, the District Court ruled that in any event respondents were immune from liability by virtue of their official position. 276 F.Supp., at 15. This question was not passed upon by the Court of Appeals, and accordingly we do not consider it here. The judgment of the Court of Appeals is reversed and the case is remanded for further proceedings consistent with this opinion.

So ordered.

Judgment reversed and case remanded.

Questions

1. What is the holding in *Bivens*?
2. Do you think this is a good or a bad decision? Why?

Some have attributed to *Bivens* the notion of qualified immunity, but as you can tell from reading the case, the Court passed on the question of immunity. Some government officials have absolute immunity. That means they cannot be sued at all in their official capacity. Judges, prosecutors, and presidents are examples.[17] Most government officials possess what is called a qualified immunity for *Bivens*-type suits. This means that sometimes they can be sued, and sometimes they are immune from suit.

In the 1950s, the acting director of the Office of Rent Stabilization (Barr) issued a press release that a jury later found to have slandered former employees (Matteo and Madigan). This was not a *Bivens*-type action but, rather, a tort suit. It was not an FTCA suit, however, because the plaintiffs were not suing the government but, instead, were suing Barr personally for an intentional tort. One of the defenses Barr raised was that even if his actions did amount to slander, because he was acting in an official capacity, he should enjoy immunity. The Supreme Court agreed, saying, "The fact that the action here taken was within the outer perimeter of petitioner's line of duty is enough to render the privilege applicable."[18]

The "privilege" the Court spoke of is official immunity (as opposed to sovereign immunity), and in saying that official immunity extended all the way to the "outer perimeter of official duty," the Court effectively created an absolute immunity for government officials.

The *Bivens* case signaled the end of absolute official immunity. Indeed, on remand to the circuit court, the *Bivens* defendants were found to have acted beyond the outer perimeter of their line of duty. The case you are about to read, though not the most recent case on federal official immunity (see *Carlson v. Green,* at the end of this chapter), is famous for its official or qualified immunity jurisprudence.

BUTZ V. ECONOMOU
438 U.S. 478 (1978)

Justice White delivered the opinion of the Court, joined by Justices Brennan, Marshall, Blackmun, and Powell. Justice Rehnquist filed an opinion concurring in part and dissenting in part, joined by Chief Justice Burger and Justices Stewart and Stevens.

This case concerns the personal immunity of federal officials in the Executive Branch from claims for damages arising from their violations of citizens' constitutional rights. Respondent filed suit against a number of officials in the Department of Agriculture claiming that they had instituted an investigation and an administrative proceeding against him in retaliation for his criticism of that agency. The District Court dismissed the action on the ground that the individual defendants, as federal officials, were entitled to absolute immunity for all discretionary acts within the scope of their authority. The Court of Appeals reversed, holding that the defendants were entitled only to the qualified immunity available to their counterparts in state government. *Economou v. U.S. Dept. of Agriculture,* 535 F.2d 688 (1976). Because of the importance of immunity doctrine to both the vindication of constitutional guarantees and the effective functioning of government, we granted certiorari. . . .

I

Respondent controls Arthur N. Economou and Co., Inc., which was at one time registered with the Department of Agriculture as a commodity futures commission merchant. Most of respondent's factual allegations in this lawsuit focus on an earlier administrative proceeding in which the Department of Agriculture sought to revoke or suspend the company's registration. On February 19, 1970, following an audit, the Department of Agriculture issued an administrative complaint alleging that respondent, while a registered merchant, had willfully failed to maintain the minimum financial requirements prescribed by the Department. After another audit, an amended complaint was issued on June 22, 1970. A hearing was held before the Chief Hearing Examiner of the Department, who filed a recommendation sustaining the administrative complaint. The Judicial Officer of the Department, to whom the Secretary had delegated his decisional authority in enforcement proceedings, affirmed the Chief Hearing Examiner's decision. On respondent's petition for review, the Court of Appeals for the Second Circuit vacated the order of the Judicial Officer. It reasoned that "the essential finding of willfulness . . . was made in a proceeding instituted without the customary warning letter, which the Judicial Officer conceded might well have resulted in prompt correction of the claimed insufficiencies." *Economou v. U.S. Department of Agriculture,* 494 F.2d 519 (1974).

While the administrative complaint was pending before the Judicial Officer, respondent filed this

lawsuit in Federal District Court. Respondent sought initially to enjoin the progress of the administrative proceeding, but he was unsuccessful in that regard. On March 31, 1975, respondent filed a second amended complaint seeking damages. Named as defendants were the individuals who had served as Secretary and Assistant Secretary of Agriculture during the relevant events; the Judicial Officer and Chief Hearing Examiner; several officials in the Commodity Exchange Authority; the Agriculture Department attorney who had prosecuted the enforcement proceeding; and several of the auditors who had investigated respondent or were witnesses against respondent. . . .

The complaint stated that prior to the issuance of the administrative complaints respondent had been "sharply critical of the staff and operations of Defendants and carried on a vociferous campaign for the reform of Defendant Commodity Exchange Authority to obtain more effective regulation of commodity trading." The complaint also stated that, some time prior to the issuance of the February 19 complaint, respondent and his company had ceased to engage in activities regulated by the defendants. The complaint charged that each of the administrative complaints had been issued without the notice or warning required by law; that the defendants had furnished the complaints "to interested persons and others without furnishing respondent's answers as well"; and that following the issuance of the amended complaint, the defendants had issued a "deceptive" press release that "falsely indicated to the public that [respondent's] financial resources had deteriorated, when Defendants knew that their statement was untrue and so acknowledge[d] previously that said assertion was untrue." . . .

The complaint then presented 10 "causes of action," some of which purported to state claims for damages under the United States Constitution. For example, the first "cause of action" alleged that respondent had been denied due process of law because the defendants had instituted unauthorized proceedings against him without proper notice and with the knowledge that respondent was no longer subject to their regulatory jurisdiction. The third "cause of action" stated that by means of such actions "the Defendants discouraged and chilled the campaign of criticism [plaintiff] directed against them, and thereby deprived the [plaintiff] of [his] rights to free expression guaranteed by the First Amendment of the United States Constitution." . . .

The defendants moved to dismiss the complaint on the ground that "as to the individual defendants it is barred by the doctrine of official immunity. . . ."

II

The single submission by the United States on behalf of petitioners is that all of the federal officials sued in this case are absolutely immune from any liability for damages even if in the course of enforcing the relevant statutes they infringed respondent's constitutional rights and even if the violation was knowing and deliberate. Although the position is earnestly and ably presented by the United States, we are quite sure that it is unsound and consequently reject it.

Bivens established that compensable injury to a constitutionally protected interest could be vindicated by a suit for damages invoking the general federal-question jurisdiction of the federal courts, but we reserved the question whether the agents involved were "immune from liability by virtue of their official position," and remanded the case for that determination. On remand the Court of Appeals for the Second Circuit, as has every other Court of Appeals that has faced the question, held that the agents were not absolutely immune and that the public interest would be sufficiently protected by according the agents and their superiors a qualified immunity. . . .

"[I]n varying scope, a qualified immunity is available to officers of the executive branch of government, the variation being dependent upon the scope of discretion and responsibilities of the office and all the circumstances as they reasonably appeared at the time of the action on which liability is sought to be based. It is the existence of reasonable grounds for the belief formed at the time and in light of all the circumstances, coupled with good-faith belief, that affords a basis for qualified immunity of executive officers for acts performed in the course of official conduct." . . .

[3] We agree with the perception of these courts that, in the absence of congressional direction to the contrary, there is no basis for according to federal officials a higher degree of immunity from liability when sued for a constitutional infringement as authorized by Bivens than is accorded state officials when sued for the identical violation under § 1983. The constitutional injuries made actionable by § 1983 are of no greater magnitude than those for which federal officials may be responsible. The

pressures and uncertainties facing decisionmakers in state government are little if at all different from those affecting federal officials. We see no sense in holding a state governor liable but immunizing the head of a federal department; in holding the administrator of a federal hospital immune where the superintendent of a state hospital would be liable; in protecting the warden of a federal prison where the warden of a state prison would be vulnerable; or in distinguishing between state and federal police participating in the same investigation. Surely, federal officials should enjoy no greater zone of protection when they violate federal constitutional rules than do state officers. . . .

[8] This is not to say that considerations of public policy fail to support a limited immunity for federal executive officials. We consider here, as we did in *Scheuer*, the need to protect officials who are required to exercise their discretion and the related public interest in encouraging the vigorous exercise of official authority. Yet *Scheuer* and other cases have recognized that it is not unfair to hold liable the official who knows or should know he is acting outside the law, and that insisting on an awareness of clearly established constitutional limits will not unduly interfere with the exercise of official judgment. We therefore hold that, in a suit for damages arising from unconstitutional action, federal executive officials exercising discretion are entitled only to the qualified immunity specified in *Scheuer*, subject to those exceptional situations where it is demonstrated that absolute immunity is essential for the conduct of the public business.

[11] We think that the Court of Appeals placed undue emphasis on the fact that the officials sued here are—from an administrative perspective—employees of the Executive Branch. Judges have absolute immunity not because of their particular location within the Government but because of the special nature of their responsibilities. . . . We think that adjudication within a federal administrative agency shares enough of the characteristics of the judicial process that those who participate in such adjudication should also be immune from suits for damages. . . .

We therefore hold that persons subject to these restraints and performing adjudicatory functions within a federal agency are entitled to absolute immunity from damages liability for their judicial acts. Those who complain of error in such proceedings must seek agency or judicial review.

[13] We also believe that agency officials performing certain functions analogous to those of a prosecutor should be able to claim absolute immunity with respect to such acts. The decision to initiate administrative proceedings against an individual or corporation is very much like the prosecutor's decision to initiate or move forward with a criminal prosecution. An agency official, like a prosecutor, may have broad discretion in deciding whether a proceeding should be brought and what sanctions should be sought.

[14] We turn finally to the role of an agency attorney in conducting a trial and presenting evidence on the record to the trier of fact. We can see no substantial difference between the function of the agency attorney in presenting evidence in an agency hearing and the function of the prosecutor who brings evidence before a court. . . .

We therefore hold that an agency attorney who arranges for the presentation of evidence on the record in the course of an adjudication is absolutely immune from suits based on the introduction of such evidence. . . .

VI

There remains the task of applying the foregoing principles to the claims against the particular petitioner-defendants involved in this case. Rather than attempt this here in the first instance, we vacate the judgment of the Court of Appeals and remand the case to that court with instructions to remand the case to the District Court for further proceedings consistent with this opinion.

So ordered.

Question

The Court here clearly establishes a qualified official immunity for federal officials. Can you describe when such officials will be liable and when they will enjoy immunity?

IMMUNITY IN THE STATES

Because sovereign immunity was the jurisprudential status quo in the United States and both the state and federal governments are sovereign entities, it follows that state governments are clothed with sovereign immunity. They cannot be sued without their consent. Today, ten states still have refused to relinquish sovereign immunity.[19] The rest have passed tort claims acts, most of which are similar to the FTCA in that they have numerous exemptions.

What about county and city governments? Because they are creatures of the state legislature, they are not sovereign and hence do not enjoy sovereign immunity. Local governments did, however, have an immunity created by the courts. Local governments could not be sued so long as they were engaged in a governmental function or activity but could be sued if engaged in a proprietary function. A *proprietary function* is a function that could be performed by a private business. The state of North Dakota for example, runs a bank and a mill and elevator, and, at one time, brewed beer. These are proprietary functions. Qualified immunity for local governments no longer hinges on governmental/proprietary functions, as you can see by the following case.

OWEN V. CITY OF INDEPENDENCE
445 U.S. 622 (1980)

Justice Brennan delivered the opinion of the Court, joined by Justices White, Marshall, Blackmun, and Stevens. Justice Powell filed a dissent, joined by Justices Stewart and Rehnquist and Chief Justice Burger.

Monell v. New York City Dept. of Social Services, 436 U.S. 658 (1978), overruled *Monroe v. Pape,* 365 U.S. 167 (1961), insofar as *Monroe* held that local governments were not among the "persons" to whom 42 U.S.C. § 1983 applies and were therefore wholly immune from suit under the statute. *Monell* reserved decision, however, on the question whether local governments, although not entitled to an absolute immunity, should be afforded some form of official immunity in § 1983 suits. In this action brought by petitioner in the District Court for the Western District of Missouri, the Court of Appeals for the Eighth Circuit held that respondent city of Independence, Mo., "is entitled to qualified

immunity from liability" based on the good faith of its officials: "We extend the limited immunity the district court applied to the individual defendants to cover the City as well, because its officials acted in good faith and without malice." 589 F.2d 335 (1978). We granted certiorari. We reverse. . . .

I

The events giving rise to this suit are detailed in the District Court's findings of fact, 421 F.Supp. 1110 (1976). On February 20, 1967, Robert L. Broucek, then City Manager of respondent city of Independence, Mo., appointed petitioner George D. Owen to an indefinite term as Chief of Police. In 1972, Owen and a new City Manager, Lyle W. Alberg, engaged in a dispute over petitioner's administration of the Police Department's property room. In March of that year, a handgun, which the records of the Department's property room stated had been destroyed, turned up in Kansas City in the possession of a felon. This discovery prompted Alberg to initiate an investigation of the management of the property room. Although the probe was initially directed by petitioner, Alberg soon transferred responsibility for the investigation to the city's Department of Law, instructing the City Counselor to supervise its conduct and to inform him directly of its findings. . . . While Alberg was away on the weekend of April 15 and 16, two developments occurred. Petitioner, having consulted with counsel, sent Alberg a letter demanding written notice of the charges against him and a public hearing with a reasonable opportunity to respond to those charges. At approximately the same time, City Councilman Paul L. Roberts asked for a copy of the investigative report on the Police Department property room. Although petitioner's appeal received no immediate response, the Acting City Manager complied with Roberts' request and supplied him with the audit report and witness statements. . . .

On the evening of April 17, 1972, the City Council held its regularly scheduled meeting. After completion of the planned agenda, Councilman Roberts read a statement he had prepared on the investigation. Among other allegations, Roberts charged that petitioner had misappropriated Police Department property for his own use, that narcotics and money had "mysteriously disappeared" from his office, that traffic tickets had been manipulated, that high ranking police officials had made "inappropriate" requests affecting the police court, and that "things have occurred causing the unusual release of felons." At the close of his statement, Roberts moved that the investigative reports be released to the news media and turned over to the prosecutor for presentation to the grand jury, and that the City Manager "take all direct and appropriate action" against those persons "involved in illegal, wrongful, or gross inefficient activities brought out in the investigative reports." After some discussion, the City Council passed Roberts' motion with no dissents and one abstention. . . .

City Manager Alberg discharged petitioner the very next day. Petitioner was not given any reason for his dismissal; he received only a written notice stating that his employment as Chief of Police was "[t]erminated under the provisions of Section 3.3(1) of the City Charter." Petitioner's earlier demand for a specification of charges and a public hearing was ignored, and a subsequent request by

his attorney for an appeal of the discharge decision was denied by the city on the grounds that "there is no appellate procedure or forum provided by the Charter or ordinances of the City of Independence, Missouri, relating to the dismissal of Mr. Owen." . . . The local press gave prominent coverage both to the City Council's action and petitioner's dismissal, linking the discharge to the investigation. As instructed by the City Council, Alberg referred the investigative reports and witness statements to the Prosecuting Attorney of Jackson County, Mo., for consideration by a grand jury. The results of the audit and investigation were never released to the public, however. The grand jury subsequently returned a "no true bill," and no further action was taken by either the City Council or City Manager Alberg.

II

Petitioner named the city of Independence, City Manager Alberg, and the present members of the City Council in their official capacities as defendants in this suit. Alleging that he was discharged without notice of reasons and without a hearing in violation of his constitutional rights to procedural and substantive due process, petitioner sought declaratory and injunctive relief, including a hearing on his discharge, back pay from the date of discharge, and attorney's fees. The District Court, after a bench trial, entered judgment for respondents. 421 F.Supp. 1110 (1976).

The Court of Appeals initially reversed the District Court. . . . Respondents petitioned for review of the Court of Appeals' decision. Certiorari was granted, and the case was remanded for further consideration in light of our supervening decision in *Monell v. New York City Dept. of Social Services,* 436 U.S. 658 (1978). The Court of Appeals on the remand reaffirmed its original determination that the city had violated petitioner's rights under the Fourteenth Amendment, but held that all respondents, including the city, were entitled to qualified immunity from liability. 589 F.2d 335 (1978).

[1] *Monell* held that "a local government may not be sued under § 1983 for an injury inflicted solely by its employees or agents. Instead, it is when execution of a government's policy or custom, whether made by its lawmakers or by those whose edicts or acts may fairly be said to represent official policy, inflicts the injury that the government as an entity is responsible under § 1983." The

Court of Appeals held in the instant case that the municipality's official policy was responsible for the deprivation of petitioner's constitutional rights: "[T]he stigma attached to [petitioner] in connection with his discharge was caused by the official conduct of the City's lawmakers, or by those whose acts may fairly be said to represent official policy. Such conduct amounted to official policy causing the infringement of [petitioner's] constitutional rights, in violation of section 1983." . . . We turn now to the reasons for our disagreement with this holding. . . .

III

[2] [3] Because the question of the scope of a municipality's immunity from liability under § 1983 is essentially one of statutory construction, see *Wood v. Strickland,* 420 U.S. 308 (1975); the starting point in our analysis must be the language of the statute itself. By its terms, § 1983 "creates a species of tort liability that on its face admits of no immunities." Its language is absolute and unqualified; no mention is made of any privileges, immunities, or defenses that may be asserted. Rather, the Act imposes liability upon "every person" who, under color of state law or custom, "subjects, or causes to be subjected, any citizen of the United States . . . to the deprivation of any rights, privileges, or immunities secured by the Constitution and laws." And *Monell* held that these words were intended to encompass municipal corporations as well as natural "persons." . . . But there is no tradition of immunity for municipal corporations, and neither history nor policy supports a construction of § 1983 that would justify the qualified immunity accorded the city of Independence by the Court of Appeals. We hold, therefore, that the municipality may not assert the good faith of its officers or agents as a defense to liability under § 1983. . . .

[6] To be sure, there were two doctrines that afforded municipal corporations some measure of protection from tort liability. The first sought to distinguish between a municipality's "governmental" and "proprietary" functions; as to the former, the city was held immune, whereas in its exercise of the latter, the city was held to the same standards of liability as any private corporation. The second doctrine immunized a municipality for its "discretionary" or "legislative" activities, but not for those which were "ministerial" in nature. A brief examination of the application and the rationale underlying each of these doctrines demonstrates that Congress could not have intended them to limit a municipality's liability under § 1983.

In sum, we can discern no "tradition so well grounded in history and reason" that would warrant the conclusion that in enacting § 1 of the Civil Rights Act, the 42d Congress *sub silentio* extended to municipalities a qualified immunity based on the good faith of their officers. Absent any clearer indication that Congress intended so to limit the reach of a statute expressly designed to provide a "broad remedy for violations of federally protected civil rights," *Monell v. New York City Dept. of Social Services,* 436 U.S., at 685, we are unwilling to suppose that injuries occasioned by a municipality's unconstitutional conduct were not also meant to be fully redressable through its sweep. . . .

[16][17] Moreover, § 1983 was intended not only to provide compensation to the victims of past abuses, but to serve as a deterrent against future constitutional deprivations, as well. See *Robertson v. Wegmann,* 436 U.S. 584 (1978); *Carey v. Piphus,* 435 U.S. 247 (1978). The knowledge that a municipality will be liable for all of its injurious conduct, whether committed in good faith or not, should create an incentive for officials who may harbor doubts about the lawfulness of their intended actions to err on the side of protecting citizens' constitutional rights. Furthermore, the threat that damages might be levied against the city may encourage those in a policy-making position to institute internal rules and programs designed to minimize the likelihood of unintentional infringements on constitutional rights. Such procedures are particularly beneficial in preventing those "systemic" injuries that result not so much from the conduct of any single individual, but from the interactive behavior of several government officials, each of whom may be acting in good faith. . . .

In *Scheuer v. Rhodes,* supra, 416 U.S., at 240, the Chief Justice identified the two "mutually dependent rationales" on which the doctrine of official immunity rested: "(1) the injustice, particularly in the absence of bad faith, of subjecting to liability an officer who is required, by the legal obligations of his position, to exercise discretion; (2) the danger that the threat of such liability would deter his willingness to execute his office with the decisiveness and the judgment required by the public good." . . .

[19] The first consideration is simply not implicated when the damages award comes not from the official's pocket, but from the public treasury. . . .

[20] It has been argued, however, that revenue raised by taxation for public use should not be diverted to the benefit of a single or discrete group of taxpayers, particularly where the municipality has at all times acted in good faith. On the contrary, the accepted view is that stated in *Thayer v. Boston*—"that the city, in its corporate capacity, should be liable to make good the damage sustained by an [unlucky] individual, in consequence of the acts thus done." 36 Mass., at 515. After all, it is the public at large which enjoys the benefits of the government's activities, and it is the public at large which is ultimately responsible for its administration. Thus, even where some constitutional development could not have been foreseen by municipal officials, it is fairer to allocate any resulting financial loss to the inevitable costs of government borne by all the taxpayers, than to allow its impact to be felt solely by those whose rights, albeit newly recognized, have been violated. . . .

The second rationale mentioned in *Scheuer* also loses its force when it is the municipality, in contrast to the official, whose liability is at issue. At the heart of this justification for a qualified immunity for the individual official is the concern that the threat of personal monetary liability will introduce an unwarranted and unconscionable consideration into the decisionmaking process, thus paralyzing the governing official's decisiveness and distorting his judgment on matters of public policy. The inhibiting effect is significantly reduced, if not eliminated, however, when the threat of personal liability is removed.

IV

In sum, our decision holding that municipalities have no immunity from damages liability flowing from their constitutional violations harmonizes well with developments in the common law and our own pronouncements on official immunities under § 1983. Doctrines of tort law have changed significantly over the past century, and our notions of governmental responsibility should properly reflect that evolution. No longer is individual "blameworthiness" the acid test of liability; the principle of equitable loss-spreading has joined fault as a factor in distributing the costs of official misconduct.

We believe that today's decision, together with prior precedents in this area, properly allocates these costs among the three principals in the scenario of the § 1983 cause of action: the victim of the constitutional deprivation; the officer whose conduct caused the injury; and the public, as represented by the municipal entity. The innocent individual who is harmed by an abuse of governmental authority is assured that he will be compensated for his injury. The offending official, so long as he conducts himself in good faith, may go about his business secure in the knowledge that a qualified immunity will protect him from personal liability for damages that are more appropriately chargeable to the populace as a whole. And the public will be forced to bear only the costs of injury inflicted by the "execution of a government's policy or custom, whether made by its lawmakers or by those whose edicts or acts may fairly be said to represent official policy."

Reversed.

The plaintiff, Owen, in the preceding case was suing the city under 42 U.S.C., § 1983, which is part of the Civil Rights Act of 1871. This law makes any state official liable in an equity suit or an action for damages for a "deprivation of any rights, privileges or immunities secured by the Constitution." Hence, the law creates a constitutional suit against state officials, just as the decision in *Bivens* created one for federal officials. Such suits are referred to as "1983 suits," and they constitute a mushrooming proportion of cases filed in federal courts.[20] Court interpretation of Section 1983 created a qualified official immunity for state officials, just as the immunity articulated in *Butz* created one for federal officials. The two cases that follow show the evolution of doctrine in state official immunity cases. The *Wood* case articulates the current constitutional test for when a state official has crossed the line from immunity to liability.

SCHEUER V. RHODES
416 U.S. 232 (1974)

Chief Justice Burger delivered the opinion for a unanimous court. Justice Douglas did not participate.

We granted certiorari in these cases to resolve whether the District Court correctly dismissed civil damage actions, brought under 42 U.S.C. § 1983, on the ground that these actions were, as a matter of law, against the State of Ohio, and hence barred by the Eleventh Amendment to the Constitution and, alternatively, that the actions were against state officials who were immune from liability for the acts alleged in the complaints. These cases arise out of the same period of alleged civil disorder on the campus of Kent State University in Ohio during May 1970 which was before us, in another context, in *Gilligan v. Morgan,* 413 U.S. 1 (1973). . . . In these cases the personal representatives of the estates of three students who died in that episode seek damages against the Governor, the Adjutant General, and his assistant, various named and unnamed officers and enlisted members of the Ohio National Guard, and the president of Kent State University. The complaints in both cases allege a cause of action under the Civil Rights Act of 1871, now 42 U.S.C. § 1983. Petitioner Scheuer also alleges a cause of action under Ohio law on the theory of pendent jurisdiction. Petitioners Krause and Miller make a similar claim, asserting jurisdiction on the basis of diversity of citizenship. . . .

The District Court dismissed the complaints for lack of jurisdiction over the subject matter on the theory that these actions, although in form against the named individuals, were, in substance and effect, against the State of Ohio and thus barred by the Eleventh Amendment. The Court of Appeals affirmed the action of the District Court, agreeing that the suit was in legal effect one against the State of Ohio and, alternatively, that the common-law doctrine of executive immunity barred action against the state officials who are respondents here. 471 F.2d 430 (1972). We are confronted with the narrow threshold question whether the District

Court properly dismissed the complaints. We hold that dismissal was inappropriate at this stage of the litigation and accordingly reverse the judgments and remand for further proceedings. We intimate no view on the merits of the allegations since there is no evidence before us at this stage.

I

The complaints in these cases are not identical but their thrust is essentially the same. In essence, the defendants are alleged to have "intentionally, recklessly, willfully and wantonly" caused an unnecessary deployment of the Ohio National Guard on the Kent State campus and, in the same manner, ordered the Guard members to perform allegedly illegal actions which resulted in the death of plaintiffs' decedents. Both complaints allege that the action was taken "under color of state law" and that it deprived the decedents of their lives and rights without due process of law. Fairly read, the complaints allege that each of the named defendants, in undertaking such actions, acted either outside the scope of his respective office or, if within the scope, acted in an arbitrary manner, grossly abusing the lawful powers of office. The complaints were dismissed by the District Court for lack of jurisdiction without the filing of an answer to any of the complaints. The only pertinent documentation before the court in addition to the complaints were two proclamations issued by the respondent Governor. The first proclamation ordered the Guard to duty to protect against violence arising from wildcat strikes in the trucking industry; the other recited an account of the conditions prevailing at Kent State University at that time. In dismissing these complaints for want of subject matter jurisdiction at that early stage, the District Court held, as we noted earlier, that the defendants were being sued in their official and representative capacities and that the actions were therefore in effect against the State of Ohio. The primary question presented is whether the District Court acted prematurely and hence erroneously in dismissing the complaints on the stated ground, thus precluding any opportunity for the plaintiffs by subsequent proof to establish a claim. . . .

Whatever the plaintiffs may or may not be able to establish as to the merits of their allegations, their claims, as stated in the complaints, given the favorable reading required by the Federal Rules of Civil Procedure, are not barred by the Eleventh Amendment. Consequently, the District Court erred in dismissing the complaints for lack of jurisdiction. . . .

III

The Court of Appeals relied upon the existence of an absolute "executive immunity" as an alternative ground for sustaining the dismissal of the complaints by the District Court. If the immunity of a member of the executive branch is absolute and comprehensive as to all acts allegedly performed within the scope of official duty, the Court of Appeals was correct; if, on the other hand, the immunity is not absolute but rather one that is qualified or limited, an executive officer may or may not be subject to liability depending on all the circumstances that may be revealed by evidence. The concept of the immunity of government officers from personal liability springs from the same root considerations that generated the doctrine of sovereign immunity. While the latter doctrine—that the "King can do no wrong"—did not protect all government officers from personal liability, the common law soon recognized the necessity of permitting officials to perform their official functions free from the threat of suits for personal liability. This official immunity apparently rested, in its genesis, on two mutually dependent rationales: (1) the injustice, particularly in the absence of bad faith, of subjecting to liability an officer who is required, by the legal obligations of his position, to exercise discretion; (2) the danger that the threat of such liability would deter his willingness to execute his office with the decisiveness and the judgment required by the public good. . . .

Under the criteria developed by precedents of this Court, § 1983 would be drained of meaning were we to hold that the acts of a governor or other high executive officer have "the quality of a supreme and unchangeable edict, overriding all conflicting rights of property and unreviewable through the judicial power of the federal govern-

ment." *Sterling v. Constantin,* 287 U.S., at 397. In *Sterling,* Mr. Chief Justice Hughes put it in these terms: "If this extreme position could be deemed to be well taken, it is manifest that the fiat of a state Governor, and not the Constitution of the United States, would be the supreme law of the land; that the restrictions of the Federal Constitution upon the exercise of state power would be but impotent phrases, the futility of which the State may at any time disclose by the simple process of transferring powers of legislation to the Governor to be exercised by him, beyond control, upon his assertion of necessity. Under our system of government, such a conclusion is obviously untenable. There is no such avenue of escape from the paramount authority of the Federal Constitution. When there is a substantial showing that the exertion of state power has overridden private rights secured by that Constitution, the subject is necessarily one for judicial inquiry in an appropriate proceeding directed against the individuals charged with the transgression." . . .

V

The documents properly before the District Court at this early pleading stage specifically placed in issue whether the Governor and his subordinate officers were acting within the scope of their duties under the Constitution and laws of Ohio; whether they acted within the range of discretion permitted the holders of such office under Ohio law and whether they acted in good faith both in proclaiming an emergency and as to the actions taken to cope with the emergency so declared. Similarly, the complaints place directly in issue whether the lesser officers and enlisted personnel of the Guard acted in good-faith obedience to the orders of their superiors. Further proceedings, either by way of summary judgment or by trial on the merits are required. The complaining parties are entitled to be heard more fully than is possible on a motion to dismiss a complaint.

We intimate no evaluation whatever as to the merits of the petitioners' claims or as to whether it will be possible to support them by proof. We hold only that, on the allegations of their respective complaints, they were entitled to have them judicially resolved.

The judgments of the Court of Appeals are reversed and the cases are remanded for further proceedings consistent with this opinion.

It is so ordered.

WOOD V. STRICKLAND
420 U.S. 308 (1975)

Justice White delivered the opinion of the Court, joined by Justices Brennan, Stewart, Marshall, and Stevens. Justice Powell filed an opinion concurring in part and dissenting in part, which was joined by Chief Justice Burger and Justices Blackmun and Rehnquist.

Respondents Peggy Strickland and Virginia Crain brought this lawsuit against petitioners, who were members of the school board at the time in question, two school administrators, and the Special School District of Mena, Ark., purporting to assert a cause of action under 42 U.S.C. § 1983, and claiming that their federal constitutional rights to due process were infringed under color of state law by their expulsion from the Mena Public High School on the grounds of their violation of a school regulation prohibiting the use or possession of intoxicating beverages at school or school activities. The complaint as amended prayed for compensatory and punitive damages against all petitioners, injunctive relief allowing respondents to resume attendance, preventing petitioners from imposing any sanctions as a result of the expulsion, and restraining enforcement of the challenged regulations, declaratory relief as to the constitutional invalidity of the regulation, and expunction of any record of their expulsion. After the declaration of a mistrial arising from the jury's failure to reach a verdict, the District Court directed verdicts in favor of petitioners on the ground that petitioners were immune from damages suits absent proof of malice in the sense of ill will toward respondents. 348 F.Supp. 244 (WD Ark. 1972). The Court of Appeals, finding that the facts showed a violation of respondents' rights to "substantive due process," reversed and remanded for appropriate injunctive relief and a new trial on the question of damages. 485 F.2d 186 (CA8 1973). A petition for rehearing en banc was denied, with three judges dissenting. Certiorari was granted to consider whether this application of due process by the Court of Appeals was warranted and whether that court's expression of a standard governing immunity for school board members from liability for compensatory damages under 42 U.S.C. § 1983 was the correct one. . . .

I

The violation of the school regulation prohibiting the use or possession of intoxicating beverages at school or school activities with which respondents were charged concerned their "spiking" of the punch served at a meeting of an extracurricular school organization attended by parents and students. At the time in question, respondents were 16 years old and were in the 10th grade. The relevant facts begin with their discovery that the punch had not been prepared for the meeting as previously planned. The girls then agreed to "spike" it. Since the county in which the school is located is "dry," respondents and a third girl drove across the state border into Oklahoma and purchased two 12-ounce bottles of "Right Time," a malt liquor. They then bought six 10-ounce bottles of a soft drink, and, after having mixed the contents of the eight bottles in an empty milk carton, returned to school. Prior to the meeting, the girls experienced second thoughts about the wisdom of their prank, but by then they were caught up in the force of events and the intervention of other girls prevented them from disposing of the illicit punch. The punch was served at the meeting, without apparent effect. . . .

Ten days later, the teacher in charge of the extracurricular group and meeting, Mrs. Curtis Powell, having heard something about the "spiking," questioned the girls about it. Although first denying any knowledge, the girls admitted their involvement after the teacher said that she would handle the punishment herself. The next day, however, she told the girls that the incident was becoming increasingly the subject of talk in the school and that the principal, P. T. Waller, would probably hear about it. She told them that her job was in jeopardy but that she would not force them to admit to Waller what they had done. If they did not go to him then, however, she would not be able to help them if the incident became "distorted." The three girls then went to Waller and admitted their role in the affair. He suspended them from school for a maximum two-week period, subject to the decision of the school board. Waller also told them that the board would meet that night, that the girls could tell their parents about the meeting, but that the parents should not contact any members of the board.

Neither the girls nor their parents attended the school board meeting that night. Both Mrs. Powell and Waller, after making their reports concerning the incident, recommended leniency. At this point, a telephone call was received by S. L. Inlow, then the superintendent of schools, from Mrs. Powell's husband, also a teacher at the high school, who reported that he had heard that the third girl involved had been in a fight that evening at a basketball game. Inlow informed the meeting of the news, although he did not mention the name of the girl involved. Mrs. Powell and Waller then withdrew their recommendations of leniency, and the board voted to expel the girls from school for the remainder of the semester, a period of approximately three months.

The board subsequently agreed to hold another meeting on the matter, and one was held approximately two weeks after the first meeting. The girls, their parents, and their counsel attended this session. The board began with a reading of a written statement of facts as it had found them. The girls admitted mixing the malt liquor into the punch with the intent of "spiking" it, but asked the board to forgo its rule punishing such violations by such substantial suspensions. Neither Mrs. Powell nor Waller was present at this meeting. The board voted not to change its policy and, as before, to expel the girls for the remainder of the semester. . . .

Petitioners as members of the school board assert here, as they did below, an absolute immunity from liability under § 1983 and at the very least seek to reinstate the judgment of the District Court. If they are correct and the District Court's dismissal should be sustained, we need go no further in this case. Moreover, the immunity question involves the construction of a federal statute, and our practice is to deal with possibly dispositive statutory issues before reaching questions turning on the construction of the Constitution. We essentially sustain the position of the Court of Appeals with respect to the immunity issue. . . .

The nature of the immunity from awards of damages under § 1983 available to school administrators and school board members is not a question which the lower federal courts have answered with a single voice. There is general agreement on the existence of a "good faith" immunity, but the courts have either emphasized different factors as elements of good faith or have not given specific content to the good-faith standard. . . .

Therefore, in the specific context of school discipline, we hold that a school board member is not immune from liability for damages under § 1983 if he knew or reasonably should have known that the action he took within his sphere of official responsibility would violate the constitutional rights of the student affected, or if he took the action with the malicious intention to cause a deprivation of constitutional rights or other injury to the student. That is not to say that school board members are "charged with predicting the future course of constitutional law." A compensatory award will be appropriate only if the school board member has acted with such an impermissible motivation or with such disregard of the student's clearly established constitutional rights that his action cannot reasonably be characterized as being in good faith. . . .

IV

Respondents' complaint alleged that their procedural due process rights were violated by the action taken by petitioners. App. 9. The District Court did not discuss this claim in its final opinion, but the Court of Appeals viewed it as presenting a substantial question. It concluded that the girls were denied procedural due process at the first school board meeting, but also intimated that the second meeting may have cured the initial procedural deficiencies. Having found a substantive due process violation, however, the court did not reach a conclusion on this procedural issue.

Respondents have argued here that there was a procedural due process violation which also supports the result reached by the Court of Appeals. But because the District Court did not discuss it, and the Court of Appeals did not decide it, it would be preferable to have the Court of Appeals consider the issue in the first instance.

The judgment of the Court of Appeals is vacated and the case remanded for further proceedings consistent with this opinion.

So ordered.

Although they do not relate so much to administrative law, the student should be aware that there are many other forms of immunity from suit.

Members of Congress and state legislators are immune from both suit and criminal prosecution under constitutional speech and debate clauses. The states can make charities immune from their torts. However, one of the rising costs for agencies at all levels of government is the cost of liability insurance to protect their employees from *Bivens*-type actions and Section 1983 suits. If you interview for a job with a state or local governmental agency, this insurance is one of the benefits you should inquire about.

You will need to think carefully at this point because you must be able to distinguish between a case involving the unintentional tort of negligence and a case involving a "constitutional tort." The former involves the existence of a legal duty (e.g., to exercise reasonable care or a duty to warn), the breach of that duty (foreseeability), harm caused by the breach of duty, and often whether the government employee who breached the duty absolved the government of liability because of the discretionary exemption (e.g., the FAA inspectors who missed the particular Boeing 707 in the *Varig* case because of the policy of "spot checks"). In negligence cases arising under the FTCA, only acts of discretion with policy implications can make the government immune.

The latter kinds of cases, *constitutional torts,* involve situations in which a government employee has taken some action that has violated a citizen's constitutional or civil rights. Here, a plaintiff can sue the individual federal or state employee (but not the government). At the city or county level, a plaintiff could sue either the individual employee or the government as Owens sued the city of Independence, Missouri. However, if a plaintiff attempts to sue city or county government, alleging that the city or county violated his or her constitutional rights, then the plaintiff would have to prove that the violation resulted from a local governmental policy (see *Pembaur v. Cincinnati* at the end of this chapter).

At the federal level, and in most cases at the state level as well (state legislatures decide what specific and peculiar exemptions will apply in suing the respective states), *policy* decisions involve immunity for government under the Tort Claims Act. That is because it is desirable to ensure that important decisions do not get put off out of fear of a lawsuit. Conversely, at the city and county levels under Section 1983 suits, those governments can only be liable if the decision or action that violates a citizen's rights was the result of a local *policy.* That is because it is not desirable to expose government to the threat of a lawsuit based on the arbitrary actions of an individual employee (a loose cannon, perhaps). Hence, only if city policy violates someone's rights can the city be sued under Section 1983.

SUMMARY

1. Both state and federal governments in the United States are clothed with sovereign immunity. They can be sued only with their consent and only under the conditions they set:

> Section 702 of the APA sanctions suits in equity against the federal government.
>
> A tort claims act is the vehicle through which most state and federal governments agree to be held liable for their torts (mostly for the unintentional tort of negligence).
>
> To pursue a successful negligence suit against the federal government, one must show that (a) a failure to exercise reasonable care occurred (foreseeability measured by the average reasonable person), (b) the failure to exercise reasonable care was the proximate cause of injuries, (c) a dollar amount can be attached to the injuries, and (d) the negligent action was not the result of the exercise of discretion with policy implications.
>
> The tort claims act absolves the individual employee of legal liability (so long as the negligence occurred in the scope of employment) and spreads the cost to the taxpayers.

2. *Official immunity* is a term used to connote that employees of the federal government can be sued for their acts that violate the constitutional rights of another but that they have a qualified immunity in that sometimes they are immune from such suits: (a) when there is a lack of malice (they acted in good faith) and (b) when they did not know and could not have known that their actions would violate the constitutional rights of another (e.g., *Butz v. Economou*).

3. State employees are exposed to liability for violating another person's rights by Section 1983 of the Civil Rights Act of 1871. They also have a qualified immunity, which is the same as for federal employees (a) when there is absence of malice and (b) when they did not know and could not have known that their actions would violate the constitutional rights of another.

4. City and county governments can also be sued under Section 1983 (*Owens v. City of Independence*). Such suits can only be successful, however, if the violation of citizens rights was the result of a local policy.

5. Notice in the two following cases (*Carlson* and *Bush*) two situations in which a plaintiff cannot maintain a successful *Bivens* actions:

Where the defendant demonstrates special factors counseling hesitation in the absence of affirmative action by Congress (see *Bush v. Lucas*)

Where the defendant shows that Congress has provided an equally effective remedy at law (see *Carlson v. Green*)

An interesting question involving individual qualified immunity was argued before the Supreme Court in spring 1997. In *Richardson v. McKnight* (117 S. Ct. 2100, 1997), the question was whether prison guards who work for a private corrections firm under contract to run Tennessee's prison system possesses a qualified immunity under Section 1983 just as public employees would. This question is important in an era of antigovernment, privatization, and downsizing. The Supreme Court refused to clothe the guards with qualified immunity.

END-OF-CHAPTER CASES

CARLSON V. GREEN
446 U.S. 14 (1980)

Justice Brennan delivered the opinion of the Court, joined by Justices White, Marshall, Blackmun, and Stevens. Justices Powell and Stewart concurred, and Chief Justice Burger dissented, joined by Justice Rehnquist.

[1][2] Respondent brought this suit in the District Court for the Southern District of Indiana on behalf of the estate of her deceased son, Joseph Jones, Jr., alleging that he suffered personal injuries from which he died because the petitioners, federal prison officials, violated his due process, equal protection, and Eighth Amendment rights (they failed to provide adequate medical attention to Jones, causing his death). Asserting jurisdiction under 28 U.S.C. § 1331(a), she claimed compensatory and punitive damages for the constitutional violations. Two questions are presented for decision: (1) Is a remedy available directly under the Constitution, given that respondent's allegations could also support a suit against the United States under the Federal Tort Claims Act? And (2) if so, is survival of the cause of action governed by federal common law or by state statutes? . . .

II

[3] *Bivens* established that the victims of a constitutional violation by a federal agent have a right to recover damages against the official in federal court despite the absence of any statute conferring such a right. Such a cause of action may be defeated in a particular case, however, in two situations. The first is when defendants demonstrate "special factors counselling hesitation in the absence of affirmative action by Congress." 403 U.S., at 396, *Davis v. Passman,* 442 U.S. 228 (1979). The second is when defendants show that Congress has provided an alternative remedy which it explicitly declared to be a substitute for recovery directly under the Constitution and viewed as equally effective. *Bivens,* supra, at 397, *Davis v. Passman,* supra, at 245-247. Neither situation obtains in this case. . . .

Second, our decisions, although not expressly addressing and deciding the question, indicate that punitive damages may be awarded in a *Bivens* suit. Punitive damages are "a particular remedial mechanism normally available in the federal courts," *Bivens,* 403 U.S., at 397, and are especially appropriate to redress the violation by a Government official of a citizen's constitutional rights. Moreover, punitive damages are available in "a proper" § 1983 action, *Carey v. Piphus,* 435 U.S. 247 (1978) (punitive damages not awarded because District Court found defendants "did not act with a malicious intention to deprive respondents of their rights or to do them other injury"), and *Butz v. Economou* suggests that the "constitutional design" would be stood on its head if federal officials did not face at least the same liability as state officials guilty of the same constitutional transgression. But punitive damages in an FTCA suit are statutorily prohibited. Thus FTCA is that much less effective than a *Bivens* action as a deterrent to unconstitutional acts. . . .

Third, a plaintiff cannot opt for a jury in an FTCA action, 28 U.S.C. § 2402, as he may in a *Bivens* suit. Petitioners argue that this is an irrelevant difference because juries have been biased against *Bivens* claimants. Significantly, however, they do not assert that judges trying the claims as FTCA actions would have been more receptive, and they cannot explain why the plaintiff should not retain the choice. . . .

Fourth, an action under FTCA exists only if the State in which the alleged misconduct occurred would permit a cause of action for that misconduct to go forward. 28 U.S.C. § 1346(b) (United States liable "in accordance with the law of the place where the act or omission occurred"). Yet it is obvious that the liability of federal officials for violations of citizens' constitutional rights should be governed by uniform rules. The question whether respondent's action for violations by federal officials of federal constitutional rights should be left to the vagaries of the laws of the several States admits of only a negative answer in the absence of a contrary congressional resolution.

Plainly FTCA is not a sufficient protector of the citizens' constitutional rights, and without a clear congressional mandate we cannot hold that Congress relegated respondent exclusively to the FTCA remedy.

III

[6] *Bivens* actions are a creation of federal law and, therefore, the question whether respondent's action survived Jones' death is a question of federal law. Petitioners, however, would have us fashion a federal rule of survivorship that incorporates the survivorship laws of the forum State, at least where the state law is not inconsistent with federal law. Respondent argues, on the other hand, that only a uniform federal rule of survivorship is compatible with the goal of deterring federal officials from infringing federal constitutional rights in the manner alleged in respondent's complaint. We agree with respondent. Whatever difficulty we might have resolving the question were the federal involvement less clear, we hold that only a uniform federal rule of survivorship will suffice to redress the constitutional deprivation here alleged and to protect against repetition of such conduct.

In short, we agree with and adopt the reasoning of the Court of Appeals, 581 F.2d, at 674-675, "The essentiality of the survival of civil rights claims for complete vindication of constitutional rights is buttressed by the need for uniform treatment of those claims, at least when they are against federal officials. As this very case illustrates, uniformity cannot be achieved if courts are limited to applicable state law. Here the relevant Indiana statute would not permit survival of the claim, while in *Beard [v. Robinson,* 563 F.2d 331 (1977)], the Illinois statute permitted survival of the *Bivens* action. The liability of federal agents for violation of constitutional rights should not depend upon where the violation occurred. . . . In sum, we hold that whenever the relevant state survival statute would abate a *Bivens*-type action brought against defendants whose conduct results in death, the federal common law allows survival of the action." . . .

Affirmed.

BUSH V. LUCAS
462 U.S. 367 (1983)

Justice Stevens delivered the opinion for a unanimous Court, with Justices Marshall and Blackmun concurring.

Petitioner asks us to authorize a new nonstatutory damages remedy for federal employees whose First Amendment rights are violated by their superiors. Because such claims arise out of an employment relationship that is governed by comprehensive procedural and substantive provisions giving meaningful remedies against the United States, we conclude that it would be inappropriate for us to supplement that regulatory scheme with a new judicial remedy.

Petitioner Bush is an aerospace engineer employed at the George C. Marshall Space Flight Center, a major facility operated by the National Aeronautics and Space Administration in Alabama. Respondent Lucas is the Director of the Center. In 1974 the facility was reorganized and petitioner was twice reassigned to new positions. He objected to both reassignments and sought formal review by the Civil Service Commission. In May and June 1975, while some of his administrative appeals were pending, he made a number of public statements, including two televised interviews, that were highly critical of the agency. The news media quoted him as saying that he did not have enough meaningful work to keep him busy, that his job was "a travesty and worthless," and that the taxpayers' money was being spent fraudulently and wastefully at the Center. His statements were reported on local television, in the local newspaper, and in a national press release that appeared in newspapers in at least three other States. . . .

In June 1975 respondent, in response to a reporter's inquiry, stated that he had conducted an investigation and that petitioner's statements regarding his job had "no basis in fact." In August 1975 an adverse personnel action was initiated to remove petitioner from his position. Petitioner was charged with "publicly mak[ing] intemperate remarks which were misleading and often false, evidencing a malicious attitude towards Management and generating an environment of sensationalism demeaning to the Government, the National Aeronautics and Space Administration and the personnel of the George C. Marshall Space Flight Center, thereby impeding Government efficiency and economy and adversely affecting public confidence in the Government service." He was also informed that his conduct had undermined morale at the Center and caused disharmony and disaffection among his fellow employees. Petitioner had the opportunity to file a written response and to make an oral presentation to agency officials. Respondent then determined that petitioner's statements were false and misleading and that his conduct

would justify removal, but that the lesser penalty of demotion was appropriate for a "first offense." He approved a reduction in grade from GS-14 to GS-12, which decreased petitioner's annual salary by approximately $9,716.

Petitioner exercised his right to appeal to the Federal Employee Appeals Authority. After a three-day public hearing, the Authority upheld some of the charges and concluded that the demotion was justified. It specifically determined that a number of petitioner's public statements were misleading and that, for three reasons, they "exceeded the bounds of expression protected by the First Amendment." First, petitioner's statements did not stem from public interest, but from his desire to have his position abolished so that he could take early retirement and go to law school. Second, the statements conveyed the erroneous impression that the agency was deliberately wasting public funds, thus discrediting the agency and its employees. Third, there was no legitimate public interest to be served by abolishing petitioner's position. . . .

Two years after the Appeals Authority's decision, petitioner requested the Civil Service Commission's Appeals Review Board to reopen the proceeding. The Board reexamined petitioner's First Amendment claim and, after making a detailed review of the record and the applicable authorities, applied the balancing test articulated in *Pickering v. Board of Education,* 391 U.S. 563 (1968). On the one hand, it acknowledged the evidence tending to show that petitioner's motive might have been personal gain, and the evidence that his statements caused some disruption of the agency's day-to-day routine. On the other hand, it noted that society as well as the individual had an interest in free speech, including "a right to disclosure of information about how tax dollars are spent and about the functioning of governmental apparatus, an interest in the promotion of the efficiency of the government, and in the maintenance of an atmosphere of freedom of expression by the scientists and engineers who are responsible for the planning and implementation of the nation's space program." Because petitioner's statements, though somewhat exaggerated, "were not wholly without truth, they properly stimulated public debate." Thus the nature and extent of proven disruption to the agency's operations did not "justify abrogation of the exercise of free speech." The Board recommended that petitioner be restored to his former position, retroactively to

November 30, 1975, and that he receive back pay. That recommendation was accepted. Petitioner received approximately $30,000 in back pay.

While his administrative appeal was pending, petitioner filed an action against respondent in state court in Alabama seeking to recover damages for defamation and violation of his constitutional rights. Respondent removed the lawsuit to the United States District Court for the Northern District of Alabama, which granted respondent's motion for summary judgment. It held, first, that the defamation claim could not be maintained because, under *Barr v. Matteo,* 360 U.S. 564 (1959), respondent was absolutely immune from liability for damages for defamation; and second, that petitioner's demotion was not a constitutional deprivation for which a damages action could be maintained. The United States Court of Appeals for the Fifth Circuit affirmed. 598 F.2d 958 (1979). We vacated that court's judgment, 446 U.S. 914, 100 S.Ct. 1846, 64 L.Ed.2d 268 (1980), and directed that it reconsider the case in the light of our intervening decision in *Carlson v. Green,* 446 U.S. 14, 100 S.Ct. 1468, 64 L.Ed.2d 15 (1980). The Court of Appeals again affirmed the judgment against petitioner. It adhered to its previous conclusion "that plaintiff had no cause of action for damages under the First Amendment for retaliatory demotion in view of the available remedies under the Civil Service Commission regulations." 647 F.2d 573, 574 (1981). It explained that the relationship between the Federal Government and its civil service employees was a special factor counselling against the judicial recognition of a damages remedy under the Constitution in this context.

We assume for purposes of decision that petitioner's First Amendment rights were violated by the adverse personnel action. We also assume that, as petitioner asserts, civil service remedies were not as effective as an individual damages remedy and did not fully compensate him for the harm he suffered. Two further propositions are undisputed. Congress has not expressly authorized the damages remedy that petitioner asks us to provide. On the other hand, Congress has not expressly precluded the creation of such a remedy by declaring that existing statutes provide the exclusive mode of redress.

[2] This much is established by our prior cases. The federal courts' statutory jurisdiction to decide federal questions confers adequate power to award damages to the victim of a constitutional violation.

When Congress provides an alternative remedy, it may, of course, indicate its intent, by statutory language, by clear legislative history, or perhaps even by the statutory remedy itself, that the Court's power should not be exercised. In the absence of such a congressional directive, the federal courts must make the kind of remedial determination that is appropriate for a common-law tribunal, paying particular heed, however, to any special factors counselling hesitation before authorizing a new kind of federal litigation.

Congress has not resolved the question presented by this case by expressly denying petitioner the judicial remedy he seeks or by providing him with an equally effective substitute. There is, however, a good deal of history that is relevant to the question whether a federal employee's attempt to recover damages from his superior for violation of his First Amendment rights involves any "special factors counselling hesitation." When those words were first used in *Bivens,* 403 U.S., at 396, we illustrated our meaning by referring to *United States v. Standard Oil Co.,* 332 U.S. 301 (1947), and *United States v. Gilman,* 347 U.S. 507 (1954). A federal employee in the competitive service may be removed or demoted "only for such cause as will promote the efficiency of the service." The regulations applicable at the time of petitioner's demotion in 1975, which are substantially similar to those now in effect, required that an employee be given 30 days' written notice of a proposed discharge, suspension, or demotion, accompanied by the agency's reasons and a copy of the charges. The employee then had the right to examine all disclosable materials that formed the basis of the proposed action, the right to answer the charges with a statement and supporting affidavits, and the right to make an oral non-evidentiary presentation to an agency official. The regulations required that the final agency decision be made by an official higher in rank than the official who proposed the adverse action. The employee was entitled to notification in writing stating which of the initial reasons had been sustained. The next step was a right to appeal to the Civil Service Commission's Federal Employee Appeals Authority [FEAA]. The Appeals Authority was required to hold a trial-type hearing at which the employee could present witnesses, cross-examine the agency's witnesses, and secure the attendance of agency officials, and then to render a written decision. An adverse decision by the FEAA was judicially reviewable in either federal district court or the Court of Claims. In addition, the employee had the right to ask the Commission's Appeals Review Board to reopen an adverse decision by the FEAA.

If the employee prevailed in the administrative process or upon judicial review, he was entitled to reinstatement with retroactive seniority. He also had a right to full back pay, including credit for periodic within-grade or step increases and general pay raises during the relevant period, allowances, differentials, and accumulated leave. Congress intended that these remedies would put the employee "in the same position he would have been in had the unjustified or erroneous personnel action not taken place."

[3] Given the history of the development of civil service remedies and the comprehensive nature of the remedies currently available, it is clear that the question we confront today is quite different from the typical remedial issue confronted by a common-law court. The question is not what remedy the court should provide for a wrong that would otherwise go unredressed. It is whether an elaborate remedial system that has been constructed step by step, with careful attention to conflicting policy considerations, should be augmented by the creation of a new judicial remedy for the constitutional violation at issue. That question obviously cannot be answered simply by noting that existing remedies do not provide complete relief for the plaintiff. The policy judgment should be informed by a thorough understanding of the existing regulatory structure and the respective costs and benefits that would result from the addition of another remedy for violations of employees' First Amendment rights.

Not only has Congress developed considerable familiarity with balancing governmental efficiency and the rights of employees, but it also may inform itself through factfinding procedures such as hearings that are not available to the courts. Nor is there any reason to discount Congress' ability to make an evenhanded assessment of the desirability of creating a new remedy for federal employees who have been demoted or discharged for expressing controversial views. Congress has a special interest in informing itself about the efficiency and morale of the Executive Branch. In the past it has demonstrated its awareness that lower-level government employees are a valuable source of information, and that supervisors might improperly attempt to curtail their subordinates' freedom of expression.

Thus, we do not decide whether or not it would be good policy to permit a federal employee to recover damages from a supervisor who has improperly disciplined him for exercising his First Amendment rights. As we did in *Standard Oil,* we decline "to create a new substantive legal liability without legislative aid and as at the common law" because we are convinced that Congress is in a better position to decide whether or not the public interest would be served by creating it.

The judgment of the Court of Appeals is Affirmed.

PEMBAUR V. CINCINNATI
475 U.S. 469 (1986)

Justice Brennan delivered the opinion of the Court with respect to Parts I, II-A, and II-C, in which Justices White, Marshall, Blackmun, Stevens, and O'Connor (except for Part II-C) joined, and an opinion with respect to Part II-B, in which Justices White, Marshall, and Blackmun joined. Justice White filed a concurring opinion, and Justices Stevens and O'Connor filed opinions concurring in part and concurring in the judgment. Justice Powell filed a dissenting opinion, in which Chief Justice Burger and Justice Rehnquist joined.

In *Monell v. New York City Dept. of Social Services,* 436 U.S. 658 (1978) the Court concluded that municipal liability under 42 U.S.C. § 1983 is limited to deprivations of federally protected rights caused by action taken "pursuant to official munici-pal policy of some nature. . . ." The question presented is whether, and in what circumstances, a decision by municipal policymakers on a single occasion may satisfy this requirement.

I

Bertold Pembaur is a licensed Ohio physician and the sole proprietor of the Rockdale Medical Center, located in the city of Cincinnati in Hamilton County. Most of Pembaur's patients are welfare recipients who rely on government assistance to pay for medical care. During the spring of 1977, Simon Leis, the Hamilton County Prosecutor, began investigating charges that Pembaur fraudulently had accepted payments from state welfare agencies for services not actually provided to patients. A grand jury was convened, and the case was assigned to Assistant Prosecutor William Whalen. In April, the grand jury charged Pembaur in a six-count indictment.

During the investigation, the grand jury issued subpoenas for the appearance of two of Pembaur's employees. When these employees failed to appear as directed, the Prosecutor obtained capiases for their arrest and detention from the Court of Common Pleas of Hamilton County. . . . On May 19, 1977, two Hamilton County Deputy Sheriffs attempted to serve the capiases at Pembaur's clinic. Although the reception area is open to the public, the rest of the clinic may be entered only through a door next to the receptionist's window. Upon arriving, the Deputy Sheriffs identified themselves to the receptionist and sought to pass through this door, which was apparently open. The receptionist blocked their way and asked them to wait for the doctor. When Pembaur appeared a moment later, he and the receptionist closed the door, which automatically locked from the inside, and wedged a piece of wood between it and the wall. Returning to the receptionist's window, the Deputy Sheriffs identified themselves to Pembaur, showed him the capiases and explained why they were there. Pembaur refused to let them enter, claiming that the police had no legal authority to be there and requesting that they leave. He told them that he had called the Cincinnati police, the local media, and his lawyer. The Deputy Sheriffs decided not to take further action until the Cincinnati police arrived.

Shortly thereafter, several Cincinnati police officers appeared. The Deputy Sheriffs explained the situation to them and asked that they speak to Pembaur. The Cincinnati police told Pembaur that the papers were lawful and that he should allow the Deputy Sheriffs to enter. When Pembaur refused, the Cincinnati police called for a superior officer. When he too failed to persuade Pembaur to open the door, the Deputy Sheriffs decided to call their supervisor for further instructions. Their supervisor told them to call Assistant Prosecutor Whalen and to follow his instructions. The Deputy Sheriffs then telephoned Whalen and informed him of the situation. Whalen conferred with County Prosecutor Leis, who told Whalen to instruct the Deputy Sheriffs to "go in and get [the witnesses]." Whalen in turn passed these instructions along to the Deputy Sheriffs.

After a final attempt to persuade Pembaur voluntarily to allow them to enter, the Deputy Sheriffs

tried unsuccessfully to force the door. City police officers, who had been advised of the County Prosecutor's instructions to "go in and get" the witnesses, obtained an axe and chopped down the door. The Deputy Sheriffs then entered and searched the clinic. Two individuals who fit descriptions of the witnesses sought were detained, but turned out not to be the right persons.

After this incident, the Prosecutor obtained an additional indictment against Pembaur for obstructing police in the performance of an authorized act. Although acquitted of all other charges, Pembaur was convicted for this offense. The Ohio Court of Appeals reversed, reasoning that Pembaur was privileged under state law to exclude the deputies because the search of his office violated the Fourth Amendment. The Ohio Supreme Court reversed and reinstated the conviction. *State v. Pembaur,* 459 N.E.2d 217 (1984). The Supreme Court held that the state-law privilege applied only to bad-faith conduct by law enforcement officials, and that, under the circumstances of this case, Pembaur was obliged to acquiesce to the search and seek redress later in a civil action for damages.

On April 20, 1981, Pembaur filed the present action in the United States District Court for the Southern District of Ohio against the city of Cincinnati, the County of Hamilton, the Cincinnati Police Chief, the Hamilton County Sheriff, the members of the Hamilton Board of County Commissioners (in their official capacities only), Assistant Prosecutor Whalen, and nine city and county police officers. Pembaur sought damages under 42 U.S.C. § 1983, alleging that the county and city police had violated his rights under the Fourth and Fourteenth Amendments. His theory was that, absent exigent circumstances, the Fourth Amendment prohibits police from searching an individual's home or business without a search warrant even to execute an arrest warrant for a third person. We agreed with that proposition in *Steagald v. United States,* 451 U.S. 204 (1981), decided the day after Pembaur filed this lawsuit. Pembaur sought $10 million in actual and $10 million in punitive damages, plus costs and attorney's fees. . . .

II

A

Our analysis must begin with the proposition that "Congress did not intend municipalities to be held liable unless action pursuant to official municipal policy of some nature caused a constitutional tort." *Monell v. New York City Dept. of Social Services,* 436 U.S., at 691. As we read its opinion, the Court of Appeals held that a single decision to take particular action, although made by municipal policymakers, cannot establish the kind of "official policy" required by *Monell* as a predicate to municipal liability under § 1983. The Court of Appeals reached this conclusion without referring to *Monell*—indeed, without any explanation at all. However, examination of the opinion in *Monell* clearly demonstrates that the Court of Appeals misinterpreted its holding. . . . The conclusion that tortious conduct, to be the basis for municipal liability under § 1983, must be pursuant to a municipality's "official policy" is contained in this discussion. The "official policy" requirement was intended to distinguish acts of the municipality from acts of employees of the municipality, and thereby make clear that municipal liability is limited to action for which the municipality is actually responsible. *Monell* reasoned that recovery from a municipality is limited to acts that are, properly speaking, acts "of the municipality"—that is, acts which the municipality has officially sanctioned or ordered.

B

Having said this much, we hasten to emphasize that not every decision by municipal officers automatically subjects the municipality to § 1983 liability. Municipal liability attaches only where the decisionmaker possesses final authority to establish municipal policy with respect to the action ordered. The fact that a particular official—even a policymaking official—has discretion in the exercise of particular functions does not, without more, give rise to municipal liability based on an exercise of that discretion. See, e.g., *Oklahoma City v. Tuttle,* 471 U.S., at 822-824. The official must also be responsible for establishing final government policy respecting such activity before the municipality can be held liable. Authority to make municipal policy may be granted directly by a legislative enactment or may be delegated by an official who possesses such authority, and of course, whether an official had final policymaking authority is a question of state law.

C

[3] Applying this standard to the case before us, we have little difficulty concluding that the Court of Appeals erred in dismissing petitioner's claim against the county. The Deputy Sheriffs who attempted to serve the capiases at petitioner's clinic found themselves in a difficult situation. Unsure of the proper course of action to follow, they sought instructions from their supervisors. The instructions they received were to follow the orders of the County Prosecutor. The Prosecutor made a considered decision based on his understanding of the law and commanded the officers forcibly to enter petitioner's clinic. That decision directly caused the violation of petitioner's Fourth Amendment rights.

Respondent argues that the County Prosecutor lacked authority to establish municipal policy respecting law enforcement practices because only the County Sheriff may establish policy respecting such practices. Respondent suggests that the County Prosecutor was merely rendering "legal advice" when he ordered the Deputy Sheriffs to "go in and get" the witnesses. Consequently, the argument concludes, the action of the individual Deputy Sheriffs in following this advice and forcibly entering petitioner's clinic was not pursuant to a properly established municipal policy.

We might be inclined to agree with respondent if we thought that the Prosecutor had only rendered "legal advice." However, the Court of Appeals concluded, based upon its examination of Ohio law, that both the County Sheriff and the County Prosecutor could establish county policy under appropriate circumstances, a conclusion that we do not question here. Ohio Rev.Code Ann. § 309.09(A) (1979) provides that county officers may "require . . . instructions from [the County Prosecutor] in matters connected with their official duties." Pursuant to standard office procedure, the Sheriff's Office referred this matter to the Prosecutor and then followed his instructions. The Sheriff testified that his Department followed this practice under appropriate circumstances and that it was "the proper thing to do" in this case. We decline to accept respondent's invitation to overlook this delegation of authority by disingenuously labeling the Prosecutor's clear command mere "legal advice." In ordering the Deputy Sheriffs to enter petitioner's clinic the County Prosecutor was acting as the final decisionmaker for the county, and the county may therefore be held liable under § 1983.

The decision of the Court of Appeals is reversed, and the case is remanded for further proceedings consistent with this opinion.

It is so ordered.

DeSHANEY V. WINNEBAGO COUNTY DEPARTMENT
OF SOCIAL SERVICES
489 U.S. 189 (1989)

Chief Justice Rehnquist delivered the opinion of the Court, joined by Justices White, Stevens, O'Connor, Scalia, and Kennedy. Justices Brennan, Marshall, and Blackmun dissented.

Petitioner is a boy who was beaten and permanently injured by his father, with whom he lived. Respondents are social workers and other local officials who received complaints that petitioner was being abused by his father and had reason to believe that this was the case, but nonetheless did not act to remove petitioner from his father's custody. Petitioner sued respondents claiming that their failure to act deprived him of his liberty in violation of the Due Process Clause of the Fourteenth Amendment to the United States Constitution. We hold that it did not.

I

The facts of this case are undeniably tragic. Petitioner Joshua DeShaney was born in 1979. In 1980, a Wyoming court granted his parents a divorce and awarded custody of Joshua to his father, Randy DeShaney. The father shortly thereafter moved to Neenah, a city located in Winnebago County, Wisconsin, taking the infant Joshua with him. There he entered into a second marriage, which also ended in divorce.

The Winnebago County authorities first learned that Joshua DeShaney might be a victim of child abuse in January 1982, when his father's second wife complained to the police, at the time of their divorce, that he had previously "hit the boy causing marks and [was] a prime case for child abuse." The Winnebago County Department of Social Services (DSS) interviewed the father, but he denied the accusations, and DSS did not pursue them further. In January 1983, Joshua was admitted to a local hospital with multiple bruises and abrasions. The examining physician suspected child abuse and notified DSS, which immediately obtained an order from a Wisconsin juvenile court placing Joshua in the temporary custody of the hospital. Three days later, the county convened an ad hoc "Child Protection Team"—consisting of a pediatrician, a psychologist, a police detective, the county's lawyer, several DSS caseworkers, and various hospital per-

sonnel—to consider Joshua's situation. At this meeting, the Team decided that there was insufficient evidence of child abuse to retain Joshua in the custody of the court. The Team did, however, decide to recommend several measures to protect Joshua, including enrolling him in a preschool program, providing his father with certain counselling services, and encouraging his father's girlfriend to move out of the home. Randy DeShaney entered into a voluntary agreement with DSS in which he promised to cooperate with them in accomplishing these goals.

Based on the recommendation of the Child Protection Team, the juvenile court dismissed the child protection case and returned Joshua to the custody of his father. A month later, emergency room personnel called the DSS caseworker handling Joshua's case to report that he had once again been treated for suspicious injuries. The caseworker concluded that there was no basis for action. For the next six months, the caseworker made monthly visits to the DeShaney home, during which she observed a number of suspicious injuries on Joshua's head; she also noticed that he had not been enrolled in school, and that the girlfriend had not moved out. The caseworker dutifully recorded these incidents in her files, along with her continuing suspicions that someone in the DeShaney household was physically abusing Joshua, but she did nothing more. In November 1983, the emergency room notified DSS that Joshua had been treated once again for injuries that they believed to be caused by child abuse. On the caseworker's next two visits to the DeShaney home, she was told that Joshua was too ill to see her. Still DSS took no action.

In March 1984, Randy DeShaney beat 4-year-old Joshua so severely that he fell into a life-threatening coma. Emergency brain surgery revealed a series of hemorrhages caused by traumatic injuries to the head inflicted over a long period of time. Joshua did not die, but he suffered brain damage so severe that he is expected to spend the rest of his life confined to an institution for the profoundly retarded. Randy DeShaney was subsequently tried and convicted of child abuse.

Joshua and his mother brought this action under 42 U.S.C. § 1983 in the United States District Court for the Eastern District of Wisconsin against respondents Winnebago County, DSS, and various individual employees of DSS. The complaint alleged that respondents had deprived Joshua of his liberty without due process of law, in violation of his rights under the Fourteenth Amendment, by failing to intervene to protect him against a risk of violence at his father's hands of which they knew or should have known. The District Court granted summary judgment for respondents.

The Court of Appeals for the Seventh Circuit affirmed, 812 F.2d 298 (1987), holding that petitioners had not made out an actionable § 1983 claim for two alternative reasons. First, the court held that the Due Process Clause of the Fourteenth Amendment does not require a state or local governmental entity to protect its citizens from "private violence, or other mishaps not attributable to the conduct of its employees." In so holding, the court specifically rejected the position endorsed by a divided panel of the Third Circuit in *Estate of Bailey by Oare v. County of York,* 768 F.2d 503 (CA3 1985), and by dicta in *Jensen v. Conrad,* 747 F.2d 185 (CA4 1984), that once the State learns that a particular child is in danger of abuse from third parties and actually undertakes to protect him from that danger, a "special relationship" arises between it and the child which imposes an affirmative constitutional duty to provide adequate protection.

Second, the court held, in reliance on our decision in *Martinez v. California,* 444 U.S. 277 (1980), that the causal connection between respondents' conduct and Joshua's injuries was too attenuated to establish a deprivation of constitutional rights actionable under § 1983. The court therefore found it unnecessary to reach the question whether respondents' conduct evinced the "state of mind" necessary to make out a due process claim after *Daniels v. Williams,* 474 U.S. 327 (1986), and *Davidson v. Cannon,* 474 U.S. 344 (1986). Because of the inconsistent approaches taken by the lower courts in determining when, if ever, the failure of a state or local governmental entity or its agents to provide an individual with adequate protective services constitutes a violation of the individual's due process rights, and the importance of the issue to the administration of state and local governments, we granted certiorari. We now affirm.

II

[1] The Due Process Clause of the Fourteenth Amendment provides that "[n]o State shall . . . de-

prive any person of life, liberty, or property, without due process of law." Petitioners contend that the State deprived Joshua of his liberty interest in "free[dom] from . . . unjustified intrusions on personal security," *Ingraham v. Wright,* 430 U.S. 651 (1977), by failing to provide him with adequate protection against his father's violence. The claim is one invoking the substantive rather than the procedural component of the Due Process Clause; petitioners do not claim that the State denied Joshua protection without according him appropriate procedural safeguards, but that it was categorically obligated to protect him in these circumstances.

[2][3][4][5] But nothing in the language of the Due Process Clause itself requires the State to protect the life, liberty, and property of its citizens against invasion by private actors. The Clause is phrased as a limitation on the State's power to act, not as a guarantee of certain minimal levels of safety and security. It forbids the State itself to deprive individuals of life, liberty, or property without "due process of law," but its language cannot fairly be extended to impose an affirmative obligation on the State to ensure that those interests do not come to harm through other means.

[6][7] Consistent with these principles, our cases have recognized that the Due Process Clauses generally confer no affirmative right to governmental aid, even where such aid may be necessary to secure life, liberty, or property interests of which the government itself may not deprive the individual. See, e.g., *Harris v. McRae,* 448 U.S. 297 (1980) (no obligation to fund abortions or other medical services) (discussing Due Process Clause of Fifth Amendment); *Lindsey v. Normet,* 405 U.S. 56 (1972) (no obligation to provide adequate housing) (discussing Due Process Clause of Fourteenth Amendment); see also *Youngberg v. Romeo,* supra, 457 U.S., at 317 ("As a general matter, a State is under no constitutional duty to provide substantive services for those within its border"). As we said in *Harris v. McRae*: "Although the liberty protected by the Due Process Clause affords protection against unwarranted government interference . . . , it does not confer an entitlement to such [governmental aid] as may be necessary to realize all the advantages of that freedom." If the Due Process Clause does not require the State to provide its citizens with particular protective services, it follows that the State cannot be held liable under the Clause for injuries that could have been averted had it chosen to provide them. As a general matter, then, we conclude

that a State's failure to protect an individual against private violence simply does not constitute a violation of the Due Process Clause.

[10] The *Estelle-Youngberg* analysis simply has no applicability in the present case. Petitioners concede that the harms Joshua suffered did not occur while he was in the State's custody, but while he was in the custody of his natural father, who was in no sense a state actor. While the State may have been aware of the dangers that Joshua faced in the free world, it played no part in their creation, nor did it do anything to render him any more vulnerable to them. That the State once took temporary custody of Joshua does not alter the analysis, for when it returned him to his father's custody, it placed him in no worse position than that in which he would have been had it not acted at all; the State does not become the permanent guarantor of an individual's safety by having once offered him shelter. Under these circumstances, the State had no constitutional duty to protect Joshua.

Judges and lawyers, like other humans, are moved by natural sympathy in a case like this to find a way for Joshua and his mother to receive adequate compensation for the grievous harm inflicted upon them.

But before yielding to that impulse, it is well to remember once again that the harm was inflicted not by the State of Wisconsin, but by Joshua's father. The most that can be said of the state functionaries in this case is that they stood by and did nothing when suspicious circumstances dictated a more active role for them. In defense of them it must also be said that had they moved too soon to take custody of the son away from the father, they would likely have been met with charges of improperly intruding into the parent-child relationship, charges based on the same Due Process Clause that forms the basis for the present charge of failure to provide adequate protection.

The people of Wisconsin may well prefer a system of liability which would place upon the State and its officials the responsibility for failure to act in situations such as the present one. They may create such a system, if they do not have it already, by changing the tort law of the State in accordance with the regular lawmaking process. But they should not have it thrust upon them by this Court's expansion of the Due Process Clause of the Fourteenth Amendment.

Affirmed.

NOTES

1. *Dalehite v. United States,* 346 U.S. 15, 47-48 (1953).

2. Ibid., 16.

3. There was an agreement among all the plaintiffs and defendants that the trial judge's findings of fact and interpretation of law as to the federal government's liability in the *Dalehite* litigation would be accepted in all the remaining suits, 346 U.S. 15, 16.

4. *Erie Railroad Company v. Tompkins,* 304 U.S. 64 (1938).

5. 346 U.S. 15, 55.

6. 28 U.S.C. 1346 and 2671-80.

7. The material on private bills comes from footnote 9 in *Dalehite v. United States,* 346 U.S. 15, 25.

8. The only available remedy for the Texas City plaintiffs was to return to the activity the FTCA was intended to stop—the private bill. By 1957, when Congress passed the last private bill from this incident, it passed 1,394 awards for a total of almost $17 million. See Donald Barry and Howard Whitcomb, *The Legal Foundations of Public Administration,* 2d ed. (St. Paul, MN: West, 1987), 268.

9. Daniel Oran, *Oran's Dictionary of the Law* (St. Paul, MN: West, 1983), 424.

10. *Kimble v. Machintosh Hemphill Company,* 59 A. 2d 68 (1948).

11. 346 U.S. 15, 35-36.

12. *Allen v. United States,* 588 F.Supp. 247, 336 (1984).

13. The material on the Giglotto and Askew raids comes from Jack Boger, Mark Gitenstein, and Paul Verkuil, "The Federal Tort Claims Act Intentional Torts Amendment: An Interpretative Analysis," *North Carolina Law Review* 54 (1976): 498.

    14. Ibid., 501, 502.

    15. Ibid., 501.

    16. Ibid.

17. But see *Forrester v. White,* 108 S.Ct. 538 (1988). A judge was held not to be immune in the execution of administrative duties, as opposed to judicial duties.

    18. *Barr v. Matteo,* 360 U.S. 564, 575 (1959).

19. Arthur Bonfield and Michael Asimow, *State and Federal Administrative Law* (St. Paul, MN: West, 1989), 640.

    20. Ibid., 645.

CHAPTER 11

SUMMARY AND CONCLUSIONS

"The field a farmer plowed typified the work setting of the agricultural society. The factory assembly line was the distinctive setting for the industrial society. Bureaucracy is the predominant work setting for the post-industrial era."[1] This book began with the proposition that we live in an era characterized by the administrative state; that is, the fourth branch of government, bureaucracy, makes policy decisions based on expertise, rather than on electoral accountability. Bureaucracy enforces its own policies and adjudicates infractions of those policies. Through the cases you have read, it may strike you that the policy choices often made by agencies do not simply involve the "filling in of details," but rather can be significant and far-reaching policy choices. Evidence was presented in Chapters 2 and 3 that neither the president nor Congress exerts significant control over the fourth branch. If all that I have previously said is true, then you and I as citizens do not exercise control over many policies, either directly or indirectly, through our elected representatives.

Think about some policy decisions that have been made by agencies. The Department of Transportation adopted a policy that, by a certain date, all vehicles manufactured in the United States would have either passive-restraint seat belts or air bags. That policy cost industry and consumers billions of dollars by the time compliance rippled through the economy. Similarly, the Department of Energy promulgated standards (adopted a policy) requiring that every major appliance manufactured in the United States operate at a certain level of efficiency.[2] In the case commonly known as the *Benzene* case,[3] discussed in Chapter 3, Congress delegated to the secretary of labor nothing less than the power to make the choice between workers' safety and industry profits. In a case discussed in Chapter 7, *Pacific Gas and Electric v. Federal Power Commission,* 506 F.2d 33 (D.C. Cir. 1974), the Federal Power Commission adopted a rule regarding the allocation of natural gas in the event of a shortage that would have voided otherwise valid contracts between buyers and sellers of natural gas. In yet another case, briefly discussed in Chapter 10, the Atomic Energy Commission (AEC; now the Nuclear Regulatory Commission) adopted policies to conduct above-ground nuclear testing and not to warn or educate those citizens who live downwind of the test site about nuclear fallout. The AEC's failure to warn has allegedly led to above-normal incidences of cancer among residents of southern Utah. (Indeed, as this book goes to press, the federal government now admits that nuclear fallout from the tests rained down all over the Midwest.) Secretary of Health and Human Services Margaret Heckler directed her agency to purge from the disability roles some individuals who were clearly disabled. When ordered by more than one U.S. circuit court of appeals to cease and desist, she adopted a policy of nonacquiescence.

Finally, to cite examples as the twentieth century moves toward closure, the Federal Communications Commission (FCC) is preparing to promulgate rules that will usher in digital television. As a classic example of how our government usually attempts to facilitate capitalism, the FCC is negotiating with digital television manufacturers and television retailers to time the phase-in of digital television in the largest markets with the Christmas shopping season.[4] State and local educational governing bodies are contemplating adopting national educational standards.[5] The Environmental Protection Agency (EPA) is preparing to tighten standards that will reduce the amount of chemicals and particles in the air. Not only will this cost business and industry billions, but one hundred million people are thought to live in cities that are currently in compliance with the Clean Air Act but that will fall out of compliance with the new standards. The EPA and advocates for the new standards argue that tens of thousands of people will be protected from illness and even death.[6]

The corollary proposition to the existence of the administrative state and lack of control over the fourth branch was that, by default, the task of controlling the fourth branch fell to the courts. What kind of job have the courts done? Although the cases presented in this text are diverse and in some instances not consistent, some broad trends can be identified, especially with regard to democracy.

Although it was ultimately reversed by an act of Congress, the Court further eroded presidential control over agency rule making through a narrow construction of the Paperwork Reduction Act (*Dole v. United Steelworkers of America,* in Chapter 2). The Constitution mandates, "The executive power shall be vested in a President of the United States of America . . . [who] shall take care that the laws be faithfully executed." It is difficult to imagine how a president can effectively exercise executive power or see to it that laws are faithfully executed without the ability to control the rule making, standard setting, or policy making of his or her own executive branch of government.

The Court has eroded the ability of Congress to control agency rule making by declaring the legislative veto to be unconstitutional (*Immigration and Naturalization Service v. Chadha,* in Chapter 3). Through more than one decision, the Court has restricted a citizen's ability to challenge agency actions in the courts. First, the Court has narrowed standing to challenge agency action. The Court has adopted a narrower, three-pronged test for standing and has refused to recognize a sufficient legal interest for certain litigants. For example, in *Allen v. Wright et al.* (Chapter 4), the Court refused to recognize the possibility of a connection between an IRS grant of tax-exempt status to discriminatory private schools and the Wrights' inability to send their children to desegregated public schools. In *City of Los Angeles v. Lyons* (Chapter 4), the Court refused to find an appropriate legal connection between the victim of police brutality and the victim's legal ability to challenge a police department policy that led to the act of brutality.

Second, consistent with court deference to agency expertise, the Court has refused to narrow estoppel against the government. As a consequence of this, the average citizen dare not rely on the advice or information provided by the agency with the expertise. The two-pronged test for estoppel against the government adopted in *Heckler v. Community Health Services* (Chapter 6) in 1984 does little to move beyond the Court's 1920 pronouncement, "Men must turn square corners when they deal with the government."[7]

A third line of cases in which the Court has inhibited a citizen's ability to challenge agency activity in the courts is in the area of due process. As was the case with standing, the Court has simply restricted the situations in which a liberty or property interest either exists or requires a due process hearing.

Bear in mind that the purpose of the due process requirement is to guard against arbitrary or mistaken deprivations of liberty or property interests by government. The following cases are representative of the Court's due process jurisprudence over the past twenty-two years: *Paul v. Davis,* 1976 (no liberty interest in the erroneous posting of plaintiff's picture as a shoplifter); *Bishop v. Wood,* 1976 (federal courts do not function to rectify the erroneous discharge of a public employee); *Ingraham v. Wright,* 1977 (no due process requirement for the administration of corporal punishment in the public schools); *Board of*

Curators of the University of Missouri v. Horowitz, 1978 (no due process required for the academic suspension of a college student); *Waters v. Churchill,* 1994 (what an employer reasonably thought was said, as opposed to what was actually said, will provide the legal basis for an employee termination under the due process clause); *National Treasury Employees Union v. Von Raab,* 1989 (no liberty interest in the compelled collection of urine samples from certain public employees); *Pacific Mutual Life Insurance v. Haslip,* 1991 (no due process violation in the apparently arbitrary jury award of punitive damages); *Collins v. City of Harker Heights,* 1992 (no liberty interest whereby city's failure to properly train and warn its employees led to employee's death).

Finally, a series of cases unrelated to citizen access to the courts allows agencies a wide swath in terms of how they deal with clients or the public. The cases referred to here involve situations in which Congress has mandated that the agencies proceed according to a specific procedure, the agency employs a different procedure, and the courts refuse to make the agency comply with the required procedure. In *National Labor Relations Board v. Bell Aerospace Company,* 1974 (Chapter 7), both Congress and the nature of the subject matter dictated that the agency use rule promulgation in decision making, but the agency used a quasi-judicial adjudication instead. The Supreme Court, deferring to agency expertise, condoned the agency's choice of a case-by-case procedure. In *Heckler v. Campbell,* 1983 (Chapter 7), the Court reaffirmed the Storer Doctrine that when an agency is required by Congress to proceed by adjudication, the agency is not precluded from promulgating a rule and denying the adjudicatory hearing to those who do not meet the rule's requirements.

Court decisions, then, have inhibited both presidential and congressional control over agency rule making and have restricted citizen access to the courts to challenge agency activity. Further, the courts seem to be willing to allow agencies to proceed any way they wish despite congressional dictates to the contrary. Before we can conclude, on the basis of the preceding review, that court decisions do not bode well for democracy and citizen control of the fourth branch, two points should be raised. First, not all of the Court's decisions can be interpreted as hostile to citizen control of agencies; and second, it is probably unrealistic to expect the undemocratic "least dangerous branch" of government, the courts, to make decisions that would ensure citizen control over the fourth branch of government.

Recent court decisions in at least one area of administrative law have broadened, rather than restricted, citizen control of agencies. Tort Claims Act jurisprudence today recognizes a much broader species of agency activity that exposes government to legal liability; that is, in the 1950s, only the "common law torts of employees of agencies" fell outside the discretionary exemption of the Tort Claims Act so that, for example, the citizen could hold an agency liable only for the negligent operation of an agency vehicle. As Justice Jackson said in dissent in *Dalehite,* "The king can only do little wrongs."[8] The Court has narrowed the definition of the discretionary exemption so that only those acts of agency discretion with policy implications will render government immune from suit. Hence, a governmental agency was liable under the Federal Tort Claims Act for the release of a tainted batch of polio vaccine in *Berkovitz v. United States* (486 U.S. 531 [1988]), and the Veterans Administration was found to be liable for the negligent, premature release of a mental patient who subsequently murdered his ex-girlfriend.[9] Although the decision was later overturned by a circuit court of appeals, a district court judge found the government liable for its failure to warn citizens downwind of nuclear tests about the dangers of radiation in *Allen v. United States,* 1984 (Chapter 10).

Also, the Court has created a whole new avenue for citizens to sue federal officials who violate a citizen's constitutional rights. Such suits were referred to as *Bivens* suits in Chapter 10, and only since the Court created this legal option in 1971 could citizens redress the actions of federal bureaucrats that infringed their constitutional rights. In *Butz v. Economou,* 1978 (Chapter 10), the Court made it easier than it had been for citizens to prevail in such suits. In *Butz,* the Court said that a citizen could successfully sue a federal official for a constitutional tort if the official knew or should have known that the official's action would violate a citizen's constitutional rights.

Finally, the Court has made it easier for citizens to sue state and local officials for a violation of citizens' rights. In Chapter 10, suits against state and local officials for constitutional violations were referred to as "Section 1983 suits," and the same "knew or should have known" criterion used against federal officials in *Bevins* was held to apply in, for example, *Wood v. Strickland,* 1975 (Chapter 10). The Court has also removed an immunity for municipalities and made them liable for constitutional torts in *Owen v. City of Independence,* 1980 (Chapter 10). Although these cases, facilitating citizen suits against the government for torts and civil rights violations, may not necessarily enhance citizen control over policy decisions, they do tend to reduce the distance between citizens and their government. There is nothing like the threat of a good lawsuit to encourage behavior in a desired direction. As the circuit court said in *Halperin v. Kissinger* (a case making the president, the national security adviser, the director of the FBI, and the president's chief of staff liable for a constitutional tort under the Fourth Amendment), "The President is the elected chief executive of our government, not an omniscient leader clothed in mystical power."[10]

Court decisions in administrative law have had inconsistent effects relative to citizen control over agency policy making. First, the *Dole* and *Chadha* cases have further insulated bureaucratic policy making from control by either branch of government that is subject to citizen control. Second, court decisions in the areas of standing, due process, and estoppel have insulated agencies from direct citizen challenge through the courts. The Court's decisions in the areas of the Tort Claims Act and constitutional torts, however, have enhanced bureaucratic accountability through the courts, but not through the ballot box.

Is it reasonable to expect the judicial branch of government to make decisions that enhance citizen control of bureaucracy? It is the role of the federal courts to interpret the Constitution, and as was discussed in Chapter 1, the Constitution is not a particularly democratic document, at least not as democracy has been defined in this book. If we wait for the courts to deliver us from the administrative state, we will wait for a very long time.

The fourth branch of government is a fact of life, and policy making by insulated bureaucrats is here to stay for the foreseeable future. The task is to at least begin the discussion about how to make the fourth branch more accountable. As Robert Reich, Professor of Economics and former Secretary of Labor under President Clinton, pointed out, volumes have been written about making judicial review compatible with democracy, but very little has been written about making the administrative state compatible with democracy.[11]

The essence of the administrative state is policy making by rule promulgation. If accountability is to be achieved, one of the elected branches needs to gain control of at least the agency rules that will have a major impact on society and the economy. I would argue that the logical branch is the executive. The president should establish a mechanism—perhaps through the Office of Management and Budget, but not necessarily—to review those agency rules having a significant impact. Rather than stretch the logic of an obscure law such as the Paperwork Reduction Act for legal authority (see *Dole v. United Steelworkers,* in Chapter 2), the president should rely on the constitutional powers of the office; that is, it is impossible to exercise executive power without the ability to control (veto) agency policy making. It is likewise difficult, if not impossible, for the president to see that the laws are faithfully executed without the ability to control agency implementation of congressional acts. The Supreme Court, in 1988, used that same logic in establishing a new doctrine for presidential removal power (see *Morrison v. Olson,* in Chapter 2). If presidential control of agency rule making were to occur, that would help restore accountability so that the voting public could hold one nationally elected official and perhaps his or her party responsible for significant fourth-branch activity. The voting public would have the responsibility of judging a Reagan/ Bush hostility to regulation or a Clinton embrace of it.

A second possibility involves leadership by agency heads. The idea is for agency heads to encourage citizen debate prior to agency action. Secretary Reich called it "civic discovery,"[12] but thirty years ago a famous political scientist, E. E. Schattschneider, referred to the same concept as the "socialization of conflict."[13]

Schattschneider argued that conflict could be either expanded (socialization of conflict) or constricted (privatization of conflict). Schattschneider's thesis was that socialization or broadening of conflict is more compatible with democracy than is the privatization of conflict. The socialization of conflict is compatible with democracy because socialization of conflict leads to citizen input on policy making through political parties via elections. The privatization of conflict, in contrast, leads to pluralism and policy making by interest groups, bureaucrats, cozy triangles, and, I would add, the administrative state.

Secretary Reich argued for a variant of Schattschneider's thesis. Rather than agencies making policy by cost-benefit analysis or in collusion with interest groups with vested interests (see the reg-neg process referred to in Chapter 7), Reich argued that agencies should open the question to citizen debate. Reich referred to this as "civic discovery," and he recounted how it worked in Tacoma, Washington.[14]

The Environmental Protection Agency (EPA) had to make the same kind of choice in Tacoma that the secretary of labor made in the *Benzene* case, in Chapter 3—that is, a choice between human life and economic well-being. A mainstay of Tacoma's economy, the American Smelting and Refining Company (ASARCO), employed 570 workers with a payroll of $23 million and local annual purchases of $12 million. ASARCO produced inorganic arsenic, as a by-product of its smelting process, which it released into the air. Inorganic arsenic is a documented cause of lung cancer, and the EPA was charged by Congress to provide an "ample margin of safety to protect the public health." Rather than make a unilateral decision within the agency, the director of the EPA, William Ruckelshaus, opened the question for public debate in a series of town meetings.

The price of copper on the world market eventually forced the plant to close, but not before the citizens of Tacoma encouraged the city policy makers to diversify the Tacoma economy.

A third possibility for restoring accountability would require unlikely court action. The action referred to is to dust off the dormant doctrine from *Hampton v. United States* (Chapter 3) and for the Court not to allow delegation of legislative power to an agency without sufficient standards and guidelines so as to channel agency discretion. This action has been urged by political scientist Theodore Lowi,[15] Chief Justice William Rehnquist,[16] and Associate Justice Antonin Scalia.[17] A court, for instance, should refuse to allow Congress to delegate to the EPA the power to promulgate rules and adopt standards to ensure an "ample margin of safety to protect the public health." Congress should decide what an "ample margin of safety" is to protect the public health, and the representatives should be prepared to explain their votes to the voters back home.

In our federal system, the states have played a role as experimental laboratories from the beginning. Several states have been taking steps to enhance the accountability of their agencies. More than two thirds of the states use sunset laws[18] (an agency has a specific life span and can be given renewed life only after some type of action by the state legislature). Although the legislative veto (Chapter 3) has been declared unconstitutional for the federal government and in eight states, it is still used in more than a third of the remaining states.[19] More than half of the states have adopted some form of zero- or reduced-based budgeting[20] (agency budgets are not determined by last year's appropriation plus inflation but, rather, must justify a percentage of last year's budget). The states have taken the lead in broadening representation on boards and commissions[21] (e.g., lay representation on licensing boards, ombudsmen office).

The point was made before in this book that the average liberal arts graduate changes careers three times in a working life. If you are taking a course in administrative law, chances are that you may find yourself in a decision-making position within a governmental agency someday. The temptation will be great to privatize the conflict and to make a decision based on the expertise of those within the agency who advise you or on the expertise of those groups with a vested interest in the decision. To be a democratic decision maker is neither easy nor efficient. Secretary Ruckelshaus, in the Tacoma example earlier, received criticism from all sides—industry, environmentalists, and organized labor. He was also criticized by the media for not unilaterally making a decision. *The New York Times* said it was "inexcusable . . . for him to impose such an impossible choice on Tacomans."[22] Whose choice should it be?

NOTES

1. Everett Carll Ladd, *The American Polity,* 5th ed. (New York: Norton, 1985), 25.

2. Leif Carter, *Administrative Law and Politics: Cases and Comments* (Boston: Little, Brown, 1983), 30.

3. *Industrial Union Department AFL-CIO v. American Petroleum Institute,* 448 U.S. 607 (1980).

4. Joel Brinkley, "F.C.C. Is Ready to Ease Timing of Digital T.V.," *The New York Times,* 3 April 1997, A1, national edition.

5. Pam Belluck, "National Standards Are Proposed for Use in New York City Schools," 5 December 1996, A1, national edition.

6. John H. Cushman Jr., "E.P.A. Advocating Higher Standards to Clean the Air," 25 November 1996, A1, national edition.

7. *Rock Island, Arkansas and Louisiana Railroad Company v. United States,* 254 U.S. 141, 143 (1920).

8. *Dalehite v. United States,* 346 U.S. 15, 60 (1953).

9. *Jablonski by Pahls v. United States,* 712 F.2d 391 (1983, 9th Cir.).

10. 606 F.2d 1192, 1213 (D.C. Cir. 1979). Appeals court decision affirmed on appeal by virtue of a divided Supreme Court. 452 U.S. 713 (1981).

11. Robert B. Reich, "Policy Making in a Democracy," in *Current Issues in Public Ad-ministration,* ed. Frederick S. Lane, 5th ed. (New York: St. Martin's, 1994), 115.

12. Ibid., 129.

13. E. E. Schattschneider, *The Semisovereign People* (Hinsdale, IL: Dryden, 1975), 7-19.

14. All the material on the EPA, ASARCO, and Tacoma comes from Reich, "Policy Making in a Democracy," 131-33.

15. Theodore Lowi, *The End of Liberalism* (New York: Norton, 1969), 287-314, esp. 298.

16. *Industrial Union Department AFL-CIO v. American Petroleum Institute,* 448 U.S. 607 (Chief Justice Rehnquist, dissenting, 671-72, 1980).

17. *Mistretta v. United States,* 488 U.S. 361 (Justice Scalia, dissenting, 416-17, 1989).

18. William T. Gormley, Jr., "Accountability Battles in State Administration" in *Current Issues in Public Administration,* Frederick S. Lane, 5th ed. (New York: St. Martin's, 1994), 141-42.

19. Ibid., 142.

20. Ibid., 143.

21. Ibid., 143-44.

22. Reich, "Policy Making in a Democracy," 132.

APPENDIX

ADMINISTRATIVE PROCEDURE ACT

Material from Parts II and III of Title 5 relating to administrative law judges has been omitted. If you were actually to use the United States Code Annotated, you would see that Subchapter III is really entitled "The Administrative Conference of the United States" (which has been omitted). There are two Subchapter IVs, one on negotiated rule making and the other on alternative dispute resolution. For simplicity, we have presented the index for you as outlined above.

UNITED STATES CODE ANNOTATED

TITLE 5. GOVERNMENT ORGANIZATION AND EMPLOYEES CHAPTER—ADMINISTRATIVE PROCEDURE

§ 552. Public Information; Agency Rules, Opinions, Orders, Records, and Proceedings

(a) Each agency shall make available to the public information as follows:

   (1) Each agency shall separately state and currently publish in the *Federal Register* for the guidance of the public—

      (A) descriptions of its central and field organization and the established places at which, the employees (and in the case of a uniformed service, the members) from whom, and the methods whereby, the public may obtain information, make submittals or requests, or obtain decisions;

      (B) statements of the general course and method by which its functions are channeled and determined, including the nature and requirements of all formal and informal procedures available;

      (C) rules of procedure, descriptions of forms available or the places at which forms may be obtained, and instructions as to the scope and contents of all papers, reports, or examinations;

      (D) substantive rules of general applicability adopted as authorized by law, and statements of general policy or interpretations of general applicability formulated and adopted by the agency; and

      (E) each amendment, revision, or repeal of the foregoing.

Except to the extent that a person has actual and timely notice of the terms thereof, a person may not in any manner be required to resort to, or be adversely affected by, a matter required to be published in the *Federal Register* and not so published. For the purpose of this paragraph, matter reasonably available to the class of persons affected thereby is deemed published in the *Federal Register* when incorporated by reference therein with the approval of the Director of the *Federal Register.*

   (2) Each agency, in accordance with published rules, shall make available for public inspection and copying—

      (A) final opinions, including concurring and dissenting opinions, as well as orders, made in the adjudication of cases;

      (B) those statements of policy and interpretations which have been adopted by the agency and are not published in the *Federal Register;* and

      (C) administrative staff manuals and instructions to staff that affect a member of the public; unless the materials are promptly published and copies offered for sale. To the extent required to prevent a clearly unwarranted invasion of personal privacy, an agency may delete identifying details when it makes available or publishes an opinion, statement of policy, interpretation, or staff manual or instruction. However, in each case the justification for the deletion shall be explained fully in writing. Each agency shall also maintain and make available for public inspection and copying current indexes providing identifying information for the public as to any matter issued, adopted, or promulgated after July 4, 1967, and required by this paragraph to be made available or published. Each agency shall promptly publish, quarterly or more frequently, and distribute (by sale or otherwise) copies of each index or supplements thereto unless it determines by order published in the *Federal Register* that the publication would be unnecessary and impracticable, in which case the agency shall nonetheless provide copies of such index on request at a cost not to exceed the direct cost of duplication. A final order, opinion, statement of policy, interpretation, or staff manual or instruction that affects a member of the public may be relied on, used, or cited as precedent by an agency against a party other than an agency only if—

(i)   it has been indexed and either made available or published as provided by this paragraph; or

(ii)   the party has actual and timely notice of the terms thereof.

(3)   Except with respect to the records made available under paragraphs (1) and (2) of this subsection, each agency, upon any request for records which (A) reasonably describes such records and (B) is made in accordance with published rules stating the time, place, fees (if any), and procedures to be followed, shall make the records promptly available to any person.

(4)(A)(i) In order to carry out the provisions of this section, each agency shall promulgate regulations, pursuant to notice and receipt of public comment, specifying the schedule of fees applicable to the processing of requests under this section and establishing procedures and guidelines for determining when such fees should be waived or reduced. Such schedule shall conform to the guidelines which shall be promulgated, pursuant to notice and receipt of public comment, by the Director of the Office of Management and Budget and which shall provide for a uniform schedule of fees for all agencies.

(ii)   Such agency regulations shall provide that—

(I)   fees shall be limited to reasonable standard charges for document search, duplication, and review, when records are requested for commercial use;

(II)   fees shall be limited to reasonable standard charges for document duplication when records are not sought for commercial use and the request is made by an educational or noncommercial scientific institution, whose purpose is scholarly or scientific research; or a representative of the news media; and

(III) for any request not described in (I) or (II), fees shall be limited to reasonable standard charges for document search and duplication.

(iii) Documents shall be furnished without any charge or at a charge reduced below the fees established under clause (ii) if disclosure of the information is in the public interest because it is likely to contribute significantly to public understanding of the operations or activities of the government and is not primarily in the commercial interest of the requester.

(iv) Fee schedules shall provide for the recovery of only the direct costs of search, duplication, or review. Review costs shall include only the direct costs incurred during the initial examination of a document for the purposes of determining whether the documents must be disclosed under this section and for the purposes of withholding any portions exempt from disclosure under this section. Review costs may not include any costs incurred in resolving issues of law or policy that may be raised in the course of processing a request under this section. No fee may be charged by any agency under this section—

(I) if the costs of routine collection and processing of the fee are likely to equal or exceed the amount of the fee; or

(II) for any request described in clause (ii)(II) or (III) of this subparagraph for the first two hours of search time or for the first one hundred pages of duplication.

(v) No agency may require advance payment of any fee unless the requester has previously failed to pay fees in a timely fashion, or the agency has determined that the fee will exceed $250.

(vi) Nothing in this subparagraph shall supersede fees chargeable under a statute specifically providing for setting the level of fees for particular types of records.

(vii) In any action by a requester regarding the waiver of fees under this section, the court shall determine the matter de novo: Provided, that the court's review of the matter shall be limited to the record before the agency.

(B) On complaint, the district court of the United States in the district in which the complainant resides, or has his principal place of business, or in which the agency records are situated, or in the District of Columbia, has jurisdiction to enjoin the agency from withholding agency records and to order the production of any agency records improperly withheld from the complainant. In such a case the court shall determine the matter de novo, and may examine the contents of such agency records in camera to determine whether such records or any part thereof shall be withheld under any of the exemptions set forth in subsection (b) of this section, and the burden is on the agency to sustain its action.

(C) Notwithstanding any other provision of law, the defendant shall serve an answer or otherwise plead to any complaint made under this subsection within thirty days after service upon the defendant of the pleading in which such complaint is made, unless the court otherwise directs for good cause shown.

[(D) Repealed. Pub.L. 98-620, Title IV, § 402(2), Nov. 8, 1984, 98 Stat. 3357]

(E) The court may assess against the United States reasonable attorney fees and other litigation costs reasonably incurred in any case under this section in which the complainant has substantially prevailed.

(F) Whenever the court orders the production of any agency records improperly withheld from the complainant and assesses against the United States reasonable attorney fees and other litigation costs, and the court additionally issues a written finding that the circumstances surrounding the withholding raise questions whether agency personnel acted arbitrarily or capriciously with respect to the withholding, the Special Counsel shall promptly initiate a proceeding to determine whether disciplinary action is warranted against the officer or employee who was primarily responsible for the withholding. The Special Counsel, after investigation and consideration of the evidence submitted, shall submit his findings and recommendations to the administrative authority of the agency concerned and shall send copies of the findings and recommendations to the officer or employee or his representative. The administrative authority shall take the corrective action that the Special Counsel recommends.

(G) In the event of noncompliance with the order of the court, the district court may punish for contempt the responsible employee, and in the case of a uniformed service, the responsible member.

(5) Each agency having more than one member shall maintain and make available for public inspection a record of the final votes of each member in every agency proceeding.

(6)(A) Each agency, upon any request for records made under paragraph (1), (2), or (3) of this subsection, shall—

(i) determine within ten days (excepting Saturdays, Sundays, and legal public holidays) after the receipt of any such request whether to comply with such request and shall immediately notify the person making such request of such determination and the reasons therefor, and of the right of such person to appeal to the head of the agency any adverse determination; and

(ii) make a determination with respect to any appeal within twenty days (excepting Saturdays, Sundays, and legal public holidays) after the receipt of such appeal. If on appeal the denial of the request for records is in whole or in part upheld, the agency shall notify the person making such request of the provisions for judicial review of that determination under paragraph (4) of this subsection.

(B) In unusual circumstances as specified in this subparagraph, the time limits prescribed in either clause (i) or clause (ii) of subparagraph (A) may be extended by written notice to the person making such request setting forth the reasons for such extension and the date on which a determination is expected to be dispatched. No such notice shall specify a date that would result in an extension for more than ten working days. As used in this subparagraph, "unusual circumstances" means, but only to the extent reasonably necessary to the proper processing of the particular request—

(i) the need to search for and collect the requested records from field facilities or other establishments that are separate from the office processing the request;

(ii) the need to search for, collect, and appropriately examine a voluminous amount of separate and distinct records which are demanded in a single request; or

(iii) the need for consultation, which shall be conducted with all practicable speed, with another agency having a substantial interest in the determination of the request or among two or more components of the agency having substantial subject-matter interest therein.

(C) Any person making a request to any agency for records under paragraph (1), (2), or (3) of this subsection shall be deemed to have exhausted his administrative remedies with respect to such request if the agency fails to comply with the applicable time limit provisions of this paragraph. If the Government can show exceptional circumstances exist and that the agency is exercising due diligence in responding to the request, the court may retain jurisdiction and allow the agency additional time to complete its review of the records. Upon any determination by an agency to comply with a request for records, the records shall be made promptly available to such person making such request. Any notification of denial of any request for records under this subsection shall set forth the names and titles or positions of each person responsible for the denial of such request.

(b) This section does not apply to matters that are—

(1)(A) specifically authorized under criteria established by an executive order to be kept secret in the interest of national defense or foreign policy and (B) are in fact properly classified pursuant to such executive order;

(2) related solely to the internal personnel rules and practices of an agency;

(3) specifically exempted from disclosure by statute (other than section 552b of this title), provided that such statute (A) requires that the matters be withheld from the public in such a manner as to leave no discretion on the issue, or (B) establishes particular criteria for withholding or refers to particular types of matters to be withheld;

(4) trade secrets and commercial or financial information obtained from a person and privileged or confidential;

(5) inter-agency or intra-agency memorandums or letters which would not be available by law to a party other than an agency in litigation with the agency;

(6) personnel and medical files and similar files the disclosure of which would constitute a clearly unwarranted invasion of personal privacy;

(7) records or information compiled for law enforcement purposes, but only to the extent that the production of such law enforcement records or information (A) could reasonably be expected to interfere with enforcement proceedings, (B) would deprive a person of a right to a fair trial or an impartial adjudication, (C) could reasonably be expected to constitute an unwarranted invasion of personal privacy, (D) could reasonably be expected to disclose the identity of a confidential source, including a State, local, or foreign agency or authority or any private institution which furnished information on a confidential basis, and, in the case of a record or information compiled by criminal law enforcement authority in the course of a criminal investigation or by an agency conducting a lawful national security intelligence investigation, information furnished by a confidential source, (E) would disclose techniques and procedures for law enforcement investigations or prosecutions, or would disclose guidelines for law enforcement investigations or prosecutions if such disclosure could reasonably be expected to risk circumvention of the law, or (F) could reasonably be expected to endanger the life or physical safety of any individual;

(8) contained in or related to examination, operating, or condition reports prepared by, on behalf of, or for the use of an agency responsible for the regulation or supervision of financial institutions; or

(9) geological and geophysical information and data, including maps, concerning wells. Any reasonable segregable portion of a record shall be provided to any person requesting such record after deletion of the portions which are exempt under this subsection.

(c)(1) Whenever a request is made which involves access to records described in subsection (b)(7)(A) and—

(A) the investigation or proceeding involves a possible violation of criminal law; and

(B) there is reason to believe that (i) the subject of the investigation or proceeding is not aware of its pendency, and (ii) disclosure of the existence of the records could reasonably be expected to interfere with enforcement proceedings, the agency may, during only such time as that circumstance continues, treat the records as not subject to the requirements of this section.

(2) Whenever informant records maintained by a criminal law enforcement agency under an informant's name or personal identifier are requested by a third party according to the informant's name or personal identifier, the agency may treat the records as not subject to the requirements of this section unless the informant's status as an informant has been officially confirmed.

(3) Whenever a request is made which involves access to records maintained by the Federal Bureau of Investigation pertaining to foreign intelligence or counterintelligence, or international terrorism, and the existence of the records is classified information as provided in subsection (b)(1), the Bureau may, as long as the existence of the records remains classified information, treat the records as not subject to the requirements of this section.

(d) This section does not authorize withholding of information or limit the availability of records to the public, except as specifically stated in this section. This section is not authority to withhold information from Congress.

(e) On or before March 1 of each calendar year, each agency shall submit a report covering the preceding calendar year to the Speaker of the House of Representatives and President of the Senate for referral to the appropriate committees of the Congress. The report shall include—

(1) the number of determinations made by such agency not to comply with requests for records made to such agency under subsection (a) and the reasons for each such determination;

(2) the number of appeals made by persons under subsection (a)(6), the result of such appeals, and the reason for the action upon each appeal that results in a denial of information;

(3) the names and titles or positions of each person responsible for the denial of records requested under this section, and the number of instances of participation for each;

(4) the results of each proceeding conducted pursuant to subsection (a)(4)(F), including a report of the disciplinary action taken against the officer or employee who was primarily responsible for improperly withholding records or an explanation of why disciplinary action was not taken;

(5) a copy of every rule made by such agency regarding this section;

(6) a copy of the fee schedule and the total amount of fees collected by the agency for making records available under this section; and

(7) such other information as indicates efforts to administer fully this section.

The Attorney General shall submit an annual report on or before March 1 of each calendar year which shall include for the prior calendar year a listing of the number of cases arising under this section, the exemption involved in each case, the disposition of such case, and the cost, fees, and penalties assessed under subsections (a)(4)(E), (F), and (G). Such report shall also include a description of the efforts undertaken by the Department of Justice to encourage agency compliance with this section.

(f)   For purposes of this section, the term "agency" as defined in section 551(1) of this title includes any executive department, military department, Government corporation, Government controlled corporation, or other establishment in the executive branch of the Government (including the Executive Office of the President), or any independent regulatory agency.

§ 553. Rule Making

(a)   This section applies, according to the provisions thereof, except to the extent that there is involved—

(1)   a military or foreign affairs function of the United States; or

(2)   a matter relating to agency management or personnel or to public property, loans, grants, benefits, or contracts.

(b)   General notice of proposed rule making shall be published in the *Federal Register,* unless persons subject thereto are named and either personally served or otherwise have actual notice thereof in accordance with law. The notice shall include—

(1)   a statement of the time, place, and nature of public rule-making proceedings;

(2)   reference to the legal authority under which the rule is proposed; and

(3)   either the terms or substance of the proposed rule or a description of the subjects and issues involved.

Except when notice or hearing is required by statute, this subsection does not apply—

(A)   to interpretative rules, general statements of policy, or rules of agency organization, procedure, or practice; or

(B)   when the agency for good cause finds (and incorporates the finding and a brief statement of reasons therefor in the rules issued) that notice and public procedure thereon are impracticable, unnecessary, or contrary to the public interest.

(c)   After notice required by this section, the agency shall give interested persons an opportunity to participate in the rule making through submission of written data, views, or arguments with or without opportunity for oral presentation. After consideration of the relevant matter presented, the agency shall incorporate in the rules adopted a concise general statement of their basis and purpose. When rules are required by statute to be made on the record after opportunity for an agency hearing, sections 556 and 557 of this title apply instead of this subsection.

(d)   The required publication or service of a substantive rule shall be made not less than 30 days before its effective date, except—

    (1)   a substantive rule which grants or recognizes an exemption or relieves a restriction;

    (2)   interpretative rules and statements of policy; or

    (3)   as otherwise provided by the agency for good cause found and published with the rule.

(e)   Each agency shall give an interested person the right to petition for the issuance, amendment, or repeal of a rule.

§ 554. Adjudication

(a)   This section applies, according to the provisions thereof, in every case of adjudication required by statute to be determined on the record after opportunity for an agency hearing, except to the extent that there is involved—

    (1)   a matter subject to a subsequent trial of the law and the facts de novo in a court;

    (2)   the selection or tenure of an employee, except an administrative law judge appointed under section 3105 of this title;

    (3)   proceedings in which decisions rest solely on inspections, tests, or elections;

    (4)   the conduct of military or foreign affairs functions;

    (5)   cases in which an agency is acting as an agent for a court; or

    (6)   the certification of worker representatives.

(b)   Persons entitled to notice of an agency hearing shall be timely informed of—

    (1)   the time, place, and nature of the hearing;

    (2)   the legal authority and jurisdiction under which the hearing is to be held; and

    (3)   the matters of fact and law asserted.

When private persons are the moving parties, other parties to the proceeding shall give prompt notice of issues controverted in fact or law; and in other instances agencies may by rule require responsive pleading. In fixing the time and place for hearings, due regard shall be had for the convenience and necessity of the parties or their representatives.

(c)   The agency shall give all interested parties opportunity for—

    (1)   the submission and consideration of facts, arguments, offers of settlement, or proposals of adjustment when time, the nature of the proceeding, and the public interest permit; and

(2)   to the extent that the parties are unable so to determine a controversy by consent, hearing and decision on notice and in accordance with sections 556 and 557 of this title.

(d)   The employee who presides at the reception of evidence pursuant to section 556 of this title shall make the recommended decision or initial decision required by section 557 of this title, unless he becomes unavailable to the agency. Except to the extent required for the disposition of ex parte matters as authorized by law, such an employee may not—

(1)   consult a person or party on a fact in issue, unless on notice and opportunity for all parties to participate; or

(2)   be responsible to or subject to the supervision or direction of an employee or agent engaged in the performance of investigative or prosecuting functions for an agency.

An employee or agent engaged in the performance of investigative or prosecuting functions for an agency in a case may not, in that or a factually related case, participate or advise in the decision, recommended decision, or agency review pursuant to section 557 of this title, except as witness or counsel in public proceedings. This subsection does not apply—

(A)   in determining applications for initial licenses;

(B)   to proceedings involving the validity or application of rates, facilities, or practices of public utilities or carriers; or

(C)   to the agency or a member or members of the body comprising the agency.

(e)   The agency, with like effect as in the case of other orders, and in its sound discretion, may issue a declaratory order to terminate a controversy or remove uncertainty.

§ 555. Ancillary Matters

(a)   This section applies, according to the provisions thereof, except as otherwise provided by this subchapter.

(b)   A person compelled to appear in person before an agency or representative thereof is entitled to be accompanied, represented, and advised by counsel or, if permitted by the agency, by other qualified representative. A party is entitled to appear in person or by or with counsel or other duly qualified representative in an agency proceeding. So far as the orderly conduct of public business permits, an interested person may appear before an agency or its responsible employees for the presentation, adjustment, or determination of an issue, request, or controversy in a proceeding, whether interlocutory, summary, or otherwise, or in connection with an agency function. With due regard for the convenience and necessity of the parties or their representatives and within a reasonable time, each agency shall proceed to conclude a matter presented to it. This subsection does not grant or deny a person who is not a lawyer the right to appear for or represent others before an agency or in an agency proceeding.

(c) Process, requirement of a report, inspection, or other investigative act or demand may not be issued, made, or enforced except as authorized by law. A person compelled to submit data or evidence is entitled to retain or, on payment of lawfully prescribed costs, procure a copy or transcript thereof, except that in a nonpublic investigatory proceeding the witness may for good cause be limited to inspection of the official transcript of his testimony.

(d) Agency subpoenas authorized by law shall be issued to a party on request and, when required by rules of procedure, on a statement or showing of general relevance and reasonable scope of the evidence sought. On contest, the court shall sustain the subpoena or similar process or demand to the extent that it is found to be in accordance with law. In a proceeding for enforcement, the court shall issue an order requiring the appearance of the witness or the production of the evidence or data within a reasonable time under penalty of punishment for contempt in case of contumacious failure to comply.

(e) Prompt notice shall be given of the denial in whole or in part of a written application, petition, or other request of an interested person made in connection with any agency proceeding. Except in affirming a prior denial or when the denial is self-explanatory, the notice shall be accompanied by a brief statement of the grounds for denial.

§ 556. Hearings; Presiding Employees; Powers and Duties; Burden of Proof; Evidence; Record as Basis of Decision

(a) This section applies, according to the provisions thereof, to hearings required by section 553 or 554 of this title to be conducted in accordance with this section.

(b) There shall preside at the taking of evidence—

    (1) the agency;

    (2) one or more members of the body which comprises the agency; or

    (3) one or more administrative law judges appointed under section 3105 of this title.

This subchapter does not supersede the conduct of specified classes of proceedings, in whole or in part, by or before boards or other employees specially provided for by or designated under statute. The functions of presiding employees and of employees participating in decisions in accordance with section 557 of this title shall be conducted in an impartial manner. A presiding or participating employee may at any time disqualify himself. On the filing in good faith of a timely and sufficient affidavit of personal bias or other disqualification of a presiding or participating employee, the agency shall determine the matter as a part of the record and decision in the case.

(c) Subject to published rules of the agency and within its powers, employees presiding at hearings may—

(1) administer oaths and affirmations;

(2) issue subpoenas authorized by law;

(3) rule on offers of proof and receive relevant evidence;

(4) take depositions or have depositions taken when the ends of justice would be served;

(5) regulate the course of the hearing;

(6) hold conferences for the settlement or simplification of the issues by consent of the parties or by the use of alternative means of dispute resolution as provided in subchapter IV of this chapter;

(7) inform the parties as to the availability of one or more alternative means of dispute resolution, and encourage use of such methods;

(8) require the attendance at any conference held pursuant to paragraph (6) of at least one representative of each party who has authority to negotiate concerning resolution of issues in controversy;

(9) dispose of procedural requests or similar matters;

(10) make or recommend decisions in accordance with section 557 of this title; and

(11) take other action authorized by agency rule consistent with this subchapter.

(d) Except as otherwise provided by statute, the proponent of a rule or order has the burden of proof. Any oral or documentary evidence may be received, but the agency as a matter of policy shall provide for the exclusion of irrelevant, immaterial, or unduly repetitious evidence. A sanction may not be imposed or rule or order issued except on consideration of the whole record or those parts thereof cited by a party and supported by and in accordance with the reliable, probative, and substantial evidence. The agency may, to the extent consistent with the interests of justice and the policy of the underlying statutes administered by the agency, consider a violation of section 557(d) of this title sufficient grounds for a decision adverse to a party who has knowingly committed such violation or knowingly caused such violation to occur. A party is entitled to present his case or defense by oral or documentary evidence, to submit rebuttal evidence, and to conduct such cross-examination as may be required for a full and true disclosure of the facts. In rule making or determining claims for money or benefits or applications for initial licenses an agency may, when a party will not be prejudiced thereby, adopt procedures for the submission of all or part of the evidence in written form.

(e) The transcript of testimony and exhibits, together with all papers and requests filed in the proceeding, constitutes the exclusive record for decision in accordance with section 557 of this title and, on payment of lawfully prescribed costs, shall be made available to the parties. When an agency decision rests on official notice of a material fact not appearing in the evidence in the record, a party is entitled, on timely request, to an opportunity to show the contrary.

§ 557. Initial Decisions; Conclusiveness; Review by Agency; Submissions by Parties; Contents of Decisions; Record

(a) This section applies, according to the provisions thereof, when a hearing is required to be conducted in accordance with section 556 of this title.

(b) When the agency did not preside at the reception of the evidence, the presiding employee or, in cases not subject to section 554(d) of this title, an employee qualified to preside at hearings pursuant to section 556 of this title, shall initially decide the case unless the agency requires, either in specific cases or by general rule, the entire record to be certified to it for decision. When the presiding employee makes an initial decision, that decision then becomes the decision of the agency without further proceedings unless there is an appeal to, or review on motion of, the agency within time provided by rule. On appeal from or review of the initial decision, the agency has all the powers which it would have in making the initial decision except as it may limit the issues on notice or by rule. When the agency makes the decision without having presided at the reception of the evidence, the presiding employee or an employee qualified to preside at hearings pursuant to section 556 of this title shall first recommend a decision, except that in rule making or determining applications for initial licenses—

    (1) instead thereof the agency may issue a tentative decision or one of its responsible employees may recommend a decision; or

    (2) this procedure may be omitted in a case in which the agency finds on the record that due and timely execution of its functions imperatively and unavoidably so requires.

(c) Before a recommended, initial, or tentative decision, or a decision on agency review of the decision of subordinate employees, the parties are entitled to a reasonable opportunity to submit for the consideration of the employees participating in the decisions—

    (1) proposed findings and conclusions; or

    (2) exceptions to the decisions or recommended decisions of subordinate employees or to tentative agency decisions; and

    (3) supporting reasons for the exceptions or proposed findings or conclusions.

The record shall show the ruling on each finding, conclusion, or exception presented. All decisions, including initial, recommended, and tentative decisions, are a part of the record and shall include a statement of—

    (A) findings and conclusions, and the reasons or basis therefor, on all the material issues of fact, law, or discretion presented on the record; and

(B) the appropriate rule, order, sanction, relief, or denial thereof.

(d)(1) In any agency proceeding which is subject to subsection (a) of this section, except to the extent required for the disposition of ex parte matters as authorized by law—

    (A) no interested person outside the agency shall make or knowingly cause to be made to any member of the body comprising the agency, administrative law judge, or other employee who is or may reasonably be expected to be involved in the decisional process of the proceeding, an ex parte communication relevant to the merits of the proceeding;

    (B) no member of the body comprising the agency, administrative law judge, or other employee who is or may reasonably be expected to be involved in the decisional process of the proceeding, shall make or knowingly cause to be made to any interested person outside the agency an ex parte communication relevant to the merits of the proceeding;

    (C) a member of the body comprising the agency, administrative law judge, or other employee who is or may reasonably be expected to be involved in the decisional process of such proceeding who receives, or who makes or knowingly causes to be made, a communication prohibited by this subsection shall place on the public record of the proceeding:

        (i) all such written communications;

        (ii) memoranda stating the substance of all such oral communications; and

        (iii) all written responses, and memoranda stating the substance of all oral responses, to the materials described in clauses (i) and (ii) of this subparagraph;

    (D) upon receipt of a communication knowingly made or knowingly caused to be made by a party in violation of this subsection, the agency, administrative law judge, or other employee presiding at the hearing may, to the extent consistent with the interests of justice and the policy of the underlying statutes, require the party to show cause why his claim or interest in the proceeding should not be dismissed, denied, disregarded, or otherwise adversely affected on account of such violation; and

    (E) the prohibitions of this subsection shall apply beginning at such time as the agency may designate, but in no case shall they begin to apply later than the time at which a proceeding is noticed for hearing unless the person responsible for the communication has knowledge that it will be noticed, in which case the prohibitions shall apply beginning at the time of his acquisition of such knowledge.

(2) This subsection does not constitute authority to withhold information from Congress.

§ 558. Imposition of Sanctions;
Determination of Applications for Licenses;
Suspension, Revocation and Expiration of Licenses

(a) This section applies, according to the provisions thereof, to the exercise of a power or authority.

(b) A sanction may not be imposed or a substantive rule or order issued except within jurisdiction delegated to the agency and as authorized by law.

(c) When application is made for a license required by law, the agency, with due regard for the rights and privileges of all the interested parties or adversely affected persons and within a reasonable time, shall set and complete proceedings required to be conducted in accordance with sections 556 and 557 of this title or other proceedings required by law and shall make its decision. Except in cases of willfulness or those in which public health, interest, or safety requires otherwise, the withdrawal, suspension, revocation, or annulment of a license is lawful only if, before the institution of agency proceedings therefor, the licensee has been given—

   (1) notice by the agency in writing of the facts or conduct which may warrant the action; and

   (2) opportunity to demonstrate or achieve compliance with all lawful requirements.

When the licensee has made timely and sufficient application for a renewal or a new license in accordance with agency rules, a license with reference to an activity of a continuing nature does not expire until the application has been finally determined by the agency.

§ 559. Effect on Other Laws;
Effect of Subsequent Statute

This subchapter, chapter 7, and sections 1305, 3105, 3344, 4301(2)(E), 5372, and 7521 of this title, and the provisions of section 5335(a)(B) of this title that relate to administrative law judges, do not limit or repeal additional requirements imposed by statute or otherwise recognized by law. Except as otherwise required by law, requirements or privileges relating to evidence or procedure apply equally to agencies and persons. Each agency is granted the authority necessary to comply with the requirements of this subchapter through the issuance of rules or otherwise. Subsequent statute may not be held to supersede or modify this subchapter, chapter 7, sections 1305, 3105, 3344, 4301(2)(E), 5372, or 7521 of this title, or the provisions of section 5335(a)(B) of this title that relate to administrative law judges, except to the extent that it does so expressly.

TITLE 5. GOVERNMENT ORGANIZATION AND EMPLOYEES

PART I—THE AGENCIES GENERALLY
CHAPTER 5—ADMINISTRATIVE PROCEDURE
SUBCHAPTER III—NEGOTIATED RULE-MAKING PROCEDURE

§ 564. Publication of Notice; Application for Membership on Committees

(a) Publication of notice.—If, after considering the report of a convener or conducting its own assessment, an agency decides to establish a negotiated rule-making committee, the agency shall publish in the *Federal Register* and, as appropriate, in trade or other specialized publications, a notice which shall include—

   (1) an announcement that the agency intends to establish a negotiated rule-making committee to negotiate and develop a proposed rule;

   (2) a description of the subject and scope of the rule to be developed, and the issues to be considered;

   (3) a list of the interests which are likely to be significantly affected by the rule;

   (4) a list of the persons proposed to represent such interests and the person or persons proposed to represent the agency;

   (5) a proposed agenda and schedule for completing the work of the committee, including a target date for publication by the agency of a proposed rule for notice and comment;

   (6) a description of administrative support for the committee to be provided by the agency, including technical assistance;

   (7) a solicitation for comments on the proposal to establish the committee, and the proposed membership of the negotiated rule-making committee; and

   (8) an explanation of how a person may apply or nominate another person for membership on the committee, as provided under subsection (b).

(b) Applications for membership or committee.—Persons who will be significantly affected by a proposed rule and who believe that their interests will not be adequately represented by any person specified in a notice under subsection (a)(4) may apply for, or nominate another person for, membership on the negotiated rule-making committee to represent such interests with respect to the proposed rule. Each application or nomination shall include—

   (1) the name of the applicant or nominee and a description of the interests such person shall represent;

   (2) evidence that the applicant or nominee is authorized to represent parties related to the interests the person proposes to represent;

(3) a written commitment that the applicant or nominee shall actively participate in good faith in the development of the rule under consideration; and

(4) the reasons that the persons specified in the notice under subsection (a)(4) do not adequately represent the interests of the person submitting the application or nomination.

(c) Period for submission of comments and applications.—The agency shall provide for a period of at least 30 calendar days for the submission of comments and applications under this section.

§ 565. Establishment of Committee

(a) Establishment.—

(1) Determination to establish committee.—If after considering comments and applications submitted under section 564, the agency determines that a negotiated rule-making committee can adequately represent the interests that will be significantly affected by a proposed rule and that it is feasible and appropriate in the particular rule-making, the agency may establish a negotiated rule-making committee. In establishing and administering such a committee, the agency shall comply with the Federal Advisory Committee Act with respect to such committee, except as otherwise provided in this subchapter.

(2) Determination not to establish committee.—If after considering such comments and applications, the agency decides not to establish a negotiated rule-making committee, the agency shall promptly publish notice of such decision and the reasons therefor in the *Federal Register* and, as appropriate, in trade or other specialized publications, a copy of which shall be sent to any person who applied for, or nominated another person for, membership on the negotiated rule-making committee to represent such interests with respect to the proposed rule.

(b) Membership.—The agency shall limit membership on a negotiated rule-making committee to 25 members, unless the agency head determines that a greater number of members is necessary for the functioning of the committee or to achieve balanced membership. Each committee shall include at least one person representing the agency.

(c) Administrative Support.—The agency shall provide appropriate administrative support to the negotiated rule-making committee, including technical assistance.

§ 566. Conduct of Committee Activity

(a) Duties of Committee.—Each negotiated rule-making committee established under this subchapter shall consider the matter proposed by the agency for consideration and shall attempt to reach a consensus concerning a proposed rule with respect to such matter and any other matter the committee determines is relevant to the proposed rule.

(b) Representatives of Agency on Committee.—The person or persons representing the agency on a negotiated rule-making committee shall participate in the deliberations and activities of the committee with the same rights and responsibilities as other members of the committee, and shall be authorized to fully represent the agency in the discussions and negotiations of the committee.

(c) Selecting Facilitator.—Notwithstanding section 10(e) of the Federal Advisory Committee Act, an agency may nominate either a person from the Federal Government or a person from outside the Federal Government to serve as a facilitator for the negotiations of the committee, subject to the approval of the committee by consensus. If the committee does not approve the nominee of the agency for facilitator, the agency shall submit a substitute nomination. If a committee does not approve any nominee of the agency for facilitator, the committee shall select by consensus a person to serve as facilitator. A person designated to represent the agency in substantive issues may not serve as facilitator or otherwise chair the committee.

(d) Duties of Facilitator.—A facilitator approved or selected by a negotiated rule-making committee shall—

   (1) chair the meetings of the committee in an impartial manner;

   (2) impartially assist the members of the committee in conducting discussions and negotiations; and

   (3) manage the keeping of minutes and records as required under section 10(b) and (c) of the Federal Advisory Committee Act, except that any personal notes and materials of the facilitator or of the members of a committee shall not be subject to section 552 of this title.

(e) Committee Procedures.—A negotiated rule-making committee established under this subchapter may adopt procedures for the operation of the committee. No provision of section 553 of this title shall apply to the procedures of a negotiated rule-making committee.

(f) Report of Committee.—If a committee reaches a consensus on a proposed rule, at the conclusion of negotiations the committee shall transmit to the agency that established the committee a report containing the proposed rule. If the committee does not reach a consensus on a proposed rule, the committee may transmit to the agency a report specifying any areas in which the committee reached a consensus. The committee may include in a report any other information, recommendations, or materials that the committee considers appropriate. Any committee member may include as an addendum to the report additional information, recommendations, or materials.

(g) Records of Committee.—In addition to the report required by subsection (f), a committee shall submit to the agency the records required under section 10(b) and (c) of the Federal Advisory Committee Act.

§ 567. Termination of Committee

A negotiated rule-making committee shall terminate upon promulgation of the final rule under consideration, unless the committee's charter contains an earlier termination date or the agency, after consulting the committee, or the committee itself specifies an earlier termination date.

§ 568. Services, Facilities, and Payment of Committee Member Expenses

(a) Services of Conveners and Facilitators.—

  (1) In general.—An agency may employ or enter into contracts for the services of an individual or organization to serve as a convener or facilitator for a negotiated rule-making committee under this subchapter, or may use the services of a Government employee to act as a convener or a facilitator for such a committee.

  (2) Determination of conflicting interests.—An agency shall determine whether a person under consideration to serve as convener or facilitator of a committee under paragraph (1) has any financial or other interest that would preclude such person from serving in an impartial and independent manner.

(b) Services and Facilities of Other Entities.—For purposes of this subchapter, an agency may use the services and facilities of other Federal agencies and public and private agencies and instrumentalities with the consent of such agencies and instrumentalities, and with or without reimbursement to such agencies and instrumentalities, and may accept voluntary and uncompensated services without regard to the provisions of section 1342 of title 31. The Federal Mediation and Conciliation Service may provide services and facilities, with or without reimbursement, to assist agencies under this subchapter, including furnishing conveners, facilitators, and training in negotiated rule making.

(c) Expenses of Committee Members.—Members of a negotiated rule-making committee shall be responsible for their own expenses of participation in such committee, except that an agency may, in accordance with section 7(d) of the Federal Advisory Committee Act, pay for a member's reasonable travel and per diem expenses, expenses to obtain technical assistance, and a reasonable rate of compensation, if—

  (1) such member certifies a lack of adequate financial resources to participate in the committee; and

(2) the agency determines that such member's participation in the committee is necessary to assure an adequate representation of the member's interest.

(d) Status of Member as Federal Employee.—A member's receipt of funds under this section or section 569 shall not conclusively determine for purposes of sections 202 through 209 of title 18 whether that member is an employee of the United States Government.

§ 569. Role of the Administrative Conference of the United States and Other Entities

(a) Consultation by Agencies.—An agency may consult with the Administrative Conference of the United States or other public or private individuals or organizations for information and assistance in forming a negotiated rule-making committee and conducting negotiations on a proposed rule.

(b) Roster of Potential Conveners and Facilitators.—The Administrative Conference of the United States, in consultation with the Federal Mediation and Conciliation Service, shall maintain a roster of individuals who have acted as or are interested in serving as conveners or facilitators in negotiated rule-making proceedings. The roster shall include individuals from government agencies and private groups, and shall be made available upon request. Agencies may also use rosters maintained by other public or private individuals or organizations.

(c) Procedures to Obtain Conveners and Facilitators.—

(1) Procedures.—The Administrative Conference of the United States shall develop procedures which permit agencies to obtain the services of conveners and facilitators on an expedited basis.

(2) Payment for services.—Payment for the services of conveners or facilitators shall be made by the agency using the services, unless the Chairman of the Administrative Conference agrees to pay for such services under subsection (f).

(d) Compilation of Data on Negotiated Rule-making; Report to Congress.—

(1) Compilation of data.—The Administrative Conference of the United States shall compile and maintain data related to negotiated rule-making and shall act as a clearinghouse to assist agencies and parties participating in negotiated rule-making proceedings.

(2) Submission of information by agencies.—Each agency engaged in negotiated rule-making shall provide to the Administrative Conference of the United States a copy of any reports submitted to the agency by negotiated rule-making committees under section 566 and such additional information as necessary to enable the Administrative Conference of the United States to comply with this subsection.

(3) Reports to congress.—The Administrative Conference of the United States shall review and analyze the reports and information received under this subsection and shall transmit a biennial report to the Committee on Governmental Affairs of the Senate and the appropriate committees of the House of Representatives that—

  (A) provides recommendations for effective use by agencies of negotiated rule making; and

  (B) describes the nature and amounts of expenditures made by the Administrative Conference of the United States to accomplish the purposes of this subchapter.

(e) Training in Negotiated Rule Making.—The Administrative Conference of the United States is authorized to provide training in negotiated rule-making techniques and procedures for personnel of the Federal Government either on a reimbursable or nonreimbursable basis. Such training may be extended to private individuals on a reimbursable basis.

(f) Payment of Expenses of Agencies.—The Chairman of the Administrative Conference of the United States is authorized to pay, upon request of an agency, all or part of the expenses of establishing a negotiated rule-making committee and conducting a negotiated rule making. Such expenses may include, but are not limited to—

  (1) the costs of conveners and facilitators;

  (2) the expenses of committee members determined by the agency to be eligible for assistance under section 568(c); and

  (3) training costs.

Determinations with respect to payments under this section shall be at the discretion of such Chairman in furthering the use by Federal agencies of negotiated rule making.

(g) Use of Funds of the Conference.—The Administrative Conference of the United States may apply funds received under section 595(c)(12) of this title to carry out the purposes of this subchapter.

§ 570. Judicial Review

Any agency action relating to establishing, assisting, or terminating a negotiated rule-making committee under this subchapter shall not be subject to judicial review. Nothing in this section shall bar judicial review of a rule if such judicial review is otherwise provided by law. A rule which is the product of negotiated rule making and is subject to judicial review shall not be accorded any greater deference by a court than a rule which is the product of other rule-making procedures.

TITLE 5.

GOVERNMENT ORGANIZATION AND EMPLOYEES
PART I—THE AGENCIES GENERALLY
CHAPTER 7—JUDICIAL REVIEW

§ 701. Application; Definitions

(a) This chapter applies, according to the provisions thereof, except to the extent that—

  (1) statutes preclude judicial review; or

  (2) agency action is committed to agency discretion by law.

(b) For the purpose of this chapter—

  (1) "agency" means each authority of the Government of the United States, whether or not it is within or subject to review by another agency, but does not include—

   (A) the Congress;

   (B) the courts of the United States;

   (C) the governments of the territories or possessions of the United States;

   (D) the government of the District of Columbia;

   (E) agencies composed of representatives of the parties or of representatives of organizations of the parties to the disputes determined by them;

   (F) court martial and military commissions;

   (G) military authority exercised in the field in time of war or in occupied territory; or

   (H) functions conferred by sections 1738, 1739, 1743, and 1744 of title 12; chapter 2 of title 41; or sections 1622, 1884, 1891-1902, and former section 1641(b)(2), of title 50, appendix; and

  (2) "person," "rule," "order," "license," "sanction," "relief," and "agency action" have the meanings given them by section 551 of this title.

§ 702. Right of Review

A person suffering legal wrong because of agency action, or adversely affected or aggrieved by agency action within the meaning of a relevant statute, is entitled to judicial review thereof. An action in a court of the United States seeking relief other than money damages and stating a claim that an agency or an officer or employee thereof acted or failed to act in an official capacity or under color of legal authority shall not be dismissed nor relief therein be denied on the ground that it is against the United States or that the United States is an indispensable party. The United States may be named as a defendant in any such action, and a judgment or decree may be entered against the United States: Provided, that any mandatory or injunctive decree shall specify the Federal officer or officers (by name or by title), and their successors in office, personally responsible for compliance. Nothing herein (1) affects other limitations on judicial review or the power or duty of the court to dismiss any action or deny relief on any other appropriate legal or equitable ground; or (2) confers authority to grant relief if any other statute that grants consent to suit expressly or impliedly forbids the relief which is sought.

§ 703. Form and Venue of Proceeding

The form of proceeding for judicial review is the special statutory review proceeding relevant to the subject matter in a court specified by statute or, in the absence or inadequacy thereof, any applicable form of legal action, including actions for declaratory judgments or writs of prohibitory or mandatory injunction or habeas corpus, in a court of competent jurisdiction. If no special statutory review proceeding is applicable, the action for judicial review may be brought against the United States, the agency by its official title, or the appropriate officer. Except to the extent that prior, adequate, and exclusive opportunity for judicial review is provided by law, agency action is subject to judicial review in civil or criminal proceedings for judicial enforcement.

§ 704. Actions Reviewable

Agency action made reviewable by statute and final agency action for which there is no other adequate remedy in a court are subject to judicial review. A preliminary, procedural, or intermediate agency action or ruling not directly reviewable is subject to review on the review of the final agency action. Except as otherwise expressly required by statute, agency action otherwise final is final for the purposes of this section whether or not there has been presented or determined an application for a declaratory order, for any form of reconsideration, or, unless the agency otherwise requires by rule and provides that the action meanwhile is inoperative, for an appeal to superior agency.

§ 705. Relief Pending Review

When an agency finds that justice so requires, it may postpone the effective date of action taken by it, pending judicial review. On such conditions as may be required and to the extent necessary to prevent irreparable injury, the reviewing court, including the court to which a case may be taken on appeal from or on application for certiorari or other writ to a reviewing court, may issue all necessary and appropriate process to postpone the effective date of an agency action or to preserve status or rights pending conclusion of the review proceedings.

§ 706. Scope of Review

To the extent necessary to decision and when presented, the reviewing court shall decide all relevant questions of law, interpret constitutional and statutory provisions, and determine the meaning or applicability of the terms of an agency action. The reviewing court shall—

    (1)   compel agency action unlawfully withheld or unreasonably delayed; and

    (2)   hold unlawful and set aside agency action, findings, and conclusions found to be—

        (A)   arbitrary, capricious, an abuse of discretion, or otherwise not in accordance with law;

        (B)   contrary to constitutional right, power, privilege, or immunity;

        (C)   in excess of statutory jurisdiction, authority, or limitations, or short of statutory right;

        (D)   without observance of procedure required by law;

        (E)   unsupported by substantial evidence in a case subject to sections 556 and 557 of this title or otherwise reviewed on the record of an agency hearing provided by statute; or

        (F)   unwarranted by the facts to the extent that the facts are subject to trial de novo by the reviewing court.

In making the foregoing determinations, the court shall review the whole record or those parts of it cited by a party, and due account shall be taken of the rule of prejudicial error.

Index

ABOUT THE AUTHOR

Steven J. Cann is a Full Professor and Prelaw Coordinator at Washburn University of Topeka, Kansas. He has published extensively in the area of substantive constitutional law, primarily in civil liberties. He received his Ph.D. in political science from Purdue University in 1977. In 1996, he was nominated for inclusion in *Who's Who Among America's Teachers.*